Hugh Johnson's

POCKET ENCYCLOPEDIA

OF WINE

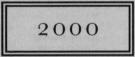

2000

A Fireside Book
Published by Simon & Schuster

Acknowledgments

This store of detailed recommendations comes partly from
my own notes and partly from those of a great number of
kind friends. Without the generous help and cooperation of
innumerable winemakers, merchants and critics, I could not
attempt it. I particularly want to thank the following for help
with research or in the areas of their special knowledge.

Colin Anderson MW
Fritz Ascher
Martyn Assirati
Jean-Claude Berrouet
Frances and Tom Bissell
Gregory Bowden
Lucy Bridgers
Michael Broadbent MW
Jim Budd
Michael Cooper
John Cossart
Michael Edwards
Len Evans
Dereck Foster
Jacqueline Friedrich
Denis Gastin
Rosemary George MW
Howard G Goldberg

James Halliday
Shirley Jones
Annie Kay
Stephen Kirkland
Chandra Kurt
Gabriel Lachmann
Tony Laithwaite
Konstantinos Lazarakis
John Livingstone-
    Learmonth
Andreas März
Richard Mayson
Maggie McNie MW
Adam Montefiore
Vladimir Moskvan
Christian Moueix
Dan Muntean
Richard Neill

Judy Peterson-Nedry
Stuart Pigott
John and Erica Platter
Carlos Read
Jan and Maite Read
Michael, Prinz zu Salm
Nellie Salvi
Lisa Shara-Hall
Joanna Simon
Stephen Skelton
Paul Strang
Marguerite Thomas
Bob Thompson
Peter Vinding-Diers
Julia Wilkinson
Simon Woods
Hilary Wright

Hugh Johnson's Pocket Encyclopedia of Wine 2000

FIRESIDE
Rockefeller Center
1230 Avenue of the Americas
New York, NY 10020

Senior Editor: Lucy Bridgers
Commissioning Editor: Rebecca Spry
Production: Karen Farquhar

Manufactured in China

10 9 8 7 6 5 4 3 2 1

ISBN 0-684-86756-7

Contents

Foreword

It is a well established convention that every thousand years (and indeed every hundred) writers of reference books do a little stock-taking and crystal-gazing. But wine calls for much shorter intervals.

You don't have to look back more than 25 years to see a totally different wine world: one where France was in firm control, indeed virtually the only producer of fine and luxurious wines. California and Australia were only just beginning to understand their potential. Italy and Spain were so little exploited or understood that their exports were limited to two or three wines apiece. Germany alone was held in more respect than her wines receive today.

Look forward 25 years and what do we see? Wines of good to fine and even luxurious quality from almost every country that makes wine at all.

This is the pace and extent of progress. What a joyous prospect.

Are there no snags? Only for people with long memories and those with a passion for the distinctive and authentic. For clearly there is a risk, and more than a risk, of all these good, fine and even luxurious wines resembling each other. They will not become identical, or even indistinguishable; but we already see certain characteristics praised by the critics in one region being imitated by producers in another. Big fruity red wines tasting of oak are only the most obvious example.

Once a region discovers that it can raise its price by abandoning its individuality, it becomes a mere fashion item. Fashions change; terroir is the one immutable – the anchor of character.

There are other changes, too. The ever-present temptation to over-produce, resulting in watery wine, is encouraged by better disease control in vineyards. Wine merchants encourage it too, by haggling for unrealistically low prices.

But the overwhelming majority of the news is good; there is scarcely a country or region in this book without aspiring and dedicated producers leading it onto higher ground.

Such giant strides in quality have been made in Spain, Italy and Portugal (also Greece) that their wines now reach markets that spurned them utterly a few years ago. Europe's giant weakling in the wine world is Germany. Her international market for anything but sugar-water has almost disappeared. But here also young ambition (not necessarily well-healed, either) is building a new edifice: modern prestige German wine.

The world tour of aspirants to quality and prestige can make you giddy. One should not make the mistake of thinking only 'new' regions can do new things. The Mediterranean is probably the general area moving fastest just now.

Another welcome trend is the planting of varieties other than the predictable few. Perhaps it takes more self-confidence to offer the world a Marsanne, a Vermentino, a Mourvèdre or even a Refosco than a Chardonnay or Cabernet. But in the continuing world-wide search for the right match of grape and ground, trying different varieties must make sense.

Meanwhile, even the most varietally-led regions are learning rapidly that you need more than just a grape name to sell wine these days. The demand that will shape the future is for a sense of place in what we drink. The game is up for those who turn their backs on terroir. The earth will open and swallow them up.

Laying aside the broader issues, though, this micro-encyclopedia looks closely at the present position in this fast-changing world. Even readers who bought the last edition (others, I'm afraid, only come back to the well at intervals of two or three) will find thousands of changes of detail, emphasis and evaluation.

This is intended to be a practical guide; theory has little place here. In essence, it compresses all the useful information you can't possibly carry in your head – and neither can I. My information is gleaned, as ever, from many sources, from tastings, visits and never-ending correspondence. Revision is a continuing process. Before you read this I will have a much scribbled-on proof for next year's edition.

The book is designed to take the panic out of buying. You are faced with a daunting restaurant wine list, or mind-numbing shelves of bottles in a store. Your mind goes blank. Out comes your little book. You can start with what you propose to eat, by turning to the wines for food section on pages 14–30, or where you are by turning up a national section, or a grape variety you like. Just establish which country a wine comes from, then look up the principal words on the label in that country's section. You should find enough information to guide your choice – and often a great deal more: the cross-references are there to help you delve further. Even after 21 editions I find I can browse for hours...

A declaration of interest
Readers should know that I have interests in the Royal Tokáji Wine Company in Hungary and Château Latour in Bordeaux. (It's hard not to be interested in many friends' vineyards, too.)

How to use this book

The top line of most entries consists of the following information:

①   **③**

Aglianico del Vulture Bas | r dr (s/sw sp) | ★★★ | 88 90' **91 92** 93' 94' 95 96 (97)

         ②   **④**

① Wine name and the region the wine comes from.

② Whether it is red, rosé or white (or brown/amber), dry, sweet or
sparkling, or several of these (and which is most important):

r	red
p	rosé
w	white
br	brown
dr	dry*
sw	sweet
s/sw	semi-sweet
sp	sparkling

( ) brackets here denote a less important wine
*assume wine is dry when **dr** or **sw** are not indicated

③ Its general standing as to quality: a necessarily rough-and-ready
guide based on its **current reputation** as reflected in its prices:

★	plain, everyday quality
★★	above average
★★★	well known, highly reputed
★★★★	grand, prestigious, expensive

So much is more or less objective. Additionally there is a subjective rating:

★ etc   Stars are coloured red for any wine which in my experience is
usually especially good within its price range. There are good everyday
wines as well as good luxury wines. This system helps you find them.

④ Vintage information: which of the recent vintages can be
recommended; of these, which are ready to drink this year, and
which will probably improve with keeping. Your choice for current
drinking should be one of the vintage years printed in **bold** type.
Buy light-type years for further maturing.

95 etc   recommended years which may be currently available
90' etc   vintage regarded as particularly successful for the
property in question
87 etc   years in **bold** should be ready for drinking (the others should
be kept)
89 etc   vintages in colour are the ones to choose first for drinking in '99 –
they should be à point. (See also Bordeaux introduction, page 78.)
(97) etc   provisional rating

The German vintages work on a different principle again: see page 136.

Other abbreviations

DYA   drink the youngest available
NV   vintage not normally shown on label; in Champagne,
means a blend of several vintages for continuity
CHABLIS   properties, areas or terms cross-referred within the section

A quick-reference vintage chart appears on page 280

Grape varieties

In the past two decades a radical change has come about in all except the most long-established wine countries: the names of a handful of grape varieties have become the ready reference to wine. In senior wine countries, above all France and Italy (between them producing nearly half the world's wine), more complex traditions prevail. All wine of prestige is known by its origin, more or less narrowly defined, not just the particular fruit-juice that fermented.

For the present the two notions are in rivalry. Eventually the primacy of place over fruit will become obvious, at least for wines of quality. But for now, for most people, grape tastes are the easy reference-point – despite the fact that they are often confused by the added taste of oak. If grape flavours were really all that mattered this would be a very short book.

But of course they do matter, and a knowledge of them both guides you to flavours you enjoy and helps comparisons between regions. Hence the originally Californian term 'varietal wine' – meaning, in principle, one grape variety.

At least seven varieties – Cabernet Sauvignon, Pinot Noir, Riesling, Sauvignon Blanc, Chardonnay, Gewürztraminer and Muscat – have tastes and smells distinct and memorable enough to form international categories of wine. To these you can add Merlot, Malbec, Syrah, Sémillon, Chenin Blanc, Pinots Blanc and Gris, Sylvaner, Viognier, Nebbiolo, Sangiovese, Tempranillo… The following are the best and/or most popular wine grapes.

Grapes for white wine

Albariño The Spanish name for N Portugal's Alvarinho, emerging as excellently fresh and fragrant wine in Galicia. One of Spain's new delights.

Aligoté Burgundy's second-rank white grape. Crisp (often sharp) wine, needs drinking in 1–3 yrs. Perfect for mixing with cassis (blackcurrant liqueur) to make a 'Kir'. Widely planted in E Europe, esp Russia.

Arinto White central Portuguese grape for crisp, fragrant dry whites.

Blanc Fumé Alias of SAUV BL, referring to its reputedly 'smoky' smell, particularly from the Loire (Sancerre and Pouilly). In California used for oak-aged Sauv and reversed to 'Fumé Blanc'. But the smoke is oak.

Bual Makes top-quality sw Madeira wines, not quite so rich as Malmsey.

Chardonnay (Chard) The white burgundy grape, the white Champagne grape, and the best white grape of the New World, partly because it is one of the easiest to grow and vinify. All regions are trying it, mostly aged (or, better, fermented) in oak to reproduce the flavours of burgundy. Australia and California make classics (but also much dross). Those of Italy, Spain, New Zealand, South Africa, New York State, Chile, Argentina, Hungary and the Midi are all coming on strong. Called Morillon in Austria.

Chasselas Prolific early-ripening grape with little aroma, mainly grown for eating. AKA Fendant in Switzerland (where it is supreme), Gutedel in Germany.

Chenin Blanc (Chenin Bl) Great white grape of the middle Loire (Vouvray, Layon, etc). Wine can be dry or sweet (or very sweet), but with plenty of acidity – hence its long life and use in warmer climates (eg California). See also Steen.

Clairette A low-acid grape formerly widely used in the S of France as a vermouth base. Being revived.

Colombard Slightly fruity, nicely sharp grape, hugely popular in California, now gaining ground in SW France, South Africa, etc.

Fendant See Chasselas.

Folle Blanche High acid/little flavour make this ideal for brandy. Called Gros Plant in Brittany, Picpoul in Armagnac. Respectable in California.

Fumé Blanc (Fumé Bl) See Blanc Fumé.

Furmint A grape of great character: the trademark of Hungary both as the principal grape in Tokay and as vivid, vigorous table wine with an appley flavour. Called Sipon in Slovenia. Some grown in Austria.

Gewürztraminer, alias Traminer (Gewürz) One of the most pungent grapes, distinctively spicy with aromas like rose petals and grapefruit. Wines are often rich and soft, even when fully dry. Best in Alsace; also good in Germany, E Europe, Australia, California, Pacific NW, NZ.

Grauburgunder See Pinot Gris.

Grechetto or Greco Ancient grape of central and S Italy: vitality and style.

Grüner Veltliner Austria's favourite (planted in almost half her vineyards). Around Vienna and in the Wachau and Weinviertel (also in Moravia) it can be delicious: light but dry, peppery and lively. The best age 5 years or so.

Hárslevelü The other main grape of Tokay (with FURMINT). Adds softness and body.

Italian Riesling Grown in N Italy and E Europe. Much inferior to Rhine RIES, with lower acidity, best in sweet wines. Alias Welschriesling, Olaszrizling (no longer legally labelled simply 'Riesling').

Kéknyelü Low-yielding, flavourful grape giving one of Hungary's best whites. Has the potential for fieriness and spice. To be watched.

Kerner The most successful of many recent German varieties, mostly made by crossing RIES and SILVANER, but in this case Ries x (red) Trollinger. Early-ripening flowery (but often too blatant) wine with good acidity. Popular in Pfalz, Rheinhessen, etc.

Loureiro The best and most fragrant Vinho Verde variety in Portugal.

Macabeo The workhorse white grape of N Spain, widespread in Rioja (alias Viura) and in Catalan cava country. Good quality potential.

Malvasia Known as Malmsey in Madeira, Malvasia in Italy, Malvoisie in France. Alias Vermentino (esp in Corsica). Also grown in Greece, Spain, W Australia, E Europe. Makes rich brown wines or soft whites, ageing magnificently with superb potential not often realized.

Marsanne Principal white grape (with Roussanne) of the N Rhône (eg in Hermitage, St-Joseph, St-Péray). Also good in Australia, California and (as Ermitage Blanc) the Valais. Soft full wines that age v well.

Müller-Thurgau (Müller-T) Dominant in Germany's Rheinhessen and Pfalz and too common on the Mosel; a cross between RIESLING and SILVANER. Ripens early to make soft aromatic wines for drinking young. Makes good sweet wines but usually dull, often coarse, dry ones. Has no place in top vineyards.

Muscadelle Adds aroma to many white Bordeaux, esp Sauternes. Also the base for Australian Liqueur Tokay. Apparently not a true MUSCAT.

Muscadet, alias Melon de Bourgogne Makes light, refreshing, very dry wines with a seaside tang round Nantes in Brittany. (California 'Pinot Bl' is this grape.)

Muscat (Many varieties; the best is Muscat Blanc à Petits Grains.) Universally grown, easily recognized, pungent grapes, mostly made into perfumed sweet wines, often fortified (as in France's vins doux naturels). Superb in Australia. The third element in Tokay Azsú. Rarely (eg Alsace) made dry.

Palomino, alias Listán Makes all the best sherry but poor table wine.

Pedro Ximénez, alias PX Makes very strong wine in Montilla and Málaga. Used in blending sweet sherries. Also grown in Argentina, the Canaries, Australia, California, South Africa.

Pinot Blanc (Pinot Bl) A cousin of PINOT N; not related to CHARD, but with a similar, milder character: light, fresh, fruity, not aromatic, to drink young; eg good for Italian spumante. Grown in Alsace, N Italy, S Germany, E Europe. Weissburgunder in Germany. See also Muscadet.

Pinot Gris (Pinot Gr) At best makes rather heavy, even 'thick', full-bodied whites with a certain spicy style. Known (formerly) as Tokay in Alsace; Ruländer (sweet) or Grauburgunder (dry) in Germany; Tocai or Pinot Grigio in Italy and Slovenia (but much thinner wine).

Pinot Noir (Pinot N) Superlative black grape (See 'Grapes for red wine') used in Champagne and occasionally elsewhere (eg California, Australia) for making white, sparkling, or very pale pink 'vin gris'.

Riesling (Ries) Germany's great grape, and at present the world's most underrated. Wine of brilliant sweet/acid balance, either dry or sweet, flowery in youth but maturing to subtle oily scents and flavours. Unlike CHARD it does not need high alcohol for character. Very good (usually dry) in Alsace (but absurdly grown nowhere else in France), Austria, Australia (widely grown), Pacific NW, Ontario, California, South Africa. Often called White-, Johannisberg- or Rhine-Riesling. Subject to 'noble rot'.

Ruländer Obsolescent German name for PINOT G used for sweeter wines.

Sauvignon Blanc (Sauv Bl) Makes v distinctive aromatic grassy – or goose-berry – sometimes rank-smelling wines; best in Sancerre. Blended with SEM in B'x. Can be austere or buxom. Pungent triumph in New Zealand, now overplanted everywhere. Also called Fumé Blanc or vice versa.

Savagnin The grape of Vin Jaune of Savoie: related to TRAMINER?

Scheurebe Spicy-flavoured German RIES x SYLVANER, very successful in Pfalz, esp for Auslesen. Can be weedy in dry wines.

Sémillon (Sém or Sem) Contributes the lusciousness to Sauternes; subject to 'noble rot' in the right conditions but increasingly important for Graves and dry white Bordeaux. Grassy if not fully ripe, but can make soft dry wine of great ageing potential. Formerly called 'Riesling' in parts of Australia where it is often blended with CHARD. Old Hunter Valley Sem can be great wine.

Sercial Makes the driest Madeira (where myth says it is really RIESLING).

Seyval Blanc (Seyval Bl) French-made hybrid of French and American vines. V hardy and attractively fruity. Popular and reasonably successful in eastern States and England but dogmatically banned by EU from 'quality' wines.

Steen South Africa's most popular white grape: good lively fruity wine. Said to be the CHENIN BL of the Loire and now often so labelled.

Silvaner, alias Sylvaner Germany's former workhorse grape: wine rarely fine except in Franken where it is savoury and ages admirably, and in Rheinhessen and the Pfalz, where it is enjoying a renaissance. Gd in the Italian Tyrol; useful in Alsace. Vg (and powerful) as 'Johannisberg' in the Valais, Switzerland.

Tokay See Pinot Gris. Also a table grape in California and a supposedly Hungarian grape in Australia. The wine Tokay (Tokáji) is made of FURMINT, HARSLEVELU and MUSCAT.

Torrontes Strongly aromatic, MUSCAT-like Argentine grape, usually dry.

Traminer See Gewürztraminer.

Trebbiano Important but mediocre grape of central Italy (Orvieto, Chianti, Soave etc). Also grown in S France as Ugni Blanc, and Cognac as St-Emilion. Mostly thin, bland wine; needs blending (or more careful growing).

Ugni Blanc (Ugni Bl) See Trebbiano.

Verdejo The grape of Rueda in Castile, potentially fine and long-lived.

Verdelho Madeira grape making excellent medium-sweet wine; in Australia, fresh soft dry wine of great character.

Verdicchio Gives its name to potentially good dry wine in central-eastern Italy.

Vermentino Close to Malvasia, but make a sprightlier wine in Liguria, Tuscany, etc – still with satisfying texture and ageing capacity.

Vernaccia Grape grown in central and S Italy and Sardinia for strong smooth lively wine, sometimes inclining towards sherry.

Viognier Rare Rhône grape, grown at Condrieu for v fine fragrant wine. Drink ASAP. Much in vogue in the Midi, California, etc, but still only a trickle.

Viura See Macabeo.

Weissburgunder See Pinot Blanc.

Welschriesling See Italian Riesling.

Grapes for red wine

Aleatico Dark Muscat variety, alias Aglianico, used the length of W Italy for fragrant sweet wines. A speciality of Elba.

Baga The main red of Bairrada, central Portugal. Dark, tannic; great potential.

Barbera Most popular of many productive grapes of N Italy, esp Piedmont, giving dark, fruity, often sharp wine. Gaining prestige in California.

Blaufränkisch Austrian reputed GAMAY but at best (in Burgenland) a considerable red. LEMBERGER in Germany, KEKFRANKOS in Hungary.

Bourboulenc This and the rare Rolle make some of the Midi's best wines.

Brunello South Tuscan form of SANGIOVESE, splendid at Montalcino.

Cabernet Franc, alias Bouchet (Cab F) The lesser of two sorts of Cab grown in Bordeaux but dominant (as 'Bouchet') in St-Emilion. The Cab of the Loire, making Chinon, Saumur, etc, and rosé. Used for blending with CAB S, etc, in California, Australia.

Cabernet Sauvignon (Cab S) Grape of great character: spicy, herby, tannic, with characteristic 'blackcurrant' aroma. The first grape of the Médoc; also makes most of the best California, S American, E European reds. Vies with Shiraz in Australia. Its wine almost always needs ageing; usually benefits from blending with eg MERLOT, CAB F or SYRAH. Makes aromatic rosé.

Cannonau GRENACHE in its Sardinian manifestation: can be v fine, potent.

Carignan By far the most common grape of France, covering hundreds of thousands of acres. Prolific with dull but harmless wine. Best from old vines in Corbières. Also common in N Africa, Spain, California.

Cinsault /Cinsaut Common bulk-producing grape of S France; in S Africa crossed with PINOT N to make PINOTAGE. Pale wine, but quality potential.

Dolcetto Source of soft seductive dry red in Piedmont. Now high fashion.

Gamay The Beaujolais grape: light, very fragrant wines, at their best young. Makes even lighter wine in the Loire Valley, in central France, and in Switzerland and Savoie. Known as 'Napa Gamay' in California.

Gamay Beaujolais Not GAMAY but a poor variety of PINOT N in California (name now banned).

Grenache, alias Garnacha, Alicante, Cannonau Useful grape for strong fruity but pale wine: good rosé and vin doux naturel, esp in S France, Spain, California. Old-vine versions are currently prized in S Australia. Usually blended (eg in Châteauneuf-du-Pape).

Grignolino Makes one of the good everyday table wines of Piedmont.

Kadarka, alias Gamza Makes healthy, sound, agreeable reds in Hungary, Bulgaria, etc.

Kékfrankos Hungarian BLAUFRANKISCH, said to be related to GAMAY; similar lightish reds.

Lambrusco Productive grape of the lower Po Valley, giving quintessentially Italian, cheerful sweet and fizzy red.

Lemberger See Blaufränkisch. Württemberg's red.

Malbec, alias Cot Minor in Bordeaux, major in Cahors (alias Auxerrois) and esp Argentina. Dark, dense and tannic wine capable of real quality.

Merlot Adaptable grape making the great fragrant and plummy wines of Pomerol and (with CAB F) St-Emilion, an important element in Médoc reds, soft and strong (and à la mode) in California, Washington. A useful adjunct in Australia, lighter but often good in N Italy, Italian Switzerland, Slovenia, Argentina etc. Grassy when not fully ripe.

Montepulciano Confusingly, a major central-eastern Italian grape of high quality, as well as a town in Tuscany.

Mourvèdre, alias Mataro Excellent dark aromatic tannic grape used mainly for blending in Provence (but solo in Bandol) and the Midi. Enjoying new interest in eg S Australia, California.

Nebbiolo, alias Spanna and Chiavennasca One of Italy's best red grapes; makes Barolo, Barbaresco, Gattinara, Valtellina. Intense, nobly fruity, perfumed wine but v tannic: needs years.

Periquita Ubiquitous in Portugal for firm-flavoured reds. Often blended with CABERNET S and also known as Castelão Francês.

Petit (and Gros) Manseng The secret weapon of the French Basque country: vital for Jurançon; increasingly blended elsewhere in the SW.

Petit Verdot Excellent but awkward Médoc grape now largely superseded.

Pinot Noir (Pinot N) The glory of Burgundy's Côte d'Or, with scent, flavour, and texture unmatched anywhere. Less happy elsewhere; makes light wines rarely of much distinction in Germany, Switzerland, Austria, Hungary. But now splendid results in California's Sonoma, Carneros and Central Coast, Oregon, Ontario, Yarra Valley, Adelaide Hills, Tasmania and NZ.

Pinotage Singular S African grape (PINOT N x CINSAUT). Can be very fruity and can age interestingly, but often jammy.

Refosco Possibly a synomym for Mondeuse of Savoie. Produces deep, flavoursome age-worthy wines, esp in warmer climates.

St-Laurent Dark, smooth and full-flavoured Austrian speciality. Also a little in the Pfalz.

Sangiovese (or Sangioveto) The main red grape of Chianti and much of central Italy. BRUNELLO is the Sangiovese Grosso. Top quality potential now in California, too.

Saperavi Makes good sharp very long-lived wine in Georgia, Ukraine etc. Blends very well with CABERNET S (eg in Moldova).

Spätburgunder German for PINOT N, but a very pale shadow of burgundy.

Syrah or Petite Sirah, alias Shiraz The great Rhône red grape, giving tannic purple peppery wine which can mature superbly. Very important as Shiraz in Australia, increasingly successful in Midi, S Africa and California. Has a rapidly growing fan club.

Tannat Raspberry-perfumed, highly tannic force behind Madiran, Tursan and other firm-structured reds from southwest France. Also for rosé.

Tempranillo The pale aromatic fine Rioja grape, called Ull de Llebre in Catalonia, Cencibel in La Mancha. Early ripening.

Touriga Nacional Top port and Douro grape, travelling further afield in Portugal for full-bodied reds.

Zinfandel (Zin) Fruity adaptable grape peculiar to California with blackberry-like, and sometimes metallic, flavour. Can be gloriously lush, but also makes 'blush' white wine.

Wine & food

The dilemma is most acute in restaurants. Four people have chosen different dishes. The host calculates. A bottle of white and then one of red is conventional, regardless of the food. The formula works. But it can be refined – or replaced with something more original, something to really bring out the flavours of both food and wine.

Remarkably little ink has been spilt on this byway of knowledge, but 22 years of experimentation and the ideas of many friends have gone into making this list. It is perhaps most useful for menu-planning at home. But used with the rest of the book, it may ease menu-stress in restaurants, too. At the very least, it will broaden your mind.

Before the meal – aperitifs

The conventional aperitif wines are either sparkling (epitomized by Champagne) or fortified (epitomized by sherry in Britain, port in France, vermouth in Italy, etc). A glass of white or rosé (or in France red) table wine before eating is presently in vogue. It calls for something light and stimulating, fairly dry but not acidic, with a degree of character; rather Riesling or Chenin Blanc than Chardonnay.

Warning: Avoid peanuts; they destroy wine flavours.

Olives are also too piquant for most wines; they need sherry or a Martini. Eat almonds, pistachios or walnuts, plain crisps or cheese straws instead.

First courses

Aïoli
A thirst-quencher is needed for its garlic heat. Rhône (★→★★), sparkling dry white; Blanquette de Limoux, Provence rosé, Minervois, Verdicchio. And marc, too, for courage.

Antipasto in Italy
Dry or med white (★★): Italian (Arneis, Soave, Pinot Grigio, Prosecco, Vermentino); light red (Dolcetto, Franciacorta, ★★ young Chianti).

Artichoke vinaigrette
Young red (★): Bordeaux, Côtes du Rhône; or an incisive dry white, eg NZ Sauv Bl or a modern Greek.
hollandaise Full-bodied slightly crisp dry white (★ or ★★): Pouilly-Fuissé, Pfalz Spätlese, or a Carneros or Yarra Valley Chardonnay (★★).

Asparagus
A difficult flavour for wine, being slightly bitter, so the wine needs plenty of its own. Sauv echoes the flavour. Sem beats Chard, esp Australian, but Chard works well with melted butter. Alsace Pinot G, even dry Muscat is gd, or Jurançon Sec. With eg a feuilletté try sw: Sauternes, Loire, Tokay.

Aubergine purée (Melitzanosalata)
Crisp New World Sauv Bl eg from Chile or NZ, or modern Greek or Sicilian dry white. Or Bardolino red or Chiaretto.

Avocado with prawns, crab etc
Dry to medium or slightly sharp white (★★→★★★): Rheingau or Pfalz Kabinett, Sancerre, Pinot Grigio; Sonoma or Australian Chard or Sauvignon, Cape Steen, or dry rosé. Or Chablis Premier Cru.

vinaigrette Manzanilla sherry.

Bisques
Dry white with plenty of body (★★): Pinot Gris, Chard. Fino or dry amontillado sherry, or Montilla. West Australian Sem.

Boudin (blood sausage)
Local Sauv Bl or Chenin – esp in the Loire. Or Beaujolais Cru, esp Morgon.

Bouillabaisse
Savoury dry white (★→★★), Marsanne from the Midi or Rhône, Corsican or Spanish rosé, or Cassis, Verdicchio, California unoaked Sauv Blanc.

Caesar Salad
California (Central Coast) Chardonnay. Top California Chenin Blanc.

Carpaccio, beef
Seems to work well with the flavour of most wines, incl ★★★ reds. Top Tuscan vino da tavola is appropriate, but fine Chards are good. So are vintage and pink Champagnes. (See also Carpaccio under fish.)
salmon Chardonnay (★★→★★★), or Champagne.

Caviar
Iced vodka. Champagne, if you must, full-bodied (eg Bollinger, Krug).

Ceviche
Australian Riesling or Verdelho (★★), Chile or NZ Sauvignon Bl.

Charcuterie
Young Beaujolais-Villages or ★★ Bordeaux Blanc, Loire reds such as Saumur, Swiss or Oregon Pinot N. Young Argentine or Italian reds.

Cheese fondue
Dry white (★★): Valais Fendant or any other Swiss Chasselas, **Roussette de Savoie**, Grüner Veltliner, Alsace Ries or Pinot Gris. Or a Beaujolais Cru.

Chowders
Big-scale white (★★), not necessarily bone dry: Pinot Gris, Rhine Spätlese, Albariño, Australian Sem, buttery Chard. Or fino sherry, dry Madeira or Marsala.

Consommé
Medium-dry amontillado sherry (★★→★★★), Sercial Madeira.

Crostini
Morellino di Scansano, Montepulciano d'Abruzzo, Valpolicella.

Crudités
Light red or rosé (★→★★, no more): Côtes du Rhône, Minervois, Chianti, Okanagan Pinot Noir; or fino sherry. Or Alsace Sylvaner or Pinot Blanc.

Dim-Sum
Classically, China tea. For fun: **fried Dim-Sum:** Pinot Grigio or Riesling; **steamed:** light red (Bardolino or Beaujolais-Villages). Or NV Champagne with either (fried or steamed).

Eggs See also Soufflés.
These present difficulties: they clash with most wines and spoil good ones. But local wine with local egg dishes is a safe bet. So ★→★★ of whatever is going. Try Pinot Bl or straightforward not too oaky Chardonnay. As a last resort I can bring myself to drink Champagne with scrambled eggs.
Quail's eggs Blanc de Blancs Champagne.
Seagull's (or gull's) eggs Mature white burgundy or vintage Champagne.

Escargots
Rhône reds (Gigondas, Vacqueyras), or St-Véran or Aligoté. In the Midi, vg
Petits-Gris go with local white, rosé or red. In Alsace, Pinot Bl or Muscat.

Fish terrine
Pfalz Riesling Spätlese Trocken, Chablis Premier Cru, Washington Sém,
Clare Valley Ries, Sonoma Chard; or manzanilla.

Foie gras
White (★★★→★★★★). In Bordeaux they drink Sauternes. Others prefer
a late-harvest Pinot Gris, Riesling (incl New World), Vouvray, Montlouis,
Jurançon Moelleux or Gewürz. Tokay Aszú is the new Lucullan choice.
Old dry amontillado can be sublime. But not on any account Chard or
Sauv Bl.

Gazpacho
A glass of fino before and after. Or Sauvignon Bl.

Goat's cheese, grilled or fried (warm salad)
Sancerre, Pouilly-Fumé or New World Sauvignon Bl. Chilled Chinon or
Saumur-Champigny or Provence rosé. Or strong red: Château Musar,
Greek, Turkish, Australian sparkling Shiraz.

Gravlax
Akvavit or iced sake. Or Grand Cru Chablis, or ★★★ California, Washington
or Margaret River Chardonnay, or Mosel Spätlese (not Trocken).

Guacamole
California Chardonnay (★★), Riesling Kabinett, dry Muscat or NV
Champagne. Or Mexican beer.

Haddock, smoked, mousse of
A wonderful dish for showing off any stylish full-bodied white,
incl Grand Cru Chablis or Sonoma or NZ Chardonnay.

Ham, raw or cured See also Prosciutto.
Alsace Grand Cru Pinot Gris or good, crisp Italian Collio white, fino
sherry or tawny port.

Herrings, raw or pickled
Dutch gin (young, not aged) or Scandinavian akvavit, and cold beer.
If wine essential, try Muscadet.

Hors d'oeuvres See also Antipasto.
Clean, fruity, sharp white (★→★★): Sancerre or any Sauvignon Bl,
Grüner Veltliner, Hungarian Leanyka, Cape Steen, English white wine;
or young light red Bordeaux, Rhône or Corbières. Or fino sherry.

Houmous
Pungent, spicy dry white, eg Hungarian or Retsina.

Mackerel, smoked
An oily wine-destroyer. Manzanilla sherry, proper dry Vinho Verde or
Schnapps, peppered or bison-grass vodka. Or good lager.

Mayonnaise
Adds richness that calls for a contrasting bite in the wine.
Côte Chalonnaise whites (eg Rully) are good. Try NZ Sauvignon Bl,
Verdicchio or a Spätlese Trocken from the Pfalz.

Melon
Strong sweet wine (if any): port (★★), Bual Madeira, Muscat de
Frontignan or vin doux naturel; or dry, perfumed Viognier or
Australian Marsanne.

Minestrone
Red (★): Grignolino, Chianti, Zinfandel, Rhône Syrah, etc. Or fino.

Mushrooms à la Grecque
Greek Mantinia, any hefty dry white, or fresh young red.

Omelettes See Eggs.

Oyster stew
California, Long Island or S Australian ★★ Chardonnay.

Oysters
White (★★→★★★): NV Champagne, Chablis Premier Cru, Muscadet, white Graves, Sancerre or Guinness.

Pasta
Red or white (★→★★) according to the sauce or trimmings:
cream sauce Orvieto, Frascati, Alto Adige Chardonnay.
meat sauce Montepulciano d'Abruzzo, Salice Salentino, Merlot.
pesto (basil) sauce Barbera, Sicilian Torbato, Ligurian Vermentino, NZ Sauv Bl, Hungarian Hárslevelü or Furmint.
seafood sauce (eg vongole) Verdicchio, Soave, top white Rioja, Cirò, Sauv Bl.
tomato sauce Sauv Bl, Barbera, S Italian red, Zin, S Australian Grenache.

Pâté
According to constituents and quality:
chicken livers Call for pungent white (Alsace Pinot Gris or Marsanne), a smooth red like a light Pomerol or Volnay, or even amontillado sherry.
with simple pâté A dry white ★★: Good vin de pays, Graves, Fumé Blanc.
with duck pâté Ch'neuf-du-Pape, Cornas, Chianti Classico, Franciacorta.

Peperonata
Dry Australian Ries, W Australian Sem or NZ Sauv Bl. Tempranillo or Beaujolais.

Pipérade
Navarra rosado, Béarn or Irouléguy rosés. Or dry Australian Riesling.

Pimentos, roasted
NZ Sauvignon, Spanish Chardonnay, or Valdepeñas.

Pizza
Any dry Italian red ★★ or Rioja ★★, Australian Shiraz or California Sangiovese. Corbières, Coteaux d'Aix-en-Provence or red Bairrada.

Prawns or shrimps
Fine dry white (★★→★★★): burgundy, Graves, NZ Chard, Washington Riesling – even fine mature Champagne.
Indian-, Thai- or Chinese-style rich Australian Hunter Valley Chardonnay. ('Cocktail sauce' kills wine, and in time, people.)

Prosciutto (also with melon, pears or figs)
Full-bodied dry or medium white (★★→★★★): Orvieto, Gambellara, Pomino, Fendant or Grüner Veltliner, Tokay Furmint, white Rioja, Australian Sem or Jurançon Sec.

Quiches
Dry full-bodied white (★→★★★): Alsace, Graves, Sauv, dry Rheingau; or young red (Beauj-Villages, Chilean Pinot N), according to ingredients.

Ravioli See Pasta.
with wild mushrooms Dolcetto or Nebbiolo d'Alba, Oregon Pinot N, red Rioja crianza.

16

Saffron sauces (eg on fish)
Pungent or full-bodied white (esp Chardonnay, Jurançon sec, Rioja, Albariño) or Provence rosé.

Salade niçoise
Very dry, ★★, not too light or flowery white or rosé: Provençal, Rhône or Corsican; Catalan white; Fernão Pires, Sauv Bl or Hungarian dry white.

Salads
As a first course, especially with blue cheese dressing, any dry and appetizing white wine. After a main course: no wine.
NB Vinegar in salad dressings destroys the flavour of wine. If you want salad at a meal with fine wine, dress the salad with wine or a little lemon juice instead of vinegar.

Salami
Barbera, top Valpolicella, sparkling Freisa d'Asti, genuine Lambrusco, young Zinfandel, Tavel or Ajaccio rosé, Vacqueyras, young Bordeaux, Chilean Cab S or New World Gamay.

Salmon, smoked
A dry but pungent white: fino sherry, Alsace Pinot Gris, Chablis Grand Cru, Pouilly-Fumé, Pfalz Ries Spätlese, vintage Champagne. If you must have red try a lighter one such as Barbera. Vodka, schnapps or akvavit.

Seafood salad
Fresh N Italian Chard or Pinot Grigio. Australian Verdelho or Clare Ries.

Shark's fin soup
Add a teaspoon of Cognac. Sip amontillado.

Soufflés
As show dishes these deserve ★★→★★★ wines.
fish Dry white: ★★★ burgundy, Bordeaux, Alsace, Chardonnay, etc.
cheese ★★★ Red burgundy or Bordeaux, Cabernet Sauvignon, etc.
spinach (tougher on wine) Mâcon-Villages, St-Véran, Valpolicella.

Spinach
A challenge here. Can make reds taste of rust. Good Cabs usually survive.

Tapenade
Manzanilla or fino, or any sharpish dry white or rosé.

Taramasalata
A rustic southern white with personality; not necessarily Retsina. Fino sherry works well. Try white Rioja or a Rhône Marsanne. The bland supermarket version goes well with fine delicate whites or Champagne.

Terrine
As for pâté, or similar r: Mercurey, St-Amour or Beaujolais-Villages, youngish St-Emilion (★★), Calif Syrah, Sangiovese; Bulgarian or Chilean Cab.

Thai-style dishes (seasoned with lemon-grass, coconut milk, ginger, etc)
Pungent Sauv Bl eg Loire, Styrian, NZ or South African, or Riesling Spätlese (Pfalz or Austrian). Or Gewürz.

Tortilla
Rioja crianza, fino sherry or white Mâcon-Villages.

Trout, smoked
Sancerre, California or South African Sauvignon Bl. Rully or Bourgogne Aligoté, Chablis or Champagne.

Vegetable terrine
Not a great help to fine wine, but California, Chilean or South African Chardonnays make a fashionable marriage, Chenin Blanc such as Vouvray a lasting one.

Fish

Abalone
Dry or medium w (★★→★★★): Sauvignon Blanc, Côte de Beaune blanc, Pinot Grigio, Muscadet sur lie. Chinese style: vintage Champagne.

Anchovies
A robust wine: red, white or rosé – try Rioja. Or Muscadet.

Bass, striped or sea
Weissburgunder from Baden or Pfalz. Vg for any fine/delicate white, eg Coonawarra dry Riesling, Chablis, white Châteauneuf-du-Pape.

Beurre blanc, fish with
A top-notch Muscadet sur lie, a Sauvignon/Sémillon blend, Chablis Premier Cru, Vouvray or a Rheingau Charta wine.

Brandade
Chablis Premier Cru or Sancerre Rouge.

Bream (esp baked in a salt crust)
Full-bodied white or rosé; Rioja, Albariño, Costières de Nîmes, Côte de Luberon or Minervois

Carpaccio of salmon or tuna
See also First courses. Puligny-Montrachet, Condrieu, (★★★) California Chardonnay or NZ Sauvignon Blanc.

Cod
Good neutral background for fine dry/medium whites: ★★→★★★ Chablis, Meursault, Corton-Charlemagne, cru classé Graves, top Muscadet; German Kabinett or dry Spätlesen, or a good light red, eg Beaune.

Crab, cioppino
Sauvignon Blanc; but West Coast friends say Zinfandel. Also California sparkling wine.
cold, with salad Alsace or Rhine Riesling, dry California or Australian Riesling, or Viognier from Condrieu.
softshell ★★★ Chardonnay or top-quality German Riesling Spätlese.
Chinese, baked with ginger and onion
German Riesling Kabinett or Spätlese Halbtrocken. Tokay Furmint, Gewürz. with Black Bean sauce A big Barossa Shiraz or Syrah.

Eel, jellied
NV Champagne or a nice cup of (Ceylon) tea.
smoked Strong/sharp wine: fino sherry, Bourgogne Aligoté. Schnapps.

Fish and chips, fritto misto (or tempura)
Chablis, ★★ white Bordeaux, Sauv Bl, Pinot Blanc, Gavi, Fino, Montilla, Koshu, tea or NV Champagne.

Fish pie (with creamy sauce)
Albariño, Soave Classico, Pinot Gris d'Alsace.

Haddock
Rich dry white (★★→★★★): Meursault, California or NZ Chard, Marsanne or Albariño.

Hake
Sauv Bl or any freshly fruity white: Pacherenc, Tursan, white Navarra.

Herrings
Need a white with some acidity to cut their richness. Rully, Bourgogne
Aligoté, Gros Plant from Brittany, dry Sauvignon Bl. Or cider.

Kedgeree
Full white, still or sparkling: Mâcon-Villages, South African Chard
or (at breakfast) Champagne.

Kippers
A good cup of tea, preferably Ceylon (milk, no sugar). Scotch? Dry
oloroso sherry is surprisingly good.

Lamproie à la Bordelaise
5-yr-old St-Emilion or Fronsac: ★★→★★★. Or Esparão or Bairrada with
Portuguese lampreys.

Lobster, richly sauced
Vintage Champagne, fine white burgundy, cru classé Graves,
California Chard or Australian Ries, Pfalz Spätlese.
salad White (★★→★★★★): NV Champagne, Alsace Riesling,
Chablis Premier Cru, Condrieu, Mosel Spätlese, Penedès Chard or Cava.

Mackerel
Hard or sharp white (★★): Sauvignon Blanc from Touraine, Gaillac,
Gros Plant, Vinho Verde, white Rioja, English white wine. Or Guinness.

Monkfish
As for cod, but often elaborate recipes suggest fuller rather than
leaner wines. Try NZ Chard.

Mullet, red
A chameleon, adaptable to good white or red, esp Pinot Noir.

Mussels
Muscadet sur lie, Chablis Premier Cru, ★★★ Chardonnay.
stuffed, with garlic See Escargots.

Perch, Sandre
Exquisite fishes for finest wines: top white burgundy, Alsace Riesling
Grand Cru or noble Mosels. Or try top Swiss Fendant or Johannisberg.

Salmon, fresh
Fine white burgundy (★★★): Puligny- or Chassagne-Montrachet,
Meursault, Corton-Charlemagne, Chablis Grand Cru; Condrieu,
California, Idaho or NZ Chard, Rheingau Kabinett/Spätlese, Australian
Ries. Young Pinot N can be good, too – Merlot or light claret not bad.

Sardines, fresh grilled
Very dry white (★→★★): Vinho Verde, Soave, Muscadet, modern Greek.

Sashimi
If you are prepared to forego the wasabi, sp wines will go, or Washington
or Tasmanian Chard, Chablis Grand Cru, Rheingau Riesling Halbtrocken,
English Seyval Bl. Otherwise, iced sake, fino sherry or beer. Recent trials
have matched 5-putt Tokáji with fat tuna, sea urchin and anago (eel).

Scallops
An inherently slightly sweet dish, best with medium-dry whites.
in cream sauces German Spätlese (★★★) a -Montrachet or top
Australian Chardonnay.
grilled or fried Hermitage Blanc, Gewürztraminer, Grüner Veltliner,
★★ Entre-Deux-Mers, Australian Riesling or vintage Champagne.

Shad and shad roe
White Graves (★★→★★★), Meursault, Pomino, Vernaccia or
Hunter Semillon.

Shellfish
Dry (★★★) white with plain boiled shellfish, richer wines with richer
sauces. Crab and Riesling are part of the Creator's plan.

Shrimps, potted
Fino sherry, (★★★) Chablis, white Rioja or Long Island Chardonnay.

Skate with brown butter
White (★★) with some pungency (eg Pinot Gris d'Alsace), or a clean
straightforward one like Muscadet or Verdicchio.

Snapper
Sauvignon Blanc if cooked with oriental flavours, white Rhône with
Mediterranean flavours.

Sole, plaice, etc: plain, grilled or fried
Perfect with fine wines: ★★★→★★★★ white burgundy, or its equivalent.
with sauce Depending on the ingredients: sharp dry wine for tomato
sauce, fairly rich for sole véronique, etc.

Sushi
Hot wasabi is usually hidden in every piece. German QbA trocken wines
or simple Chablis or NV brut Champagne. Or, of course, sake or beer.

Swordfish
Full-bodied dry (★★) white of the country. Nothing grand.

Trout
Delicate white wine, eg ★★★ Mosel (esp Saar or Ruwer), Alsace Pinot Bl.
smoked See First Courses.

Tuna, grilled
White, red or rosé (★★) of fairly fruity character; a top St-Véran or
white Hermitage, or Côtes du Rhône would be fine. Pinot Noir and
Merlot are the best reds to try.

Turbot
Your best rich dry white: ★★★ Meursault or Chassagne-Montrachet,
mature Chablis or its California, Australian or NZ equivalent. Condrieu.
Mature Rheingau, Mosel or Nahe Spätlese or Auslese (not trocken).

Whitebait
Crisp dry whites: Muscadet, Touraine Sauvignon Bl, Verdicchio or
fino sherry.

Meat, poultry, etc

Barbecues
Red (★★) with a slight rasp, therefore young: Shiraz, Chianti, Navarra,
Zinfandel, Turkish Buzbag. Bandol for a real treat.

Beef, boiled
Red (★★): Bordeaux (Bourg or Fronsac), Roussillon, Australian Shiraz.
Gevrey-Chambertin, Côte-Rôtie. Or top-notch beer.
roast An ideal partner for fine red wine ★★→★★★★ of any kind.

Beef stew
Sturdy red (★★→★★★): Pomerol or St-Emilion, Hermitage, Cornas,
Barbera, Shiraz, Napa Cabernet, Torres Gran Coronas.

Beef Stroganoff
Dramatic red (★★→★★★): Barolo, Valpolicella Amarone, Cahors, Hermitage, late-harvest Zin – even Moldovan Negru de Purkar.

Boudin Blanc
Loire Chenin Bl (★★→★★★) esp when served with apples: dry Vouvray, Saumur, Savennières. Mature red Côtes de Beaune, if without apple.

Cabbage, stuffed
Hungarian Cab Franc/Kadarka; village Rhônes; Salice Salentino and other spicy S Italian reds. Or Argentine Malbec.

Cajun food
Fleurie, Brouilly or Sauv Bl. With gumbo: amontillado or Mexican beer.

Cassoulet
Red (★★) from SW France (Gaillac, Minervois, Corbières, St-Chinian or Fitou), or Shiraz. But best of all Beaujolais Cru or young red Navarra.

Chicken/turkey/guinea fowl, roast
Virtually any wine, incl very best bottles of dry/med white and finest old reds (esp burgundy). The meat of fowl can be adapted with sauces to match almost any fine wine (eg coq au vin with red or white burgundy). Try sparkling Shiraz with strong, sweet or spicy stuffings and trimmings. Avoid sauces which include tomato if you want to taste any good bottles.

Chicken casserole
Lirac, St-Joseph, or ★★ Bordeaux or Chilean Pinot Noir.
Kiev Alsace Riesling, Collio, Chardonnay, Bergerac Rouge.

Chilli con carne
Young red (★→★★): Gattinara, Beaujolais, Navarra, Zinfandel, Argentine Malbec.

Warning notice:
Tomatoes (with anything): the acidity of tomatoes is no friend to fine wines. Chefs should take note and not add them at random for a splash of colour. If they do Sauvignon Blanc is the white to try. For reds, try Chianti.

Chinese food, Canton or Peking style
Dry to med-dry white (★★→★★★) – Mosel Ries Kabinett or Spätlese trocken – can be good throughout a Chinese banquet. Gewürz, often suggested but rarely works yet Chasselas and Pinot Gris are attractive alternatives. Dry or off-dry sparkling (esp cava) cuts the oil and matches sweetness. Eschew sweet/sour dishes but try an 89/90 St-Emilion ★★ (or Le Pin?), New World Pinot N, or Châteauneuf-du-Pape with duck. I often serve both white and red wines concurrently during Chinese meals.
Szechuan style Muscadet, Alsace Pinot Blanc or v cold beer.

Choucroute garni
Alsace, Pinot Blanc, Pinot Gris or Riesling or beer.

Cold meats
Generally better with full-flavoured white than red. Mosel Spätlese or Hochheimer and Côte Chalonnaise are very good. And so is Beaujolais.

Confit d'oie/de canard
Young tannic red B'x Cru Bourgeois (★★→★★★) California Cab and Merlot, and Priorato help cut richness. Alsace Pinot Gris or Gewürz matches it.

Coq au vin
Red burgundy (★★→★★★★). In an ideal world, one bottle of Chambertin in the dish, two on the table.

Curry
Medium-sw w (★→★★), very cold: Orvieto abboccato, California Chenin Bl, Slovenian Traminer, Indian sp, cava and NV Champagne. Or emphasize the heat with a tannic Barolo or Barbaresco, or deep-flavoured reds such as Chât'neuf-du-Pape, Cornas, Shiraz-Cab or Valpolicella Amarone.

Duck or goose
Rather rich white (★★★): Pfalz Spätlese or Alsace réserve exceptionelle; or mature gamey red: Morey-St-Denis or Côte-Rôtie or ★★★ Bordeaux or burgundy. With oranges or peaches, the Sauternais propose drinking Sauternes, others Monbazillac or Riesling Auslese.
Peking See Chinese food.
wild duck Big-scale red (★★★): Hermitage, Bandol, California or S African Cab, Australian Shiraz – Grange if you can find it.
with olives Top-notch Chianti or Tuscan VdT.

Frankfurters
German (★→★★), NY Riesling, Beaujolais, light Pinot Noir. Or Budweiser.

Game birds, young birds plain-roasted
The best red wine you can afford.
older birds in casseroles ★★→★★★ Red (Gevrey-Chambertin, Pommard, Santenay or Grand Cru St-Emilion, Napa Valley Cabernet or Rhône).
well-hung game Vega Sicilia, great red Rhône, Château Musar.
cold game Mature vintage Champagne.

Game pie
hot Red (★★★): Oregon Pinot Noir.
cold Equivalent white or Champagne.

Goulash
Flavoursome young red (★★): Zinfandel, Bulgarian Cabernet or Mavrud, Hungarian Kadarka, young Australian Shiraz, Copertino.

Grouse See Game birds – but push the boat right out.

Haggis
Fruity red, eg young claret, New World Cabernet or Châteauneuf-du-Pape. Or of course malt whisky.

Ham
Softer red burgundies (★★→★★★): Volnay, Savigny, Beaune; Chinon or Bourgueil; slightly sweet German white (Rhine Spätlese); Czech Frankova; lightish Cabernet (eg Chilean), or California Pinot Noir. And don't forget the heaven-made match of ham and sherry.

Hamburger
Young red (★→★★): Beaujolais or Bulgarian Cabernet, Chianti, Zinfandel, Kadarka from Hungary. Or Coke or Pepsi (not 'Diet', but 'Max').

Hare
Jugged hare calls for ★★→★★★ flavourful red: not-too-old burgundy or Bordeaux, Rhône (eg Gigondas), Bandol, Barbaresco, Rib del Duero, Rioja reserva. The same for saddle. Australia's Grange would be an experience.

Kebabs
Vigorous red (★★): Greek Nemea or Naoussa, Turkish Buzbag, Corbières, Chilean Cabernet, Zinfandel or Barossa Shiraz.

Kidneys
Red (★★→★★★): St-Emilion or Fronsac: Nuits-St-Georges, Cornas, Barbaresco, Rioja, Spanish or Australian Cabernet, Portuguese Bairrada.

Lamb, cutlets or chops
As for roast lamb, but a little less grand.
roast One of the traditional and best partners for very good red Bordeaux – or its Cabernet equivalents from the New World. In Spain, the partner of the finest old Rioja and Ribera del Duero reservas.

Liver
Young red (★★): Beaujolais-Villages, St-Joseph, Médoc, Italian Merlot, Breganze Cabernet, Zinfandel, Portuguese Bairrada.
Calf's Red Rioja crianza, Salice Salentino Riserva, Fleurie.

Meatballs
Tangy medium-bodied red (★★→★★★): Mercurey, Crozes-Hermitage, Madiran, Rubesco, Dão, Zinfandel or Cabernet.
Spicy Indian-style Dry Muscat; even Viognier.

Moussaka
Red or rosé (★→★★): Naoussa from Greece, Chianti, Corbières, Côtes de Provence, Ajaccio or Patrimonio, Chilean Pinot Noir.

Osso buco
Low tannin, supple red, eg Dolcetto d'Alba or Pinot Noir.

Oxtail
Rather rich red (★★→★★★): St-Emilion, Pomerol, Pommard, Nuits-St-Georges, Barolo or Rioja reserva, California or Coonawarra Cabernet, Châteauneuf-du-Pape; or a dry Rheingau Riesling Spätlese.

Paella
Young Spanish red (★★), dry white or rosé: Penedès, Somontano, Navarra or Rioja.

Pigeons
Lively reds (★★→★★★): Savigny, Chambolle-Musigny; Crozes-Hermitage, Chianti Classico or California Pinot. Or try Franken Silvaner Spätlese.

Pork, roast
A good rich neutral background to a fairly light red or rich white. It deserves ★★★ treatment – Médoc is fine. Portugal's famous sucking pig is eaten with Bairrada garrafeira, Chinese is good with Pinot Noir.

Pot au feu, bollito misto, cocido
Rustic red wines from the region of origin; Sangiovese di Romagna, Chusclan, Lirac, Rasteau, Portuguese Alentejo and Yecla and Jumilla from Spain.

Quail As for squab. Carmignano, Rioja Reserva, mature claret, Pinot N.

Rabbit
Lively medium-bodied young Italian red (★→★★★) or Aglianico del Vulture or Chiroubles, Chinon, Saumur-Champigny or Rhône rosé.

Risotto
Pinot Gr from Friuli, Gavi, youngish Sém, Dolcetto or Barbera d'Alba.
with mushrooms Cahors, Madiran, Barbera.
with fungi porcini Finest mature Barolo or Barbaresco.

Satay
Australia's McLaren Vale Shiraz or Alsace or NZ Gewürztraminer.

Sauerkraut
Lager or stout. (But see also Choucroute garni.)

Sausages See also Frankfurters, Salami.
The British banger requires a young Malbec from Argentina (or a red wine, anyway).

Shepherd's pie
Rough-and-ready red (★→★★) seems most appropriate, eg Barbera, but beer or dry cider is the real McCoy.

Squab
Fine white or red Burgundy, Alsace Riesling Grand Cru or mature claret.

Steak, au poivre
A fairly young ★★★ Rhône red or Cabernet.
tartare Vodka or ★★ light young red: Beaujolais, Bergerac, Valpolicella.
Korean Yuk Whe (the world's best steak tartare) Sake.
filet or tournedos Any ★★★ red (but not old wines with béarnaise sauce).
T-bone Reds of similar bone structure (★★→★★★): Barolo, Hermitage, Australian Cabernet or Shiraz.
fiorentina (bistecca) Chianti Classico Riserva or Brunello.

Steak and kidney pie or pudding
Red Rioja reserva Dão or Bairrada or mature ★★→★★★ Bordeaux.

Stews and casseroles
★★★ Burgundy such as Chambolle-Musigny or Bonnes-Mares if fairly simple; otherwise lusty full-flavoured red: young Côtes du Rhône, Toro, Corbières, Barbera, Shiraz, Zinfandel, etc.

Sweetbreads
A grand dish, so grand wine: Rhine Riesling (★★★) or Franken Silvaner Spätlese, Alsace Grand Cru Pinot Gris or Condrieu, depending on sauce.

Tandoori chicken
Sauvignon Blanc, or young ★★ red Bordeaux or light N Italian red served cool. Also cava and NV Champagne.

Thai food
Ginger and lemongrass call for Sauvignon Bl or Australian Riesling.
coconut curries Hunter Valley and other ripe, oaked Chards; Alsace Pinot Bl for refreshment. And of course cava or NV Champagne.

Tongue
Good for any red or white of abundant character, esp Italian. Also Beaujolais, Loire reds and full dry rosés.

Tripe
Red (★→★★), eg Corbières, Roussillon or rather sweet white (eg German Spätlese). Better: W Australian Sem-Chard, or cut with pungent dry white such as Pouilly-Fumé or fresh red eg Saumur-Champigny.

Veal, roast
A good neutral background dish for any fine old red which may have faded with age (eg a Rioja reserva) or a ★★★ German or Austrian Riesling or Vouvray or Alsace Pinot Gris.

Venison
Big-scale red (★★★) incl Mourvèdre (Mataro) solo as in Bandol, or in blends, Rhône, Bordeaux or California Cab of a mature vintage; or rather rich white (Pfalz Spätlese or Alsace Pinot Gr).

Vitello tonnato
Full-bodied white esp Chard; light red (eg Valpolicella) served cool.

> **Urgent notice: sherry, port, Madeira and food**
> By a quirk of fashion, the wines of Jerez, Madeira and to some
> extent the ports of the Douro Valley are currently being left on the
> sidelines by a world increasingly hypnotized by a limited range of
> 'varietal' wines. Yet these regions include wines of every quality of
> 'greatness', and far more gastronomic possibilities than anyone
> seems to remember. It is notorious that for the price of a bottle of
> top white burgundy you can buy three of the finest fino sherry,
> which with many dishes will make an equally exciting partner.
> Mature Madeiras give the most lingering farewell of any wine to a
> splendid dinner. Tawny port is a wine of many uses, especially
> wonderful at sea. Perhaps it is because the New World cannot rival
> these Old World classics that they are left out of the headlines.

Vegetarian dishes

Baked pasta dishes
Pasticcio, lasagne and canneloni with elaborate vegetarian fillings and
sauces: an occasion to show of a grand wine esp finest Tuscan vdt, but
also ★★★ Claret and Burgundy. Also Gavi and vintage Tunina from Italy.

Bean and vegetable stew with herb dumplings
Bairrada from Portugal, Toro from Spain.

Bubble-and-squeak
Beer, stout, or Beaujolais Nouveau.

Cauliflower cheese with gratin topping
Crisp aromatic white: Sancerre, Riesling Spätlese, Muscat, English
Seyval Blanc or Schönburger

Couscous with spiced vegetables
Young red with a bite: Shiraz, Corbières, Minervois or well chilled rosé
from Navarra or Somontano.

Fennel-based dishes
Sauv Bl: Pouilly-Fumé or one from NZ; English Schönburger or Seyval
Blanc or a Beaujolais.

Grilled Mediterranean vegetables
Brouilly, Barbera or Cab-Shiraz.

Kidney bean and roast vegetable salad
Red Rioja reserva, New World Merlot, Provence red such as Bandol.

'Meaty' aubergine, lentil or mushroom bakes
Corbières, Zinfandel, Shiraz-Cabernet.

Mezze
Hot and cold vegetable dishes. Cava is a good all-purpose choice as is
rosé from Languedoc or Provence.

Mushrooms (in most contexts)
Fleshy red; eg ★★★ Pomerol, California Merlot, Rioja reserva or Vega Sicilia.
on toast Your best claret.
wild mushroom risotto (ceps are best for wine) Ribera del Duero,
Barolo or Chianti Rufina, or top claret: Pauillac or St-Estèphe.

Onion/leek tart
Fruity off-dry or dry white (★→★★★): Alsace Pinot Gr or Gewürz,
Canadian Riesling, English Whites, Jurançon, Australian Ries. Or
Beaujolais or Loire red.

Peppers or aubergines (eggplant), stuffed
Vigorous red wine(★★): Nemea, Italian Chianti or Dolcetto, California Zinfandel, Bandol, Vacqueyras.

Pumpkin/Squash ravioli or risotto
Full-bodied fruity dry or off-dry white: white Rhône (Viognier or Marsanne); demi-sec Vouvray, Gavi, Pomino or South African Chenin.

Ratatouille
Vigorous young red (★★): Chianti, Bulgarian Cabernet or Merlot; young red Bordeaux or Gigondas or Coteaux du Languedoc.

Spinach, ricotta and pasta bake
Valpolicella (its bitterness helps); Greco di Molise, or w Sicilian/Sardinian.

Desserts

Apple pie, strudel or Tarte Tatin
Sweet (★★→★★★) German, Austrian, Loire white, Tokáji Aszú or Canadian Ice Wine.

Apples, Cox's Orange Pippins
Vintage port (55 60 63 66 70 75 82).

Bread and butter pudding
Fine 10-yr-old Barsac, Tokáji Azsú or Australian botrytised Sem.

Cakes and gâteaux see also Chocolate, Coffee, Ginger, Rum
Bual or Malmsey Madeira, oloroso or cream sherry.

Cheesecake
Sweet white: Vouvray or Anjou or fizz, refreshing but nothing special.

Chocolate flavours
Generally only powerful flavours can compete. Bual, California orange Muscat, Tokay Azsú, Australian liqueur Muscat, 10-yr-old tawny port; Asti for light, fluffy mousses. Experiment with rich, ripe reds: Syrah, Zinfandel even sparkling Shiraz. Banyuls for a weightier partnership. Or a tot of good rum.

Christmas pudding, mince pies
Tawny port, cream sherry, or liquid Christmas pudding itself, Pedro Ximénez sherry. Asti or Banyuls.

Coffee flavours
Sweet Muscat incl Australia liqueur Muscats or Tokáji Aszú.

Creams, custards, fools, syllabubs see also Chocolate, Coffee, Ginger, Rum
Sauternes, Loupiac, Ste-Croix-du-Mont, Monbazillac.

Crème brûlée
★★★→★★ Sauternes or Rhine Beerenauslese, best Madeira or Tokáji. (With concealed fruit, a more modest sweet wine.)

Crêpes Suzette
Sweet Champagne, Orange Muscat or Asti spumante.

Fruit
fresh Sweet Coteaux du Layon, light sweet or liqueur Muscat.
stewed, ie apricots, pears, etc Sweet Muscatel: try Muscat de Beaumes-de-Venise, Moscato di Pantelleria or Spanish dessert Tarragona.
dried fruit (and compotes) Banyuls, Rivesaltes, Maury.
flans and tarts Sauternes, Monbazillac or sweet Vouvray or Anjou: ★★★.

salads, orange salad
A fine sweet sherry, or any Muscat-based wine.

Ginger flavours
Sweet Muscats, New World botrytised Riesling and Semillon.

Ice-cream and sorbet
Fortified wine (Australian liqueur Muscat, Banyuls); sweet Asti spumante or sparkling Moscato. Amaretto liqueur with vanilla; rum with chocolate.

Meringues
Recioto di Soave, Asti or Champagne doux.

Mille feuille
Delicate sweet sparkling white, eg Moscato d'Asti, demi-sec Champagne.

Nuts
Finest oloroso sherry, Madeira, vintage or tawny port (nature's match for walnuts), Vin Santo, Setúbal Moscatel.

Orange flavours
Experiment with old Sauternes, Tokáji Aszú or California Orange Muscat.

Panettone
Jurançon moelleux, late-harvest Riesling, Barsac, Tokáji Aszú.

Pears in red wine
A pause before the port. Or try Rivesaltes, Banyuls or Ries Beerenauslese.

Pecan pie
Orange Muscat or liqueur Muscat.

Raspberries (no cream, little sugar)
Excellent with fine reds that themselves taste of raspberries: young Juliénas, Regnié.

Rum flavours (baba, mousses, ice-cream)
Muscat – from Asti to Australian liqueur, according to weight of dish.

Strawberries, wild (no cream)
Serve with ★★★ red Bordeaux (most exquisitely Margaux) poured over.

Strawberries and cream
Sauternes (★★★) or similar sweet Bordeaux, Vouvray Moelleux (90) or Jurançon Vendange Tardive.

Summer pudding
Fairly young Sauternes of a good vintage (83 85 86 88 89 90).

Sweet soufflés
Sauternes or Vouvray moelleux. Sweet (or rich) Champagne.

Tiramisú
Vin Santo, young tawny port, Beaumes-de-Venise or Sauternes and Australian liqueur muscats.

Trifle
Should be sufficiently vibrant with its internal sherry.

Zabaglione
Light-gold Marsala or Australian botrytised Semillon or Asti.

Wine & cheese

The notion that wine and cheese were married in heaven is not born out by experience. Fine red wines are slaughtered by strong cheeses: only sharp or sweet white wines survive.

Principles to remember, despite exceptions, are first: the harder the cheese the more tannin the wine can have. And the creamier it is the more acidity is needed in the wine. The main exception constitutes a third principle: wines and cheeses of a region usually sympathize.

Cheese is classified by its texture and the nature of its rind, so its appearance is a guide to the type of wine to match it. Individual cheeses mentioned below are only examples taken from the hundreds sold in good cheese shops.

Fresh, no rind – cream cheese, crème fraîche, Mozzarella
Light crisp white – Côtes de Duras, Bergerac, Vinho Verde, English unoaked whites; or pink – Anjou, Rhône; or very light, v young, v fresh red Bordeaux, Bardolino or Beaujolais.

Hard cheeses, waxed or oiled, often showing marks from cheesecloth – Gruyère family, Manchego and other Spanish cheeses, Parmesan, Cantal, Comté, old Gouda, Cheddar and most 'traditional' English cheeses
Particularly hard to generalize here; Gouda, Gruyère, some Spanish and a few English cheeses complement fine claret or Cab and great Shiraz/Syrah wines, but strong cheeses need less refined wines, preferably local. Sugary, granular old Dutch red Mimolette or Beaufort are good for finest mature Bordeaux. Also for Tokáji Aszú.

Blue cheeses
Roquefort can be wonderful with Sauternes, but don't extend the idea to other blues. It is the sweetness of Sauternes, especially old, which complements the saltiness. Stilton and port, preferably tawny, is a classic. Intensely flavoured old oloroso, amontillado, Madeira, Marsala and other fortified wines go with most blues.

Natural rind (mostly goat's cheese) with bluish-grey mould (the rind becomes wrinkled when mature), s'times dusted with ash – St-Marcellin Sancerre, Valençay, light fresh Sauvignon, Jurançon, Savoie, Soave, Italian Chard, lightly oaked English whites.

Bloomy rind soft cheeses, pure white rind if pasteurized, or dotted with red: Brie, Camembert, Chaource, Bougon (goat's milk 'Camembert') Full dry white burgundy or Rhône if cheese is white, immature; powerful, fruity St-Emilion, E European Pinot, young Australian (or Rhône) Shiraz/ Syrah if mature.

Washed-rind soft cheeses, with rather sticky orange-red rind – Langres, mature Epoisses, Maroilles, Carré de l'Est, Milleens, Munster Local reds, especially for Burgundy cheeses; vigorous Languedoc, Cahors, Côtes du Frontonnais, Corsican, southern Italian, Sicilian, Bairrada. Also powerful whites, esp Alsace Gewurztraminer and Muscat.

Semi-soft cheeses, grey-pink thickish rind – Livarot, Pont l'Evêque, Reblochon, Tomme de Savoie, St-Nectaire
Powerful w Bordeaux, Chard, Alsace Pinot G, dryish Riesling, southern Italian and Sicilian w, aged w Rioja, dry oloroso sherry. But the strongest of these cheeses kill most wines.

Food & finest wine

With very special bottles, the wine sometimes guides the choice of food rather than the usual way around. The following suggestions are based largely on the gastronomic conventions of the wine regions producing these treasures, plus much diligent research. They should help bring out the best in your best wines.

Red wines

Red Bordeaux
and other Cabernet Sauvignon-based wines
(very old, light and delicate: eg pre-59, with exceptions such as 45)
Leg or rack of young lamb, roast with a hint of herbs (but not garlic); entrecôte; roast partridge or grouse, sweetbreads; or cheese soufflé after the meat has been served.

Fully mature great vintages (eg Bordeaux 59 61)
Shoulder or saddle of lamb, roast with a touch of garlic, roast ribs or grilled rump of beef.

Mature but still vigorous (eg 82 70 66)
Shoulder or saddle of lamb (incl kidneys) with rich sauce, eg béarnaise. Fillet of beef marchand de vin (with wine and bone-marrow). Avoid Beef Wellington: pastry dulls the palate.

Merlot-based Bordeaux (Pomerol, St-Emilion)
Beef as above (fillet is richest) or venison.

Côte d'Or red burgundy
(Consider the weight and texture, which grow lighter/more velvety with age. Also the character of the wine: Nuits is earthy, Musigny flowery, great Romanées can be exotic, Pommard renowned for its four-squareness, etc.) Roast chicken, or better, capon, is a safe standard with red burgundy; guinea-fowl for slightly stronger wines, then partridge, grouse or woodcock for those progressively more rich and pungent. Hare and venison (chevreuil) are alternatives.

Great old reds
The classic Burgundian formula is cheese: Epoisses (unfermented). A fabulous cheese but a terrible waste of fine old wines.

Vigorous younger burgundy
Duck or goose roasted to minimize fat.

Great Syrahs: Hermitage, Côte-Rôtie, Grange; or Vega Sicilia
Beef, venison, well-hung game; bone-marrow on toast; English cheese (esp best farm Cheddar) but also the newer hard goat's milk and ewe's milk cheese such as Berkswell and Ticklemore.

Rioja Gran Reserva, Pesquera...
Richly flavoured roasts: wild boar, mutton, saddle of hare, whole suckling pig.

Barolo, Barbaresco
Cheese risotto with white truffles; pasta with game sauce (eg pappardelle alle lepre); porcini mushrooms; Parmesan.

White wines

Very good Chablis, white burgundy, other top quality Chardonnays
White fish simply grilled or meunière with Doria garnish of sautéed cucumber. Dover sole, turbot, Rex sole are best. (Sea-bass is too delicate; salmon passes but does little for the finest wine.)

Supreme white burgundy (Le Montrachet, Corton-Charlemagne) or equivalent Graves
Roast veal, organic chicken stuffed with truffles or herbs under the skin, or sweetbreads; richly sauced white fish or scallops as above. Or lobster or wild salmon.

Condrieu, Château-Grillet or Hermitage Blanc
Very light pasta scented with h erbs and tiny peas or broad beans.

Grand Cru Alsace, Riesling
Truite au bleu, smoked salmon or choucroute garni.
Pinot Gris Roast or grilled veal.
Gewurztraminer Cheese soufflé (Munster cheese).
Vendange Tardive Foie gras or Tarte Tatin.

Sauternes
Simple crisp buttery biscuits (eg Langue-de-Chat), white peaches, nectarines, strawberries (without cream). Not tropical fruit. Pan-fried foie-gras. Experiment with cheeses.

Supreme Vouvray moelleux, etc
Buttery biscuits, apples, apple tart.

Beerenauslese/TBA
Biscuits, peaches, greengages. Desserts made from rhubarb, gooseberries, quince or apples.

Tokay Aszú (4–6 putts)
Foie gras is thoroughly recommended. Fruit desserts, cream desserts, even chocolate can be wonderful.

Finest old amontillado/oloroso
Pecans.

Great vintage port or Madeira
Walnuts or pecans. A Cox's Orange Pippin and a digestive biscuit is a classic English accompaniment.

Old vintage Champagne (not Blanc de Blancs)
As an aperitif, or with cold partridge, grouse or woodcock.

The 1998 vintage

Eccentric weather is a well-worn excuse for all sorts of anomalies, but in 1998 it was the rule rather than the exception. Floods, gales and heatwaves were all put down to El Niño. Everyone had a story to tell.

Those who were in northern Europe in August all tell the same one: a mid-month scorcher, temperatures over 40°C for several days; enough to grill grapes exposed to the sun. The weather before and after was on the whole cool-to-medium, and rain arrived in mid-vintage over the northern half of France and Germany. But the August heat had already resulted in thick-skinned grapes boosted towards ripeness. Nobody was to have a bad vintage, and with luck and skill many excellent wines were made almost everywhere.

In Bordeaux Merlot had the advantage: St-Emilion and Pomerol produced some of their best wines for years; even great ones. In the Médoc Cabernet picked after rain was tricky, but on the whole (and with new techniques for getting rid of surplus liquid), certainly better than 1997. A good year. The Graves, with more Merlot, did well – and so did many in Sauternes.

Grilling, then soaking, is not ideal treatment for Pinot Noir either. A fine spell in mid-September allowed a dry Burgundy harvest, certainly of good wines, if not great. A fairly good, if facile vintage in Chablis (hail fell on the Grands Crus in May).

The Midi, the southern Rhône and Provence had a splendid vintage; the northern Rhône a good (but small) one. In the Loire there is excellent Muscadet and good Sancerre, but Anjou and Touraine broke their exceptional run of luck. Alsace had a fine vintage, with Gewurztraminer in particular plentiful and ripe. Champagne made large quantities, at least some of it good enough to produce vintage bottles.

Italy also felt the August heat, then the north had rain, the south drought. Tuscany in the middle probably did best, though reports from Piedmont to Friuli are good, and the newly ambitious Mezzogiorno has some concentrated wines.

Spain felt the August heat, too. Here the east was spared harvest rain, while Rioja and points west felt more of the El Niño effect (which deprived Portugal of half its crop). Rain also plagued the Germans, Austrians and Hungarians at vintage time. Everyone was surprised at how ripe Riesling was, and how much top-quality wine emerged.

California knew all about El Niño, from floods in winter and spring to vintage rain which stretched out the harvest to its longest ever, finishing in mid-November. They argue that long 'hang-time' produces finer flavours; we shall see. There is no doubt about the northwest, though: Washington had its biggest and best vintage ever and Oregon had a good small one.

Chile and Argentina, closest to El Niño, were wet – Mendoza almost drowned. Australia was, in general, moderately cool, with fine results. New Zealand, by contrast, was uncharacteristically hot and dry and may have made its best reds yet...

France

Heavier shaded areas are the
wine growing regions

The following abbreviations
of regional names
are used in the text:

Al	Alsace
Beauj	Beaujolais
Burg	Burgundy
B'x	Bordeaux
Champ	Champagne
Lo	Loire
Prov	Provence
Pyr	Pyrenees
N/S Rh	North/South Rhône
SW	Southwest

Le Havre○

Caen ○

○Brest

LOIRE

Loire

Nantes
○
Muscadet

Anjou-
Saumur

○ La Rochelle

BORDEAU

Médoc

Bordeaux○

Pomerol
St-Emilic

Entre-
Deux-

Graves

Sauternes

Buz

Côtes du
Marmandais

Côtes c
St-Mo

Tursan

Madira
○
Biarritz

Jurançon

Will the 21st Century take the crown from France? In the
19th and 20th Centuries she set the standards by which
all the world's best wines are judged. At a humble level, too,
whether with simple varietal wines or the renaissance of almost-
forgotten local specialities, France has little to learn. But as more
and more countries and regions raise their game her age-old
complacency has been shaken.

Unless the _fonctionnaires_ who run the system of Appellations
Contrôlées abandon nit-picking restrictions and apply their minds
to quality, the danger of fossilization combined with
commercialization is a sombre prospect. The French genius for
taste and style is on trial.

Appellations remain the key to French wine. An appellation
defines a type. It may apply to a single small vineyard or to a large
district. Burgundy, on the whole, has the most precise and smallest

appellations, Bordeaux the widest and most general. An appellation is the first thing to look for on a label. But more important is the name of the maker. The best growers' and merchants' names are a vital ingredient of these pages. Regions without the overall quality and traditions required for an appellation can be ranked as vins délimités de qualité supérieure (VDQS), a shrinking category as its members gain AC status. Their place is being taken by the relatively new and highly successful vins de pays. Vins de pays are almost always worth trying. They include some brilliant originals and often offer France's best value for money – which still (and especially since the 'franc fort' disappeared) means the world's.

Recent vintages of the French classics

Red Bordeaux

Médoc/red Graves For some wines bottle-age is optional: for these it is indispensable. Minor châteaux from light vintages need only 2 or 3 yrs, but even modest wines of great years can improve for 15 or so, and the great châteaux of these years need double that time.

1998 Rain at vintage *again*. But August heat ripened (even roasted) grapes. Good to very good.

1997 Uneven flowering and summer rain were a double challenge. Cabernet Sauvignon ripened best. Some good wines for the canny.

1996 Cool summer, fine harvest, esp Cabernet. Good to excellent. Now–2020.

1995 Heatwave and drought; saved by rain. Good to excellent. Now–2020+.

1994 Hopes of a supreme year; then heavy vintage rain. The best very good, but be careful. Now–2010.

1993 Ripe grapes but a wet vintage. Tannic wines; maybe too tannic. Now–2015.

1992 Rain at flowering, in August and at vintage. A huge crop; light wines, but some easy drinking. Now–2005.

1991 Frost in April halved crop and rain interrupted vintage. The northern Médoc did best. Drink soon. Now–2010?

1990 A paradox: a drought year with a threat of over-production. Self-discipline was essential. Its results are magnificent. To 2020+.

1989 Early spring and splendid summer. The top wines will be classics of the ripe dark kind with elegance and length. Small ch'x are uneven. To 2020.

1988 Generally very good; tannic, balanced, beginning to open, but keep top wines. To 2020.

1987 Much more enjoyable than seemed likely. Drink up.

1986 Another splendid, huge, heatwave harvest. Better than 85 in Pauillac and St-Julien; a long-term prospect. Now–2020.

1985 Vg vintage, in a heatwave. V fine wines now accessible. Now–2010.

1984 Poor. Originally overpriced. Avoid.

1983 A classic vintage, esp in Margaux: abundant tannin with fruit to balance it. But many wines need drinking. To 2010?

1982 Made in a heatwave. Huge, rich, strong wines which promise a long life but are developing unevenly. Top châteaux will run to 2015.

1981 Admirable despite rain. Not rich, but balanced and fine. Now–2005.

1980 Small late harvest: ripe but rained-on. Drink up.

1979 Abundant harvest of above average quality. Drink soonish.

1978 A miracle vintage: magnificent long warm autumn. Now at full stretch.

1976 Hot, dry summer; rain just before vintage. The best vg; all now ready.

1975 V fine vintage but excess of tannin is *still* the problem. Time to drink.

1970 Big, excellent vintage with scarcely a failure. Now–2010+.

Older fine vintages: 66 62 61 59 55 53 52 50 49 48 47 45 29 28.

St-Emilion/Pomerol

1998 Merlot, earlier ripening than Cabernet, largely escaped the rain. Some excellent wines.

1997 The Merlot vintage suffered in the rain. But growers are getting better at handling problems. Good for supple wines. Now–2010.

1996 Cool fine summer, vintage rain on Merlot. Less consistent than Médoc. Now–2020.

1995 Perhaps even better than Médoc/Graves. Now–2015.

1994 Less compromised by rain than Médoc. Vg, esp Pomerol. Now–2015.

1993 As in the Médoc, but generally better, esp in Pomerol; good despite terrible vintage weather.

1992 Very dilute but some charming wines to drink quickly. Drink up.

1991 A sad story. Many wines not released.

1990 Another chance to make great wine or a lot of wine. Now–2020.

1989 Large, ripe, early harvest; an overall triumph. To 2020.

1988 Generally excellent; ideal conditions. But some châteaux over-produced. Pomerol best. Now–2005.

1987 Some v adequate wines (esp in Pomerol). Drink soon.

1986 A prolific vintage; but top St-Emilions have long life ahead.

1985 One of the great yrs, with a long future. To 2010+.

1984 A sad story. Most of the crop wiped out in spring. Avoid.

1983 Less impressive than it seemed. Drink soon.

1982 Enormously rich and concentrated wines, most excellent. Now–2005.

1981 A vg vintage, if not as great as it first seemed. Now or soon.

1979 A rival to 78, but not developing as well as hoped. Now or soon.

1978 Fine wines, but some lack flesh. Drink soon.

1976 V hot, dry summer, but vintage rain. Some excellent. Drink soon.

1975 Most St-Ems gd, the best: superb. Pomerol splendid. Drink now or soon.

1971 On the whole better than Médocs, but now ready.

1970 Beautiful wines with great fruit and strength. V big crop. Now.

Older fine vintages: 67 66 64 61 59 53 52 49 47 45.

Red burgundy

Côte d'Or Côte de Beaune reds generally mature sooner than the bigger wines of the Côte de Nuits. Earliest drinking dates are for lighter commune wines, eg Volnay, Beaune; latest for the biggest wines of eg Chambertin, Romanée. But even the best burgundies are much more attractive young than the equivalent red Bordeaux.

1998 Wet September had a diluting/softening effect on a v ripe harvest. Not for very long keeping.

1997 Again the gods smiled. Very ripe grapes, with low acidity the main potential problem. Lovely wines for medium term, to 2010+.

1996 Fine summer and vintage. Superb ripe wines for keeping. 2002–2020.

1995 Small, excellent crop, despite vintage rains. Grapes were very ripe.

1994 Ripe grapes compromised by vintage rain. Côte de Nuits better. Generally lean, but exceptions in Côte de Nuits. Now–2005.

1993 An excellent vintage – concentrated. Now–2010.

1992 Ripe, plump, pleasing. No great concentration. Now–2005.

1991 Very small harvest; some wines v tannic. Côte de Nuits best. Now–2010.

1990 Great vintage: perfect weather compromised only by touches of drought and some over-production. Long life ahead but start to enjoy. To 2020.

1989 A year of great charm, not necessarily for very long maturing, but will age. Now–2015.

1988 Very good but tannic. Now–2020 (but only the best).

1987 Small crop with ripe fruit flavours, esp in Côte de Beaune. Now–2005.

1986 Aromatic but rather dry wines: generally lack flesh. Drink up.

1985 At best a great vintage. Concentrated wines are splendid. Now–2010.

1984 Lacks natural ripeness; tends to be dry and/or watery. Now – if at all.

1983 Powerful, vigorous, tannic and attractive vintage dreadfully compromised by rot. Be very careful. Now–2005.

1982 Big vintage, pale but round and charming. Côte de Beaune best. Drink up.

1978 A small vintage of outstanding quality. The best will live to 2005+.

Older fine vintages: 71 69 66 64 62 61 59 (all mature).

White burgundy

Côte de Beaune Well-made wines of good vintages with plenty of acidity as well as fruit will improve and gain depth and richness for some years – anything up to 10. Lesser wines from lighter vintages are ready for drinking after 2 or 3 years.

1998 Whites more successful than reds: some rich and potent wines (again).
1997 Overall excellent: it will be a joy to develop these alongside 96 and 95.
1996 A great vintage to lay down. Now–2020.
1995 A potentially great vintage, diluted in places. Now–2015.
1994 Patchy; top growers made v fine potent wines – but not for long keeping. Now or soon.
1993 September rain on ripe grapes. Easy wines, pleasant young but far behind reds. Soon.
1992 Ripe, aromatic and charming. Mostly ready. Now–2010.
1991 Mostly lack substance. Frost problems. For early drinking. Now.
1990 Very good, even great, but with a tendency to fatness. Now–2005.
1989 At best ripe, tense, structured and long. Now–2010.
1988 Extremely good, some great wines but others rather dilute. Drink soon.
1987 V disappointing, though a few exceptions emerged. Avoid.
1986 Powerful wines; most with better acidity/balance than 85. Now or soon.
1985 V ripe; those that still have balance have aged v well. Soon.

The white wines of the Mâconnais (Pouilly-Fuissé, St-Véran, Mâcon-Villages) follow a similar pattern, but do not last as long. They are more appreciated for their freshness than their richness.

Chablis Grand Cru Chablis of vintages with both strength and acidity can age superbly for up to 10 years; Premiers Crus proportionately less.

1998 Cool weather and some hail. Wines fair but lack acidity: not for keeping.
1997 Another fine vintage; perhaps drink before the 96 vintage.
1996 Ideal harvest but hail on top v'yds. Classic keeping Chablis. Now–2015.
1995 Very good to very very good. Now–2010.
1994 Downpours on a ripe vintage. Easy wines; drink up.
1993 Fair to good quality; nothing great. Soon.
1992 Ripe and charming wines. Grands Crus splendid. Now–2005 at least.
1991 Generally better than Côte d'Or. Useful wines. Now.
1990 Grands Crus will be magnificent; other wines may lack intensity and acidity. Now–2005.
1989 Excellent vintage of potent character. Soon.
1988 Almost a model: great pleasure now. Soon.

Beaujolais 98: v gd, if patchy. Best Crus will keep. 97: excellent and will keep. 96: v satisfactory, but not for keeping. 95: excellent. 94 vg; drink. 93: Fine Crus to drink up. 90: drink up. Older wines should be finished.

Alsace 98 good despite heatwaves and rain early on during harvest; much more Gewurz than previous years. 97 superlative vintage. Concentrated dry wines and marvellous VT and SGN. 96 excellent for dry wines, but not much Gewurz. 95 gd wines from those who harvested late, esp Riesling. 94 some variation between growers but generally gd. 93 very gd and fruity, smaller harvest. 92 reasonably gd; matured quickly. 91 respectable. 90 outstanding esp for Riesling. 89 and 88 both made wines of top quality. 87s and 86s finished. 85s drink up.

Abel-Lepitre Brut NV; Brut 85 88 90; Cuvée 134 BL DE BLANCS NV; Réserve BL DE BLANCS CUVEE 'C' 85 88 90; Rosé 88 90 Middle-rank CHAMP house.

Abymes Savoie w ★ DYA Hilly little area nr Chambéry; light mild Vin de Savoie AC from the Jacquère grape has alpine charm. SAVOIE has a score of such local crus for local pleasure.

Ackerman-Laurance Classic-method sparkling house of the Loire, oldest in SAUMUR. Improving still wines under guidance of Jacques Lurton.

Agenais SW France r p (w) ★ DYA VDP of Lot-et-Garonne, mostly from coops at Goulens, Donzac, Monflanquin and Mézin. Also from Marmandais coops.

Ajaccio Corsica r p w ★→★★ 91 92 93 94 95 96 97 98 The capital of CORSICA. AC for some vg Sciacarello reds. Top grower: Peraldi (try his Vermentino). Also Clos Capitoro, Jean Courrèges (Dom de Pratavone).

Alain Thienot Brut NV; Brut 88 90; Brut Rosé 88 89 90; Luxury Grande Cuvée 85 90. Broker-turned-merchant; dynamic force for gd in CHAMP. Grande Cuvée: one of best luxury cuvées. Also owns Marie Stuart CHAMP, Ch Ricaud in LOUPIAC.

Aligoté Second-rank burgundy white grape and its wine. Should be pleasantly tart and fruity with local character when young. BOUZERON is the one commune to have an all-Aligoté appellation. The shining example is de Villaine's, but try others from good growers. NB PERNAND-VERGELESSES.

Aloxe-Corton Burg r w ★★→★★★ 78' 85' 87 88' 89' 90' 91 92 93' 94 95 96 97 98 Village at N end of COTE DE BEAUNE famous for its two GRANDS CRUS: CORTON (red), CORTON-CHARLEMAGNE (white). Village wines much lighter but to try.

Alsace Al w (r sp) ★★→★★★ 88 89 90' 92 93 94 95 96 97 98 Region comprising E foothills of Vosges mts, esp Strasbourg–Mulhouse. Unique wines: aromatic, fruity, full-strength, usually dry and expressive of each grape variety. Some sw made; see Vendange Tardive, Sélection des Grains Nobles. Mostly sold by grape variety (PINOT Bl, Ries, GEWURZ etc). Matures well (except Pinot Bl, MUSCAT) up to 5, even 10 yrs; GRAND CRU even longer. Gd-quality and -value CREMANT. PINOT N can have gd varietal character but not widely sold outside region. (See below.)

Alsace Grand Cru w ★★★→★★★★ 76 85 88 89' 90 91 92 93 94 95 96 97 98 AC restricted to 50 of the best named v'yds (approx 4,000 acres, 1,680 in production) and four noble grapes (Ries, PINOT Gr, GEWURZ, MUSCAT) mainly dry, some sw. Not without controversy but generally vg and expressive of terroir.

> **Fifteen good Alsace producers**
> Among many good growers offering reliability, value for money and tastes varying from scintillating to sumptuous, NB Léon Beyer, Marcel Deiss, Dopff 'Au Moulin', Hugel (Special cuvées), Marc Kreydenweiss, Kuentz-Bas, Albert Mann, Muré-Clos St-Landelin, Rolly-Gassmann, Charles Schleret, Dom Schoffit, Doms Schlumberger, Dom Trimbach, Dom Weinbach, Zind-Humbrecht.

Ampeau, Robert Exceptional grower and specialist in VOLNAY; also POMMARD, etc. Perhaps unique in only releasing long-matured bottles.

André, Pierre NEGOCIANT at Ch Corton-André, ALOXE-CORTON; 95 acres of v'yds in CORTON, SAVIGNY, GEVREY-CHAMBERTIN, etc. Also owns REINE PEDAUQUE.

d'Angerville, Marquis Top burgundy grower with immaculate 35-acre estate in VOLNAY. Top wines: Champans and intense, potent CLOS des Ducs.

Anjou Lo p r w (sw dr sp) ★→★★★★ Both region and Loire AC. Wide spectrum of styles: light reds incl AC Anjou GAMAY; improving dry whites. Gd red (CAB) ANJOU-VILLAGES, strong dry SAVENNIERES; luscious COTEAUX DU LAYON whites of CHENIN BLANC.

France entries also cross-refer to Châteaux of Bordeaux section, pages 78–103.

37

Anjou-Coteaux de la Loire Lo w s/sw sw ★★→★★★ 89' 90' 93 94 95' 96 97 98 Tiny AC for some forceful CHENIN whites. DEMI-SEC or sw not as rich as COTEAUX DU LAYON, esp Musset-Roullier, Ch de Putille, Doms du Fresche, de Putille.

Anjou-Villages Lo r ★→★★ 89 90 93 95 96 97 98 Superior central ANJOU AC for reds (mainly CAB F, some CAB S). Juicy, quite tannic young; gd value esp: Bablut, RICHOU, Rochelles, Pierre-Bise, Ogereau, Montigilet, Ch'x de Coulaine, de Tigné (Gérard Dépardieu's domaine). New sub-AC to watch: Anjou-Villages-Brissac.

Appellation Contrôlée (AC or AOC) Government control of origin and production (not quality) of all the best French wines (see Introduction).

Apremont Savoie w ★★ DYA One of the best villages of SAVOIE for pale delicate whites, mainly from Jacquère grapes, but recently incl CHARD.

Arbin Savoie r ★★ Deep-coloured lively red from MONDEUSE grapes, rather like a good Loire CABERNET. Ideal après-ski. Drink at 1–2 yrs.

Arbois Jura r p w (sp) ★★→★★★ Various good and original light but tasty wines; speciality is VIN JAUNE. On the whole, DYA except excellent Vin Jaune.

l'Ardèche, Coteaux de Central France r p (w) ★→★★ DYA Area W of Rhône given impetus by G DUBOEUF of BEAUJOLAIS. Bargain fresh country reds; best from pure SYRAH, GAMAY, CAB. Powerful, almost burgundian CHARD 'Ardèche' by LOUIS LATOUR (keep 1–2 yrs); Grand Ardèche: oaked. Also Dom du Colombier.

l'Arlot, Domaine de Outstanding producer of excellent NUITS-ST-GEORGES, esp CLOS de l'Arlot, red and white. Owned by AXA Insurance.

Armagnac SW France The alternative brandy; more tasty, rustic and peppery than COGNAC. Table wines: COTES DE GASCOGNE, GERS, TERROIRS LANDAIS.

Armand, Comte Excellent POMMARD wines, esp Clos-des-Epeneaux.

Aube Southern extension of CHAMP region. See Bar-sur-Aube.

Aujoux, J-M Substantial grower/merchant of BEAUJOLAIS. Swiss-owned.

Auxey-Duresses Burg r w ★★→★★★ 85 87 88 89 90' 91 92 93 94 95 96 97 98 2nd-rank (but v pretty) COTE DE BEAUNE village: affinities with VOLNAY, MEURSAULT. Best estates: Diconne, HOSPICES DE BEAUNE (Cuvée Boillot), LEROY, M Prunier, R Thévenin. Drink whites in 3–4 yrs. Top wine: Leroy's Les Boutonniers.

Avize Champ ★★★★ One of the top Côte des Blancs villages. All CHARDONNAY.

Aÿ Champ ★★★★ One of the best PINOT N-growing villages of CHAMP.

Ayala NV; Demi-Sec NV; Brut 89 90; Château d'Aÿ 85 88; Grande Cuvée 85 88 90; Blanc de Blancs 88 92; Brut Rosé NV Once-famous AY-based old-style CHAMP firm. Deserves more notice for its fresh appley wines.

Bahuaud, Donatien ★★→★★★ Leading Loire wine merchant. Le Master de Donatien is the top MUSCADET. Ch de la Cassemichère also good.

Bandol Prov r p (w) ★★★ 79 82 83 85' 86 87 88 89 90 91 92 93 94 95 96 97 98 Little coastal region near Toulon producing Provence's best wines; splendid vigorous tannic reds predominantly from MOURVEDRE; esp DOM OTT, Dom de Pibarnon, Ch Pradeaux, Mas de la Rouvière, DOM TEMPIER.

Banyuls Pyr br sw ★★→★★★ One of best VINS DOUX NATURELS, chiefly from GRENACHE (Banyuls GRAND CRU: over 75% Grenache, aged for 2 yrs+): a distant relation of port. The best are RANCIOS eg those from Doms la Rectorie, du Mas Blanc (★★★), Vial Magnères (Blanc), at 10–15 yrs old. Cheap NV wines end up in bars.

Barancourt One of many CHAMP marques bought by the acquisitive Paul-François VRANKEN. PINOT N-led Champagnes, esp Cuvée des Fondateurs. Gd BOUZY ROUGE.

Barrique The Bordeaux (and Cognac) term for an oak barrel holding 225 litres (300 bottles). Barrique-ageing to flavour almost any wine with oak was craze of late '80s, with some sad results. The current price of oak enjoins discretion.

Barsac B'x w sw ★★→★★★★ 70 71' 75 76' 78 79' 80' 81 82 83' 85 86' 88' 89' 90' 91 93 95 96 97 98 Neighbour of SAUTERNES with similar superb golden wines from different soil; generally less rich and more racy. Richly repays long ageing. Top ch'x: CLIMENS, COUTET, DOISY-DAENE, DOISY-VEDRINES.

Barthod-Noëllat, Ghislaine Domaine for impressive range of CHAMBOLLE-MUSIGNY.

Barton & Guestier BORDEAUX shipper since 18th C, now owned by Seagram.

Bâtard-Montrachet Burg w ★★★★ 78 79 85 86' 88 89' 90' 91 92 93 94 95 96 97 98 Larger (55-acre) n'bour of M'RACHET. Should be v long-lived: intense flavours, rich texture. Bienvenues-B-M: separate adjacent 9-acre GRAND CRU, 15 owners, thus no substantial bottlings; v rare. Seek out: BOUCHARD PERE, J-M BOILLOT, CARILLON, DROUHIN, Gagnard, L LATOUR, LEFLAIVE, Lequin-Roussot, MOREY, RAMONET, SAUZET.

Baumard, Domaine des ★★→★★★★ Leading grower of ANJOU wine, esp SAVENNIERES, COTEAUX DU LAYON (CLOS Ste-Catherine) and QUARTS DE CHAUME.

Baux-en-Provence, Coteaux des Prov r p ★→★★★ Formerly joined with COTEAUX D'AIX now AC in its own right for red and pink, but not white. Best wine: DOM DE TREVALLON (CAB-SYRAH) is VDP: without GRENACHE it does not conform to AC(!) Also Mas Gourgonnier, Romanin, Terres Blanches, Dom Hauvette.

Béarn SW France r p w ★→★★ w p DYA r 95' 96 97 (98) Low-key Basque AC centred on coop at Bellocq. Also ★★ Dom de Guilhémas. JURANCON red (esp Clos Mirabel, Dom Nigri) and MADIRAN rosé must be sold as Béarn or VDP PYRENEES-ATLANTIQUES.

Rather absurdly, the best wines of the Beaujolais region are not identified as Beaujolais at all on their labels, despite the fact that they exhibit all the best characteristics of the region. They are known simply by the names of their 'crus': Brouilly, Chénas, Chiroubles, Côte de Brouilly, Fleurie, Juliénas, Morgon, Moulin-à-Vent, Regnié, St-Amour. See entries for each of these. They can be some of the best-value wines in the whole of France.

Beaujolais Beauj r (p w) ★ DYA Simple AC of the v big Beaujolais region: light short-lived fruity red of GAMAY grapes. Beaujolais Supérieur is little different.

Beaujolais de l'année The BEAUJOLAIS of the latest vintage, until the next.

Beaujolais Primeur (or Nouveau) Same as above, made in a hurry (often only 4–5 days fermenting) for release at midnight on the third Wednesday in November. Ideally soft, pungent, fruity and tempting; too often crude, sharp, too alcoholic. BEAUJ-VILLAGES should be a better bet.

Beaujolais-Villages Beauj r ★★ 96 97 98 Wines from better (N) half of BEAUJOLAIS; should be much tastier than plain BEAUJOLAIS. The 10 (easily) best 'villages' are the 'CRUS': FLEURIE etc (see box above). Of the 30 others the best lie around Beaujeu. Crus cannot be released EN PRIMEUR before December 15th. Best kept until spring (or considerably longer).

Beaumes-de-Venise S Rh br (r p) ★★→★★★ DYA Widely regarded as France's best dessert MUSCAT, from S COTES DU RHONE; can be highly flavoured, subtle, lingering (eg from CHAPOUTIER, Dom de Coyeux, Dom Durban, JABOULET, VIDAL-FLEURY). Red wines from Ch Redortier, Dom du Fenouillet and coop are also good.

Beaune Burg r (w) ★★★ 78' 85' 88 89' 90' 91 92 93 94 95 96 97 98 Historic wine capital of Burgundy: walled town hollow with cellars. Wines are classic burgundy – but no GRAND CRU. Many fine growers. NEGOCIANTS' CLOS wines (usually PREMIER CRU) often best; eg DROUHIN's superb Clos des Mouches (esp white), JADOT's Clos des Ursules. Beaune du Château is a BOUCHARD PERE brand. Best v'yds: Bressandes, Fèves, Grèves, Marconnets, Teurons.

Becker, Caves J Proud old family firm at Zellenberg, ALSACE. Classic RIESLING Hagenschlauf and GRAND CRU Froehn MUSCAT. Second label: Gaston Beck.

Bellet Prov p r w ★★★ Fashionable much-above-average local wines from nr Nice. Serious producers: Ch de Bellet, Dom de la Source. Pricey.

Bergerac Dordogne r w p dr sw ★★ (r) 89 90' 94 95 96 97 98 Effectively, but not politically, an eastward extension of B'x with no clear break in style/quality. Top properties incl La Tour des Gendres, Dom de Gouyat, Ch'x Grinou, de la Jaubertie, du Constant, les Eyssards, de la Mallevieille, les Marais, le Paradis, le Raz, la Tour de Grangemont and CLOS des Verdots; brand-named Julien de Savignac. Also MONBAZILLAC, MONTRAVEL, ROSETTE, SAUSSIGNAC and PECHARMANT.

Besserat de Bellefon Grande Tradition NV; Cuvée des Moines Brut and Rosé NV; Grande Cuvée NV; Brut and Rosé 85 85 89 90 93 Now in Epernay, CHAMP house known for fine, light wines. Owned by MARNE ET CHAMPAGNE.

Beyer, Léon Ancient ALSACE family firm at Eguisheim. Forceful dry wines needing 5–10 yrs esp Comtes d'Eguisheim GEWURZ, Comtes d'Eguisheim RIES from GRAND CRU Pfersigberg. Beyer is militant against GRAND CRU restrictions.

Bichot, Maison Albert One of BEAUNE's biggest growers and merchants. V'yds (32-acre Dom du CLOS Frantin: excellent): CHAMBERTIN, RICHEBOURG, CLOS DE VOUGEOT, etc; Dom Long-Depaquit in CHABLIS; also many other brand names.

Billecart-Salmon NV; Rosé NV; Brut 85 86 88 89; Nicolas François Billecart (88 89 90 91); Bl de Blancs 85 88 90; Elisabeth Salmon Rosé (88 89 90); Grande Cuvée 85 88 90 One of the very best CHAMP houses, founded in 1818, still family-owned. Exquisite fresh-flavoured wines age beautifully. A new single v'yd Clos St-Hilaire (BLANC DE NOIRS) will come on stream in early 21st Century.

Bize, Simon Admirable red burgundy grower with 35 acres at SAVIGNY-LES-BEAUNE. Usually model wines in the racy and elegant Savigny style.

Blagny Burg r w ★★→★★★ (w) 86' 88 89 90' 91 92 93 94 95 96 97 98 Hamlet between MEURSAULT and PULIGNY-M'RACHET: whites have affinities with both (and sold under both ACS), reds with VOLNAY (sold as AC Blagny). Good ones need age; esp AMPEAU, JOBARD, LATOUR, LEFLAIVE, MATROT, G Thomas.

Blanc de Blancs Any white wine made from white grapes only, esp CHAMP (usually both red and white). Not an indication of quality but should be of style.

Blanc de Noirs White (or slightly pink or 'blush') wine from red grapes.

Blanck, Paul et Fils Versatile ALSACE grower at Kientzheim. Good PINOT Bl and GRANDS CRUS Furstentum (GEWURZ, Pinot Gr, esp RIES), SCHLOSSBERG (Ries).

Blanquette de Limoux Midi w sp ★★ Gd value fizz from nr Carcassonne with long local history. V dry, clean; increasingly tasty: CHARD and Chenin now added to basic Mauzac, esp in newer AC CREMANT de Limoux.

Blaye B'x r w ★ 88 89 90 93 94 95 96 97 98 Your daily BORDEAUX from E of the Gironde. PREMIERES COTES DE BLAYE is the AC of the better wines.

Boillot, J-M POMMARD-based domaine: also v fine PULIGNY-M'RACHET, BATARD-M, etc and recently remarkable MONTAGNY.

Boisset, Jean-Claude Far and away the biggest burgundy merchant and grower, based in NUITS-ST-GEORGES. Owner of Bouchard-Aîné, Lionel Bruck, F Chauvenet, Delaunay, Jaffelin, Morin Père et Fils, de Marcilly, Pierre Ponnelle, Thomas-Bassot, Vienot, CELLIER DES SAMSONS (BEAUJOLAIS), MOREAU (CHABLIS) and a share in MOMMESSIN. Predictable standards.

Bollinger NV 'Special Cuvée'; Grande Année 76 79 82 83 85 88 89 90; Rosé 81 82 83 85 88 Top CHAMP house, at AY. Luxury wines: RD (73 75 76 79 81 82 85), VIEILLES VIGNES Françaises (75 79 80 81 82 85 88 89) from ungrafted Pinot vines. Pioneered Charter of Quality ('91). Investor in Petaluma, Australia.

Bonneau du Martray, Domaine Biggest grower (with 22 acres) of CORTON-CHARLEMAGNE of highest quality; also red GRAND CRU CORTON all on a high since '90. Cellars at PERNAND-VERGELESSES. White wines have often outlived reds.

Bonnes-Mares Burg r ★★★→★★★★★ 78' 79 80 85' 87 88 89 90' 91 92 93 94 95 96 97 98 37-acre GRAND CRU between CHAMBOLLE-MUSIGNY and MOREY-ST-DENIS. V sturdy long-lived wines, less fragrant than MUSIGNY; can rival CHAMBERTIN. Top growers: DUJAC, GROFFIER, JADOT, MUGNIER, ROUMIER, DOM DES VAROILLES, DE VOGUE.

Bonnezeaux Lo w sw ★★★→★★★★ 76' 78 85' 86 88' 89' 90' 93' 94 95' 96 97 98
Velvety, structured, complex sw CHENIN, potentially the best of COTEAUX DU LAYON. Esp Angeli, Ch de Fesles, Dom du Petit Val. Ages well, but v tempting young.

Bordeaux B'x r w (p) ★→★★ 90 93 94 95 96 97 98 (for ch'x see pages 78–103)
Catch-all AC for low-strength B'x wine. Not to be despised: it may be light but its flavour cannot be imitated. If I had to choose one simple daily wine this would be it.

Bordeaux Supérieur ★→★★ As above, with slightly more alcohol.

Borie-Manoux Admirable B'x shipper, château-owner owned by Castéja family. Ch'x incl BATAILLEY, BEAU-SITE, DOM DE L'EGLISE, HAUT-BAGES-MONPELOU, TROTTEVIEILLE.

Bouchard Père et Fils Important burgundy shipper (est 1731) and grower; excellent v'yds (232 acres), mainly COTE DE BEAUNE; cellars at Ch de Beaune. Owned since '95 by HENRIOT with radical steps to upgrade quality and image.

Bouches-du-Rhône Prov r p w ★ VINS DE PAYS from Marseille environs. Robust reds from southern varieties, CAB S, SYRAH and Merlot.

Bourg B'x r (w) ★★ 86' 88' 89' 90' 93 94 95 96 97 98 Un-fancy claret from E of the Gironde. For ch'x see Côtes de Bourg.

Bourgeois, Henri 89 90 93 95 96 97 98 Leading SANCERRE grower/merchant in Chavignol; also owns Laporte. Also POUILLY-FUME. Top wines incl: Etienne Henri, MD de Bourgeois, La Bourgeoise.

Bourgogne Burg r w (p) ★★ 90' 93 94 95 96' 97 98 Catch-all Burgundy AC, with higher standards than basic B'x. Light often gd flavour, best at 2–4 yrs. Top growers make bargain beauties from fringes of COTE D'OR villages; do not despise. BEAUJOLAIS CRUS can also be labelled Bourgogne.

Bourgogne Grand Ordinaire Burg r (w) ★ DYA Lowest B'y AC, also allowing GAMAY. Rare. White may incl ALIGOTE, PINOT BI, Melon de Bourgogne.

Bourgogne Passe-Tout-Grains Burg r (p) ★ Age 1–2 yrs, junior burgundy: minimum 33% PINOT N, the balance GAMAY, mixed in the vat. Often enjoyable. Not as heady as BEAUJOLAIS.

Bourgueil Lo r (p) ★★→★★★(★) 76' 85 86' 88 89' 90' 93' 95' 96 97 98 Normally delicate fruity TOURAINE red (mainly CAB F). Deep-flavoured, ageing like B'x in top yrs. ST-NICOLAS-DE-B'GUEIL often lighter. Esp from Amirault, Audebert, Billet, Breton, Caslot, Cognard, Delaunay, Druet, Gambier, Lamé-Delisle-Boucard, Mailloches.

Bouvet-Ladubay Major producer of sp SAUMUR, controlled by TAITTINGER. Wines incl vintage BRUT Saphir, CREMANT Excellence and oak-fermented deluxe Trésor (white, rosé), with 2 yrs age. Also good sw Grand Vin de Dessert.

Bouzeron Village of the COTE CHALONNAISE distinguished for the only single-village AC ALIGOTE. Top grower: de Villaine. Also NB BOUCHARD PERE.

Bouzy Rouge Champ r ★★★ 85 89 90 96 97 Still red of famous CHAMP PINOT village. Like v light burgundy, but can last well in sunny vintages.

Brana, Domaine 90' 94' 95' 96 (97') Pioneering IROULEGUY property perched high above St-Jean-Pied-du-Port. Outstanding wines and eaux-de-vie.

Brand ALSACE GRAND CRU hot spot nr Turkheim. PINOT Gris does extremely well here; also excellent GEWURZ from ZIND-HUMBRECHT.

Brédif, Marc One of the most important growers and traders of VOUVRAY, esp sparkling (METHODE TRADITIONELLE and PETILLANT). Owned by LADOUCETTE.

Bricout Brut NV (Rés, Prestige, Cuvée Spéciale Arthur Bricout); Rosé NV; Brut 85 90 93 AVIZE CHAMP house associated with stars of French showbiz. First-rate CUVEE Prestige, mainly CHARD.

Brocard, J-M CHABLIS grower to note for fine value, crisp and typical wines, incl Montmains, Montée de Tonnerre. A confirmed terroiriste.

Brouilly Beauj r ★★ 94 95 96 97 98 Biggest of the 10 CRUS of BEAUJOLAIS: fruity, round, refreshing wine, can age 3–4 yrs. CH DE LA CHAIZE is largest estate. Top growers: Michaud, Dom de Combillaty, Dom des Grandes Vignes.

FRANCE

Brumont, Alain Best-known producer of MADIRAN and PACHERENC DU VIC-BILH. Owns Ch'x MONTUS, Bouscassé. Also Dom Meinjarre. Likes oaky wines.

Bruno Paillard Brut Première Cuvée NV; Rosé Première Cuvée; CHARD Réserve Privée, Brut **85 89 90** Sm prestigious young CHAMP house; v high standards. Paillard also force behind Boizel-Chanoine group (ABEL LEPITRE and PHILIPPONNAT).

Brut Term for the dry classic wines of CHAMP. Brut Ultra/Zéro: a recent term for bone-dry wines.

Buisse, Paul Quality Montrichard merchant: range of Loire, esp TOURAINE wines.

Bugey Savoie r p w sp ★→★★★ DYA VDQS for light sp, still or half-sp wines from Roussette (or Altesse) and CHARD (gd). Best from Montagnieu; also Rosé de Cerdon, mainly GAMAY.

Burguet, Alain Superb GEVREY-CHAMBERTIN; esp his VIEILLES VIGNES village wine.

Buxy Burg w ★★ Village in AC MONTAGNY with gd coop for CHARD.

Buzet SW France r (w p) ★★ **90' 93 94 95' 96 97 98** Region just SE of B'X; similar wines, s'times a bit pruney. Dynamic coop has bulk of production, incl some single properties (eg Ch'x de Gueyze, Mazelières). More local character from (independent) Dom de Pech, Ch'x du Frandat, Sauvagnères and Tournelles.

Cabardès Midi r (p w) ★→★★★ 88 89 90 91 92 93 **94** 95 96 97 98 New AC N of Carcassonne. MIDI and B'X grapes show promise at Ch Pennuaties, Ch des Hautes-Caunettes, Ch Ventenac, Dom de Cabrol, Coop de Conques sur Orbiel.

Cabernet See Grapes for red wine (pages 11–13).

Cabernet d'Anjou Lo p s/sw ★→★★ DYA Delicate, grapey, med-sw rosé. Traditionally: sw, age-worthy; a few venerable bottles survive. Esp from Bablut.

Cabrières Midi p (r) ★★ DYA COTEAUX DU LANGUEDOC.

Cahors SW France r ★→★★★ 82 83' 85' 86' 88 89' 90' **92' 93** 94 95' 96 97 98 Historically 'black' and tannic wines, mostly from Malbec (here 'Cot'). Now range from conc, tannic, to quick-drinking. Best incl CLOS DE GAMOT, Coutale, Ch'x du Cayrou, La Coustarelle, La Caminade, Lamartine, Pech de Jammes, La Reyne, du Cèdre, Les Ifs, Latuc, Doms de la Bérangeraie, Paillas, Pineraie, Savarines, Eugénie.

Cairanne S Rh r p w ★★ 88 89 90' 93 **94 95'** 96' 97 98' One of best COTES DU RHONE-VILLAGES: solid, robust esp from Doms Alary, Ameillaud, Brusset, l'Oratoire St-Martin, Rabasse-Charavin, Richaud. Some improving whites.

Canard-Duchêne Brut NV; Demi-Sec NV; Rosé NV; Charles VII NV; Brut **85 88 90 93** CHAMP house connected with VEUVE CLICQUOT, ie same group as MOET & CHANDON. Fair prices for lively, PINOT-tasting wines. Improved quality recently.

Canon-Fronsac B'x r ★→★★★ 82 83' 85' 86 88 89' 90' **92 94 95** 96 97 98 Full tannic reds of increasing quality from small area W of POMEROL. Need less age than formerly. Eg Ch'x: CANON, CANON-DE-BREM, CANON-MOUEIX, Coustolle, La Dauphine, La Fleur Caillou, Junayme, Mazeris-Bellevue, Moulin-Pey-Labrie, Toumalin, La Truffière, Vraye-Canon-Boyer. See also Fronsac.

Cantenac B'x r ★★★ Village of HAUT-MEDOC entitled to the AC MARGAUX. Top ch'x include BRANE-CANTENAC, PALMER, etc.

Cap Corse Corsica w br ★★→★★★ CORSICA'S wild N cape. Splendid MUSCAT from CLOS Nicrosi in Rogliano, and rare soft dry Vermentino white. Vaut le détour, if not le voyage.

Caramany Pyr r (w) ★ **90 92 93 94 95** 96 97 98 Notionally superior AC for single-village COTES DU ROUSSILLON-VILLAGES.

Carillon, Louis Leading PULIGNY-M domaine now in top league. Esp PREMIER CRU Referts, Perrières and a tiny amount of GRAND CRU Bienvenues-Bâtard.

Cassis Prov w (r p) ★★ DYA Seaside village E of Marseille known for dry white wine with a certain character, drunk with bouillabaisse (eg Dom de la Ferme Blanche). Not to be confused with cassis: blackcurrant liqueur made in Dijon.

Cave Cellar, or any wine establishment.

Cave coopérative Wine-growers' cooperative winery; over half of all French production. Almost all now well-run, well-equipped and their wine reasonable value for money.

Cellier des Samsons BEAUJOLAIS/MACONNAIS coop at Quincié with 2,000 grower-members. Wines widely distributed; now owned by BOISSET.

Cépage Variety of vine, eg CHARD, Merlot.

Cérons B'x w dr sw ★★ 83' 85' 86' 88' 89' 90 91 92 93 94 95 96 97 98 Neighbour of SAUTERNES with some gd sweet wine, eg Ch'x de Cérons et de Calvimont, Grand Enclos, Haura. Ch Archambeau makes vg dry GRAVES.

Chablis

There is no better expression of the all-conquering Chardonnay than the full but tense, limpid but stony wines it makes on the heavy limestone soils of Chablis. Chablis terroir divides cleanly into 3 quality levels with great consistency. Best makers use little or no new oak to mask the precise definition of variety and terroir. They incl: Bessin*, Billaud-Simon, J-M Brocard, J Collet *, D Dampf, R & V Dauvissat*, J Dauvissat*, B, D et E, and J Defaix, Droin, Drouhin*, Durup, Fèvre, Geoffroy, J-P Grossot, Laroche, Long-Depaquit, Dom des Malandes, L Michel*, La Moutonne, Pic, Pupillon, Raveneau*, G Robin*, Servin, P Testut*, Tribut, Vocoret. Simple unqualified 'Chablis' may be thin; best is premier or grand cru (see below). The coop, La Chablisienne, has high standards (esp Grenouille*) and many different labels (it makes 1 in every 3 bottles). (* = outstanding)

Chablis Burg w ★★ ·→★★★ 90 92 93 94 95 96' 97 98 Unique flavoursome dry minerally wine of N Burgundy, CHARD only; 10,000 acres (doubled since '85).

Chablis Grand Cru Burg w ★★★ ·→★★★★ 78 83 85 86 88 89 90 91 92 93 94 95' 96' 97 98 In maturity a match for greatest white burgundy: forceful but often dumb in youth, at best with age combines mineral 'cut' with a gentle hint of SAUTERNES. 7 v'yds: Blanchots, Bougros, CLOS, Grenouilles, Preuses, Valmur, Vaudésir. See also Moutonne.

Chablis Premier Cru Burg w ★★★ 85 86 88 89 90 91 92 93 94 95' 96' 97 98 Technically second-rank but at best excellent, more typical of CHABLIS than its GRANDS CRUS. Often outclasses more expensive MEURSAULT and other COTE DE BEAUNE. Best v'yds incl Côte de Léchet, Fourchaume, Mont de Milieu, Montée de Tonnerre, Montmains, Vaillons. See above for producers.

Chai Building for storing and maturing wine, esp in BORDEAUX.

Chambertin Burg r ★★★★ 78' 79 80 83 85' 87 88 89 90' 91 92 93 94 95 96' 97 98 32-acre GRAND CRU; some of the meatiest, most enduring, best red burgundy, 15 growers, incl BOUCHARD, Camus, Damoy, DROUHIN, MORTET, PONSOT, Rebourseau, Rossignol-Trapet, ROUSSEAU, Tortochot, Trapet.

Chambertin-Clos de Bèze Burg r ★★★★ 78' 79 80 83 85 87 88 89 90' 91 92 93 94 95 96' 97 98 37-acre neighbour of CHAMBERTIN. Similarly splendid wines. May legally be sold as Chambertin. 10 growers incl B CLAIR, Clair-Dau, Damoy, DROUHIN, Drouhin-Laroze, FAIVELEY, JADOT, ROUSSEAU.

Chambolle-Musigny Burg r (w) ★★★ ·→★★★★ 78' 85' 87 88 89 90' 91 92 93 94 95 96 97 98 420-acre COTE DE NUITS village: fabulously fragrant, complex, never heavy wine. Best v'yds: Les Amoureuses, part of BONNES-MARES, Les Charmes, MUSIGNY. Growers to note: BARTHOD-NOELLAT, DROUHIN, FAIVELEY, HUDELOT-NOELLAT, JADOT, Moine-Hudelot, MUGNERET, MUGNIER, RION, ROUMIER, Serveau, DE VOGUE.

Champagne Sparkling wine of PINOTS Noir and Meunier and/or CHARD, and its region (70,000⁺ acres 90 miles E of Paris); made by METHODE TRADITIONELLE. Bubbles from elsewhere, however gd, cannot be Champagne.

Champy Père et Cie Oldest burgundy NEGOCIANT, in BEAUNE, rejuvenated by Meurgey family (also brokers 'DIVA'). Range of v well-chosen wines.

Chandon de Briailles, Domaine Small burgundy estate at SAVIGNY. Makes wonderful CORTON (and Corton Blanc) and vg PERNAND-VERGELESSES.

Chanson Père et Fils Old grower-NEGOCIANT family co at BEAUNE (110 acres). Esp BEAUNE CLOS des Fèves, SAVIGNY, PERNAND-VERGELESSES, CORTON. Fine quality.

Chapelle-Chambertin Burg r ★★★ 78' 85 87 88 89' 90' 91 92 93 94 95 96' 97 98 13-acre neighbour of CHAMBERTIN. Wine more 'nervous', not so meaty. Top producers: Damoy, JADOT, Rossignol-Trapet, Trapet.

Chapoutier Long-est'd grower and trader of full Rhônes; bio-dynamic principles. Best: special CUVEES CH'NEUF Barbe Rac (all GRENACHE), HERMITAGE: Le Pavillon (red) and Cuvée d'Orée (white, late-picked Marsanne), also CROZES red Les Varonniers. New holdings in BANYULS, CTX DU TRICASTIN and CTX D'AIX-EN-PROVENCE promising.

Chardonnay See Grapes for white wine (pages 7–11). Also the name of a MACON-VILLAGES commune. Hence Mâcon-Chardonnay.

Charlopin, Philippe Perfectionist GEVREY-CHAMBERTIN estate. To watch.

Charmes-Chambertin Burg r ★★★ 78' 85' 87 88 89' 90' 91 92 93 94 95 96' 97 98 76-acre CHAMBERTIN neighbour, incl AC MAZOYERES-C. 'Suppler', rounder wines; esp from Bachelet, Castagnier, DROUHIN, DUJAC, LEROY, ROTY, ROUMIER, ROUSSEAU.

Chassagne-Montrachet Burg r w ★★★→★★★★ r (★★★) 78' 85 87 88 89' 90' 91 92 93 94 95 96' 97 98; w 78' 83 85 86 88 89' 90 91 92 93 94 95 96' 97 98 750-acre COTE DE BEAUNE village. Sterling hefty r; excellent rich dry w rarely win quite the finesse of PULIGNY next door but often cost less. Best v'yds incl part of M'RACHET, BATARD-M, Boudriottes (r w), Caillerets, CRIOTS-BATARD-M, Morgeot (r w), Ruchottes, CLOS ST-JEAN (r). Growers incl Amiot-Bonfils, Blain-Gagnard, COLIN-DELEGER, Delagrange-Bachelet, DROUHIN, Fontaine-Gagnard, J-N Gagnard, GAGNARD-DELAGRANGE, Lamy-Pillot, MAGENTA, Ch de la Maltroye, MOREY, Niellon, RAMONET.

Château

Means an estate, big or small, good or indifferent, particularly in Bordeaux (see pages 78–103). Elsewhere in France château tends to mean, literally, castle or great house, as in most of the following entries. In Burgundy 'domaine' is the usual term.

Château d'Arlay Major JURA estate; 160 acres in skilful hands with wines incl vg VIN JAUNE, VIN DE PAILLE, PINOT N and MACVIN.

Château de Beaucastel S Rh r w ★★★ 78' 79 81' 83 85 86' 88 89' 90' 92 93' 94' 95' 96' 98' One of biggest (173 acres), best-run CH'NEUF-DU-PAPE estates with cult following. Deep-hued, complex wines; unusual varietal mix incl ⅓ MOURVEDRE. Drink well young, too. Sm amount of wonderful Roussanne w: keep 5–14 yrs. Also leading COTES DU RHONE Coudoulet de Beaucastel (r and w – part Viognier); improving Ch du Grand Prébois. Also Beaucastel Estate, Paso Robles, California.

Château de la Chaize Beauj r ★★★ 94 95 96 97 Best-known BROUILLY estate.

Château Corton-Grancey Burg r ★★★ 78 85 88 89 90 91 92 93 95 96 97 98 Famous ALOXE-CORTON estate; property of LOUIS LATOUR: benchmark wines.

Château Fortia S Rh r (w) ★★★ 78' 79 81' 83 84 85 86 86 88 90 94 95' 96' Trad 72-acre CHATEAUNEUF property. The owner's father, Baron Le Roy, also fathered the APPELLATION CONTROLEE system in '20s. Not at top form, but signs of revival.

Château Fuissé Burg w ★★★ The ultimate POUILLY-FUISSE estate. The Vincent's Pouilly-F VIEILLES VIGNES is ★★★★, and sumptuous with age; though recent wines have needed less time. Also ST-VERAN, MACON-VILLAGES (value).

Château de Meursault Burg r w ★★★ 150-acre estate owned by PATRIARCHE, with good v'yds and wines in BEAUNE, MEURSAULT, POMMARD, VOLNAY. Splendid cellars open to the public for tasting.

Château de Montaigne Dordogne w (sw) ★★ Home of great philosopher Michel de M, now making sw COTES DE MONTRAVEL; part-owns CH PALMER (MARGAUX).

Château Montus ★★★ SW France 89' 90' **92** 95 96 (97) Top MADIRAN estate. Some wines 100% Tannat, long vinification, slow-maturing. Owner: A BRUMONT.

Château La Nerthe S Rh r (w) ★★★ 78' 79 81' 85 86 88 89' 90' 93 94 95'96' 98' Renowned imposing 222-acre CHATEAUNEUF estate. Solid modern-style wines, esp special CUVEES Cadettes (r) and oaked Beauvenir (w).

Château Rayas S Rh r (w) ★★★ 78' 79 81' 83 85 86 88' 89 90' 91 93 94'95' 96' 97 Famous old-style property of only 37 acres in CH'NEUF-DU-PAPE. Talented, eccentric owner Jacques Reynaud died in '97. Concentrated wines entirely GRENACHE, yet can age superbly. White Rayas can be vg. Pignan is 2nd label. Also vg Ch Fonsalette, COTES DU RHONE (NB CUVEE SYRAH and whites).

Château Routas Prov r p w ★★ Recent estate created by dynamic Swiss Canadian, making its mark in COTEAUX VAROIS. Wines incl SYRAH, CAB S, CHARD-Viognier, both AC and VDP.

Château de Selle Prov r p w ★★→★★★ 100-acre estate of OTT family nr Cotignac, Var. Pace-setters for PROVENCE. Cuvée Spéciale is largely CAB S.

Château Simone Prov r p w ★★ Age 2–6 yrs or longer. Famous old property synonymous with AC PALETTE, nr Aix-en-Provence. The red is best: smooth but herby and spicy. White is good too and repays bottle age.

Château de la Tour Fashionably dark, oaky CLOS DE VOUGEOT.

Château Val-Joanis Prov r p w ★★→★★★ Beautiful estate; v full COTES DU LUBERON.

Château Vignelaure Prov r ★★★ 82' 83' 85 86 87 88 89 90 91 92 93 94 95 96 97 98 135-acre Provençal estate nr Aix: exceptional more-or-less B'x-style wine with CAB S, SYRAH and GRENACHE grapes.

Château de Villeneuve Loire r w ★★★ Dynamic SAUMUR estate. Exciting Saumur Blanc (esp Les Cormiers) and S-CHAMPIGNY (esp VIEILLES VIGNES, Grand Clos).

Château-Chalon Jura w ★★★ Not a CHATEAU but AC and village. Unique dry yellow sherry-like wine. Develops flor while ageing in barrels for min 6 yrs. Ready to drink when when bottled, but ages forever. A curiosity.

Château-Grillet N Rh w ★★★★ 94' 95 96 97' 98 9-acre terraced v'yd of Viognier; one of France's smallest ACS. Absurdly over-expensive, but shows signs of revival in the '90s. Less floral aromas than CONDRIEU. Drink young – or don't bother.

Châteaumeillant Lo r p ★→★★ DYA Tiny VDQS area nr SANCERRE. GAMAY and PINOT N for light reds and rosés. Top producer: Lanoix.

Châteauneuf-du-Pape S Rh r (w) ★★★ 78' 79 81' 83 85 86 88 89' 90' 93 94 95' 96' 98' 8,200 acres near Avignon with core of 30 or so domaines for very fine wines (quality more variable over remaining 90). Mix of up to 13 varieties led by GRENACHE, SYRAH, MOURVEDRE. The best are dark, strong, exceptionally long-lived. Whites either fruity and zesty or rather heavy: mostly now 'DYA'. Top growers incl Ch'x DE BEAUCASTEL, FORTIA, Gardine, MONT-REDON, LA NERTHE, RAYAS; Doms de Beaurenard, Le Bosquet des Papes, Les Cailloux, Font-de-Michelle, Grand Tinel, VIEUX TELEGRAPHE; Henri Bonneau, Clos du Mont-Olivet, Clos des Papes, Clos St-Jean, Le Vieux Donjon etc.

Châtillon-en-Diois Rh r p w ★ DYA Small AC of mid-Rhône. Adequate largely GAMAY reds; white (some ALIGOTE) mostly made into CLAIRETTE DE DIE.

Chave, Gérard To many the superstar grower (with his son Jean-Louis) of HERMITAGE, with 25 acres red, 12 acres white – spread over 9 hillside v'yds. V long-lived red and white (esp vg red ST-JOSEPH), and also VIN DE PAILLE. Interesting new J L Chave brand wine at St-Joseph bought from growers.

To decipher codes, please refer to 'Key to symbols' on front flap of jacket, or to 'How to use this book' on page 6.

45

Chavignol Village of SANCERRE with famous v'yd, Les Monts Damnés. Chalky soil gives vivid wines that age 4–5 yrs; esp from BOURGEOIS and Cotat.

Chénas Beauj r ★★★ 90 91 92 93 94 95 96 97 98 Smallest BEAUJOLAIS CRU and one of the weightiest; neighbour to MOULIN-A-VENT and JULIENAS. Growers incl Benon, Champagnon, Charvet, Ch Chèvres, DUBOEUF, Lapière, Robin, Trichard, coop.

Chenin Blanc See Grapes for white wine (pages 7–11).

Chenonceau, Ch de Lo ★★ Architectural jewel of Loire makes good to v good AC TOURAINE SAUV BL, CAB and CHENIN, still and sparkling.

Chéreau-Carré Makers of some of top domaine MUSCADETS (esp Ch'x du Chasseloir, du Coing). A name to follow.

Chevalier-Montrachet Burg w ★★★★ 78 83 85' 86 88 89' 90 91 92 93 95 96' 97 98 17-acre neighbour of M'RACHET making similar luxurious wine, perhaps less powerful. Incl 2.5-acre Les Demoiselles. Growers incl LATOUR, JADOT, BOUCHARD PERE, CHARTRON, COLIN-DELEGER, LEFLAIVE, Niellon, PRIEUR.

Cheverny Lo r p w ★→★★ Loire AC nr Chambord. Dry crisp whites from SAUV BL and CHARD. Also GAMAY, PINOT N or CAB reds; generally light but tasty. 'Cour Cheverny' uses the local Romorantin grape. Sparkling wines use CREMANT DE LOIRE AC. Esp Cazin, Huards, OISLY ET THESEE, Dom de la Desoucherie.

Chevillon, R 32-acre estate at NUITS-ST-GEORGES; a name to watch.

Chignin Savoie w ★ DYA Light soft white from Jacquère grapes for alpine summers. Chignin-Bergeron (with Roussanne grapes) is best and liveliest.

Chinon Lo r (p w) ★★→★★★★ 76 85 86' 88 89' 90' 93' 95' 96 97 98 Juicy, variably rich CAB F from TOURAINE. Drink cool, young; treat exceptional yrs like B'x. Small quantity of crisp dry white from CHENIN. Top growers: Bernard Baudry, Alliet, COULY-DUTHEIL (CLOS de l'Echo), Druet, Ch de la Grille, Joguet, Raffault.

Chiroubles Beauj r ★★★ 95 96 97 98 Good but tiny BEAUJOLAIS CRU next to FLEURIE; freshly fruity silky wine for early drinking (1–3 yrs). Growers incl Bouillard, Cheysson, DUBOEUF, Fourneau, Passot, Raousset, coop.

Chorey-lès-Beaune Burg r (w) ★★ 85 88 89 90' 91 92 93 94 95 96' 97 98 Minor AC on flat land N of BEAUNE: 3 fine growers: Arnoux, Germain (Ch de Chorey) and esp TOLLOT-BEAUT.

Chusclan S Rh r p w ★→★★ 93 94 95' 96' 98' Village of COTES DU RHONE-VILLAGES with able coop. Labels incl Cuvée de Marcoule, Seigneurie de Gicon. Also Dom de Lindas and special CUVEES from André Roux.

Cissac HAUT-MEDOC village just west of PAUILLAC.

Clair, Bruno Leading MARSANNAY estate. Vg wines from there and GEVREY-CHAMBERTIN (esp CLOS DE BEZE), FIXIN, MOREY-ST-DENIS, SAVIGNY.

Clairet Very light red wine, almost rosé. Bordeaux Clairet is an AC.

Clairette Traditional white grape of the MIDI. Its low-acid wine was a vermouth base. Revival by Terrasses de Landoc is full and zesty.

Clairette de Bellegarde Midi w ★ DYA Small AC nr Nîmes: plain neutral white.

Clairette de Die Rh w dr s/sw sp ★★ NV Popular dry or (better) semi-sweet MUSCAT-flavoured sparkling wine from pre-Alps in E Rhône; or straight dry CLAIRETTE white, surprisingly ageing well 3–4 yrs. Worth trying.

Clairette du Languedoc Midi w ★ DYA Nr Montpellier. Neutral white variety and its wine; improving with late harvest grapes, barrel ageing. Ch'x La Condamine Bertrand, St-André and Cave d'Adissan looking good.

Clape, La Midi r p w ★→★★ CRU to note of AC COTEAUX DU LANGUEDOC. Full-bodied wines from limestone hills between Narbonne and sea. Red gains character after 2–3 yrs, Bourboulenc white even longer. Esp from Ch'x Rouquette-sur-Mer, Mire l'Etang, Pech-Céléyran, Pech-Redon, Dom de l'Hospitalet.

Claret Traditional English term for all red BORDEAUX.

Climat Burgundian word for individually named v'yd, eg BEAUNE Grèves.

Clos A term carrying some prestige, reserved for distinct (walled) v'yds, often in one ownership (esp Burgundy and ALSACE). Les Clos is CHABLIS' Grandest Cru.

Clos de Bèze See Chambertin-Clos de Bèze.

Clos de Gamot ★★★ SW France 70' 78' 82' 83' 85' 88 89 90 92 94 (95') (96) Famous CAHORS estate. Ultra-traditional long-lived benchmark wines.

Clos des Lambrays Burg r ★★★ 15-acre GRAND CRU vineyard at MOREY-ST-DENIS. Changed hands *again* in '96. Great potential here.

Clos des Mouches Burg r w ★★★ Splendid PREMIER CRU BEAUNE v'yd, largely owned by DROUHIN. White and red, spicy and memorable – and consistent.

Clos de la Roche Burg r ★★★ 78' 85' 86 87 88 89' 90 91 92 93' 94 95 96' 97 98 MOREY-ST-DENIS GRAND CRU (38-acres). Powerful and complex like CHAMBERTIN. Esp BOUCHARD PERE, Bourée, Castagnier, DUJAC, Lignier, PONSOT, REMY, ROUSSEAU.

Clos du Roi Burg r ★★★ Part of GRAND CRU CORTON. Also a BEAUNE PREMIER CRU.

Clos Rougeard Lo r (sw) Controversial SAUMUR-CHAMPIGNY; cult following. Intense wines aged in new (or nearly new) B'x barrels. Also tiny amount of luscious COTEAUX DE SAUMUR.

Clos St-Denis Burg r ★★★ 78 79 82 85' 87 88 89' 90' 91 92 93' 94 95 96' 97 98 16-acre GRAND CRU at MOREY-ST-DENIS. Splendid sturdy wine growing silky with age. Growers incl DUJAC, Lignier, PONSOT.

Clos Ste-Hune Al w ★★★★ V fine austere RIES from TRIMBACH; perhaps ALSACE'S best. Needs 5⁺ yrs age; doesn't need GRAND CRU status.

Clos St-Jacques Burg r ★★★ 78' 85' 86 87 88 89' 90' 91 92 93' 94 95 96' 97 98 17-acre GEVREY-CHAMBERTIN PREMIER CRU. Excellent powerful velvety long-ager, often better (and dearer) than some GRANDS CRUS, esp by ESMONIN and ROUSSEAU.

Clos St-Jean Burg r ★★★ 78 85' 88 89' 90' 91 92 93 94 95 96' 97 98 36-acre PREMIER CRU of CHASSAGNE-M'RACHET. Vg red, more solid than subtle, from eg Ch de la Maltroye. NB domaine RAMONET.

Clos de Tart Burg r ★★★ 85' 88'89' 90' 92 93 94 95 96' 97 98 GRAND CRU at MOREY-ST-DENIS, owned by MOMMESSIN. At best wonderfully fragrant, young or old.

Clos de Vougeot Burg r ★★★ 78 85' 88 89' 90' 91 92 93 94 95 96' 97 98 124-acre COTE DE NUITS GRAND CRU with many owners. Variable, occasionally sublime. Maturity depends on the grower's philosophy, technique and position on hill. Top growers incl Clair-Dau, CH DE LA TOUR, DROUHIN, ENGEL, FAIVELEY, GRIVOT, GROS, HUDELOT-NOELLAT, JADOT, LEROY, Chantal Lescure, MEO-CAMUZET, MUGNERET, ROUMIER.

Coche-Dury 21-acre MEURSAULT domaine (and 1 acre+ of CORTON-CHARLEMAGNE) with high reputation for oak-perfumed wines. Also vg ALIGOTE.

Cognac Town and region of the Charentes, W France, and its brandy.

Colin-Deléger Leading CHASSAGNE-M estate. Superb rare PULIGNY-M-Les Caillerets.

Collines Rhodaniennes S Rh r w p ★ Popular Rhône VIN DE PAYS. Mainly reds: Merlot, SYRAH, GAMAY. Some Viognier and CHARD in white.

Collioure Pyr r ★★ 85 86 88 89 90 91 92 93 94 95' 96 97 98 Strong dry red from BANYULS area. Tiny production. Top growers incl Cellier des Templiers, Les CLOS de Paulilles, Cave L'Etoile, Doms du Mas Blanc, de la Rectorie, La Tour Vieille, Vial-Magnères.

Comté Tolosan SW r p w ★ DYA Covers multitude of sins and whole of southwest. Mostly coop wines. Pioneering ★★ DOM DE RIBONNET (Christian Gerber, S of Toulouse) for range of varietal wines, some long keepers.

Condrieu N Rh w ★★★★ DYA Soft fragrant white of great character (and price) from Viognier. Can be outstanding but rapid growth of v'yd (now 250 acres worked by 90 growers) has made quality variable. Increased use of young oak (eg GUIGAL's Doriane CUVEE and Cuilleron) is a doubtful move. Best growers: Y Cuilleron, DELAS, GUIGAL, JABOULET, André Perret, Niéro-Pinchon, Vernay (esp Coteau de Vernon), Verzier, Villard. CHATEAU-GRILLET: similar. Don't even try ageing it. Dubious move to VENDANGE TARDIVE by some growers.

Confuron, Jean-Jacques Tiny NUITS-ST-GEORGES estate to follow closely.

Corbières Midi r (p w) ★★ →★★★ 89 90 91 92 93 94 95' 96 97 98 Vigorous bargain reds. Best growers incl Ch'x Aiguilloux, Lastours, des Ollieux, Les Palais, de la Voulte Gasparet, Doms de Fontsainte, du Vieux Parc, de Villemajou, and coops de Embrès et Castelmaure, Camplong, St-Laurent-Cabrerisse, etc.

Cordier, Ets D Important BORDEAUX shipper and château-owner with wonderful track-record, now owned by Groupe Suez. Over 600 acres. Incl Ch'x CANTEMERLE, CLOS DES JACOBINS, LAFAURIE-PEYRAGUEY, MEYNEY, etc.

Cornas N Rh r ★★ →★★★ 78' 83' 85' 86 88' 89' 90' 91' 93 94' 95' 96 97 98' Sturdy v dark SYRAH wine from 215-acre steep granite v'yds S of HERMITAGE. Needs to age 5–15 yrs but always keeps its rustic character. Top: Allemand, Colombo (beware: new oak), Clape, Courbis, DELAS, Juge, Lionnet, JABOULET (esp St-Pierre CUVEE), Tardieu-Laurent (modern), N Verset.

Corrèze Dordogne r ★ DYA VDP from Coop de Branceilles, between Brive and Beaulieu. Also Dom de la Mégénie.

Corsica (Corse) Strong wines of all colours. ACS are: AJACCIO and PATRIMONIO and better crus Cap Corse and Calvi. VIN DE PAYS: ILE DE BEAUTE.

Corton Burg r ★★★ →★★★★ 78' 85' 88 89' 90' 91 92 93 94 95 96' 97 98 The only GRAND CRU red of the COTE DE BEAUNE. 200 acres in ALOXE-C incl CLOS DU ROI, Les Bressandes. Rich and powerful, should age well. Many good growers.

Corton-Charlemagne Burg w ★★★★ 78' 85' 86' 87 88 89' 90' 91 92 93 94 95 96' 97 98 White section (⅓) of CORTON. Rich spicy lingering; ages magnificently – like a red. Top growers: BONNEAU DU MARTRAY, Chapuis, COCHE-DURY, Delarche, Dubreuil-Fontaine, FAIVELEY, HOSPICES DE BEAUNE, JADOT, LATOUR, Rapet.

Costières de Nîmes S Rh r p w ★ →★★ DYA Rhône delta. Large new AC; fast-improving quality. Formerly Costières du Gard. NB Ch'x de Campuget, Mourgues du Gres, de Nages, de la Tuilerie, Mas des Bressades, Dom du Vieux Relais.

Côte(s) Means hillside; generally a superior v'yd to those on the plain. Many ACs are prefixed by 'Côtes' or 'Coteaux', meaning the same. In St-Emilion distinguishes valley slopes from higher plateau.

Côte de Beaune Burg r w ★★ →★★★★★ Used geographically: the southern half of the COTE D'OR. Applies as an AC only to parts of BEAUNE itself.

Côte de Beaune-Villages Burg r w ★★ 89' 90' 91 92 93 94 95 96' 97 98 Regional APPELLATION for secondary wines of classic area. Cannot be labelled 'Côte de Beaune' without either '-Villages' or village name appended.

Côte de Brouilly Beauj r ★★ 95 96 97 98 Fruity rich BEAUJ CRU. One of best. Esp from: Dom de Chavanne, G Cotton, Ch Delachanel, J-C Nesme, Ch Thivin.

Côte Chalonnaise Burg r w sp ★★ V'yd area between BEAUNE and MACON. See also Givry, Mercurey, Montagny, Rully. Alias 'Région de Mercurey'.

Côte de Nuits Burg r (w) ★★ →★★★★★ N half of COTE D'OR. Mostly red wine.

Côte de Nuits-Villages Burg r (w) ★★ 90 91 92 93 94 95 96' 97 98 A junior AC for extreme N and S ends of COTE DE N; well worth investigating for bargains.

Côte d'Or Département name applied to the central and principal Burgundy v'yd slopes: COTE DE BEAUNE and COTE DE NUITS. The name is not used on labels.

Côte Roannaise Central France r p ★ →★★ 95 96 97 Recent ('94) AC W of Lyon. Silky, focused GAMAY. Demon, Lapandéry, Doms du Pavillon, des Millets.

Côte-Rôtie N Rh r ★★★ →★★★★★ 78' 83' 85' 86 88' 89' 90' 91' 94' 95' 96' 97 98' Potentially finest Rhône red, from S of Vienne, mainly SYRAH; can achieve rich, complex softness and finesse with age (esp 5 to 10⁺ years). Top growers incl Barge, Bernard, Burgaud, Champet, CHAPOUTIER, Clusel-Roch (improving fast), DELAS, J-M Gérin, GUIGAL (long oak-ageing, different and fuller), JABOULET, Jamet, Jasmin, Ogier, ROSTAING (oak here, too), VIDAL-FLEURY.

Coteaux d'Affreux Aspiring to VDP status. Should perhaps use grapes as base.

Coteaux d'Aix-en-Provence Prov r p w ★→★★★ AC on the move. Est'd CH VIGNELAURE now challenged by Ch'x Revelette and Calissanne, also Les Matines (CHAPOUTIER-owned). See also Baux-en-Provence.

Coteaux d'Ancenis Lo r p w (sw) ★ DYA VDQS E Of Nantes. Light GAMAY reds and rosés, sharpish dry whites (CHENIN). Semi-sw from Malvoisie (ages well). Esp Guindon (Malvoisie).

Coteaux de l'Ardèche See l'Ardèche.

Coteaux de l'Aubance Lo w sw ★★→★★★★ 88' 89' 90' 93' 94' 95' 96 97 98 Similar to C'X DU LAYON, improving sw wines from CHENIN. A few SELECTION DES GRAINS NOBLES. Esp from Bablut, Montgilet, RICHOU, Rochelles.

Coteaux des Baronnies S Rh r p w ★ DYA Rhône VIN DE PAYS. SYRAH, Merlot, CAB S, CHARD, plus trad grapes. Promising. Dom du Rieu-Frais (incl gd Viognier) and Dom Rosière (incl gd Syrah) worth noting. Drink young.

Côteaux de Chalosse SW France r p w ★ DYA. Good country wines from coop at Mugron (Landes).

Coteaux Champenois Champ r w (p) ★★★ DYA (whites) AC for non-sp CHAMP. Vintages (if mentioned) follow those for Champ. Not worth inflated prices.

Coteaux du Giennois Lo r p w ★ DYA Sm area N of POUILLY promoted to AC in 98. Light red: blend of GAMAY and PINOT; SAUV à la SANCERRE. Top grower: Paulat.

Coteaux de Glanes SW France r ★ DYA Lively VDP from nr Bretenoux (Lot). Coop only producer. Mostly found in local restaurants.

Coteaux du Languedoc Midi r p w ★★★ Scattered well-above-ordinary MIDI AC areas. Best reds (eg LA CLAPE, FAUGERES, St-Georges-d'Orques, Quatourze, ST-CHINIAN, Montpeyroux, PIC ST-LOUP) age for 2–4 yrs. Now also some good whites. Standards rising dizzily.

Coteaux du Layon Lo w s/sw sw ★★→★★★★ 75 76 85' 86 88' 89' 90' 93' 94 95 96 97 98 The heart of ANJOU, S of Angers: sw CHENIN; admirable acidity, ageing almost forever. New AC SELECTION DES GRAINS NOBLES; cf ALSACE. 7 villages can add name to AC. Top ACs: BONNEZEAUX, C du Layon-Chaume, QUARTS DE CHAUME. Growers incl BAUMARD, Cady, Delesvaux, des Forges, Ogereau, Papin (Pierre-Bise), Jo Pithon, Robineau, Yves Soulez (Genaiserie), P-Y Tijou (Soucherie), Ch'x de Fesles, du Breuil.

Coteaux du Loir Lo r p w dr sw ★→★★★ 76 85 88' 89' 90' 92 93' 95 96 97 98 Sm region N of Tours, incl JASNIERES. S'times fine CHENIN, GAMAY, Pineau d'Aunis, CAB. Top growers: de Rycke, Fresneau, Gigou. The Loir is a tributary of the Loire.

Coteaux de la Loire See Anjou-Coteaux de la Loire.

Coteaux du Lyonnais Beauj r p (w) ★ DYA Junior BEAUJOLAIS. Best EN PRIMEUR.

Coteaux de Peyriac Midi r p ★ DYA One of the most-used VIN DE PAYS names of the Aude département. Huge quantities.

Coteaux de Pierrevert S Rh r p w sp ★ DYA Minor southern VDQS nr Manosque. Well-made coop wine, mostly rosé, with fresh whites.

Coteaux du Quercy SW France r ★→★★ Area S of CAHORS recently promoted to VDQS. Private growers working alongside vg coop near Monpezat incl Doms de la Garde, d'Aries, de Guyot, de Lafage and de Merchien. Three years ageing usually enough but best need more time.

Coteaux de Saumur Lo w sw ★★→★★★ 89 90 93 95' 96 97 98 Rare potentially fine s/sw CHENIN. VOUVRAY-like sw (MOELLEUX) best. Esp CLOS ROUGEARD, Legrand, Vatan.

Coteaux et Terrasses de Montauban SW France r p ★→★★ Dominated by coop at LAVILLEDIEU-LE-TEMPLE. Also Doms de Biarnès and de Montels.

Coteaux du Tricastin S Rh r p w ★★ 90' 92 94 95' 96 97 98' Fringe COTES DU RHONE of increasing quality. Attractive red can age 8 yrs. Dom de Grangeneuve, Dom de Montine, Dom St-Luc and Ch La Décelle among the best.

FRANCE

Coteaux Varois Prov r p w ★→★★ Substantial new AC zone: California-style Dom de St-Jean de Villecroze makes vg red, also Chx Routas, la Calisse, Doms les Alysses, du Deffends.

Coteaux du Vendômois Lo r p w ★→★★ DYA Fringe Loire VDQS west of Vendôme. Pineau d'Aunis is the key grape alone or with others, in rosés and reds and with CHENIN in whites.

Côtes d'Auvergne Central France r p (w) ★→★★ DYA Flourishing small VDQS. Mainly GAMAY; also PINOT N, CHARD. Producers incl Boulin-Constant, Bellard, Cave St-Verny.

Côtes de Blaye B'x w ★ DYA Run-of-the-mill B'x white from BLAYE.

Côtes de Bordeaux St-Macaire B'x w dr sw ★ DYA Everyday B'x white from E of SAUTERNES.

Côtes de Bourg B'x r ★→★★ 85' 86' 88' 89' 90 **93 94 95** 96 97 98 APPELLATION used for many of the better reds of BOURG. Ch'x incl DE BARBE, La Barde, DU BOUSQUET, Brûlesécaille, La Croix de Millorit, Falfas, Font Guilhem, Grand-Jour, de la Grave, La Grolet, Guerry, Guionne, Haut-Maco, Lalibarde, Lamothe, Mendoce, Peychaud, Rousset, Tayac, de Thau.

Côtes du Brulhois SW France r p (w) ★→★★ Nr Agen. Mostly centred on Goulens and Donzac coops. Also Dom de Coujétou-Peyret.

Côtes de Castillon B'x r ★→★★ 89' 90' **92 93 94 95'** 96' 97 98 Flourishing region just E of ST-EMILION producing tempting, often lighter wines. Best ch'x incl Beauséjour, La Clarière-Laithwaite, Fonds-Rondes, Haut-Tuquet, Lartigue, Moulin-Rouge, PITRAY, Rocher-Bellevue, Ste-Colombe, Thibaud-Bellevue.

Côtes de Duras Dordogne r w p ★→★★ **90 94 95'** 96 97 98 B'x satellite; mostly lighter wines. Top producers incl Doms de Laulan (gd Sauv), de Durand, de la Salle, du Vieux Bourg, Amblard, Clos du Cadaret and Ch La Grave Béchade. Also Berticot and Landerrouat coops (now merged).

Côtes du Forez Lo r p (sp) ★ DYA Uppermost Loire VDQS (GAMAY), around Boën, N of St-Etienne, but hardly worth bothering with.

Côtes de Francs B'x r w ★★ 85 86' 88' 89' 90' **92 93 94 95** 96 97 98 Fringe BORDEAUX from E of ST-EMILION. Increasingly attractive tasty wines, esp from Ch'x de Belcier, La Claverie, de Francs, Lauriol, PUYGUERAUD, La Prade.

Côtes du Frontonnais SW France r p ★★ 95 96' **97** 98 S'times called the 'BEAUJOLAIS of Toulouse'. Mostly DYA, ('96 excellent; against trend) but some reds with CAB need longer. Gd growers like Doms de Caze, Joliet, du Roc and Ch'x Bellevue-la-Forêt, Cahuzac and Plaisance give the gd coop a hard time keeping up.

Côtes de Gascogne SW w (r p) ★ DYA VIN DE PAYS branch of ARMAGNAC. Remarkably popular, led by Plaimont coop and Grassa family. Best-known for fresh fruity whites based on the Colombard grape, often with some Gros Manseng. Also Doms de Papolle, Bergerayre, Sancet and Ch Monluc.

Côtes du Jura Jura r p w (sp) ★ DYA Various light tints/tastes. ARBOIS more substantial.

Côtes du Lubéron Prov r p w sp ★→★★ 88 89 90 93 94 95' 96 97 98 Spectacularly improved country wines from N PROVENCE. Actors and media-magnates among owners. Star is Ch de la Canorgue, with vg largely SYRAH red, and whites as well. Others incl CHX VAL-JOANIS, de l'Isolette and Cellier de Marrenon a reliable coop.

Côtes de la Malepère Midi r ★ DYA Rising star VDQS on frontier of MIDI and SW, nr Limoux using grape varieties from both. Watch for fresh eager reds.

Côtes du Marmandais Dordogne r p w ★→★★ Light wines. Cocumont coop better than Beaupuy. Ch de Beaulieu and Dom des Geais better still.

For key to grape variety abbreviations, see pages 7–13.

Côtes de Montravel Dordogne w dr sw ★★ DYA Part of BERGERAC; traditionally med-sw, now often drier. Gd from Ch'x de Montaigne, Pique-Sègue, La Raye, La Resssaudie, Doms de Golse, de Perreau. Montravel SEC is dry, HAUT-MONTRAVEL SW.

Côtes de Provence Prov r p w ★→★★★ Wines of Provence; revolutionized by new attitudes and investment. Castel Roubine, Commanderie de Peyrassol, Doms Bernarde, de la Courtade, OTT, des Planes, Rabiéga, Richeaume are leaders. 75% rosé, 20% red, 5% white. See also Coteaux d'Aix, Côtes de Lubéron, Bandol, etc.

Côtes du Rhône S Rh r p w ★ 90' 93 94 95' 96 98' Basic Rhône AC. Best drunk young – even as PRIMEUR. Wide variations of quality: some heavy over-production. Look for estate bottlings. See Côtes du Rhône-Villages.

> **Top Côtes du Rhône producers:** Ch'x La Courançonne, l'Estagnol, Fonsalette, Montfaucon, St-Esteve and Trignon (incl Viognier white); Clos Simian; Coops Chantecotes (Ste-Cécile-les-Vignes), Villedieu (esp white); Doms Coudoulet de Beaucastel (red and white), Cros de la Mûre, Gourget, Gramenon (Grenache, Viognier), Janasse, Jaume, Réméjeanne, St-Georges, Vieux Chêne; Guigal, Jaboulet.

Côtes du Rhône-Villages S Rh r p w ★→★★ 88 89' 90' 93 94 95' 96' 97 98' Wine of the 17 best S Rhône villages. Substantial and mainly reliable; s'times delicious. Base is GRENACHE; but more SYRAH and MOURVEDRE now used. See Beaumes-de-Venise, Cairanne, Chusclan, Laudun, Rasteau, Sablet, Séguret, St-Gervais, etc. Sub-category with non-specified village name: gd value eg Doms Cabotte, Montbayon, Rabasse-Charavin, Renjarde, Ste-Anne.

Côtes du Roussillon Pyr r p w ★→★★ 88 89 90 91 93 94 95 96 97 98 E Pyrenees AC. Hefty Carignan r best, can be v tasty (eg Gauby). Some w: sharp VINS VERTS.

Côtes du Roussillon-Villages Pyr r ★★ 90 91 92 93 94 95 96 97 98 The region's best reds, from 28 communes including CARAMANY, LATOUR DE FRANCE, LESQUERDE. Best labels are Coop Baixas, Cazes Frères, Doms des Chênes, la Cazenove, Gauby (incl full, exotic white), Château de Jau, Coop Lesquerde, Dom Piquemal, Coop Les Vignerons Catalans. Some now choose to renounce AC status and make varietal VINS DE PAYS.

Côtes de St-Mont SW France r w p ★★ Highly successful Gers VDQS seeking AC status, imitating MADIRAN, PACHERENC. Coop Plaimont all-powerful (Hauts de Bergelle range and Ch de Sabazan). Private growers incl Ch de Bergalasse.

Côtes du Tarn SW France VDP r p w ★ DYA overlaps GAILLAC; from same growers esp coops, Ch de Vigné-Lourac, Doms de Labarthe and d'Escausses.

Côtes de Thongue Midi r w ★ DYA Popular VIN DE PAYS from the HERAULT. Some gd wines esp from Doms Arjolle, les Chemins de Bassac, COUSSERGUES, Croix Belle, Montmarin.

Côtes de Toul E France p r w ★ DYA V light VDQS wines from Lorraine; mainly VIN GRIS (rosé).

Côtes du Ventoux S Rh r p (w) ★★ 94 95' 96 97 98' Booming (15,000-acre) AC between the Rhône and PROVENCE for tasty reds (from café-style to much deeper flavours) and easy rosés. La Vieille Ferme, owned by J-P Perrin of CH DE BEAUCASTEL, is top producer; Coop Villes-St-Auzon, domaine Anges, Ch'x Pesquié, Valcombe and PAUL JABOULET are gd too.

Côtes du Vivarais S Rh r p w ★ DYA Ardèche VDQS. 2,500 acres across several villages on W bank S of ST-PERAY. Improving simple CUVEES; more substantial oak-aged reds. Best producers: Boulle, Gallety, Dom de Belvezet.

Coulée de Serrant Lo w dr sw ★★★★ 76' 78 79' 81 82 83' 85' 86 88 89' 90' 91 92 93 95' 96 97 98 16-acre CHENIN v'yd on Loire's N bank at SAVENNIÈRES run on ferociously organic principles. Intense strong fruity/sharp wine, good aperitif and with fish. Ages almost for ever.

Couly-Dutheil Lo r p w ★★ Major grower and merchant in CHINON; range of reliable wines – CLOS d'Olive and l'Echo are top wines.

Courcel, Dom de Mme de Leading POMMARD estate with top PREMIER CRU Rugiens.

Coussergues, Domaine de Midi r w p ★ DYA Large estate with Australian winemakers nr Beziers. CHARD, SYRAH, etc: bargains.

Crémant In CHAMP means 'creaming' (half-sparkling). Since '75, an AC for quality classic-method sparkling from ALSACE, Loire, BOURGOGNE and most recently LIMOUX – often a bargain. No longer used in Champagne.

Crémant de Loire w sp ★★→★★★ NV High-quality sparkling wine from ANJOU, especially SAUMUR and TOURAINE. Esp BAUMARD Berger, Delhumeau, LANGLOIS-CHATEAU, Nerleux, OISLY ET THESEE, Passavant.

Crépy Savoie w ★★ DYA Light soft Swiss-style white from S shore of Lake Geneva. 'Crépitant' has been coined for its faint fizz.

Criots-Bâtard-Montrachet Burg w ★★★ 78' 79 85 86 88 89 90 91 92 93 94 95' 96' 97 98 4-acre neighbour to BATARD-MONTRACHET. Similar without the extreme pungency.

Crozes-Hermitage N Rh r (w) ★★ 85' 88 89' 90' 91' 94 95' 96' 97' 98' Nr HERMITAGE: larger v'yds, SYRAH wine with fewer dimensions. Some is fruity, early-drinking (2$^+$ yrs); some cask-aged (wait 4–8 yrs). Gd examples from Belle, Ch Curson, Combier, Desmeure, Doms du Colombier, des Entrefaux, du Pavillon, de Thalabert of JABOULET, CHAPOUTIER, Fayolle et Fils, Alain Graillot. Jaboulet's Mule Blanche is vg white.

Cruse et Fils Frères Senior BORDEAUX shipper. Now owned by Pernod-Ricard. The Cruse family (not the company) owns CH D'ISSAN.

Cunac SW France ★ r DYA Part of GAILLAC area. Light fruity quaffable reds.

Cussac Village S of ST-JULIEN. (AC HAUT-MEDOC.) Top ch'x: BEAUMONT, LANESSAN.

Cuve Close Short-cut method of making sparkling wine in a tank. Sparkle dies away in glass much quicker than with METHODE TRADITIONELLE wine.

Cuvée Wine contained in a cuve or vat. A word of many uses, incl synonym for 'blend' and first-press wines (as in CHAMP); in Burgundy interchangeable with 'cru'. Often just refers to a 'lot' of wine.

Dagueneau, Didier ★★★ Top POUILLY-FUME producer. Pouilly's enfant terrible has created new benchmarks for the AC and for SAUV. Top CUVEE is barrel-fermented Silex. Serge D, another top producer, is Didier's uncle.

Daumas Gassac See Mas de Daumas Gassac.

De Castellane Brut NV; Blanc de Blancs; Brut 89 90 93; Cuvée Commodore Brut 85 88 89; Prestige Florens de Castellane 88 90; Traditional Epernay CHAMP house linked with LAURENT-PERRIER. Fine wine museum. Best for v'tage wines esp Commodore.

Degré alcoolique Degrees of alcohol, ie percent by volume.

Deiss, Domaine Marcel Fine ALSACE grower at Bergheim with 50 acres, wide range incl splendid RIES (GRAND CRU Schoenenberg), GEWURZ (Altenburg de Bergheim), good SELECTION DES GRAINS NOBLES and VIN DE PAILLE.

Delamotte Brut; Bl de Blancs (90); Cuvée Nicolas Delamotte Fine small CHARD-dominated CHAMP house at Le Mesnil, owned by LAURENT-PERRIER.

Delas Frères Old and worthy firm of Rhône wine specialists with vineyards at CONDRIEU, COTE-ROTIE, HERMITAGE. Top wines: Condrieu, Marquise de Tourette Hermitage (red and white). Owned by ROEDERER.

Delbeck Small fine CHAMP house reborn '91. Plenty of PINOT N in blend. Excellent vintage wines (85). Value.

Delorme, André Leading COTE CHALONNAISE merchants and growers. Specialists in vg CREMANT DE BOURGOGNE and excellent RULLY, etc.

Demi-Sec Half-dry: in practice more than half sweet (eg of CHAMP).

Des Guelasses, Dom Source of much restaurant house wine, most in pubs and all in theatre bars.

Deutz Brut Classic NV; Rosé NV; Brut 79 81 82 85 88 90; Rosé 88 90; Bl de Bls 85 88 89 90 One of top sm CHAMP houses, ROEDERER-owned. V dry classic wines. Superb luxury CUVEE William Deutz (82 85 88 90). Also German Sekt.

Dirler, J-P ALSACE producer of GRAND CRUS Kessler, Saering. Spiegel; esp for RIES.

Dom Pérignon, Cuvée 71 73 75' 76' 78 82' 83 85' 88 90' 92 93; Rosé 78 82 85 88 Luxury CUVEE of MOET & CHANDON (launched 1936), named after the legendary abbey cellarmaster who first blended CHAMP (but emphatically did NOT put the bubbles in). Astonishing consistent quality and creamy character, esp with 10–15 yrs bottle-age.

Domaine Property, particularly in Burgundy and the south.

Dopff & Irion Famous Riquewihr (ALSACE) business. Esp MUSCAT les Amandiers, RIES Les Murailles, GEWURZ Les Sorcières, PINOT Gr Les Maquisards: long-lived. Good CREMANT d'Alsace. Now part of PFAFFENHEIM coop.

Dopff au Moulin Ancient top-class family wine house at Riquewihr, ALSACE. Best: GEWURZ: GRAND CRUS BRAND and Sporen, RIES SCHOENENBOURG, Sylvaner de Riquewihr. Pioneers of Alsace sp wine; good CUVEES: Bartholdi and Julien.

Dourthe Frères B'X merchant with wide range: good CRUS BOURGEOIS, incl BELGRAVE, MAUCAILLOU, TRONQUOY-LALANDE. Beau-Mayne is well-made brand.

Doux Sweet.

Drappier, André Leading AUBE region CHAMP house (esp Bl de Noirs). Family-run. Vinous NV, Brut Zéro, Rosé Saignée, Carte d'Or 88 89 90 93, Signature Bl de Bl 90 93, Sumptuous prestige CUVEE Grande Sendrée 83 85 89 90 93.

DRC See Romanée-Conti, domaine de la.

Drouhin, J & Cie Deservedly prestigious burgundy grower (150 acres) and merchant with highest standards. Cellars in BEAUNE; v'yds in Beaune, CHABLIS, CLOS DE VOUGEOT, MUSIGNY, etc, and Oregon, USA. Top wines incl (esp) BEAUNE-CLOS DES MOUCHES, CHABLIS LES CLOS, CORTON-CHARLEMAGNE, GRIOTTE-CHAMBERTIN, PULIGNY-M'RACHET-Les Folatières. Majority share now held by a Tokyo co.

Duboeuf, Georges The Grand Fromage of BEAUJOLAIS. Top-class merchant at Romanèche-Thorin. Region's leader in every sense; huge range of admirable wines. Also MOULIN-A-VENT atypically aged in new oak, white MACONNAIS, etc.

Dubos High-level BORDEAUX NEGOCIANT.

Duclot BORDEAUX NEGOCIANT; top-growth specialist. Linked with J-P MOUEIX.

Dujac, Domaine Burgundy grower (Jacques Seysses) at MOREY-ST-DENIS with vineyards in that village and BONNES-MARES, ECHEZEAUX, GEVREY-CHAMBERTIN, etc. Splendidly vivid and long-lived wines. Now also buying grapes in MEURSAULT, and new venture with CAB in COTEAUX VAROIS.

Dulong Highly competent BORDEAUX merchant. Breaking all the rules with unorthodox Rebelle blends. Also VINS DE PAYS.

Durup, Jean One of the biggest CHABLIS growers with 375 acres, including Domaine de l'Eglantière and admirable Ch de Maligny.

Duval-Leroy Fleur de Champagne Brut NV and Rosé NV; Extra Brut; Fleur de C Brut 88 90 93; Bl de Blancs 90; Prestige Cuvée des Rois 86 88 90; Cuvée Spéciale 'Fin de Siècle'. Rising Côtes des Blancs star; fine quality, good value.

Echezeaux Burg r ★★★ 78' 82 85' 87 88 89' 90' 91 92 93 94 95 96 97 98 74-acre GRAND CRU between VOSNE-ROMANEE and CLOS DE VOUGEOT. Can be superlative, fragrant, without great weight, eg Confuron-Cotetidot, ENGEL, Gouroux, GRIVOT, A F GROS, MONGEARD-MUGNERET, MUGNERET, DRC, ROUGET.

Edelzwicker Alsace w ★ DYA Modest blended light white.

53

Eguisheim, Cave Vinicole d' Vg ALSACE coop: fine GRAND CRUS Hatschbourg, Hengst, Ollwiller and Spiegel. Owns Willm. Top label: WOLFBERGER (65% of production). Best ranges: Grande Réserve and Sigillé. Good CREMANT and PINOT.

Eichberg Eguisheim (ALSACE) GRAND CRU. A warm patch, with the lowest rainfall in Colmar area: good for vg KUENTZ-BAS VENDANGE TARDIVE.

Engel, R Top-class grower of CL DE VOUGEOT, ECHEZEAUX, GRANDS-ECH'X, VOSNE-ROM.

Entraygues SW France r p w DYA ★ Fragrant country VDQS. Esp F Avallon's bone-dry white.

Entre-Deux-Mers B'x w ★→★★ DYA Improving dry white B'x from between Rivers Garonne and Dordogne (aka E-2-M). Esp Ch'x BONNET, Gournin, Latour-Laguens, Moulin de Launay, Séguin, Thieuley, Turcaud, etc.

Esmonin, Michel et Fille V classy GEVREY-CHAMBERTIN esp CLOS ST-JACQUES made by daughter Sylvie since '89.

Estaing SW France r p w ★ DYA Neighbour of ENTRAYGUES and similar in style.

L'Estandon Brand name of everyday wine of Nice (AC COTES DE PROVENCE): all colours.

l'Etoile Jura w dr sp (sw) ★★ Subregion of the Jura known for stylish whites, incl VIN JAUNE, similar to CHATEAU-CHALON; good sparkling.

Champagne: a handful of good small houses

Alain Robert – perfectionist Le Mesnil grower-maker; superlative Cuvée Mesnil Tradition.

Boizel – Epernay family house; brilliant Blanc de Blancs fairly priced.

Daniel Dumont – nurseryman-grower in Rilly-la-Montagne; first-rate Grande Réserve NV and luxury Cuvée d'Excellence.

René Geoffroy – grower-maker at Cumières; vibrant fruity NV, vg oak-fermented vintages and Cumières rouge.

Pierre Gimmonet – leading Côte des Blancs grower at Cuis. Delicate dry Cuvée Gastronome ideal with oysters.

Henri Mandois – Pierry. Elegant wines from Meunier and Chard blends.

Lamandier-Bernier – Vertus; top-flight Blanc de Blancs grower-maker esp Cramant Grand Cru.

A R Lenoble – tiny low-key house at Damery. V high quality, esp Chard-led cuvées.

R & L Legras – bijou house at Chouilly with fine range of Blanc de Blancs esp bone dry Brut Intégral and luxury Cuvée St-Vincent.

Ployez Jacquemart – Ludes. Excellent NV and wood-fermented Cuvée d'Harbonville in exceptional years.

Jacques Selosses – Avize; top oak-fermented Blanc de Blancs producer.

Jean-May Tarlant – Oeuilly; subtly oaked Champagnes incl Krug-like Cuvée Louis.

Faiveley, J Family-owned growers and merchants at NUITS-ST-GEORGES, with v'yds (270 acres) in CHAMBERTIN-CLOS DE BEZE, CHAMBOLLE-MUSIGNY, CORTON, MERCUREY, NUITS (74 acres). Consistent high quality (rather than charm).

Faller, Théo/Domaine Weinbach Top ALSACE grower (Kaysersberg) run by Mme Colette Faller and her two daughters. Concentrated wines needing long ageing, up to 10 yrs. Esp GRAND CRUS SCHLOSSBERG (RIES), Furstentum (GEWURZ).

Faugères Midi r (p w) ★★ 88 89 90 91 92 93 94 95 96 97 98 Isolated COTEAUX DU LANGUEDOC village with above-average wine and exceptional terroir. Gained AC status '82. Esp Dom Alquier, Dom des Estanilles, Ch La Liquière.

Fessy, Sylvain Dynamic BEAUJOLAIS merchant with wide range.

Fèvre, William CHABLIS grower with the biggest GRAND CRU holding Dom de la Maladière (45 acres). But spoils some of his top wines with new oak. One whimsy wine he calls Napa Vallée de France. Bought '98 by HENRIOT.

Fiefs Vendéens Lo r p w ★ DYA Up-and-coming vDQS for light wines from the Vendée, just S of MUSCADET on the Atlantic coast. Wines from CHARD, CHENIN, Colombard, Grolleau, Melon (whites), CAB, PINOT N and GAMAY for reds and rosés. Esp Coirier, Ferme des Ardillers.

Filliatreau, Domaine Lo r ★★→★★★ Paul Filliatreau put SAUMUR-CHAMPIGNY on map and in Paris restaurants. Supple, fruity drinkable Jeunes Vignes. Other CUVÉES aged 2 to 5 years (Vieille Vignes and La Grande Vignolle).

Fitou Midi r ★★ 88 89 90 91 92 93 94 95 96 97 98 Superior CORBIÈRES-style red wines; powerful, ageing well. Best from coops at Cascastel, Paziols and Tuchan. Interesting experiments with Mourvèdre grapes in Leucate. Good estates, incl Ch Nouvelles, Dom Lerys, Rolland.

Fixin Burg r ★★★ 88' 89' 90' 91 92 93 94 95 96' 97 98 Worthy and under-valued northern neighbour of GEVREY-CHAMBERTIN. Often splendid reds. Best v'yds: CLOS du Chapitre, Les Hervelets, Clos Napoléon. Growers incl Bertheau, R Bouvrier, CLAIR, FAIVELEY, Gelin, Gelin-Molin, Guyard.

Fleurie Beauj r ★★★ 94 95 96 97 98 The epitome of a BEAUJOLAIS CRU: fruity, scented, silky, racy wines. Esp from Chapelle des Bois, Chignard, Depardon, Després, DUBOEUF, Ch de Fleurie, the coop.

Floc de Gascogne SW France r p w ARMAGNAC'S answer to PINEAU DES CHARENTES. Aperitif from unfermented grape juice blended with Armagnac.

Fortant de France Midi r p w ★→★★ VDP D'OC brand (dressed to kill) of remarkable quality single-grape wines from Sète neighbourhood. See Skalli.

Frais Fresh or cool.

Frappé Ice-cold.

Froid Cold.

Fronsac B'x r ★→★★★ 85' 86' 88' 89' 90' 93 94 95 96 97 98 Picturesque area; increasingly fine often tannic r just W of ST-ÉM. Ch'x incl de Carles, DALEM, LA DAUPHINE, Fontenil, Mayne-Vieil, Moulin-Haut-Laroque, LA RIVIÈRE, La Rousselle, La Valade, La Vieille Cure, Villars. Give them time. See also smaller Canon-Fronsac.

Frontignan Midi br sw ★★ NV Strong sweet liquorous MUSCAT of ancient repute. Quality steadily improving, esp from Ch'x Stony and La Peyrade.

Gagnard-Delagrange, Jacques Estimable small (12-acre) grower of CHASSAGNE-M'RACHET, including some M'RACHET. Look out also for his daughters' estates, Blain-Gagnard and Fontaine-Gagnard.

Gaillac SW France r p w dr sw sp ★→★★ mostly DYA except oaked reds (**94 95 96 97** 98), sw whites. Gd all-rounders: Dom de Labarthe, Mas Pignou, d'Aurel, Barreau, d'Escausses, the three coops esp Cave Técou (best of three, esp 'Passion' range). White sl fizzy 'perlé' (Dom de Salmes and Rabastens coops), sw and dr local varietals (Robert Plageoles and Dom de la Ramaye). Red PRIMEURS often beat BEAUJOLAIS for medals (vg Dom de Labarthe). Vg sw whites (Ch de Mayragues, Doms de Long Pech and Bicary). NB also dry whites from Dom des Perches and white sp from Doms René Rieux and Canto Perlic.

Gamay See Grapes for red wine (pages 11–13).

Gard, Vin de Pays du Languedoc ★ The Gard département at the mouth of the Rhône is a centre of gd VINS DE PAYS production, incl Coteaux Flaviens, Pont du Gard, SABLES DU GOLFE DU LION, Salavès, Uzège and Vaunage. To follow, eg Dom de Baruel (incl SYRAH).

Gers r w p ★ DYA Indistinguishable from nearby CÔTES DE GASCOGNE.

Gevrey-Chambertin Burg r ★★★ 78 85' 88 89' 90' 91 92 93 94 95 96' 97 98 Village containing the great CHAMBERTIN, its GRAND CRU cousins and many other noble v'yds (eg PREMIERS CRUS Cazetiers, Combe aux Moines, CLOS ST-JACQUES, Clos des Varoilles), as well as much more commonplace land. Growers incl Boillot, Damoy, DROUHIN, Dugat, Esmonin, FAIVELEY, Dom Harmand-Geoffroy, JADOT, Leclerc, LEROY, MORTET, ROTY, ROUMIER, ROUSSEAU, Serafin, TRAPET, VAROILLES.

Gewurztraminer Speciality grape of ALSACE: one of 4 allowed for specified GRAND CRU wines. The most aromatic of Alsace grapes: at best like rose-petals to smell, grapefruit and/or lychees to taste.

Gigondas S Rh r p ★★ →★★★ **78 81' 83 85 86 88 89' 90' 93** 94 95' 96 97 98' Worthy neighbour to CH'NEUF-DU-PAPE. Strong full-bodied s'times peppery wine, largely GRENACHE; eg Ch de Montmirail, Dom du Cayron, Font-Sane, Goubert, Gour de Chaulé, Grapillon d'Or, Les Hauts de Montmirail, Les Pallieroudas, Pesquier, les Pallières, Raspail-Ay, Sta-Duc, St-Gayan, des Travers, du Trignon.

Ginestet Long-established B'X NEGOCIANT now owned by Jacques Merlaut, said to be second in turnover. Merlaut's empire incl Ch'x CHASSE-SPLEEN, HAUT-BAGES-LIBERAL, LA GURGUE, FERRIERE.

Gisselbrecht, Louis High-quality ALSACE growers and merchants at Dambach-la-Ville. RIES and GEWURZ best. Cousin Willy Gisselbrecht's wines are v competitive.

Givry Burg r w ★★ **89' 90' 91 92 93 94 95** 96' 97 98 Underrated COTE CHALONNAISE village: light but tasty and typical burgundy from eg DELORME, Dom Joblot, L LATOUR, T Lespinasse, CLOS Salomon, BARON THENARD.

Gorges et Côtes de Millau SW France r p w ★ DYA Locally popular country wines. Reds best. Coop at Aguessac dominant .

Gosset Brut NV; Brut **81 82 83** 85 88 90; Grande Réserve; Grand Millésime Brut **79 82 83** 85 89; Grand Rosé 85 88 V old small CHAMP house at AY. Excellent full-bodied wine (esp Grand Millésime). Gosset Celebris (**90**) is prestige CUVEE, launched '95 by ambitious new owners, Cointreau family of COGNAC Frapin.

Gouges, Henri Reinvigorated estate for rich complex NUITS-ST-GEORGES.

Goulaine, Château de The ceremonial showplace of MUSCADET; a noble family estate and its wine. Adequately good rather than excellent.

Goût Taste, eg goût anglais: as the English like it (ie dry, or, differently for CHAMP, well-aged).

Grand Cru One of top Burgundy v'yds with its own APPELLATION CONTROLEE. In ALSACE one of the 50 top v'yds covered by Alsace Grand Cru AC, but more vague elsewhere. In ST-EMILION the third rank of ch'x, incl about 200 properties.

Grande Champagne The AC of the best area of COGNAC. Nothing fizzy about it.

Grande Rue, La Burg r ★★★ 89' 90' **91 92 93 94** 95 96' 97 98 Recently promoted VOSNE-R GRAND CRU, neighbour to ROMANEE-CONTI. Owned by Dom Lamarche.

Grands-Echezeaux Burg r ★★★★ **78' 82 85' 87 88' 89' 90' 91' 92 93 94** 95 96' 97 Superlative 22-acre GRAND CRU next to CLOS DE VOUGEOT. Wines not weighty but aromatic. Viz: DROUHIN, ENGEL, MONGEARD-MUGNERET, DRC.

Gratien, Alfred and Gratien & Meyer Brut NV; Cuvée Paradis Brut; Brut **79 82 83** 85' 88; Prestige Cuvée Paradis Rosé. Excellent smaller family CHAMP house with top traditional standards. Fine v dry long-lasting wine is made in barrels. Gratien & Meyer is counterpart at SAUMUR. (Vg Cuvée Flamme.)

Graves B'x r w ★★→★★★★ Region S of Bordeaux city with excellent soft earthy reds, dry whites (SAUV-Sém) reasserting star status. PESSAC-LEOGNAN is inner zone.

Graves de Vayres B'x r w ★ DYA Part of ENTRE-D-M; no special character.

Grenache See grapes for red and white wine (pages 7–13).

Griotte-Chambertin Burg r ★★★★ **78' 85' 87 88' 89' 90' 91 92 93 94** 95 96' 97 98 14-acre GRAND CRU adjoining CHAMBERTIN. Similar wine, but less masculine, more 'tender'. Growers incl DROUHIN, PONSOT.

Grivot, Jean 35-acre COTE DE NUITS domaine, in 5 ACS incl RICHEBOURG, Nuits PREMIERS CRUS, VOSNE-ROMANEE, CLOS DE VOUGEOT etc. Top quality.

Groffier, Robert Pure, elegant GEVREY-C, CHAMBOLLE-M esp Les Amoureuses.

Gros, Domaines An excellent family of vignerons in VOSNE-ROMANEE comprising (at least) Domaines Jean, Michel, Anne et François, Anne-François Gros and Gros Frère et Soeur.

Gros Plant du Pays Nantais Lo w ★ DYA Junior vDQS cousin of MUSCADET, sharper, lighter; from the COGNAC grape, aka Folle Blanche, Ugni Bl etc.

Guffens-Heynen Belgian POUILLY-FUISSE grower. Tiny quantity, top quality. Also heady GAMAY and COTE D'OR wine (bought-in grapes) – also VERGET. To follow.

Guigal, Ets E Celebrated grower (COTE-ROTIE) and merchant of CONDRIEU, Côte-Rôtie, HERMITAGE and S Rhône. Since '85 owner of VIDAL-FLEURY. By ageing single-vineyard Côte-Rôtie (La Mouline, La Landonne and La Turque) for 42 months in new oak; Guigal breaks local tradition to please (esp) American palates. His standard wines are good value, esp the red COTES DU RHONE. Special CONDRIEU CUVEE La Doriane (since '95) – full, oaky.

Haut-Poitou Lo w r ★→★★ DYA Up-and-coming VDQS S of ANJOU. Vg whites (CHARD, SAUV, CHENIN) from CAVE linked with DUBOEUF. Improving reds: GAMAY, CAB, best age 4–5 yrs. Has rejected restrictions of AC status for freedom of choice.

Haut-Benauge B'x w ★ DYA AC for a limited area in ENTRE-DEUX-MERS.

Haut-Médoc B'x r ★★→★★★★ 70 78 81 82' 83' 85' 86' 88' 89' 90' 93 94 95 96 97 98 Big AC incl best parts of MEDOC. Most of zone has communal ACS (eg MARGAUX, PAUILLAC). Some excellent ch'x (eg LA LAGUNE): simply AC HAUT-MEDOC.

Haut-Montravel Dordogne w sw ★★ 90' 94' 95' 96 97 98 Rare BERGERAC sweet white; rather like MONBAZILLAC. Look for Ch'x Le Bondieu, Moulin Caresse, Puy-Servain-Terrement and Roque-Peyre, also Dom de Libarde.

Hautes-Côtes de Beaune Burg r w ★★ 85 88 89' 90' 91 92 93 94 95 96' 97 98 AC for a dozen villages in the hills behind the COTE DE BEAUNE. Light wines, worth investigating. Top growers: Cornu, Mazilly.

Hautes-Côtes de Nuits Burg r w ★★ 85 88 89' 90' 91 92 93 94 95 96' 97 98 As above, for COTE DE NUITS. An area on the way up. Top growers: C Cornu, Jayer-Gilles, M GROS. Also has large BEAUNE coop; good esp from GEISWEILER.

Heidsieck, Charles Brut Réserve NV; Brut 83 85 90; Rosé 81 83 85 89 Major Reims CHAMP house, now controlled by Rémy Martin; also incl Trouillard, de Venoge. Luxury brand Bl des Millénaires (83 85 90). Fine quality recently esp new BRUT Réserve Mis en Cave range; NV: real bargain. See also Piper-Heidsieck.

Heidsieck, Monopole Brut NV Blue Top; Red Top. Once illustrious CHAMP house now owned by VRANKEN group. Red Top CUVEE virtually Blanc de Noirs. Luxury brand Diamant Bleu (76 85) is excellent.

Hengst Wintzenheim (ALSACE) GRAND CRU. Excels with top-notch GEWURZ from Albert Mann; also Pinot-Auxerrois, Chasselas (esp JOSMEYER'S) and PINOT Noir (esp A Mann's) with no GRAND CRU status.

Henriot Brut Souverain NV; Blanc de Blancs de CHARD NV; Brut 85 88 89 90; Brut Rosé 85 88 89 90; Luxury Cuvée: Cuvée des Enchanteleurs 85 88 Old family CHAMP house; regained independence in '94. V fine fresh creamy style. Also owns BOUCHARD PERE (since '95) and FEVRE.

Hérault Midi Biggest v'yd département in France: 980,000 acres of vines. Chiefly VIN DE TABLE but some gd AC COTEAUX DU LANGUEDOC and pioneering Vins de Pays de l'Hérault.

Hermitage N Rh r w ★★★→★★★★ 61 66 70 72 78' 83' 85' 87 88 89' 90' 91' 94 95' 96' 97' 98' By tradition, the 'manliest' wine of France: dark powerful and profound. Truest example of SYRAH from 309 hillside acres on E bank of Rhône, granite plus clay-chalk. Needs long ageing. White (Marsanne, some Roussanne) is heady and golden; now usually made for early drinking, though best wines mature for up to 25 yrs; can be better than red (eg 93). Top makers: Belle, CHAPOUTIER, CHAVE, DELAS, Faurie, Grippat, GUIGAL, JABOULET, Sorrel, DE VALLOUIT. TAIN coop also useful and improving.

Hospices de Beaune Historic hospital and charitable institution in BEAUNE, with excellent v'yds (known by 'CUVEE' names) in BEAUNE, CORTON, MEURSAULT, POMMARD, VOLNAY. Wines are auctioned on the third Sunday of each November.

FRANCE

Hudelot-Noëllat, Alain Under-appreciated VOUGEOT estate producing some excellent wines.

Huët 47' 59' 76' **85' 88'** 89' **90'** 93 95' 96 97 98 (SEC and DEMI-SEC) Leading top-quality estate in VOUVRAY, run on biodynamic principles. Wines for long ageing. Single v'yard wines best: Le Haut Lieu, Le Mont, Clos du Bourg.

Hugel et Fils The best-known ALSACE CO; founded at Riquewihr in 1639 and still in the family. 'Johnny' H (ret'd '97) is the region's beloved spokesman (Etienne H is now in charge). Quality escalates with Tradition and then Jubilée Réserve ranges. Hugels are militantly against Alsace GRAND CRU system. SELECTIONS DES GRAINS NOBLES: Hugel pioneered this style and still makes some of finest examples. Also occasionally VIN DE PAILLE.

Hureau, Ch de ★★→★★★ Dynamic SAUMUR estate: quality SAUMUR-CHAMPIGNY, Saumur Blanc, COTEAUX DE SAUMUR.

Ile de Beauté Name given to VINS DE PAYS from CORSICA. Mostly red.

Impériale BORDEAUX bottle holding 8.5 normal bottles (6.4 litres).

Irancy ('Bourgogne Irancy') Burg r (p) ★★ 85 88 89 90 **91 92** 93 **94** 95 96' 97 98 Good light red made nr CHABLIS from PINOT N and the local César. The best vintages are long-lived and mature well. To watch. Growers incl Colinot.

Irouléguy SW France r p (w) ★★ Agreeable local wines of Basque country. Mainly rosé; also dark dense Tannat/CAB reds to keep 5 yrs⁺. Gd from Doms Ilarria, BRANA, Arretxea, Etchegaraya and Abotia and coop. A future MADIRAN?

Jaboulet Aîné, Paul Old family firm at Tain, leading grower of HERMITAGE (esp La Chapelle ★★★★), CROZES Thalabert (vg value), Roure; merchant of other Rhône wines – esp CORNAS (St-Pierre), COTES DU RHONE Parallèle 45, COTES DU VENTOUX.

Jacquart Brut NV, Brut Rosé NV (Carte Blanche and Cuvée Spéciale); Brut 89 90 93 Relatively new ('62) coop-based CHAMP marque; in quantity the sixth-largest. Fair quality. Luxury brands: CUVEE Nominée Blanc 88 90, CN Rosé 88 90. Vg Mosaïque BL DE BLANCS 90, Mosaïque Rosé 90.

Jacquesson Excellent small Dizy CHAMP house. Vg vintage BL DE BLANCS (**90** 93); exquisite barrel-fermented Signature luxury CUVEES: both w (88 90) and rosé (90). Also Dégorgement Tardif (75 82) and new millennium cuvée 'Mémoire du XXième Siècle'.

Jadot, Louis Top-quality burgundy merchant house with v'yds (155 acres) in BEAUNE, CORTON, Ch des Jacques (MOULIN A VENT), etc. Wines to bank on.

Jardin de la France Lo w r p DYA One of France's four regional VINS DE PAYS. Covers Loire Valley: mostly single grape (esp CHARD, GAMAY, SAUV).

Jasnières Lo w dr (sw) ★★★ 76 **78 79** 83 85 86 88' 89' 90' 92 93' 95' 96 97 98 Rare and almost immortal dry VOUVRAY-like wine (CHENIN) of N TOURAINE. Esp Aubert de Rycke, Boulay, Gigou.

Jayer, Henri See Rouget, Emmanuel.

Jeroboam In BORDEAUX a 6-bottle bottle (holding 4.5 litres) or triple MAGNUM; in CHAMP, a double magnum.

Jobard, François Small MEURSAULT domaine; classic slow-evolving wines.

Joseph Perrier Cuvée Royale Brut NV; Cuvée Royale Bl de Blancs NV; Cuvée Royale Rosé NV; Brut 82 83 85 90 Family-run CHAMP house at Chalons with good v'yds in Marne Valley. Supple fruity style; vg prestige Cuvée Joséphine, mainly CHARD 85 90. Part-owned since '98 by ALAIN THIENOT.

JosMeyer Family house at Wintzenheim, ALSACE. Vg long-ageing wines, esp GEWURZ and Pinot Bl. Fine RIES from GRAND CRU Hengst. Wide range.

Juliénas Beauj r ★★★ 95 96 97 98 Leading CRU of BEAUJOLAIS: vigorous fruity wine to keep 2–3 yrs. Growers incl Ch'x du Bois de la Salle, des Capitans, de Juliénas, des Vignes; Doms Bottière, R Monnet, coop.

Jura See Côtes du Jura.

Jurançon SW France w sw dr ★★→★★★★ 85' 89' 90' 94' 95' 96 97' 98 Rare highly flavoured long-lived speciality of Pau in Pyrenean foothills, at best like wildflower SAUTERNES. Not to be missed. Both sw and dr should age. Top growers: Dom du Bellegarde, Barrère, Bordenave, du Cinquau, Dom Cauhapé, Gaillot, Guirouilh, Jolys, Lamouroux, Lapeyre, Larredya, Nigri, de Rousse. Also coop's dry Grain Sauvage, Brut d'Ocean and Peyre d'Or.

Kaefferkopf Alsace w dr sw ★★★ Ammerschwihr v'yd famous for blends rather than single-variety wines and denied GRAND CRU status for this reason.

Kientzheim-Kayserberg, Cave Vinicole de Important ALSACE coop for quality as well as size. Esp GEWURZ, RIES GRAND CRU Schlossberg and CREMANT.

Kientzler, André Fine ALSACE RIES specialist in Geisburg GRAND CRU, esp VENDANGE TARDIVE and SGN. Equally gd from GCs Kirchberg de Ribeauvillé for GEWURZ, Osterberg for occasional 'vins de glaces' (Eisweins). Also vg Auxerrois, Chasselas.

Kreydenweiss Fine ALSACE grower: 24 acres at Andlau, esp for PINOT Gr (vg GRAND CRU Moenchberg), Pinot Bl and RIES. Top wine: Grand Cru Kastelberg (Ries ages 20 yrs); also fine Auxerrois 'Kritt Klevner' and gd VENDANGE TARDIVE. One of first in Alsace to use new oak. Good Ries-Pinot Gr blend 'Clos du Val d'Eléon'.

Vins du Sudouest: où les trouver?

Cahors Restaurant Le Balandre, 5 av Charles-de-Freycinet, tel 05 65 30 01 97. Wines: all Cahors. Also Restaurant Le Gindreau, St-Médand de Cahors, tel 05 65 36 22 27.

Villefranche-de-Rougergue Shop: La Maison du Vin, 32 rue Sénéchal. Wines: Estaing (Mme Fages, dry white), Domaine du Clos (red Marcillac), François Avallon (Entraygues, dry white), Domaine Rotier (Gaillac), wines of A Brumont).

Gaillac La Maison des Vins, Abbaye St-Michel. The shop of the local Comité Interprofessionnel des Vins de Gaillac.

Biarritz Le Cellier des Halles, 8 rue des Halles, tel 05 59 24 21 64.

Périgueux Les Caves St-Front, tel 05 53 53 39 24.

Sarlat and Le Bugue St-Julien de Savignac, 05 53 31 29 29.

Toulouse L'Epicerie, tel 05 61 52 26 67.

Kriter Popular sparkler processed in Burgundy by PATRIARCHE. See the fountain on the Autoroute du Soleil.

Krug Grande Cuvée; Vintage 79 81 82 85 88 89; Rosé; Clos du Mesnil (Bl de Blancs) 79 81 82 83 85 88; Krug Collection 62 64 66 69 71 73 76 79 Small and supremely prestigious CHAMP house. Dense full-bodied v dry wines: long ageing, superlative quality. Owned since '99 by MOET-Hennessy.

Kuentz-Bas Top-quality ALSACE grower/merchant at Husseren-les-Châteaux, esp for PINOT Gr, GEWURZ. Also good VENDANGES TARDIVES.

Labouré-Roi Reliable, dynamic merchant at NUITS. Mostly whites. Many fine domaine wines, esp René Manuel's MEURSAULT, Chantal Lescure's Nuits.

Ladoix-Serrigny Burg r (w) ★★ Northernmost village of COTE DE BEAUNE below hills of CORTON. To watch for bargains.

Ladoucette, de ★★→★★★★ Leading producer of POUILLY-FUME, based at Ch de Nozet. Luxury brand Baron de L can be wonderful (but at a price). Also SANCERRE Comte Lafond and La Poussie (and PIC, CHABLIS).

Lafarge, Michel 25-acre COTE DE BEAUNE estate with excellent VOLNAYS.

Lafon, Domaine des Comtes 34-acre top burgundy estate in MEURSAULT, LE M'RACHET, VOLNAY. Glorious intense whites; extraordinary dark reds.

Laguiche, Marquis de Largest owner of LE M'RACHET. Magnificent wines made by DROUHIN.

Lalande de Pomerol B'x r ★★ **85 86' 88' 89' 90' 93 94 95** 96 97 98 Neighbour to POMEROL. Wines similar, but less mellow. Top ch'x: Les Annereaux, DE BEL-AIR, Belles-Graves, Bertineau-St-Vincent, La Croix Bellevue, La Croix-St-André, Hauts-Conseillants, Hauts-Tuileries, Moncets, SIAURAC, TOURNEFEUILLE. To try.

Langlois-Château One of top SAUMUR sp houses (esp CREMANT). Controlled by BOLLINGER. Also range of Loire still wines, esp Saumur Bl VIEILLES VIGNES.

Lanson Père & Fils Black Label NV; Rosé NV; Brut **88 89 90 93** Imp't improving CHAMP house with cellars at Reims. Long-lived luxury brand: Noble Cuvée (**81 85 88**). Black Label is reliable fresh and appley NV. New CUVEE: BL DE BLS **83 90**.

Laroche Important grower (190 acres) and dynamic CHABLIS merchant, incl Domaines La Jouchère and Laroche. Top wines: Blanchots (esp Réserve de l'Obédiencerie ★★★★) and CLOS VIEILLE VIGNES. Also blends gd non-regional CHARD and now ambitious MIDI range, Dom La Chevalière.

Latour, Louis Famous burgundy merchant and grower with v'yds (120 acres) in BEAUNE, CORTON, etc. Among the v best for white: CHEVALIER-M'RACHET Les Demoiselles, CORTON-CHARLEMAGNE, M'RACHET, gd-value MONTAGNY and ARDECHE CHARD etc. Also PINOT N Valmoissine from the Var.

Latour de France r (w) ★→★★ **90 91 92 93 94 95** 96 97 98 Supposedly superior village in AC COTES DE ROUSSILLON-VILLAGES.

Latricières-Chambertin Burg r ★★★ **78' 85' 88' 89' 90' 91 92 93 94** 95 96' 97 98 17-acre GRAND CRU neighbour of CHAMBERTIN. Similar wine but lighter and 'prettier', eg from FAIVELEY, LEROY, PONSOT, TRAPET.

Laudun S Rh w r p ★ Village of COTES DU RHONE-VILLAGES (west bank). Attractive wines from the coop incl fresh whites. Dom Pelaquié is best, esp white.

Laurent-Perrier Brut NV; Rosé NV; Brut **88 90** Dynamic highly successful family-owned CHAMP house at Tours-sur-Marne. Excellent luxury brands: Cuvée Grand Siècle (NV and **85 88**), CGS Alexandra BRUT Rosé (**85 88**). Also Ultra Brut. Owns SALON, DELAMOTTE, DE CASTELLANE.

Lavilledieu-du-Temple SW France r p w ★ DYA Fruity wines from coop nr Montauban. Also VDP from COTEAUX DU QUERCY, COTEAUX ET TERRASSES DE MONTAUBAN.

Leflaive, Domaine S'times considered the best of all white burgundy growers, at PULIGNY-M'RACHET. Best v'yds: Bienvenues-, Chevalier-M, Clavoillons, Pucelles and (since '91) Le M'rachet. Increasingly organic methods; ever-finer wines.

Leflaive, Olivier NEGOCIANT at PULIGNY-M'RACHET since '84, nephew of the above, now with 19 acres of his own. Reliable whites and reds, incl less famous ACS, have upgraded seriously since '90. Now ★★★.

Léognan B'x r w ★★★→★★★★ Top village of GRAVES with its own AC: PESSAC-LEOGNAN. Best ch'x: DOM DE CHEVALIER, HAUT-BAILLY.

Leroy The ultimate NEGOCIANT-ELEVEUR at AUXEY-DURESSES with a growing domaine and the finest stocks of old wines in Burgundy. Part-owners of DOM DE LA ROMANEE-CONTI. In '88 bought the 35-acre Noëllat estate in CLOS VOUGEOT, NUITS, ROMANEE-ST-VIVANT, SAVIGNY, etc. Leroy's whole range (from AUXEY whites to CHAMBERTIN and neighbours) is simply Burgundy's best. ★★★★ all round.

Lesquerde ★★ **90 91 92 93 94 95** 96 97 98 New superior AC village of COTES DU ROUSSILLON-VILLAGES.

Lichine, Alexis & Cie BORDEAUX merchants (once of the late Alexis Lichine). No connection with CH PRIEURE-LICHINE.

Lie, sur On the lees. MUSCADET is often bottled straight from the vat, for maximum zest and character.

Limoux Pyr r w ★★ Burgeoning AC for sp BLANQUETTE DE LIMOUX or better CREMANT de Limoux, oak-aged CHARD for Limoux AC and PINOT N for VDP as well as traditional grapes. Growers incl Dom de l'Aigle.

Liquoreux Term for a very sweet wine: eg SAUTERNES, top VOUVRAY, JURANCON, etc.

Lirac S Rh r p w ★★ **89' 90' 91 93 94' 95'** 96' 98' Next to TAVEL. Approachable often soft red (can age 5 yrs). Red overtaking rosé, esp Doms Cantegril, Devoy-Martine, Maby (Fermade), André Méjan, de la Mordorée, Sabon, Ch de Bouchassy, Ségriès. Greater use of MOURVEDRE: firming some reds. Gd whites too.

Listel Midi r p w ★→★★ DYA Vast (4,000-acre[+]) historic estate on sandy beaches of the Golfe du Lion. Owned by VAL D'ORBIEU group. Pleasant light 'vins des sables' incl sparkling. Dom du Bosquet-Canet is a fruity CAB, Dom de Villeroy fresh BLANC DE BLANCS SUR LIE, and CHARD. Also fruity almost non-alcoholic PETILLANT, Ch de Malijay COTES DU RHONE, Abbaye de Ste-Hilaire COTEAUX VAROIS, Ch La Gordonne COTES DE PROVENCE.

Listrac-Médoc B'x r ★★→★★★★ Village of HAUT-MEDOC next to MOULIS. Best ch'x: CLARKE, FONREAUD, FOURCAS-DUPRE, FOURCAS-HOSTEN.

Livinière, La Midi r (p w) ★→★★★ High-quality MINERVOIS village. The first cru of the AC. Best growers: Abbaye de Tholomies, Combe Blanche, Ch de Gourgazaud, Laville Bertrou, Doms Maris, Ste-Eulalie, Vallière, Coop La Livinière.

Long-Depaquit Vg CHABLIS domaine (esp MOUTONNE), owned by BICHOT.

Lorentz, Gustave ALSACE grower and merchant at Bergheim. Esp GEWURZ, RIES from GRAND CRUS Altenberg de Bergheim, Kanzlerberg. Also owns Jerome Lorentz.

Loron & Fils Big-scale grower and merchant at Pontanevaux; specialist in BEAUJOLAIS and sound VINS DE TABLE.

Loupiac B'x w sw ★★ **79' 83 85 86' 88' 89 90 91 93 95** 96 97 98 Across River Garonne from SAUTERNES. Top ch'x: CLOS-Jean, Haut-Loupiac, LOUPIAC-GAUDIET, RICAUD, Rondillon.

Lugny See Mâcon-Lugny.

Lussac-St-Emilion B'x r ★★ **85 86' 88' 89' 90' 92 93 94 95** 96 97 98 NE neighbour to ST-EMILION. Top ch'x incl Barbe Blanche, BEL AIR, DU LYONNAT, Tour de Grenat, Villadière. Coop (at PUISSEGUIN) makes pleasant Roc de Lussac.

Macération carbonique Traditional fermentation technique: whole bunches of unbroken grapes in a closed vat. Fermentation inside each grape eventually bursts it, giving vivid fruity mild wine, not for ageing. Esp in BEAUJOLAIS; now much used in the MIDI and elsewhere, even CHATEAUNEUF-DU-PAPE.

> **The Mâconnais**
> The hilly zone just north of Beaujolais has outcrops of limestone where Chardonnay gives full, if not often fine, wines. The village of Chardonnay here may (or may not) be the home of the variety. Granite soils give strong Gamay reds. The top Mâconnais AC is Pouilly-Fuissé, then St-Véran, then Mâcon-Villages with a village name. The potential is here to produce lower-priced, richly typical Chardonnays to out-do the New World (and indeed the S of France). Currently, most wines are less than extraordinary.

Mâcon Burg r w (p) ★★ **95 96 97** 98 Sound, usually unremarkable reds (GAMAY best), tasty dry (CHARD) whites. Almost DYA.

Mâcon-Lugny Burg r w sp ★★ **94 95 96 97** 98 Village next to VIRE with huge and vg coop (4M bottles). Les Genevrières is sold by LOUIS LATOUR.

Mâcon-Villages Burg w ★★→★★★ **93 94 95 96** 97 98 Increasingly well-made typical white burgundies (when not over-produced). Named for their villages, eg M-Chardonnay, -Clessé, -Lugny, -Prissé, -Viré, -Uchizy. Best coop is probably Prissé, biggest Lugny. Top growers: Vincent (Fuissé), THEVENET (Clessé), Bonhomme (Viré), Merlin (La Roche Vineuse).

Mâcon-Viré Burg w ★★ **93 94 95** 96 97 98 One of the best white wine villages of MACON. Esp A Bonhomme, CLOS du Chapitre, JADOT, Ch de Viré, coop.

Macvin Jura w sw ★★ AC for 'traditional' MARC and grape-juice aperitif.

Madiran SW France r ★★→★★★ 88 89' 90' 94 95' 96 97' 98 Dark vigorous red from s of ARMAGNAC, like tough fruity MEDOC with a fluid elegance of its own. Needs age. Try ch'x MONTUS, Bouscassé, Doms Berthoumieu, Barréjat, Laplace (Ch d'Aydie), Chapelle Lenclos, Labranche-Laffont, Peyros, Pichard, Laffitte-Teston, Capmartin and coop's Ch Crouseilles. White is AC PACHERENC DU VIC BILH.

Magenta, Duc de Recently revamped fine Burgundy estate (30 acres), half red, half white, based at CHASSAGNE-M'RACHET, managed by JADOT.

Magnum A double bottle (1.5 litres).

Mähler-Besse First-class Dutch NEGOCIANT in B'X. Has share in CH PALMER and owns Ch Michel de Montaigne. Brands incl Cheval Noir. (Total: 250 acres.)

Mailly-Champagne Top CHAMP coop. Luxury wine: CUVÉE des Echansons.

Maire, Henri The biggest grower/merchant of JURA wines, with half of the entire AC. Some top wines, many cheerfully commercial. Fun to visit.

Maranges Burg r ★★ AC for 600-odd acres of S COTE DE BEAUNE, beyond SANTENAY: one-third PREMIER CRU. Top NEGOCIANTS: DROUHIN, Jaffelin.

Marc Grape skins after pressing; also the strong-smelling brandy made from them (the equivalent of Italian 'Grappa').

Marcillac SW France r p ★→★★ DYA Became AC in '90. Violet-hued with grassy red-fruit character. Gd if rustic from Valady coop, Dom du Cros, J-L Matha.

Margaux B'x r ★★→★★★★ 70 78 79 81 82' 83' 85 86' 87 88' 89 90' 92 93 94 95 96 97 98 Village of HAUT-MEDOC. Some of most 'elegant' and fragrant red BORDEAUX. AC incl CANTENAC and several other villages. Top ch'x incl MARGAUX, RAUSAN-SEGLA, LASCOMBES etc.

Marionnet, Henry Leading TOURAINE property specializing in GAMAY and Sauv. Top CUVÉE Le M de Marionnet. Now making wine in Chile: Terra Noble.

Marne et Champagne Recent but huge-scale CHAMP house, owner (since '91) of LANSON and many smaller brands, incl BESSERAT DE BELLEFON. Alfred Rothschild brand v gd CHARD-based wines.

Marque déposée Trademark.

Marsannay Burg p w (r) ★★★ 89' 90' 91 92 93 95 96 97 98 (rosé DYA) Village with fine light red and delicate PINOT N rosé. Incl villages of Chenôve, Couchey, Dijon University. Growers: Charlopin, CLAIR, Dijon University, JADOT, ROTY, TRAPET.

Mas de Daumas Gassac Midi r w p ★★★ 82 83 85 86 87 88 89 90 91 92 93 94' 95 96 97 98 The one 'first-growth' estate of the LANGUEDOC, producing potent largely CAB S on apparently unique soil. Extraordinary quality. Also Rosé Frisant and a rich fragrant white of blended CHARD, Viognier, Petit Manseng etc to drink at 2–3 yrs. Also a good quick-drinking red, Les Terrasses de Guilhem, from a nearby coop and trad Languedoc varietals (Clairette, Cinsaut, Aramon etc) from v old vines under Terrasses de Landoc label. VIN DE PAYS status. New fun fizz: Terrasses du Lido. From '98 intriguing new sw wine: Vin de Laurence (Sém, Muscats and Sercial!).

Maury Pyr r sw ★★ NV Red VIN DOUX NATUREL of GRENACHE from ROUSSILLON. Taste the terroir. Much recent improvement, esp at Mas Amiel.

Mazis (or Mazy) Chambertin Burg r ★★★ 78' 83 85' 87 88' 89' 90' 91 92 93 94 95 96' 97 98 30-acre GRAND CRU neighbour of CHAMBERTIN, s'times equally potent. Best from FAIVELEY, HOSPICES DE BEAUNE, LEROY, Maume, ROTY.

Mazoyères-Chambertin See Charmes-Chambertin.

Médoc B'x r ★★ 85 86' 88' 89' 90' 93 94 95 96 97 98 AC for reds of the less-good (northern) part of BORDEAUX's biggest and best district. Flavours tend to earthiness. HAUT-MEDOC is much better. Top ch'x include LA CARDONNE, GREYSAC, LOUDENNE, LES ORMES-SORBET, POTENSAC, LA TOUR-DE-BY.

Meffre, Gabriel The biggest S Rhône estate, based at GIGONDAS. Variable quality. Often in French supermarkets. Also bottles and sells for small CHATEAUNEUF-DU-PAPE domaines, eg Guy Jullian, Dom de Baban.

Mellot, Alphonse ★★→★★★ Leading SANCERRE grower and merchant. Especially for La Moussière and wood-aged CUVEE Edmond; also MENETOU-SALON.

Menetou-Salon Lo r p w ★★(★) DYA Highly attractive similar wines from W of SANCERRE: SAUV BL white full of charm, PINOT N red. Top growers: Clément, Henri Pellé, Jean-Max Roger.

Méo-Camuzet V fine domaine in CLOS DE VOUGEOT, NUITS, RICHEBOURG, VOSNE-ROMANEE. HENRI JAYER inspires winemaking. Esp: V-R Cros Parantoux.

Mérode, Domaine Prince de A top domaine for CORTON and a little POMMARD.

Mesnil-sur-Oger, Le Champ ★★★★ One of top Côtes des Blancs villages; Structured CHARD for v long ageing.

Mercier & Cie, Champagne Brut NV; Brut Rosé NV; Brut **85 88 90 93** One of biggest CHAMP houses at Epernay. Controlled by MOET & CHANDON. Gd commercial quality, sold mainly in France. Good powerful PINOT-led CUVEE du Fondateur and rich, supple BLANC DE NOIRS (**93**).

Mercurey Burg r w ★★→★★★ **90' 91 92 93 94 95** 96' 97 98 Leading red wine village of COTE CHALONNAISE. Gd middle-rank burgundy incl improving whites. Try Ch de Chamirey, Chanzy, FAIVELEY, M Juillot, Dom de Suremain.

Mercurey, Région de The up-to-date name for the COTE CHALONNAISE.

Métaireau, Louis ★★→★★★ The ringleader of a group of top MUSCADET growers. Expensive well-finished wines: Number One and CUVEE LM.

Méthode champenoise Traditional laborious method of putting bubbles into CHAMP by refermenting wine in its bottle. Must use terms 'classic method' or 'méthode traditionelle' outside region. Not mentioned on Champ labels.

Méthode traditionelle See entry above.

Meursault Burg w (r) ★★★→★★★★ **85 86 88** 89' 90' **91 92 93 94 95** 96' 97 98 COTE DE BEAUNE village with some of world's greatest whites: savoury, dry but nutty and mellow. Best v'yds: Charmes, Genevrières, Perrières; also: Goutte d'Or, Meursault-Blagny, Poruzots, Narvaux, Tillets. Producers incl AMPEAU, J-M BOILLOT, M Bouzereau, Boyer-Martenot, CH DE MEURSAULT, COCHE-DURY, Fichet, Grivault, P Javillier, JOBARD, LAFON, LATOUR, O LEFLAIVE, LEROY, Manuel, Matrot, Michelot-Buisson, P MOREY, G ROULOT, Tesson. See also neighbouring Blagny.

Meursault-Blagny See Blagny.

Michel, Louis CHABLIS domaine with model, unoaked, v long-lived wines, incl superb LES CLOS, vg Montmains, MONTEE DE TONNERRE.

Midi General term for S of France W of Rhône delta. Improving reputation; brilliant promise. Top wines often based on grape variety rather than AC. A melting-pot.

Minervois Midi r (p w) br sw ★ →★★ **86 88 89 90** 91 **92 93 94** 95 96 97 98 Hilly AC region; gd lively, full wines, esp from Ch du Donjon, Fabas, Dom Laurent Fabre, coops LA LIVINIERE, de Peyriac, Pouzols; La Tour Boisée, de Violet, CLOS Centeilles. Sw Minervois Noble being developed. See also St-Jean de Minervois.

Mis en bouteille au château/domaine Bottled at the château, property or estate. NB 'dans nos caves' (in our cellars) or 'dans la région de production' (in the area of production) are often used but mean little.

Moelleux 'With marrow': creamy sweet. Used of the sw wines of VOUVRAY, COTEAUX DU LAYON, etc.

Moët & Chandon Brut NV; Rosé **81 82 85 86 88 90 92 93**; Brut Imperial **76 78 81 82 83 85 86 88 90 92 93** Much the biggest CHAMP merchant and grower with cellars in Epernay; branches in Argentina, Australia, Brazil, California, Germany, Spain. Consistent high quality, esp in vintage wines. Coteaux Champenois Saran: still wine. Prestige CUVEE: DOM PERIGNON. Links with CLICQUOT, MERCIER, POMMERY, RUINART and since '99 KRUG.

Moillard Big family firm (Domaine Thomas-Moillard) of growers and merchants in NUITS-ST-GEORGES, making full range, incl dark and v tasty wines.

Mommessin, J Major BEAUJOLAIS merchant, merged with THORIN. Owner of CLOS DE TART. White wines less successful than red.

Monbazillac Dordogne w sw ★★→★★★★ 76' 85' 89' 90' 94' 95' 96 (97') (98) Golden SAUTERNES-style wine from BERGERAC, now back on top form. Can age well. Wines like fine Sauternes as at Tirecul-la-Gravière. Top producers: L'Ancienne Cure, Ch'x de Belingard-Chayne, Bellevue, La Borderie, Treuil-de-Nailhac, Le Fagé, Haut-Bernasse, Poulvère, Theulet, Dom de la Haute-Brie et du Caillou, Clos Fontindoule and La Grande Maison stand out among 120 growers. Also Coop de Monbazillac (Ch'x de Monbazillac and Septy).

Mondeuse Savoie r ★★ DYA Red grape of SAVOIE. Potentially good vigorous deep-coloured wine. Perhaps the same as NE Italy's Refosco.

Monopole V'yd under sole ownership.

Mont-Redon, Ch de S Rh r w ★★★ 85 86 88 89 90' 93' 94' 95' 96 97 98' Outstanding 235-acre CH'NEUF-DU-PAPE estate. Fine complex r; vg aromatic, s'times substantial w (eg **94**). Also wines from Cantegril v'yd (LIRAC).

Montagne-St-Emilion B'x r ★★ 85 86' 88' 89' 90' 93 94 95 96 97 NE neighbour and largest 'satellite' of ST-EMILION: similar wines and AC regulations; becoming more important each year. Top ch'x: Calon, Faizeau, Haut-Gillet, Roudier, St-André-Corbin, Teyssier, DES TOURS, VIEUX-CH-ST-ANDRE.

Montagny Burg w (r) ★★ 89' 90 92 93 94 95 96' 97 98 COTE CHALONNAISE village. Between MACON and MEURSAULT, both geographically and gastronomically. Top producers: Cave Coop de Buxy, LOUIS LATOUR, Michel, Ch de la Saule.

Montée de Tonnerre Burg w ★★★ 90 91 92 93 94 95 96' 97 98 Famous excellent CHABLIS PREMIER CRU. Esp from BROCARD, Duplessis, L MICHEL, Raveneau, Robin.

Monthelie Burg r (w) ★★→★★★ 89' 90' 91 92 93 94 95 96' 97 98 Little-known VOLNAY neighbour, s'times almost equal. Excellent fragrant reds, esp BOUCHARD PERE, COCHE-DURY, LAFON, DROUHIN, Garaudet, Ch de Monthelie (Suremain).

Montille, Hubert de VOLNAY and POMMARD domaine to note.

Montlouis Lo w dr sw (sp) ★★→★★★ 85' 88' 89 90' 93' 95' 96 97 98 (sec) Neighbour of VOUVRAY. Similar sweet, or long-lived dry wines; also sparkling. Top growers: Berger, Chidaine, Deletang, Moyer, Taille aux Loups.

Montrachet Burg w ★★★★ 71 78 79 82 83 85' 86' 88 89' 90 91 92 93 94 95 96' 97 98 (Both 't's in the name are silent.) 19-acre GRAND CRU v'yd in both PULIGNY- and CHASSAGNE-M'RACHET. Potentially the greatest white burgundy: strong, perfumed, intense, dry yet luscious. Top wines from LAFON, LAGUICHE (DROUHIN), LEFLAIVE, RAMONET, DOM DE LA ROMANEE-CONTI, THENARD.

Montravel Dordogne ★★ w DYA Similar to dry white BERGERAC. Good examples from Doms de Krevel, Gouyat, Perreau, ch'x Péchaurieux and Pique-Sègue. Separate ACS for semi sw COTES DE MONTRAVEL and sw HAUT-MONTRAVEL.

Moreau & Fils CHABLIS merchant and grower with 100 acres. Also major table wine producer. Best wine: CLOS des Hospices (GRAND CRU).

Morey, Domaines 50 acres in CHASSAGNE-M'RACHET. Vg wines made by family members, esp Bernard, incl BATARD-M'RACHET. Also Pierre M in MEURSAULT.

Morey-St-Denis Burg r ★★★ 78 85' 88 89' 90' 91 92 93 94 95 96' 97 98 Small village with four GRANDS CRUS between GEVREY-CHAMBERTIN and CHAMBOLLE-MUSIGNY. Glorious wine often overlooked. Incl Amiot, Castagnier, DUJAC, Lignier, Moillard-Grivot, Perrot-Minot, PONSOT, ROUSSEAU, Serveau.

Morgon Beauj r ★★★ 90 91 93 94 95 96 97 98 The 'firmest' cru of BEAUJOLAIS, needing time to develop its rich savoury flavour. Growers incl Aucoeur, Ch de Bellevue, Desvignes, Lapièrre, Ch de Pizay. DUBOEUF excellent.

France entries also cross-refer to Châteaux of Bordeaux section, pages 78–103.

Morot, Albert BEAUNE domaine: wines with distinct individual characters.

Mortet, Denis Splendid perfectionist GEVREY domaine. Super wines since '93, incl a range of village Gevreys and excellent PREMIER CRU Lavaux St-Jacques.

Moueix, J-P et Cie Legendary leading proprietor and merchant of ST-EMILION, POMEROL and FRONSAC. Ch'x incl LA FLEUR-PETRUS, MAGDELAINE and part of PETRUS. Also in California: see Dominus.

Moulin-à-Vent Beauj r ★★★ **90 91 93 94 95 96** 97 98 The 'biggest' and potentially best wine of BEAUJOLAIS; can be powerful, meaty and long-lived, eventually can even taste like fine Rhône or burgundy. Many good growers, esp Ch du Moulin-à-Vent, Ch des Jacques, Dom des Hospices, Janodet.

Moulis B'x r ★★→★★★ H-MEDOC village with several Crus Exceptionnels: CHASSE-SPLEEN, MAUCAILLOU, POUJEAUX (THEIL) etc. Good hunting ground.

Mourvèdre See grapes for red wine pages 11-13.

Mousseux Sparkling.

Mouton Cadet Popular brand of blended red and white BORDEAUX.

Moutonne CHABLIS GRAND CRU honoris causa (between VAUDESIR and Preuses), owned by BICHOT.

Mugneret/Mugneret-Gibourg Superb reds from top COTE DE NUITS sites.

Mugnier, J-F 10-acre Ch de Chambolle estate with first-class delicate CHAMBOLLE-MUSIGNY Les Amoureuses and MUSIGNY. Also BONNES-MARES.

Mumm, G H & Cie Cordon Rouge NV; Mumm de Cramant NV; Cordon Rouge 89 **90**; Rosé NV Major CHAMP grower and merchant. Seagram-owned. Luxury brands: René Lalou (**79 82 85 90**), Grand Cordon (85 90). Also in Napa, California; Chile, Argentina; S Africa ('Cape Mumm').

Muré, Clos St-Landelin Fine ALSACE grower and merchant at Rouffach with v'yds in GRAND CRU Vorbourg. Full-bodied wines: ripe (unusual) PINOT N, big RIES and MUSCAT VENDANGES TARDIVES.

Muscadet Lo w ★★→★★★ DYA Popular, gd-value, often delicious v dry wine from nr Nantes at the mouth of the Loire. Should never be sharp but should have a faint iodine tang (like the bilge of a trawler). Perfect with fish and seafood. Best are from zonal ACS: COTEAUX DE LA LOIRE, M COTES DE GRAND LIEU, SEVRE ET MAINE. Choose a SUR LIE – on the lees.

Muscadet Côtes de Grand Lieu Recent zonal AC ('95) for MUSCADET around the eponymous lake. Best are SUR LIE, from eg Bâtard, Luc Choblet, Malidain.

Muscadet Coteaux de la Loire Lo w Small MUSCADET zone E of Nantes, best are SUR LIE, esp Guindon, Luneau-Papin, Les Vignerons de la Noëlle.

Muscadet de Sèvre-et-Maine Wine from central (best) part of area. Top growers incl Guy Bossard, CHEREAU-CARRE, Douillard, Landron, Luneau-Papin, METAIREAU.

Muscat Distinctively perfumed grape and its (usually sweet) wine, often fortified as VIN DOUX NATUREL. Made dry and not fortified in ALSACE.

Muscat de Beaumes-de-Venise See Beaumes-de-Venise.

Muscat de Frontignan See Frontignan.

Muscat de Lunel Midi br sw ★★ NV Ditto. A small area but good, making recent progress. Look for Dom CLOS Bellevue, Lacoste.

Muscat de Mireval Midi br sw ★★ NV Ditto, from nr Montpellier.

Muscat de Rivesaltes Midi br sw ★★ NV Sweet MUSCAT wine from large zone near Perpignan. Especially good from Cazes Frères, Château de Jau.

Musigny Burg r (w) ★★★★ **82 85' 88' 89' 90' 91 92 93 94** 95 96' 97 98 25-acre GRAND CRU in CHAMBOLLE-MUSIGNY. Can be the most beautiful, if not the most powerful, of all red burgundies (and a little white). Best growers: DROUHIN, JADOT, LEROY, MUGNIER, PRIEUR, ROUMIER, DE VOGUE.

Napoléon Brand-name of family-owned Prieur CHAMPAGNE house at Vertus. Excellent Carte d'Or NV and first-rate vintages, esp 89.

Nature Natural or unprocessed – esp of still CHAMP.

Négociant-éleveur Merchant who 'brings up' (ie matures) the wine.

Nicolas, Ets Paris-based wholesale and retail wine merchant controlled by Castel Frères. One of the biggest in France and one of the best.

Noble Joué p ★→★★ Ancient but recently revived rosé from three Pinots (Gris, Meunier, Noir) just S of Tours. Esp from Rousseau and Sard.

Nuits-St-Georges Burg r ★★→★★★★ 78' 82 83 85' 86 87 88' 89' 90' 91 92 93 94 95 96' 97 98 Important wine town: wines of all qualities, typically sturdy, relatively tannic, needing time. Name often shortened to 'Nuits'. Best v'yds incl Les Cailles, CLOS des Corvées, Les Pruliers, Les St-Georges, Vaucrains, etc. Many growers and merchants esp DOM DE L'ARLOT, Ambroise, J Chauvenet, Chevillon, CONFURON, FAIVELEY, GOUGES, GRIVOT, Lechemeaut, LEROY, Machard de Gramont, Michelot, RION, THOMAS-MOILLARD.

d'Oc Midi r p w ★ →★★ Regional VIN DE PAYS for Languedoc and ROUSSILLON. Esp single-grape wines and VINS DE PAYS PRIMEURS. Tremendous technical advances recently. Top growers: VAL D'ORBIEU, SKALLI, Jeanjean.

Oisly & Thesée, Vignerons de ★ Go-ahead coop in E TOURAINE (Loire), with good SAUV BL (esp Cuvée Excellence), CAB, GAMAY, Cot and CHARD. Blends labelled Baronnie d'Aignan and good domaine wines. Value.

Orléanais, Vin de l' Lo r p w ★ DYA Small VDQS for light but fruity wines, based on Pinots Meunier and Noir, CAB and CHARD. Esp CLOS St-Fiacre.

Ostertag Sm ALSACE domaine (Epfig). Uses new oak for gd PINOT N; best RIES, Pinot Gr of GRAND CRU Muenchberg. GEWURZ from lieu-dit Fronholz is worth ageing.

Ott, Domaines Top high-quality producer of PROVENCE, incl CH DE SELLE (rosé, red), CLOS Mireille (white), BANDOL Ch de Romassan.

Pacherenc du Vic-Bilh SW France w dr sw ★★→★★★ The white wine of MADIRAN, in three styles: dry, sw unwooded (both DYA) and sw oaked (allow to age for 5 years). Ch Laffitte-Teston, Doms Capmartin, Crampilh, Barréjat, Laplace and Berthoumieu often best, but listed MADIRAN producers are generally all gd.

Palette Prov r p w ★★ Near Aix-en-Provence. Full-bodied reds, solid rosés and fragrant whites from CHATEAU SIMONE.

Parigot-Richard Producer of vg CREMANT DE BOURGOGNE at SAVIGNY.

Pasquier-Desvignes V old firm of BEAUJOLAIS merchants nr BROUILLY.

Patriarche One of the bigger firms of burgundy merchants. Cellars in BEAUNE; also owns CH DE MEURSAULT (150 acres), sparkling KRITER etc.

Patrimonio Corsica r w p ★★ →★★★ 91 92 93 94 95 96 97 Wide range from dramatic chalk hills in N CORSICA. Fragrant reds from Nielluccio, crisp whites. Top growers: Gentile, Leccia, Arena.

Pauillac B'x r ★★★→★★★★★ 66' 70' 75 78' 79 81' 82' 83' 85' 86 88' 89' 90' 91 92 93 94 95' 96 97 98 The only B'x (HAUT-MEDOC) village with 3 first growths (CH'X LAFITE, LATOUR, MOUTON) and many other fine ones, famous for high flavour; v varied in style.

Pécharmant Dordogne r ★★ 85 90' 93 94 95 96 Inner AC for best BERGERAC reds, needing ageing. Best: La Métairie, Doms du Haut-Pécharmant, des Costes des Bertranoux; Ch'x Champarel, Terre Vieille, Les Grangettes and de Tiregand. Also (from Bergerac coop at Le Fleix) Doms Brisseau-Belloc, du Vieux Sapin and Ch le Charmeil. A name to watch.

Pelure d'oignon 'Onion skin' – tawny tint of certain rosés.

Perlant or Perlé Very slightly sparkling.

Pernand-Vergelesses Burg r (w) ★★★ 88' 89' 90 91 92 93 94 95 96' 97 98 Village next to ALOXE-CORTON containing part of the great CORTON and C-CHARLEMAGNE v'yds and one other top v'yd: Ile des Vergelesses. Growers incl BONNEAU DU MARTRAY, CHANDON DE BRIAILLES, CHANSON, Delarche, Dubreuil-Fontaine, JADOT, LATOUR, Rapet.

Perrier-Jouët Brut NV; Blason de France NV; Blason de France Rosé NV; Brut **76 79 82 85 88 90 92** Excellent CHAMP grower at Epernay, the first to make dry Champagne and once the smartest name of all now best for vintage wines. Luxury brands: Belle Epoque (**79 82 83 85 86 88 89 90**) in a painted bottle. Also Belle Epoque Rosé (**79 82 85 88 89**).

Pessac-Léognan B'x Relatively recent AC for the best part of N GRAVES, incl the area of most of the GRANDS CRUS.

Pétillant Normally means slightly sparkling; but half-sparkling speciality in TOURAINE esp VOUVRAY and MONTLOUIS.

Petit Chablis Burg w ★ DYA Wine from fourth-rank CHABLIS v'yds. Not much character but can be pleasantly fresh. Best: coop La Chablisienne.

Pfaffenheim Top ALSACE coop with 500 acres. Strongly individual wines incl good Sylvaner and vg PINOTS (N, Gr, Bl). GRANDS CRUS: Goldert, Steinert and Hatschbourg. Hartenberger CREMANT d'Alsace is vg. Also owns DOPFF & IRION.

Pfersigberg Eguisheim (ALSACE) GRAND CRU with two parcels; v aromatic wines. GEWURZ does v well. RIES esp Paul Ginglinger, BRUNO SORG and LEON BEYER Comtes d'Eguisheim. Top grower: KUENTZ-BAS.

Philipponnat NV; Rosé NV; Réserve Spéciale **82 85 88**; Grand Blanc Vintage **76 81 82 85 88 89 90**; CLOS des Goisses **76 78 79 82 85 86 88** Small family-run CHAMP house producing well-structured wines, esp remarkable single-v'yd CLOS des Goisses and charming rosé. Also Le Reflet BRUT NV.

Piat Père & Fils Big-scale merchant of BEAUJOLAIS and MACON wines at Mâcon, now controlled by Diageo.

Pic, Albert Fine CHABLIS producer, controlled by DE LADOUCETTE.

Pic St-Loup Midi ★→★★★ r (p) Notable COTEAUX DU LAN'DOC commune. Top growers: Ch'x de Cazeneuve, de Lancyre, Lascaux, Mas Bruguière, Dom de l'Hortus.

Picpoul de Pinet Midi w ★→★★ Improving AC exclusively for the old variety Picpoul. Best growers: Dom Gaujal, Coop Pomérols.

Pineau des Charentes Strong sweet aperitif: white grape juice and COGNAC.

Pinot See Grapes for white and red wine (pages 7–13).

Piper-Heidsieck Brut NV; Brut Rosé NV; Brut **76 79 82 85 89 90** CHAMP-makers of old repute at Reims, now owned by Rémy-Cointreau. Rare (**76 79 85 88 90**) and Brut Sauvage (**79 82 85 90**) are best, but non-vintage CUVEES much improved. See also Piper Sonoma, California.

Plageoles, Robert Brilliant GAILLAC winemaker. Outstanding wines from Mauzac grape incl sp, VIN JAUNE. Also SAUV, GAMAY, Muscadelle and rare Ondenc.

Pol Roger Brut White Foil NV; Brut **75 76 79 82 85' 88 90'**; Rosé **75 79 82 85 88 90**; Blanc de CHARD **79 82 85 88 90** Top-ranking family-owned CHAMP house at Epernay, much loved in Britain. Esp gd silky NV White Foil, Rosé, Réserve PR (**88 90**) and CHARD. Sumptuous CUVEE: Sir Winston Churchill (**75 79 82 85 88 90**).

Pomerol B'x r ★★★→★★★★ **70 75' 81' 82' 83 85 86 88 89' 90' 92 93 94 95** 96 97 98 Next village to ST-EM: similar but more plummy, creamy wines, often maturing sooner, reliable, delicious. Top ch'x incl: CERTAN-DE-MAY, L'EVANGILE, LA FLEUR, LA FLEUR-PETRUS, LATOUR-A-POMEROL, PETRUS, LE PIN, TROTANOY, VIEUX CH CERTAN etc.

Pommard Burg r ★★★ **78' 85' 86 87 88' 89' 90 91 92 93 94** 95 96' 97 98 The biggest COTE D'OR village. Few superlative wines, but many potent and often tannic ones to age 10 yrs+. Best v'yds: Epenots, HOSPICES DE BEAUNE CUVEES, Rugiens. Growers incl COMTE ARMAND, G Billard, Billard-Gonnet, J-M BOILLOT, DE COURCEL, Gaunoux, LEROY, Machard de Gramont, DE MONTILLE, A Mussy, Ch de Pommard, Pothier-Rieusset.

Pommery Brut NV; Rosé NV; Brut **82 83 85 87 88 89 90 91** V big CHAMP house at Reims owned by MOET since '91. Wines much improved. Outstanding luxury CUVEE Louise (**81 82 83 85 87 88 90**). Cuvée Louise Rosé (**82 83 85 88 89**). Also Flacons d'Exception, late-disgorged older vintages in MAGNUM (**79**).

Ponsot, J M 25-acre MOREY-ST-DENIS estate. Many high quality GRANDS CRUS, incl CHAMBERTIN, CHAPELLE-C, LATRICIERES-C, CLOS DE LA ROCHE, CLOS ST-DENIS.

Pouilly-Fuissé Burg w ★★→★★★ 89' 90' 91 92 **93 94 95** 96 97 98 The best white of the MACON region, potent and dense. At its best (eg Ch Fuissé VIEILLES VIGNES) outstanding, but usually over-priced compared with (eg) CHABLIS. Top growers: Ferret, Forest, GUFFENS-HEYNEN, Luquet, Noblet, Valette, Vincent.

Pouilly-Fumé Lo w ★★→★★★ **90' 91' 92' 93' 94 95' 96 97 98** 'Gun-flinty', fruity, often sharp white from upper Loire, nr SANCERRE. Grapes must be SAUV BL. Best CUVEES can improve 5–6 yrs. Top growers incl Cailbourin, Chatelain, DAGUENEAU, Ch de Favray, Edmond and André Figeat, LADOUCETTE, Masson-Blondelet, Redde, Tinel Blondelet, Cave de Pouilly-sur-Loire.

Pouilly-Loché Burg w ★★ POUILLY-FUISSE's neighbour. Similar, cheaper; scarce.

Pouilly-sur-Loire Lo w ★ DYA Neutral wine from the same v'yds as POUILLY-FUME but different grapes (Chasselas). Rarely seen today.

Pouilly-Vinzelles Burg w ★★ 92 **93 94 95 96** 97 98 Neighbour of POUILLY-FUISSE. Similar wine, worth looking for. Value.

Pousse d'Or, Domaine de la 32-acre estate in POMMARD, SANTENAY and esp VOLNAY, where its MONOPOLES Bousse d'Or and CLOS des 60 Ouvrées are powerful, tannic, and justly famous. Sadly Gérard Potel died in '97.

Premier Cru First growth in B'x; second rank of v'yds (after GRAND CRU) in Burgundy.

Premières Côtes de Blaye B'x r w ★→★★ 86 88' 89' 90' **93 94 95** 96 97 Restricted AC for better BLAYE wines; greater emphasis on r. Ch'x incl BARBE, LE BOURDIEU, Charron, l'Escadre, Haut-Sociondo, Le Menaudat, La Rose-Bellevue, Segonzac, La Tonnelle.

Premières Côtes de Bordeaux B'x r w (p) dr sw ★→★★ Large hilly area east of GRAVES across the River Garonne: gd bet for quality and value, upgrading sharply. Largely Merlot. Ch'x incl Bertinerie (esp), Carsin, La Croix de Roche, Fayau, Fontenil, Gardera, HAUT-BRIGNON, du Juge, Laffitte (sic), Lamothe, Peyrat, Plaisance, REYNON, Tanesse. To watch, esp in gd vintages.

Prieur, Domaine Jacques Splendid 40-acre estate all in top Burgundy sites, incl PREMIER CRU MEURSAULT, VOLNAY, PULIGNY- and even LE M'RACHET. Now 50% owned by RODET and quality rejuvenated, esp since '89.

Primeur 'Early' wine for refreshment and uplift; esp from BEAUJOLAIS; VINS DE PAYS too. Wine sold 'En Primeur' is offered for sale still in barrel for future delivery.

Prissé See Mâcon-Villages.

Propriétaire-récoltant Owner-manager.

Provence See Côtes de Provence.

Puisseguin St-Emilion B'x r ★★ 82 85 86 88' 89' 90' **92 93 94 95** 96 97 98 E neighbour of ST-EMILION, its smallest 'satellite'; wines similar – not so fine or weighty but often value. Ch'x incl La Croix de Berny, LAURETS, Puisseguin, Soleil, Teyssier, Vieux-Ch-Guibeau. Also Roc de Puisseguin from coop.

Puligny-Montrachet Burg w (r) ★★★★ 85' 86' 88 89' 90' 91 92 **93 94 95** 96' 97 98 Bigger neighbour of CHASSAGNE-M: potentially even finer, more vital and complex rich dr wine. (But apparent finesse can be result of over-production.) Best v'yds: BATARD-M, Bienvenues-Bâtard-M, Caillerets, Champ-Canet, CHEVALIER-M, Clavoillon, Les Combettes, M'RACHET, Pucelles etc. Top growers incl Amiot-Bonfils, AMPEAU, J-M BOILLOT, BOUCHARD PERE, L CARILLON, CHARTRON, H Clerc, DROUHIN, JADOT, LATOUR, DOM LEFLAIVE, O LEFLAIVE, Pernot, SAUZET.

Pyrénées-Atlantiques SW France DYA VDP for wines not qualifying for local ACS MADIRAN, PACHERENC DU VIC BILH or JURANCON.

Quarts de Chaume Lo w sw ★★★→★★★★★ 75 76 78' 79' 82 85' 86 88' 89' **90'** 91 92 93' 94 95 96 97 98 Famous COTEAUX DU LAYON plot. CHENIN grapes grown for immensely long-lived intense rich golden wine. Esp from BAUMARD, Bellerive, Claude Papin, Suronde.

Quatourze Midi r w (p) ★ **91** 92 93 94 95 96 97 Minor cru of COTEAUX DE LANGUEDOC. Best wines from Dom Notre Dame du Quatourze.

Quincy Lo w ★→★★ DYA Small area: v dry SANCERRE-style wine of SAUV BL. Worth trying. Growers: Domaine Mardon, Sorbe.

Ramonet, Domaine Leading (indeed legendary) estate in CHASSAGNE-M'RACHET with 42 acres, incl some M'RACHET. Vg whites, and red CLOS ST-JEAN.

Rancio The delicious nutty tang of brown wood-aged fortified wine eg VDN, esp BANYULS. Indicates exposure to oxygen and/or heat: a fault in table wine.

Rangen V high-class ALSACE GRAND CRU in Thann and Vieux Thann. Owes much of its reputation to ZIND-HUMBRECHT. Esp for PINOT Gr, GEWURZ, RIES.

Rasteau S Rh r br sw (p w dr) ★★ 86 88 **89** 90' 93 94 95' 96' 97 98' Village for sound, robust reds, especially Beaurenard, Cave des Vignerons, Ch du Trignon, Doms Didier Charavin, Rabasse-Charavin, Girasols, St-Gayan, Soumade. Strong sweet GRENACHE dessert wine is (declining) speciality.

Ratafia de Champagne Sweet aperitif made in CHAMP of 67% grape juice and 33% brandy. Not unlike PINEAU DES CHARENTES.

Récolte Crop or vintage.

Regnié Beauj r ★★ 96 97 98 BEAUJ village between MORGON and BROUILLY, promoted to cru in '88. About 1,800 acres. Try DUBOEUF's or Aucoeur's.

Reine Pédauque, La Long-est'd burgundy grower-merchant at ALOXE-CORTON. V'yds in ALOXE-CORTON, SAVIGNY, etc, and COTES DU RHONE. Owned by PIERRE ANDRE.

Remoissenet Père & Fils Fine burgundy merchant (esp for whites and THENARD wines) with a tiny BEAUNE estate (5 acres). Give his reds time. Also broker for NICOLAS.

Rémy Pannier Important Loire wine merchant at SAUMUR.

Reuilly Lo w (r p) ★★ N'bour of QUINCY. Similar whites; rising reputation. Also rosés (PINOTS N, Gr), reds (PN). Esp from Claude Lafond, Beurdin, Sorbe, Vincent.

Muscadet: formerly the darling of Paris bistrots, then démodé, Muscadet has come roaring back with fabulous wines since '95. Good estate wines may now be France's very best value in their proper salty context. NB Esp from M Bahuaud, Ch de Chasseloir, Chéreau-Carré, Ch de la Mercredière, Ch la Noë, Sauvion, etc.

Ribonnet, Domaine de ★★ SW France Christian Gerber makes pioneering range of varietals (r p w) without benefit of APPELLATION; s of Toulouse.

Riceys, Rosé des Champ p ★★★ DYA Minute AC in AUBE for a notable PINOT N rosé. Principal producers: A Bonnet, Jacques Defrance.

Richebourg Burg r ★★★★ 78' 82 83 85' 88' 89' 90' 91 92 93' 94 95 96' 97 98 19-acre VOSNE-ROMANEE GRAND CRU. Powerful perfumed fabulously expensive wine, among Burgundy's finest. Top growers: BICHOT, GRIVOT, J GROS, LEROY, MEO-CAMUZET, DRC.

Richou, Dom Long-est'd, quality ANJOU estate for wide range of wines, esp ANJOU-VILLAGES VIEILLES VIGNES, COTEAUX DE L'AUBANCE Les Trois Demoiselles.

Riesling See Grapes for white wine (pages 7–11).

Rion, Daniel et Fils 48-acre domaine in Prémeaux (NUITS). Excellent VOSNE-ROMANEE (Les Chaumes, Les Beaumonts), Nuits PREMIER CRU Les Vignes Rondes and CHAMBOLLE-MUSIGNY-Les Charmes. NB Also Michelle et Patrice Rion.

Rivesaltes Midi r w br dr sw ★★ NV Fortified wine of east Pyrenees. A tradition v much alive, if struggling these days. Top producers: Doms Cazes, Sarda-Malet, Vaquet, des Schistes, Château de Jau. See Muscat de Rivesaltes.

Roche-aux-Moines, La Lo w sw ★★★ 76' **78 79 82 83 85 86 88'** 89' 90' 93' 94 95' 96 97 98 60-acre v'yd in SAVENNIERES, ANJOU. Intense strong fruity/ sharp wine, needs long ageing or drinking fresh.

FRANCE

Rodet, Antonin Substantial quality burgundy merchant with large (332-acre) estate, esp in MERCUREY (Ch de Chamirey). See also Prieur.

Roederer, Louis Brut Premier NV; Rich NV; Brut **75 76 78 79 81 83 85 90**; Blanc de Blancs **90 91** 93; Brut Rosé **85 88 91** Top-drawer family-owned CHAMP-grower and merchant at Reims. Vanilla-rich NV with plenty of flavour. Sumptuous Cristal may be greatest of all prestige CUVÉES (**79 82 83 85 88 89 90**) and Cristal Rosé (**88 90**). Also owns Champ house DEUTZ and CHATEAU DE PEZ in Bordeaux. See also Roederer Estate, California.

Rolly Gassmann Distinguished ALSACE grower at Rorschwihr, esp for Auxerrois and MUSCAT from lieu-dit Moenchreben.

Romanée, La Burg r ★★★★ 78' **85' 88' 89' 90' 91 92** 93 94 95 96' 97 98 2-acre GRAND CRU in VOSNE-ROMANEE, just uphill from ROMANEE-CONTI. MONOPOLE of Liger-Belair, sold by BOUCHARD PERE.

Romanée-Conti Burg r ★★★★ 66' 76 78' **80' 82 83 85' 86 87 88' 89' 90' 91 92** 93' 94 95 96' 97 98 4.3-acre MONOPOLE GRAND CRU in VOSNE-ROMANEE; 450 cases pa. The most celebrated and expensive red wine in the world, with reserves of flavour beyond imagination. See next entry.

Romanée-Conti, Domaine de la (DRC) The grandest estate in Burgundy. Incl the whole of ROMANEE-CONTI and LA TACHE and major parts of ECHEZEAUX, GRANDS ECH'X, RICHEBOURG and ROMANEE-ST-VIVANT. Also tiny parts of M'RACHET and VOSNE-ROMANEE. Crown-jewel prices (if you can buy them at all). Keep top DRC vintages for decades.

Romanée-St-Vivant Burg r ★★★★ 78' 80' 82 **85' 87 88' 89' 90' 91 92** 93' 95 96' 97 98 23-acre GRAND CRU in VOSNE-ROMANEE. Similar to ROMANEE-CONTI but lighter and less sumptuous. Top growers: DRC and LEROY.

Rosé d'Anjou Lo p ★ DYA Pale slightly sw rosé. CAB D'ANJOU should be better.

Rosé de Loire Lo p ★→★★ DYA Wide-ranging AC for dr Loire rosé (ANJOU is sw).

Rosette Dordogne w s/sw ★★ DYA Pocket-sized AC for charming aperitif wines, eg CLOS Romain, Ch Puypezat-Rosette and Dom de la Cardinolle.

Rostaing Growing 17-acre COTE-ROTIE estate with prime plots, notably La Blonde (soft, elegant wines) and fuller, firmer La Viaillère and La Landonne (15–20 years). Style is polished, v accomplished, some new oak. CONDRIEU also.

Roty, Joseph Small grower of classic GEVREY-CHAMBERTIN, esp CHARMES- and MAZIS-CHAMBERTIN. Long-lived wines.

Rouget, Emmanuel Inheritor (nephew) of the legendary 13-acre estate of Henri Jayer in ECHEZEAUX, NUITS-ST-GEORGES and VOSNE-ROMANEE. Top wine: Vosne-R-Cros Parantoux. Jayer (who retired '88) still consults here and at MEO-CAMUZET.

Roulout, Domaine G Excellent range of 7 (only 2 PREMIER CRU) distinctive MEURSAULTS.

Roumier, Georges Christophe R makes exceptional long lasting wines from BONNES-MARES, CHAMBOLLE-MUSIGNY-Amoureuses, MUSIGNY etc. Excellent standards.

Rousseau, Domaine A Major burgundy grower famous for CHAMBERTIN etc, of v highest quality. Wines are intense, long-lived and mostly GRAND CRU.

Roussette de Savoie Savoie w ★★ DYA Tastiest of the fresh whites from S of Lake Geneva.

Roussillon Midi Top region for VINS DOUX NATURELS (eg MAURY, RIVESALTES, BANYULS). Lighter MUSCATS are taking over from darker heavier wines. See Côtes du Roussillon for table wines.

Ruchottes-Chambertin Burg r ★★★★ 78' **85' 87 88' 89' 90' 91 92** 93' 94 95 96' 97 98 7.5-acre GRAND CRU neighbour of CHAMBERTIN. Similar splendid lasting wine of great finesse. Top growers: LEROY, MUGNERET, ROUMIER, ROUSSEAU.

Ruinart Père & Fils 'R' de Ruinart Brut NV; 'R' de Ruinart Rosé NV; 'R' de Ruinart Brut **88 90 92** Oldest CHAMP house, now owned by MOET-Hennessy, with markedly elegant yet vinous wines, esp luxury brands: Dom Ruinart BLANC DE BLANCS (**83 85 88** 90), Dom Ruinart Rosé (**86 88 90**). Also new 'R' de Ruinart rosé.

Rully Burg r w (sp) ★★ 90' 91 92 93 94 95 96' 97 98 COTE CHALONNAISE village famous for CREMANT. Still white and red are light but tasty, good value, esp whites. Growers incl DELORME, FAIVELEY, Dom de la Folie, Jacquesson, A RODET.

Sables du Golfe du Lion Midi p r w ★ DYA VIN DE PAYS from Mediterranean sand-dunes: esp Gris de Gris from Carignan, GRENACHE, Cinsault. Dominated by LISTEL.

Sablet S Rh r w (p) ★★ 89 90' 93 94 95' 96 97 98' Admirable, improving COTES DU RHONE village, esp Dom de Boissan, Les Goubert, Piaugier, Ch du Trignon, Dom de Verquière. Whites to try, too.

St-Amour Beauj r ★★ 95 96 97 98 Northernmost CRU of BEAUJOLAIS: light, fruity, irresistible. Growers to try: Janin, Patissier, Revillon.

St-André-de-Cubzac B'x r w ★→★★ 90' 93 94 95 96 97 98 Town 15 miles NE of B'x, centre of minor Cubzaguais region. Sound reds have AC B'X SUPERIEUR. Incl: Dom de Beychevelle, Ch'x du Bouilh, TERREFORT-QUANCARD, TIMBERLAY.

St-Aubin Burg w (r) ★★ 90 91 92 93 94 95 96' 97 98 Little-known n'bour of CHASSAGNE-M, up a side-valley. Several PREMIERS CRUS: light firm quite stylish wines; fair prices. Also sold as COTE DE BEAUNE-VILLAGES. Top growers incl JADOT, J Lamy, Lamy-Pillot, H Prudhon, Roux, Thomas.

St-Bris Burg w (r) ★ DYA Village west of CHABLIS known for fruity ALIGOTE, but chiefly for SAUVIGNON DE ST-BRIS. Also good CREMANT.

St-Chinian Midi r ★→★★ 89 90 91 92 93 94 95 96 97 98 Hilly area of growing reputation in COTEAUX DU LANGUEDOC. AC since '82. Tasty southern reds, esp at Berlou and Roquebrun, and from Chx de Viranel, Coujan.

St-Emilion B'x r ★★→★★★★ 70' 75 79 81 82' 83' 85' 86' 88' 89' 90' 93 94 95 96 97 98 The biggest top-quality BORDEAUX district (13,000 acres); solid rich tasty wines from hundreds of ch'x, incl AUSONE, CANON, CHEVAL BLANC, FIGEAC, MAGDELAINE, etc. Also a gd coop.

St-Estèphe B'x r ★★→★★★★ 78' 81 82' 83' 85' 86 88' 89' 90' 91 92 93 94 95' 96 97 98 N village of HAUT-MEDOC. Solid, structured, sometimes superlative wines. Top ch'x: COS D'ESTOURNEL, MONTROSE, CALON-SEGUR, etc, and more notable CRUS BOURGEOIS than any other HAUT-MEDOC commune.

St-Gall Brut NV; Extra Brut NV; Brut Blanc de Blancs NV; Brut Rosé NV; Brut Blanc de Blancs 90; Cuvée Orpale Blanc de Blancs 88 90 Brand name used by Union-Champagne: top CHAMP growers' coop at AVIZE. Cuvée Orpale exceptionally gd value.

St-Georges-St-Emilion B'x r ★★ 82 83' 85' 86' 88' 89' 90' 93 94 95 96 97 98 Part of MONTAGNE-ST-EM with high standards. Best ch'x: Belair-Montaiguillon, Marquis-St-G, ST-GEORGES, Tour du Pas-St-G.

St-Gervais S Rh r (w) ★ West bank S Rhône village. Sound coop, excellent Dom Ste-Anne reds (marked MOURVEDRE flavours); whites incl a Viognier.

St-Jean de Minervois Min w sw ★★ Perhaps top French MUSCAT: sw and fine. Much recent progress esp Dom de Barroubio, Michel Sigé, coop.

St-Joseph N Rh r w ★★ 88' 89 90' 94' 95' 96 97 98' AC stretching whole length of N Rhône (40 miles). Delicious, fruit-packed wines at its core, around Tournon; elsewhere quality variable. Often better, more structure than CROZES-HERMITAGE, esp from CHAPOUTIER (Les Granits) B Gripa, Grippat; also CHAVE, Chèze, Coursodon, Faury, Gaillard, JABOULET, Marsanne, Paret, Perret, Trollat. Gd whites, too (mainly Marsanne grape).

St-Julien B'x r ★★★→★★★★ 70' 75 78' 79 81' 82' 83' 85' 86' 87 88' 89' 90' 91 92 93 94 95' 96 97 98 Mid-MEDOC village with a dozen of BORDEAUX's best ch'x, incl three LEOVILLES, BEYCHEVELLE, DUCRU-BEAUCAILLOU, GRUAUD-LAROSE, etc. The epitome of harmonious, fragrant and savoury red wine.

To decipher codes, please refer to 'Key to symbols' on front flap of jacket, or to 'How to use this book' on page 6.

St-Nicolas-de-Bourgueil Lo r p ★★→★★★ 85' 86 88 89' 90' 93' 95' 96 97 98 The next village to BOURGUEIL: the same lively and fruity CAB F red. Top growers: Amirault, Cognard, Mabileau, Taluau.

St-Péray N Rh w sp ★★ NV Rather heavy w Rhône (Marsanne grape), much of it sp. Curiosity worth trying once. Top names: J-F Chaboud, B Gripa, J-L Thiers.

St-Pourçain-sur-Sioule Central France r p w ★→★★ DYA Niche wine of the centre of France. Red and rosé from GAMAY and/or PINOT N, white from Tressalier and/or CHARD (increasingly popular) or SAUV. Recent vintages improved. Growers incl: Ray, Dom de Bellevue, D Barbara and gd coop.

St-Romain Burg r w ★★ (w) 90' **91 92 93 94 95 96'** 97 98 Overlooked village just behind COTE DE BEAUNE. Value, esp for firm fresh whites. Reds have a clean 'cut'. Top growers: FEVRE, Jean Germain, Gras, LATOUR, LEROY, Thévenin-Monthelie.

St-Véran Burg w ★★ 92 **93 94 95 96** 97 98 Next-door AC to POUILLY-FUISSE. Similar wines, better value, with real character from best slopes of MACON-VILLAGES. Try DUBOEUF, Doms des Deux Roches, des Valanges, Demessey, des FUISSE.

Ste-Croix-du-Mont B'x w sw ★★ 75 76' **82 83** 86' 88' **89** 90 **91 92 93** 95' 96 97 98 Neighbour to SAUTERNES with similar golden wine. No superlatives but well worth trying, esp CLOS des Coulinats, Ch Loubens, Ch Lousteau Vieil, Ch du Mont. Often a bargain, esp with age.

Salon 71 **73** 76 **79** 82 **83** 85 88 90 The original BLANC DE BLANCS CHAMP, from Le Mesnil in the Côte de Blancs. Superlative intense v dry wine with long keeping qualities. Tiny quantities. Bought in '88 by LAURENT-PERRIER.

Sancerre Lo w (r p) ★★→★★★ **89** 90' 93' 95' 96 97 98 The world's model for fragrant SAUV BL, almost indistinguishable from POUILLY-FUME, its neighbour across River Loire. Top wines can age 5 yrs[+]. Also light PINOT N red (best drunk at 2–3 yrs) and rosé (do not over-chill). Occasional vg VENDANGES TARDIVES. Top growers incl BOURGEOIS, Cotat Frères, Lucien Crochet, André Dezat, Jolivet, MELLOT, Vincent Pinard, Roger, Vacheron.

Santenay Burg r (w) ★★★ 85' **88'** 89' 90 **91 92 93 94** 95 96 97 98 Sturdy reds from village S of CHASSAGNE. Best v'yds: La Comme, Les Gravières, CLOS de Tavannes. Top growers: Lequin-Roussot, MOREY, POUSSE D'OR.

Saumur Lo r w p sp ★→★★★ Fresh fruity whites plus a few more serious, vg CREMANT and Saumur MOUSSEUX (producers incl BOUVET-LADUBAY, CAVE des Vignerons de Saumur, GRATIEN ET MEYER, LANGLOIS-CHATEAU), pale rosés and increasingly good CAB F (see next entry).

Saumur-Champigny Lo r ★★→★★★ **82 85** 86' **88 89'** 90' 93' 95' 96 97 98 Flourishing nine-commune AC for fresh CAB F ageing remarkably in sunny years. Look for CH DU HUREAU, Ch de Villeneuve, domaines FILLIATREAU, Legrand, Nerleux, Roches Neuves, Val Brun, CLOS ROUGEARD, coop St-Cyr.

Saussignac Dordogne w sw ★★→★★★ 90' **93** 95' 96 **97** (98) MONBAZILLAC-style age-worthy wines. Producers of new ultra-sw style incl Dom de Richard, Ch'x les Miaudoux, Tourmentine, le Payral, le Chabrier and Clos d'Yvigne.

Sauternes B'x w sw ★★→★★★★ 67' **71'** 75 76' **78** 79' **80** 81 **82 83' 85** 86' **88' 89' 90' 91** 92 95' 96 97 98 District of 5 villages (incl BARSAC) which make France's best sw wine, strong (14%[+] alcohol), luscious and golden, 10 yrs demanding to be aged. Top ch'x are D'YQUEM, CLIMENS, COUTET, GUIRAUD, SUDUIRAUT, etc. Dry wines cannot be sold as Sauternes.

Sauvignon Blanc See Grapes for white wine (pages 7–11).

Sauvignon de St-Bris Burg w ★★ DYA A baby VDQS cousin of SANCERRE, from nr CHABLIS. To try. 'Dom Saint Prix' from Dom Bersan is good.

Sauvion & Fils Ambitious and well-run MUSCADET house, based at the Ch de Cléray. Top wine: Cardinal Richard.

Sauzet, Etienne Top-quality white burgundy estate at PULIGNY-M'RACHET. Clearly-defined, well-bred wines, at best superb.

Savennières Lo w dr sw ★★★→★★★★ 75 76' 78' **82 83** 85 86' 88 **89' 90'** 93 95' 96 97 98 Small ANJOU district of pungent long-lived whites, incl Baumard, Ch de Chamboureau, Ch de Coulaine, Closel, Ch d'Epiré. Top sites: COULÉE DE SERRANT, ROCHE-AUX-MOINES, CLOS du Papillon.

Savigny-lès-Beaune Burg r (w) ★★★ 85' **87** 88' **89'** 90' **91** 92 **93 94 95** 96' 97 98 Important village next to BEAUNE; similar balanced mid-weight wines, often deliciously lively, fruity. Top v'yds: Dominode, Les Guettes, Marconnets, Serpentières, Vergelesses; growers: BIZE, Camus, CHANDON DE BRIAILLES, CLAIR, Ecard, Girard-Vollot, LEROY, Pavelot, TOLLOT-BEAUT.

Savoie E France r w sp ★★ DYA Alpine area with light dry wines like some Swiss or minor Loires. APREMONT, CREPY and SEYSSEL are best-known whites, ROUSSETTE is more interesting. Also good MONDEUSE red.

Schaller, Edgard ALSACE grower (dry style wines) in Mandelburg GRAND CRU, Mittelwihr; esp for RIES 'Mandelberg VIEILLES VIGNES' (needs time) and 'Les Amandiers' (younger-drinking).

Schlossberg V successful ALSACE GRAND CRU for RIES in two parts: Kientzheim and small section at Kayserberg. Top growers: FALLER/DOM WEINBACH and PAUL BLANCK.

Loire wines: buying sur place
Try the small chain of wine shops called 'Fief de Vigne' in Nantes, Angers, Cholet and Les Sables d'Olonne.
    Alternatively try restaurants Auberge du Porc Valières in Port Valières nr Fondettes (Touraine) and the Michelin-starred Lion d'Or at Romorantin-Lanthenay (south of Orléans).

Schlumberger, Domaines ALSACE growers at Guebwiller. Unusually rich wines incl luscious GEWURZ GRAND CRUS Kessler and Kitterlé (also SGN and VT). Fine RIES from GRAND CRUS Kitterlé and Saering. Also good PINOT Gr.

Schlumberger, Robert de SAUMUR sp wine made by Austrian method: fruity and delicate.

Schoffit, Domaine Colmar ALSACE house with GRAND CRU RANGEN PINOT Gr, GEWURZ of top-quality. Chasselas is unusual everyday delight.

Schröder & Schÿler Old BORDEAUX merchant, co-owner of CH KIRWAN.

Schoenenbourg V rich successful Riquewihr GRAND CRU (ALSACE): RIES, Tokay-PINOT Gr, v fine VT and SGN. Esp from MARCEL DEISS and DOPFF AU MOULIN. Also vg MUSCAT.

Sciacarello Original grape of CORSICA for red and rosé, eg AJACCIO, Sartène.

Sec Literally means dry, though CHAMP so-called is medium-sweet (and better at breakfast, tea-time and weddings than BRUT).

Séguret S Rh r w ★ Good S Rhône village nr GIGONDAS. Peppery, quite full red, rounded clean white. Esp Ch La Courançonne, Dom de Cabasse.

Sélection des Grains Nobles (SGN) Description coined by HUGEL for ALSACE equivalent to German Beerenauslese. Grains nobles are individual grapes with 'noble rot' (see page 102).

Sèvre-et-Maine The delimited zone containing the best v'yds of MUSCADET.

Seyssel Savoie w sp ★★ NV Delicate pale dry Alpine white, v pleasant sp.

Sichel & Co One of BORDEAUX most respected merchant houses. Sadly, Peter A Sichel died in '98; his five sons continue with the family's interests in Chx D'ANGLUDET and PALMER, in CORBIERES as B'x merchants.

Silvaner See Grapes for white wine (pages 7–11).

Sipp, Jean and Louis ALSACE growers in Ribeauvillé (Louis is also a NEGOCIANT). Both produce vg RIES GRAND CRU Kirchberg, Jean's: youthful elegance (smaller v'yd, own vines only); Louis': firmer when mature. Louis also makes vg GEWURZ, esp Grand Cru Osterberg.

Sirius Serious oak-aged blended BORDEAUX from Maison SICHEL.

Skalli Revolutionary producer of top VINS DE PAYS D'OC from CAB s, Merlot, CHARD etc, at Sète in the Languedoc, inspired by Mondavi. FORTANT DE FRANCE is standard brand. Style and value. Watch this name wherever it turns up.

Sorg, Bruno First-class sm ALSACE grower at Eguisheim for GRAND CRUS Florimont (RIES) and PFERSIGBERG (MUSCAT). Also v good Auxerrois.

Sparr, Pierre Sigolsheim ALSACE grower/producer, as good at CUVEES of several grapes (eg Symphonie) as rich GRANDS CRUS.

Sur Lie See Lie and Muscadet.

Syrah See Grapes for red wine (pages 11–13).

Tâche, La Burg r ★★★★ 78' 80' 82 83 85' 86 87 88' 89' 90' 91 92 93' 94 95 96' 97 98 15-acre (1,500 case) GRAND CRU of VOSNE-ROMANEE and one of best v'yds on earth: big perfumed luxurious wine. See DOMAINE DE LA ROMANEE-CONTI.

Tain, Cave Coopérative de, 425-members in northern Rhône ACs; owns ¼ HERMITAGE. Making increasingly good red Hermitage since '91. Good value.

Taittinger Brut NV; Rosé NV; Brut 82 83 85 86 88 89 90; Collection Brut 78 81 82 83 85 86 88 Fashionable Reims CHAMP grower and merchant; wines have distinctive silky flowery touch. Luxury brand: Comtes de Champagne BLANC DE BLANCS (79 81 82 83 85 86 88 90 91), also vg Rosé (79 83 85 86). See also Domaine Carneros, California.

Tardy, Jean Impressive fledgeling VOSNE-R domaine (since '85); vines leased from MEO-CAMUZET. To follow.

Tastevin, Confrèrie des Chevaliers du Burgundy's colourful successful promotion society. Wine with their Tastevinage label has been approved by them and is usually of a fair standard. A tastevin is the traditional shallow silver wine-tasting cup of Burgundy.

Tavel Rh p ★★★ DYA France's most famous, though not her best, rosé: strong and dry. Best growers: Ch d'Aquéria, Dom Corne-Loup, GUIGAL, Maby, Dom de la Mordorée, Prieuré de Montézargues, Roc-Epine, Ch de Trinquevedel.

Tempier, Domaine ★★★★ The top grower of BANDOL: noble reds and rosé.

Terroirs Landais Gascony r p w ★ VDP an extension in the département of Landes of the COTES DE GASCOGNE. Domaine de Laballe is most seen example.

Thénard, Domaine The major grower of the GIVRY appellation, but best known for his substantial portion (4+ acres) of LE MONTRACHET. Could still try harder with this jewel.

Thevenet, Jean Dom de la Bongrand at Clessé stands out for rich concentrated (even sweet!) white MACON.

Thézac-Perricard SW France r p ★ VDP W of CAHORS. Same grapes but lighter style. All made by coop at Thézac and incl a 100% Malbec multi-prizewinner.

Thomas-Moillard Underrated NUITS-ST-GEORGES estate for slow-emerging wines; sister co is Moillard-Grivot NEGOCIANT house.

Thorin, J Grower and major merchant of BEAUJOLAIS.

Thouarsais, Vin de Lo w r p ★ DYA Light CHENIN (20% CHARD permitted), GAMAY and CAB from tiny VDQS S of SAUMUR. Esp Gigon.

Tokay d'Alsace Old name for PINOT Gris in ALSACE in imitation of Hungarian Tokay. Now changed to Tokay-Pinot-Gris. Will be just Pinot Gris.

Tollot-Beaut Stylish and consistent burgundy grower with 50 acres in the COTE DE BEAUNE, including v'yds at Beaune Grèves, CORTON, SAVIGNY- (Les Champs Chevrey) and at his CHOREY-LES-BEAUNE base.

Touchais, Moulin Proprietary name of a selected COTEAUX DU LAYON released onto the market after about 10 years' cellaring. Vintages back to the '20s are like creamy honey and not over-priced.

For key to grape variety abbreviations, see pages 7–13.

Touraine Lo r p w dr sw sp ★ ★★★ Big mid-Loire region with immense range, incl dry white SAUV BL, dry and sweet CHENIN (eg VOUVRAY), red CHINON and BOURGUEIL. Also large AC with light CAB F, GAMAYS, gutsy Cot, or increasing a blend of these; grassy Sauv Bl and MOUSSEUX; often bargains. Amboise, Azay-le-Rideau and Mesland are sub-sections of the AC.

Trévallon, Domaine de Provence r w ★★★ 88 89 90 91 **92 93 94** 95 96' 97 98 Highly fashionable estate at Les Baux. Rich intense CAB-SYRAH blend to age.

Trimbach, F E Distinguished ALSACE grower and merchant at Ribeauvillé with supremely elegant if at times austere house style. Best wines incl RIES CLOS STE-HUNE, Cuvée Frédéric-Emile (grapes mostly from GRAND CRU Osterberg). Also GEWURZ. Opposed to GRAND CRU system like HUGEL.

Turckheim, Cave Vinicole de A first-class coop in ALSACE. Many fine wines, incl GRANDS CRUS from 790 acres, eg vg PINOT GR from GRAND CRU Hengst.

Tursan SW France r p w ★ VDQS aspiring to AOC. Easy drinking holiday-style wines. Mostly from coop at Geaune, but Ch de Bachen (★★) belongs to master-chef Michel Guérard, who makes one-off, atypical whites in a New-World style. Also Dom de Perchade-Pourrouchet (recent investment).

Vacqueyras S Rh r ★★ 85 86 88' **89' 90' 93** 94 95' 96' 97 98' Full, peppery GRENACHE-based neighbour to GIGONDAS – finer structure and often cheaper. Try JABOULET's, Ch de Montmirail, Ch des Tours, Dom Archimbaud-Vache, Le Couroulu, La Fourmone, Montvac, Pascal Frères, Le Sang des Cailloux.

The vin de pays revolution

The junior rank of country wines. No one should overlook this category, the most dynamic in France today. More than 140 vins de pays names have come into active use in the past few years, mainly in the Midi. They fall into three categories: regional (eg Vin de Pays d'Oc for the whole Midi); departmental (eg Vin de Pays du Gard for the Gard département near the mouth of the Rhône), and vins de pays de zone, the most precise, usually with the highest standards. Single-grape vins de pays and vins de pays primeurs (reds and whites, all released on the third Thursday in November) are especially popular. Well-known zonal vins de pays include Coteaux de l'Uzège, Côtes de Gascogne, Val d'Orbieu. Don't hesitate to try them. There are some real gems among them, and a great many charming trinkets.

Val d'Orbieu, Vignerons du Association of some 200 top growers and coops in CORBIERES, COTEAUX DU LANGUEDOC, MINERVOIS, ROUSSILLON etc, marketing a first-class range of selected MIDI AC and VDP wines.

Valençay Lo r p w ★ DYA VDQS in E TOURAINE, S of Cher; light easy-drinking sometimes sharpish wines from similar range of grapes as Touraine, esp SAUV BL.

Vallée du Paradis Midi r w p ★ Popular VDP of local red varieties in CORBIERES.

Valréas S Rh r (p w) ★★ 88 90' 93 94 **95'** 96 97 98' COTES DU RHONE village with big coop. Gd mid-weight reds (more sap than CAIRANNE, RASTEAU), improving whites. Esp Romain Bouchard, Dom des Grands Devers, Ch la Décelle.

Varichon & Clerc Principal makers and shippers of SAVOIE sparkling wines.

Vaudésir Burg w ★★★★ 85' 86 88 88' 89' 90 91 92 93 94 95 96 97 98 Arguably the best of seven CHABLIS GRANDS CRUS (but then so are the others).

VDQS Vin Délimité de Qualité Supérieure (see page 33).

Vendange Harvest.

Vendange Tardive Late harvest. ALSACE equivalent to German Auslese, but usually higher alcohol.

Verget The NEGOCIANT business of J-M GUFFENS-HEYNEN with admirable range from MACON to MONTRACHET. Intense wines, often models, from bought-in grapes.

Veuve Clicquot Yellow label NV; White Label Demi-Sec NV; Gold Label **76 78 79 82 83** (since '85 called Vintage Réserve: 85 **88** 89 90); Rosé Reserve **83 85** 88 Historic CHAMP house of highest standing, now owned by LVMH. Full-bodied, almost rich: one of Champ's surest things. Cellars at Reims. Luxury brands: La Grande Dame (**79 83 85 88** 89 90), new Rich Réserve (**89**) released '95 and La Grande Dame Rosé (**88**), launched '97.

Veuve Devaux Premium CHAMPAGNE of powerful Union Auboise coop in Bar-sur-Seine. Vg well-aged Grande Réserve NV and Oeil de Perdrix Rosé.

Some vins de pays for 2000

1 **Vin de Pays d'Oc** – A great diversity of grapes for some of the best value vins de pays: some traditional (Carignan, Grenache, Syrah), some new to the region (Chardonnay, Viognier, Cabernet, Merlot), and usually mentioned on label. Input from New World winemakers galvanizes local talent.

2 **Vin de Pays du Comté Tolosan** – A wider area of the southwest for red wine from Cabernets, Merlot, Tannat (and there are whites from Sauvignon, Sémillon, Chardonnay and others).

3 **Vin de Pays des Côtes de Thongue** – A compact VDP in the Hérault with more than its fair share of innovative producers. Blends as well as single varietals. Look for Arjolle, Chemin de Bassac, Croix-Belle, Prieuré d'Armailhac.

4 **Vin de Pays de l'Hérault** – Some of the best and worst vins de pays are from this large Midi area; a demonstration of the extremes of tradition and innovation both in grape varieties and technique.

5 **Vin de Pays des Côtes de Gascogne** – Decline in sales of Armagnac has been to the benefit of the local table wines: fragrant dry Colombard and Ugni Blanc are refreshing but perhaps less interesting than experiments with the local Gros and Petit Manseng.

6 **Vin de Pays des Sables du Golfe de Lion** – Pioneering Domaines Listel is virtually sole producer here on S coast, renowned for its rosé.

Vidal-Fleury, J Long-established GUIGAL-owned shipper of top Rhône wines and grower of COTE-ROTIE. Steady quality.

Vieille Ferme, La S Rh r w ★★ Vg brand of COTES DU VENTOUX (red) and COTES DU LUBERON (white) made by the Perrins, owners of CH DE BEAUCASTEL.

Vieilles Vignes Old vines – therefore the best wine. Used by many, esp by BOLLINGER, DE VOGUE and CH FUISSE.

Vieux Télégraphe, Domaine du S Rh r w ★★★ 78' 79 81' 82 83 85 86 88 89' 90 92 93 94' 95' 96' 97 98' A leader in fine, vigorous, modern red CHATEAUNEUF-DU-PAPE, and usually fresh whites, which age well in lesser yrs. New second wine: Vieux Mas des Papes. Second dom: de la Roquette. Bought GIGONDAS Dom des Pallières in '96 with US importer Kermit Lynch.

Vigne or vignoble Vineyard, vineyards. **Vigneron** V'yd worker.

Vin de l'année This year's wine. See Beaujolais, Beaujolais-Villages.

Vin Doux Naturel (VDN) Sweet wine fortified with wine alcohol, so the sweetness is 'natural', not the strength. The speciality of ROUSSILLON. based on GRENACHE or MUSCAT. A staple in French bars, but top wines remarkable.

Vin de garde Wine that will improve with keeping. The serious stuff.

Vin Gris 'Grey' wine is v pale pink, made of red grapes pressed before fermentation begins – unlike rosé, which ferments briefly before pressing. Oeil de Perdrix means much the same; so does 'blush'.

Vin Jaune Jura w ★★★ Speciality of ARBOIS: odd yellow wine like fino sherry. Normally ready when bottled (after at least 6 yrs). Best is CH-CHALON.

Vin Nouveau See Beaujolais Nouveau.

Vin de Paille Wine from grapes dried on straw mats, consequently v sweet, like Italian passito. Esp in the JURA. See also Chave.

Vin de Table Standard everyday table wine, not subject to particular regulations about grapes and origin. Choose VINS DE PAYS instead.

Vin Vert Very light acidic refreshing white wine, a speciality of ROUSSILLON (and v necessary in summer in those torrid parts).

Vinsobres S Rh r (p w) ★★ 89 90' 93 94 95' 96 97 98' Contradictory name of gd S Rhône village. Potentially substantial reds, rounded and fruity, but many ordinary. Best producers incl Doms les Aussellons, Bicarelle, du Moulin.

Viré See Mâcon-Viré.

Visan S Rh r p w ★★ 90' 93 94 95' 96 97 98 Village for far better medium-weight reds than whites. Note: Dom des Grands Devers.

Viticulteur Wine-grower.

Vogüé, Comte Georges de ('Dom les Musigny') First-class 30-acre BONNES-MARES and MUSIGNY domaine at CHAMBOLLE-MUSIGNY. At best, esp since '90, the ultimate examples.

Volnay Burg r ★★★ → ★★★★ 78 85' 88' 89' 90' 91 92 93 94 95 96' 97 98 Village between POMMARD and MEURSAULT: often the best reds of the CÔTE DE BEAUNE, not dark or heavy but structured and silky. Best v'yds: Caillerets, Champans, CLOS des Chênes, Clos des Ducs, etc. Best growers: D'ANGERVILLE, J M BOILLOT, HOSPICES DE BEAUNE, LAFARGE, LAFON, DE MONTILLE, POUSSE D'OR, Rossignol-Changarnier.

Volnay-Santenots Burg r ★★★ Excellent red wine from MEURSAULT is sold under this name. Indistinguishable from other PREMIER CRU VOLNAY. Best growers: AMPEAU, LAFON, LEROY.

Vosne-Romanée Burg r ★★★→★★★★ 78' 85' 87 88' 89' 90' 91 92 93 94 95 96' 97 98 Village with Burgundy's GRANDEST CRUS (ROMANEE-CONTI, LA TACHE etc). There are (or should be) no common wines in Vosne. Many good growers include Arnoux, Castagnier, Chevigny, DRC, ENGEL, GRIVOT, GROS, JAYER, LATOUR, LEROY, MEO-CAMUZET, MONGEARD-MUGNERET, Mugneret, RION.

Vougeot See Clos de Vougeot.

Vouvray Lo w dr sw sp ★★→★★★★ 76' 79 82 83 85' 86 88' 89' 90' 93 95' 96 97 98 (sec and demi-sec) 4,350-acre AC just E of Tours: v variable wines, increasingly gd, reliable. DEMI-SEC is classic style but in great years MOELLEUX can be intensely sw, almost immortal. Gd dry sp – look out for PETILLANT. Best producers: Allias, Champalou, Foreau, Fouquet, Ch Gaudrelle, HUET, Pinon, Poniatowski, Vigneau-Chevreau.

Vranken, Champagne With impressive Epernay HQ: ever-more powerful CHAMP group created in '76 by Belgian marketing man. CHARD-led wines of gd quality. Leading brand Demoiselle. Acquired HEIDSIECK MONOPOLE in '96.

Wolfberger Principal label of Eguisheim coop. Exceptional quality for such a large-scale producer.

'Y' (pronounced 'ygrec') 78' 79' 80' 84 85 86 87 88 89 90 94 95 96 Intense dry wine produced occasionally at CH D'YQUEM. Most interesting with age.

Zind-Humbrecht, Domaine Outstanding 74-acre ALSACE estate in Wintzenheim, Thann, Turckheim. First-rate single-v'yd wines (esp CLOS St-Urbain), and v fine from GRANDS CRUS Goldert (GEWURZ and MUSCAT), HENGST and RANGEN (RIES, Gewurz and PINOT Gris).

Châteaux of Bordeaux

The following abbreviations of regional names are used in the text:

B'x	Bordeaux
E-Deux-Mers	Entre-Deux-Mers
H-Méd	Haut-Médoc
Mar	Margaux
Méd	Médoc
Pau	Pauillac
Pessac-L	Pessac-Léognan
Pom	Pomerol
St-Em	St-Emilion
St-Est	St-Estèphe
St-Jul	St-Julien
Saut	Sauternes

Heavier shaded areas are the wine growing regions

Gironde

MEDOC

St-Estèphe
Pauillac
St-Julien
Listrac
Moulis
Margaux

Côtes de Blaye

Côtes de Bourg

Dronne

Isle

HAUT-MEDOC

POMEROL
Fronsac
Lalande de Pomerol
St-Emilion Satellites
Libourne
Côtes de Castillon
ST-EMILION
Dordogne

Bordeaux

Premières Côtes de Bordeaux

Ste-Foy-Bordeaux

PESSAC-LEOGNAN

Garonne

ENTRE-DEUX-MERS

GRAVES
Loupiac
Cérons
Côtes de Bordeaux/St-Macaire
BARSAC
Ste-Croix-du-Mont

SAUTERNES
Langon

I n 1998 Bordeaux has at last produced a better vintage at a lower price than the last, to everyone's delight. It was not especially easy.

Winter was mild and wet and April very wet. May and June were fine for flowering. July was warm and dull. Then in August 'la canicule' (heatwave), arrived, grilling exposed grapes and suddenly thickening the skins of the whole crop. For the rest of the month it was dry and vines started flagging. But at this point it looked like a great vintage.

In September rain fell on the Médoc from the 2nd to the 15th, then sun from the 16th to the 23rd. St-Emilion and Pomerol were able to pick their precocious Merlot in prime condition, but waiting for the Cabernet Sauvignon to ripen in the Médoc was nail-biting. What saved it was the thick skins formed in August. Ripeness, no rot; just too much water. There are very great Pomerols and St-Emilions this year. For the rest the quality varies as always with the grower's skill. There will be tannic wines and weak ones. But the ripeness is there. White Bordeaux was a big success, both in its dry and sticky modes.

In this listing I have picked out in colour the vintages which proprietors themselves will be serving this year as their first choices: their own wines in the state of maturity they prefer. Their choices, for older or younger wines or both, remind us that there are no absolutes – least of all in the glorious diversity of Bordeaux.

d'Agassac H-Méd r ★★ 82' **83' 85' 86 88** 89' **90' 93 94** 95 96 97 98 Sleeping Beauty 14th-C moated fort. 86 acres v nr Bordeaux suburbs. Wine popular in Holland. Investment '98. New owners since '96.

Andron-Blanquet St-Est r ★★ **82 83 85' 86 87** 88 89' **90 91 92 93** 94 95 96 97 98' Sister château to COS-LABORY. 40 acres. Toughish wines showing more charm lately.

L'Angélus St-Em r ★★★★ **83' 85' 86 87** 88 89' 90' **91 92 93'** 94' 95 96 97 98' 57-acre classed growth on ST-EMILION COTES. A current star with some sumptuous wines. Promoted to Premier Grand Cru Classé status in '96.

d'Angludet Cantenac-Mar r ★★★ 82 **83' 85 86 87** 88' **89' 90 91 92 93 94** 95 96' 97' 98' 75-acre CRU EXCEPTIONNEL of classed growth quality owned by the late PETER SICHEL's family. New equipment '98. Lively long-living MARGAUX of great style. Value.

d'Archambeau Graves r w dr (sw) ★★ (r) 85 **86 88 89 90** 91 **93 94 95** 96 97 98 (w) **90' 92' 93 95 96** 97 98 Up-to-date 54-acre property at Illats. Vg fruity dry white; since '85 fragrant barrel-aged reds (¾ of v'yd).

d'Arche Saut w sw ★★ 82 **83' 85 86' 88' 89' 90 91 93** 94 **95** 96 97 98 Classed growth of 88 acres rejuvenated since '80. Modern methods. Rich juicy wines to follow with pleasure.

d'Arcins Central Méd r ★★ 86 88 89 90 **93 94 95** 96 97 98 185-acre Castel family property (Castelvin: famous VIN DE TABLE). Sister to next-door Barreyres (160 acres).

d'Armailhac Pau r ★★★ 82' **83 85** 86' 88' 89 **90**' 91 **92** 93 **94** 95' 96' 97 98 Formerly CH MOUTON-BARONNE-PHILIPPE. Substantial fifth growth nurtured by the late Baron Philippe de Rothschild. 125 acres: wine much less rich and luscious than MOUTON-ROTHSCHILD, but outstanding in its class.

l'Arrosée St-Em r ★★★ 82 83 85' **86'** 88 89' **90' 92 93** 94' 95 96 97 98 24-acre COTES estate. Name means diluted, but wine is top-flight: opulent, structured. Modern cuvier; 100% new barrels.

Ausone St-Em r ★★★★ **75 76** 78' **79 81 82'** 83' **85 86'** 87 88 89 90 **92** 93 94 95 96 97 98 Illustrious first growth with 17 acres (about 2,500 cases) in the best position on the COTES with famous rock-hewn cellars. The most expensive ST-EMILION, but for a long time behind CHEVAL BLANC or FIGEAC in performance. Partial change of owners in '97 and considerable new investment. To watch.

Bahans-Haut-Brion Graves r ★★★ NV and **82 83 85 86'** 88 89' 90 92 93 94 95 96' 97 98 The second-quality wine of CH HAUT-BRION. Worthy of its noble origin; softly earthy yet intense.

Balestard-la-Tonnelle St-Em r ★★ 83 85 86' 88' 89 90' **93 94 95** 96 97 98' Historic 30-acre classed growth on the plateau. Big flavour; more finesse since '85. NEW CHAI in '95 and further investment since.

de Barbé Côtes de Bourg r (w) ★★ 88 89 90 **93 94 95 96 97** 98 The biggest (148 acres), best-known château of BOURG. Light fruity Merlot.

Baret Pessac-L r w ★★ (r) 85 86 88 89' 90' 95 96 97 98 Famous name recovered from a lull. Now run by BORIE-MANOUX. White well-made too.

Bastor-Lamontagne Saut w sw ★★ **82 83 85 86 87** 88' 89' 90' **94** 95 96' 98' Large Bourgeois Preignac sister-château to CH BEAUREGARD. classed growth quality; excellent rich wines. Second label: Les Remparts de Bastor (**92 93**). Also Ch St-Robert at Pujols: red and white GRAVES. 10,000 cases.

Batailley Pau r ★★★ 70 78' **81 82' 83'** 85' 86 **88'** 89' 90' **91** 93 94 95 96 97 98 The bigger of the famous pair of fifth growths (with HAUT-BATAILLEY) on the borders of PAUILLAC and ST-JULIEN. 110 acres. Fine, firm, strong-flavoured and good value Pauillac, to age. Home of the Castéja family of BORIE-MANOUX.

Beaumont Cussac (Haut-Méd) r ★★ **82 85 86'** 88 89' 90' 92 93' **94** 95 96 97 98' 200-acre+ CRU BOURGEOIS, well known in France for easily enjoyable wines from maturing vines. Second label: Ch Moulin d'Arvigny. 35,000 cases. New equipment '98. In the same hands as CH BEYCHEVELLE.

Beauregard Pom r ★★★ **82' 83 85 86** 88 89' **90'** 92 93 94' 95' 96' 97 98' 42-acre v'yd; fine 17th-C château nr LA CONSEILLANTE. Top-rank rich wines. Advice from Michel Rolland; cellar extended and re-equipped '96. Second label: Benjamin de Beauregard.

Beau-Séjour-Bécot St-Em r ★★★ 70 78 82' 83 85 86' 88' 89' **90' 92 93** 94 95' 96 97 98' Other half of BEAUSEJOUR-DUFFAU; 45 acres. Controversially demoted in class in '85 but properly re-promoted to 1er Grand Cru Classé in '96. The Bécots also own GRAND-PONTET. Now also La Gomerie: 1,000 cases, 100% Merlot.

Beau-Site St-Est r ★★ 82 83 85 86' **88 89' 90** 92 93 94 95 96 97 98 55-acre CRU BOURGEOIS EXCEPTIONNEL in same hands as CH BATAILLEY etc. Quality and substance typical of ST-ESTEPHE.

Beauséjour-Duffau St-Em r ★★★ 82 83 85 86 88 89' 90' 92 93' 94 95 96 97 98 Part of the old Beau-Séjour Premier Grand Cru estate on W slope of the COTES. 17 acres in old family hands; only 2,000+ cases of firm-structured, concentrated, even hedonistic wine.

de Bel-Air Lalande de Pom r ★★ 82' 85 **86** 88' 89' **90 93** 94' 95 96 97 98 The best-known estate of L de P, just N of POMEROL. Similar wine. 37 acres.

Bel-Air-Marquis-d'Aligre Soussans-Mar r ★★ **82'** 85 86 **88** 89 90 95 96 97 98' Organically run CRU EXCEPTIONNEL with 42 acres of old vines giving only 3,500 cases. Concentrated, but supple; a sleeper.

Bel-Orme-Tronquoy-de-Lalande St-Seurin-de-Cadourne (H-Méd) r ★★ 83 85 86 88 89 90 91 92 93 94 95 96 97′ 98 60-acre CRU BOURGEOIS N of ST-ESTEPHE. Old v'yd previously known for tannic wines. More tempting since new manager and new equipment in '97.

Belair St-Em r ★★★ 75′ 78 79′ 82′ 83′ 85′ 86′ 88′ 89′ 90′ 93 94′ 95 96 97 98 Neighbour of AUSONE. Wine is simpler; less tightly wound. Also NV Roc-Blanquant (magnums only). Biodynamic approach since '98.

Belgrave St-Laurent r ★★ 82 83 85 86′ 88 89 90′ 96′ 97′ 98 Little-seen fifth growth managed by DOURTHE in ST-JULIEN's back-country. 107 acres. Second label: Diane de Belgrave. Re-equipped '96-7.

Bellegrave Listrac r ★★ 82 83 85 86 88 89 90 92 93 94 95 96 97 98 38-acre CRU BOURGEOIS making full-flavoured wine with advice from PICHON-LALANDE.

Belles Graves Lalande de P r ★★ Confusing name, but one of the reasons to watch Lalande de Pomerol.

Berliquet St-Em r ★★ 82 83 85 86 88 89′ 90 92 93 94 95 96 97 98 23-acre Grand Cru Classé recently v well run. Investment '97.

Bertineau St-Vincent Lalande de Pom r ★★ 10 acres owned by top oenologist Michel Rolland (see also Le Bon Pasteur).

Beychevelle St-Jul r ★★★ 70′ 78 81 82′ 83 85 86′ 88 89′ 90′ 91 92 93 94′ 95 96 97 98 170-acre fourth growth with historic mansion, owned by an insurance company; now also Suntory. Wine should have elegance and power, just below top-flight ST-JULIEN. Re-equipped '99. Second wine: Amiral de Beychevelle.

Biston-Brillette Moulis r ★★ 88 89 90 93 94 95 96′ 97 98 Another attractive MOULIS. 7,000 cases.

Le Bon Pasteur Pom r ★★★ 82′ 83 85 86′ 87 88 89′ 90′ 92 93′ 94′ 95 96′ 97 98′ Excellent small property on ST-EM boundary, owned by consultant oenologist Michel Rolland. Concentrated, even creamy wines can be virtually guaranteed.

Bonalgue Pom r ★★ 89 90 91 92 93 94 95 96′ 97 98′ Ambitious little estate to watch. Les Hautes-Tuileries is sister château. Wines age 5-10 yrs. Re-equipped '98.

Bonnet E-Deux-Mers r w ★★ (r) 90 93 94 95 96 97 98′ (w) DYA Owned by Lurton family. Big producer (600 acres!) of some of the best ENTRE-DEUX-MERS.

Le Boscq St-Est r ★★ 85 86 88 89′ 90 92 93 95′ 96′ 97 98 Leading CRU BOURGEOIS giving excellent value in tasty ST-ESTEPHE. Re-equipped '97, '98.

Le Bourdieu-Vertheuil H-Méd r ★★ 82 83 85 86 88 89 90′ 92 93′ 94 95 96 97 98 Vertheuil CRU BOURGEOIS with sister château Victoria (134 acres in all); ST-ESTEPHE-style wines. New owners, equipment and effort since '90.

Bourgneuf-Vayron Pom r ★★ 82 83 85′ 86 88 89′ 90 92 94 95′ 96 97 98 22-acre v'yd on sandy gravel soil, its best wines with typically plummy POMEROL perfume. New equipment '98. 5,000 cases.

Bouscaut Graves r w ★★ (r) 82′ 83 85 86′ 88 89 90 92 93 95 96 97 98 (w) 94 96 97 98 Classed growth at Cadaujac bought in '80 by Lucien Lurton of BRANE-CANTENAC etc. 75 acres red (largely Merlot); 15 white. Never yet brilliant, but surely Lurtons can make it. New investment '98.

du Bousquet Côtes de Bourg r ★★ 82 85 86 88 89 90′ 92 93 95 96 97 98 Reliable estate with 148 acres making attractive solid wine.

Boyd-Cantenac Mar r ★★★ 78′ 82′ 83′ 85 86′ 88 89 90 91 94′ 95 96′ 97 98 44-acre third growth often producing attractive wine, full of flavour, if not of third growth class. Wines now aged in 50% new oak. See also Ch Pouget.

Branaire-Ducru St-Jul r ★★★ 79′ 81 82′ 83 85 86 88 89′ 90′ 91 92 93′ 94 95 96 97 98 Fourth growth of 125 acres. Notably spicy and flavoury wine in the '70s. Late '80s saw a full-scale revival. New owners since '88 are doing well. Second label: Duluc.

Brane-Cantenac Cantenac-Mar r ★★★ 78' **82' 83 85** 86' **88** 89 **90** 94 95 96 97 98 Big (211-acre) second growth. At (rare) best rich, even gamey wines of strong character. New equipment '97. Same owners as CH'X BOUSCAUT, CLIMENS, DURFORT-VIVENS, VILLEGEORGE etc. Second labels: ch'x Baron de Brane, Notton. Should do better.

du Breuil Cissac r ★★ 89 **90 92** 93 **95** 96 97 98 Historic château being restored by owners of CISSAC. Vines replanted after purchase in '87 now bearing fruit. To follow.

Brillette Moulis r ★★ **82 83 85' 86 88 89' 90 91 92** 93 95 96 97 98 70-acre CRU BOURGEOIS. Reliable and attractive. Second label: Berthault Brillette.

La Cabanne Pom r ★★ **81 82' 83 88'** 89' **90' 92 93 94'** 95 96 97 98' Well-regarded 25-acre property nr the great TROTANOY. Recently modernized. Second wine: Dom de Compostelle. See also CH HAUT-MAILLET.

Cadet-Piola St-Em r ★★ **82 83' 85' 86 88 89' 90 92 93'** 94' 95 96 97 98 Distinguished sm property (17.5 acres) N of ST-EMILION town. 3,000 cases of tannic wine. FAURIE-DE-SOUCHARD: same owner; less robust. New equipment '97.

Caillou Saut w sw ★★ 75 76 78 81 **82 83 85 86 87 88' 89' 90' 91 92** 94 **95** 96 97 98 Well-run second-rank 37-acre BARSAC v'yd for firm fruity wine. Private CUVÉE (**81 83 85** 86 88 89') is a top selection. To follow...

Calon-Ségur St-Est r ★★★ 78 81 82' **83** 85 86' **88' 89' 90 91** 93 94 95 96 97 98 Big (123-acre) third growth of great reputation. Hearty tannic wines; less stylish than v top ST-EST's but currently on gd form. Second label: Marquis de Ségur.

Cambon-la-Pelouse H-Méd r ★★ **93 94 95 96'** 97 98 Big accessible CRU BOURGEOIS. A sure bet for fresh typical MEDOC. Change of ownership '96; cellar fully re-equipped in '97 incl 350 new barrels.

Camensac St-Laurent r ★★ **82' 85** 86' **88 89 90 93** 95 96' 97' 98' 149-acre fifth growth. Quite lively if not exactly classic wines. New vat-house in '94. Second label: La Closerie de Camensac.

Canon Canon-Fronsac r ★★→★★★ **82 83 85** 86' **88 89' 90 92** 93 94 95 96 97 98 Tiny property of CHRISTIAN MOUEIX. Long-ageing wine.

Canon St-Em r ★★★★ 79' 80 81 82' **83 85'** 86 **88' 89' 90' 92** 93' 94 95 96 97 98' Famous first-classed growth with 44+ acres on plateau W of the town bought in '96 by (Chanel) owners of RAUZAN-SEGLA. Conservative methods, immaculate kit: v impressive wine, among ST-EM's best. Second label (in '91): Clos J Kanon.

Canon-de-Brem Canon-Fronsac r ★★ **82' 83 85 86 88 89' 90** 93 94 95 96 97 98 One of the two FRONSAC v'yds for vigorous wine. MOUEIX property.

Canon-la-Gaffelière St-Em r ★★★ **82 83** 85 86' **88' 89' 90' 92** 93' 94' 95 96 97 98 47-acre classed growth on lower slopes of COTES. German owners. Total renovation in '85. Stylish, up front impressive wines.

Canon-Moueix Canon-Fronsac r ★★ **82 83** 85 86 **88 89'** 90 92 93 94 95 96 97 98 Important MOUEIX investment in this rising AC. V stylish wine. NB also sister chx CANON-DE-BREM, CANON (Canon-Fronsac).

Cantegril Graves r ★★ **93 94 95** 96 97 98 Good earthy red from CH DOISY-DAENE.

Cantemerle Macau r ★★★ **82 83'** 85 **88 89'** 90 **92 93** 94 95 96 97 98 Romantic southern MEDOC estate, a château in a wood with 150 acres of vines. Fifth growth capable of great things (eg '89). Problems in the late '70s, but since '81 CORDIER management has restored to potential. New cellars and oak vats in '90. Second label: Villeneuve de Cantemerle.

Cantenac-Brown Cantenac-Mar r ★★→★★★ 70 81 **82 83** 85 86' **88 89' 90' 92 93** 94 95 96 97 98 Formerly old-fashioned 77-acre third growth. New owners (same as PICHON-LONGUEVILLE) investing heavily; direction from J-M Cazes and promising since '94. Tannic wines. 2nd label: Canuet.

Châteaux entries also cross-refer to France section, pages 32–77.

Cap-de-Mourlin St-Em r ★★ 82' 83 85 86 88 89 90 93 94 95 96 97 98' Well-known 37-acre property of the Cap-de-Mourlin family, owners of CH BALESTARD and CH ROUDIER, MONTAGNE-ST-EM. Rich tasty ST-EMILION.

Capbern-Gasqueton St-Est r ★★ 82 83 85 86 88 89 90 92 93 94 95 96 97 98 Good 85-acre CRU BOURGEOIS; same owner as CALON-SEGUR.

Carbonnieux Graves r w ★★★ 82 83 85 86' 88 89' 90' 91 92 93 94 95 96 97 98 Historic estate at LEOGNAN for sterling (and improving) red and white. The whites, 65% Sauv (eg 90 91 92' 93 94' 95 96 97), have the structure to age 10 yrs. Ch'x Le Pape and Le Sartre are also in the family. Second label: La Tour-Léognan.

Cardaillan Graves r ★★ 92 93 94 95 96 97 98 The trusty red wine of the distinguished CHATEAU DE MALLE (SAUTERNES).

La Cardonne Blaignan (Méd) r ★★→★★★ 93 94 95 96 97 98 Fairly large (125 acre) CRU BOURGEOIS of northern MEDOC. Rothschild-owned 1973–90. Big changes and improvements since.

de Carles Fronsac r ★★ 86 88 89 90 92 93 94 95 96 97' 98 Steadily well-made quite juicy FRONSACS. New investment '97.

Les Carmes-Haut-Brion Graves r ★★ 81' 82' 83 85 86 88' 89 90' 91 93' 94 95 96 97 98 Small (11-acre) neighbour of HAUT-BRION with higher-than-Bourgeois standards. Old vintages show its potential. Produces only 1,500 cases.

Caronne-Ste-Gemme St-Laurent r ★★→★★★ 61 66 81 82' 83 85 86 87 88 89' 90 92 93' 94' 95 96 97 98 CRU BOURGEOIS EXCEPTIONNEL (100 acres). Steady stylish quality repays patience. At minor CRU CLASSE level. New investment '97, '98.

Carsin Premières Côtes r w ★★ (r) 95 96 97 98 (w) 95 96 97 98 Ambitious enterprise: Finish-owned, Australian winemaker. V attractive wines. To follow.

Carteau St-Em ★★ 85 88 89 90 93 94 95 96' 97 98' Emerging 5,000-case GRAND CRU; to follow for full-flavoured wines maturing fairly early. Investment '97; new gear '98.

Castera Méd r ★★ 85 86 88 89 90' 93 94' 95 96' 97 98 Historic property at St-Germain (N MEDOC). Recent investment; tasty but not tannic wine.

Certan-Giraud Pom r ★★ 82 83' 85 86 88 89' 90' 92 93' 94 95 96 97 98 Small (17-acre) property next to PETRUS. Has underperformed but was bought in '99 by J-P MOUEIX. Watch this space.

Certan-de-May Pom r ★★ 75 79 81 82' 83' 85' 86 87 88' 89' 90' 92 93 94 95 96 97 98 Neighbour of VIEUX CHATEAU CERTAN. Tiny property (1,800 cases) with full-bodied, rich, tannic wine.

Chambert-Marbuzet St-Est r ★★ 70 78 81 82 83 85 86 87 88 89' 90' 91 92 93 94' 95 96 97 98 Tiny (20-acre) sister château of HAUT-MARBUZET. Vg predominantly Cab, aged v tastily in new oak. M Duboscq, likes his wines well hung.

Chantegrive Graves r w ★★ 85 88 89 90 93 94 95 96' 97 98' 215-acre estate, half white, half red; modern GRAVES of v fair quality. CUVEE Caroline is top white selection (89 90 93 94 95 96 97 98'), Cuvée Edouard top red (82 83 85 88 89 90 91 93 94 95 96 97 98). Other labels incl Mayne-Lévêque, Mayne-d'Anice, Bon-Dieu-des-Vignes.

Chasse-Spleen Moulis r ★★★ 70 75' 78' 79 81' 82' 83' 85 86 87 88 89' 90' 91 92 93 94 95 96 97 98' 180-acre CRU EXCEPTIONNEL at classed growth level. Consistently good, often outstanding, long-maturing wine. Second label: Ermitage de C-S. One of the surest things in Bordeaux. See also La Gurgue and Haute-Bages-Libéral.

Chauvin St Em r ★★ 88 89 90 92 93 94 95 96 97 98' Steady performer with a certain following.

Chéret-Pitres Graves r w ★→★★ 91 92 93 94 95 96 97 98 Substantial estate in the notable village of Portets. Drink young or keep.

Cheval Blanc St-Em r ★★★★ 75' 76 78 79 81' 82' 83' 85' 86 87 88 89 90' 92 93 94 95' 96' 97 98 This and AUSONE are the 'first growths' of ST-EMILION. Cheval Bl is consistently richer, more full-blooded, intensely vigorous and perfumed, from 100 acres. Delicious young; lasts a generation. For many *the* first choice in Bordeaux. New owners '98 (Albert Frères and LVMH chairman Bernard Arnault). 2nd wine: Le Petit Cheval.

Chevalier, Domaine de Graves r w ★★★★ 66' 70' 78' 81' 83' 85 86' 87 88' 89' 90' 91 92 93 94' 95' 96' 97 98' Superb estate of 94 acres at LEOGNAN. The red is stern at first, softly earthy with age. The white matures slowly to rich flavours (83' 85' 87' 88 89 90' 91 92 93 94 95 96' 97 98'). New equipment '98. Second wine: Esprit de Chevalier. Also look out for Domaine de la Solitude, PESSAC-LEOGNAN.

Cissac Cissac-Médoc r ★★ 70' 75' 78' 81 82' 83' 85 86' 88 89 90 91 92 93 94' 95 96' 97 98 Pillar of the bourgeoisie. 80-acre CRU GRAND BOURGEOIS EXCEPTIONNEL: steady record for tasty, v long-lived wine. Cellar expanded in '97 and '98. Second wine: Les Reflets du Ch Cissac. Also, since '87, CH DU BREUIL.

Citran Avensan (H-Méd) r ★★ 82 85 86 88 89' 90' 93 94' 95 96 97 98 CRU EXCEPTIONNEL of 178 acres, back in possession of Villars-Merlaut family since '96 after a Japanese interlude of dark, tannic wines. Major works. Second label is Moulins de Citran. To watch.

Clarke Listrac r (p w) ★★ 82 83 85' 86' 88 89' 90' 93 94 95 96' 97 98 Huge (350-acre) CRU BOURGEOIS Rothschild development, incl visitor facilities and neighbouring ch'x Malmaison and Peyrelebade. Also a unique sweet white 'Le Merle Blanc du Ch Clarke'. M Rolland consulting from '98.

Clerc-Milon Pau r ★★★ 82' 83 85 86' 88 89' 90' 91 92 93 94 95 96' 97 98' Once-forgotten fifth growth bought by the late Baron Philippe de Rothschild in '70. Now 73 acres. Not thrilling in the '70s (except 70), but vg 85, 86 (esp), and now a top performer, weightier than ARMAILHAC.

Climens Saut w sw ★★★★ 71' 73 75' 76 78 79 80' 81 82 83' 85' 86' 88' 89 90' 95 96 97 98 74-acre BARSAC classed growth making some of the world's most stylish wine (but not the v sweetest) for a good 10 yrs' maturing. (Occasional) second label: Les Cyprès. Same owner as CH BRANE-CANTENAC etc.

Clinet Pom r ★★★★ 82 83 85 86 88' 89' 90' 91 92 93' 94 95 96 97 98 17-acre property in central POMEROL making intense sumptuous wines from old vines. Since '88 one of the models for POMEROL.

Clos l'Eglise Pom r ★★★ 75 81 83 85 86 88 89 90' 93 94 95 96 97 98 15-acre v'yd on one of the best sites in POMEROL. Fine wine without great muscle or flesh. M Rolland consults. The same family owns CH HAUT-BERGEY.

Clos Floridène Graves r w ★★ (r) 89 90' 93' 94 95 96 97 98' (w) 93 94 95 96' 97 98' A sure thing from one of B'dx's best white winemakers, Denis Dubourdieu. Oak-fermented Sauv-Sém to keep 5 yrs; fruity red. See also Ch Reynon.

Clos Fourtet St-Em r ★★★ 79 81 82' 83 85 86 88 89 90 93 94 95 96 97 98 Well-placed 42-acre first growth on the plateau, cellars almost in town. Back on form after a middling patch: André Lurton now winemaker; more changes to come. Same owners as BRANE-CANTENAC, CLIMENS, etc. Second label: Dom de Martialis.

Clos Haut-Peyraguey Saut w sw ★★ 75 76 79 82 83 85 86' 88' 89 90' 93 94 95' 96 97 98 Tiny production of excellent medium-rich wine. Haut-Bommes is the second label. New equipment '98.

Clos des Jacobins St-Em r ★★ 75' 79 81 82' 83' 85 86 87 88' 89' 90' 93 94 95 96 97 98 Well-known and well-run little (18-acre) classed growth owned by CORDIER. Wines of roundness and style.

Clos du Marquis St-Jul r ★★ →★★★ 82 83 85 86' 88 89' 90 91 92 93 94 95 96 97 98 The second wine of LEOVILLE-LAS-CASES, cut from the same cloth and regularly a match for many highly classed growths.

Clos de l'Oratoire St-Em r ★★ Steady performer on the plateau nr CH FIGEAC.

Clos René Pom r ★★ **75** 82' 83 85 **86** 88 89 90 **92 93 94** 95 96 97 98 Leading château west of POMEROL. 38 acres. Increasingly concentrated wines. New vats in '96. Alias Ch Moulinet-Lasserre.

La Closerie-Grand-Poujeaux Moulis r ★★ 85 86 88 **89 90 93** 94' 95 96 97 98' Small but respected middle-MEDOC property modernized in '92/'93. Emphatic wines. Also owners of neighbouring ch'x Bel-Air-Lagrave and Haut-Franquet.

La Clotte St-Em r ★★ 82 83' 85 86 88 89 90' 93' 94 95' 96' 97 98' Tiny COTES GRAND CRU: pungent supple wine. Drink at owners' restaurant, Logis de la Cadène, in ST-EM. Cellar extended '98. Second label: Clos Bergat Bosson (93 94 95 96 97 98).

Colombier-Monpelou Pau r ★★ 82 83 85 86' 88 89 90' 93 94 95 96 97 98 Reliable small CRU BOURGEOIS; fair standard. New equipment '98.

La Conseillante Pom r ★★★★ 70' **75' 76** 79 81' 82' 83 84 85 86 87 88 89 90' **91 92 93 94** 95' 96' 97 98' 29-acre historic property on the plateau between PETRUS and CHEVAL BLANC. Some of the noblest and most fragrant POMEROL, worthy of its superb position; drinks well young or old.

Corbin (Giraud) St-Em r ★★ **79 81** 82' 83 85 86 88 89 90' 93 94 95 96 97 98 28-acre classed growth in N ST-EMILION where a cluster of Corbins occupy the plateau edge. Top vintages are v rich. Same owner as CERTAN-GIRAUD.

Corbin-Michotte St-Em r ★★ 82 83 85 88 89' 90 93 94' 95 96 97 98' Well-run modernized 19-acre property; 'generous' POMEROL-like wine.

Cordeillan-Bages Pau r ★★ A mere 1,000 cases of rather lean PAUILLAC from the vg château-hotel of J-M Cazes (see Lynch-Bages).

Cos-d'Estournel St-Est r ★★★★ 75' **79 81'** 82' 83' 85' 86' **87 88' 89' 90' 91 92** 93' 94 95 96' 97' 98' 140-acre second growth with eccentric chinoiserie tower overlooking CH LAFITE. Most refined ST-EST and regularly one of best wines of the MEDOC. New equipment '97. Second label: Les Pagodes de Cos-d'Estournel. Sold to Belgian group, but still managed by Guillaume, son of Bruno Prats.

Cos-Labory St-Est r ★★ 82 83 85 86 87 88 89' 90' 91 92 93 94 95 96' 97' 98 Little-known fifth growth neighbour of COS-D'ESTOURNEL with 37 acres. Efforts since '85 have raised it steadily to classed growth form (esp since '90). ANDRON-BLANQUET is sister château.

Coufran St-Seurin-de-Cadourne (H-Méd) r ★★ 82' 83 85 86' 87 88 89 90 92 93 94 95 96' 97 98 Coufran and CH VERDIGNAN, in the extreme N of the HAUT-MEDOC, are co-owned. Coufran is mainly Merlot for supple wine. New equipment in '97. 148 acres. CH SOUDARS is another, smaller sister.

Couhins-Lurton Graves w ★★→★★★ 93 94 95 96 97' 98' Tiny quantity of v fine oaky Sauv Bl for maturing. Classed growth château; cellar being reconstructed.

Couspaude, La St Em r ★★ 89 90 91 93 94 95 96 97 98 Another to watch closely. Modern methods and full-flavoured wine. New oak barrels '98.

Coutet Saut w sw ★★★ 71' 75' 76 81' 82 83' 85 85 86' 87 88' 89' 90' (no 93 94) 95 96 97 98 Traditional rival to CH CLIMENS; 91 acres in BARSAC. Usually slightly less rich; at its best equally fine. Cuvée Madame is a v rich selection in the best vintages. A dry GRAVES is sold under the same name.

To decipher codes, please refer to 'Key to symbols' on front flap of jacket, or to 'How to use this book' on page 6.

Couvent des Jacobins St-Em r ★★→★★★ 82' 83 85 86 87 88 89 90 92 93 94 95 96' 97 98' Well-known 22-acre v'yd on E edge of town. Among the best of its kind. Splendid cellars; further investment '97. Second label: Ch Beau-Mayne.

Le Crock St-Est r ★★ 81 82 83 85 86 88 89 90' 92 93 95 96 97 98 Outstanding CRU BOURGEOIS of 74 acres in the same family as CH LEOVILLE-POYFERRE. Among the best Crus Bourgeois of the commune.

La Croix Pom r ★★ 75' 79' 81 82 83 85' 86 88 89 90 92 93 94 95 96 97 98 Well-reputed property of 32 acres. Appealing plummy POMEROL. Also La C-St-Georges, La C-Toulifaut, Castelot, Clos des Litanies and HAUT-SARPE (St-Em).

La Croix-de-Gay Pom r ★★★ 81 82' 83' 85 86 88' 89 90 91 92 93 94' 95 96 97 98 30 acres in best part of the commune. Recently on fine form. Has underground cellars (rare in POMEROL). LA FLEUR-DE-GAY is the best selection.

La Croix du Casse Pom r ★★ 89 90 93 94 95 96 97 98 Up-and-coming property to look out for.

Croizet-Bages Pau r ★★ 82' 85 86 88 89 90' 93 94 95 96' 97 98' 52-acre fifth growth (lacking a château or a reputation). Same owners as CH RAUZAN-GASSIES. New manager in '94 and new Cab S plantings in '97 indicate better things to come.

Croque-Michotte St-Em r ★★ 75 81 82' 83 85 86 88 89' 90' 91 93 94 95 96 97 98 35-acre Grand Cru on the POMEROL border. Good steady wines but apparently not grand enough to be classé.

de Cruzeau Graves r w ★★ (r) 86 88 89 90 92 93 94 95 96 97 98 100-acre PESSAC-LEOGNAN v'yd recently developed by André Lurton of LA LOUVIERE etc. V high standards; to try. Oak-fermented white keeps 2–5 years.

Curé-Bon St-Em r ★★ 82' 83 85 86 88 89 90 92 93 94 95 96 97 98 Tiny little-known (12-acre) property between AUSONE and CANON.

Dalem Fronsac r ★★ 85 86 88 89 90 93 94 95 96 97 98' Leading full-blooded FRONSAC. 36 acres: 85% Merlot. Investment '97; new barrel cellar '98.

Dassault St-Em r ★★ 82 83 85 86 88 89 90 93 94 95 96 97 98' Consistent, early-maturing middle-weight GRAND CRU. 58 acres. New owners in 95. Could be more exciting.

La Dauphine Fronsac ★★ 85 86 88 89' 90' 93 94 95 96 97 98' Old star rejuvenated by J-P MOUEIX.

Dauzac Labarde-Mar r ★★→★★★ 82' 85 86 88' 89' 90' 93' 94 95 96 97 98' 120-acre fifth growth nr the river south of MARGAUX; underachiever for many years. New owner (insurance company) in '89; direction since '92 by André Lurton. New cuvier in '94. Second wine: La Bastide Dauzac.

Desmirail Mar r ★★ 82 83' 85 86 88 89 90 93 94 95' 96' 97 98 Third growth, now 45 acres. A long-defunct name revived in '81 by Lucien Lurton of BRANE-CANTENAC. So far wines for drinking fairly young, but higher ambitions on stream. Re-equipped '97.

Doisy-Daëne Barsac w (r) sw dr ★★★ 76' 80 81 82 83 85 86 88' 89' 90' 91 94 95 96 97 98 Forward-looking, even experimental, 34-acre estate for crisp oaky dry white and red CH CANTEGRIL as well as notably fine (and long-lived) sweet BARSAC. L'Extravagance (**90**) was a super-CUVÉE.

Doisy-Dubroca Barsac w sw ★★ 75' 76 78 79 81 83 85 86 87 88' 89 90' 95 96 97 Tiny (8.5-acre) BARSAC classed growth allied to CH CLIMENS.

Doisy-Védrines Saut w sw ★★★ 70 75' 76' 78 79 80 81 82' 83' 85 86 88' 89' 90 92 93 95 96 97 98' 50-acre classed growth at BARSAC, nr CLIMENS and COUTET, re-equipped '98. Delicious, sturdy, rich: for keeping. See the '89.

La Dominique St-Em r ★★★ 79 81 82' 83 86' 87 88' 89' 90' 92 93 94 95 96 97 98 45-acre classed growth next to CH CHEVAL BLANC for fruity, nose-catching wines. Second label: St Paul de Dominique (91). New ownership in '97.

Ducluzeau Listrac r ★★ **82 83 85 86 88 89 90 91 92 93 94** 95 96' 97 Tiny sister property of DUCRU-BEAUCAILLOU. 10 acres, unusually 90% Merlot.

Ducru-Beaucaillou St-Jul r ★★★★ 61 62 66' **70' 75' 78' 81 82' 83' 85' 86' 87 88 89 90 91 92 93 94** 95 96' 97 98 Outstanding second growth; 120 acres overlooking the river. Classic cedar-scented claret for long ageing. The devoted J-E Borie died in '98; family goes on. See also Grand-Puy-Lacoste, Haut-Batailley, Lalande-Borie. New cellar being built '97/8.

Duhart-Milon-Rothschild Pau r ★★★ 81 82' **83 85 86 87 88 89 90 91 92 93** 95 96' 97 98 Fourth growth neighbour of LAFITE, under same management. Maturing vines; increasingly fine quality and reputation. 110 acres. Second label: Moulin de Duhart.

Duplessis-Fabre Moulis r ★★ **82 85 86 88' 89 90 92** 93 95 96 97 98 Former sister château of FOURCAS-DUPRE; since '89 owned by DOURTHE.

Durfort-Vivens Mar r ★★★ **78' 79' 81 82' 83 85' 86 87 88' 89' 90 93** 95 96 97 98 Relatively small (49-acre) second growth owned by Lurton family. Recent wines have structure (lots of Cab S) and class. Investment in '97, '98.

Dutruch-Grand-Poujeaux Moulis r ★★ **75 81 82' 83 85 86 88 89 90 91 93 94** 95 96' 97 98' One of the leaders of MOULIS making full-bodied and tannic wines. 60 acres. Cellar extended '98.

de l'Eglise, Domaine Pom r ★★ 79' 82' **83 85 86 88 89 90 92 93** 95 96 97 98 Small property: stylish resonant wine distributed by BORIE-MANOUX.

L'Eglise-Clinet Pom r ★★★ 79 81 **82' 83' 84 85' 86 88' 89 90' 91 93'** 94 95 96 97 98 11 acres. Ranked v nr top; full fleshy wine. Changed hands in '82; '86 '90 noble. 1,700 cases. Second label: La Petite Eglise.

L'Enclos Pom r ★★★ **70 75 79 82' 83 85 86 87 88 89' 90' 91 92 93 94 95** 96 97 98' Respected 26-acre property on west side of POMEROL, nr CLOS RENE. Usually big well-made long-flavoured wine. New kit in '97.

L'Evangile Pom r ★★★★ **75' 82' 83' 85' 86 88' 89' 90' 92 93** 95' 96' 97 98' 33 acres between PETRUS and CHEVAL BLANC. Deep-veined but elegant style in a POMEROL classic. In the same area and class as LA CONSEILLANTE. Bought in '90 by Domaines (LAFITE) Rothschild.

de Fargues Saut w sw ★★★ **70' 71' 75' 76' 78 79 80 81 83 85' 86 87 88 89 90** 95 96 97 98 25-acre v'yd by ruined château in same ownership as CH D'YQUEM. Fruity and extremely elegant wines, maturing earlier than Yquem.

Faurie-de-Souchard St-Em r ★★ 85 **86 88 89 90 92 93 94 95** 96 97 98' Small GRAND CRU CLASSE château on the COTES, now tightening its grip. See also Château Cadet-Piola.

de Ferrand St-Em ★★→★★★ 85 86 **87 88 89 90' 92** 93' 95 96 97 98 Big (75-acre) plateau estate. Rich oaky wines, with plenty of tannin.

Ferrand-Lartigue St-Em ★★★ New perfectionist 5-acre property. First wine (93) v promising in dense rich style.

Ferrande Graves r (w) ★★ **85 86 88 89 90 93 94 95** 96 97 98 Major estate of Castres: 100⁺ acres. Easy enjoyable red and good white wine, at their best at 1–4 yrs.

Ferrière Mar r ★★ **89 90 93 94** 95 96 97' 98 Up until '92 a phantom third growth; only 20 acres; part of LASCOMBES. Now in same capable hands as CHASSE-SPLEEN, LA GURGUE and HAUT-BAGES-LIBERAL.

Feytit-Clinet Pom r ★★ **82' 83 85' 86 88' 89' 90' 93** 94 95 96 97' 98 Little property nr LATOUR-A-POM managed by J-P MOUEIX. At best fine lightish wines.

Fieuzal Graves r (w) ★★★ **75 79 81 82' 83 85' 86' 88 89 90' 91 92** 93 94 95 96' 97 98' 75-acre classed growth at LEOGNAN. Finely made, memorable wines of both colours. Classic whites since '85 are 4–10-yr keepers. New owners in '94. Ch Le Bonnat is sister château vinified at Fieuzal. Further investment '97.

87

Figeac St-Em r ★★★★ 70' 75 76 81**82' 83** 85' 86' 88 89' 90' **92 93 94' 95'** 96 97 98 First growth neighbour of CHEVAL BLANC. 98-acre gravelly vineyard gives one of Bordeaux's most stylish, rich but elegant wines, lovely to drink relatively quickly but lasting indefinitely. Second label: Grangeneuve.

Filhot Saut w sw dr ★★ 82' 83' 85 86' **87 88'** 88 91 92 93 94 95 96 97 98 Second-rank classed growth with splendid château, 148-acre v'yd. Lightish rather simple (Sauv) sweet wines for fairly early drinking, a little dry, and red. Vg 'Crème de Tête' (**90** extremely rich).

La Fleur St-Em r ★★ **82' 83** 85 86 88 89' 90' **92** 93 94 95 96 97 98 16-acre CÔTES estate; deliciously fruity wines. Now owned by J-P MOUEIX.

La Fleur-de-Gay Pom r ★★★★ 1,000-case super-CUVÉE of CH LA CROIX DE GAY.

La Fleur-Pétrus Pom r ★★★★ 70 75' 78 79 81' 82 83' 85 86 87 88' 89' 90' 92 94 95 96' 97 98 32-acre v'yd flanking PÉTRUS and under same management. Exceedingly fine densely plummy wines; POMEROL at its most stylish (and expensive).

Fombrauge St-Em r ★★ 82' 83 85 86 87 88' 89 90 **92** 93 94' 95 96 97 98 120 acres at St-Christophe-des-Bardes, E of ST-EMILION; Danish connections. Mainstream St-Emilion making great efforts. Second label: Ch Maurens.

Fonbadet Pau r ★★ 70 78 81' **82' 83** 85 86 87 88 89 90' **91 92** 93 94 95 96' 97 98' CRU BOURGEOIS of solid reputation. 50 acres next to PONTET-CANET. Old vines; wine needs long bottle-age. Continued investment. Value.

Fonplégade St-Em r ★★ 82' 83 85 86 **88 89 90'** 93 94 95 96 97 98 48-acre GRAND CRU CLASSÉ on the CÔTES W of ST-EMILION. Firm and long-lasting.

Fonréaud Listrac r ★★ 82' **83** 85' **86' 88** 89 90 **92** 93 94 95 96 97 98 One of the bigger (96 acres) and better CRUS BOURGEOIS of its area. Further investment '98. Now also 5 acres of white: Le Cygne, barrel-fermented. See also Ch Lestage.

Fonroque St-Em r ★★★ 75' 78 **82 83' 85' 86 87 88** 89' 90' **92** 93 94 95 96 97 98 48 acres on the plateau N of ST-EMILION. J-P MOUEIX property. Big deep dark wine: drink or (better) keep.

Fontmarty Pom r ★★ 82 83 85 86 **88'** 89 90 92 **93** 94 95' 96 97 98' Small property owned by Bernard Moueix group (also TAILLEFER); 1,500 cases.

Les Forts de Latour Pau r ★★★ 70' 75 78' 79 81 82' **83** 85 86 87 88 89' 90' 91 92 93 94 95' 96' 97 98 The second wine of CH LATOUR; the authentic flavour in (slightly) lighter format. Until '90 unique in being bottle-aged at least 3 yrs before release; now offered EN PRIMEUR.

Fourcas-Dupré Listrac r ★★ 82' 83' 85' 86' 88 89' 90 91 92 93 94 95 96' 97 98' Top-class 100-acre CRU BOURGEOIS EXCEPTIONNEL making consistent wine in the tight LISTRAC style. New equipment '98. To follow. Second label: Ch Bellevue-Laffont.

Fourcas-Hosten Listrac r ★★ →★★★ 81 82' 83' 85 86' 87 88 89 90 **91 92** 93 94 95' 96' 97 98' 96-acre CRU BOURGEOIS often the best of its (underestimated) commune. Firm wine with a long life. New gear '98.

Franc-Mayne St-Em r ★★ 85 86 88 89' 90' 93 94 **95** 96 97 98' 18 acre-GRAND CRU CLASSÉ. Ambitious new owners '96. Michel Rolland consults. To watch.

de France Pessac-L r w ★★ (r) 88 89 90' **93** 94 95' 96' 97 98 (w) **95 96 97** 98 Well-known GRAVES property with Michel Rolland consulting. Try a top vintage. More investment '98.

La Gaffelière St-Em r ★★★ 82' 83' 85 86' 88' **89'** 90' **92 93** 94 95 96 97 98 61-acre first growth at the foot of the CÔTES below CH BELAIR. Elegant, not rich wines; worthy of its rank since '82. Re-equipped '98.

NB The vintages printed in colour are the ones you should choose first for drinking in 2000.

Galius St-Em r ★★★ 85 86 **88 89** 90 93 94 95 96 97 98 Oak-aged selection from ST-EMILION coop, to a high standard. Formerly Haut Quercus.

La Garde Graves r (w) ★★ **81 82' 83' 84 85 86 88 89** 90 **91 92 93 94 95'** 96' 97' 98' Substantial property; reliable red. Réserve du Château is grand stuff.

Le Gay Pom r ★★★ 75' 76' 79 82' 83' 85 86 88 89' 90' 92 95 96 97 98 Fine 14-acre v'yd on N edge of POMEROL. Same owner as CH LAFLEUR; under J-P MOUEIX management since '85. Impressive tannic wines.

Gazin Pom r ★★★ 82 83 85 **86 87' 88 89' 90' 93** 94' 95 96 97 98 Large property (for POMEROL): 58 acres alongside PETRUS. Inconsistent up to '85; now back on magnificent form. Distributed by J-P MOUEIX. Second label: Ch l'Hospitalet.

BORDEAUX

Gilette Saut w sw ★★★ 37 49 53 55 59 61 62 70 76 Extraordinary small Preignac château stores its sumptuous wines in cask to a great age. Only about 5,000 bottles of each. Ch Les Justices is the sister château (**88 89 90**).

Giscours Labarde-Mar r ★★★ 70 71' 75' 78' 82 85 88 89' 90 92' 93 94 95 96' 97 98 Splendid 182-acre third growth property south of CANTENAC. Excellent vigorous wine in '70s; '80s v wobbly; revival during '90s esp under new owner since '95. Second labels: ch'x Cantelaude, Grand Goucsirs (!) and La Sirène de Giscours. Ch La Houringue is baby sister.

du Glana St-Jul r ★★ 85 86 **88 89** 90 93 **94 95** 96 97' 98 Big CRU BOURGEOIS. Undemanding; undramatic; value. Second wine: Ch Sirène.

Gloria St-Jul r ★★→★★★ 79 81 82 83 85 86 88 89 90 91 92 93 94 95' 96 97 98 CRU BOURGEOIS with wine of vigour. 110 acres. In '82 the owner bought ST-PIERRE. Recent return to long-maturing style. 2nd label: Peymartin.

Grand-Barrail-Lamarzelle-Figeac St-Em r ★★ 85 86 88 89 90 92 93 94 95 96 97 98 48-acre property S of FIGEAC, incl Ch La Marzelle. Well-reputed and popular, if scarcely exciting. Now also a smart hotel. Change of owner '97.

Grand-Corbin-Despagne St-Em r ★★→★★★ 70 75 79 82' 83 85 88 **89 90' 91 92 93** 94 95 96 97 98 One of biggest and best GRANDS CRUS on CORBIN plateau. New generation (of the founding Despagnes, since 1812) in '93. New equipment '98. Also Ch Maison Blanche, MONTAGNE ST-EM.

Grand-Mayne St-Em ★★→★★★ 82 83 85 86 88 **89' 90' 93** 94 95 96 97 98 40-acre GRAND CRU CLASSE on W COTES. Noble old château with wonderfully rich tasty wines recently.

Grand-Pontet St-Em r ★★ 82' 85 86' 88 89 **90'** 93 94 95' 96 97 98 35 acres beside CH BEAU-SEJOUR-BECOT; both have been revitalized since '85. Do not hesitate to try.

Grand-Puy-Ducasse Pau r ★★★ 81 82' 83 85 86 87 88 89' 90 91 92 93 94 95 96' 97 98' Fifth growth enlarged to 90 acres under expert management, but remains way behind the next entry. Investment '97. Second label: Ch Artiges-Arnaud.

Grand-Puy-Lacoste Pau r ★★★ 70' 75 78' 79' 81' 82' 83 85' 86' 88' 89' 90' 91 92 93 94 95 96' 97 98 Leading fifth growth famous for excellent full-bodied vigorous examples of PAUILLAC. 110 acres among the 'Bages' châteaux, owned by the Borie family (see DUCRU-BEAUCAILLOU). New cellar '97. Second label: Lacoste-Borie.

Gravas Saut w sw ★★ 83' 85 86 88 89' 90' 91 92 93 94 95 96 97 98 Small BARSAC property; impressive firm sweet wine. NB CUVÉE Spéciale.

La Grave à Pomerol Pom r ★★★ 81' 82' 83 85 86' 88 89' 90 92 93 94 95 96 97 98' Verdant château with small but first-class v'yd owned by CHRISTIAN MOUEIX. Beautifully structured POMEROL of medium richness.

Gressier-Grand-Poujeaux Moulis r ★★·›★★★ 75' 78 79' 81 82 83' 85 86 87 88 89 90 91 92 93 94 95 96 97 98 Vg CRU BOURGEOIS, neighbour of CHASSE-SPLEEN. Fine firm wine with good track record. Repays patient cellaring.

Greysac Méd r ★★ 88 89 90 93 94 95 96 97 98 Elegant 140-acre property. Easy early-maturing wines popular in US.

Gruaud-Larose St-Jul r ★★★ 61 70 75 78' 79 82' 83' 85 86' 88' 89 90' 91 92 93 94 95 96' 97 98 One of the biggest and best-loved second growths. 189 acres. Smooth rich stylish claret, year after year; ages for 20⁺ years. Owned by Societé Bernard Taillan since '97. New equipment '94 and '96. Vg second wine: Sarget de Gruaud-Larose.

Guadet-St-Julien St-Em ★★ 82 83 85 86 88 89 90' 93 94 95 96' 97 98 Extremely well-made wines from v small GRAND CRU CLASSÉ.

Guiraud Saut w (r) sw (dr) ★★★67 79 80 81 82 83' 84 85 86' 87 88' 89' 90' 92 93 94 95 96' 97' 98 Restored classed growth of top quality. 250+ acres. At best excellent sweet wine of great finesse; also small amount of red and dry white. New cellar '99.

Guiteronde du Hayot Saut ★★ 75-acres in BARSAC; known for finesse, value.

La Gurgue Mar r ★★ 82 83' 85' 86 87 88 89' 90 93 94 95' 96' 97' 98 Small, well-placed 25-acre property, for MARGAUX of the fruitier sort. From owners of CHASSE-SPLEEN and HAUT-BAGES-LIBÉRAL. To watch.

Hanteillan Cissac r ★★ 85' 86 88' 89 90' 91 92 93 94 95' 96' 97' 98' Huge vineyard: v fair CRU BOURGEOIS, conscientiously made. Ch Laborde is the second label. New equipment '98.

Haut-Bages-Averous Pau r ★★ 81 82' 83 85' 86 87 88 89' 90 91 92 93 94 95 96 97 The second wine of CH LYNCH BAGES. Should be tasty drinking.

Haut-Bages-Libéral Pau r ★★★ 75' 81 82' 83 85 86' 88 89 90' 92 93 94' 95 96' 97' 98 Lesser-known fifth growth of 70 acres (next to LATOUR) in same stable as CHASSE-SPLEEN. Results are excellent, full of PAUILLAC vitality.

Haut-Bages-Monpelou Pauillac r ★★ 85 86 88 89' 90 92 93 94 95 96 97 98 25-acre CRU BOURGEOIS stable-mate of CH BATAILLEY on former DUHART-MILON land. Good minor PAUILLAC.

Haut-Bailly Graves r ★★★ 79 81' 82 83 85' 86 87 88' 89' 90' 92 93' 94 95 96 97 98' 70-acres+ at LEOGNAN American-owned since '98, but old family still directing. Since '79 some of the best savoury, round, intelligently made red GRAVES have come from this château. Second label is La Parde de Haut-Bailly.

Haut-Batailley Pau r ★★★ 66 70' 75' 78 79 82' 83 85 90' 93 94 95 96' 97 98 Smaller part of divided fifth growth BATAILLEY: 49 acres. Gentler than sister château GRAND-PUY-LACOSTE. Second wine: La Tour-d'Aspic.

Haut-Bergey Pessac-L r ★★ 65 acres, largely Cab; fragrant delicate GRAVES.

Haut-Bommes See Clos Haut-Peyraguey.

Haut-Brion Pessac (Graves) r (w) ★★★★ 59' 61' 66' **70' 71' 75' 76** 78' **79'** 80 81 82' **83' 85' 86' 87** 88' 89' 90' 91 92 93 94 95 96' 97 98' The oldest great château of BORDEAUX and the only non-MEDOC first growth of 1855. 108 acres. Deeply harmonious, never-aggressive wine with endless soft earthy complexity. Consistently great (and modestly priced) since '75. A little full dry white in 78 **81 82 83 85 87 88 89' 90 91** 92 93 94 95 96 97 98. See Bahans-Haut-Brion, La Mission-Haut-Brion.

Haut-Maillet Pom ★★ 86 **88 89 90 93 94 95** 96 97 98' 12-acre sister château of LA CABANNE. Well-made gentle wines.

Haut-Marbuzet St-Est r ★★ ·★★★ **78'** 82' 83' 85' **86' 88 89' 90' 93'** 94 95 96' 97 98 The best of many good ST-ESTEPHE CRUS BOURGEOIS. Monsieur Dubosq has reassembled the ancient Dom de Marbuzet, in total 175 acres. Haut-M is 60% Merlot. Also owns CHAMBERT-MARBUZET, MACCARTHY, MacCarthy-Moula, Tour de Marbuzet. New oak gives them a distinctive, if not subtle, style of great appeal.

Haut-Pontet St-Em r ★★ Reliable 12-acre v'yd of the COTES deserving its GRAND CRU status. 2,500 cases.

Haut-Sarpe St-Em r ★★ 82 83' **85 86 88** 89 90' 92 **93 94 95** 96 97 98 GRAND CRU CLASSE (6,000 cases) with elegant château and park, 70% Merlot. Same owner as CH LA CROIX, POMEROL.

Hortevie St-Jul r ★★ 82 83 85' **86 88 89' 90' 91 92 93** 94 95 96 97 98 One of the few ST-JULIEN CRUS BOURGEOIS. This tiny v'yd and its bigger sister TERREY-GROS-CAILLOU are shining examples. Now hand-harvesting only.

Houissant St-Est r ★★ 82 83 85 **86 88 89' 90' 91** 92 93 94 95 96 97 98 Typical robust well-balanced ST-ESTEPHE CRU BOURGEOIS also called Ch Leyssac; well-known in Denmark.

d'Issan Cantenac-Mar r ★★★ 70 83' **85 86 88 89 90'** 93 **93** 94 95 96' 97 98 Beautifully restored moated château nr the Garonne with 75-acre third growth v'yd; but recent vintages have been wobbly. Second label: Ch de Candale.

Kirwan Cantenac-Mar r ★★★ **82' 83' 85 86 88 89'** 90' 93' 94 95 96 97 98 86-acre third growth; from '97 majority owned by SCHRODER & SCHYLER with new investment. Mature v'yds recently giving tastier wines (esp '95).

Labégorce Mar r ★★ **82' 83'** 85 86 88 **89' 90'** 93 94 95 96 97 98 Substantial 95-acre property N of MARGAUX; long-lived wines of true Margaux quality. New owner since '89; re-equipped '96; strict controls in v'yd from '98.

Labégorce-Zédé Mar r ★★ ·★★★ **78 82' 83' 85 86' 88 89' 90' 91 92 93** 94 95 96' 97 98 CRU BOURGEOIS on road N from MARGAUX. 62 acres. Typically delicate, fragrant; truly classic since '81. Same family as VIEUX CH CERTAN. Second label: Dom Zédé. Also 23 acres of AC Bordeaux: 'Z'.

Lacoste-Borie The second wine of CH GRAND-PUY-LACOSTE.

Lafaurie-Peyraguey Saut w sw ★★★ 78 80 82 83' **85 86' 87 88' 89' 90' 91 92 93 94** 95 96' 97 98 Fine classed growth of only 49 acres at Bommes, belonging to CORDIER. Now one of best buys in SAUTERNES. 2nd wine: La Chapelle de Lafaurie. New equipment '99.

Lafite-Rothschild Pau r ★★★★ 59 76' 78 79 81' 82' 83 84 85 86' 87 88' 89' **90' 91 92 93** 94 95 96' 97 98 First growth of famous elusive perfume and style in its great vintages, which keep for decades. Resplendent since '76. Amazing circular cellars opened '87. Joint ventures in Chile ('88), California ('89), Portugal ('92). Second wine: Carruades de Lafite. 225 acres. Also OWNS CH'x DUHART-MILON, L'EVANGILE, RIEUSSEC.

Lafleur Pom r ★★★★ 70' 75' 79' 81 82' **83 85' 86' 88' 89' 90' 92** 93 94 95 96 97 98 Superb 12-acre property just N of PETRUS. Resounding wine of the turbo-charged, tannic, less 'fleshy' kind for long maturing/investment. Same owner as LE GAY. Second wine: Les Pensées de Lafleur.

Lafleur-Gazin Pom r ★★ 75' 82' 83 85' 86 88' 89 90 92 93 94 95 96 97 98
Distinguished small J-P MOUEIX estate on the NE border of POMEROL.

Lafon-Rochet St-Est r ★★★ 70' 82 83' 85 86 88' 89' 90' 91 92 93 94 95 96' 97
98 Fourth growth neighbour of COS D'ESTOURNEL, restored in '60s and again
recently. 110 acres. Good hard full-bodied ST-ESTEPHE, slow to 'give'. New cellar
equipment '96. Same owner as CH PONTET-CANET. New equipment '98. Second
label: Numéro 2.

Lagrange Pom r ★★ 70' 75' 81 82' 83 85' 86 88 89' 90' 92 93 94 95 96 97
98 20-acre vineyard in the centre of POMEROL run by the ubiquitous house of
J-P MOUEIX. Rising profile for flavour/value.

Lagrange St-Jul r ★★★ 70 82 83 85' 86' 88' 89' 90' 91 92 93 94 95 96 97 98
Formerly neglected third growth inland from ST-JULIEN, bought by Suntory
('83). 280 acres now in tiptop condition with wines to match (and lots of
oak). Second wine: Les Fiefs de Lagrange (85 86 88 89 90 91 92 93 94 95
96 97 98).

La Lagune Ludon r ★★★ 78' 82' 83' 85 86' 88' 89' 90' 91 92 93 94 95 96'
97 98 Ultra-modern 160-acre third growth in southernmost MEDOC.
Attractively rich wines with marked oak; steadily high quality. Owned
by CHAMPAGNE AYALA.

Lalande-Borie St-Jul r ★★ 81 82 85 86 88 89 90' 93 94 95 96' 97 98 A baby
brother of the great DUCRU-BEAUCAILLOU created from part of the former v'yd
of CH LAGRANGE. Gracious, easy drinking.

Lamarque Lamarque (H-Méd) r ★★ 82 83' 85 86' 88 89 90' 93 94 95 96 97
98 Splendid medieval fortress in central MEDOC with 113 acres giving
admirable wine of high Bourgeois standard. Second wine: Donjon de L.

Lamothe Bergeron H-Méd r ★★ 88 89 90 93 94 95 96' 97 98' 150 acres at
CUSSAC making 25,000 cases of reliable claret. Run by GRAND-PUY-DUCASSE.

Lanessan Cussac (H-Méd) r ★★→★★★ 78' 81 82 83 85 86' 88' 89' 90' 91 92
93 94 95 96' 97 98 Distinguished 108-acre CRU BOURGEOIS EXCEPTIONNEL just S
of ST-JULIEN. Fine rather than burly but ages well. Same family owns châteaux
de Ste-Gemme, Lachesnaye, La Providence.

Langoa-Barton St-Jul r ★★★ 78' 81 82' 83 85 86' 88' 89' 90' 91 92 93 94' 95
96 97 98 49-acre third growth sister château to LEOVILLE-BARTON. V old
Barton-family estate with impeccable standards and generous value.
Second wine: Lady Langoa.

Larcis-Ducasse St-Em r ★★ 81 82' 83 84 85 86 88' 89' 90' 92 93 94 95 96 97
98' Top property of St-Laurent, eastern neighbour of ST-EMILION, on COTES next
to CH PAVIE. 30 acres in a fine situation; wines could be better.

Larmande St-Em r ★★★ 81 82 83' 85 86 88' 89' 90' 92 93 94 95' 96 97 98'
Substantial 60-acre property related to CAP-DE-MOURLIN. Replanted, re-equipped
and now making rich strikingly scented wine, silky in time. Second label:
Ch des Templiers.

Laroque St-Em r ★★→★★★ 75' 81 82' 83 85 86 88 89 90 92 93 94 95 96 97
98 Important 108-acre v'yd on the ST-EMILION COTES in St-Christophe.
Promoted to GRAND CRU CLASSE in '96. New equipment in '97.

Larose-Trintaudon St-Laurent r ★★ 86 88 89 90' 91 92 93 94' 95 96' 97 98
The biggest v'yd in the MEDOC: 425 acres. Modern methods make reliable
fruity and charming CRU BOURGEOIS wine to drink young. Second label:
Larose St-Laurent.

Laroze St-Em r ★★ 88' 89 90' 93 94 95 96' 97 98' Large v'yd (74 acres) on
western COTES. Fairly light wines from sandy soils; approachable when
young. New equipment '98.

Châteaux entries also cross-refer to France section, pages 32–77.

Larrivet-Haut-Brion Graves r (w) ★★ 75' 81 82' 83 85 86 87 88 89 90 92 93 94 95 96' 97 98' Little LEOGNAN property with perfectionist standards. Also 500 cases of fine, barrel-fermented white (88 89 90 91 92 93 94 95 96' 97 98').

Lascombes Mar r (p) ★★★ 70' 82 83 85 86 88' 89' 90' 91 92 93 94 95 96' 97 98' 240-acre second growth owned by British brewer Bass-Charrington; lavishly restored. Has re-emerged as a serious contender since '86 with robust vigorous wines. Second wine: Ch Segonnes.

Latour Pau r ★★★★ 49 59 61 62 64 66 67 70' 71 73 75' 76 78' 79 81 82' 83 84 85 86' 87 88' 89' 91' 92 93' 94' 95' 96 97 98' First growth considered the grandest statement of the MEDOC. Profound, intense, almost immortal wines in great yrs; even weaker vintages have the characteristic note of terroir and run for many years. 150 acres sloping to R Gironde. Latour always needs 10 yrs to show its hand. British-owned from '63 to '93, now again in (private) French hands. 2nd wine: LES FORTS DE LATOUR; 3rd, Pauillac.

Latour-Martillac Graves r w ★★ (r) 82' 85' 88' 89 90 91 92 93 94 95 96 97 98' Small but serious property at Martillac. 10 acres of white grapes; 37 of black. The white can age admirably (89 90 91 92 93' 94' 95 96 97 98').

Latour-à-Pomerol Pom r ★★★★ 61' 70' 76 79 81 82 83 83 85' 86 87 88' 89' 90' 91 92 93 94 95 96 97 98' Top growth of 19 acres under MOUEIX management. POMEROL of great power and perfume, yet also ravishing finesse.

des Laurets St-Em r ★★ 89' 90' 93 94 95 96 97 98 Major property in PUISSEGUIN-ST-EMILION and MONTAGNE-ST-EMILION (to the E) with 160 acres of v'yd on the COTES (40,000 cases). Sterling wines sold by J-P MOUEIX.

Médoc: the class system

The Médoc has 60 crus classés, ranked in 1855 in five classes. In a separate classification it has 18 Crus Grands Bourgeois Exceptionnels, 41 Crus Grands Bourgeois (which must age their wine in barrels), and 68 Crus Bourgeois. (The old terms Grand Bourgeois and Exceptionnel – like so many traditional and useful things – are not acceptable to the EC, and are therefore no longer used on labels.)

Apart from the first growths, the five classes of 1855 are now hopelessly jumbled in quality, with some second growths at fifth growth level and vice versa. They also overlap in quality with the Crus Exceptionnels. (Besides the official 18, another 13 châteaux are unofficially acknowledged as belonging to this category.) The French always do things logically.

Laville-Haut-Brion Graves w ★★★★ 83 85' 86 87 88 89' 90 92 93' 94 95' 96 97 98 A tiny production of the v best white GRAVES for long succulent maturing, made at CH LA MISSION-HAUT-BRION. The 89, 95, 96 are off the dial.

Léoville-Barton St-Jul r ★★★·★★★★ 78 81 82' 83 85' 86' 88' 89' 90' 91 92 93' 94' 95 96' 97 98 90-acre portion of the great second growth LEOVILLE v'yd in Anglo-Irish hands of the Barton family for over 150 years. Powerful classic claret; traditional methods, v fair prices. Major investment has raised already high standards to 'super-second'. See also Langoa-Barton.

Léoville-Las-Cases St-Jul r ★★★★ 66' 75' 76 78' 79 81' 82' 83' 84 85' 86' 87 88 89' 90' 91 92 93' 94 95 96 97 98 The largest LEOVILLE. Next to LATOUR; 210 acres with daunting reputation. Elegant complex powerful austere wines, for immortality. Second label CLOS DU MARQUIS also outstanding.

Léoville-Poyferré St-Jul r ★★★ 81 82' 83' 85 86' 87 88 89' 90' 91 92 93 94 95 96 97 98 For years the least outstanding of the LEOVILLES; high potential rarely realised. Michel Rolland now makes the wine; things should be better. 156 acres. Second label: Ch Moulin-Riche.

Lestage Listrac r ★★ 81 82 85 86' 87 88 89' 90' 93 94 95 96 97 98 130-acre CRU BOURGEOIS in same hands as CH FONREAUD. Light stylish wine, oak-aged since '85. Re-equipped '97, '98. Second wine: Ch Caroline. Also La Mouette (white).

Lilian-Ladouys St-Est ★★ 89 90 91 92 93 94 95 96 97 98 Recent creation: a 50-acre CRU BOURGEOIS with high ambitions and early promise. There have been problems, but the early wines are looking good.

Liot Barsac w sw ★★ 75' 76 82 83 85 86 88 89' 90' 92 94 95 96 97 98 Consistent fairly light golden wines from 50 acres. How they last!

Liversan St-Sauveur r ★★ 82' 83 85 86' 88' 89' 90' 91 92 93 94 95 96 97 98 116-acre GRAND CRU BOURGEOIS inland from PAUILLAC. Since '84 the Polignac family have had steadily high standards. Now managed by owners of PATACHE D'AUX. New equipment '97. Second wine: Ch Fonpiqueyre.

Livran Méd r ★★ 82' 83 85 86 88' 89' 90' 91 92 93 94' 95 96 97 98 Big CRU BOURGEOIS at St-Germain in the N MEDOC. Consistent round wines (half Merlot).

Loudenne St-Yzans (Méd) r ★★ 82' 83 85 86' 88 89' 90' 91 92 93 94 95 95 96' 97 98 Beautiful riverside château owned by Gilbeys since 1875 but sadly now up for sale. Well-made CRU BOURGEOIS red and Sauvignon white from 155 acres. The new oak-scented white is best at 2–4 yrs (92' 93 94 95 96 97 98).

Loupiac-Gaudiet Loupiac w sw ★★ 85 86 88 89 90 91 92 93 94 95 96 97 98' Reliable source of good-value 'almost-SAUTERNES', just across R Garonne.

La Louvière Graves r w ★★★ (r) 82' 83 85 86' 88' 89' 90' 91 92 93' 94' 95 96' 97 98' (w) 90' 92 93' 94 95' 96' 97' 98' 135-acre LEOGNAN estate with classical mansion restored by ubiquitous Lurton family. Excellent white and red of classed growth standard.

de Lussac St-Em r ★★ 85 86 88 89' 90 93 94 95 96 97 98 One of the best estates in LUSSAC-ST-EMILION (to the NE).

Lynch-Bages Pau r (w) ★★★→★★★★ 61 70 81 82' 83' 84 85' 86' 87 88' 89' 90' 91 92 93' 94 95 96 97 98 Always popular, now a regular star. 200 acres. Rich robust wine: deliciously dense, brambly; aspiring to greatness. See also Haut-Bages-Averous. From '90, intense oaky white. Owner J-M Cazes also directs CH PICHON-LONGUEVILLE, etc, for AXA Insurance.

Lynch-Moussas Pau r ★★ 82 85 86 88 89 90' 91 92 93 94 95' 96' 97 98 Fifth growth restored by the director of CH BATAILLEY. Now 60⁺ acres are making serious wine, gaining depth as the vines age.

du Lyonnat Lussac-St-Em r ★★ 85 86' 88 89 90' 92 93 94 95 96 97 98 120-acre estate with well-distributed reliable wine.

MacCarthy St-Est r ★★ 88 89 90 91 92 93 94 95 96 97 98 The second label of CH CHAMBERT-MARBUZET.

Macquin-St-Georges St-Em r ★★ 85 86' 88 89 90' 91 92 93 94 95 96 97 98 Steady producer of delicious, not weighty, 'satellite' ST-EMILION at ST-GEORGES.

Magdelaine St-Em r ★★★ 70' 71' 75 78 82' 83' 85 86 88 89' 90' 92 93' 94 95 96 97 98' Leading COTES first growth: 28 acres next to AUSONE owned by J-P MOUEIX. Top-notch, Merlot-led wine; recently powerful and fine. Substantial rebuilding promises even better things.

Magence Graves r w ★★ Go-ahead 93-acre property in S GRAVES. Sauv Bl-flavoured dry white and fruity red. Both age well 2–6 yrs.

Malartic-Lagravière Graves r (w) ★★★ (r) 82' 83 85 86' 88 89 90' 93 94 95 96 97 98 (w) 89 90 91 92 93 94 95 96 97 98 LEOGNAN classed growth of 53 acres. Rather hard red wine and a little long-ageing Sauv Bl white. New Belgian owner ('96). Significant investment '97; M Rolland and D Dubourdieu now consulting. To watch.

Malescasse Lamarque (H-Méd) r ★★ 82 83 85 86 88 89 90 93' 94 95' 96 97 98 Renovated CRU BOURGEOIS with 100 well-situated acres. Second label: Le Tana de M. Same owners as GRUAUD-LAROSE. Investment in '97. To watch.

Malescot-St-Exupéry Mar r ★★★ 59 61 70 82' 83' 86 88 89 90' 91 92 93 94 95 96 97 98' Third growth of 59 acres. Often tough when young, eventually fragrant MARGAUX. M Rolland consulting since '90.

de Malle Saut w r sw dr ★★★ (w sw) 75 76 78 79 81' 82' 83 85 86' 87 88 89' 90' 91 94 95 96' 97 98' Beautiful Preignac château. 124 acres. Vg SAUTERNES; also M de Malle dr w (92 93 95 96' 97 98). See also Ch du Cardaillan.

de Malleret H-Méd r ★★ 82 83 85 86 88 89' 90 91 92 93 94 95 96 97 98 The Marquis du Vivier makes 25,000 cases of fine gentlemanly claret at Le Pian, among forests just N of Bordeaux.

Marbuzet St-Est r ★★ 85 86 88 89 90 93 94 95' 96' 97 98 Second label of COS-D'ESTOURNEL until '94 when it became a CRU BOURGEOIS in its own right. Both sold in '98 to a Belgian group.

Margaux Mar r (w) ★★★★ 53 61' 78' 79 80 81' 82' 83' 84 85' 86' 87 88' 89' 90' 91 92 93' 94 95' 96' 97' 98' First growth (209 acres), the most seductive and fabulously perfumed of all in its (v frequent) best vintages. Pavillon Rouge (82' 83 85 86 88 89 90' 91 92 93 94 95 96 97 98) is second wine. Pavillon Blanc is best white (Sauv) of MEDOC: keep 5 yrs plus (88 89 90 91 92 93 94 95 96 97 98).

Marquis-d'Alesme-Becker Mar r ★★ 82 83 85 86 88' 89 90 94 95 96 97 98 Tiny (17-acre) third growth. A lost CRU CLASSE, once highly regarded. Potential here for classic Margaux. Re-equipped '98.

Marquis-de-Terme Mar r ★★ →★★★ 82 83' 85 86' 88' 89' 90' 93 95 96 97 98 Renovated fourth growth of 84 acres. Fragrant, fairly lean style has developed since '85, with more Cab S and more flesh.

Martinens Mar r ★★ 82 83 85 86 88 89 90 92 93 94' 95 96 97 98 Worthy 75-acre CRU BOURGEOIS of the mayor of CANTENAC. Re-equipped '98.

Maucaillou Moulis r ★★ 82 83' 85' 86' 88' 89' 90' 91 92 93 94' 95 97 96 97 98' 130-acre CRU BOURGEOIS with high standards, property of DOURTHE family. Richly fruity Cap de Haut-Maucaillou is second wine.

Mazeyres Pom r ★★ 93 94 95 96' 97' 98' Consistent, charming, typical lesser POMEROL. 50 acres.

Méaume B'x Supérieur r ★★ An Englishman's domaine, N of POMEROL. Since '80 has built solid reputation for vg daily claret to age 4–5 yrs. 7,500 cases.

Meyney St-Est r ★★ →★★★ 82' 83 85 86' 87 88' 89' 90' 91 92 93 94 95 96 97 98 Big (125-acre) riverside property next door to CH MONTROSE in a superb situation; one of the best of many steady long-lived CRUS BOURGEOIS in ST-ESTEPHE. Owned by CORDIER. Second label: Prieur de Meyney.

Millet Graves r w (p) ★★ (r) 89 90' 92 93 94 95 96 97 98 Useful GRAVES. Second label, Clos Renon: drink young. Cuvée Henri: oak-aged white.

La Mission-Haut-Brion Graves r ★★★★ 59' 61' 66' 75' 78' 79 81 82' 83 85' 86 87 88 89' 90' 91 92 93' 94' 95 96' 97 98' N'bour and long-time rival to CH HAUT-BRION; since '84 in same hands. Consistently grand-scale full-blooded long maturing wine; even 'bigger' wine than H-B and s'times more impressive. 30 acres. Second label is La Chapelle de la Mission. White is LAVILLE-H-B.

Monbousquet St-Em r ★★ 82 83 85' 86 88' 89' 90' 93 94 95 96 97 98 Attractive early-maturing wine from deep gravel soil: lasts well. Second label: Ch Caperot.

Monbrison Arsac-Mar r ★★ →★★★ 81 82 83 84 85 86 87 88' 89' 90 91 93 94 95 96' 97 98 A name to follow. High standards (lavish with new oak) make it Margaux's most modish CRU BOURGEOIS. 4,000 cases and 2,000 of second label, Ch Cordet.

Mondotte, La St-Em r ★★★ →★★★★ 96' 97' Intense wines from micro-property owned by Comte Stefan Von Neipperg (CANON-LA GAFFELIERE, CLOS DE L'ORATOIRE).

Montrose St-Est r ★★★→★★★★ 61 **64** 70' 75' 82' **83** 85 **86' 87 88** 89' 90' 91 **92** 93 94 95 96' 97 98 158-acre family-run second growth famous for deeply coloured forceful old-style claret. Vintages '79–'85 (except '82) were lighter, but recent Montrose is almost ST-ESTEPHE'S answer to CH LATOUR. Second wine: La Dame de Montrose.

Moulin du Cadet St-Em r p ★★ 83 85 86 **88** 89' 90' **92 93** 94 95 96 97 98 Little v'yd on the COTES, owned by J-P MOUEIX. Fragrant medium-bodied wines.

Moulin de la Rose St-Julien r ★★ Tiny CRU BOURGEOIS; high standards. To watch.

Moulin-Pey-Labrie Canon-Fronsac r ★★ **88** 89 90 **92 93** 94 95 96 97 98' Increasingly well-made drinker-friendly Fronsac. To follow.

Moulin-à-Vent Moulis r ★★ 82' **83** 85' **86 88** 89 90' 91 **92** 93 94 95 96' 98 60-acre property in the forefront of this booming AC. Lively forceful wine. LA TOUR-BLANCHE (MEDOC) has the same owners.

Moulinet Pom r ★★ 85 86 88 89' 90 **92 93 94** 95 96 97 98 One of POMEROL'S bigger châteaux; 45 acres on lightish soil, wine lightish too.

Mouton-Baronne-Philippe See d'Armailhac.

Mouton-Rothschild Pau r (w) ★★★★ 59 61 62' 66' **70' 75'** 76 78 81 82' 83' 85' 86' **87** 88' 89' 90' **91 92 93'** 94 95' 96' 97 98' Officially a first growth only since '73, though in reality far longer. 175 acres (87% Cab S) make majestic rich wine, often MEDOC'S most opulent (also, from '91, white Aile d'Argent). Artists' labels and the world's greatest museum of art relating to wine. Baron Philippe, the foremost champion of the MEDOC, died in '88. His daughter Philippine now reigns. See also Opus One, California.

Nairac Saut w sw ★★ 76' 80 81 82 **83' 85 86'** 87 **88** 89 90' 91 **92 93'** 94 95' 96 97 98 Perfectionist BARSAC classed growth. 2,000 cases of oak-fermented wine to lay down for a decade.

Nenin Pom r ★★ 70' 75' **82 83 85'** 86 87 88' 89 90 93 94' 95 96 97 98 Well-known 66-acre estate, one of Pomerol's biggest; on a (v necessary) but slow upswing since '85.

Olivier Graves r w ★★★ (r) 82 **83** 85 86 88 89' 90' 91 92 93 94 95 96 97 (w) **85 86** 88 89 90 91 92 **93 94** 95 96 97 98 90-acre classed growth, surrounding a moated castle at LEOGNAN. 9,000 cases oaky red, 6,000 oaky white. '95 seems to promise more charm. Re-equipped '97 and '98.

Les Ormes-de-Pez St-Est r ★★→★★★ 81' 82' 83' 85 **86' 88** 89' 90' 91 92 93 94 95 96 97 98 Outstanding 72-acre CRU BOURGEOIS owned by CH LYNCH-BAGES. Consistently one of the most likeable ST-ESTEPHES.

Les Ormes-Sorbet Méd r ★★ 78 81 82' 83 85' 86' 87 88 89 90' 91 92 93 94 95 96 97 98' 10,000-case producer of good stylish red aged in new oak at Couquèques. A leader of the N MEDOC. Second label: Ch de Conques. Tighter grape selection from '98.

Palmer Cantenac-Mar r ★★★★ 61' 62 66' **70 71' 75'** 76 78' 79' 82 83' 84 85 86' 87 88' 89 90 91 92 93 94 95 96' 97 98' The star of CANTENAC: a third growth occasionally outshining first growths. Wine of power, flesh, delicacy and much Merlot. New cellar in '95. 110 acres with Dutch, British (the SICHEL family) and French owners. Second wine: Réserve du Général (a steal).

Pape-Clément Graves r (w) ★★★ 70 75' 83 85 86' 88' 89' 90' **91 92** 93' 94' 95 96 97 98 Ancient PESSAC v'yd; record of seductive, scented, not ponderous reds. Early '80s not so gd: dramatic quality (and more white) since '85. New gear '97. Watch very closely.

de Parenchère r (w) ★★ **88** 89 90 91 92 93 94 95 96 97 98 Steady supply of useful AC Ste-Foy Bordeaux from handsome château with 125 acres.

Patâche d'Aux Bégadan (Méd) r ★★ 85 86 88 89' 90' 93 **94** 95 96 97 98 90-acre CRU BOURGEOIS of the N MEDOC. Fragrant largely Cab wine with the earthy quality of its area. See also Ch Liversan.

Paveil (de Luze) Mar r ★★ 82' 83' 85 86' 87 88' 89' 90 91 92 93 **94 95** 96' 97
Old family estate at Soussans. Small but highly regarded. Investment '97.

Pavie St-Em r ★★★ 78 79' 81 82' 83' **85** 86' 87 88' 89' 90' 91 93' 94 95 96 97
98 Splendidly sited first growth; 92 acres mid-slope on the CÔTES. Great track
record, wobbly since '89. PAVIE-DECESSE and La Clusière are in same family.

Pavie-Decesse St-Em r ★★ →★★★ 82 83 85 86 87 88 89 90 92 93 94 95 96 97
98 24 acres. Brother to the above and also wobbly.

Pavie-Macquin St-Em r ★★→★★★ 82 83 85' 86 87 88 89' 90' 92 93 94 95
96' 97 98' Another PAVIE; this time the neighbours up the hill. 25-acre CÔTES
v'yd E of ST-EMILION. Steadily fine organic winemaking by a son of VIEUX CH
CERTAN. Second label: Les Chênes.

Pavillon Rouge (Blanc) du Château Margaux See Ch Margaux.

Pedesclaux Pau r ★★ **81** 82' **83** 85 86 87 88 89' 90' 91 92 93 **94** 95' 96' 97'
98 50-acre fifth growth on the level of a CRU BOURGEOIS. Wines mostly go to
Belgium. Second labels: Bellerose, Grand-Duroc-Milon. Perhaps new
resolve in '98?

Petit-Village Pom r ★★★ 75' 82' 83 85' 86 88 89' 90' 91 92 93 94' 95 96 97 98
Top property revived. 26 acres next to VIEUX-CHATEAU-CERTAN, same owner
(AXA) as CH PICHON-LONGUEVILLE since '89. Powerful plummy wine.

Pétrus Pom r ★★★★ 61 62 64 66 67 70' 71' 73 75' 76 78 79' 81 82' 83 84 85'
86 87 **88'** 89' 90 92 93' 94 95' 96 97 98' The (unofficial) first growth of
POMEROL: Merlot solo in excelsis. 28 acres of gravelly clay giving 5,000 cases
of massively rich and concentrated wine, on allocation to the world's
millionaires. Each vintage adds lustre (NB no 91 produced).

Peyrabon St-Sauveur r ★★ 82' 83 85 86' 87 88 89' 90' 93 94 95 96 97 98
Serious 132-acre CRU BOURGEOIS popular in the Low Countries. Also La Fleur-
Peyrabon (only 12 acres).

Peyre-Labade r p Listrac ★★ Second label of CH CLARKE.

Peyreau St-Em r ★★ Sister-château of CLOS DE L'ORATOIRE.

de Pez St-Est r ★★ 70' 75' 76 78' 79 81 82' 83 85 86' 87 88 89' 90' 91 92 93'
94 95' 96' 97 98' Outstanding CRU BOURGEOIS of 60 acres. As reliable as any
of the classed growths of the village, though not so fine. Bought in '95 by
CHAMPAGNE house ROEDERER. To follow.

Phélan-Ségur St-Est r ★★→★★★ 75' 81 82' 85 86 87 88' 89' 90' 91 92 93 94 95
96' 97 98 Big and important CRU BOURGEOIS (125 acres): rivals the last as one of
ST-ESTEPHE's best. No '83 or '84, but from '86 has gone from strength to
strength. You can bank on it.

Pibran Pau r ★★ 88 89' 90' 93 94 95 96 97 98 Small CRU BOURGEOIS allied to
PICHON-LONGUEVILLE. Should be classy wine with PAUILLAC drive.

Pichon-Lalande (formerly Pichon-Longueville, Comtesse de Lalande)
Pau r ★★★★ 61 62 66 70' 75' 76 78' 79' 81 82' 83' 85' 86' 87 88' 89' 90' 91
92 93 94 95 96 97 98 'Super-second' growth neighbour to CH LATOUR. 148
acres. Consistently among v top performers; long-lived wine of fabulous
breed for those who like it luscious, even in lesser yrs. Second wine: Réserve
de la Comtesse. Rivalry across the road (next entry) is worth watching. Taste
the dreamy '82, '83, '85. Other property Ch Bernadotte.

Pichon-Longueville (formerly Baron de Pichon-Longueville) Pau r ★★★★
79' 82' 83 85 86' **88' 89'** 90' 91 92 93 94' 95 96 97 98 77-acre second
growth. Since '87 owned by AXA Insurance, run by J-M Cazes (LYNCH-
BAGES). Revitalized winemaking matches aggressive new buildings. Second
label: Les Tourelles de Longueville.

Le Pin Pom r ★★★★ 81 82 83 85 86 87 88 89 90' **91** 92 **93** 94 95 96 97 98'
A mere 500 cases of Merlot, with same owners as VIEUX-CHATEAU-CERTAN.
Almost as rich as its drinkers, but prices well beyond PETRUS are ridiculous.

Pindefleurs St-Em r ★★ 82' 83 85 86 88 89 90' 93' 94 95 96' 97 98 Steady 23-acre v'yd on light soil. Second label: Clos Lescure.

de Pitray Castillon r ★★ 83 85 86 88 89 90 93 94 95 96' 97 98' Large (77-acre) v'yd on COTES DE CASTILLON E of ST-EM. Flavoursome wines, the best-known of the APPELLATION.

Plince Pom r ★★ 75 79 81 82 83 85 86 88 89' 90 92 93 94 95 96 97 98' Reliable 20-acre property nr Libourne. Lightish wine from sandy soil.

La Pointe Pom r ★★→★★★ 89' 90 92 93 94 95 96 97 98 Prominent 63-acre estate; wines recently plumper and more pleasing. New cellar '98. LA SERRE is in the same hands.

Pontac-Monplaisir Graves r (w) ★★ 89 90 92 93 94 95 96 97 98' Another GRAVES property offering useful white and fragrant light red. New equipment '98.

Pontet-Canet Pau r ★★★ 82' 85 86' 88 89' 90 92 93 94' 95 96' 97 98 182-acre neighbour to MOUTON-ROTHSCHILD. Dragged its feet for many yrs. Owners (same as LAFON-ROCHET) have done better since '86. Should make v fine wines, but hardness is an old problem. Vintages since '94 promise better things. Second label: Les Hauts de Pontet.

Potensac Méd r ★★ 82' 85' 86 88 89' 90' 92 93 94 95 96 97 98 Biggest and best-known CRU BOURGEOIS of N MEDOC. N'bouring ch'x Lassalle, Gallais-Bellevue and super-second LEOVILLE-LAS-CASES all owned by Delon family. Class shows.

Pouget Mar ★★ 82' 83 85 86 88 89 90 91 92 93 94 95 96 97 98' 27-acre fourth growth attached to BOYD-CANTENAC. Sharing owners since 1906. Similar wines.

Poujeaux (Theil) Moulis r ★★ 70' 75' 76 78 79' 81 82' 83' 85' 86 87 88' 89' 90' 91 92 93' 94' 95' 96' 97 98 Family-run CRU EXCEPTIONNEL of 120 acres. 20,000-odd cases of characterful tannic and concentrated wine for a long life, year after year. Second label: La Salle de Poujeaux. Also Ch Arnauld.

Prieuré-Lichine Cantenac-Mar r ★★★ 78' 82' 83' 85 86' 87 88 89' 90' 91 92 93' 94' 95 96 97 98' 143-acre fourth growth brought to the fore by the late Alexis Lichine, now owned by his son Sacha and advised by Michel Rolland. Full fragrant MARGAUX currently on form. Re-equipped '98. Second wine: Clairefont. A good Bordeaux Blanc, too.

Puy-Blanquet St-Em r ★★ 82' 83 85 86 88 89' 90' 92 93 94 95 96 97 98 The major property of St-Etienne-de-Lisse, E of ST-EMILION, with 50 acres.

Puygueraud Côte de Francs r ★★ 85 86 88 89' 90 92 93 94 95' 96 97 98 Leading château of this rising district. Wood-aged wines of surprising class. Ch Laclaverie and Les Charmes-Godard follow the same lines. Same winemaker as CH PAVIE-MACQUIN (ST-EM).

Rabaud-Promis Saut w sw ★★→★★★ 83' 85 86' 87 88' 89' 90 94 95 96 97 98 74-acre classed growth at Bommes. Since '86 near top rank. Rich stuff.

Rahoul Graves r w ★★ (r) 82 85 86 88 89' 90' 91 92 93 94 95 96 97 98' 37-acre v'yd at Portets is still a sleeper despite long record of gd red (80%) and vg (Sémillon) white (90 91 94 95 96 97 98).

Ramage-la-Bâtisse H-Méd r ★★ 89' 90 91 92 93 94 95 96' 97 98 Potentially outstanding CRU BOURGEOIS; 130 acres at ST-SAUVEUR, N of PAUILLAC. Ch Tourteran: second wine.

Rauzan-Gassies Mar r ★★ 88 89' 90' 91 94 95 96 97 98 75-acre second growth neighbour of the last with little to report for two decades. But '96 could be the new leaf.

Rauzan-Ségla Mar r ★★★★ 70' 82 83' 85 86' 88' 89' 90' 91 92 93 94' 95 96 97 98 106-acre second growth famous for its fragrance; a great MEDOC name back at the top. New owners in '94 (Chanel) have rebuilt the château and CHAIS. Second wine: Ségla. This should be the top second growth of all. Ancient vintages can be superb and latest ones are splendid.

Smaller Bordeaux châteaux to watch for:
The detailed list of ch'x on these pages is limited to the prestigious classified parts of the Bordeaux region. But this huge v'yd by the Atlantic works on many levels. Standard Bordeaux AC wine is claret at its most basic – but it is still recognizable. The areas and representative châteaux listed below are an important resource; they are potentially distinct and worthwhile variations on the claret theme to be investigated and enjoyed.

Bordeaux Supérieur Ch Dôme Ile de Margaux, de Seguin, Trocard

Canon-Fronsac Chx Barrabaque, Coustolle, Croix Canon, La Fleur Caillou, Grand Renouil, Junayme, Mazeris-Bellevue, La Roche-Gaby, Toumalin, Vraye-Canon-Boyer

Côtes de Bourg Chx Brûlésécaille, Guerry, Guionne, Haut-Maco, Mendoce, Mercier, Peychaud, Roc de Cambes, Rousset, Tayac Cuvée Prestige, Tour-de-Tourteau

Côtes de Castillon Chx d'Aiguilhe, Belcier, Cap de Faugères, Castegens (Fontenay), Chante-Grive, La Clarière-Laithwaite, de Clotte, L'Estang, Haut-Tuquet, Lardit, Moulin-Rouge, Puycarpin, Robin, Rocher-Bellevue, Ste-Colombe, Thibaud-Bellevue

Côtes de Francs Chx de Belcier, Les Charmes Godard, de Francs, Laclaverie, Lauriol, La Prade, Puygueraud

Entre-Deux-Mers Chx Fondarzac, Fongrave, L'Hoste-Blanc, Jonqueyres, Launay, Moulin de Launay, de la Rose, de Sours, Tertre-Launay, Tour de Mirambeau, Turcaud

Fronsac Chx Fontenil, Jeandeman, Mayne-Vieil, Moulin-Haut-Laroque, Rouet, La Valade, La Vieille Cure, Villars, Vrai-Canon-Bouché

Lalande de Pomerol Chx Les Annereaux, du Chapelaine, La Croix-St-André, La Fleur St-Georges, Grand Ormeau, Les Hauts Conseillants aka Les Hauts-Tuileries, Moncets, Sergant, de Viaud

Lussac St-Emilion Chx Bel Air, Mayne-Blanc

Montagne St-Emilion Chx Calon, Faizeau, Maison Blanche, Roudier

Premières Côtes de Blaye Chx Barbé, Bertinerie, Charron, l'Escadre, Haut-Sociando, Le Menaudat, Pérenne, Peybonhomme Les Tours, La Rose-Bellevue, Segonzac, La Tonnelle

Premières Côtes de Bordeaux Chx Bertinerie (vg), La Croix de Roche, Dudon-Cuvée Jean-Baptiste, Fayau, Fontenil, Gardera, de Haut, Haux Frère, Jonqueyrès, du Juge, Laffitte (sic), Lafitte-Laguens, Lamothe, Peyrat, Plaisance, de Plassan, Prieuré-Ste-Anne, Recougne, Reynon, Suau, Tanesse

Ste-Croix du Mont Chx Clos des Coulinats, Loubens, Lousteau-Vieil, du Mont, La Rame

Raymond-Lafon Saut w sw ✱✱✱ 75' 76 78 79 80' 81 82 83' 85 86' 87 88 89' 90' 91 92 93 94 95 96' 97 98 Serious little SAUTERNES estate (44 acres) owned by YQUEM ex-manager. Splendid wines for ageing. Ranks among v top Sauternes.

de Rayne-Vigneau Saut w sw ✱✱ 76' 83 85 86' 88' 89 90' 91 92 94 95 96 97 98 164-acre classed growth at Bommes. Standard sw wine and dry Rayne SEC.

Respide-Médeville Graves w (r) ✱✱ (w) 86 88 89 90 91 92' 93 94 95' 96' 97 98 One of the better unclassified properties. Full-flavoured wines for ageing. (NB CUVÉE Kauffman.) Drink the reds at 4–6 yrs.

Reynon Premières Côtes r w ✱✱→✱✱✱ 100 acres for fragrant white from old Sauv vines (VIEILLES VIGNES) (92 93' 93' 94 95 96 97 98); also serious red (86 88' 89 90 91 92 93 94 95 96 97 98). Second wine (red): Ch Reynon-Peyrat. From '98 Ch Reynon Cadillac liquoreux, too. See also Clos Floridène.

Reysson Vertheuil (H-Méd) r ★★ 82' 83 85 86 87 88 89' 90' 91 92 93 94 95 96 97 98 Recently replanted 120-acre CRU BOURGEOIS; same owners as GRAND-PUY-DUCASSE.

Ricaud Loupiac w sw (r dr) ★★ (w) 83' 85 86' 88 89 90 91 92 94 95 96 97 98 Substantial grower of SAUTERNES-like age-worthy wine just across the river.

Rieussec Saut w sw ★★★★ 67 71' 75' 79 81 82 83' 85 86' 87 88' 89' 90' 91 92 93 94 95 96' 97' 98' Worthy neighbour of CH D'YQUEM with 136 acres in Fargues, bought in '84 by the (LAFITE) Rothschilds. Vinified in oak since '96. Fabulous opulent wine. Also dry 'R' and super-wine Crème de Tête.

Ripeau St-Em r ★★ 82 83 85 86 88 89 90 93 94 95 96 97 98 Steady GRAND CRU with the right idea in the centre of the plateau. 40 acres.

de la Rivière Fronsac r ★★ 82 83 85' 86 88' 89 90 91 94 95 96' 97 98' The biggest and most impressive FRONSAC property with a Wagnerian castle and cellars. Formerly big tannic wines seem to have lightened recently.

de Rochemorin Graves r (w) ★★→★★★ 88 89' 90' 91 92 93 95 96 97 98' An important restoration at Martillac by the Lurtons of CH LA LOUVIÈRE: 165 acres of maturing vines. Oaky whites to keep 4–5 yrs.

Rouet Fronsac r ★★ 90 93 95 96 97 98 A gentlemanly Fronsac, full of life and fruit.

Rouget Pom r ★★ 82' 83 85' 86 88 89' 90 92 93 94 95 96 97 98 Attractive old estate on the N edge of POMEROL. New owners in '92. Track-record is for solid long-agers.

Royal St-Emilion Brand name of the important and dynamic growers' coop. See also Berliquet, Galius.

Ruat-Petit-Poujeaux Moulis r ★★ 82 85 86 88 89 90 92 93 94 95 96 97 98 45-acre v'yd with local reputation for vigorous wine, keep for 5–6 yrs.

St-André-Corbin St-Em r ★★ 82' 85' 86 88 89 90 93 94 95 96 97 98 54-acre estate in MONTAGNE- and ST-GEORGES-ST-EMILION: above-average wines.

St-Bonnet Méd r ★★ 85 86 88 89 90 93 94 95 96 97 98 Big N MEDOC estate at St-Christoly. Flavoursome wine.

St-Estèphe, Marquis de St-Est r ★ 86 88 89 90 93 94 95 96 97 98 The growers' coop; bigger but not as interesting as formerly.

St-Georges St-Georges-St-Em r ★★ 82 83 85' 86 87 88' 89' 90' 92 93 94 95' 96' 97 98' Noble 18th-C château overlooking the ST-EMILION plateau from the hill to the north. 125 acres. Vg wine sold direct to the public.

St-Georges-Côte-Pavie St-Em r ★★ 82 83' 85' 86 88' 89' 90' 93 94 95 96' 97' 98' Perfectly placed little v'yd on the COTES. Run with dedication.

St-Pierre St-Jul r ★★★ 70' 78' 82' 83' 85 86' 88' 89' 90' 91 92 93 94 95' 96' 97 98 Small (42-acre) fourth growth. V stylish and consistent classic ST-JULIEN.

de Sales Pom r ★★★ 82' 83 85 86 88 89' 90' 92 93 94 95 96 97 98 Biggest v'yd of POMEROL (116 acres), attached to grandest château. Never poetry: recently below form. Second labels: ch'x Chantalouette, du Delias.

Saransot-Dupré Listrac r (w) ★★ 85 86 88 89 90 91 92 93 94 95 96' 97 98' Small property performing well since '86. Also one of LISTRAC's little band of whites. New cellar '99.

Sénéjac H-Méd r (w) ★★ 82' 83' 85 86' 88 89' 90' 91 92 93 94 95 96 97 98 60-acre CRU BOURGEOIS in S MEDOC. Tannic reds to age and unusual all-Sém white, also to age (90 91 92 93 94 95 96 97 98). Second label: Artigue de Sénéjac.

La Serre St-Em r ★★ 82 83 85 86 88' 89 90 92 93 94 95 96 97 98 Small GRAND CRU, same owner as LA POINTE. Renovation of cellars '98. Increasingly tasty.

Sigalas-Rabaud Saut w sw ★★★ 76' 80 81 82 83 85 86 87 88 89' 90' 91 92 95' 96' 97 98 The smaller part of the former RABAUD estate: 34 acres in Bommes run by CORDIER. At best v fragrant and lovely.

Siran Labarde-Mar r ★★→★★★ 82' 83 85 86 88 89' 90' 92 93 95 96 97 98
77-acre property of passionate owner who resents lack of classé rank.
To follow for full-flavoured wines to age. Continually striving.

Smith-Haut-Lafitte Graves r (w p) ★★★ (red) **82' 85 86 89' 90' 91 92 93 94
95** 96 97 98, (white) **92 93 94 95 96 97** 98 Classed growth at Martillac: 122
acres (14 acres white). Ambitious owners (since '90) have spent hugely to
spectacular effect. Watch closely. Second label: Les Hauts de Smith.

Sociando-Mallet H-Méd r ★★→★★★ 82' 83 85' 86' 88' 89' 90' **91 92 93**
94 95 96' 97 98 Splendid CRU GRAND BOURGEOIS at St-Seurin. 65 acres.
Conservative big-boned wines to lay down for yrs. Second wine: Demoiselles
de Sociando.

Soudars H-Méd r ★★ 86 89 90 **92 93 94** 95 96' 97 98 Sister to COUFRAN; new
CRU BOURGEOIS doing v well.

Soutard St-Em r ★★★ **70' 82' 83 85' 86 88' 89' 90' 92 93** 94 95 96 97 98'
Excellent 48-acre classed growth, 60% Merlot. Potent wines: long-lived for
Anglo-Saxon drinking; exciting young to French palates. Second label: Clos
de la Tonnelle. Re-equipped '97.

St-Emilion: the class system
St-Emilion has its own class system, last revised in 1996. At the
top are two Premiers Grands Crus Classés 'A': Châteaux Ausone and
Cheval Blanc. Then come 11 Premiers Grands Crus Classés 'B'. 55
châteaux were elected as Grands Crus Classés. Another 170-odd are
classed simply as Grands Crus, a rank renewable each year after official
tastings. St-Emilion Grand Cru is therefore the very approximate
equivalent of Médoc Crus Bourgeois and Grand Bourgeois.

Suduiraut Saut w sw ★★★★ 67 75 76' **78 79'** 81 82 83 85 86 88' 89' 90' 94 95
96 97 98 One of the best SAUTERNES, in its best vintages supremely luscious.
173 acres potentially of top class. Now in AXA control. See Pichon-
Longueville.

du Tailhas Pom r ★★ **82 89 90 93** 94 **95** 96' 97 98' 5,000 cases. POMEROL of
the lighter kind, near FIGEAC. New gear '98.

Taillefer Pom r ★★ **82 83 85 86 88' 89 90 92 93** 94 95' 96 97 98' 28-acres on
the edge of POMEROL in the Bernard Moueix family (see also Fontmarty).

Talbot St-Jul r (w) ★★★ **78' 82' 83' 85' 86' 88' 89' 90' 92** 93 94 95 96 97 98
Important 240-acre fourth growth, for many yrs younger sister to GRUAUD-
LAROSE. Wine similarly attractive: rich, consummately charming, reliable; gd
value. Vg second label: Connétable Talbot. White: 'Caillou Blanc'. Oenologist
also oversees TOUR DE MONS.

Tayac Soussans-Mar r ★★ **83 85 86 88 89** 90 92 93 **94** 95 96 97 98 MARGAUX'S
biggest CRU BOURGEOIS. Reliable if not noteworthy.

de Terrefort-Quancard B'x r w ★ **89 90 91 92 93 94** 95 96 97 98 Huge
producer of good-value wines at ST-ANDRE-DE-CUBZAC on the road to Paris.
Very drinkable quality. 33,000 cases.

Terrey-Gros-Caillou St-Jul ★★ **82' 85 86' 88 89** 90 93 **94** 95 96 97 98 Sister
château to HORTEVIE; at best, equally noteworthy and stylish.

du Tertre Arsac-Mar r ★★★ **70' 79' 81 82' 83' 85 86 88' 89' 90' 91 92 93** 94
95 96' 97 98' Fifth growth isolated S of MARGAUX. Fragrant and fruity wines
seriously undervalued. Since '97, same owner as Ch GISCOURS. To watch.

Tertre-Daugay St-Em r ★★★ **82' 83' 85 86 88' 89' 90' 92 93** 94 95 96 97 98
Small, spectacularly sited GRAND CRU. Currently being restored to good order.
Potent and stylish wines.

Tertre-Rôteboeuf St-Em ★★★ 81 85 86 87 88' 89' 90' 91 93 94 95 96 97 98' A cult star making concentrated, even dramatic, largely Merlot wine since '83. The 'roast beef' of the name gives the right idea. Also Côte de Bourg property, Roc de Cambes.

Thieuley E-Deux-Mers r p w ★★ Substantial supplier esp of clairet (rosé) and grapey Sauv. But reds are aged in oak.

Toumilon Graves r w ★★ 96 97 98 Little château in St-Pierre-de-Mons to note. Fresh and charming red and white. V'yd extended '98.

La Tour-Blanche Saut w (r) sw ★★★ 81' 82 83' 85 86 87 88' 89' 90' 91 92 93 94 95 96 97 98 Historic leader of SAUTERNES, now a gov't wine college. Coasted in '70s; hit historic form again in '88. New cellar '98.

La Tour-de-By Bégadan (Méd) r ★★ 82' 85' 86 88' 89' 90' 93 94 95 96' 97 98 V well-run 182-acre CRU BOURGEOIS in N MEDOC with a name for the most attractive sturdy wine of the area.

La Tour-Carnet St-Laurent r ★★ 82 83 85 86 89' 90 93' 94' 95 96 97 98 Fourth growth with medieval fortress, long neglected. Light wine; bolder since '88. Second wine: Sire de Comin.

La Tour-Figeac St-Em r ★★ 75 81 82' 83 85 86 88 89' 90' 92 93 94' 95 96' 97' 98 36-acre GRAND CRU CLASSE between CH FIGEAC, POMEROL. California-style ideas since '94; keep an eye on this.

Rotting with style

Botrytis cinerea (French pourriture noble, German Edelfäule, English noble rot) is a form of mould that attacks the skins of ripe grapes in certain vineyards in warm and misty autumn weather.

Its effect, instead of rotting the grapes, is to wither them. The skin grows soft and flaccid, the juice evaporates through it, and what is left is a super-sweet concentration of everything in the grape except its water content.

The world's best sweet table wines are all made of 'nobly rotten' grapes. They occur in good vintages in Sauternes, the Rhine and the Mosel (where wine made from them is called Trockenbeerenauslese), in Tokáji in Hungary, in Burgenland in Austria, and elsewhere – California and Australia included. The danger is rain on pulpy grapes already far gone in botrytis. All too often the growers' hopes are dashed by the weather.

La Tour-Haut-Brion Graves r ★★★ 70 78 82' 85 88 89 90 91 92 93 94 95 96' 97 98 Formerly second label of CH LA MISSION-HAUT-BRION. Up to '83, a plainer, v tannic wine. Now a separate 12-acre v'yd: wines v stylish.

La Tour-Haut-Caussan Méd r ★★ 88 89 90 91 92 93 94 95 96 97 98' Ambitious 40-acre estate at Blaignan to watch for full firm wines.

La Tour-du-Haut-Moulin Cussac (H-Méd) r ★★ 82' 83 85' 86' 88' 88' 89' 90' 91 92 93 94 95 96 97 98 Conservative grower: intense CRU BOURGEOIS to mature.

La Tour-de-Mons Soussans-Mar r ★★ 82' 83 85 86 88 89 90' 93 94 95 96' 97 98' Famous CRU BOURGEOIS of 87 acres, 3 centuries in the same family. A long dull patch but new ('95) TALBOT-influence is returning to the old fragrant, vigorous, age-worthy style.

Tour du Pas St-Georges St-Em r ★★ 85 86 88 89 90 93 94 95 95 96 97 98 Wine from 40 acres of ST-GEORGES-ST-EMILION made by AUSONE winemaker. V stylish; to follow.

La Tour-du-Pin-Figeac St-Em r ★★ 26-acre GRAND CRU worthy of restoration.

La Tour-du-Pin-Figeac-Moueix St-Em r ★★ 82 83 85 86 88' 89' 90' 93 94 95 96 97 98 Another 26-acre section of the same old property, owned by the Armand Moueix family. Splendid site; powerful wines.

La Tour-St-Bonnet Méd r ★★ 85 86 **88** 89' 90' **93** 94 95 96 97 98 Consistently well-made potent N MEDOC from St-Christoly. 100 acres.

Tournefeuille Lalande de Pom r ★★ 82' 83' 85 86 **88** 88 89 90' **93 94** 95' 96 97 98' Best-known Néac château. 43 acres; gd near-POMEROL. Also Ch de Bourg.

des Tours Montagne-St-Em r ★★ 85 86 88 89 90 **93 94 95** 96 97 98 Spectacular château with modern 170-acre v'yd. Sound easy wine.

Tronquoy-Lalande St-Est r ★★ **82'** 85 86 88 **89 90** 93 **94 95** 96 97 98 40-acre CRU BOURGEOIS: high-coloured wines to age, but no thrills. DOURTHE-distributed.

Troplong-Mondot St-Em r ★★★ 82'83 85' **86 88' 89'** 90' 91 92 93 94 95 96' 97 98' 75 acres well-sited on the COTES above CH PAVIE (and in same family). Run since '88 with passion and new barrels. One of St-Emilion's hottest things. Second wine: Mondot.

Trotanoy Pom r ★★★★ 61' 70' 71' 75' 82' 85 88 89 90' 92 **93 94** 95 96 97 98' Potentially the second POMEROL, after PETRUS, from the same stable. Only 27 acres; but at best (eg 82) a glorious fleshy perfumed wine. Ten wobbly years since; now resurgence under J-P MOUEIX control.

Trottevieille St-Em r ★★★ 82' 85 86 **88** 89' **90 92** 93 94 95 96 97 98 GRAND CRU of 27 acres on the COTES. Dragged its feet for yrs. Same owners as BATAILLEY have raised their game since '86.

Le Tuquet Graves r w ★★ (r) **93 94 95** 96' 97 98' (w) **93 94 95 96 97 98'** Big estate at Beautiran. Light fruity wines; white better. (Cuvée Spéciale oak-aged.)

Valandraud St-Em r ★★★★ **91 92 93 95** 96 97 98 New 'garagiste' micro-château with aspirations to glory. Silly prices for thick wine chewy with oak. V'yds expanded '98.

Verdignan Méd r ★★ 86 88 89' 90 92 93 94 95' 96 97 98 Substantial Bourgeois sister to CH COUFRAN. More Cab than Coufran.

Vieux-Château-Certan Pom r ★★★ 78 79 81 82' 83' 85 86' 88' 89 90' 92 93 94 95' 96' 97 98 Traditionally rated close to PETRUS in quality, but totally different in style; almost HAUT-BRION build. 34 acres. Same (Belgian) family owns LABEGORCE-ZEDE and tiny LE PIN. See also Château Puygueraud.

Vieux-Château-St-André St-Em r ★★ 82' 83 85' 86 88' **89' 90'** 91 92 **93'** 94' 95 97 98 Small v'yd in MONTAGNE-ST-EMILION owned by the winemaker of PETRUS. To follow. 2,500 cases.

Villegeorge Avensan r ★★ 82 83' 85 86 **88** 89 90 91 92 **93** 94 95 96' 97 98' 24-acre CRU BOURGEOIS N of MARGAUX. Enjoyable rather tannic wine. Sister-château: Duplessis (Hauchecorne).

Villemaurine St-Em r ★★ 82' 85' 86 88 89 90 92 94 95 96 97 98 Small GRAND CRU with splendid cellars well-sited on the COTES by the town. Firm wine with a high proportion of Cab.

Vray-Croix-de-Gay Pom ★★ 75' 82' 83 85 86 **88** 89 90 92 93 94 95 96 97 98 V small ideally situated v'yd in the best part of POMEROL. Could do better.

Yon-Figeac St-Em r ★★ 85 86 88 89 90 **93 94** 95 96 97 98 59-acre GRAND CRU for savoury supple wine at best.

d'Yquem Saut w sw (dr) ★★★★ 67' 71' 73 75' 76' 77 78 79 80' 81' 82' 83' 84 85 86' 87 88' 89' 90' (91 93 94 95 96' 97 98 to come) The world's most famous sweet-wine estate. 250 acres; only 500 bottles per acre of v strong intense luscious wine, kept 4 yrs in barrel. Most vintages improve for 15 yrs+; some live 100yrs+ in transcendent splendour. Sadly, after centuries in the Lur-Saluces family, in '98 they surrendoured control to Bernard Arnault of LVMH (see Cheval Blanc). Also makes dry Ygrec ('y').

Italy

Heavier shaded areas are
the wine growing regions

The following abbreviations are used in the text:

Ab	Abruzzi	Pie	Piedmont
Ap	Apulia	Sar	Sardinia
Bas	Basilicata	Si	Sicily
Cal	Calabria	T-AA	Trentino-
Cam	Campania		Alto Adige
E-R	Emilia-Romagna	Tus	Tuscany
F-VG	Friuli-	Umb	Umbria
	Venezia Giulia	VdA	Valle d'Aosta
Lat	Latium	Ven	Veneto
Lig	Liguria		
Lom	Lombardy	fz	frizzante
Mar	Marches	pa	passito

If Italy were able to achieve anything approaching the tidiness and
predictability of France's AC system, her wines would be far more
prominent on the world's wine lists. No other country produces such a
variety of original and delectable red wines – and there are signs that
the old Italian disdain for white is becoming a thing of the past.

The formulaic factory wine that gushes from many young wine
countries used to be the curse of Italy, too – but recent years have seen
a renaissance. And while the famous regions polish their acts, former
laggards of the south have started giving them serious competition.

The genius of Italy tends to be private and idiosyncratic, revealing
itself in beauty amid ugliness, kindness and wit among people with
little to spare. It also rears its head in the steady defiance with which
wine growers raise their personal stakes despite the failings of the
legislation around them. The price is confusion. It is frequently hard to
decide, from the plethora of words on an Italian label, what the wine
is actually called (the old complaint about German wines).

When the 1992 Wine Law was introduced, I suggested that
it would eventually make everything orderly and intelligible.
I outlined its 'pyramid' system with the humble vino da tavola at
the bottom, narrowing to the lofty and exclusive Vigna wine from
a DOCG region at the top. Yet it seems to have done little to help.

What is more important, though, is quality: the growing sacrifice
of quantity in favour of quality; the attention to clones and vineyard
management; the modernization of cellars – and perhaps most of all,
Italy's genius for style applied almost for the first time to her wines.
The denominations of northern Italy are all well-established; the
difference is Soave, for example, instead of being ordinary white with
a world-famous name, is discovering its real identity. Verdicchio, too.
From Friuli to Piedmont, across the north, everything is in place.

Tuscany now realizes that Chianti can cohabit with the more exotic red blends (which are throwing off the affectation of 'Vino da Tavola' for the safer, if boring, Indicazione Geografica Tipica or IGT).

For the moment Tuscany may be the most happening region, but further east and south, especially in the Marches, Abruzzi, Molise, Apulia and Sicily are to be followed closely, and good judges are talking with excitement about the future of Sardinia. For all this, and all the variety now worth tasting, one should remember that in the Italian mind, wine belongs beside (or slightly behind) food. It is the second, not the first, item in the great Italian feast.

Abbazia di Rosazzo ★★★ Major estate of COLLI ORIENTALI. White Ronco delle Acacie and Ronco di Corte. See Filliputti, Walter.

Abboccato Semi-sweet.

Adami ★★→★★★ Producer of top PROSECCO DI CONEGLIANO-VALDOBBIADENE (Vigneto Giardino).

Adanti ★★ →★★★ Umbrian producer of pleasant red SAGRANTINO DI MONTEFALCO, ROSSO DI MONTEFALCO, and Rosso d'Arquata (vg blend of BARBERA, CAB S and MERLOT). Good value.

Aglianico del Vulture Bas DOC r dr (s/sw sp) ★★★ **90' 92 93 94'** 95 97' 98 Among the best wines of S Italy. Ages well to rich aromas. Called VECCHIO after 3 yrs, RISERVA after 5. Top growers: D'ANGELO (also makes vg pure Aglianico VDT Canneto), PATERNOSTER, Basilium and Consorzio Viticoltori Associati Vulture.

Alba Major wine city of PIEDMONT, on River Tanaro, S of Turin.

Albana di Romagna E-R DOCG w dr s/sw (sp) ★★ DYA Italy's first DOCG for white wine, though it is hard to see why. Albana is the (undistinguished) grape. FATTORIA PARADISO makes some of the best. AMABILE is usually better than dry. ZERBINA's botrytis-sweet PASSITO (Scacco Matto) is outstanding.

Alcamo Si DOC w ★ Soft neutral whites. Rapitalà is the best brand.

Aleatico Excellent red Muscat-flavoured grape for sweet aromatic strong wines, chiefly of the S. Aleatico di Puglia DOC (best grower is CANDIDO) is better and more famous than Aleatico di Gradoli (Latium) DOC. ELBA makes a little, but good.

Alezio Ap DOC p (r) ★★ DYA Recent DOC at Salento, especially for delicate rosé. Top grower is Calò Michele (who also makes good barrel-aged NEGROAMARO VDT, Vigna Spano is ★★★).

Allegrini ★★★ Top-quality producer of Veronese wines, incl outstanding single v'yd VALPOLICELLA (Grola and Palazzo della Torre), top single v'yd Poja (pure Corvina) and gd AMARONE.

Altare, Elio ★★★ Small producer of good, v modern BAROLO. Look for Barolo Vigna Arborina and BARBERA VDT Vigna Larigi.

Altesino ★★ →★★★ Producer of BRUNELLO DI MONTALCINO and VDT Palazzo Altesi.

Alto Adige T-AA DOC r p w dr sw sp ★→★★★ Alto Adige or Südtirol DOC incl almost 50 types of wines: different grapes of different zones (incl varietals of VALLE ISARCO/EISACKTAL, TERLANO/TERLANER, Val Venosta/Vinschgau, AA STA MAGDALENA, AA Bozner Leiten, AA MERANESE DI COLLINA/Meraner).

Ama, Castello di, (or Fattoria di Ama) ★★★ →★★★★ One of the best, most consistent modern CHIANTI CLASSICO estates, nr Gaiole. La Casuccia and Bellavista: top single-v'yd wines. Also gd VDTS, CHARD, SAUV, MERLOT (Vigna L'Apparita), PINOT N (Il Chiuso).

Amabile Means semi-sweet, but usually sweeter than ABBOCCATO.

Amaro Bitter. When prominent on label, contents are not wine but 'bitters'.

Amarone della Valpolicella (formerly Recioto della Valpolicella Amarone) Ven DOC r ★★★ →★★★★ **83' 85 86' 88' 90 93** 94 95' 97' 98 Dry version of RECIOTO DELLA V: concentrated, long-lived, v impressive; from air-dried grapes. Top producers: Accordini, Serègo Alighieri, ALLEGRINI, Begali, BERTANI, BOLLA BOSCAINI, Brunelli, Bussola, Campagnola, DAL FORNO, Domini Veneti, GUERRIERI-RIZZARDI, Il Sestante, LE RAGOSE, MASI, Montresor (esp Capitel della Crosara), Novaia, QUINTARELLI, Ramondi-Monteleone, LE SALETTE, Speri, TEDESCHI, Trabucchi, Venturini, Viviani, Zenato. NB high alcohol content.

Ambra, Fattoria di Two unconnected producers with identical names, one in CARMIGNANO (TUS) with vg Carmignano DOCG, the second nearby in Arezzo (Tus) produces gd CHIANTI and VDT Gavignano (CAB-SANGIO blend).

Anghelu Ruju ★★★ ('Red Angel') Port-like version of Sardinian CANNONAU wine from SELLA & MOSCA. Well worth trying.

Angoris ★★ One of the few larger wineries in FRIULI (325 acres). Vg DOC COLLIO, ISONZO and COLLI ORIENTALI.

Anselmi, Roberto ★★★ A leader in SOAVE with his single-v'yd Capitel Foscarino and exceptional sweet dessert RECIOTO i Capitelli.

Antinori, Marchesi L & P ★★ ·★★★★ Immensely influential long-est'd Florentine house of highest repute, now wholly owned by Piero A, sharing management with daughters. Famous for first-rate CHIANTI CLASSICO (esp PEPPOLI, Tenute Marchese Antinori and Badia a Passignano), Umbrian (CASTELLO DELLA SALA) and PIEDMONT (PRUNOTTO) wines. Pioneer of new VDT, eg TIGNANELLO, SOLAIA (TUSCANY), CERVARO DELLA SALA (Umbria). Marchese Piero A was the 'Voice of Italy' in world wine circles in '70s and '80s. Now he is busy expanding into in S Tuscan Maremma, MONTEPULCIANO, MONTALCINO (La Braccesca), Pitigliano, in PIEDMONT, in ASTI (for BARBERA) and in APULIA. Also vg DOC BOLGHERI Guardo al Tasso (Cab-Merlot). See also Prunotto.

Antonelli ★★★ Vg DOCG SAGRANTINO and ROSSO DI MONTEFALCO.

Antoniolo ★★·★★★ Vg GATTINARA DOCG.

Apulia Puglia. Italy's heel, producing about a fifth of all Italian wine, but mostly bottled in north Italy/France. A region to follow in increasing quality/value. Best DOC: CASTEL DEL MONTE, PRIMITIVO DI MANDURIA, SALICE SALENTINO. Producers are: Botromagno, CALO MICHELE, CANDIDO, Coop COPERTINO, Conte Zecca, Fatalone, Felline, I Pástini, LEONE DE CASTRIS, Lomazzi & Sarli, Masseria Monaci, Pervini, RIVERA, ROSA DEL GOLFO, TAURINO, Torrevento, Vallone.

Aquileia F-VG DOC r w ★ ·★★ (r) **94 95 96** 97 12 single-grape wines from around the town of Aquileia on the Slovenian border. Good REFOSCO.

Argiano ★★★ Top MONTALCINO producer.

Argiolas, Antonio ★★·★★★ Important Sardinian producer. Astonishing quality. Vg: CANNONAU, NURAGUS, VERMENTINO and red VDT Turriga (★★★).

Armani ★★·★★★ Vg DOC VALDADIGE and TRENTINO CHARD.

Arneis Pie w ★★ DYA At last, a fairly gd white from BAROLO country: the revival of an ancient grape to make fragrant light wine. DOC: ROERO Arneis, a zone N of Alba, and LANGHE Arneis. Good from Almondo, Ca' du Russ, Correggia, Costa Antonio, Deltetto, BRUNO GIACOSA, Malvirà and Gianni Voerzio (Roero A); CASTELLO di Neive (Langhe A). Often too expensive.

Artimino Tusc r ★★·★★★ Ancient hill-town W of Florence. Fattoria di Artimino produces top DOCG CARMIGNANO.

Assisi Umb r (w) ★·★★ DYA VDT IGT ROSSO and BIANCO di Assisi: v attractive. Try cool.

Asti Major wine centre of PIEDMONT.

Asti (Spumante) Pie DOCG w sw sp ★·★★ NV Unfortunately, the big Asti houses are not remotely interested in making their production of 80M bottles better than routine. Despite its unique potential, Asti is a cheap, fairly proper product for supermarket shelves. Only a few producers care: WALTER BERA, Dogliotti-Caudria, Cascina Fonda, Vignaioli di Santo Stefano.

Attems, Conti Famous old COLLIO estate with wide range of good typical wines (esp PINOT GRIGIO). Now run by COLLAVINI.

Avignonesi ★★★ Noble MONTEPULCIANO house with highly ambitious and v fine range: VINO NOBILE, blended red Grifi, CHARD, SAUV, MERLOT and superlative VIN SANTO (★★★★).

Azienda agricola/agraria A farm producing crops, often incl wine.

Azienda/casa vinicola Wine firm using bought-in grapes and/or wines.

Azienda vitivinicola A (specialized) wine estate.

Badia a Coltibuono ★★·★★★ Fine CHIANTI-maker in pretty old abbey at Gaiole with a restaurant and collection of old vintages. Also produces VDT SANGIOVETO.

Badia di Morrona ★★·★★★ Nr Pisa (Tus). Vg DOCG CHIANTI RESERVA, outstanding VDT N'Antia (CAB S-SANGIO) and VDT Vigna Alta (Sangio-Canaiolo).

Banfi (Castello or Villa) ★★ →★★★ Space-age CANTINA of biggest US importer of Italian wine. Huge plantings at MONTALCINO, mostly SANGIO; also Syrah, PINOT N, CAB S, CHARD, SAUV, etc: part of a drive for quality plus quantity. BRUNELLO gd but 'Poggio all'Oro' is ★★★. Centine is ROSSO DI M. In PIEDMONT also produces vg Banfi Brut, Principessa GAVI, BRACCHETTO D'ACQUI, PINOT GR. See also Eastern States US.

Banti, Eric ★★ Makes fair DOC MORELLINO DI SCANSANO.

Barbacarlo Lom r dr sw sp ★ →★★ Traditional light wines with typical bitter-almond taste, from OLTREPO PAVESE.

Barbaresco Pie DOCG r ★★ →★★★★ 85' 88' 89' 90' 93 95' 96' 97' 98' Neighbour of BAROLO; the other great NEBBIOLO wine. Perhaps marginally less sturdy. At best palate-cleansing, deep, subtle, fine. At 4 yrs becomes RISERVA. Producers incl Ca' del Baio, CERETTO, CIGLIUTI, GAJA, BRUNO GIACOSA, MARCHESI DI GRESY, Lano, Cascina Luisin, MOCCAGATTA, Nada Ada, Fiorenzo Nada, Giorgio Pelissero, Poderi Colla, PIO CESARE, Produttori del B, PRUNOTTO, Alfredo Roagna, Albino Rocca, BRUNO ROCCA, Sottimano, Veraldo.

Barbatella, Cascina La ★★★ Top producer of BARBERA D'ASTI: excellent single-v'yd Sonvico and dell'Angelo.

Barbera d'Alba Pie DOC r ★★ →★★★ 90' 93' **94 95'** 96' 97' 98' Tasty tannic fragrant red. SUPERIORE can age 7+ yrs. Round ALBA, NEBBIOLO is s'times added to make a VDT. Best producers of BAROLO and BARBARESCO also produce reliable and gd Barbera d'Alba.

Barbera d'Asti Pie DOC r ★★ →★★★ 90' 91 93' **94 95'** 96' 97' 98' For real BARBERA-lovers: Barbera alone, tangy and appetizing, drunk young or aged up to 7–10 yrs or longer. Top growers: LA BARBATELLA, BAVA, ALFIERO BOFFA, BRAIDA, Bricco Mondalino, Cantina Sociale Vinchio e Vaglio, CASCINA CASTLET, Michele Chiarlo, Colle Manora, Contratto, COPPO, La Lune del Rospo, Livio Pavese, Marchesi Alfieri, Martinetti, La Morandina, Neirano, Occhetti, Rovero, Scrimaglio, La Tenaglia, TERRE DA VINO, Trinchero, Viarengo.

Barbera del Monferrato Pie DOC r ★ →★★ DYA Easy-drinking BARBERA from Alessandria and ASTI. Pleasant, slightly fizzy, s'times sweetish. Delimited area is almost identical to BARBERA D'ASTI, but regulations are more relaxed.

Barberani ★★ →★★★ Leading ORVIETO producer.

Barbi, Fattoria dei ★★ Traditional BRUNELLO and ROSSO DI MONTALCINO.

Barco Reale Tus DOC r ★ →★★ DOC for jnr wine of CARMIGNANO; same grapes.

Bardolino Ven DOC r (p) ★ →★★ DYA Pale summery sl bitter red from E shore of Lake Garda. Bardolino CHIARETTO: paler and lighter. Top makers: BOSCAINI GUERRIERI-RIZZARDI, MONTRESOR, Le Vigne di San Pietro, Villabella, Zenato, Fratelli Zeni.

A Barole of honour

The great classic style of Barolo: Bruno Giacosa, Giacomo Borgogno, Ceretto, Aldo Conterno, Giacomo Conterno, Bartolo Mascarello, Giuseppe Mascarello, Giuseppe Rinaldi and few others

A promising new generation of Barolos: Elio Altare, Azelia, Boglietti, Brezza, Cappellano, M Chiarlo, Elvio Cogno, Conterno Fantino, Renato Corino, Rocca Costamagna, Domenico Cerico, Angelo Gaja, Elio Grasso, Silvio Grasso, Oddero, Parusso, Prunotto, Principiano, Renato Ratto, Rocche dei Manzoni, Luciano Sandrone, Paolo Scavino, Fratelli Seghesio, Aldo Vajra, Vietti, Gianni Voerzio, Roberto Voerzio and many others.

Barolo Pie DOCG r ★★★ →★★★★ 85' 88' 89' 90' 93 95' 96' 97' 98' Small area S of ALBA with one of Italy's supreme reds: rich, tannic, alcoholic (min 13%), dry but wonderfully deep and fragrant (also crisp and clean) in the mouth. From NEBBIOLO grapes. Ages for up to 15 yrs (RISERVA after 5).

Barolo Chinato A dessert wine made from BAROLO DOCG, alcohol, sugar, herbs, spices and Peruvian bark. Producers: Guilio Cocchi, Cappellano.

Bava ★★ ·★★★ Vg DOC BARBERA D'ASTI, oaky Barbera d'Asti Stradivario, vg DOC Castelnuovo don Bosco, BAROLO CHINATO; the Bava family controls the old firm Guilio Cocchi in Asti where they produce gd sp METHODO CLASSICO.

Bellavista ★★★ FRANCIACORTA estate with brisk SPUMANTE (Gran Cuvée Franciacorta is top). Also Crémant. Terre di Franciacorta DOC and Sebino IGT Solesine (both Cab-Merlot blends).

Bera, Walter ★★ ·★★★ Sm estate nr BARBARESCO. Vg MOSCATO D'ASTI and ASTI.

Berlucchi, Guido Italy's biggest producer of sp METODO CLASSICO. Quality steady.

Bersano Historic wine house in Nizza MONFERRATO with most of the PIEDMONT DOC wines incl BAROLO, BARBARESCO, BARBERA D'ASTI, sp Moscato.

Bertani ★★★ Well-known producer of good quality VERONESE wines, esp old style AMARONE.

Bertelli ★★ Good small PIEDMONT producer: BARBERA D'ASTI, VDT CAB, CHARD.

Bianco White.

Bianco di Custoza Ven DOC w (sp) ★ ·★★ DYA Twin of SOAVE from VERONA's other side (W). Corte Sant'Arcadio, Le Tende, Le Vigne di San Pietro, MONTRESOR all gd.

Bianco di Pitigliano Tus DOC w ★ DYA A dry white from extreme S of TUSCANY. New interest (e.g. ANTINORI). To watch.

Bigi Famous producer of ORVIETO and other wines of Umbria and TUSCANY. Bigi's Torricella v'yd produces vg dry Orvieto.

Biondi-Santi ★★ ·★★★★ The original producer of BRUNELLO DI MONTALCINO, from 45-acre Il Greppo v'yd. Prices can be absurd, but old vintages are unique.

Bisol ★★★ Vg PROSECCO DI VALDOBBIADENE. Also top MET CLASS SPUMANTE.

Boca Pie DOC r ★★ 90' 91' 93 95 96' 97' 98' Another NEBBIOLO from N of PIEDMONT. Look for Poderi ai Valloni (Vigneto Cristiana ★★★).

Boffa, Alfiero ★★ ·★★★ Sm property: top BARBERA D'ASTI. Esp single-v'yd wines.

Bolgheri Tus DOC r p w (sw) ★★ ·★★★★ On the coast S of Livorno. Incl 7 types of wine: BIANCO, VERMENTINO, SAUVIGNON BLANC, ROSSO, ROSATO, VIN SANTO and Occhio di Pernice. Newish DOC Bolgheri Rosso: CAB-MERLOT-SANGIO blend. Top producers: Le Macchiole: DOC Paleo, Toscana IGTS Scrio (Syrah), Messorio (MERLOT); ORNELLAIA: DOC Ornellaia, Toscana IGT Masseto (Merlot); SAN GUIDO: DOC SASSICAIA; ANTINORI: DOC Guado al Tasso; Meletti-Cavallari: DOC Grattamacco; Michele Satta: DOC Piastraia, Toscana IGT Vigna al Cavaliere (SANGIO).

Bolla ★★ ·★★★ Famous Verona firm for VALPOLICELLA, AMARONE, SOAVE, etc. Top wines: Castellaro, Creso (red and white), Jago. And vg RECIOTO

Bonarda Minor red grape (alias Croatina) widely grown in PIEDMONT, Lombardy, Emilia-Romagna and blended with BARBERA.

Bonarda Lom DOC r ★★ Soft fresh often red FRIZZANTE from S of Pavia.

Borgo del Tiglio ★★★ FRIULI estate for one of NE Italy's top MERLOTS: VDT ROSSO della Centa; also good sp COLLIO CHARD, TOCAI and BIANCO.

Boscaini Ven★★ ·★★★ VERONA producer of VALPOLICELLA, AMARONE, SOAVE.

Boscarelli, Poderi ★★★ Small estate with vg VINO NOBILE DI MONTEPULCIANO, barrel-aged VDT Boscarelli and good ROSSO DI M.

Brachetto d'Acqui Pie DOCG r sw (sp) ★★ DYA Sweet sparkling red with enticing Muscat scent. Much better than it sounds. Best producer: BANFI.

Braida ★★★ The late Giacomo Bologna's estate; for top BARBERA D'ASTI (BRICCO della Bigotta and Barbera VDT BRICCO DELL'UCCELLONE).

Bramaterra Pie DOC r ★★ 90' 93 95' 96' 97 98' Neighbour to GATTINARA. NEBBIOLO grapes predominate in a blend. Good producers: Perazzi, Sella.

Breganze Ven DOC ★ ·★★★ (r) 93 94 95' 96 97' 98 Catch-all for many varieties nr Vicenza. CAB and PINOT BL are best. Top producers: B Bartolomeo, MACULAN.

Bricco Term for a high (and by implication vg) ridge v'yd in PIEDMONT.

Bricco Manzoni Pie r ★★★ V successful blend of NEBBIOLO and BARBERA from Monforte d'Alba.

Bricco dell'Uccellone Pie r ★★★ Barrique-aged BARBERA from BRAIDA the estate of the late Giacomo Bologna. Bricco della Bigotta and Ai Suma are others.

Brindisi Ap DOC r ★★ Strong NEGROAMARO. Esp Vallone's Vigna Flaminia.

Brolio, Castello di ★★→★★★ After a sad period under foreign ownership, the RICASOLI family has taken this legendary estate in hand again. The results are heartening. Vg CHIANTI CLASSICO and VDT Castelferro (SANGIO).

Brunelli ★★→★★★ Vg quality of AMARONE and VALPOLICELLA (esp Pa' Riondo).

Brunello di Montalcino Tus DOCG r ★★★→★★★★ 88' 90' 91 93 95' (96) 97' 98 With BAROLO, Italy's most celebrated red: strong, full-bodied, high-flavoured, tannic and long-lived. 4 yrs' ageing; after 5 becomes RISERVA. Quality ever-improving. Montalcino is 25 miles S of Siena.

Bukkuram Si br ★★★ Celebrated MOSCATO DI PANTELLERIA from De Bartoli.

Ca' del Bosco ★★★→★★★★ FRANCIACORTA estate; some of Italy's best sparklers (outstanding DOCG Annamaria Clementi ★★★★), vg CHARD and excellent reds: a CAB blend (Maurizio Zanella), PINOT NERO (Pinèro).

Cabernet Sauvignon in Italy

Cabernet has been overused in Italy in the past as a way of improving even classic wines (like Chianti Classico, Valpolicella, Amarone, etc) and consequently has been widely planted. But it is becoming clearer that Cabernet only ripens in particular areas and vintages sufficiently to lose its strident varietal character. Cabernet, therefore, can decisively alter the characteristic aroma and tannin structure of native Italian grape varieties in a blend. Some winemakers rejected it in favour of the less dominant Merlot. Others prefer to increase quality with a somewhat antiquated system – they simply reduce their yields!

Cacchiano, Castello di ★★★ First-rate CHIANTI CLASSICO estate at Gaiole, owned by RICASOLI cousins.

Cafaggio, Villa ★★→★★★ CHIANTI CLASSICO estate. Solid red VDT: Solatio Basilica.

Calatrasi SI ★★→★★★ Good producer of r and w VDT labels, esp Pelavet (★★★ CAB, Syrah, Nero d'Avola), d'Istinto (esp Syrah), Terre di Ginestra.

Caldaro (Lago di Caldaro) T-AA DOC r ★ DYA Alias KALTERERSEE. Light soft bitter-almond red from SCHIAVA grapes. From a huge area. CLASSICO from a smaller area is better.

Calò, Michele ★★★ Top producer of Salento wines; look for DOC ALEZIO ROSSO and VDT Vigna Spano.

Caluso Passito Pie DOC w sw (fz) ★★ Made from Erbaluce grapes; delicate scent, velvety taste. Tiny production. Best from Bianco, Ferrando.

Candido, F ★★★ Top grower of Salento, APULIA; gd reds: Duca d'Aragona, Cappello i Prete, SALICE SALENTINO; also vg dessert wine: ALEATICO DI PUGLIA.

Canevel ★★→★★★ Vg producer of PROSECCO DI CONEGLIANO-VALDOBBIADENE.

Cannonau di Sardegna Sar DOC r (p) dr s/sw ★★ 94 95 96 97 98 Cannonau (Grenache) is S's basic red grape. Ranges from v potent to fine and mellow: Arcadu Tonino, CS di Jerzu, Giuseppe Gabbas, Loi, Gigi Picciau, SELLA & MOSCA.

Cantalupo, Antichi Vigneti di ★★→★★★ Top GHEMME wines – esp single-v'yd Breclemae and Carellae.

Cantina Cellar or winery.

Cantina Sociale (CS) Growers' coop.

Capannelle ★★★ Good producer of VDT (formerly CHIANTI CLASSICO), nr Gaiole.

Caparzo, Tenuta ★★★ MONTALCINO estate. Excellent BRUNELLO La Casa; also vg ROSSO DI M (esp La Caduta), red blend Ca' del Pazzo and white blend Le Grance.

Capezzana, Tenuta di (or Villa) ★★★ The TUSCAN estate (W of Florence) of the Contini Bonacossi family. Excellent CHIANTI Montalbano and CARMIGNANO. Also vg Bordeaux-style red, GHIAIE DELLA FURBA.

Caprai ★★★ Widely copied, v oaky DOCG SAGRANTINO, vg ROSSO DI MONTEFALCO.

Capri Cam DOC r p w ★→★★ Legendary island with widely abused name. Only interesting wines are from La Caprense.

Cardizze Famous, frequently too expensive and too sweet DOC PROSECCO of top v'yd nr VALDOBBIADENE.

Carema Pie DOC r ★★→★★★ 89' 90' 91 93 94 95 96' 97' 98 Old speciality of N PIEDMONT. Best from Luigi Ferrando (or the CANTINA SOCIALE).

Carignano del Sulcis Sar DOC r p ★★→★★★ 90 91 93 94 95 96 97' 98 Well-structured, ageworthy red. Best is Terre Brune from CANTINA SOCIALE di Santadi.

Carmignano Tus DOCG r ★★★ 85' 86 88' 90' 92' 93 95' 96' 97' 98 Region W of Florence. CHIANTI grapes plus 10% CAB s make distinctive, reliable, even excellent reds. Best incl AMBRA, CAPEZZANA, Farnete, Poggiolo and Vittorio Contini Bonacossi's Villa Trefiano.

Carpenè Malvolti Leading producer of classic PROSECCO and other sp wines at Conegliano, Veneto. Seen everywhere in Venice.

Carpineto ★★ Producer of CHIANTI CLASSICO in N part of region.

Carso F-VG DOC r w ★★→★★★ (r) 90 91' 93 94 96 97' 98 DOC nr Trieste incl good MALVASIA. Terrano del C is a REFOSCO red. Top grower: EDI KANTE.

Casa fondata nel... Firm founded in...

Casalte, Fattoria Le ★★★ Vg VINO NOBILE DI MONTEPULCIANO; also r and w VDT Celius.

Casanova di Neri ★★★ BRUNELLO DI MONTALCINO (and vg ROSSO DI M) from Neri family.

Case Basse ★★★ Small estate with v impressive BRUNELLO and VDT Intistieti.

Case Bianche, Le ★★ Reliable estate nr Conegliano (Ven) for PROSECCO, SAUV and surprising red Wildbacher (from ancient Austrian grape). Also SPUMANTE of growing reputation.

Castel del Monte Ap DOC r p w ★★→★★★ (r) 93' 94 95 96 97' 98 Dry fresh well-balanced southern wines. The red is RISERVA after 3 yrs. Rosé most widely known. RIVERA'S Il Falcone and Torrevento's Vigna Pedale are outstanding.

Good Brunello di Montalcino producers include:

Altesino, Argiano, Banfi, Barbi, Biondi-Santi, Campogiovanni, Canalicchio di Sopra, Capanna-Cencioni, Caparzo, Casanova di Neri, Case Basse, Castelgiocondo, Le Chiusa di Sotto, Col d'Orcia, Costanti, Eredi Fuligni, Gorelli, Lisini, Marchesato degli Aleramici, Marroneto, Mastrojanni, Siro Pacenti, Ciacci Piccolomini, Pieve di Santa Restituta, Poggio Antico, Poggione, Le Prata, Salvioni-Cerbaiola, Talenti, and Tiezzi.

Castelgiocondo ★★★ FRESCOBALDI estate in MONTALCINO: vg BRUNELLO; gd VDT MERLOT Lamaïone.

Castell' in Villa ★★★ Vg CHIANTI CLASSICO estate. Also VIN SANTO.

Castellare ★★→★★★ Small but admired CHIANTI CLASSICO producer. First-rate SANGIO VDT I Sodi di San Niccoló and sprightly GOVERNO di Castellare: old-style CHIANTI updated. Also SAUV, CHARD, CAB.

Castello Castle. (See under name: eg Albola, Castello d'.)

Castello della Sala See Antinori.

Castello di Albola See Zonin.

Castelluccio ★★→★★★ Best SANGIO of Emilia-Romagna: VDT RONCO dei Cigliegi and Ronco della Simia.

Castlet, Cascina ★★→★★★ Producers of concentrated BARBERA PASSITO, VDT Passum, vg BARBERA D'ASTI.

Caudrina-Dogliotti Redento ★★★ Top MOSCATO D'ASTI: La Galeisa and Caudrina.

Cavalleri ★★★ Vg reliable FRANCIACORTA producer. Esp sparkling.

Cavallotto ★★ →★★★ Reliable BAROLO estate: esp Barolo Vigna San Giuseppe.

Cavicchioli Large Emilia-Romagna producer of LAMBRUSCO and other sparkling: Lambrusco di Sorbara Vigna del Cristo is best. Also TERRE DI FRANCIACORTA

Ca'Vit (Cantina Viticoltori) Group of quality coops nr Trento. Wines incl MARZEMINO, CAB, PINOTS N, BL, GR, NOSIOLA. Top wines: Brume di Monte (r and w) and sp Graal.

Cecchi Large-scale producer and bottler of TUSCAN wines.

Cerasuolo Ab DOC p ★★ The ROSATO version of MONTEPULCIANO D'ABRUZZO.

Cerasuolo di Vittoria Si DOC p ★★ Pink, full-bodied, aromatic (Frappato and Nero d'Avola grapes); can be interesting, esp from Valle dell'Acate and COS.

Ceretto ★★★ Vg grower of BARBARESCO (BRICCO Asili), BAROLO (Bricco Rocche, Brunate, Prapò), top BARBERA D'ALBA (Piana), CHARD (La Bernardina), DOLCETTO and ARNEIS. Also vg METHODO CLASSICO SPUMANTE La Bernardina.

Cervaro See Castello della Sala.

Chardonnay Has recently joined permitted varieties for several N Italian DOCS (eg T-AA, FRANCIACORTA, F-VG, PIEDMONT). Some of the best (eg from ANTINORI, FELSINA, GAJA, LUNGAROTTI) are still only VDT.

Chianti Tus DOCG r ★ →★★★ 93' 94 95' 96 97' 98 Chianti Annata DYA The lively local wine of Florence and Siena. At best fresh fruity and tangy. Of the subdistricts, RUFINA (★★ →★★★) and Colli Fiorentini (★ →★★★) can make CLASSICO-style RISERVAS. Montalbano, COLLI Senesi, Aretini and Pisani: lighter wines. New subdistrict since '97 is Chianti Montespertoli; wines similar to Colli Fiorentini.

Chianti Classico Tus DOCG r ★★ →★★★★ 90 93 94 95' 96 97' 98 (Reserve and single v'yd) 88' 90' 93 95 96 97' 98 Senior CHIANTI from central area. Its old pale astringent style is now rarer as top estates opt for either darker tannic wines or softer and fruitier ones. Some are among the best wines of Italy. Members of the CONSORZIO use the badge of a black rooster, but not all top firms belong.

Who makes really good Chianti Classico?
Ama, Antinori, Bibbiano, Brolio, Cacchiano, Carobbio, Casa Emma, Casaloste, Castel Ruggero, Castellare, Castell'in Villa, Le Cinciole, Coltibuono, Corti, Felsina, Le Filigare, Le Fonterutoli, Fontodi, Isole e Olena, Querciabella, Lilliano, La Massa, Le Masse di San Leolino, Giovanna Morganti, Monterinaldi, Nittardi, Palazzino, Paneretta, Petroio-Lenzi, Poggerino, Poggio al Sole, Querceto, Rampolla, Riecine, Rocca di Montegrossi, Rodano, San Felice, San Giusto, Valtellina, Vecchie Terre di Montefili, Verrazzano, Villa Cafaggio, Volpaia.

Chianti Putto Tus DOCG r ★ →★★ DYA From a league of producers outside the CLASSICO zone. The neck-label, a pink cherub, is now rarely seen.

Chiarli Producer of Modena LAMBRUSCO (look for Generale Cialdini label).

Chiarlo, Michele ★★ →★★★ Good PIEDMONT producer. (BAROLOS Cerequio, Cannubi, GAVI and BARBERA D'ASTI are vg.) Also BARBARESCO and DOLCETTO.

Chiaretto Rosé (the word means 'claret') produced esp around Lake Garda. See Bardolino, Riviera del Garda.

Chiesa di Santa Restituta See Pieve di Santa Restituta.

Chionetti ★★ →★★★ Makes best DOLCETTO di Dogliani (look for Briccolero).

Ciacci Piccolomini ★★★ Vg BRUNELLO DI MONTALCINO (esp Vigna di Pianrosso) and ROSSO DI M.

Cigliuti, Renato ★★★ Small high-quality estate for BARBARESCO and BARBERA D' ALBA.

Cinqueterre Lig DOC w dr sw pa ★★ Fragrant fruity white from precipitous coast nr La Spezia. PASSITO is known as SCIACCHETRA (★★ →★★★). Good from De Batte, Coop Agricola di Cinqueterre, Forlini & Cappellini.

Cinzano Major Vermouth co also known for its ASTI. Now owned by Diageo.

Cirò Cal DOC r (p w) ★→★★★ 88 89 90' 91 93 94' 96 97 98 V strong r from Gaglioppo grapes; light fruity w (DYA). Best: LIBRANDI (Duca San Felice ★★★), San Francesco (Donna Madda, Ronco dei Quattroventi), Caparra & Siciliani.

Classico Term for wines from a restricted area within the limits of a DOC. By implication, and often in practice, the best of the district. Applied to sp wines it denotes the classic method (as for Champagne).

Clerico, Domenico ★★★ Constantly evolving PIEDMONT wines; the aim is for international flavour. Esp good for BAROLO.

Cocci Grifoni ★★→★★★ Vg DOC ROSSO PICENO (look for Vigna Messieri).

Col d'Orcia ★★★ Top MONTALCINO estate; interesting VDT. Best wine is BRUNELLO.

Collavini An important new FRIULI house. Good quality COLLIO and GRAVE wines, SPUMANTE (best is METODO CLASSICO Applauso).

Colle Picchioni ★★ Estate S of Rome making MARINO white; also red (CAB-MERLOT) VDT, Vigna del Vassallo.

Colli Hills. Occurs in many wine names.

Colli Berici Ven DOC r p w ★★ Hills S of Vicenza. CAB: best wine. Top producer Villa Dal Ferro.

Colli Bolognesi E-R DOC r p w ★★ (w) DYA SW of Bologna. 8 wines, 5 grape varieties. TERRE ROSSE: top estate (★★★). Other gd producers are Tenuta Bonzara and Santarosa (esp VDT Giò Rosso).

Colli Euganei Ven DOC r w dr s/sw (sp) ★→★★★ DYA DOC SW of Padua for 7 wines. Adequate r; w, sp soft, pleasant. Best producers: Vignalta, Ca' Lustra.

Colli Orientali del Friuli F-VG DOC r w dr sw ★★→★★★★ (r) 88 90' 94 95 96' 97' Hills E of Udine. 20 wines (18 named after their grapes). Whites esp are vg. Top growers: Cantarutti, Dal Fari, DORIGO, Ermacora, Gigante, Le Viarte, LIVIO FELLUGA, Meroi, Miani, Perusini, Petrucco, Petrussa, Rocca Bernarda, Rochi dio Manzano, Rodaro, Ronchi di Cialla, Ronco dei Rosetti, RONCO DEL GNEMIZ, Ronco delle Betulle, Scubla, Specogna, VIGNE DAL LEON, Visentini, VOLPE PASINI, WALTER FILIPUTTI, Zamò & Zamò, Zof.

Colli Piacentini E-R DOC r p w ★→★★ DYA DOC incl traditional GUTTURNIO and Monterosso Val d'Arda among 11 types grown S of Piacenza. Good fizzy MALVASIA. Most wines FRIZZANTE. New French and local reds: La Stoppa, La Tosa, Marchese Malaspina, Villa Peirano.

Colli Romani The wooded hills S of Rome: ancient summer resort and source of FRASCATI, MARINO, etc.

Colli del Trasimeno Um DOC r w ★→★★ (r) 95 96 97 98 Lively wines from Perugia. Best: Casale dei Cucchi (formerly Morolli), Marella, Pieve del Vescovo.

Colline Novaresi Pie DOC r w ★→★★ DYA New DOC for old region in Novara province. 7 different wines: BIANCO, ROSSO, NEBBIOLO, BONARDA, Vespolina, Croatina and BARBERA. Incl declassified BOCA, GHEMME, FARA and SIZZANO.

Collio F-VG DOC r w ★★→★★★ 88 90 93 94 95 96 97 19 wines, 17 named after their grapes, from nr Slovenian border. Vg whites, esp SAUV, PINOTS B and GR from: BORGO DEL TIGLIO, Ca' Ronesca, Castello di Spessa, Colmello di Grotta, Edi Keber, MARCO FELLUGA, Fiegl, GRAVNER, La Castellada, La Rajade, LIVON, Picech, Primosic, Princic, Ronco dei Tassi, RUSSIZ SUPERIORE, SCHIOPETTO, Subida di Monte, Toròs, Venica & Venica, Vigna del Lauro, VILLA RUSSIZ, Villanova.

Consorzio In Italy there are two types of associations recognised by wine law. One is dedicated to the observance of DOC regulations (eg Consorzio Tutela del CHIANTI CLASSICO). The second is to promote the wines of their members (eg Consorzio del Marchio Storico di Chianti Classico, previously Gallo Nero).

Conterno, Aldo ★★★★ Legendary grower of BAROLO, etc, at Monforte d'Alba. Good GRIGNOLINO, FREISA, vg CHARD Printanier and Bussia d'Oro. Best BAROLOS are Gran Bussia, Cicala and Colonello. Barrel-aged NEBBIOLO VDT Favot vg.

Conterno, Giacomo ★★★★ Top grower of BAROLO etc at Monforte d'Alba. Monfortino Barolo is long-aged, rare, outstanding.

Conterno-Fantino ★★★ 3 young families for vg BAROLO etc at Monforte d'Alba.

Contini, Attilio ★·★★★ Famous producer of VERNACCIA DI ORISTANO; best is vintage blend 'Antico Gregori'.

Contucci, Conti ★★ Ancient esteemed maker of VINO NOBILE DI MONTEPULCIANO.

Copertino Ap DOC r (p) ★★ **95 96** 97 98 Savoury age-able red of NEGROAMARO from the heel of Italy. Look for CANTINA SOCIALE's RISERVA and Tenuta Monaci.

Coppo ★★·★★★ Ambitious producers of BARBERA D'ASTI (eg 'Pomorosso').

Cordero di Montezemolo-Monfalletto ★★ Tiny maker of good BAROLO.

Cortese di Gavi See Gavi. (Cortese is the grape.)

Corzano & Paterno, Fattoria di ★★★ Dynamic CHIANTI COLLI Fiorentini estate. Vg RISERVA, red VDT Corzano and outstanding VIN SANTO.

COS ★★★ Tiny estate: 3 friends making top Sicilian wines esp VDT Vigne di Cos white (CHARD) and red (CAB).

Costanti, Conti ★★★ Tiny estate for top-quality BRUNELLO DI MONTALCINO.

D'Ambra ★★ Top producer of ISCHIA wines, esp excellent white DOC Biancolella ('Piellero' and single-v'yd 'Frassitelli').

D'Angelo ★★·★★★ Leading producers of admirable DOC AGLIANICO DEL VULTURE. Barrel-aged Aglianico VDT Canneto also vg.

Dal Forno, Romano ★★★★ Very high-quality VALPOLICELLA and AMARONE from perfectionist grower, bottling only best: 14,000 bottles from 20 acres.

Darmagi Pie r ★★★★ CAB S from GAJA in BARBARESCO is one of PIEDMONT's most discussed (and expensive) VDT reds.

Denominazione di Origine Controllata (DOC) Means the same as Appellation d'Origine Contrôlée (qv France).

Denominazione di Origine Controllata e Garantita (DOCG) Like DOC but with an official guarantee of origin shown by an officially numbered neck-label on the bottle indicating limited production.

Decugnano dei Barbi ★★ Top ORVIETO estate with an ABBOCCATO known as 'Pourriture Noble', and a good red VDT.

Di Majo Norante ★★·★★★ Lone star of Molise on the Adriatic with vg Biferno DOC MONTEPULCIANO and white Falanghina.

DOC, DOCG See Denominazione di Origine Controllata (e Garantita).

Italy's DOCG wines: the complete list (for what it's worth)
Albana di Romagna, Asti and Moscato d'Asti, Barbaresco, Barolo, Brachetto d'Acqui, Brunello di Montalcino, Carmignano, Chianti, Chianti Classico, Franciacorta, Gattinara, Ghemme, Montefalco Sagrantino, Soave Recioto, Taurasi, Torgiano, Valtellina Superiore, Vermentino di Gallura, Vernaccia di San Gimignano, and Vino Nobile di Montepulciano.

Dolce Sweet.

Dolceacqua See Rossese di Dolceacqua.

Dolcetto ★·★★★ PIEDMONT's earliest-ripening grape, for v attractive everyday wines: dry youthful fruity and fresh with deep purple colour. Gives its name to several DOCs: D d'Acqui, D d'Asti, D delle Langhe Monregalesi, D di Diano d'Alba (also Diano DOC), D di Dogliani (esp from CHIONETTI, San Fereolo, San Romano, Poderi Luigi Einaudi, Pecchenino) and D di Ovada (best from La Guardia, Abbazia di Vallechiara). D d'Alba: made by most BAROLO and BARBARESCO growers.

Donnafugata Si r w ★★ Zesty Sicilian whites (best from Vigna di Gabri). Also sound red. Was VDT, now in DOC Contessa Entellina.

Dorigo, Girolamo ★★★ Top COLLI ORIENTALI DEL FRIULI producer for outstanding white VDT Ronc di Juri, CHARD, dessert VERDUZZO and PICOLIT, red Pignolo (★★★★), REFOSCO, Schioppettino, and VDT Montsclapade.

Duca Enrico See Duca di Salaparuta.

Duca di Salaparuta ★★ AKA Vini Corvo. Popular Sicilian wines. Sound dry reds; pleasant soft whites. Excellent Duca Enrico (★★★) is one of Sicily's best reds. Valguarnera is premium oak-aged white.

Elba Tus r w (sp) ★→★★ DYA The island's white is drinkable with fish. Try Acquabona. Napoléon in exile here loved the sweet red ALEATICO. Me, too.

Enoteca Wine library. There are many, the impressive original being the Enoteca Italiana of Siena. Also used for wine shops or restaurants.

Erbaluce di Caluso See Caluso Passito.

Eredi Fuligni ★★★ Vg producer of BRUNELLO and ROSSO DI MONTALCINO.

Est! Est!! Est!!! Lat DOC w dr s/sw ★ DYA Unextraordinary white from Montefiascone, N of Rome. Trades on its oddball name.

Etna Si DOC r p w ★ →★★ (r) **93 94 95** 96 97 98 Wine from volcanic slopes. Red: big, ageworthy; white: grapey. Top producers: Benanti, Russo, Scammacca.

Falchini ★★★ Producer of good DOCG VERNACCIA DI SAN GIMIGNANO and the best reds of the district, eg VDT Campora (★★★) and BIANCO Selva d' Oro.

Falerno del Massico Cam DOC r w ★★ (r) 90 93 **94 95** 96 97' 98 As in Falernum, the best-known wine of ancient times. Times change. Strong red from AGLIANICO, fruity white from Falanghina. Good producer: VILLA MATILDE.

Fara Pie DOC r ★★ **90' 93 95'** 96' 97' 98 Good NEBBIOLO from Novara, N PIEDMONT. Fragrant; worth ageing; esp Dessilani's Caramino.

Farneta, Tenuta ★★ →★★★ Nr Siena but outside CHIANTI CLASSICO, an estate for pure SANGIO VDT: eg Bongoverno (★★★) and Bentivoglio.

Farnetella, Castello di ★★→★★★ Estate nr MONTEPULCIANO where Giuseppe Mazzocolin of FELSINA makes vg SAUV and CHIANTI COLLI Senesi. Also vg PINOT N 'Nero di Nubi' and Poggio Granoni (SANGIO-Syrah-CAB-MERLOT blend).

Faro Si DOC r ★★ (95) (96) 97 98 Quite interesting tannic red from Messina. Gd producer: Palari.

Fattoria TUSCAN term for a wine-growing property, traditionally noble.

Favorita Pie w ★→★★ DYA Dry youthful fruity white making friends in BAROLO country.

Fazi-Battaglia ★★ Well-known producer of VERDICCHIO, etc. White Le Moie VDT is pleasant. Also owns Fassati (producer of VINO NOBILE DI MONTEPULCIANO).

Felluga ★★★ Brothers Livio and Marco (RUSSIZ SUPERIORE) have separate companies in COLLIO and COLLI ORIENTALI. Both are highly esteemed.

Felsina-Berardenga ★★★★ CHIANTI CLASSICO estate; famous RISERVA Vigna Rancia, VDT Fontalloro; the simple Annata-Chianti Classico and RISERVA: less fashionable, less expensive and have more terroir-taste. Also vg Mastro Raro (CAB).

Ferrari ★★→★★★ Cellars making some of Italy's best dry sparkling wines nr Trento, TRENTINO-ALTO ADIGE. Giulio Ferrari RISERVA is best.

Fiano di Avellino Cam w ★★→★★★ (DYA) Considered the best white of Campania, esp from new VITICOLTORI PLD-TERRE DORA DI PAOLO estate. Can be intense, slightly honeyed, memorable. Also gd: MASTROBERARDINO, Vadiaperti, Feudi di S Gregorio, Struzziero, Vega, Viticoltori PLD-Terre Dora di Paolo.

Filiputti, Walter ★★→★★★ Since 1997, tenant of the vineyards of ABBAZIA DI ROSAZZO (owner is the court of Udine) again. Produces vg white and red COLLI ORIENTALI wines under the label 'Walter Filiputti'.

Florio The major volume producer of MARSALA, controlled by Illva-Saronno.

Foianeghe T-AA vdt r (w) ★★ Brand of Conti Bossi Fedrigotti. TRENTINO CAB-MERLOT red to age 7–10 yrs. White is PINOT BL-CHARD-TRAMINER.

Folonari Large run-of-the-mill merchant of Lombardy. See also GIV.

Fontana Candida ★·★★ One of the biggest producers of FRASCATI. Single-v'yd Santa Teresa stands out. See also GIV.

Fontanafredda ★★·★★★ Big historic producer of PIEDMONT wines on former royal estates, incl BAROLO from single v'yds and a range of ALBA DOCS. Also very good DOCG ASTI and SPUMANTE Brut (esp ★★★ Vigna Gattinera).

Fonterutoli ★★★ Historic CHIANTI CLASSICO estate of the Mazzei family at Castellina. Noted VDT Concerto while splendid RISERVA Ser Lapo now replaced by new RISERVA 'Castello di Fonterutoli' (dark, oaky, fashionable Chianti).

Fontodi ★★★ Top Panzano CHIANTI CLASSICO esp Chianti and RISERVA, esp Vigna del Sorbo; also red VDT Flaccianello (SANGIO), vg VDT Case Via (Syrah).

Foradori ★★★ Elizabetta F makes very best TEROLDEGO (Morei, Sgarzon). Also oak-aged Teroldego Granato, vg CHARD.

Forteto della Luja ★★★ Number 1 for LOAZZOLO; vg BARBERA-PINOT N 'Le Grive'.

Franciacorta Lom DOCG w (p) sp ★★·★★★★ Small sp wine centre fast growing in quality and renown. Wines exclusively bottle-fermented. Top producers: BELLAVISTA, CA' DEL BOSCO, Castelveder, CAVALLERI, Faccoli, Gatti, Guarischi, Lo Sparviere, UBERTI, Villa; also vg: Contadi Gastaldi, Cornaleto, Ferghettina, Il Mosnel, Monte Rossa, Castellino-Bonomi. For w and r, see Terre di Franciacorta.

Frascati Lat DOC w dr s/sw sw (sp) ★·★★ DYA Best-known wine of Roman hills: should be soft, limpid, golden, tasting of whole grapes. Most is disappointingly neutral today: look for Conte Zandotti, Villa Simone, or Santa Teresa from FONTANA CANDIDA. Sweet is known as Cannellino. The best place to drink it is from the jug in a trattoria in Trastevere, Rome.

Freisa Pie r dr s/sw sw (sp) ★★ DYA Usually v dry (except nr Turin), often FRIZZANTE red, said to taste of raspberries and roses. With enough acidity it can be highly appetizing, esp with salami. Gd wines from CIGLIUTI, CONTERNO, Cozzo, Gilli, PARUSSO, Pecchenino, Pelissero, Sebaste, Trinchero, VAJRA and VOERZIO.

Frescobaldi ★★·★★★ Ancient noble family, leading CHIANTI pioneers at NIPOZZANO, E of Florence. Also white POMINO and PREDICATO SAUV BL (Vergena) and CAB (Mormoreto). See also Montesodi. Also owns Castelgiocondo (★★★), a big estate for BRUNELLO DI M and vg VDT MERLOT Lamaïone. From '97: joint TUSCAN venture with Mondavi of California nr MONTALCINO producing LUCE.

Friuli-Venezia Giulia The NE region on the Slovenian border. Many wines; the DOCS COLLIO and COLLI ORIENTALI include most of the best.

Friuli vintages

1998 Very hot summer; good whites, but then September rains damaged reds, esp Cabernets.

1997 Long, warm and dry autumn; results not as homogenous as in other regions; good whites and possibly superb reds.

1996 Rains from mid-August to mid-October. Whites have surprising body and aroma; reds: not bad.

1995 Promising year, then heavy rains in August and September. Light whites, better reds.

1994 Wet spring and September, hot between. Whites can lack acidity; reds better.

Frizzante (fz) Semi-sparkling. Used to describe wines such as LAMBRUSCO.

Gaja ★★★★ Old family firm at BARBARESCO under meteoric direction of Angelo G. Top-quality – and price – wines, esp BARBARESCO (single v'yds SORI Tildin, Sorí San Lorenzo, Costa Russi), BAROLO Sperss. Also sets trends with excellent CHARD (Gaia & Rey), CAB DARMAGI. Latest acquisition: Marengo-Marenda estate (BAROLO), commercial Gromis label, PIEVE DI SANTA RESTITUTA (BRUNELLO) and recently planted new v'yd at BOLGHERI.

Galestro Tus w ★ V light white from eponymous shaley soil in CHIANTI country. Current moves to upgrade (v necessary).

Gambellara Ven DOC w dr s/sw (sp) DYA Neighbour of SOAVE. Dry wine similar. Sweet (RECIOTO DI G) nicely fruity. Also VIN SANTO.

Gancia Famous ASTI house also producing vermouth and dry sparkling. Also vg single-v'yd BAROLO, 'Cannubi' (★★★), since '89.

Garganega Principal white grape of SOAVE and GAMBELLARA.

Garofoli, Gioacchino ★★ →★★★ Quality leader of the Marches (nr Ancona). Notable style in VERDICCHIO Podium, Macrina and Serra Fiorese; also vg sparkling. ROSSO CONERO Piancarda and vg Grosso Agontano.

Gattinara Pie DOCG r ★★★ 88' 89' 90' 95 96' 97' 98 V tasty BAROLO-type red (from NEBBIOLO, locally known as Spanna). Best are TRAVAGLINI (RISERVA), Antoniolo (single-v'yd wines). Others incl Bianchi, Le Colline-Monsecco, Nervi.

Gavi Pie DOCG w ★★ →★★★ DYA At (rare) best, subtle dry white of CORTESE grapes. LA SCOLCA is best known, vg are BANFI (esp Vigna Regale), Castellari Bergaglio, TERRE DA VINO. Castello di Tassarolo and Villa Sparina are v fair; also fair: CHIARLO, PODERE Saulino, Cascina degli Ulivi, La Zerba.

Ghemme Pie DOCG r ★★ →★★★ 86 88' 89 90' 93 95 96 97' 98 Neighbour of GATTINARA but not as good. Best is Antichi Vigneti di Cantalupo.

Ghiaie della Furba Tus r ★★★ Bordeaux-style VDT CAB blend from the admirable TENUTA DI CAPEZZANA, CARMIGNANO.

Giacosa, Bruno ★★★★ Inspired loner: outstanding BARBARESCO, BAROLO and PIEDMONT wines at Neive. Remarkable ARNEIS white and PINOT N sparkling.

GIV (Gruppo Italiano Vini) Complex of coops and wineries incl BIGI, Conti Serristori, FOLONARI, FONTANA CANDIDA, LAMBERTI, Macchiavelli, MELINI, Negri, Santi and since '97 controls Ca' Bianca (PIEDMONT) and Vignaioli di San Floriano (FRIULI); interests now moving into south.

Goldmuskateller Aromatic ALTO ADIGE grape made into irresistible dry white, esp by TIEFENBRUNNER.

Governo Old TUSCAN custom, enjoying mild revival with some producers, in which dried grapes or must are added to young wine to induce second fermentation and give a slight prickle – sometimes instead of using must concentrate to increase alcohol.

Gradi Degrees (of alcohol), ie percent by volume.

Grappa Pungent spirit made from grape pomace (skins etc after pressing).

Grasso, Elio ★★★ Hard-working, reliable quality producer at Monforte d'Alba: outstanding BAROLO (look for Gavarini and Casa Maté), potent barrel-aged BARBERA D'ALBA Vigna Martina, DOLCETTO D'ALBA and CHARD Educato, etc.

Grattamacco ★★★ Top TUSCAN producer on coast outside classic centres (nr SASSICAIA S of Bolgheri). Vg Grattamacco SANGIO-CAB blend, r and w BOLGHERI.

Grave del Friuli F-VG DOC r w ★★ (r) 90' 93 94 95 96 97 DOC covering 15 different wines, 14 named after their grapes, from nr the Slovenian border. Good MERLOT and CAB. Best producers: Borgo Magredo, Di Lenardo, Le Fredis, Le Monde, Plozner, Vicentini-Orgnani, Villa Chiopris.

Gravner, Josko ★★★ →★★★★ Together with MARIO SCHIOPETTO, spiritual leader of COLLIO: estate with range of excellent whites, led by CHARD and SAUV.

Grechetto White grape with more flavour than the ubiquitous TREBBIANO, increasingly used in Umbria.

Greco di Bianco Cal DOC w sw ★★ An original smooth and fragrant dessert wine from Italy's toe; worth ageing. Best from Ceratti. See Mantonico.

Greco di Tufo Cam DOC w (sp) ★★ →★★★ (DYA) One of the best white wines from the S of the country: fruity and slightly wild in flavour. A character. Best: Vignadangelo by MASTROBERARDINO and VITICOLTORI PLD-TERRE DORA DI PAOLO. Also vg from Vadiaperti, Di Meo, Feudi di S Gregorio, Vega.

Gresy, Marchesi de (Cisa Asinari) ★★★ Consistent LANGHE producer of fine BARBARESCO; also vg SAUV, CHARD and MOSCATO D'ASTI.

Grevepesa Reliable CHIANTI CLASSICO coop.

Grignolino d'Asti Pie DOC r ★ DYA Lively standard light red of PIEDMONT.

Guerrieri-Gonzaga ★★★ Top producer in TRENTINO; esp VINO DA TAVOLA San Leonardo, a ★★★ CAB-MERLOT blend.

Guerrieri-Rizzardi ★★→★★★ Top producer of AMARONE, BARDOLINO, SOAVE TRENTINO CHARD and VALPOLICELLA from various family estates.

Gutturnio dei Colli Piacentini E-R DOC r dr ★→★★ DYA BARBERA-BONARDA blend from the hills of Piacenza, often FRIZZANTE.

Haas, Franz ★★★ Very good ALTO ADIGE MERLOT and PINOT NERO.

Hofstätter ★★★ SUDTIROL producer of top PINOT NERO; look for S Urbano.

IGT (Indicazione Geografica Tipica) New category: between VDT and DOC.

Ischia Cam DOC w (r) ★→★★ DYA Wine of the island off Naples. Slightly sharp white SUPERIORE is the best of the DOC. Top producer D'AMBRA makes single v'yd DOC Biancolella: Piellero and excellent Frassitelli.

Isole e Olena ★★★→★★★★ Top CHIANTI CLASSICO estate of great beauty with fine red VDT Cepparello. Vg VIN SANTO, CAB, CHARD, and L'Eremo Syrah.

Isonzo F-VG DOC r w ★★★ (r) **90 93 94 95** 96 97' DOC covering 19 wines (17 varietals) in NE. Best w and CAB compare with COLLIO wines. Best from Lis Neris-Pecorari, Lorenzon, PIERPAOLO PECORARI, Puiatti, Ronco del Gelso, VIE DI ROMANS.

Jermann, Silvio ★★★→★★★★ Family estate in COLLIO: top white VDT, incl singular VINTAGE TUNINA oak-aged white blend and lighter Vinnae. Also fresh Capo Martino (**91**) and CHARD 'WHERE THE DREAMS HAVE NO END...'

Kalterersee German (and local) name for LAGO DI CALDARO.

Kante, Edi ★★★ Lone star of CARSO with outstanding DOC CHARD, SAUV, MALVASIA and vg red Terrano.

Lacryma (or Lacrima) Christi del Vesuvio Cam r p w dr (sw fz) ★→★★ DYA Famous but ordinary range of wines in great variety from Vesuvius. (DOC Vesuvio.) MASTROBERARDINO produces the only good example.

Lageder, Alois ★★→★★★ The lion of Bolzano (ALTO A). Exciting wines, incl oak-aged CHARD and CAB Löwengang. Single-v'yd SAUV is Lehenhof, PINOT BL Haberlehof, PINOT GR Benefizium Porer.

Lago di Caldaro See Caldaro.

Lagrein, Südtiroler T-AA DOC r p ★★→★★★ **85' 88' 90 93 94** 95' 96 97' A Tyrolean grape with a bitter twist. Good fruity wine – at best very appetizing. The rosé is 'Kretzer', the dark 'Dunkel'. Best from Gries, SCHRECKBICHL, St Magdalena, Tramin coops and Kössler, Muri Gries, NIEDERMAYR estates.

Lamberti ★→★★ Large producers of SOAVE, VALPOLICELLA, BARDOLINO, etc at Lazise on the E shore of Lake Garda. NB LUGANA and VDT Turà. See also GIV.

Lambrusco E-R DOC (or not) r p d s/sw ★→★★ DYA Popular fizzy red, best known in industrial s/sw version. Best is SECCO, traditional is with second fermentation in bottle (yeast sediment on bottom). DOCs are L Grasparossa di Castelvetro, L Salamino di Santa Croce and L di Sorbara. Best from: Bellei, Caprari, Casali, CAVICCHIOLI, Franco FERRARI, Graziano, Lini Oreste, Medici Ermete (esp Concerto), Rinaldo Rinaldini, VENTURINI BALDINI.

La Morandina ★★★ Small family estate with top MOSCATO and BARBERA D'ASTI.

Langhe The hills of central PIEDMONT, home of BAROLO, BARBARESCO, etc. Has become name for recent DOC (r w ★★→★★★) for 8 different wines: ROSSO, BIANCO, NEBBIOLO, DOLCETTO, FREISA, ARNEIS, CHARD and CHARD. Barolo and Barbaresco can now be declassified to DOC Langhe Nebbiolo.

La Scolca ★★→★★★ Famous GAVI estate for good Gavi and SPUMANTE.

Latisana F-VG DOC r w ★→★★ (r) **94 95** 96' 97' DOC for 13 varietal wines from 50 miles NE of Venice. Esp good TOCAI FRIULANO.

Le Macchiole ★★★ Outstanding red DOC BOLGHERI Paleo, TOSCANA IGTS Scrio (Syrah) and Messorio (MERLOT).

Le Pupille ★★★ Top producer of MORELLINO DI SCANSANO. outstanding VDT CAB-MERLOT blend Saffredi.

Le Salette ★★★ Small VALPOLICELLA producer: look for vg AMARONE Pergole Vece and RECIOTO Le Traversagne.

Leone de Castris ★★ Large, reliable producer to follow of APULIAN wines. Estate at SALICE SALENTINO, near Lecce. See also Locorotondo

Lessona Pie DOC r ★★ 90 93 94 95 96' 97' 98 Soft dry claret-like wine from Vercelli province. NEBBIOLO, Vespolina, BONARDA grapes. Best producer Sella.

Librandi ★★→★★★ Top Calabria producer. Vg red CIRO (RISERVA Duca San Felice is ★★★) and VDT Gravello (CAB-Gaglioppo blend).

Lilliano, Castello di ★★→★★★ Old CHIANTI CLASSICO estate pulling its weight again in the '90s. Also good Chianti COLLI.

Liquoroso Means strong, usually sweet and always fortified.

Lisini ★★★ Small estate for some of the finest recent vintages of BRUNELLO.

Livon ★★★ Top COLLIO producer, also some COLLI ORIENTALI wines like VERDUZZO.

Loazzolo Pie DOC w sw ★★★ 90 91 93 94 95 96' 97' 98' New DOC for MOSCATO dessert wine from botrytised air-dried grapes: expensive and sweet. Esp from Forteto della Luja.

Locorotondo Ap DOC w (sp) ★→★★ DYA Pleasantly fresh southern white. To try. See Leone de Castris

Lugana Lom and Ven DOC w (sp) ★★ DYA Whites of S Lake Garda: can be fragrant, smooth, full of body and flavour. Good from Ca' dei Frati, Zenato.

Luce ★★★★ Typically ambitious Mondavi (cf California) joint venture (launched '98) with FRESCOBALDI. SANGIO-MERLOT blend. Could become Italy's Opus One.

Lungarotti ★★→★★★ The leading producer of TORGIANO wine, with cellars, hotel and wine museum nr Perugia. Also some of Italy's best CHARD (Miralduolo and Vigna I Palazzi) and PINOT GR. See Torgiano.

Maculan ★★→★★★ The top producer of DOC BREGANZE. Also Torcolato, dessert VDT (★★★) and Prato di Canzio (CHARD, PINOT BL and PINOT GR).

Malvasia Important underrated grape grown throughout Italy; chameleon character: w or r, sp or still, strong or mild, sw or dry, aromatic or rather neutral, often VDT, s'times DOC.

Italian producers to look for in the early 2000s

Gini Soave and Recioto (Veneto)
Felline Primitivo di Manduria (Puglia)
Antonelli Montefalco Sagrantino (Umbria)
Cascina Ballarin Barolo (Piedmont)
Guarischi Franciacorte (Lombardy)
Marroneto Brunello di Montalcino (Tuscany)

Manduria (Primitivo di) Ap DOC r s/sw ★★→★★★ 93 94 95 96 97' (98) Dark red, naturally strong, sometimes sweet from nr Taranto. Good producers: Felline, Pervini, coop Sava, coop Manduria, Madrigale.

Mantonico Cal w dr sw fz ★★ Fruity deep amber dessert wine from Reggio Calabria. Can age remarkably well. Ceratti's is gd. See also Greco di Biano.

Marchesi di Barolo ★★ Important ALBA house: BAROLO, BARBARESCO, DOLCETTO D'ALBA, BARBERA, FREISA D'ASTI and GAVI.

Marino Lat DOC w dr s/sw (sp) ★→★★ DYA A neighbour of FRASCATI with similar wine; often a better buy. Look for COLLE PICCHIONI brand.

NB Vintages in colour are those you should choose first for drinking in 2000.

Marsala Si DOC br dr s/sw sw fz ★★→★★★ NV Sicily's sherry-type wine, invented by the Woodhouse Bros from Liverpool in 1773; excellent aperitif or for dessert, but mostly used in the kitchen for zabaglione, etc. The dry ('virgin'), s'times made by the solera system, must be 5 yrs old. Top producers: FLORIO, Pellegrino, Rallo, VECCHIO SAMPERI. V special old vintages ★★★★.

Martini & Rossi Vermouth and sparkling wine house now controlled by Bacardi group. (Has a fine wine-history museum in Pessione, nr Turin.)

Marzemino (Trentino) T-AA DOC r ★→★★ 95' 96 97 Pleasant local red. Fruity, slightly bitter. Esp from Bossi Fedrigotti, Casata Monfort, CA'VIT, De Tarczal, Gaierhof, Letrari, Simoncelli, Vallarom, Vallis Agri.

Mascarello The name of two top producers of BAROLO, etc: Bartolo M and Giuseppe M & Figli. Look for the latter's BAROLO Monprivato (★★★★).

Masi ★★→★★★ Well-known, conscientious, reliable VALPOLICELLA, AMARONE, RECIOTO, SOAVE, etc, incl fine r Campo Fiorin. Also excellent barrel-aged r VDT Toar.

Mastroberardino ★★→★★★ Campania's leading wine producing family has split into two parts: M and VITICOLTORI PLD-TERRE DORA DI PAOLO, but with v few changes. Wines incl FIANO DI AVELLINO, GRECO DI TUFO, LACRYMA CHRISTI and TAURASI (look for Radici).

Melini ★★ Long-est'd producers of CHIANTI CLASSICO at Poggibonsi. Good quality/price; look for single-v'yd C Classico Selvanella. See also GIV.

Meranese di Collina T-AA DOC r ★ DYA Light red of Merano, known in German as Meraner Hügel.

Merlot Adaptable red B'x grape widely grown in N (esp) and central Italy. MERLOT DOCS are abundant. Best growers are: HAAS, La Vis (Merlot Ritratti), SCHRECKBICHL, Baron Widman in T-AA, Torre Rosazza (L'Altromerlot), BORGO DEL TIGLIO, Livio FELLUGA (Sossò) and SCHIOPETO (Merlot Collio) in F-VG, Bonzara (Rocca di Bonacciara) in Emilia-Romagna, La Palazzola in Umbria, Falesco (Montiano) in Latium and TUSCAN Super-VDTS of AMA (L'Apparita), ORNELLAIA (Masseto), Macchiole (Messorio), AVIGNONESI (Toro Desiderio), FRESCOBALDI (Lamaione), Ghizzano (Nambrot), Casa Emma (Soloìo).

Metodo classico or tradizionale Now the mandatory terms to identify classic method sp wines. 'Metodo Champenois' banned since '94 and now illegal. (See also Classico.)

Mezzacorona Huge TRENTINO coop with gd DOC TEROLDEGO and MC sp Rotari.

Moccagatta ★★→★★★ Specialist in impressive single-v'yd BARBARESCO: Basarin, Bric Balin (★★★) and Vigna Cole. Also BARBERA D'ALBA and LANGHE.

Monacesca, La ★★★ Top producer of vg VERDICCHIO DI MATELICA. Top wine: Mirus.

Moncaro MARCHES coop: good VERDICCHIO DEI CASTELLI DI JESI.

Monferrato Pie DOC r w sw p ★★ The hills between the River Po and the Apennines give their name to a new DOC; incl ROSSO, BIANCO, CHIARETTO, DOLCETTO, Casalese and FREISA CORTESE.

Monica di Sardegna Sar DOC r ★ DYA Monica is the grape of light dry red.

Monsanto ★★→★★★ Esteemed CHIANTI CLASSICO estate, esp for Il Poggio v'yd.

Montalcino Small town in province of Siena (TUSCANY), famous for concentrated, v expensive BRUNELLO and more approachable, better value ROSSO DI M.

Monte Vertine ★★★→★★★★ Top estate at Radda in CHIANTI. VDT Le Pergole Torte (100% SANGIO) is one of TUSCANY's best. Also Sodaccio (SANGIOVETO plus Canaiolo) and fine VIN SANTO.

Montecarlo Tus DOC w r ★★ DYA (w) White wine area nr Lucca in N TUSCANY: smooth neutral blend of TREBBIANO with a range of better grapes. Now applies to a CHIANTI-style red too. Good producers: Buonamico (esp VDT 'Il Fortino'), Carmignani (vg VDT 'For Duke'), Michi.

Montefalco (Rosso di) Umb DOC r ★★→★★★ 93 94 95 96 97' 98 SANGIO-TREBBIANO-SAGRANTINO blend. For gd producers, see Montefalco Sagrantino.

Montefalco Sagrantino Umb DOCG r dr (sw) ★★★ →★★★★ 90 91 92 93 **94**
95' (96) 97' 98 Strong, v interesting SECCO or sw PASSITO r from Sagrantino
grapes only. Gd from: ADANTI, Antonelli, Caprai-Val di Maggio, Colpetrone.

Montellori, Fattoria di ★★ →★★★ TUSCAN producer making admirable SANGIO-
CAB VDT blend 'Castelrapiti Rosso', Cab-MERLOT blend 'Salamartano', CHARD VDT
'Castelrapiti Bianco' and vg MC SPUMANTE.

Montepulciano An important red grape of central-east Italy as well as the
famous TUSCAN town (see next entries).

Montepulciano d'Abruzzo Ab DOC r p ★ →★★★ 90 91 92 93 94 95 97' 98'
At (rare) best one of Italy's tastiest reds, full of flavour and warmth, from
Adriatic coast nr Pescara. Best: VALENTINI, Barone Cornacchia, Bosco Nestore,
Bove, Illuminati, Masciarelli, Montori, Nicodemi, Tenuta del Priore, La
Valentina and Zaccagnini. See also Cerasuolo.

Montepulciano, Vino Nobile di See Vino Nobile di Montepulciano.

Montescudaio Tus DOC r w ★★ New DOC nr Pisa. Terriccio is gd producer, esp
of VDT MERLOT-CAB S blends Lupicaia and Tassinaia (both ★★★).

Montesodi Tus r ★★★ Tip-top CHIANTI RUFINA RISERVA from FRESCOBALDI.

An Italian choice for 2000

Franciacorta Blanc de Blancs, Cavalleri, Erbusco (Lombardy)

Riserva Brut Millesimato Bisol, S Stefano (Veneto)

Barolo Cascina Ballarin, La Morra (Piedmont)

Dolcetto di Dogliani San Fereolo, Dogliani, Piedmont

Lagrein Riserva Baron Carl Eyrl, Gries coop, Bolzano (Alto Adige)

Chianti Classico Poggio al Sole, Badia a Passignano (Tuscany)

Brunello di Montalcino Nardi, Montalcino (Tuscany)

Soave Superiore Gini, Monteforte d'Alpone (Veneto)

Amarone Capitel della Crosara , Montresor, Verona (Veneto)

Verdicchio di Matelica La Monacesca, Civitanova Marche, (Marches)

Aglianico del Vulture Valle del Trono, Basilium, Acerenza (Basilicata)

Primitivo di Manduria Dolce Naturale Terra di Miele, Sava coop (Apulia)

Cirò Riserva Duca Sanfelice, Librandi, Cirò (Calabria)

Montevetrano ★★★ Tiny CAMPANIA producer; superb VDT Montevetrano (CAB S-
MERLOT-AGLIANICO).

Montresor ★★ VERONA wine house: gd LUGANA, BIANCO DI CUSTOZA, VALPOLICELLA.

Morellino di Scansano Tus DOC r ★★ →★★★ 90' 91 93 94 95 96 97 98 Local
SANGIO of the Maremma, the S TUSCAN coast. Cherry-red, lively and tasty
young or matured. Fattorie LE PUPILLE, MORIS FARMS are best.

Moris Farms ★★★ Top producer of MORELLINO DI SCANSANO nr Grosseto; look for
RISERVA and super-concentrated CAB S-Morellino blend Avvoltore.

Moscadello di Montalcino Tus DOC w sw (sp) ★★ DYA Traditional wine of
MONTALCINO, much older than BRUNELLO. Sw white fizz, and sweet to high-
octane PASSITO MOSCATO. Gd producers: BANFI, Capanna-Cencioni, POGGIONE.

Moscato Fruitily fragrant ubiquitous grape for a diverse range of wines:
sparkling or still, light or full-bodied, but always sweet.

Müller-Thurgau Makes wine to be reckoned with in TRENTINO-ALTO ADIGE and
FRIULI, esp TIEFENBRUNNER's Feldmarschall.

Murana, Salvatore ★★ →★★★ Vg MOSCATO di PANTELLERIA and PASSITO di P.

Nebbiolo The best red grape of PIEDMONT. Also the grape of VALTELLINA (Lombardy).

Nebbiolo d'Alba Pie DOC r dr (s/sw sp) ★★ 89 90 93 95 96 97 98 From ALBA (but
not BAROLO, BARBARESCO). Often like a lighter BAROLO but more approachable.
Best from Correggia, MASCARELLO, PRUNOTTO, Ratti, Roagna. See also Roero.

ITALY

Negroamaro Literally 'black bitter'; APULIAN red grape with potential for quality. See Copertino and Salice Salentino.

Nepente di Oliena Sar r ★★ Strong fragrant CANNONAU red; a touch bitter. Good from Arcadu Tonino.

Niedermayr ★★ →★★★ Vg DOC ALTO ADIGE, esp LAGREIN DI GRIEST RISERVA, ST MAGDALENER SCHIAVA, CAB Riserve, PINOT N Riserve.

Nipozzano, Castello di ★★★ FRESCOBALDI estate east of Florence making MONTESODI CHIANTI. The most important outside the CLASSICO zone.

Nittardi ★★ →★★★ Up-and-coming little CHIANTI CLASSICO estate.

Nosiola (Trentino) T-AA DOC w dr sw ★★ DYA Light fruity white from dried Nosiola grapes. Also good VIN SANTO. Best from Pravis: Le Frate.

Nozzole ★★ →★★★ Famous estate, owned by RUFFINO, in the heart of CHIANTI CLASSICO, N of Greve. Also good CAB.

Nuragus di Cagliari Sar DOC w ★ DYA Lively Sardinian white.

Oberto, Andrea ★★ Small La Morra producer: top BAROLO and BARBERA D'ALBA.

Oltrepò Pavese Lom DOC r w dr sw sp ★ →★★★ DOC applicable to 14 wines from Pavia province, mostly named after their grapes. S'times astonishing PINOT N and M-C-SPUMANTE. Top growers incl Agnes, Anteo, Ca' di Frara, Cabanon, Casa Re, Doria, Frecciarossa, Le Fracce, Monsupello, Vercesi del Castellazzo.

Ornellaia Tus ★★★ →★★★★ Newish 130-acre ANTINORI estate nr Bolgheri on the tuscan coast. Watch for VDT Ornellaia (CAB-MERLOT), vg straight VDT Masseto (MERLOT) and vg VDT SAUV Poggio delle Gazze.

Orvieto Umb DOC w dr s/sw ★ →★★★ DYA The classical Umbrian golden white: smooth and substantial; formerly very dull but recently more interesting, esp in sweet versions. Orvieto CLASSICO is better. Only the finest examples (eg BARBERANI, BIGI, DECUGNANO DEI BARBI) age well. But see Castello della Sala.

Pacenti, Siro ★★★ Vg BRUNELLO DI MONTALCINO and ROSSO DI M.

Pagadebit di Romagna E-R DOC w dr s/sw ★ DYA Pleasant traditional 'payer of debts' from around Bertinoro.

Palazzino, Podere Il ★★★ Small estate with admirable CHIANTI CLASSICO and VDT Grosso Sanese. Also VIN SANTO.

Panaretta, Castello della ★★ →★★★ To follow for fine CHIANTI CLASSICO.

Pancrazi, Marchese ★★ →★★★ Estate nr Florence: some of Italy's top PINOT NERO.

Panizzi ★★ →★★★ Makes top VERNACCIA DI SAN GIMIGNANO. Also CHIANTI COLLI Senesi.

Pantelleria See Moscato.

Paradiso, Fattoria ★★ →★★★ Old family estate near Bertinoro (E-R). Gd ALBANA, PAGADEBIT, unique r Barbarossa. Vg SANGIO. Also TREBBIANO di Romagna.

Parrina Tus r w ★★ Grand estate nr the classy resorts of Argentario, S TUSCANY. Light red and white from Maremma coast.

Parusso ★★★ Tiziana and Marco Parusso make top-level BAROLO (eg single-v'yd Bussia, Mariondino), also vg BARBERA D'ALBA and DOLCETTO, etc.

Pasolini Dall'Onda Noble family with estates in CHIANTI COLLI Fiorentini and Romagna, producing traditional-style wines.

Pasqua, Fratelli ★★ Good level producer and bottler of Verona wines: VALPOLICELLA, AMARONE, SOAVE. Also BARDOLINO and RECIOTO.

Passito (pa) Strong sweet wine from grapes dried on the vine or indoors.

Paternoster ★★ →★★★ Top AGLIANICO DEL V producer. Also SPUMANTE di Gualita.

Patriglione ★★★ →★★★★ Concentrated, strong red VDT from NEGROAMARO and MALVASIA Nera grapes. See Taurino.

Pecorari, Pierpaolo ★★★ Vg DOC ISONZO wines; best are CHARD and SAUV.

Peppoli ★★★ Estate owned by ANTINORI producing excellent CHIANTI CLASSICO in a full, round, youthful style.

Per'e Palummo Cam r ★ Appetizing light tannic red from island of ISCHIA.

Perrone, Elio ★★★ Sm estate for top MOSCATO D'ASTIS, BARBERA D'ASTI Pighlin.

Piave Ven DOC r w ★ →★★ (r) **95** 96 97 (w) DYA Flourishing DOC NW of Venice covering 8 wines, 4 red and 4 white, named after their grapes. CAB, MERLOT and RABOSO reds can all age. Good from Molon-Traverso.

Picolit (Colli Orientali del Friuli) F-VG DOC w s/sw sw ★★ →★★★ **94 95** 96 97 Delicate dessert wine; exaggerated reputation. A little like Jurançon. Ages up to 6 yrs, but v overpriced. Best: DORIGO, Dri, LIVIO FELLUGA, Graziano Specogna.

Piedmont (Piemonte) The most important Italian region for top-quality wine. Turin is the capital, ASTI and ALBA the wine centres. See Barbaresco, Barbera, Barolo, Dolcetto, Grignolino, Moscato, etc.

Piemonte Pie DOC r w p (sp) ★ →★★ New all-PIEDMONT blanket-DOC incl BARBERA, BONARDA, BRACHETTO, CORTESE, GRIGNOLINO, CHARD, SPUMANTE, MOSCATO.

Pieropan ★★★ Outstanding SOAVE and RECIOTO: for once deserving its fame esp Soave La Rocca and sweet PASSITO della Rocca.

Pieve di Santa Restituta ★★★ →★★★★ Estate for admirable BRUNELLO DI MONTALCINO, vg ROSSO DI M and red VDT Pian de Cerri. Links with GAJA.

Pigato Lig DOC w ★★ DOC under Riviera Ligure di Ponente. Often out-classes VERMENTINO as Liguria's finest white, with rich texture and structure. Good from: Anfossi, COLLE dei Bardellini, Feipu, Lupi, TERRE ROSSE, Vio.

Pighin, Fratelli ★★ →★★★ One of biggest FRIULI producers. Reliable COLLIO, Goriziano, FRIULI and GRAVE reds and whites.

Pinot Bianco (Pinot Bl) Popular grape in NE for many DOC wines, generally bland and dry. Best from ALTO ADIGE ★★ (top growers: CS St-Michael, LAGEDER, Elena Walch), COLLIO ★★ (vg from Keber, Mangilli, Picech, Princic) and COLLI ORIENTALI ★★ →★★★ (best from Rodaro and VIGNE DAL LEON).

Pinot Grigio (Pinot Gr) Tasty low-acid white grape popular in NE. Best from DOCS ALTO ADIGE (LAGEDER, Kloster Muri-Gries, Schwanburg) and COLLIO (Caccese, SCHIOPETTO). Vg Pinot Grigio VALDADIGE DOC from ARMANI.

Pinot Nero (Pinot Noir) Planted in much of NE Italy. DOC status in ALTO ADIGE (HAAS, SCHRECKBICHL, St-Michael-Eppan coop, Niedrist, HOFSTATTER, coop Girlan, coop Kurtatsch, coop Kaltern, NIEDERMAYR, LAGEDER) and in OLTREPO PAVESE (Vercesi del Castellazzo, Ruiz de Cardenas). Promising trials elsewhere eg TUSCANY (BANFI, FONTODI, AMA, Pancranzi, RUFFINO). Also fine sp from several regions: TRENTINO (Maso Cantanghel, POJER & SANDRI), Lombardy (CA' DEL BOSCO), Umbria (ANTINORI).

Piedmont vintages

1998 Very good whites, excellent reds. The fourth lucky year for Piedmont after four poor ones.

1997 Long, warm and dry autumn, most likely the Barolo vintage of the century; the same for Nebbiolo and Barbera wines. Dolcetto, Moscato and whites: not as good.

1996 Again promising. Quality of Barbera and Nebbiolo is v high: vintage could turn out to be better than '95.

1995 V promising vintage: average quality white and Dolcetto, good Barbera. Some excellent Barolos.

1994 Hot summer; but vintage rains prevented excellence.

1993 Hot summer, good Dolcetto and Barbera, but September rains disrupted Nebbiolo harvest and severe selection was necessary for Barolo and Barbaresco.

1992 Rainly year. Whites good. Nebbiolo wines not so lucky.

Pio Cesare ★★ →★★★ Long-est' PIEDMONT producer. All red, incl BAROLO.

Planeta ★★★ One of the top Sicilian producers. Look for Segreta BIANCO (blend of Greganico, Catarratto, CHARD), Segreta ROSSO (Nero d'Avola-MERLOT blend), also outstanding Chard and CAB.

Podere TUSCAN term for a wine-farm; smaller than a FATTORIA.

Poggio Antico (Montalcino) ★★★ Admirably consistent top-level BRUNELLO, ROSSO and red VDT Altero.

Poggione, Tenuta II ★★★ Perhaps the most reliable estate for BRUNELLO, ROSSO and MOSCADELLO DI MONTALCINO.

Pojer & Sandri ★★★ Top TRENTINO producers: reds and whites, incl SPUMANTE.

Poliziano ★★★ Federico Carletti makes vg VINO NOBILE DI MONT (esp Asinone, Caggiole), VDT Elegia (CAB, SANGIO) and wonderful VIN SANTO. Vg value.

Pomino Tus DOC w (r br) ★★★ r 93 94 95 96 97 98 Fine white, partly CHARD (esp Il Benefizio), and a SANGIO-CAB-MERLOT-PINOT N blend. Also VIN SANTO. Esp from FRESCOBALDI and SELVAPIANA.

Predicato Name for 4 VDT from central TUSCANY, illustrating current rush from tradition. P del Muschio: CHARD and PINOT BL; P del Selvante: SAUV BL; P di Biturica: CAB with SANGIO; P di Cardisco: SANGIO straight. Esp RUFFINO's Cabreo brand.

Primitivo Vg red grape of far S, now identified with California's Zinfandel. Of few producers, Coppi, Sava, Savese and Felline are best. See Manduria.

Primitivo Gioia del Colle Ap DOC r ★★ →★★★ Strong, full-bodied red from nr Bari. Best from Fatalone.

Produttori del Barbaresco ★★ →★★★ Coop and one of DOCG's most reliable producers. Often outstanding single-v'yd wines (Ovello, Rabajà, Pajé, etc).

Prosecco White grape making light v dry sp wine popular in Venice. Next is better.

Prosecco di Conegliano-Valdobbiàdene Ven DOC w s/sw sp (dr) ★★ DYA Slight fruity bouquet, the dry pleasantly bitter, the sw fruity; the sweetest (and most expensive) are known as Superiore di Cartizze. CARPENE-MALVOLTI is best-known producer, now challenged by ADAMI, Bisol, Bortolotti, Bortolin, Canevel, Le Colture, Col Vetoraz, Dea, Gregoletto, Nino Franco, Foss Marai, Ruggeri.

Prunotto, Alfredo ★★★ Very serious ALBA company with top BARBARESCO, BAROLO, NEBBIOLO, etc. Since 1999 Prunotto (now controlled by ANTINORI) also produces BARBERA D'ASTI (look for Costamiole).

Puiatti ★★ V reliable, important producer of COLLIO; also METODO CLASSICO SPUMANTE. Puiatti also owns a FATTORIA in CHIANTI CLASSICO (Casavecchia).

Querciabella ★★★ Up-and-coming CHIANTI CLASSICO estate with excellent red VDT Camartina and an admirable Chianti Classico RISERVA.

Quintarelli, Giuseppe ★★★★ True artisan producer of VALPOLICELLA, RECIOTO and AMARONE, at the top in both quality and price.

Raboso del Piave (now DOC) Ven r ★★ 93 94 95 96 97 Powerful sharp interesting country red; needs age. Look for Molon-Traverso.

Ragose, Le ★★★ Family estate, one of VALPOLICELLA's best. AMARONE and RECIOTO top quality; CAB and Valpolicella vg too.

Ramandolo See Verduzzo Colli Orientali del Friuli.

Ramitello See Di Majo Norante.

Rampolla, Castello dei ★★★ Fine CHIANTI CLASSICO estate at Panzano; also excellent CAB-based VDT Sammarco.

Recioto
Wine made of half-dried grapes. Speciality of Veneto since the days of the Venetian empire; has roots in classical Roman wine, Raeticus. Always sw; s'times sp (drink young). Sw, concentrated, can be kept for a long time.

Recioto di Gambellara Ven DOC w sw (sp s/sw DYA) ★ Mostly half-sparkling and industrial. Best is strong and sweet.

Recioto di Soave Ven DOCG w s/sw (sp) ★★★ 90 91 92 93 94 95 96 97 SOAVE made from selected half-dried grapes: sweet fruity fresh, slightly almondy; high alcohol. Outstanding from ANSELMI, Gini and PIEROPAN.

Recioto della Valpolicella Ven DOC r s/sw (sp) ★★ ⇢★★★ Strong and s'times sp red. Vg from Accordini, ALLEGRINI, BOLLA, Brigaldara, Corte Sant'Alda, DAL FORNO, Degani, Nicolis, Serègo Alighieri, LE RAGOSE, LE SALETTE, SAN RUSTICO, Speri, TEDESCHI.

Recioto della Valpolicella Amarone See Amarone.

Refosco r ★★ ⇢★★★ 93 94 95 96 97' Interesting full-bodied dark tannic red, needs ageing. The same grape as the Mondeuse of Savoie (France)? It tastes like it. Best comes from F-VG DOC COLLI ORIENTALI, GRAVE and CARSO (where known as Terrano). Vg from Bosco Romagno, Villa Belvedere, DORIGO, EDI KANTE, Le Fredis, LIVON, VOLPE PASINI. Often value.

Regaleali ★★★ ⇢★★★★ Perhaps best Sicilian producer owned by noble family of Tasca d'Almerita (between Palermo and Caltanissetta to the SE). Vg VDT r, w and p Regaleali, red Rosso del Conte and CAB. Also v impressive CHARD.

Ribolla (Colli Orientali del Friuli and Collio) F-VG DOC w ★⇢★★ DYA Thin NE white. The best comes from COLLIO. Top estates: La Castellada, GRAVNER, Krapez, Radikon, Venica & Venica, VILLA RUSSIZ.

Ricasoli Famous TUSCAN family, 'inventors' of CHIANTI, whose C CLASSICO is named after their BROLIO estate and castle. Also ORVIETO, VERNACCIA DI SAN GIMIGNANO.

Riecine Tus r (w) ★★ ⇢★★★ First-class CHIANTI CLASSICO estate at Gaiole, created by its English owner, John Dunkley. Also VDT La Gioia SANGIO.

Riesling Formerly used to mean Italian Ries (Ries Italico or Welschriesling). German (Rhine) Ries, now ascendant, is called Ries Renano. Best are DOC ALTO ADIGE ★★ (esp coop Kurtatsch, Ignaz Niedrist, coop La Vis, Elena Walch) and DOC OLTREPO PAVESE LOM ★★ (Brega, Cabanon, Doria, Frecciarossa, coop La Versa), also astonishing from RONCO del Gelso (DOC ISONZO).

Ripasso VALPOLICELLA re-fermented on AMARONE grape skins to make a more complex, longer-lived and fuller wine. First-class is MASI's Campo Fiorin.

Riserva Wine aged for a statutory period, usually in barrels.

Riunite One of the world's largest coop cellars, nr Reggio Emilia, producing huge quantities of LAMBRUSCO and other wines.

Rivera ★★ ⇢★★★ Reliable winemakers at Andria, near Bari (APULIA), with v good red Il Falcone and CASTEL DEL MONTE. Also Vigna al Monte label.

Rivetti, Giorgio (La Spinetta) ★★★ Top MOSCATO d'Asti, vg BARBERA, v interesting VDT Pin (Barbera-NEBBIOLO). Also BARBARESCO.

Riviera del Garda Bresciano Lom DOC w p r (sp) ★★★ Simple, s'times charming cherry-pink CHIARETTO, neutral w from SW Garda. Gd producers: Ca'dei Frati, Comincioli, Costaripa, Monte Cigogna.

Rocca, Bruno ★★★ Young producer with admirable BARBARESCO (Rabajà).

Rocca di Castagnoli ★★⇢★★★ Recent producer of vg CHIANTI CLASSICO.

Rocca delle Macìe ★⇢★★ Large CHIANTI CLASSICO winemaker nr Castellina.

Rocche dei Manzoni, Valentino ★★★ Go-ahead estate at Monforte d'Alba. Excellent BAROLO (best: Vigna Big), BRICCO MANZONI (outstanding NEBBIOLO-BARBERA blend VDT), ALBA wines, CHARD (L'Angelica) and Valentino Brut sp.

Rodano ★★★ Enrico Pozzesi makes mild but typical CHIANTI CLASSICO at Castellina. Both Annata and RISERVA vg.

Roero Pie DOC r ★★ 93 94 95 96 97 98 Evolving former drink-me-quick NEBBIOLO from Roeri hills nr ALBA. Can be delicious. Best: Correggia, Deltetto, Malabaila, Malvirà.

Roero Arneis See Arneis.

Ronco Term for a hillside v'yd in FRIULI-VENEZIA GIULIA.

Ronco del Gnemiz ★★★ Tiny property. Superb COLLI ORIENTALI DOCS, VDT CHARD.

Rosa del Golfo ★★⇢★★★ Mino Calò's ROSATO DEL SALENTO is one of the best. Also vg red VDT Portulano.

Rosato Rosé.

Rosato del Salento Ap p ★★ DYA From nr BRINDISI and v like COPERTINO and SALICE SALENTINO ROSATOS; can be strong, but often really juicy and good. See Copertino, Salice Salentino for producers.

Rossese di Dolceacqua Lig DOC r ★★ DYA Well-known fragrant light red of the Riviera. Good from Giuncheo, Guglielmi, Lupi, Perrino, Terre Bianche.

Rosso Red.

Rosso Cònero Mar DOC r ★★ ·★★★ **90' 92 93 94 95** 96 97' Some of the best MONTEPULCIANO (varietal) reds of Italy, eg GAROFOLI'S Grosso Agontano, Moroder's RC Dorico, UMANI RONCHI's Cumaro and San Lorenzo. Also vg from Conte Dittajuti, E Lanari Leardo, Le Terrazze, Marchetti.

Rosso di Montalcino Tus DOC r ★★ ·★★★ **90 93 94 95** 96 97' 98 DOC for younger wines from BRUNELLO grapes. For growers see Brunello di Montalcino.

Rosso di Montepulciano Tus DOC r ★★ **95' 96** 97' 98 Equivalent of the last for junior VINO NOBILE, but yet to establish a consistent style. For growers see Vino Nobile di M. While Rosso di Montalcino is increasingly expensive, Rosso di Montepulciano stills offers value.

Rosso Piceno Mar DOC r ★★ **90 91 93 95** (96) 97' 98' Stylish Adriatic red. SUPERIORE from classic zone near Ascoli. Best include Bucci, Le Caniette, Cocci Grifoni, Velenosi Ercole, San Giovanni, Saladini Pilastri, Villamagna.

Rubesco ★★ The excellent popular red of LUNGAROTTI; see Torgiano.

Ruchè (also Rouchè or Rouchet) A rare old grape (French origin); fruity, fresh, rich bouqueted red wine (s/sw). Ruchè di Castagnole Monferrato: recent DOC; Piero Bruno best producer. SCARPA'S Rouchet Briccorosa: dr, excellent (★★★).

Ruffino ★ ·★★★ CHIANTI merchant at Pontassieve. RISERVA Ducale Oro and Santedame: top wines. NB new PREDICATO wines (r and w Cabreo), CAB Il Pareto. Also owns estate in MONTEPULCIANO (Ludola Nuova) for DOCG VINO NOBILE DE M.

Rufina ★ ·★★★ Important subregion of CHIANTI in the hills E of Florence. Best wines from Basciano, CASTELLO DI NIPOZZANO (FRESCOBALDI), SELVAPIANA.

Russiz Superiore (Collio) See Felluga, Marco.

Sagrantino di Montefalco See Montefalco.

St-Michael-Eppan Top SUDTIROL coop: look for St-Valentin (★★★), SAUV, vg SPUMANTE, PINOT N, PINOT BIANCO, Gewürz and even vg RIES Renano.

Sala, Castello della ★★ ·★★★ ANTINORI's estate at ORVIETO. Borro is the regular white. Top wine is Cervaro della Sala: CHARD and GRECHETTO aged in oak. Muffato della S is one of Italy's best botrytis wines.

Salice Salentino Ap DOC r ★★ ·★★★ **93 94' 95** 96 97' 98 Resonant but clean and quenching red from NEGROAMARO grapes. RISERVA after 2 years. Top makers: CANDIDO, De Castris, TAURINO, Vallone.

San Felice ★★ ·★★★ Rising star in CHIANTI with fine CLASSICO Poggio ROSSO. Also red VDT Vigorello, PREDICATO di Biturica and BRUNELLO DI MONTALCINO.

San Gimigniano Famous TUSCAN city of towers and its dry white VERNACCIA.

San Giusto a Rentennano One of the best CHIANTI CLASSICO producers (★★★). Delicious but v rare VIN SANTO. Excellent VDT red Percarlo.

San Guido, Tenuta ★★★★ See Sassicaia.

San Polo in Rosso, Castello di ★★★ CHIANTI CLASSICO estate with first-rate red VDT Cetinaia (aged in big casks, not barriques).

Sandrone, Luciano ★★★ Exponent of new-style BAROLO vogue with vg Barolo Cannubi Boschis, DOLCETTO and BARBERA D'ALBA.

Sangiovese (Sangioveto) Principal red grape of Italy. Top performance only in TUSCANY, where its many forms incl CHIANTI, VINO NOBILE, BRUNELLO, MORELLINO, etc. Very popular is S di Romagna (EMILIA-ROMAGNA DOC r ★ ·★★), a pleasant standard red. Vg from PARADISO, Trerè, ZERBINA. Outstanding ★★★ VDTS RONCO dei Cigliegi, R delle Ginestre from CASTELLUCCIO. Sometimes gd from ROSSO PICENO (Marches).

Santa Maddalena (or St-Magdalener) T-AA DOC r ★ →★★★ DYA Typical SCHIAVA AA red, s'times lightish with bitter aftertaste or warm, smooth and fruity esp from: Cantina Sociale St-Magdalena (eg Huck am Bach), Gojer, Brigl (Ihlderhof), Rottensteiner (Premstallerhof), Untermoser, Unterganzner.

Santa Margherita Large Veneto (Portogruaro) merchants: Veneto (Torresella), A-A (Kettmeir), TUSCAN (Lamole di Lamole, Vistarenni), Lombardy (CA' DEL BOSCO).

Saracco, Paolo ★★★ Small estate with top MOSCATO D'ASTI.

Sartarelli ★★ →★★★ One of top VERDICCHIO DEI CASTELLI DI JESI producers, (Tralivio), outstanding, rare Verdicchio VENDEMMIA Tardiva (Contrada Balciana).

Sassicaia Tus r ★★★★ 85' 88' 89 90' 91 92 93 94 95' 96 97' 98 Outstanding pioneer CAB, Italy's best and great wine by any standards, from the Tenuta San Guido of the Incisa family, at Bolgheri nr Livorno. 'Promoted' from SUPER-TUSCAN VDT to DOC BOLGHERI in '94.

Satta, Michele ★★★ Vg DOC BOLGHERI.

Sauvignon Sauvignon Blanc is working v well in the northeast, best from DOCS ALTO ADIGE, COLLIO, COLLI ORIENTALI, ISONZO.

Savuto Cal DOC r p ★★ 93 94 95 96' 97' 98 Fragrant juicy wine from the provinces of Cosenza and Catanzaro. Best producer is Odoardi.

Scarpa ★★ →★★★ Old-fashioned house with BARBERA D'ASTI (La Bogliona), rare ROUCHET (RUCHÈ), vg DOLCETTO, BAROLO, BARBARESCO.

Scavino, Paolo ★★★ Successful modern-style BAROLO producer. Sought-after single-v'yd wines: Bric del Fiasc and Cannubi; also oak-aged BARBERA.

Schiava High-yielding red grape of TRENTINO-ALTO ADIGE with characteristic bitter aftertaste, used for LAGO DI CALDARO, SANTA MADDALENA, etc.

Schiopetto, Mario ★★★ →★★★★ Legendary COLLIO pioneer with brand-new 20,000-case winery; vg DOC SAUV, PINOT GR, TOCAI, VDT blend Bl de Rosis, etc.

Schreckbichl (or Colterenzio CS) ★★ →★★★ No 1 SUDTIROL CANTINA SOCIALE. Admirable ALTO ADIGE CAB S, Gewürz, PINOT N (look for Schwarzhaus RISERVA), CHARD, PINOT BL, PINOT GR, SAUV (look for Lafoa), red VDT Cornelius, etc.

Sciacchetrà See Cinqueterre.

Secco Dry.

Sella & Mosca ★★ →★★★ Major Sardinian growers and merchants at Alghero. Their port-like Anghelu Ruju (★★★) is excellent. Also pleasant white TORBATO and delicious light fruity VERMENTINO Cala Viola (DYA). Also outstanding red Alghero DOC Marchese di Villamarina (CAB).

Selvapiana ★★★ Top CHIANTI RUFINA estate. Best wine is RISERVA Bucerchiale.

Sforzato See Valtellina.

Sizzano Pie DOC r ★★ 90 91' 93 94 95 96' 97' Full-bodied red from Sizzano, (Novara); mostly NEBBIOLO. Ages up to 10 yrs. Esp from: Bianchi, Dessilani.

Soave Ven DOC w ★ →★★★ DYA Famous Veronese white, widely available. Should be fresh with smooth, limpid texture. Standards rising (at last). Soave CLASSICO: better, more restricted. Esp from PIEROPAN; also ANSELMI, La Cappuccina, Gini, GUERRIERI-RIZZARDI, Inama, Portinari, TEDESCHI, Ca' Rugate, Zenato.

Solaia Tus r ★★★★ V fine B'x-style VDT of CAB S and a little SANGIO from ANTINORI; first made in '78. Extraordinarily influential in shaping VDT (and Italian) philosophy.

Solopaca Cam DOC r w ★★ 94 95 96 97 98 Rather sharp red; soft dry white from nr Benevento. Some promise: esp Antica Masseria Venditti.

Sorì Term for a high S, SE or SW oriented v'yd in PIEDMONT.

Spanna See Gattinara.

Spumante Sparkling, as in sw ASTI or many gd dry wines, incl both METODO CLASSICO (best from TRENTINO, A ADIGE, FRANCIACORTA, PIEDMONT, some vg also from FRIULI and Veneto) and tank-made cheapos.

Stravecchio Very old.

Südtirol The local name of German-speaking ALTO ADIGE.

Super-Tuscans Term coined for curious varietal novelties from TUSCANY, usually involving CAB, barriques, and frequently fancy bottles and prices.

Superiore Wine that has undergone more ageing than normal DOC and contains 0.5–1% more alcohol.

Tasca d'Almerita See Regaleali.

Taurasi Cam DOCG r ★★★ 90' 92 93' 94' 94' 95 96 97' 98 The best Campanian red, from MASTROBERARDINO of Avellino. Harsh when young. RISERVA after 4 yrs. Radici (since '86) is Mastroberardino's top estate bottling.

Taurino, Cosimo ★★★ Tip-top producer of Salento-APULIA, vg SALICE SALENTINO, VDT Notarpanoro and PATRIGLIONE ROSSO.

Tedeschi, Fratelli ★★★ V reliable and vg producer of VALPOLICELLA, AMARONE, RECIOTO and SOAVE. Vg Capitel San Rocco red and white VDT.

Terlano T-AA w ★★→★★★ DYA Terlano DOC recently incorporated into ALTO ADIGE. AA Terlano DOC is applicable to 8 varietal whites, esp SAUV. Terlaner in German. Esp from CS Andrian, CS Terlan, LAGEDER.

Teroldego Rotaliano T-AA DOC r p ★★→★★★ 93 94 95 96 97 Attractive blackberry-scented red; slightly bitter aftertaste; can age v well. Esp FORADORI'S. Also gd from CA'VIT, Dorigati, Sebastiani and MEZZACORONA'S RISERVA.

Terre di Franciacorta Lom DOC r w ★★ 94 95 96 97 98 Usually pleasant reds (blends of CAB, BARBERA, NEBBIOLO, MERLOT); quite fruity and balanced whites (CHARD, PINOTS BIANCO, NERO). Best producers: see Franciacorta DOCG.

Terre Rosse ★★★ Distinguished small estate nr Bologna. Its CAB, CHARD, SAUV, PINOT GR, RIES, even Viognier etc, are the best of the region.

Terre da Vino ★→★★★ Association of 27 PIEDMONT coops and private estates incl most local DOCS. Best: BARBERA D'ASTI La Luna e i Falo and GAVI Ca' da Bosio.

Teruzzi & Puthod (Fattoria Ponte a Rondolino) ★★→★★★ Innovative SAN GIMIGNANO producers. Vg VERNACCIA DI SAN G, white VDTS Terre di Tufi, Carmen.

Tiefenbrunner ★★→★★★ Leading grower of some of the very best ALTO ADIGE white and red wines at Schloss Turmhof, Cortaccio (Kurtatsch).

Tignanello Tus r ★★★→★★★★ Pioneer and still leader of the new style of Bordeaux-inspired TUSCAN reds, made by ANTINORI.

Tocai Mild smooth white (no relation of Hungarian Tokay) of NE. DOC also in Ven and Lom (★→★★), but producers are most proud of it in F-VG (esp COLLIO and COLLI ORIENTALI): (★★→★★★). Best producers: BORGO DEL TIGLIO, Keber, Picech, Princic, Raccaro, RONCO del Gelso, RONCO DI GNEMIZ, SCHIOPETTO, Scubla, Specogna, Castello di Spessa, Toros, Venica & Venica, VILLA RUSSIZ, VOLPE PASINI.

Torbato di Alghero Sar w ★★ DYA Good N Sardinian table wine. Leading brand is SELLA & MOSCA.

Torgiano Umb DOC r w p (sp) ★★→★★★ and **Torgiano, Rosso Riserva** Umb DOCG r ★★★ 90 93 94 95 96 97 98 (3 yrs ageing) Top r from nr Perugia, comparable with vg CHIANTI CL. RUBESCO: standard. RISERVA VIGNA Monticchio can be outstanding; keep up to 10 yrs.

Toscana See Tuscany.

Traminer Aromatico T-AA DOC w ★★→★★★ DYA (German: Gewürztraminer) Delicate, aromatic, soft. Best from: CANTINA SOCIALE Girlan/Cornaiano, CS St-Michael, CS SCHRECKBICHL/COLTERENZIO, Hofkellerei, HOFSTATTER, Laimburg, Plattenhof, Stiftskellerei Neustift.

Travaglini ★★★ Very reliable producer of top DOCG GATTINARA.

Trebbiano Principal white grape of TUSCANY, found all over Italy. Ugni Blanc in French. Sadly a waste of good v'yd space, with v rare exceptions.

Trebbiano d'Abruzzo Ab DOC w ★→★★ DYA Gentle, neutral, sl tannic w from round Pescara. VALENTINI is much the best producer (also MONTEPULCIANO D'A).

Trefiano ★★★ One of the best CARMIGNANO DOCG produced by Vittorio Contini Bonacossi on a small AZIENDA at Carmignano.

Trentino T-AA DOC r w dr sw ★→★★★ DOC for as many as 20 different wines, mostly named after their grapes. Best are CHARD, PINOT BL, MARZEMINO, TEROLDEGO. The region's capital is Trento.

Triacca ★★→★★★ Vg producer of VALTELLINA; also owns estates in TUSCANY (CHIANTI CLASSICO: La Madonnina; MONTEPULCIANO: Santavenere. All ★★).

Trinoco, Tenuta di Tus VDT Isolated and exceptional red wine estate (B'x varieties) in Val d'Orcia nr Chiàncino Terme. Early wines jaw-dropping.

Tuscany (Toscana) Italy's central wine region, incl DOCS CHIANTI, MONTALCINO, MONTEPULCIANO etc, regional IGT Toscana and of course 'SUPER TUSCANS'.

Tuscany vintages

1998 Summer was too hot and too dry, followed by autumn rains at harvest time. Some good reds, but none excellent.

1997 Long, dry, warm autumn, early ripening; very concentrated reds, billed to be the vintage of the century The omens are good.

1996 Some autumn rain fell after a fine summer; despite this, grapes ripened quite well (esp those whose growers held out longest before picking). Result: a relatively good vintage for reds.

1995 Much autumn rain, worse even than 1992. Top estates made good wines if they waited for a warm, dry October. Otherwise dull.

1994 Dry summer, showers in September; good to very good wines.

1993 A hot summer followed by October rains; nevertheless, Chianti Classico quite good, Brunello and Vino Nobile di Montepulciano vg.

1992 Promise of a top-quality vintage dispelled for reds by rain. The whites had better luck.

Uberti ★★★ Top producer of DOCG FRANCIACORTA, also vg white TERRE DI F.

Umani Ronchi ★→★★★ Leading Marches merchant; gd quality notably VERDICCHIO (Casal di Serra, Villa Bianchi), ROSSO CONERO (Cumaro, San Lorenzo).

Vajra, Giuseppe Domenico ★★★ Vg consistent BAROLO producer, esp for BARBERA, BAROLO, DOLCETTO LANGHE, etc. Also an interesting (not fizzy) FREISA.

Val di Cornia Tus DOC r p w ★→★★★ New DOC nr Livorno; some good producers: Ambrosini, Tua Rita, Gualdo del Re.

Valcalepio Lom DOC r w ★→★★ From nr Bergamo. Pleasant red; lightly scented fresh white. Good from Bonaldi, Il Calepino and Tenuta CASTELLO.

Valdadige T-AA DOC r w dr s/sw ★→★★ Name for the simple wines of the ADIGE Valley – in German 'Etschtaler'. Best producer: ARMANI.

Valentini, Edoardo ★★★→★★★★ The best traditionalist maker of TREBBIANO and MONTEPULCIANO D'ABRUZZO.

Valgella See Valtellina.

Valle d'Aosta VdA DOC Regional DOC for more than 20 Alpine wines incl Premetta, Fumin, Blanc de Morgex et de La Salle, Chambave, Nus Malvoisie, Arnad Montjovet, Torrette, Donnas, Enfer d'Arvier.

Valle Isarco (Eisacktal) T-AA DOC w ★★ DYA Recently this DOC was incorporated into ALTO ADIGE DOC. AA Valle Isarco DOC is appicable to 7 varietal wines made NE of Bolzano. Gd MULLER-T, Silvaner. Top producers: CS Eisacktaler, Kloster Neustift and Kuenhof.

Vallechiara, Abbazia di ★★→★★★ Young PIEDMONT estate, owned by actress Ornella Muti, with astonishingly good wines, eg DOC DOLCETTO di Ovada and Dolcetto-based VDTS Due Donne and Torre Albarola.

Valpolicella Ven DOC r ★→★★★ (Superiore) 93 94 95 96 97 98 (others) DYA Attractive r from nr VERONA; best young. Recent quality improvement. V best can be conc, complex and merit higher prices. Delicate nutty scent, sl bitter taste, (none true of junk sold in big bottles). CLASSICO more restricted; SUPERIORE has

12% alcohol and 1 yr of age. Gd esp from Accordini, ALLEGRINI, Cecilia Beretta, Bertani, Brunelli, Corte Sant Alda, GUERRIERI-RIZZARDI, LE RAGOSE, LE SALETTE, Speri, TEDESCHI, CANTINA SOCIALE Valpolicella, MASI, Sant' Antonio, Michele Castellani, Zenato. DAL FORNO and QUINTARELLI make the best (★★★). Interesting VDTS on the way to a new Valpolicella style: MASI's Toar and Osar, ALLEGRINI's La Poja (★★★).

Valtellina Lom DOC r ★★ →★★★ 88 89 90 94 **95** 96 97 98 DOC for tannic wines: mainly from Chiavennasca (NEBBIOLO) grapes in Alpine Sondrio province, N Lombardy. Vg SUPERIORE (since 1998 DOCG) from Grumello, Inferno, Sassella, Valgella v'yds. Best from: Conti Sertoli-Salis, Fay, TRIACCA, Nera, Arturo Pelizzatti Perego, Nino Negri, Rainoldi. Sforzato is most concentrated type of Valtellina; similar to AMARONE (Rainoldi's vg).

Vecchio Old.

Vecchio Samperi Si ★★★ MARSALA-like VDT from outstanding estate. The best is barrel-aged 20 years, not unlike amontillado sherry. The owner, Marco De Bartoli, also makes the best DOC Marsalas.

Vendemmia Harvest or vintage.

Venegazzù Ven r w sp ★★ →★★★ Rustic Bordeaux-style red produced from CAB grapes near Treviso. Rich bouquet and soft warm taste. Della Casa and Capo di Stato are best quality. Also makes v fair sparkling.

Verdicchio dei Castelli di Jesi Mar DOC w (sp) ★★ →★★★ DYA Ancient fresh pale w from nr Ancona. Current revivial; result: fruity, well-structured gd value wines. Also CLASSICO. Esp from Bonci-Vallerosa, Brunori, Bucci, Casalfarneto, Cimarelli, Coroncino, GAROFOLI, Lucangeli Aymerich di Laconi, Mancinelli, Sta Barbara, SARTARELLI, UMANI RONCHI, La Vite, Zaccagnini; also FAZI-BATTAGLIA.

Verdicchio di Matelica Mar DOC w (sp) ★★ →★★★ DYA Similar to the last, smaller and less well-known. Esp from Belisario, Bisci, San Biagio, and La Monacesca (outstanding).

Verduno Pie DOC r ★★ (DYA) Pale red with spicy perfume, from Pelaverga grape. Good producers: Alessandria, Castello di Verduno.

Verduzzo (Colli Orientali del Friuli) F-VG DOC w dr s/sw sw ★★ →★★★ Full-bodied w from a native grape. The best sw: called Ramandolo. Top makers: Dario Coos, DORIGO, Giovanni Dri.

Verduzzo (del Piave) Ven DOC w ★ DYA A dull little white wine.

Vermentino Lig w ★★ DYA Best seafood white wine of Italian Riviera: esp from Pietra Ligure and San Remo. DOC is Riviera Ligure di Ponente. See Pigato. Particularly gd from Anfossi, Colle dei Bardellini, Lambruschi, Lupi, Cascina dei Peri.

Vermentino di Gallura Sar DOCG w ★★ →★★★ DYA Soft dry strong white of N Sardinia. Especially from CS di Gallura, CS Del Vermentino, Capichera.

Vernaccia di Oristano Sar DOC w dr (sw fz) ★ →★★★ 71' 80' 85' 86' 87 88 **90'** 91' 92 93' 94' 95' 96' 97' 98 Sardinian speciality, like light sherry, a touch bitter, full-bodied and interesting. SUPERIORE with 15.5% alcohol and 3 yrs of age. Top producer: CONTINI.

Vernaccia di San Gimignano Tus DOCG w ★ →★★ DYA Once Michelangelo's favourite, then ordinary tourist wine. Much recent improvement, now newly DOCG with tougher production laws. Best from FALCHINI, Montenidoli, Palagetto, PANIZZI, Rampa di Fugnano, TERUZZI & PUTHOD, Vagnoni.

Vernatsch German for SCHIAVA.

Verona Capital of the Veneto region (home of VALPOLICELLA, BARDOLINO, SOAVE etc) and seat of Italy's splendid annual April Wine fair 'Vinitaly'.

Verrazzano, Castello di ★★ →★★★ Vg CHIANTI CLASSICO estate near Greve.

Vicchiomaggio CHIANTI CLASSICO estate near Greve.

VIDE An association of better-class Italian producers for marketing their estate wines from many parts of Italy.

Vie di Romans ★★★→★★★★ A young wine genius, Gianfranco Gallo, has built up his father's ISONZO estate to top FRIULI status within a few years. Unforgettable Isonzo CHARD and SAUV; excellent TOCAI and PINOT GR.

Vietti ★★★ Excellent producer of characterful PIEDMONT wines, incl BAROLO and BARBARESCO and BARBERA D'ALBA, at Castiglione Falletto in BAROLO region.

Vigna or vigneto A single vineyard (but unlike elsewhere, higher quality than that for generic DOC is not required in Italy).

Vignalta ★★★ Top producer in COLLI EUGANEI nr Padova (VENETO); vg Colli Euganei CAB RISERVA and VDT MERLOT-Cab 'Gemola'.

Vignamaggio ★★ →★★★ Historic, beautiful, vg CHIANTI CLASSICO estate nr Greve.

Vigne dal Leon ★★★ Vg producer of COLLI ORIENTALI (FRIULI).

Villa Matilde ★★ Top Campania producer: vg FALERNO and white Falanghina.

Villa Russiz ★★★ Impressive white DOC COLLIO Goriziano from Gianni Menotti: eg SAUV (look for 'de la Tour'), PINOT BL, TOCAI, etc.

Vin Santo or Vinsanto, Vin(o) Santo Term for certain strong sweet wines esp in TUSCANY: usually PASSITO. Can be v fine, esp in TUSCANY and TRENTINO.

Vin Santo Toscano Tus w s/sw ★→★★★ Aromatic rich and smooth. Aged in v small barrels called caratelli. Can be as astonishing as expensive, but a gd one is v rare and top producers are always short of it. Best from AVIGNONESI, CAPEZZANA, CORZANO & PATERNO, ISOLE E OLENA, POLIZIANO, SAN GIUSTO A RENTENNANO, SELVAPIANA.

Vino da arrosto 'Wine for roast meat' – ie good robust dry red.

Vino Nobile di Montepulciano Tus DOCG r ★★★ 88' 90 91 93 **94** 95' 96 97' 98 Impressive SANGIO r with bouquet and style, rapidly making its name and fortune. RISERVA after 3 yrs. Best estates incl AVIGNONESI, Bindella, BOSCARELLI, Canneto, LE CASALTE, Casella, Fattoria del Cerro, CONTUCCI, Crociani, Dei, Innocenti, Macchione, Paterno, POLIZIANO, Salcheto, Trerose, Valdipiatta and Vecchia Cantina (look for the RISERVA). So far reasonably priced.

Vino novello Italy's equivalent of France's primeurs (as in Beaujolais).

Vino da tavola (vdt) 'Table wine': intended to be the humblest class of Italian wine, with no specific geographical or other claim to fame. See IGT.

Vintage Tunina F-VG w ★★★ A notable blended white from JERMANN estate.

Vivaldi-Arunda ★★★ Winemaker Josef Reiterer makes top SUDTIROLER sp. Best: Extra Brut RISERVA, Cuvée Marianna.

Viticoltore PLD-Terre Dora di Paolo ★★★ Founded after split of MASTROBERARDINO family estate. Walter M and sons make FIANO and GRECO from 300 acres.

Voerzio, Roberto ★★★ Young BAROLO pace-setter: Brunate is new-style best.

Volpaia, Castello di ★★→★★★ First-class CHIANTI CLASSICO estate at Radda. Elegant, rather light Chianti. VDT r Balifico (CAB); COLTASSALA: all SANGIO.

Volpe Pasini ★★★ Ambitious COLLIO ORIENTALI DEL FRIULI estate, esp for gd SAUV.

VQPRD Often found on the labels of DOC wines to signify Vini di Qualità Prodotti in Regioni Delimitati.

Where the dreams have no end... ★★★ A memorable VDT CHARD from JERMANN.

Zanella, Maurizio Creator of CA' DEL BOSCO. His name is on his top CAB-MERLOT blend, one of Italy's best.

Zardetto ★★ Vg producer of PROSECCO DI CONEGLIANO-VALDOBBIADENE.

Zerbina, Fattoria ★★★ New leader nr Ravenna with best ALBANA DOCG to date (a rich PASSITO called Scacco Matto), good SANGIO and a barrique-aged Sangio-CAB VDT called Marzeno di Marzeno.

Zibibbo Si w sw ★★ Fashionable MOSCATO from island of PANTELLERIA. Gd producer: Murana.

Zonin ★→★★ One of Italy's biggest privately owned estates and wineries, based at GAMBELLARA, with DOC and DOCG VALPOLICELLA, etc. Others are at ASTI and in CHIANTI CLASSICO (Castello di Albola), SAN GIMIGNANO, FRIULI, now in Sicily and throughout Italy. Also at Barboursville, Virginia (USA).

Germany

Heavier shaded areas are the wine growing regions

North Sea

Hamburg

Bremen

Berlin

Hannover

Elbe

Rhine

Weser

SAALE-UNSTRUT
Leipzig

SACHSEN

Dresden

Bonn

AHR MITTELRHEIN

Koblenz

MOSEL-
SAAR-
RUWER

RHEINGAU

Frankfurt

FRANKEN

RHEINHESSEN

Worms

Würzburg

Trier

NAHE

HESSISCHE-
BERGSTRASSE

PFALZ

Nürnberg

Neckar

WURTTEMBERG

Stuttgart

Main

Baden Baden

Danube

BADEN

München

Freiburg

L Bodensee

The following abbreviations
of regional names
are used in the text:

Bad   Baden
Frank   Franken
M-M   Mittelmosel
M-S-R   Mosel-Saar-Ruwer
Na   Nahe
Rhg   Rheingau
Rhh   Rheinhessen
Pfz   Pfalz
Würt   Württemberg

German wines should be enjoying a worldwide boom today. New ideas, easier labelling on many wines, reasonable prices and an unprecedented string of 12 fine vintages are all in their favour. Yet outside Germany they are a hard sell. What is wrong? Pure, penetrating flavours and low-to-moderate alcohol should be ideal for modern tastes. Instead, Germany has everyone confused: there are too many variations on the theme; producers make too many styles. Kabinett, Spätlese and Auslese might all be sweet, dry or in the middle. Their appellations might mean single vineyards, whole communes or entire regions. A clear lead is sorely needed.

This is a pivotal time in the politics of German wine. The much-criticized Wine Law of 1971 is under sustained challenge from the most responsible producers. The VDP, the association of the great majority of top-quality growers, has put its weight behind a long-overdue (though still unofficial) classification of the German vineyards. Most of the best (referred to here as 'First Class') are on steep land whose cultivation demands sacrifice. They are now rightly being described as National Cultural Monuments in the same way as abbeys or castles; an attempt to persuade a chronically hesitant government to recognize and protect their status. At long last a dialogue has begun which could lead to a new law, but progress is deathly slow.

The problem is that, officially, German wines are still only classified according to grape ripeness levels. Most wines (like most from France) need sugar added before fermentation to make up for missing sunshine. But unlike in France, German wine from grapes ripe enough not to need extra sugar is made and sold as a separate product: Qualitätswein mit Prädikat, or QmP. Within this top category, natural sugar content is expressed by traditional terms in ascending order of ripeness: Kabinett, Spätlese, Auslese, Eiswein, Beerenauslese, Trockenbeerenauslese.

QbA (Qualitätswein bestimmter Anbaugebiete), the second level, is for wines that needed additional sugar. The third level, Tafelwein, like Italian vino da tavola, is free of restraints. Officially it is the lowest grade, but impatience with the outdated law can make it the logical resort for innovative producers who set their own high standards.

Though there is much more detail in the laws, this is the gist of the quality grading. It differs completely from other countries' systems in ignoring geographical differences. In theory, all any German vineyard has to do to make the best wine is to grow the ripest grapes – even of inferior varieties – which is patent nonsense.

The law does distinguish between degrees of geographical exactness – but in a way that just leads to confusion. In labelling 'quality' wine growers or merchants are given a choice. They can (and generally do) label their best wines with the name of a single vineyard or Einzellage. Germany has about 2,600 Einzellage names. Obviously, only a relative few are famous enough to help sell the wine. So the 1971 law created a second class of vineyard name: the Grosslage. A Grosslage is a group of Einzellagen of supposedly similar character. Because there are fewer Grosslage names, and far more wine from each, they have the advantage of familiarity – a poor substitute for hard-earned fame. This is a law that must change.

Thirdly, growers or merchants may choose to sell their wine under a Bereich or regional name. To cope with demand for 'Bernkasteler', 'Niersteiner' or 'Johannisberger' these famous names were made legal for large districts. 'Bereich Johannisberg' covers the entire Rheingau: another avenue to consumer disappointment that must be closed.

Leading growers are now simplifying labels to avoid confusion and clutter. Some use the village name only, or indeed sell top wines under a brand name alone, as in Italy. But before German wine can fully recover its rightful place, two additional things are needed: the banning of inferior grapes from top areas, and the development of an official vineyard classification on similar lines to unofficial ones which already exist for the Rheingau, the Nahe and the Mosel. First Class vineyards are named here and mapped in the 4th edition of *The World Atlas of Wine*.

Recent vintages

Mosel-Saar-Ruwer

Mosels (including Saar and Ruwer wines) are so attractive young that, their keeping qualities are not often enough explored, and wines older than about 8 years are unusual. But well-made Riesling wines of Kabinett class gain from at least 5 years in bottle–often much more–Spätlese from 10 to 20, and Auslese and Beerenauslese, anything from 10 to 30 years.

As a rule, in poor years the Saar and Ruwer make sharp lean wines, but in the best years, above all with botrytis, they can surpass the whole world for elegance and thrilling steely 'breed'.

1998   Riesling grapes came through rainy autumn to give astonishingly good results on the Middle Mosel; Saar and Ruwer less lucky with most QbA.

1997   A generous vintage of consistently fruity, elegant wines for the entire region, but there was little botrytis so top Auslese, BA and TBA are rare.

1996   A very variable vintage with fine Spätlese and Auslese from top sites, but only QbA and Tafelwein elsewhere. Many excellent Eisweins.

1995   Excellent vintage, mainly of Spätlese and Auslese of firm structure and long ageing potential. Try to resist drinking too early.

1994   Another v good vintage, mostly QmP with unexceptional QbA and Kabinett, but many Auslese, BA and TBA. Rich fruit and high acidity. Start drinking them.

1993   Small excellent vintage: lots of Auslese/botrytis; nr perfect harmony. Start to drink except top Auslese.

1992   A very large crop. Mostly good QbA, but 30% QmP, some exceptional in the Mittelmosel. Now at their best.

1991   A mixed vintage. Bad frost damage in Saar and Ruwer, many tart QbA wines but also fine Spätlesen. To drink soonish.

1990   Superb vintage, though small. Many QmP wines were the finest for 20 years. Try to resist drinking them all too soon.

1989   Large and often outstanding, with noble rot giving many Auslesen etc. Saar wines best; the Mittelmosel overproduced causing some dilution. Except for top Auslese, ready to drink.

1988   Excellent vintage. Much ripe QmP, esp in Mittelmosel. For long keeping. Lovely now but no hurry.

1985 A modest summer but beautiful autumn. 40% of harvest was QmP.
Riesling vintage from best v'yds, incl Eiswein. Most are ideal now.

1983 The best between '76 and '88; 31% Spätlese; Auslesen few but fine.
Now at their best, but no hurry to drink. Beautiful now.

1979 A patchy vintage after bad winter frost damage. But many excellent
Kabinetts and better. Light but well-balanced wines should be drunk up.

1976 Vg small vintage, with some superlative sweet wines and almost no dry.
Most wines ready; only the best will keep.

1971 Superb, with perfect balance. At its peak – but no hurry for best wines.

Older fine vintages: 69 64 59 53 49 45 37 34 21.

Rheinhessen, Nahe, Pfalz, Rheingau

Even the best wines can be drunk with pleasure when young, but
Kabinett, Spätlese and Auslese Riesling gain enormously in character by
keeping for longer. Rheingau wines tend to be longest-lived, improving
for 15 years or more, but best wines from the Nahe and Pfalz can last as
long. Rheinhessen wines usually mature sooner, and dry Franken and
Baden wines are generally best at 3–6 years.

1998 An excellent vintage of rich, balanced wines in the Pfalz, more variable
further north, but also many good Spätlesen.

1997 Very clean, ripe grapes gave excellent QbA, Kabinett, Spätlese in dry
and classic styles. Rare botrytis means Auslese and higher qualities rare.

1996 An excellent vintage in the Pfalz and the Rheingau with many
fine Spätlesen, but only good in other regions. Some great Eisweins.

1995 Slightly variable, but some excellent Spätlese and Auslese maturing
well – like the 90s. Weak in the Pfalz due to harvest rain.

1994 Good vintage, mostly QmP, with abundant fruit and firm structure.
Some superb Auslese, BA and TBA. No hurry.

1993 A small vintage of v good to excellent quality. Plenty of Spätlese and
Auslese wines, which are just beginning to reach their peak.

1992 Very large vintage, would have been great but for October cold and rain.
A third QmP wines of rich stylish quality. Most drinking well now.

1991 A good middling vintage, though light soils in Pfalz suffered from
drought. Some fine wines are emerging. Beginning to drink well.

1990 Small but exceptionally fine. High percentage of QmP will keep well
beyond 2000.

1989 Summer storms reduced crop in Rheingau. Vg quality elsewhere,
up to Auslese level. Maturing more quickly than expected. Soonish.

1988 Not quite so outstanding as the Mosel, but similarly good as '83.
Drinking well now.

1986 Well-balanced Rieslings, mostly QbA but some Kabinett and Spätlese.
Good botrytis-affected wines in Pfalz. Drink soonish.

1985 Sadly small crops, of variable quality, esp Riesling. Average 65% QmP.
Best in the Pfalz. Enjoy soon

1983 Vg Rieslings, esp in the Rheingau and central Nahe. Generally about
half QbA, but plenty of Spätlesen, now excellent to drink.

1976 The richest vintage since '21 in places. Very few dry wines. Generally
mature now.

1971 A superlative vintage, now at its peak.

Older fine vintages: 69 67 64 59 53 49 45 37 34 21.

> **NB On the German vintage notation**
>
> Vintage notes after entries in the German section are given in a different form from those elsewhere, to show the style of the vintage as well as its quality. Three styles are indicated:
>
> Bold type (eg **93**) indicates classic, super-ripe vintages with a high proportion of natural (QmP) wines, including Spätlese and Auslese.
>
> Normal type (eg 92) indicates 'normal' successful vintages with plenty of good wine but no great preponderance of sweeter wines.
>
> Italic type (eg *91*) indicates cool vintages with generally poor ripeness but a fair proportion of reasonably successful wines, tending to be over-acidic. Few or no QmP wines, but correspondingly more selection in the QbA category. Such wines sometimes mature more favourably than expected.
>
> Where no mention is made the vintage is generally not recommended, or most of its wines have passed maturity.

Achkarren Bad w (r) ★★ Village on the KAISERSTUHL, known esp for RULANDER. First Class vineyard: Schlossberg. Good wines: DR HEGER and coop.

Ahr Ahr r ★→★★ **88 89 90** 91 *92* **93 94 95** 96 **97** 98 Traditional specialized red wine area, south of Bonn. Light, pale SPATBURGUNDER, esp from Adeneuer, Deutzerhof, Kreuzberg, MEYER-NAKEL, Nelles, Stodden.

Amtliche Prüfungsnummer See Prüfungsnummer.

Anheuser, Paul Well-known NAHE grower (★★) at BAD KREUZNACH.

APNr Abbreviation of AMTLICHE PRUFUNGSNUMMER.

Assmannshausen Rhg r ★→★★★ **76 85 88 89 90** *91 92* **93** 94 **95 96 97** 98 RHEINGAU village known for its usually pale, light reds, incl AUSLESEN. First Class v'yd: Höllenberg. Grosslagen: Steil and Burgweg. Growers incl AUGUST KESSELER, Robert König, Hotel Krone, Von Mumm, and the STATE DOMAIN.

Auslese Wines from selective harvest of super-ripe grapes, the best affected by 'noble rot' (Edelfäule) and correspondingly unctuous in flavour. Dry Auslesen are usually too alcoholic for me.

Avelsbach M-S-R (Ruwer) w ★★★ **71** 75 76 83 85 88 **89 90** *91 92* **93** 94 95 96 **97** *98* Village nr TRIER. At (rare) best, lovely delicate wines. Esp BISCHOFLICHE WEINGUTER, STAATLICHE WEINBAUDOMANE (see Staatsweingut). Grosslage: Römerlay.

Ayl M-S-R (Saar) w ★★★ **71 75 76 83** 85 88 **89 90** *91 92* **93** 94 95 96 **97** *98* One of the best villages of the SAAR. First Class v'yd: Kupp. Grosslage: SCHARZBERG. Growers incl BISCHOFLICHE WEINGUTER, Lauer, DR WAGNER.

Bacchus Modern, perfumed, even kitsch, grape. Best for KABINETT wines.

Bacharach ★→★★★ Principal wine town of MITTELRHEIN just downstream from RHEINGAU. Now part of the new BEREICH LORELEY. Racy, austere RIESLINGS, some v fine. First Class v'yards: Hahn, Posten, Wolfshöhle. Growers include FRITZ BASTIAN, TONI JOST, Randolph Kauer, Helmut Mades, RATZENBERGER.

Bad Dürkheim Pfz w (r) ★★→★★★ 76 83 85 86 88 **89 90** *91 92* **93** 94 95 **96 97** 98 Main town of MITTELHAARDT, with the world's biggest barrel (so big it serves as a tavern) and an ancient September wine festival, the 'Würstmarkt'. First Class v'yds: Michelsberg, Spielberg. Grosslagen: Feuerberg, Hochmess, Schenkenböhl. Growers: Kurt Darting, Fitz-Ritter, Karst, Karl Schäfer.

Bad Kreuznach Nahe w ★★→★★★ 75 76 79 **83 85** 86 88 **89 90** *91* 92 **93** 94 95 96 **97** 98 Agreeable spa town of many fine vineyards. First Class: Brückes, Kahlenberg and Krötenpfuhl. Grosslage: Kronenberg. Growers include ANHEUSER, Finkenauer, VON PLETTENBERG.

Baden Huge SW area of scattered v'yds but rapidly growing reputation. Style is substantial, generally dry but supple, good for meal-times. Fine Pinots, SPATBURGUNDER, RIES, GEWURZ. Best areas: KAISERSTUHL, ORTENAU.

Badische Bergstrasse/Kraichgau (Bereich) Widespread district of N BADEN. WEISSBURGUNDER and RULANDER make best wines.

Badischer Winzerkeller Germany's (and Europe's) biggest coop, at BREISACH; 25,000 members with 12,000 acres, producing almost half of BADEN's wine: dependably unambitious.

German producers redrawing the map

Seeing that Germany's politicians are too busy trying to knock the taxation and pension systems into shape, in order to do anything about the flawed wine law, some of the nation's leading estates have taken the initiative themselves and put proposals on the table. As part of this endeavour, several of them have printed documents which prove that Germany already had a classification system a century and more ago.

Reinhard Löwenstein of the **Heymann-Löwenstein** estate in Winningen, on the Lower or 'Terrace Mosel' was the first of them, in 1995 reprinting a vineyard classification map of his region originally published by the Prussian government in 1897. It proved that this little-known area of the Mosel-Saar-Ruwer has many vineyard sites with excellent potential. Since the beginning of the 1990s, Löwenstein dry and dessert Rieslings from the First Class Röttgen and Uhlen sites of Winnigen add liquid proof.

Armin Diel of **Schlossgut Diel** of Burg Layen on the Nahe followed in 1996 with a reprinting of the Prussian government's vineyard classification map of his vineyard from 1901. Diel is a journalist as well as a winegrower, and has actively promoted the cause of vineyard classification in his books and articles as well as in his elegant Rieslings from the three First Class sites of Dorsheim: Burgberg, Goldloch and Pittermännchen.

Christian von Guradze of the famous **Dr Bürklin-Wolf** estate of the Wachenheim area of the Pfalz went a step further. He employed Beate Hoffmann and Gisela Winterling to assemble a map from the hitherto unpublished vineyard classification for the Mittelhaardt undertaken by the Bavarian Royal Surveyors office in 1832. Since 1994, von Guradze has implemented a radical internal classification of the wines at Dr Bürklin-Wolf, and the estate's dry Rieslings from the First Class vineyards of Forst, Ruppertsberg and Wachenheim have become some of the most sought-after wines in the region.

Badisches Frankenland See Tauberfranken.

Barriques Small new oak casks arrived tentatively in Germany 15 yrs ago. Results are mixed. The oak smell can add substance to the white Pinots, SPATBURGUNDER and LEMBERGER. It usually spoils RIESLING.

Bassermann-Jordan ★★★ 104-acre MITTELHAARDT family estate with many of the best v'yds in DEIDESHEIM, FORST, RUPPERTSBERG, etc. New winemaker Ulrich Mell has put this historic estate back on top since superb 1996 vintage.

Bastian, Weingut Fritz ★★ 12-acre BACHARACH estate. Racy, austere RIESLINGS with MOSEL-like delicacy, best from the First Class Posten v'yd.

Becker, J B ★★→★★★ Dedicated family estate and brokerage house at WALLUF. 30 acres in ELTVILLE, MARTINSTHAL, Walluf. Specialist in dry RIES.

Beerenauslese Luscious, honeyed sw wine from exceptionally ripe individual berries (sugar and flavour usually concentrated by 'noble rot'). Rare, expensive.

Bensheim See Hessische Bergstrasse.

Bercher ★★★ KAISERSTUHL estate; 40 acres of white and red Pinots at Burkheim. Excellent Chardonnay etc and some of Germany's best SPATBURGUNDER.

Warning notice: Bereich
District within an Anbaugebiet (region). The word on a label should be treated as a flashing red light. Do not buy. See Introduction and under Bereich names, eg Bernkastel (Bereich).

Bernkastel M-M w ★→★★★★ 71 75 76 79 83 85 86 88 89 90 91 92 93 94 95 96 97 98 Top wine town of the MITTELMOSEL; the epitome of RIES. Great First Class v'yd: Doctor, 8 acres; First Class v'yds: Graben, Lay. Grosslagen: Badstube, Kurfürstlay. Top growers incl HERIBERT KERPEN, DR LOOSEN, Markus Molitor, DR PAULY-BERGWEILER, J J PRUM, Studert-Prüm, THANISCH, WEGELER-DEINHARD.

Bernkastel (Bereich) Wide area of deplorably dim quality and superficial flowery character. Mostly MULLER-T. Includes all the MITTELMOSEL. Avoid.

Biffar, Josef ★★★ Rising star DEIDESHEIM estate. 40 acres (also WACHENHEIM) of RIES. Intense classic wines.

Bingen Rhh w ★→★★★ 76 83 85 88 89 90 91 92 93 94 95 96 97 98 Rhine/NAHE town; fine v'yds: First Class: Scharlachberg. Grosslage: St-Rochuskapelle.

Bingen (Bereich) District name for west RHEINHESSEN.

Bischöfliche Weingüter ★★ Famous M-S-R estate at TRIER, a union of the cathedral properties with 2 other famous charities, the Bischöfliches Priesterseminar and the Bischöfliches Konvikt. 240 acres of top v'yds, esp in SAAR and RUWER. Recent vintages returning to former fine form.

Blue Nun Famous but fading brand of LIEBFRAUMILCH from SICHEL.

Bocksbeutel Flask-shaped bottle used for FRANKEN wines.

Bodenheim Rhh w ★★ Village nr NIERSTEIN with full earthy wines. Top grower: Kühling-Gillot.

Bodensee (Bereich) Idyllic district of S BADEN, on Lake Constance.

Boppard ★→★★★ 76 83 88 90 91 92 93 94 95 96 97 98 Important wine town of MITTELRHEIN where quality is rapidly improving. Best sites all belong to amphitheatre of vines called Boppader Hamm. Growers: Heinrich Müller, August Perll, Weingart.

Braun, Weingut Heinrich ★★ 60-acre NIERSTEIN estate. Dry and sweet RIES of variable quality from First Class v'yds of Nierstein, esp Pettenthal.

Brauneberg M-M w ★★★★ 71 75 76 83 85 86 87 88 89 90 91 92 93 94 95 96 97 98 Top M-S-R village nr BERNKASTEL (750 acres), unbroken tradition for excellent full-flavoured RIES – Grand Cru if anything on the Mosel is. Great First Class v'yd: Juffer-Sonnenuhr. First Class v'yd is Juffer. Grosslage: Kurfürstlay. Growers: Bastgen, FRITZ HAAG, WILLI HAAG, Paulinshof, M F RICHTER.

Breisach Frontier town on Rhine nr KAISERSTUHL. Seat of the largest German coop, the BADISCHER WINZERKELLER.

Breisgau (Bereich) Little-known BADEN district. Good reds and pink WEISSHERBST.

Breuer, Weingut Georg ★★★ Family estate of 36 acres in RUDESHEIM, a CHARTA leader: 6 acres of Berg Schlossberg, also 12.5-acre monopole RAUENTHALER Nonnenberg. Superb quality in recent years, esp full-bodied elegant dry RIES. New ideas incl sparkling Ries-Pinot Bl-Pinot Gr blend.

Buhl, Reichsrat von ★★★ Historic PFALZ family estate, returning to historic form as of '94. 160 acres (DEIDESHEIM, FORST, RUPPERTSBERG...). Leased by Japanese firm.

Bundesweinprämierung The German State Wine Award, organized by DLG (see below): gives great (grosse), silver or bronze medallion labels.

Bürgerspital zum Heiligen Geist ★★★ Ancient charitable WURZBURG estate. 275 acres: W'bg, RANDERSACKER etc. Rich dry wines, esp SILVANER, RIES; can be vg.

Bürklin-Wolf, Dr ★★★ ·★★★★ Famous PFALZ family estate. 222 acres in FORST, DEIDESHEIM, RUPPERTSBERG and WACHENHEIM. Excellent quality since 94 vintage shows the estate is back on top form.

Castell'sches Fürstlich Domänenamt ★★ ·★★★ Historic 142-acre princely estate in STEIGERWALD. SILVANER, RIESLANER, also SEKT. Noble dessert wines.

Chardonnay Can now be grown legally throughout Germany but total planted area remains less than 300 acres.

Charta Organization of top RHEINGAU estates making forceful dry RIES to far higher standards than dismally permissive laws require.

Christoffel, J J ★★★ Tiny domain in ERDEN, URZIG. Polished elegant RIES.

Clevner (or Klevner) Synonym in WURTTEMBERG for Blauer Frühburgunder red grape, supposedly a mutation of Pinot N or Italian Chiavenna (early-ripening black Pinot). Confusingly also ORTENAU (BADEN) synonym for TRAMINER.

Crusius ★★ ·★★★★ 30-acre family estate at TRAISEN, NAHE. Vivid RIES from Bastei, Rotenfels and SCHLOSSBOCKELHEIM. Top wines age v well. Also good SEKT and freshly fruity SPATBURGUNDER dry rosé.

Deidesheim Pfz w (r) ★★ ·★★★★ 71 76 83 85 86 **88 89 90** 91 **92** 93 94 95 **96** 97 **98** Biggest top-quality village of the PFALZ (1,000 acres). Richly flavoured lively wines. Also SEKT. First Class v'yds: Grainhübel, Hohenmorgen, Kalkofen, Kieselberg, Langenmorgen, Leinhöhle. Grosslagen: Mariengarten, Hofstück. Esp BASSERMANN-JORDAN, BIFFAR, V BUHL, BURKLIN-WOLF, DEINHARD, WOLF.

Deinhard ★ In '97 the Wegeler family sold the 200-year-old merchant house and SEKT producer Deinhard to sparkling-wine giant Henkell-Söhnlein of Schierstein on the Rhine. But the splendid Deinhard estates remain in family ownership (see Wegeler-Deinhard).

Deinhard, Dr ★★ Fine 62-acre family estate: some of DEIDESHEIM's best v'yds.

Deutscher Tafelwein Officially the term for v humble German wines. Now confusingly the flag of convenience for some costly novelties as well (eg BARRIQUE wines). As in Italy, the law will have to change.

Deutsches Weinsiegel A quality seal (ie neck label) for wines which have passed a statutory tasting test. Seals are: yellow for dry, green for medium-dry, red for medium-sweet. Means little; proves nothing.

Diel, Schlossgut ★★★ Fashionable 30-acre NAHE estate; made its name by ageing RULANDER and WEISSBURGUNDER in French BARRIQUES. But its traditional RIES is among finest Nahe wines. Stunning AUSLESE and EISWEIN.

DLG (Deutsche Landwirtschaftgesellschaft) The German Agricultural Society at Frankfurt. Awards national medals for quality – generously.

Dom German for 'cathedral'. Wines from the famous TRIER cathedral properties have 'Dom' before the v'yd name.

Domäne German for 'domain' or 'estate'. Sometimes used alone to mean the 'State domain' (STAATSWEINGUT or Staatliche Weinbaudomane).

Dönnhoff, Weingut Hermann ★★★★ 23-acre leading NAHE estate with exceptionally fine RIES from NIEDERHAUSEN, Oberhausen etc.

Dornfelder New red grape making deep-coloured everyday wines in the PFALZ.

Durbach Baden w (r) ★★ ·★★★ 76 83 85 88 **89 90** 91 92 **93 94** 95 **96 97** 98 Village with 775 acres of v'yds incl a handful of First Class sites. Top growers: A LAIBLE, H Männle, SCHLOSS STAUFENBERG, WOLFF METTERNICH. Choose their KLINGELBERGERS (RIES) and CLEVNERS (TRAMINER). Grosslage: Fürsteneck.

Edel Means 'noble'. Edelfäule means 'noble rot': see page 100.

To decipher codes, please refer to 'Key to symbols' on front flap of jacket, or to 'How to use this book' on page 6.

Egon Müller zu Scharzhof ★★★★ Top saar estate of 32 acres at wiltingen. Its rich and racy scharzhofberger ries in auslesen vintages is among the world's greatest wines; best are given gold capsules. 93s, 95s and 97s are sublime, honeyed, immortal. Le Gallais is a second estate in wiltinger Braune Kupp.

Eiswein Dessert wine made from frozen grapes with the ice (ie water content) discarded, thus v concentrated in flavour, acidity and sugar – of beerenauslese ripeness or more. Alcohol content can be as low as 5.5%. V expensive. S'times made as late as Jan/Feb of following year.

Eitelsbach M-S-R (Ruwer) w ★★ ·★★★★ 71 75 76 83 85 88 89 90 *91* 92 **93** 94 **95** *96* **97** 98 ruwer village now part of trier, incl superb Great First Class karthauserhofberg vineyard site. Grosslage: Römerlay.

Elbe Important wine-river of eastern Germany. See Sachsen.

Elbling Traditional grape widely grown on upper mosel. Can be sharp and tasteless; but capable of real freshness and vitality in the best conditions (eg at Nittel or schloss thorn in the obermosel).

Eltville Rhg w ★★ ·★★★ 71 75 76 83 85 86 88 **89 90** *91* 92 **93** 94 **95** 96 **97** 98 Major wine town with cellars of rheingau state domain, fischer and von simmern estates. First Class v'yd: Sonnenberg. Grosslage: Steinmächer.

Enkirch M-M w ★★ ·★★★ 71 76 83 85 88 89 90 91 **93** 94 95 *96* **97** 98 Little-known mittelmosel village, often overlooked but with lovely light tasty wine. Grosslage: Schwarzlay. Best v'yds: Batterieberg, Zeppwingert.

Erbach Rhg w ★★★ ·★★★★ 71 76 83 85 86 88 **89 90** *91* **92 93** 94 **95** 96 **97** 98 Top rhg area: big, perfumed age-worthy wines, incl superb First Class v'yds Hohenrain, marcobrunn, Siegelsberg, Steinmorgen, Schlossberg. Major estates: schloss reinhartshausen, schonborn. Also becker, knyphausen, von simmern etc.

Erben Word meaning 'heirs', often used on old-established estate labels.

Erden M-M w ★★★ 71 75 76 83 85 86 *87* 88 89 90 *91* 92 **93** 94 **95** 96 **97** 98 Village between Urzig and Kröv: noble full-flavoured vigorous wine (different in style from nearby bernkastel and wehlen but equally long-living). Great First Class v'yds: Prälat, Treppchen. Grosslage: Schwarzlay. Growers incl bischofliche weinguter, j j christoffel, dr loosen, Meulen-hoff, Mönchhof, Peter Nicolay.

Erstes Gewächs Literally translates as 'first growth'. A new classification for the top vineyards of the rheingau. Has applied since '92 vintage, but not yet legally recognized.

Erzeugerabfüllung Bottled by producer. Being replaced by 'gutsabfullung'.

Escherndorf Frank w ★★ ·★★★ 76 83 **88** *89* **90** *91* **92 93** 94 95 96 97 98 Important wine town near wurzburg. Similar tasty dry wine. Top v'yd: First Class Lump. Grosslage: Kirchberg. Growers incl juliusspital, Egon Schäffer, Horst Sauer.

Eser, Weingut August ★★ 20-acre rheingau estate at oestrich. V'yds also in hallgarten, rauenthal (esp Gehrn, Rothenberg), winkel. Variable wines.

Filzen M-S-R (Saar) w ★★ ·★★★ **76 83 85** 88 **89 90** *91* 92 **93** 94 **95** 96 **97** 98 Small saar village nr wiltingen. First Class v'yd: Pulchen. Grower to note: Piedmont.

Fischer Erben, Weingut ★★★ 18-acre rheingau estate at eltville with high traditional standards. Long-lived, classic wines.

Forschungsanstalt See Hessische Forschungsanstalt.

Forst Pfz w ★★ ·★★★★ 71 76 83 85 86 88 **89 90** 91 92 **93** 94 95 *96* **98** mittelhaardt village with 500 acres of Germany's best v'yds. Ripe, richly fragrant, full-bodied but subtle wines. First Class vineyards: Jesuitengarten, Kirchenstück, Pechstein, Ungeheuer. Grosslagen: Mariengarten, Schnepfenflug. Top growers incl bassermann-jordan, burklin-wolf, deinhard, g mosbacher, Eugen Müller, Spindler, Werlé, j l wolf.

Franken Franconia Region of excellent distinctive dry wines, esp SILVANER, always bottled in round-bellied flasks (BOCKSBEUTEL). The centre is WURZBURG. Bereich names: MAINDREIECK, STEIGERWALD. Top producers: BURGERSPITAL, CASTELL, Fürst, JULIUSSPITAL, LOWENSTEIN, WIRSCHING, etc.

Freiburg Baden w (r) ★ →★★ DYA Wine centre in BREISGAU, N of MARKGRAFLERLAND. Good GUTEDEL.

Germany's quality levels

The official range of qualities in ascending order are as follows:

1 Deutscher Tafelwein: sweetish light wine of no special character. (Unofficially, can be very special.)

2 Landwein: dryish Tafelwein with some regional style.

3 Qualitätswein: dry or sweetish wine with sugar added before fermentation to increase its strength, but tested for quality and with distinct local and grape character.

4 Kabinett: dry or dryish natural (unsugared) wine of distinct personality and distinguishing lightness. Can be very fine.

5 Spätlese: stronger, often sweeter than Kabinett. Full-bodied. The trend today is towards drier or even completely dry Spätlese.

6 Auslese: sweeter, sometimes stronger than Spätlese, often with honey-like flavours, intense and long. Occasionally dry and weighty.

7 Beerenauslese: v sweet and usually strong, intense; can be superb.

8 Eiswein: (Beeren- or Trockenbeerenauslese) concentrated, sharpish and very sweet. Can be v fine or too extreme, unharmonious.

9 Trockenbeerenauslese: intensely sweet and aromatic; alcohol slight. Extraordinary and everlasting.

Friedrich-Wilhelm Gymnasium ★★★ Important 82-acre charitable estate based in TRIER with v'yds in BERNKASTEL, GRAACH, OCKFEN, TRITTENHEIM, ZELTINGEN etc, all M-S-R. Since '95 much improved after poor patch.

Fuhrmann See Pfeffingen.

Fürst Rudolf ★★★ Small estate in Bürgstadt making some of the best wines in FRANKEN, particularly Burgundian SPATBURGUNDER and oak-aged WEISSBURGUNDER.

Gallais Le See Egon Müller.

Geisenheim Rhg w ★★ →★★★ 71 76 83 85 86 88 89 90 91 92 93 94 95 96 97 98 Village famous for Germany's best-known wine school and vg aromatic wines. First Class v'yds: Kläuserweg, Rothenberg. Grosslagen: Burgweg, Erntebringer. Top growers: JOHANNISHOF, SCHLOSS SCHONBORN, WEGELER-DEINHARD, VON ZWIERLEIN.

Gemeinde A commune or parish.

Gewürztraminer (or Traminer) 'Spicy' grape, speciality of Alsace, also giving some impressive wines in Germany, esp in PFALZ, BADEN and WURTTEMBERG.

Gimmeldingen Pfz w ★★ 76 83 85 87 88 89 90 91 92 93 94 95 96 97 98 Village just S of MITTELHAARDT. At best, rich, succulent wines. Grosslage: Meerspinne. Growers incl: Christmann, MULLER-CATOIR.

Graach M-M w ★★★ 71 75 76 83 85 86 88 89 90 91 92 93 94 95 96 97 98 Small village between BERNKASTEL and WEHLEN. First Class v'yds: Domprobst, Himmelreich, Josephshofer. Grosslage: Münzlay. Many top growers, eg: VON KESSELSTATT, DR LOOSEN, J J PRUM, WILLI SCHAEFER, SELBACH-OSTER, WEINS-PRUM.

Grans-Fassian ★★ Fine 25-acre MOSEL estate at Leiwen. V'yds there and in TRITTENHEIM.

Remember that vintage information for German wines is given in a different form from the ready/not ready distinction applying to other countries. Read the explanation at the top of page 136.

Grauburgunder Synonym of RULANDER or Pinot Gris.

Grosser Ring Group of top (VDP) MOSEL-SAAR-RUWER estates, whose annual September auction regularly sets world-record prices.

Grosslage See Introduction, pages 133–134.

Gunderloch ★★★★ 30-acre NACKENHEIM estate making some of the finest RIES on the entire Rhine. The undisputed number one in RHEINHESSEN. Recently purchased well-known Balbach estate in NIERSTEIN.

Guntrum, Louis ★★ Large (67-acre) family estate in NIERSTEIN, OPPENHEIM etc. Good SILVANERS and GEWURZTRAMINER as well as RIESLING.

Gutedel German word for the Chasselas grape, used in S BADEN.

Gutsabfüllung Estate-bottled. A new term limited to qualified estates.

Gutsverwaltung Estate administration.

Haag, Weingut Fritz ★★★★ 12-acre top estate in BRAUNEBERG run by Wilhelm Haag, president of GROSSER RING. MOSEL RIES of crystalline purity and racy brilliance for long ageing. Haag's son runs the Schloss LIESER estate.

Haag, Weingut Willi ★★ 7-acre BRAUNEBERG estate. Full 'old-style' RIES. Some fine AUSLESE. Improving quality since '95.

Haart, Reinhold ★★★ The best estate in PIESPORT, and growing rapidly in repute. Refined aromatic wines, capable of long ageing.

Halbtrocken Medium-dry (literally 'semi-dry'). Containing fewer than 18 but more than 9 grams per litre unfermented sugar. Popular category of wine intended for meal-times, usually better balanced than TROCKEN.

Hallgarten Rhg w ★★→★★★ **71 76 83 85** 88 **89 90** 91 **92 93** 94 **95 96** 97 98 Small wine town behind HATTENHEIM. Robust full-bodied wines, seldom seen. Dominated by coops (unusual for RHEINGAU). NB Weingut Fred Prinz.

Hattenheim Rhg w ★★→★★★★ **71 75 76 83 85** 88 **89 90** 91 **92 93** 94 **95 96** 97 98 Superlative 500-acre wine town. First Class v'yds are Engelmannsberg, Mannberg, Pfaffenberg, Nussbrunnen, Wisselbrunnen and most famously STEINBERG (ORTSTEIL). Grosslage: Deutelsberg. MARCOBRUNN: on ERBACH boundary. Estates incl KNYPHAUSEN, RESS, SCHLOSS SCHONBORN, VON SIMMERN, STATE DOMAIN etc.

Henkell See Deinhard.

Heger, Dr ★★★ Leading estate of BADEN with excellent dry WEISSBURGUNDER, GRAUBURGUNDER and impressive oak-aged SPATBURGUNDER reds.

Heilbronn Würt w r ★→★★ **88 89 90** 92 **93** 94 95 **96 97** Wine town with many small growers and a good coop. Best wines are RIES and LEMBERGERS. Seat of DLG competition. Top growers: Amalienhof, Drautz-Able, Heinrich.

Hessen, Prinz von ★★→★★★ Famous 75-acre estate in JOHANNISBERG, KIEDRICH and WINKEL. Rapidly improving quality since '95 vintage.

Hessische Bergstrasse w ★★→★★★ **76 88** 89 90 91 **92 93** 94 95 96 **97** 98 Smallest wine region in western Germany (1,000 acres), N of Heidelberg. Pleasant RIES from STATE DOMAIN v'yds at BENSHEIM, Bergstrasser Coop, Heppenheim and Stadt Bensheim.

Hessische Forschungsanstalt für Wein-Obst & Gartenbau Famous wine school and research establishment at GEISENHEIM, RHEINGAU. Good wines incl reds. The name on the label is Forschungsanstalt.

Heyl zu Herrnsheim ★★★ Leading 72-acre NIERSTEIN estate, 60% RIES. Since fine '96 vintage owned by Ahr family. Wines of classical elegance.

Heymann-Löwenstein ★★★ Young estate in Lower or 'Terrace Mosel' with most consistent dry RIES in MOSEL-SAAR-RUWER and some remarkable AUSLESE, TBA.

Hochgewächs Supposedly superior level of QBA RIES, esp in MOSEL-SAAR-RUWER.

Hochheim Rhg w ★★→★★★★ **71 75 76** 79 **83 85** 86 **88 89 90** 91 **92 93** 94 95 **96 98** 600-acre wine town 15 miles E of main RHEINGAU area, once thought of as best on Rhine. Similar fine wines with an earthy intensity and fragrance of their own. First Class v'yds: Domdechaney,

Hölle, Kirchenstück, Königin Viktoria Berg (12-acre monopoly of Hupfeld of OESTRICH). Grosslage: Daubhaus. Growers incl Hupfeld, FRANZ KUNSTLER, SCHLOSS SCHONBORN, STAATSWEINGUT, WERNER.

Hock Traditional English term for Rhine wine, derived from HOCHHEIM.

Hoensbroech, Weingut Reichsgraf zu ★★★ Top KRAICHGAU estate. 37 acres. Superb dr WEISSBURGUNDER, GRAUBURGUNDER, SILVANER, eg Michelfelder Himmelberg.

Hohenlohe-Oehringen, Weingut Fürst zu ★★ Noble 47-acre estate in Oehringen and WURTTEMBERG. Substantial dry RIES and powerful reds from SPATBURGUNDER and LEMBERGER grapes.

Hövel, Weingut von ★★★ Very fine SAAR estate at OBERMOSEL (Hütte is 12-acre monopoly) and in SCHARZHOFBERG. Superb wines since '93.

Huber, Bernard ★★★ Rising star of Breisgau area of BADEN with powerful oak-aged SPATBURGUNDER reds and Burgundian-style WEISSBURGUNDER, CHARDONNAY.

Huxelrebe Modern aromatic grape variety, best for dessert wines.

Ihringen Bad r w ★ ·★★★ **86** 87 88 **89 90** 91 92 **93** 94 95 **96 97 98** One of the best villages of the KAISERSTUHL, BADEN. Proud of its SPATBURGUNDER red, WEISSHERBST and GRAUBURGUNDER. Top growers: DR HEGER, Stigler.

Ilbesheim Pfz w ★ ·★★ **89 90** 91 92 **93** 94 95 **96 97** 98 Base of vast growers' coop of SUDLICHE WEINSTRASSE 'Deutsches Weintor'. See also Schweigen.

Ingelheim Rhh r w ★★ 89 **90** 91 92 **93** 94 95 96 **97** 98 Town opposite RHEINGAU historically known for its SPATBURGUNDER. Top v'yds are Horn, Pares, Sonnenberg and Steinacker.

Iphofen Frank w ★★ ·★★★ 76 79 83 85 *87* 88 *89 90 91* 92 **93** 94 95 *96 97* 98 Village nr WURZBURG. Superb First Class v'yds: Julius-Echter-Berg, Kalb. Grosslage: Burgweg. Growers: JULIUSSPITAL, Ruck, WIRSCHING.

Jahrgang Year – as in 'vintage'.

Johannisberg Rhg w ★★ ·★★★★ **71** 75 **76 83 85** 86 *87* 88 **89 90** 91 92 **93** 94 **95 96 97** 98 260-acre classic RHEINGAU village with superlative subtle RIES. First Class v'yds: Hölle, Klaus, SCHLOSS JOHANNISBERG. Grosslage: Erntebringer. Top growers: JOHANNISHOF, SCHLOSS JOHANNISBERG.

Johannisberg (Bereich) District name for the entire RHEINGAU. Avoid.

Johannishof ★★★ JOHANNISBERG family estate, aka HH Eser. 45 acres. RIESLINGS that justify the great Johannisberg name. Since '96 also RUDESHEIM wines.

Johner, Karl-Heinz ★★★ Small BADEN estate at Bischoffingen, in the front line for new-look SPATBURGUNDER and oak-aged WEISSBURGUNDER.

Josephshofer First Class v'yd at GRAACH, the sole property of VON KESSELSTATT.

Jost, Toni ★★★ Perhaps the top estate of the MITTELRHEIN. 25 acres, mainly RIES, in BACHARACH and also in the RHEINGAU.

Juliusspital ★★★ ·★★★★ Ancient WURZBURG religious charity with 374 acres of top FRANKEN v'yds and many top wines. Look for its dry SILVANERS and RIES.

Kabinett The term for the lightest category of natural, unsugared (QMP) wines. Low in alcohol (RIES averages 7–9%) but capable of sublime finesse. Drink young or with several yrs' age.

Kaiserstuhl (Bereich) One of the top BADEN districts, with notably warm climate and volcanic soil. Villages incl ACHKARREN, IHRINGEN. Grosslage: Vulkanfelsen.

Kallfelz, Albert Useful producer of light MOSELS at ZELL and Merl.

Kallstadt Pfz w (r) ★★ ·★★★ **76 83 85** 86 88 **89 90** 91 92 **93** 94 **95 96** 97 98 Village of N MITTELHAARDT. Often underrated fine rich wines. First Class v'yd: Saumagen. Grosslages: Feuerberg, Kobnert. Growers incl Henninger, KOEHLER-RUPRECHT, Schüster.

Kammerpreismünze See Landespreismünze.

Kanzem M-S-R (Saar) w ★★★ **71** 75 **76 83 88 89 90** 91 92 **93** 94 **95** 96 97 *98* Small neighbour of WILTINGEN. First Class v'yd: Altenberg. Grosslage: SCHARZBERG. Growers incl Othegraven, Reverchon. Best is J P Reinert.

Karlsmühle ★★★ Small estate with Lorenshofer monopoly site in RUWER making classic Ruwer RIES, also wines from First Class Kasel v'yds sold under Patheiger label.

Karthäuserhofberg ★★★★ Top RUWER estate of 46 acres at Eitelsbach. Easily recognized by bottles with only a neck-label. Since 1993 estate has been back on top form. Also good TROCKEN wines.

Kasel M-S-R (Ruwer) w ★★ ·★★★ **71 75 76 83 85** 86 **88 89 90** 91 92 **93** 94 **95** 96 **97** 98 Stunning flowery Römerlay wines. First Class v'yds: Kehrnagel, Nies'chen. Top growers: KARLSMUHLE, VON KESSELSTATT, WEGELER-DEINHARD.

Keller Wine cellar. **Kellerei** Winery.

Kerner Modern aromatic grape variety, earlier-ripening than RIES, of fair quality but without Riesling's inbuilt grace and harmony.

Kerpen, Weingut Heribert ★★ Tiny estate in BERNKASTEL, GRAACH, WEHLEN.

Kesseler, Weingut August ★★ 35-acre estate making the best SPATBURGUNDER reds in ASSMANNSHAUSEN. Also good off-dry RIES.

Kesselstatt, von ★★★ The biggest private MOSEL estate, 600 yrs old. Now belonging to Reh family. Some 150 acres in GRAACH, KASEL, PIESPORT, WILTINGEN etc, producing aromatic, generously fruity MOSELS. Consistent high quality, magnificent wines from JOSEPHSHOFER monopoly v'yd.

Kesten M-M w ★ ·★★★ **71 75 76 83 85** 86 88 89 90 91 **92 93** 94 **95** 96 **97** 98 Neighbour of BRAUNEBERG. Best wines (from Paulinshofberg v'yd) similar. Grosslage: Kurfürstlay. Top growers: Bastgen, Paulinshof.

Kiedrich Rhg w ★★ ·★★★★ **71 76 83 85** 88 89 **90** 91 **92 93** 94 **95 96 97** 98 Neighbour of RAUENTHAL; almost as splendid and high-flavoured. First Class v'yds: Gräfenberg, Wasseros. Grosslage: Heiligenstock. Growers incl FISCHER, KNYPHAUSEN. R WEIL now top estate.

Klingelberger ORTENAU (BADEN) term for RIESLING, esp at DURBACH.

Kloster Eberbach Glorious 12th-C Cistercian Abbey in HATTENHEIM forest. Monks planted STEINBERG, Germany's Clos de Vougeot. Now STATE DOMAIN-owned; HQ of German Wine Academy.

Klüsserath M-M w ★·★★★ **76 83 85 88 90** 91 92 **93** 94 **95** 96 97 98 Little-known MOSEL village whose winegrowers have joined forces to classify its top site, Brüderschaft. Growers: Bernhard Kirsten, FRIEDRICH-WILHELM-GYMNASIUM, Regnery.

Knyphausen, Weingut Freiherr zu ★★★ Noble 50-acre estate on former Cistercian land (see Kloster Eberbach) in ELTVILLE, ERBACH, HATTENHEIM, KIEDRICH and MARCOBRUNN. Classic RHEINGAU wines, many dry.

Koehler-Ruprecht ★★★★ Highly rated estate (22-acre) going from strength to strength; top KALLSTADT grower. V traditional winemaking; v long-lived, memorable dry RIES from K Saumagen. Since '91 outstanding Pinot N.

Kohl, Helmut Also a small producer of gd dry SEKT at Bauenheim, PFALZ.

Königin Viktoria Berg See Hochheim.

Kraichgau Small BADEN region S of Heidelberg. Top grower: HOENSBROECH.

Kröv M-M w ★·★★★ **88 89 90** 91 92 **93** 94 95 96 97 98 Popular tourist resort famous for its Grosslage name: Nacktarsch, or 'bare bottom'. Be very careful.

Künstler, Franz ★★★·★★★★ HOCHHEIM estate recently expanded to 50 acres by purchase of well-known Aschrott estate. Superb dry RIES, esp from First Class H Hölle and Kirchenstück, also excellent AUSLESE.

Laible, Weingut Andreas ★★ 10-acre DURBACH estate. Fine sw and dr RIES, SCHEUREBE, GEWURZ (First Class Plauelrain v'yd). 'Klingelberger' can be utter joy.

Landespreismünze Prizes for quality at state, rather than national, level.

Landwein A category of better-quality TAFELWEIN (the grapes must be slightly riper) from 20 designated regions. It must be TROCKEN OR HALBTROCKEN. Similar in intention to France's vin de pays but without the buzz.

Leitz, J ★★★ Fine little RUDESHEIM family estate for elegant dry RIES. A rising star.

Lemberger Red grape variety imported from Austria – where it is known as Blaufränkisch. Deep-coloured, tannic wines; can be excellent. Or rosé.

Liebfrauenstift 26-acre v'yd in city of Worms; origin of 'LIEBFRAUMILCH'.

Liebfraumilch
Much abused name, accounting for 50% of all German wine exports – to the detriment of Germany's better products. Legally defined as a QBA 'of pleasant character' from RHEINHESSEN, PFALZ, NAHE or RHEINGAU, of a blend with at least 51% RIESLING, SILVANER, KERNER or MULLER-T. Most is mild, semi-sweet wine from Rheinhessen and the Pfalz. Rules now say it must have more than 18 grams per litre unfermented sugar. S'times v cheap and of inferior quality, depending on brand or shipper. Its definition makes a mockery of the legal term 'Quality Wine'.

Lieser M-M w ★★ 71 76 83 85 86 **88 89 90** 91 92 **93** 94 **95** 96 **97** 98 Little-known neighbour of BERNKASTEL. Lighter wines. First Class v'yd: Niederberg-Helden. Grosslage: Kurfürstlay. Top grower: Schloss Lieser.

Lingenfelder, Weingut ★★ Small, innovative Grosskarlbach (PFALZ) estate: good dry and sweet SCHEUREBE, full-bodied RIES, etc.

Loewen, Carl ★★★ Top grower of Leiwen on MOSEL making ravishing AUSLESE from town's First Class Laurentiuslay site and superb EISWEIN.

Loosen, Weingut Dr ★★★★ Dynamic 24-acre St-Johannishof estate in BERNKASTEL, ERDEN, GRAACH, URZIG, WEHLEN. Deep intense RIESLINGS from old vines in great First Class v'yds. Superlative quality since '90.

Lorch Rhg w (r) ★→★★ 71 76 83 85 88 **89 90** 91 92 **93** 94 **95** 96 **97** 98 At extreme W of RHEINGAU. Some fine light MITTELRHEIN-like RIESLING. Best grower: von Kanitz.

Loreley (Bereich) New BEREICH name for RHEINBURGENGAU and BACHARACH.

Löwenstein, Fürst ★★★ Top FRANKEN estate. 66 acres. Intense savoury Sylvaners from Homberger Kallmuth, one of Germany's most dramatic slopes. 45-acre H'GARTEN estate long rented by SCHLOSS VOLLRADS, independent again since '97.

Maindreieck (Bereich) District name for central FRANKEN, incl WURZBURG.

Marcobrunn Historic RHEINGAU v'yd; one of Germany's v best. See Erbach.

Markgräflerland (Bereich) District S of FREIBURG, BADEN. Typical GUTEDEL wine can be delicious refreshment when drunk v young, but best wines are the -BURGUNDERS: WEISS-, GRAU- and SPAT-. Also SEKT.

Maximin Grünhaus M-S-R (Ruwer) w ★★★★ 71 75 76 79 **83** 85 86 87 **88 89 90** 91 **92 93** 94 **95** 96 **97** 98 Supreme RUWER estate of 80 acres at Mertesdorf. Wines of firm elegance and great subtlety to mature 20 yrs+.

Meyer-Näkel, Weingut ★★ (internationally) ★★★★ (Germany) 15-acre AHR estate. Fine SPATBURGUNDERS in Dernau and Bad Neuenahr exemplify modern oak-aged German reds.

Mittelhaardt The north-central and best part of the PFALZ, incl DEIDESHEIM, FORST, RUPPERTSBERG, WACHENHEIM, largely planted with RIESLING.

Mittelhaardt-Deutsche Weinstrasse (Bereich) District name for the northern and central parts of the PFALZ.

Mittelmosel The central and best part of the MOSEL, incl BERNKASTEL, PIESPORT, WEHLEN, etc. Its top sites are (or should be) entirely RIESLING.

Mittelrhein Northern Rhine area of domestic importance (and great beauty), incl BACHARACH and BOPPARD. Some attractive steely RIESLING.

Morio-Muskat Stridently aromatic grape variety now on the decline.

Mosbacher, Weingut ★★★ Fine 23-acre estate for some of best dry and sweet RIES of FORST. Three stars on label indicate superior Reserve bottlings.

GERMANY

Mosel The TAFELWEIN name of the area. All quality wines from the Mosel must be labelled MOSEL-SAAR-RUWER. (Moselle is the French – and English – spelling.)

Mosel-Saar-Ruwer (M-S-R) 31,000-acre QUALITATSWEIN region between TRIER and Koblenz; incl MITTELMOSEL, RUWER and SAAR. The natural home of RIESLING.

Moselland, Winzergenossenschaft Huge M-S-R coop, at BERNKASTEL, incl Saar-Winzerverein at WILTINGEN. Its 5,200 members produce 25% of M-S-R wines (incl classic method SEKT), but little above average.

Müller zu Scharzhof, Egon See Egon Müller.

Müller-Catoir, Weingut ★★★★ Outstanding 40-acre NEUSTADT estate. Very aromatic powerful wines (RIESLING, SCHEUREBE, RIESLANER, GEWURZTRAMINER, WEISSBURGUNDER, GRAUBURGUNDER and MUSKATELLER). Consistent quality and good value; dry/sweet equally impressive.

Müller-Thurgau Fruity early ripening, usually low-acid grape; most common in PFALZ, RHEINHESSEN, NAHE, BADEN and FRANKEN; increasingly planted in all areas, incl MOSEL. Should be banned from all top v'yds by law.

Münster Nahe w ★ ·★★★ 71 75 76 83 85 88 **89 90** 91 92 **93** 94 95 **96 97** 98 Best N NAHE village; fine delicate wines. First Class v'yds: Dautenpflänzer, Kapellenberg, Pittersberg. Grosslage: Schlosskapelle. Top growers: Kruger-Rumpf, STATE DOMAIN.

Muskateller Ancient aromatic white grape with crisp acidity. A rarity in the PFALZ, BADEN and WURTTEMBERG, where it is mostly made dry.

Nackenheim Rhh w ★ ·★★★★ 76 83 **88 89 90** 91 **92 93** 94 95 **96 97 98** NIERSTEIN neighbour also with top Rhine terroir; similar best wines (esp 1st-class Rothenberg). Grosslagen: Spiegelberg, Gutes Domtal. Top grower: GUNDERLOCH.

Nahe Tributary of the Rhine and high-quality wine region. Balanced, fresh, clean but full-bodied, even minerally wines; RIES best. BEREICH: NAHETAL.

Nahetal (Bereich) BEREICH name for amalgamated BAD KREUZNACH and SCHLOSS-BOCKELHEIM districts.

Neckar The river with many of WURTTEMBERG's finest v'yds, mainly between Stuttgart and Heilbronn.

Neckerauer, Weingut Klaus ★★ Interesting, out-of-the-way 40-acre estate at Weissenheim-am-Sand, on sandy N PFALZ soil. Unpredictable.

Neef M-S-R w ★★ 71 76 83 **89 90** 91 92 **93** 94 95 96 **97** 98 Village of lower MOSEL with one fine v'yd: Frauenberg.

Neipperg, Graf von ★★★ Noble 70-acre estate in Schwaigern, WURTTEMBERG: elegant dry RIES and TRAMINER, and trad-style reds, esp from LEMBERGER.

Neumagen-Dhron M-M w ★★ Neighbour of PIESPORT: fine but sadly neglected.

Neustadt Central town of PFALZ with a famous wine school. Top growers: MULLER-CATOIR, Weegmüller.

Niederhausen Nahe w ★★ ·★★★★ 71 75 76 83 85 86 87 88 **89 90** 91 **93** 94 **95** 96 **97 98** Neighbour of SCHLOSSBOCKELHEIM. Graceful powerful wines. First Class v'yds incl Felsensteyer, Hermannsberg, Hermannshöhle. Grosslage: Burgweg. Esp from CRUSIUS, DONNHOFF, Hehner-Kilz, STATE DOMAIN.

Nierstein Rhh w ★ ·★★★★ 71 75 76 83 85 86 87 **88 89 90** 91 **92 93** 94 95 **96** 97 98 Famous but treacherous village name. 1,300 acres. Superb First-Class v'yds: Brüdersberg, Glöck, Heiligenbaum, Hipping, Oelberg, Orbel, Pettenthal. Grosslagen: Auflangen, Rehbach, Spiegelberg. Ripe aromatic elegant wines. Beware Grosslage Gutes Domtal: a supermarket deception. Try GUNDERLOCH, GUNTRUM, HEYL ZU HERRNSHEIM, ST-ANTONY, G A Schneider, Strub, Wehrheim.

Nierstein (Bereich) Large E RHEINHESSEN district of ordinary quality.

To decipher codes, please refer to 'Key to symbols' on front flap of jacket, or to 'How to use this book' on page 6.

Nierstein Winzergenossenschaft The leading NIERSTEIN coop, with above-average standards. (Formerly Rheinfront.)

Nobling New white grape: light fresh wine in BADEN, esp MARKGRAFLERLAND.

Norheim Nahe w ★ →★★★ 71 76 79 **83 85** 86 87 88 **89 90 91 92 93** 94 95 96 **97 98** Neighbour of NIEDERHAUSEN. First Class v'yds: Dellchen, Kafels, Kirschheck. Grosslage: Burgweg. Growers: DONNHOFF, CRUSIUS, Mathern.

Oberemmel M-S-R (Saar) w ★★ →★★★ 71 75 76 **83 85** 86 88 **89 90** 91 92 **93 94 95** 96 97 98 Next village to WILTINGEN. V fine wines from First Class v'yd Hütte etc. Grosslage: SCHARZBERG. Top growers: VON HOVEL, VON KESSELSTATT.

Obermosel (Bereich) District name for the upper MOSEL above TRIER. Generally uninspiring wines from the ELBLING grape, unless v young.

Ockfen M-S-R (Saar) w ★★ →★★★ 71 75 76 **83 85** 86 87 **88 89 90** 91 92 93 94 **95** 96 **97** 98 Superb fragrant austere wines. 1st-class v'yd: Bockstein. Grosslage: SCHARZBERG. Growers: DR FISCHER, Jordan & Jordan, WAGNER, ZILLIKEN.

Oechsle Scale for sugar content of grape juice (see page 272).

Oestrich Rhg w ★★ →★★★ 71 75 76 **83 85** 86 **88 89 90** 91 92 93 94 95 96 97 98 Big village; variable but some splendid RIES AUSLESE. 1st-class v'yds: Doosberg, Lenchen. Grosslage: Gottesthal. Top growers: AUGUST ESER, WEGELER-DEINHARD.

Offene weine Wine by the glass: the way to order it in wine villages.

Oppenheim Rhh w ★ →★★★ 76 **83 85** 86 **88 89 90** 91 **92 93** 94 95 96 **97** 98 Town S of NIERSTEIN; spectacular 13th-C church. 1st-class Herrenberg and Sackträger v'yds: top wines. Grosslagen: Guldenmorgen (★), Krötenbrunnen. Growers incl GUNTRUM, C Koch, Kühling-Gillot. None of these, though, are presently at full potential.

Ortenau (Bereich) District just S of Baden-Baden. Good KLINGELBERGER (RIES), SPATBURGUNDER and RULANDER. Top village: DURBACH.

Ortsteil Independent part of a community allowed to use its estate v'yd name without the village name, eg SCHLOSS JOHANNISBERG, STEINBERG.

Palatinate English for PFALZ.

Pauly-Bergweiler, Dr ★★ Fine 27-acre BERNKASTEL estate. V'yds there and in WEHLEN etc. Peter Nicolay wines from URZIG and ERDEN are usually best.

Perlwein Semi-sparkling wine.

Pfalz 56,000-acre v'yd region S of RHEINHESSEN (see Mittelhaardt and Südliche Weinstrasse). Warm climate: grapes ripen fully. The classics are rich wines, with TROCKEN and HALBTROCKEN increasingly fashionable and well made. Biggest RIES area after M-S-R. Formerly known as Rheinpfalz.

Pfeffingen, Weingut ★★★ Messrs Fuhrmann and Eymael make very good RIES and SCHEUREBE on 26 acres of UNGSTEIN.

Piesport M-M w ★ →★★★★ 71 75 76 **83 85** 86 **88 89 90** 91 **92 93** 94 **95** 96 **97** 98 Tiny village with famous vine amphitheatre: at best glorious rich aromatic RIES. Great First Class v'yds: Goldtröpfchen and Domherr. Treppchen far inferior. Grosslage: Michelsberg (mainly MULLER-T; avoid). Esp R HAART, Kurt Hain, KESSELSTATT, Reuscher-Haart, Weller-Lehnert.

Plettenberg, von ★★ →★★★ 100-acre estate at BAD KREUZNACH. Mixed quality.

Portugieser Second-rate red-wine grape now often used for WEISSHERBST.

Prädikat Special attributes or qualities. See QmP.

Prüfungsnummer The official identifying test-number of a quality wine.

Prüm, J J ★★★★ Superlative and legendary 34-acre MOSEL estate in BERNKASTEL, GRAACH, WEHLEN, ZELTINGEN. Delicate but long-lived wines, esp in Wehlener SONNENUHR: 81 KABINETT is *still* young.

Qualitätswein bestimmter Anbaugebiete (QbA) The middle quality of German wine, with sugar added before fermentation (as in French 'chaptalisation'), but controlled as to areas, grapes, etc.

Qualitätswein mit Prädikat (QmP) Top category, for all wines ripe enough to be unsugared (KABINETT TO TROCKENBEERENAUSLESE). See pages 133 and 141.

Randersacker Frank w ★★·★★★ 76 83 86 87 **88** 89 **90** 91 92 **93** 94 **95** 96 **97** 98 Leading village for distinctive dry wine. First Class v'yds: Marsberg, Pfülben, Sonnenstuhl. Grosslage: Ewig Leben. Growers incl BURGERSPITAL, Göbel, STAATLICHER HOFKELLER, JULIUSSPITAL, Robert Schmitt, Schmitt's Kinder.

Ratzenberger, Jochen ★★ 17-acre estate making racy dry and off-dry RIES in BACHARACH; best from First Class Posten and Steeger St-Jost v'yds.

Rauenthal Rhg w ★★★·★★★★ 71 75 76 83 85 86 *87* 88 **89** 90 *91* 92 93 94 95 96 97 Supreme village: spicy complex wine. First Class v'yds: Baiken, Gehrn, Nonnenberg, Rothenberg, Wülfen. Grosslage: Steinmächer. Top grower: BREUER. Others incl BECKER, ESER, S REINHARTSHAUSEN, S SCHONBORN, VON SIMMERN, STATE DOMAIN.

Rebholz ★★★ Top SUDLICHE WEINSTRASSE grower. Many varieties on 25 acres.

Ress, Balthasar ★★ R'GAU estate (74 good acres), cellars in HATTENHEIM. Also runs SCHLOSS REICHARTSHAUSEN. Variable wines; original artists' labels.

Restsüsse Unfermented grape sugar remaining in (or in cheap wines added to) wine to give it sweetness. TROCKEN wines have v little, if any.

Rheinburgengau (Bereich) District name for MITTELRHEIN v'yds around the Rhine Gorge. Wines with 'steely' acidity needing time to mature.

Rheingau Best v'yd region of Rhine, W of Wiesbaden. 7,000 acres. Classic substantial but subtle RIES, yet on the whole recently eclipsed by brilliance elsewhere. BEREICH name for whole region: JOHANNISBERG.

Rheinhessen Vast region (61,000 acres of v'yds) between Mainz and Worms, bordered by River NAHE, mostly second-rate, but incl top RIESLINGS from NACKENHEIM, NIERSTEIN, OPPENHEIM, etc.

Rheinhessen Silvaner (RS) New uniform label for dry wines from SILVANER – designed to give a modern quality image to the region.

Rheinpfalz See Pfalz.

Rhodt SUDLICHE WEINSTRASSE village: esp Rietburg coop; agreeable fruity wines.

Richter, Weingut Max Ferd ★★★ Top 37-acre MITTELMOSEL family estate, based at Mülheim. Fine barrel-aged RIES from: BRAUNEBERG (Juffer-SONNENUHR), GRAACH, Mülheim (Helenenkloster), WEHLEN (Sonnenuhr) usually models.

Rieslaner Cross between SILVANER and RIES; makes fine AUSLESEN in FRANKEN, where most is grown. Also superb from MULLER-CATOIR.

Riesling The best German grape: fine, fragrant, fruity, long-lived. Only CHARDONNAY can compete as the world's best white grape.

Rosewein Rosé wine made from red grapes fermented without their skins.

Rotwein Red wine.

Rüdesheim Rhg w ★★·★★★★ 71 75 76 79 *81* 82 **83** 84 **85** 86 87 88 **89** **90** 91 **92 93** 94 95 **96 97** 98 Rhine resort with excellent v'yds; the three best called Rüdesheimer Berg–. Full-bodied wines, fine-flavoured, often remarkable in 'off' years. Grosslage: Burgweg. Most top RHEINGAU estates own some Rüdesheim v'yds. Best growers: G BREUER, JOHANNISHOF, August Kesseler, J LEITZ, SCHLOSS SCHONBORN, STATE DOMAIN.

Rüdesheimer Rosengarten RUDESHEIM is also the name of a NAHE village near BAD KREUZNACH. Do not be misled by the ubiquitous blend going by this name. It has nothing to do with RHEINGAU Rüdesheim. Avoid.

Ruländer Pinot Gris: grape giving soft full-bodied wine, alias (as dry wine) GRAUBURGUNDER. Best in BADEN and southern PFALZ.

Ruppertsberg Pfz w ★★·★★★ 83 85 86 88 89 **90** 91 92 **93** 94 95 **96 97** 98 Southern village of MITTELHAARDT. First Class v'yds incl Hoheburg, Linsenbusch, Nussbien, Reiterpfad, Spiess. Grosslage: Hofstück. Growers incl BASSERMANN-JORDAN, BIFFAR, VON BUHL, BURKLIN-WOLF, DEINHARD.

Ruwer Tributary of MOSEL nr TRIER. V fine delicate but highly aromatic and well-structured wines. Villages incl EITELSBACH, KASEL, MERTESDORF.

Saale-Unstrut Region in former E Germany, 1,000 acres around confluence of these two rivers at Naumburg, nr Leipzig. Terraced v'yds of WEISSBURGUNDER, SILVANER, RIESLING, GEWÜRZ etc and red PORTUGIESER have Cistercian origins. Quality leader: Lützkendorf.

Saar Hill-lined tributary of MOSEL S of RUWER. The most brilliant austere 'steely' RIES of all. Villages incl AYL, OCKFEN, Saarburg, SERRIG, WILTINGEN (SCHARZHOFBERG). Grosslage: SCHARZBERG. Many fine estates.

Saar-Ruwer (Bereich) District covering these 2 regions.

Sachsen Former E-German region (750 acres) in ELBE Valley around Dresden and Meissen. MULLER-T dominant, but WEISSBURGUNDER, GRAUBURGUNDER, TRAMINER, RIES give dry wines with real character. Best growers: SCHLOSS PROSCHWITZ, Vincenz Richter, Klaus Seifert, Klaus Zimmerling.

St-Antony, Weingut ★★★ Excellent 50-acre estate. Rich, intense dry and off-dry RIES from First Class v'yds of NIERSTEIN.

St-Ursula Well-known merchants at BINGEN.

Salm, Prinz zu Owner of SCHLOSS WALLHAUSEN in NAHE and Villa Sachsen in RHEINHESSEN. President of VDP.

Salwey, Weingut ★★ Leading BADEN estate at Oberrotweil, esp for RIESLING, WEISSBURGUNDER and RULANDER.

Samtrot Red WURTTEMBERG grape. Makes Germany's closest shot at Beaujolais.

Schaefer, Willi ★★★ The finest grower of GRAACH (but only 5 acres).

Scharzberg Grosslage name of WILTINGEN and neighbours.

Scharzhofberg M-S-R (Saar) w ★★★★ 71 75 76 83 85 86 **88 89 90** 91 92 **93** 94 95 96 **97** 98 Superlative 67-acre SAAR v'yd: austerely beautiful wines, the perfection of RIESLING, best in AUSLESEN. Do not confuse with the previous entry. Top estates: BISCHOFLICHE WEINGUTER, EGON MULLER, VON HOVEL, VON KESSELSTATT.

Schaumwein Sparkling wine.

Scheurebe Aromatic grape of high quality (and RIESLING parentage), esp used in PFALZ. Excellent for botrytis wine (BA, TBA).

Schillerwein Light red or rosé QBA; speciality of WURTTEMBERG (only).

Schloss Johannisberg Rhg w ★★★ 76 79 **83** 85 86 87 **88 89 90** 91 92 93 94 95 **96** 97 98 Famous R'GAU estate of 86 acres owned by Princess Metternich and the Oetker family. The original Rhine 'first growth'. Wines incl fine SPATLESE, KABINETT TROCKEN. Since '96 there has been a dramatic return to top form.

Schloss Lieser ★★★ Small estate run by Thomas Haag, from FRITZ HAAG estate, making pure, racy RIESLINGS from underrated v'yds of Lieser.

Schloss Proschwitz ★★ Resurrected princely estate at Meissen, leading former E Germany in quality, esp with dry WEISSBURGUNDER.

Schloss Reichartshausen 10-acre HATTENHEIM v'yd run by RESS.

Schloss Reinhartshausen ★★★ Fine 175-acre estate in ERBACH, HATTENHEIM, KIEDRICH, etc. Changed hands in '88. Model RHEINGAU RIESLING. The mansion beside the Rhine is now a luxury hotel.

Schloss Saarstein ★★★ SERRIG estate of 25 acres with consistently fine RIES.

Schloss Schönborn ★★★ One of biggest RHEINGAU estates, based at HATTENHEIM. Full-flavoured wines, variable, at best excellent. Also vg SEKT.

Schloss Staufenberg ★★ 69-acre DURBACH estate. KLINGELBERGER is best wine.

Schloss Thorn Ancient OBERMOSEL estate, remarkable ELBLING, RIES and castle.

Schloss Vollrads Rhg w ★★★ 71 76 **83** 85 86 **88 89** 90 91 92 93 94 95 96 **97 98** Since the sudden death of owner Erwein Count Matuschka in August 97, the future of this famous estate hangs in the balance.

For key to grape variety abbreviations, see pages 7–13.

Schloss Wallhausen ★★★ The 25-acre NAHE estate of the PRINZ ZU SALM, one of Germany's oldest. 65% RIES. Vg TROCKEN (esp).

Schlossböckelheim Nahe w ★★ →★★★★ 71 75 76 79 **83 85** 86 88 **89 90** 91 92 **93** 94 **95** 96 **97** 98 Village with top NAHE v'yds, including First Class Felsenberg, In den Felsen, Königsfels, Kupfergrube. Firm yet delicate wine. Grosslage: Burgweg. Top growers: CRUSIUS, DONNHOF.

Schneider, Weingut Georg Albrecht ★★ Impeccably run 32-acre estate. Classic off-dry and sweet RIES in NIERSTEIN, the best from First Class Hipping.

Schoppenwein Café (or bar) wine: ie wine by the glass.

Schubert, von Owner of MAXIMIN GRUNHAUS.

Schwarzer Adler, Weingut ★★ →★★★ Franz Keller and his son make top BADEN dry GRAU-, WEISS- and SPATBURGUNDER on 35 acres at Oberbergen.

Schweigen Pfz w r ★ →★★ **85** 86 87 88 **89 90** 91 **92 93** 94 95 **96 97** 98 S PFALZ village. Grosslage: Guttenberg. Best growers: Fritz Becker, esp for SPAT-BURGUNDER, Bernhart.

Sekt German (QBA) sparkling wine, best when label specifies RIES, WEISS-BURGUNDER or SPATBURGUNDER. Sekt bA is the same but from specified area.

Selbach-Oster ★★★ 15-acre ZELTINGEN estate among MITTELMOSEL leaders.

Serrig M-S-R (Saar) w ★★ →★★★ 71 75 76 83 **85** 86 **88 89 90** 91 **93** 94 **95** 96 **97** 98 Village for 'steely' wines, excellent in sunny yrs. First Class v'yds: Herrenburg, Saarstein, Schloss Saarstein, WURZBERG. Grosslage: SCHARZBERG. Top growers: SCHLOSS SAARSTEIN, BERT SIMON.

Silvaner The third most-planted German white grape, usually underrated; best in FRANKEN. Worth looking for in RHEINHESSEN and KAISERSTUHL too.

Simmern, Langwerth von ★★★ Famous ELTVILLE family estate. Famous v'yds: Baiken, Mannberg, MARCOBRUNN. However, disappointing quality since beginning of '90s. Erstwhile elegance of R'GAU RIESLING is lacking.

Simon, Weingut Bert ★★ One of largest SAAR estates. 60 acres: KASEL, SERRIG. Traditional style combines fruit and steel.

Sonnenuhr Sundial. Name of several v'yds, esp First Class one at WEHLEN.

Spätburgunder Pinot Noir: the best red-wine grape in Germany – esp in BADEN and WURTTEMBERG and, increasingly, PFALZ – generally improving quality, but most still pallid and underflavoured.

Spätlese Late harvest. One better (stronger, usually sweeter) than KABINETT. Wines to age at least 5 yrs. TROCKEN Spätlesen can be v fine.

Staatlicher Hofkeller ★★★ The Bavarian STATE DOMAIN. 287 acres of finest FRANKEN v'yds with spectacular cellars under the great baroque Residenz at WURZBURG. Quality improving rapidly since '95 vintage.

Staatsweingut (or Staatliche Weinbaudomäne) The state wine estates or domains; esp KLOSTER EBERBACH, TRIER.

State Domain See Staatsweingut.

Steigerwald (Bereich) District name for E part of FRANKEN.

Steinberg Rhg w ★★★ 71 75 76 79 **83 85** 86 88 89 **90** 91 92 **93** 94 **95** 96 97 98 Famous 79-acre HATTENHEIM walled v'yd, planted by Cistercians 700 yrs ago. Now owned by STATE DOMAIN, ELTVILLE. Some glorious wines; some feeble.

Steinwein Wine from WURZBURG's best v'yd, Stein.

Stuttgart Chief city of WURTTEMBERG, producer of some fine wines (esp RIES).

Südliche Weinstrasse (Bereich) District name for S PFALZ. Quality improved tremendously in last 25 yrs. See Ilbesheim, Schweigen.

Tafelwein Table wine. The vin ordinaire of Germany. Frequently blended with other EU wines. But DEUTSCHER TAFELWEIN must come from Germany alone and may be excellent. (See also Landwein.)

Tauberfranken (Bereich) New name for minor Badisches Frankenland BEREICH of N BADEN: FRANKEN-style wines.

Thanisch, Weingut Wwe Dr H ★★ BERNKASTEL estate, incl part of Doctor v'yd.

Traben-Trarbach M-M w **★★ 76 83 85 88 89 90** 91 92 **93** 94 95 96 **97**
Major wine town of 800 acres, 87% of it RIESLING. Top vineyards: Ungsberg,
Würzgarten. Grosslage: Schwarzlay. Top grower: MAX FERD RICHTER.

Traisen Nahe w **★★★ 71 75 76** 79 **83 85** 86 87 **88 89 90** 91 92 **93** 94 **95 96
97** Small village incl First Class Bastei and Rotenfels v'yds, capable of
making RIES of great concentration and class. Top grower: CRUSIUS.

Traminer See Gewürztraminer.

Trier M-S-R w **★★ ·★★★** Great wine city of Roman origin, on MOSEL, nr RUWER,
now also incl AVELSBACH and EITELSBACH. Grosslage: Römerlay. Big Mosel
charitable estates have cellars here among imposing Roman ruins.

Trittenheim M-M w **★★ 71 75 76 85** 88 **89 90** 91 92 **93** 94 95 96 97 98
Attractive S MITTELMOSEL light wines. Top v'yds were Altärchen, Apotheke, but
now incl second-rate flat land: First Class v'yds are Felsenkopf, Leiterchen.
Grosslage: Michelsberg (avoid). Growers incl E Clüsserath, GRANS-FASSIAN, Milz.

Trocken 'Dry'. By law trocken means max 9 grams per litre unfermented
sugar. Some are highly austere, others (better) have more body and alcohol.

Trockenbeerenauslese Sweetest, most expensive category of German wine,
extremely rare, with concentrated honey flavour. Made from selected
shrivelled grapes affected by 'noble rot' (botrytis). TBA for short. See also
Edel. Edelbeerenauslese would be a less-confusing name.

Trollinger Common (pale) red grape of WURTTEMBERG; locally v popular.

Germany: three Lucullan resorts

Stuttgart Wielandshöne where Vincent Klink serves modern cooking
with an exceptional purity of flavour, and star sommelier Bernd Kreis
matches it with one of the nation's great wine lists. Look out for the dry
Rieslings from Wöhrwag and reds from Albert Schwegler.

Rheingau The longest est'd is the Hotel Krone in Assmannshausen –
one of the region's great cultural monuments. Not only the rooms but
the cooking are Belle Epoque and the list of mature Rheingau Rieslings is
unsurpassed. Since 1995, the hotel's wine estate has made fine
Spätburgunders.

The best is Marcobrunn in Hotel Schloss Reinhartshausen. This is
modern cuisine of great sophistication, and sommelier Marie-Helen
Krebs is the ideal guide to the long list of wines from around the world
and around the corner (incl the estate's own).

Ungstein Pfz w **★★ ·★★★ 71 76 83 85** 86 **88 89 90** 91 92 **93** 94 **95 96** 97 **98**
MITTELHAARDT village with fine harmonious wines. First Class v'yds: Herrenberg,
Weilberg. Top growers: Darting, FITZ-RITTER, PFEFFINGEN, Karl Schäfer. Grosslagen:
Honigsäckel, Kobnert.

Urzig M-M w **★★★★ 71 75 76 83 85** 87 **88 89 90** 91 **92 93** 94 95 96 **97 98**
Village on red sandstone famous for firm, full, spicy wine unlike other
MOSELS. First Class v'yd: Würzgarten. Grosslage: Schwarzlay. Growers incl
J J CHRISTOFFEL, DR LOOSEN, Mönchhof, WEINS-PRUM.

Valckenberg, P J Major merchants and growers at Worms, with Madonna
LIEBFRAUMILCH. Also dry RIES.

VDP Verband Deutscher Prädikats und Qualitätsweingüter. The pace-making
association of premium growers. Look for their black eagle insignia.
President: PRINZ ZU SALM.

Vereinigte Hospitien ★★ 'United Hospices'. Ancient charity at TRIER with
large holdings in PIESPORT, SERRIG, TRIER, WILTINGEN, etc; but wines recently well
below their wonderful potential.

GERMANY

Verwaltung Administration (of property/estate etc).

Wachenheim Pfz w ★★★ ›★★★★ **71 76 83 85** 86 *87* 88 **89 90** *91* 92 **93** 94 95 **96 97 98** 840 acres, including exceptionally fine RIESLING. First Class v'yds: Gerümpel, Goldbächel, Rechbächel etc. Top growers: BURKLIN-WOLF, BIFFAR, WOLF. Grosslagen: Mariengarten, Schenkenböhl, Schnepfenflug.

Wagner, Dr ★★★ Saarburg estate. 20 acres of RIES. Fine wines incl TROCKEN.

Walluf Rhg w ★★★ **75 76** 79 **83 85 88 89 90** *91* 92 **93** 94 95 96 **97** 98 Neighbour of ELTVILLE; formerly Nieder- and Ober-Walluf. Underrated wines. First Class v'yd: Walkenberg. Grosslage: Steinmächer. Growers incl BECKER.

Walporzheim Ahrtal (Bereich) District name for the whole AHR Valley.

Wawern M-S-R (Saar) w ★★ ›★★★ **71 75 76 83** 85 88 **89 90** *91* 92 **93** 94 95 96 97 **98** Sm village, fine RIES. First Class v'yd: Herrenberg. Grosslage: SCHARZBERG.

Wegeler-Deinhard ★★★ After selling merchant house of DEINHARD in '97, the Wegeler family has begun restructuring its 3 wine estates. With 136 acres, the RHEINGAU estate in OESTRICH remains one of the region's quality leaders. 46 acres in MITTELHAARDT area of the PFALZ are also highly regarded for drier wines. The MITTELMOSEL estate in BERNKASTEL is being slimmed down, although quality here is currently highest of the three.

Wehlen M-M w ★★★ ›★★★★ **71 75 76 83 85** 86 **88 89 90** 91 92 **93** 94 95 96 **97** 98 Neighbour of BERNKASTEL with equally fine, somewhat richer wines. Location of great First Class v'yd: SONNENUHR. Grosslage: Münzlay. Top growers: DR LOOSEN, J J PRUM, S A Prüm, Studert-Prüm, WEGELER-DEINHARD, WEINS-PRUM.

New German names to watch for in the early 2000s
Thomas Haag Weingut Schloss Lieser, Mosel-Saar-Rüwer
Reinhard Löwenstein Weingut Heymann-Löwenstein, Mosel-Saar-Rüwer
Udo Lützkendorf Weingut Lützkendorf, Saale-Unstrut
Matthias Müller Weingut Heinrich Müller, Mittelrhein
Klaus Zimmerling, Sachsen

Weil, Weingut Robert ★★★★ Outstanding 95-acre estate in KIEDRICH; now owned by Suntory of Japan. Superb QMP, EISWEIN, BA, TBA; standard wines also vg since '92. Widely considered RHEINGAU's No 1.

Weinbaugebiet Viticultural region. For TAFELWEIN (eg MOSEL, RHEIN, SAAR).

Weingut Wine estate.

Weinkellerei Wine cellars or winery. See Keller.

Weins-Prüm, Dr ★★ ›★★★ Classic MITTELMOSEL estate; 12 acres at WEHLEN. WEHLENER SONNENUHR is top wine.

Weinstrasse Wine road. Scenic route through v'yds. Germany has several.

Weintor, Deutsches See Schweigen.

Weissburgunder Pinot Blanc. Most reliable grape for TROCKEN wines: low acidity, high extract. Also much used for SEKT.

Weissherbst Usually pale pink wine of QBA standard or above, from a single variety, occasionally BEERENAUSLESE; the speciality of BADEN, PFALZ and WURTTEMBERG.

Werner, Domdechant ★★★ Fine family estate on best HOCHHEIM slopes.

Wiltingen M-S-R (Saar) w ★★ ›★★★★ **71 75 76 83** 85 86 **88 89 90** 91 92 **93** 94 **95** 96 **97** 98 The centre of the SAAR. 790 acres. Beautiful subtle austere wine. Great First Class v'yd is SCHARZHOFBERG (ORTSTEIL); and First Class are Braune Kupp, Hölle. Grosslage (for the whole SAAR): SCHARZBERG. Top growers: EGON MULLER, LE GALLAIS, VON KESSELSTATT etc.

Winkel Rhg w ★★★ **71 75 76 83 85** 86 **88 89 90** *91* 92 **93** 94 **95 96** 97 98 Village famous for full fragrant wine, incl SCHLOSS VOLLRADS. First Class v'yds incl Hasensprung, Jesuitengarten, Klaus, SCHLOSS VOLLRADS, Schlossberg. Grosslagen: Erntebringer, Honigberg. Growers incl DEINHARD, PRINZ VON HESSEN, Von Mumm, BALTHASAR RESS, SCHLOSS SCHONBORN, etc.

Winningen M-S-R w ★★ Lower MOSEL town nr Koblenz: unusually full RIES for region. First Class v'yds: Uhlen.

Wintrich M-M w ★★ ›★★★ **71 75 76 83 85** 86 **88 89 90** 91 **92 93** 94 **95** *96* 97 Neighbour of PIESPORT; similar wines. Top vineyards: Ohligsberg. Grosslage: Kurfürstlay. Top grower: REINHOLD HAART.

Winzergenossenschaft Wine-growers' cooperative, often making sound and reasonably priced wine. Referred to in this text as 'coop'.

Winzerverein The same as the above.

Wirsching, Hans ★★★ Leading estate in IPHOFEN, and indeed FRANKEN. Wines firm, elegant and dry. 100 acres in 1st-class v'yds: Julius-Echter-Berg, Kalb etc.

Wonnegau (Bereich) District name for S RHEINHESSEN.

Wolf ★★ Run down estate in WACHENHEIM recently acquired by consortium headed by Ernst Loosen (see DR LOOSEN) of Bernkastel. From first vintage (1996) PFALZ wines with a Mosel-like delicacy. An estate to watch.

Wolff Metternich ★★ ›★★★ Noble DURBACH estate: some of BADEN's best RIES.

Württemberg Vast S area, little known for wine outside Germany despite some vg RIES (esp NECKAR Valley) and frequently unrealized potential to make good reds: LEMBERGER, TROLLINGER, SAMTROT.

Würzburg Frank ★★ ›★★★★ **71 76 79 81 83 85** 86 **88 89 90** 91 92 **93** 94 95 *96* **97** 98 Great baroque city on the Main, centre of FRANKEN wine: fine, full-bodied, dry. 1st-class vineyards: Abtsleite, Innere, Leiste, Stein. No Grosslage. See Maindreieck. Growers: BURGERSPITAL, JULIUSSPITAL, STAATLICHER HOFKELLER.

Zell M-S-R w ★ ›★★★ **76 83 88** 89 90 *91* 92 **93** 94 **95** 96 **97** The best-known lower MOSEL village, esp for its awful Grosslage: Schwarze Katz ('Black Cat'). RIES on steep slate gives aromatic light wines. Top grower: ALBERT KALLFELZ.

Zell (Bereich) District name for whole lower MOSEL from Zell to Koblenz.

Zeltingen M-M w ★★ ›★★★★ **71 75 76** 79 **83 85** 86 **88 89 90** *91* 92 **93** 94 **95** 96 *97* 98 Top MOSEL village nr WEHLEN. Lively crisp RIES. First Class v'yd: SONNENUHR. Grosslage: Münzlay. Top growers: JJ PRUM, SELBACH-OSTER.

Zilliken, Forstmeister Geltz ★★★ Former estate of Prussian royal forester at Saarburg and OCKFEN, SAAR. Racy minerally RIESLINGS, incl AUSLESE, EISWEIN with excellent ageing potential.

Zwierlein, Freiherr von ★★ 55-acre family estate in GEISENHEIM. 100% RIES.

Luxembourg

Luxembourg has 3,285 acres of v'yds on limestone soils on the Moselle's left bank. High-yielding Elbling and Rivaner (Müller-T) vines dominate, but there are also significant acreages of Ries, Gewürz and (usually best) Auxerrois, Pinot Bl and Pinot Gr. These give light to medium-bodied (10.5–11.5%) dry Alsace-like wines. The Vins Moselle coop makes 70% of the total. Domaine et Tradition estates association, founded in '88, promotes quality from noble varieties. The following vintages were all good; 89 90 92 95; 97 outstanding, 98 average. Best from: Aly Duhr et Fils, M Bastian, Caves Gales, Bernard Massard (surprisingly good Cuvée de l'Ecusson classic method sparkling), Clos Mon Vieux Moulin, Ch de Schengen, Sunnen-Hoffmann.

Spain & Portugal

The following abbreviations are used in the text:

Amp   Ampurdán-Costa Brava
Alen   Alentejo
Bair   Bairrada
Cos del S Costers del Segre
El B   El Bierzo
Est   Estremadura
La M   La Mancha
Mont-M   Montilla-Moriles
Nav   Navarra
Pen   Penedès
Pri   Priorato
Rib del D Ribera del Duero
R Ala   Rioja Alavesa
R Alt   Rioja Alta
RB   Rioja Baja
Som   Somontano
Set   Setúbal
U-R   Utiel-Requena
VV   Vinhos Verdes

g   vino generoso
res   reserva

MADEIRA (off west coast of Africa)

Funchal

S pain and Portugal joined the EU (and, as far as most of their wine is concerned, the 20th century) only 14 years ago. Both made rapid progress, Eurogrants allowing massive re-equipping. The continuing state of ferment is highly productive: many splendid new wines are appearing both in the few traditional quality areas and in former bulk-wine regions. But some makers are asking silly prices.

Currently in Spain (apart from sherry country), the north, Rioja, Navarra, Galicia, Rueda, Catalonia and Ribera del Duero hold most interest; those in Portugal (apart from the port vineyards and Madeira) are the Douro, Ribatejo, Alentejo, the central coast and the north. In Portugal especially, newly delimited areas have successfully challenged old, traditional appellations. Even Dão has made good progress through single quintas and huge investment by Portugal's largest winemaker, Sogrape.

The following list includes the best and most interesting makers, types and regions of each country, whether legally delimited or not. Geographical references (see map above) are to demarcated regions (DOs and DOCs), autonomies and provinces.

Bay of Biscay

Bilbao

Logroño○ *Ebro* Navarra

Rioja Somontano

Ampurdán-Costa Brava

Cigales Campo de Borja Costers del Segre Conca de Barbera

Valladolid *Duero* Calatayud Cariñena Priorato Alella

Ribera del Duero Penedès Barcelona

Rueda Tarragona

Madrid Vinos de Madrid

Mentrida Utiel-Requena Valencia Binassalem

La Mancha ○Valencia Palma

Almansa Valencia

uadalqui Valdepeñas Jumilla Alicante

Yecla ○Alicante

Montilla Moriles Heavier shaded areas are the wine growing regions

Málaga

○Málaga

Mediterranean Sea

SPAIN

Sherry, port and Madeira, even now still the greatest glories of Spain and Portugal, have a chapter to themselves on pages 172–179.

Spain

Agramont See Príncipe de Viana, Bodegas.

Albariño High-quality aromatic white grape of GALICIA, in legend at least descended from Alsace Riesling, and its wine, now perhaps Spain's most highly regarded white. See Rías Baixas, Cervera, Gran Bazán, Pazo de Barrantes.

Albor See Campo Viejo, Bodegas.

Alella r w (p) dr sw ★★ Small demarcated region just N of Barcelona. Pleasantly fruity wines. (See Marfil, Marqués de Alella, Parxet.)

Alicante r (w) ★ DO. Wines still earthy and overstrong.

Alión Rib del D r ★★★ **91 92 93 94' 95** Since discontinuing the 3-yr-old VALBUENA, VEGA SICILIA has acquired this second BODEGA to make CRIANZAS with 100% Tempranillo; impressive results. Vigorous and gd short- to mid-term keeping.

Allende, Finca R Ala r ★★→★★★ Much praised newish ('94) bodega making an elegant oak-aged Tempranillo under the same name.

155

Almendralejo E Spain r w ★ Wine centre of Extremadura. Much of its wine is distilled to make the spirit for fortifying sherry. See Lar de Lares.

Aloque La M r ★ DYA Light-coloured VALDEPEÑAS speciality, from r and w grapes.

Alta Pavina, Bodegas Castilla y León r ★★ 91 92 94 95 96 Good non-DO Cab S, Tinto Fino: oak-aged, spicy, dark and dense. Variable Pinot Noir.

Alvaro Palacios Pri r ★★★ 93 94 95' 96' Gifted emigré from Rioja making some of the most expensive and fashionable red wine in Spain, incl Finca Dolfi, L'Ermita and Les Terrasses.

Ampurdán, Cavas del Amp r w p ★→★★ Producers of big-selling white Pescador, red Cazador.

Ampurdán-Costa Brava Amp r w p ★→★★ Demarcated region abutting Pyrenees. Mainly coop-made rosés, reds. See also last entry.

Año Year: 4° Año (or Años) means 4 yrs old when bottled. Was common on labels, now largely discontinued in favour of vintages, or terms such as CRIANZA.

Arco Bodegas Unidas See Berberana Bodegas.

Artadi See Cosecheros Alaveses.

Arzuaga, Bodegas Ribera del Duero r ★★★ 94 95 Architecturally spectacular new bodega with 370 acres aiming for luscious modern wines.

Bach, Masía Pen r w p dr sw res ★★→★★★ 92 93 94 95 96 Stately villa-winery nr SAN SADURNI DE NOYA, owned by CODORNIU. Speciality is white Extrísimo, both sweet and oaky, and dry. Also good red RESERVAS.

Barbier, René Pen r w res ★★ 85 87 91 93 96 Owned by FREIXENET, known for fresh white Kraliner, red RB RESERVAS.

Barón de Ley RB r (w) res ★★★ 85 86 87 91 94 Newish RIOJA BODEGA linked with EL COTO: good single-estate wines.

Barril, Masía Pri r br res ★★★ 85 87 91 93 94 95 96 Old-fashioned, powerful, fruity, often tarry reds and unusual herbalised RANCIO. Bought in 1998 by Cavas HILL and renamed Mas d'eh Gil. New, more modern styles imminent.

Baso r w ★★ Brand name for reliable Garnacha from NAVARRA made by gifted young winemaker Telmo Rodríguez of LA GRANJA REMELLURI.

Berberana, Bodegas R Alt r (w) res ★★→★★★ 87 88 90 91 92 94 95 96 Recently rechristened Arco Bodegas Unidas, now incorporating BERBERANA, MARQUES DE GRIÑON, MARQUES DE MONISTROL, Lagunilla, Vinícola del Mediterraneo and Bodegas Hispano Argentinas. Fruity full-bodied reds best: young Carta de Plata, Carta de Oro CRIANZA, velvety RESERVAS.

Berceo, Bodegas R Alt r w p res ★★→★★★ 87 89 92 93 94 95 Cellar in HARO with good Gonzalo de Berceo GRAN RESERVA.

Beronia, Bodegas R Alt r w res ★★→★★★ 89 91 93 94 95 Small modern BODEGA making reds in traditional oaky style and fresh 'modern' whites. Owned by González-Byass (see page 175).

Bilbaínas, Bodegas R Alt r w (p) dr sw sp res ★★ 87 89 91 93 94 95 Long-established RIOJA house, whose traditional styles – including dark Viña Pomal, light Viña Zaco and elegantly intense VENDIMIA Especial Reservas – are no longer as reliable as they were. Will new owners CODORNIU rev them up?

Binissalem r w ★★ Best-known MAJORCA DO. See also Franja Roja.

Blanco White.

Bodega Spanish term for (i) a wineshop; (ii) a concern occupied in the making, blending and/or shipping of wine; and (iii) a cellar.

Bodegas y Bebidas Formerly Savin. One of largest Spanish wine companies; owns wineries all over Spain. Mainly good-quality and value brands. Also controls various prestigious firms, eg AGE, CAMPO VIEJO, MARQUES DEL PUERTO.

Bornos, Palacio de Bornos Rueda w sp ★★★ DYA See Cuetas de Castilla.

Bretón, Bodegas R Alt r res ★★→★★★ 89 90 91 94 95 96 Respectable Loriñon range and little-seen, expensive, concentrated Dominio de Conté 90 91 94 (comparable with CONTINO).

Calatayud ★→★★ Aragón DO (of 4): esp Garnacha. Coop San Isidro holds sway.

Campillo, Bodegas R Ala r (p) res ★★★ 82 85 87 88 89 91 92 94 Affiliated with FAUSTINO MARTÍNEZ, a young BODEGA with good wines.

Campo Viejo, Bodegas R Alt r (w) res ★→★★★ 89 92 94 95 96 Big-selling Albor wines, a fresh white and Beaujolais Nouveau-style red; 100% Temp Alcorta; also big fruity red RESERVAS, esp Marqués de Villamagna. See Bodegas y Bebidas.

Can Rafols dels Caus Pen r w ★★ 89 90 91 96 Young small PENEDES BODEGA: own-estate fruity Cab, pleasant Chard-Xarel-lo-Chenin; Gran Caus and less expensive Petit Caus ranges. Best is Caus Lubis 100% Merlot (91).

Canary Islands (Islas) r w p g ★→★★ Until recently there were few wines of any quality other than dessert Malvasías (Bodegas El Grifo and Bodegas Mozaga on Lanzarote). No fewer than 8 DOs have now been created and modernised BODEGAS esp on TENERIFE are making better and lighter wines. The tourist trade may keep prices high, but the flavours have real interest. To investigate.

Caralt, Cavas Conde de Pen r w sp res ★★→★★★ CAVA wines from outpost of FREIXENET, esp good vigorous Brut NV; also pleasant still wines.

Cariñena r (w p) ★ Coop-dominated DO: large-scale supplier of strong everyday wine. Being invigorated (and wines lightened) by new technology.

Casa Castillo Jumilla r (w p) ★★→★★★ 95 96 97 Some of the best wines from JUMILLA made by Julia Roch e Hijos, incl fruity Monastrell (97), Tempranillo (97) with a touch of oak, and CRIANZA Monastrell/Cab S/Tempranillo (95).

Spanish producers to look for in the early 2000s

Bodegas Roda Rioja Alta

Finca Allende Rioja Alta

Cosecheros Alaveses Rioja Alavesa

Finca Valpiedra Rioja Alta

Alión Ribera del Duero

Clos Martinet Priorato

Casa de la Viña Valdepeñas r (w p) ★★ 90 92 97 BODEGAS Y BEBIDAS-owned estate, since '80s: sound and fruity Cencibel wines. Drink young.

Casar de Valdaiga El B r w ★ Fruity red from Pérez Carames, N of LEON.

Castaño, Bodegas Yecla (w dr) r res ★★ 93 95 96 97 Trail blazer in remote YECLA making sound and pleasant Cab S (97), Merlot (96) and blends of Tempranillo/Monastrell and Monastrell/Cab S/Merlot (93 96) under the names of Castaño, Colección, Hecula and Pozuelo.

Castell de Remei Cos de S r w p ★★→★★★ 90 91 93 94 95 96 97 98 Historic v'yds/winery revived, re-equipped, replanted since '83. Gd Cab-Tempranillo, Merlot 93 94.

Castellblanch Pen w sp ★★ PENEDES CAVA firm, owned by FREIXENET. Look for Brut Zero (94) and Gran Castell GRAN RESERVAS (93).

Castillo de Monjardín Nav r w ★★→★★★ 93 94 95 96 Newish winery making excellent fragrant oaky Chard (95) and vg reds esp Merlot (94).

Castillo de Ygay R Alt r w ★★★★ (r) 25 34 42 52 59 64 68 70 75 78 82 85 87 89 (Current white vintage is 92) The 64 is still superb. See Marqués de Murrieta.

Castillo del Perelada, Caves Amp r w p res sp ★★ 92 93 94 Large range of both still wines and CAVA, including Chard, Sauv B, Cab S 94 and sp Gran Claustro extra brut.

NB Vintages in colour are those you should choose first for drinking in 2000.

157

Cava Official term for any classic method Spanish sparkling wine, and the DO covering the areas up and down Spain where it is made.

Cenalsa See Príncipe de Viana, Bodegas.

Cenicero Wine township of Roman origin in RIOJA ALTA.

Centro Españolas, Bodegas La M r w p ★★ 91 92 93 97 Large modern BODEGA best known for creditable red Allozo made from 100% Tempranillo.

Cepa Wine or grape variety.

Cervera, Lagar de Rías Baixas w ★★★ DYA Maker of one of best ALBARINOS: flowery and intensely fruity with subdued bubbles and a long finish.

Chacolí País Vasco w (r) ★ DYA Alarmingly sharp, often sp wine from Basque coast; 2 DOs for all 395 acres! 9–11% alcohol. Best producer: Txomín Etxaníz.

Chivite, Bodegas Julián Nav r w (p) dr sw res ★★ →★★★ 88 89 90 92 94 96 The biggest and best NAVARRA BODEGA. Now some of Spain's top reds, deep-flavoured, v long-lived; flowery well-balanced white esp Chivite Colección 125 (96) and vg 97 rosé. See Gran Feudo.

Cigales r p ★→★★ Recently demarcated region north of Valladolid, esp for light reds (traditionally known as CLARETES).

Clarete Traditional term, now banned by EC, for light red wine (or dark rosé).

Clos Mogador Pri r ★★★ 92 93 94 95' Outstation of RENE BARBIER producing a new-wave Clos Mogador PRIORATO.

Codorníu Pen w sp ★★→★★★ One of the two largest firms in SAN SADURNI DE NOYA making gd CAVA: v high tech, 10M bottles ageing in cellars. Mature Non Plus Ultra, fresh Anna de Codorníu or premium Jaume de Codorníu RESERVA. Also owns RAIMAT, BILBAINAS.

Compañía Vinícola del Norte de España (CVNE) R Alt ★★→★★★ 87 88 89 90 91 92 93 94 95 Famous RIOJA bodega. In spite of (or because of?) a revolutionary new vinification plant, young wines are less good than formerly, though some of the older Viña Real and Imperial RESERVAS are spectacular. See also CONTINO.

Con Class, Bodegas Rueda w ★★ →★★★ DYA Despite the dreadful name: exciting Verdejo/Viura and Sauv Bl, esp RUEDA Superior (96).

Conca de Barberá Pen w (r p) Catalan DO region growing Parellada grapes for making CAVA. Its best wine is TORRES MILMANDA Chard. See also SANTARA.

Condado de Haza Rib del D r ★★★ 94 95 96 Alejandro Fernandez's new BODEGA. Pure Tinto Fino aged in oak. Similar to PESQUERA: first three vintages are winners.

Condado de Huelva DO See Huelva.

Conde de Valdemar See Martínez-Bujanda.

Consejo Regulador Official organization for the control, promotion and defence of a DENOMINACION DE ORIGEN.

Contino R Ala r res ★★★ 87 88 89 91 94 95 Very fine single-v'yd red made by a subsidiary of COMPANIA VINICOLA DEL NORTE DE ESPANA.

Cosecha Crop or vintage.

Cosecheros Alaveses R Ala r (w p) ★★ →★★★ 90 91 92 93 94 95 97 Now excellent new 100% Graciano (96). Up-and-coming RIOJA coop, esp for gd young unoaked red Artadi, and Viñas de Gain, Vina El Pisón, Pagos Viejo RESERVAS.

Costers del Segre Cos del S r w p sp Small demarcated area around the city of Lleida (Lérida), famous for the v'yds of RAIMAT.

Costers del Siurana Pri r (sw) ★★★→★★★★ 92 93 94 96' Carlos Pastrana makes the prestigious Clos de l'Obac, Misere and Usatges from Garnacha/ Cab S, sometimes plus Syrah, Merlot, Tempranillo and Cariñena. Wonderful sweet Dolç de l'Orbac (96).

CoViDes Pen r w p sp res ★★→★★★ 89 91 92 93 97 Large former coop making gd Duc de Foix w and Cab S, Cab S-Tempranillo; also first-rate Duc de Foix CAVA.

Criado y embotellado por... Grown and bottled by...

Crianza Literally 'nursing'; the ageing of wine. New or unaged wine is 'sin crianza' or 'joven' (young). Reds labelled 'crianza' must be at least 2 yrs old (with 1yr in oak, in some areas 6 months), and must not be released before the third yr.

Cuevas de Castilla Rueda w dr sp ★★→★★★ DYA the enterprising Sanz fanily produce some of RUEDA'S liveliest whites under a variety of labels (eg Palacio de BORNOS and CON CLASS) using Verdejo, Viura and Sauv B. Reds include concentrated oaky Almirantazgo de Castilla from VT. Medina del Campo and new wines from recently built bodega in DO TORO.

Cumbrero See Montecillo, Bodegas.

De Muller Tarragona br (r w) ★★ Venerable TARRAGONA firm formerly making sumptuous v old SOLERA-aged dessert wines. Under new management; current wines undistinguished.

Denominación de Origen (DO) Official wine region (see page 154).

Denominación de Origen Calificada (DOCa) Classification for wines of the highest quality; so far only RIOJA benefits (since '91).

Domecq R Ala r (w) res ★★→★★★ 90 91 92 93 94 RIOJA outpost of sherry firm. Inexpensive Viña Eguía and excellent Marqués de Arienzo CRIANZAS and RESERVAS, fragrant and medium bodied.

Don Darias/Don Hugo Alto Ebro r w ★ Huge-selling, modestly priced wines, v like RIOJA, from undemarcated Bodegas Vitorianas. Sound red, white.

Dulce Sweet.

El Bierzo DO since '90, N of León. See Casar de Valdaiga.

El Coto, Bodegas R Ala r (w) res ★★ 91 94 BODEGA best known for light, soft, red El Coto and Coto de Imaz.

Elaborado y añejado por... Made and aged by...

Enate Somontano DO r w p res ★★→★★★ 92 93 94' 95 96 Good wines from SOMONTANO in the north: light, clean, fruity incl barrel-fermented Chard (96) and Cab S blends (the CRIANZA is full and juicy). Avoid the Gewürz.

Espumoso Sparkling (but see Cava).

EVENA Nav Gov't research station revolutionizing NAVARRA.

Fariña, Bodegas Toro r w res ★★ 87 89 90 91 92 94 95 97 Rising star of new DO TORO: good spicy reds. Gran Colegiata is cask-aged; Colegiata not. Good red Primero (96) bursting with fruit.

Faustino, Bodega R Ala r w (p) res ★★→★★★ 87 89 90 91 93 94' Long-estatablished BODEGA formerly F Martínez, with good reds. GRAN RESERVA is Faustino I. Do not be put off by the repellent fake-antique bottles.

Fillaboa, Granxa Rías Baixas w ★★★ DYA Small firm making delicately fruity ALBARIÑO.

Franja Roja Majorca r res ★★ 89 91 92 93 94 95 Best-known MAJORCA BODEGA at Binissalem making somewhat old-fashioned José L Ferrer wines.

Freixenet, Cavas Pen w sp ★★→★★★ Huge CAVA firm, rivalling CODORNIU in size. Range of good sparklers, notably bargain Cordón Negro in black bottles, Brut Barroco, Reserva Real and Premium Cuvée DS (90). Also owns Gloria Ferrer in California, Champagne Henri Abelé (Reims) and a sparkling wine plant in Mexico. Paul Cheneau is low-price brand.

Galicia Rainy NW Spain: esp for fresh aromatic, not cheap whites, eg ALBARIÑO.

Generoso (g) Aperitif or dessert wine rich in alcohol.

Granbazán Agro de Bazán produces a classic fragrant ALBARIÑO with mouth-cleansing acidity.

Gran Feudo Nav w res ★★→★★★ 88 89 90 92 94 95 Brand name of fragrant white, refreshing rosé 97; soft plummy red; the best-known wines from CHIVITE.

Gran Reserva See Reserva.

Gran Vas Pressurized tanks (French cuves closes) for making cheap sparkling wines; also used to describe this type of wine.

Grandes Bodegas Rib del D r ★→★★ 94 95 96 97 Reorganized and with own extensive v'yds, this BODEGA (in notoriously highly priced region) makes affordable, unoaked Marqués de Velilla. More intense CRIANZAS, RESERVAS: pricier.

Guelbenzu, Bodegas Nav r (w) res ★★→★★★ 90 92 93 94 95 96 97 89 Family estate making conc full-bodied reds. Watch for new 96 Jardin from 40-yr-old Garnacha and top wine Lautus (**96**).

Guitán Godello Valdeorras w ★★★→★★★★ 95 96 97 Made by Bodegas Tapada, these splendidly fruity fragrant and complex 100% Godello wines, rated among the top whites in Spain, typify renaissance of native grapes in Galicia. The barrel-fermented type has the edge.

A Spanish choice for 2000

Ana de Codorníu Brut Reserva Cava
Hidalgo Pastrana Manzanilla Pasada sherry
Torres Fransola Sauvignon Blanc '96 Penedès
Jean León Chardonnay '96 Penedès
Condado de Haza '96 Ribera del Duero
Alión '94/'95 Ribera del Duero
Artadi Pagos Viejos Reserva '94 Rioja Alta
Torre Muga '94 Bodegas Muga Rioja Alta
Finca Valpiedra '94, Martínez-Bujanda Rioja Alta

Gutiérrez de la Vega Alicante r w ★★ Eccentric grower in ALICANTE DO. Rare expensive wines, rarely leaving Spain; sold as 'Casta Diva'. Moscatel 'Cosecha Miel' (97) tastes of satsuma, quince and honey!

Haro Wine centre of the RIOJA ALTA, a small but stylish old city.

Hill, Cavas Pen w r sp res ★★→★★★ 88 89 91 93 94 95 96 97 Old PENEDES firm: fresh dry w Blanc Cru, gd Gran Civet and Gran Toc reds, first-rate young Masía Hill Tempranillo and delicate RESERVA Oro Brut CAVA.

Huelva Condado de Huelva (DO) r w br ★→★★ W of Cádiz. White table wines and sherry-like GENEROSOS; formerly imp't source of 'Jerez' for blending.

Joven (vino) Young, unoaked wine.

Jumilla r (w p) ★→★★ DO in mountains N of Murcia. Its overstrong (up to 18%) wines are being lightened by earlier picking and better winemaking. Esp fruity r Mayoral (97) from García Carrión; extraordinary Dulce Monastrell 96 from tiny Bodegas Olivares.

Juvé y Camps Pen w sp ★★★ Family firm. Top quality CAVA, from free-run juice only, esp Reserva de la Familia (94) and Gran Juvé y Camps (93).

Laguardia Picturesque walled town at the centre of the RIOJA ALAVESA.

LAN, Bodegas R Alt r (p w) res ★★ 89 91 92 94 95 Huge modern BODEGA. Recently reorganized and now producing improved w Lan and r Lanciano (91 94).

Lanzarote Canary Island with v fair dry Malvasía, eg El Grifo.

Lar de Lares SW r res ★★ 91 92 93 94 96 Meaty GRAN RESERVA from Bodegas InViOSA, in remote Extremadura (in SW). And younger, lighter Lar de Barros.

León, Jean Pen r w res ★★★ 82 85 86 87 90 91 95 Sm firm; TORRES-owned since '95. Gd oaky Chard (96). Earlier Cab: huge, repaid long ageing; since '90 lighter.

Logroño First town of RIOJA region. HARO has more charm (and BODEGAS).

López de Heredia R Alt r w (p) dr sw res ★★→★★★★ 54 57 61 64 68 70 73 76 78 81 86 87 88 89 90 91 92 93 Old-est'd HARO BODEGA: v long-lasting, v trad wines. Best are really old RESERVAS from '54 onwards; marvellous w 64.

López Hermanos Málaga ★★ Large BODEGA for commercial MALAGA wines, incl popular Málaga Virgen and Moscatel Gloria.

Los Llanos Valdepeñas r (p w) res ★★ 90 91 93 94 95 One of growing number of VALDEPENAS BODEGAS to age wine in oak. RESERVA, GRAN RESERVA; premium Pata Negra Gran Reserva: 100% Cencibel (Tempranillo). Clean fruity w, Armonioso.

Málaga br sw ★★→★★★ Demarcated region around city of Málaga, much depleted by the 1996 closure of its best BODEGA, Hermanos Scholtz. At their best Málaga dessert wines can resemble tawny port.

Majorca FRANCA ROJA, Herens de Ribas, Miguel Oliver and Jaume Mesquida make island's only wines of interest (eg Chard) – otherwise, drink ROSADOS or Catalan.

Mancha, La La M r w ★→★★ Vast demarcated region N and NE of VALDEPENAS. Mainly white wines, the reds lacking the liveliness of the best Valdepeñas but showing signs of improvement. To watch.

Marfil Alella w (p) ★★ Brand of ALELLA Vinícola (oldest-est'd producer in Alella). Means 'ivory'. Now for lively, rather pricey, new-style dry whites.

Marqués de Alella Alella w (sp) ★★→★★★ 95 96 97 (DYA) Light, fragrant w ALELLA wines from PARXET, some Chard (incl barrel-fermented Allier). Also CAVA.

Marqués de Cáceres, Bodegas R Alt r p w res ★★→★★★ 86 87 89 90 91 92 93 Good red RIOJAS made by modern French methods; also surprisingly light, fragrant white (DYA), barrel-fermented Antea 95 and sweet Satinela.

Marqués de Griñón La M r w ★★★ 92 93 94 95 96 Enterprising nobleman initiated v fine Cab, delicious new (96) Syrah nr Toledo, S of Madrid, a region not known for wine. Fruity wines to drink fairly young. Also gd RIOJAS (89 90 91 92 94 95 96) and Durius, r from RIB DEL DUERO area. Owned by BERBERANA.

Marqués de Monistrol, Bodegas Pen p r sp dr sw res ★★→★★★ 89 90 91 92 93 95 Old BODEGA now owned by BERBERANA. Reliable CAVAS. Fresh Merlot (93).

Marqués de Murrieta R Alt r p w res ★★★→★★★★★ 34 42 52 59 62 64 68 70 78 83 85 87 89 90 91 92 93 96 Historic, revered BODEGA nr LOGRONO, formerly for some of best RIOJAS. Also famous for r CASTILLO DE YGAY, old-style oaky w, wonderful old-style ROSADO RESERVA. Except Rosado: quality variable; but back on form with brandy-scented 89. New r and w Colección 2001.

Marqués del Puerto R Alt r (p w) res ★★→★★★ 85 87 88 89 91 93 95 Small firm, was Bodegas López Agos, now owned by Marie Brizard. Reliable.

Marqués de Riscal R Ala r (p w) res ★★★ 81 86 87 89 90 91 92 94 Best-known RIOJA ALAVESA BODEGA. Fairly light, dry reds. Old vintages: v fine, some more recent ones variable; now right back on form. Barón de Chirel, 50% Cab S (94) is magnificent. RUEDA w incl vg Sauv 97, oak-aged RESERVA Limousin (95).

Martínez-Bujanda R Ala r p w res ★★★ 87 89 90 91 92 93 94 95 96 97 Refounded ('85) family-run RIOJA BODEGA, remarkably equipped. Superb wines, incl fruity Sin CRIANZA, irresistible ROSADO; noble Valdemar RESERVAS (90) 100% Garnacha and premium 100% Tempranillo single v'yd Finca Valpiedra (94).

Mascaró, Cavas Pen r p w sp ★★→★★★ 88 89 90 91 92 Top brandy maker, gd CAVA; fresh lemony dry white Viña Franca, and Anima Cab S.

Mas Martinet Pri r ★★★→★★★★ 92 93 94 95 96 Maker of Clos Martinet and a pioneer of the exclusive boutique Prioratos.

Mauro, Bodegas nr Valladolid r ★★→★★★ 87 89 90 91 92 93 94 96 Young BODEGA in Tudela del Duero; vg round fruity Tinto del País (Tempranillo) red and excellent Tereus (96). Not DO, as some of the fruit is from outside RIBERA DEL D.

Méntrida La M r w DO west of Madrid, source of everyday red wine.

Milmanda ★★★ See Conca de Barberà, Torres.

Monopole See Compañía Vinícola del Norte de España (CVNE).

Montecillo, Bodegas R Alt r w (p) ★★ 87 89 90 91 94 95 RIOJA BODEGA owned by OSBORNE. Old GRAN RESERVAS are magnificent. Now reds are appealing when young but recent vintages fragile.

Monterrey Gal r ★ Region nr N border of Portugal; strong VERIN-like wines.

Muga, Bodegas R Alt r (w sp) res ★★★ 81 85 **89 90 91 93** Small family firm in HARO, known for some of RIOJA's best strictly trad reds. Wines are light but highly aromatic, with long complex finish. Best is Prado Enea and now extraordinary concentrated Torre Muga (91 94). Whites and CAVA less good.

Navajas, Bodegas R Alt r w res ★★ →★★★ 89 **90 91 92 93 94 95 96 97** Small firm: bargain reds, CRIANZAS, RESERVAS, fruity and well-balanced. Also excellent oak-aged white Viura and cherry/vanilla-ish ROSADO CRIANZA.

Navarra Nav r p (w) ★★ →★★★ Demarcated region. Stylish Tempranillo and Cab reds, increasingly rivalling RIOJAS in quality and trouncing many in value. See Chivite, Guelbenzu, Palacio de la Vega, Ochoa, Príncipe de Viana.

Nuestro Padre Jésus del Perdón, Coop de La M r w ★→★★ 93 **94 95 96 97** Bargain fresh white Lazarillo and more-than-drinkable Yuntero; 100% Cencibel (alias Tempranillo) and Cencibel-Cab S aged in oak.

Ochoa Nav r p w res ★★ →★★★ 87 88 **89** 90 91' 92' **93** 94 **97** Small family BODEGA; excellent Moscatel, but better known for well-made red and rosés, incl 100% Tempranillo and 100% Merlot (94 **95**). Outstanding early vintages.

Pago de Carraovejas Rib del D res ★★→★★★ **92 93** 94 **95** 96 New estate; some of the region's most stylish, densely fruity Tinto Fino/Cabernet.

Palacio, Bodegas R Ala r p w res ★★★ **89** 90 91 93 **94'** 95 96 Since this old family firm parted company with Seagram in '87, its wines have regained their former reputation. Esp Glorioso RESERVA 91 94 and Cosme Palacio (95).

Palacio de Fefiñanes Rías Baixas w dr ★★★ 95 97 Oldest-est'd of the BODEGAS in RIAS BAIXAS, now making excellent, modern-style ALBARINOS.

Palacio de la Vega Nav r p w res ★★ →★★★ **91 92** 93 94 95 New BODEGA with juicy Tempranillo JOVEN, Cab S, Merlot and much promise.

Parxet Alella w p sp ★★→★★ Excellent fresh, fruity, exuberant CAVA (only one produced in ALELLA): esp Brut Nature. Also elegant w Alella: 'MARQUES DE ALELLA'.

Paternina, Bodegas R Alt r w (p) dr sw res ★→★★ Known for its standard red brand Banda Azul. Conde de los Andes label was fine, but the much lauded 78 is strictly for fans of oak/volatile acidity, and recent vintages, as of their other RIOJAS, are disappointing. Most consistent is Banda Dorada white (DYA).

Pazo Ribeiro r p w ★★ DYA Brand name of the RIBEIRO coop, whose wines are akin to VINHOS VERDES. Rasping red is local favourite. Pleasant slightly fizzy Pazo whites are safer; white Viña Costeira and Amadeus have quality.

Pazo de Barrantes Rías Baixas w ★★★ DYA New ALBARINO from RIAS BAIXAS; estate owned by late Conde de Creixels of MURRIETA. Delicate, exotic, top quality.

Penedès Pen r w sp ★→★★★ Demarcated region including Vilafranca del Penedès, SAN SADURNI DE NOYA and Sitges. See also Torres.

Pérez Pascuas Hermanos Rib del D r res ★★★ 89 90 91 92' 94' 95' Immaculate tiny family BODEGA in RIBERA DEL D. In Spain its fruity and complex r Viña Pedrosa is rated one of the country's best. Magnificent Pérez Pascuas Gran Selección (91).

Pesquera Rib del D r ★★★ 86 87 88 89 90 91 92 **93** 94' 95' Sm quantities of RIBERA DEL D from Alejandro Fernández. Robert Parker has rated it level with finest B'x. Janus (86 94) is special (even more expensive) bottling. Also CONDADO DE HAZA.

Piedmonte S Coop, Bodegas Nav ★★→★★★ 93 **94 95 96** 97 Up-and-coming coop making first-rate Oligitum Cab S-Tempranillo and Merlot.

Piqueras, Bodegas Almansa r (w dr p) ★★ 83 **85** 86 88 89 90 **91 93** Small family BODEGA. Some of LA MANCHA's best reds: Castillo de Almansa CRIANZA, Marius GRAN RESERVA.

Pirineos, Bodega Som w p r ★★ **90 91 93 94** 95 97 Former coop and SOMONTANO pioneer. Best: Montesierra range and oak-aged Señorío de Lazán RESERVA.

162

Príncipe de Viana, Bodegas Nav r w p ★★ **90 91 92 93 94 95 96** 97 Large firm (formerly 'Cenalsa'), blending and maturing coop wines and shipping a range from NAVARRA, incl flowery new-style white and fruity red, Agramont.

Priorato Pri br r ★★★ **87 88 89 91 92 93 94** 95 **96 97** DO enclave of TARRAGONA, known for alcoholic RANCIO and splendidly full-bodied almost black r, often used for blending. At brambly best one of Spain's triumphs. See Barril, De Muller, Scala Dei. Tiny boutique BODEGAS; v pricey wines: Amadis, Clos Martinet, CLOS MOGADOR, L'Ermita, Clos de l'Obac rightly ranked among Spain's stars.

Protos, Bodegas Rib del D r w res ★★→★★★ 86 **88 89 91 92 94 95** 97 Formerly Peñafiel's coop and region's second oldest BODEGA. Originally privatized '91 as 'Bodegas Ribera del Duero'. Much improved but still with problems.

Puig Roca Pen ★★→★★★ 93 94 95 96 Superior Augustus Chard (**97**), Cab S and Merlot.

Raïmat Cos del S r w p sp ★★→★★★ (Cab) **86 87 88 89 90 91 92 94 95** Clean, structured wines from DO nr Lérida, planted by CODORNIU with Cab, Chard, other foreign vines. Good 100% Chard CAVA. Value.

Rancio Maderized (brown) white wine of nutty flavour.

Raventós i Blanc Pen w sp ★★→★★★ Excellent CAVA aimed at top of market, also fresh El Preludi white and 100% Chard.

Remelluri, La Granja R Ala r res ★★★ 89 **90 91 92 93 94 95** Small estate (since '70), making vg traditional red RIOJAS and improving all the time.

Reserva (res) Good quality wine matured for long periods. Red reservas must spend at least 1 year in cask and 2 in bottle; Gran Reservas 2 in cask and 3 in bottle. Thereafter many continue to mature for years.

Rías Baixas w ★★→★★★ NW DO embracing subzones Val do Salnés, O Rosal and Condado de Tea, now for some of the best (and priciest) cold-fermented Spanish whites, mainly from ALBARIÑO grapes.

Ribeiro r w (p) ★→★★ Demarcated region on N border of Portugal: wines similar in style to Portuguese VINHOS VERDES – and others.

Ribera del Duero Rib del D **88 89 90 91 94 95 96 97** Fashionable fast-expanding DO east of Valladolid, (the Duero becomes the Portuguese Douro). Excellent for TINTO Fino (Tempranillo) reds. But prices are high and quality dodgy. See Arzuaga, Pago de Carraovejas, Pérez Pascuas, Pesquera, Torremilanos, Vega Sicilia. Also Mauro.

Important note:

An extended range of vintages is printed for a number of Rioja bodegas. But remember that the quality of older RESERVAS and GRAN RESERVAS depends on proper cellarage. Old wines kept in the racks of a warm restaurant soon deteriorate. Riojas do not now last as long as their oakier predecessors – some of the 85s 86s 87s and 90s are already drying out – but depending upon the bodega, an older vintage from the '60s or early '70s may well be memorable. Currently 91 92 94 95 and 96 are the safest choices.

Rioja r p w sp **64 70 75 78 81 82 85 89 91 92 94 95 96** N upland region along River Ebro for many of Spain's best red table wines in some 60 BODEGAS de exportación. Tempranillo predominates. Other grapes and/or oak included depending on fashion and vintage. Subdivided into 3 areas:

Rioja Alavesa N of the R Ebro, produces fine red wines, mostly light in body and colour but particularly aromatic.

Rioja Alta S of the R Ebro and W of LOGRONO, grows most of the finest, best-balanced red and white wines; also some rosé.

Rioja Baja Stretching E from LOGRONO, makes coarser red wines, high in alcohol and often used for blending.

La Rioja Alta, Bodegas R Alt r w (p) dr (sw) res ★★★ 82 85 87 88 89 **91 92 93** 94 Excellent RIOJAS, esp red CRIANZA Viña Alberdi, velvety Ardanza RESERVA, lighter Araña RESERVA, splendid RESERVA 904 and marvellous RESERVA 890 (85) – but drink it soonish; these wines are not lasting as long as they used to.

Riojanas, Bodegas R Alt r (w p) res ★★→★★★ 64 73 75 81 85 87 88 89 91 92 93 95 96 97 Old BODEGA. Trad Viña Albina; big mellow Monte Real RESERVAS (88).

Rosado Rosé.

Rotllan Torra Pri r (r&w sw) ★★★ 96 Premium Amadis, Balandra, sweet Amadis Dolç and Moscatell Reserva Especial PRIORATOS.

Rovellats Pen w p sp ★★→★★★ 92 93 94 95 Small family firm making only good (and expensive) CAVAS, stocked in some of Spain's best restaurants.

Rueda br w ★→★★★ Sm historic DO W of Valladolid. Traditional FLOR-growing, sherry-like wines up to 17% alcohol; now for fresh whites, esp MARQUES DE RISCAL. Secret weapon is the Verdejo grape.

Ruiz, Santiago Rías Baixas w ★★→★★★ DYA Small prestigious RIAS BAIXAS CO, now owned by LAN: fresh lemony ALBARINOS, not quite up to former standards.

San Sadurní de Noya Pen w sp ★★→★★★ Town S of Barcelona, hollow with CAVA cellars. Standards can be v high, though the flavour (of Parellada and other grapes) never gets close to Champagne.

San Valero, Bodegas Cariñena r p w res ★→★★ 90 91 95 96 Large former coop. Good r Monte Ducay; fresh ROSADO with slight spritz; stylish w barrel-fermented Marqués de Tosos (96).

Sangre de Toro Brand name for a rich-flavoured red from TORRES.

Sangría Cold red wine cup traditionally made with citrus fruit, fizzy lemonade, ice and brandy. But too often repulsive commercial fizz.

Sanlúcar de Barrameda Centre of the Manzanilla district (see Sherry).

Sarría, Bodega de Nav r (p w) res ★★→★★★ 87 90 91 92 94 Quality remains high, though Duarte family's departure and death of oenologist Francisco Morriones dimmed the lustre of this model estate's international reputation.

Scala Dei, Cellers de Pri r w p res ★★→★★★ 87 88 91 92 94 95 96 An original PRIORATO BODEGA, improving; enlarged v'yds. Cartoixa RESERVAS, conc blackberry-rich young Negre. Savoury oak-fermented Garnacha Blanca Blanc Prior (97).

Schenk, Bodegas Valencia r w p ★★ 88 92 93 94 95 96 97 Decent Estrella Moscatel, gd Monastrell/Garnacha 'Cavas Murviedro' and Los Monteros.

Seco Dry.

Segura Viudas, Cavas Pen w sp ★★→★★★ CAVA from SAN SADURNI (FREIXENET-owned). Buy the Brut Vintage 94, Aria or esp RESERVA Heredad.

Siglo R Alt r res ★→★★ Best-known of the big-selling wines of AGE, an outpost of BODEGAS Y BEBIDAS.

Solís, Felix Valdepeñas r ★★ BODEGA in VALDEPENAS making sturdy oak-aged reds, Viña Albali, RESERVAS (87 89 91 93 97) and fresh white.

Somontano Som Pyrenees foothills DO. Fashionable but unreliable DO. Given the cool conditions, future could lie with w and Pinot N. Best-known BODEGAS: old French-est'd Lalanne (esp Viña San Marcos r: Moristel-Tempranillo-Cab S; w Macabeo, Chard), BODEGA PIRINEOS, new VINAS DEL VERO. Also Viñedos y Crianzas del Alto Aragón (excellent ENATE range).

Tarragona r w br dr sw ★→★★★ (i) Table wines from demarcated region (DO); of little note. (ii) Old dessert wines from the firm of DE MULLER.

Tenerife r w ★→★★ DYA Now 4 DOs; s'times much more than merely drinkable young wines. Best bodegas: Flores, Monje, Insulares (Viña Norte label).

Tinto Red.

Spain entries also cross-refer to Sherry, Port & Madeira, pages 172–179.

Toro r ★→★★★ DO 150 miles NW of Madrid. Formerly for over-powerful (up to 16%) reds, now often tasty and balanced. See Bodegas Fariña.

Torremilanos Rib del D r (p) res ★→★★★ 89 90 91 92 94' Label of Bodegas Peñalba López, a fast-expanding family firm nr Aranda de Duero. Tinto Fino (Tempranillo) is smoother, more RIOJA-like than most.

Torres, Miguel Pen r w p dr s/sw res ★★→★★★★ 87 88 89 90 92 93 94 95 96 World-famous family company for many of the best PENEDES wines; a flagship for all Spain. Wines are flowery w Viña Sol 97, Green Label Fransola Sauv (96), Gran Viña Sol (97) Parellada, MILMANDA oak-fermented Chard (96), off-dry aromatic Esmeralda, Waltraud Ries (97), r Sangre de Toro, Gran Sangre de Toro, vg Gran Coronas (Cabernet Sauvignon) RESERVAS (89 93' 94'), fresh soft Las Torres Merlot 96 and Viña Magdala Pinot. Mas Borrás (93): 100% Pinot N. New Grandes Muralles (96'), full-bodied, made from native grapes incl reintroduced Garrut. Also in Chile, California and China.

Utiel-Requena U-R r p (w) Demarcated region W of VALENCIA. Sturdy reds and thick hyper-tannic wines for blending; also light fragrant rosé.

Valbuena Rib del D r ★★★ 84 85 86 88 89 90 91 92 93 94 Formerly made with the same grapes as VEGA SICILIA but sold when 5 yrs old. Best at about 10 yrs. Some prefer it to its elder brother. 88 is outstanding. But see Alión.

Valdeorras Gal r w ★→★★★ DO E of Orense. Fresh dry wines; at best Godellos are now rated among top white wines in Spain. See Guitán Godello.

Valdepeñas La M r (w) ★→★★ Demarcated region nr Andalucían border. Mainly red wines, high in alcohol but surprisingly soft in flavour. Best wines (eg LOS LLANOS, FELIX SOLIS and CASA DE LA VINA) now oak-matured.

Valdevimbre-Los Oteros r p w ★→★★ 91 92 94 95 96 N region to watch: fruity dry refreshing wines, esp from Vinos de León (aka VILE): eg young Coyanza, more mature Palacio de los Guzmanes; full-blooded Don Suero RESERVA (91 92).

Valduero, Bodegas Rib del D r (w p) ★★→★★★ 86 91 94 95 Now more than 10 yrs old; firm reputation for well-made wine and vg value RESERVAS.

Valencia r w ★ Demarcated region exporting vast quantities of clean and drinkable table wine; also refreshing whites, esp Moscatel.

Vega Sicilia Rib del D res ★★★★ 41 48 53 59 60 61 62 64 66 67 69 70 72 73 74 75 76 79 80 81 82 83 85 86 Top Spanish wine: full fruity piquant rare and fascinating. Up to 16% alcohol; best at 12-15 yrs. RESERVA Especial: a blend, chiefly of 62 and 79(!). Also VALBUENA, ALION. Now investing in Tokáji, Hungary.

Vendimia Vintage.

Viña Literally, a vineyard. But wines such as Tondonia (LOPEZ DE HEREDIA) are not necessarily made only with grapes from the v'yd named.

Viña Pedrosa See Pérez Pascuas.

Viñas del Vero Som w p r res ★★→★★★ 91 92 93 94' 95' 96 97 New SOMONTANO estate. Gd varietal wines: Chard, Ries, Gewürz. Best r Val de Vos Cab (92).

Vinícola de Castilla La M r p w ★★ 92 93 94 95 96 97 One of largest LA MANCHA firms. Red and white Castillo de Alhambra are palatable. Top are Cab, Cencibel (Tempranillo), Señorío de Guadianeja GRAN RESERVAS.

Vinícola Navarra Nav r p w res ★★ 91 92 93 94 95 Old-est'd firm, now part of BODEGAS Y BEBIDAS, but still thoroughly traditional. Best wines Castillo de Tiebas (92), Las Campañas (91) and Viña del Recuerdo (94).

Vinival, Bodegas Valencia r p w ★ Huge Valencian consortium marketing the most widely drunk wine in the region, Torres de Quart (rosé best).

Vino común/corriente Ordinary wine.

Yecla r w ★ DO north of Murcia. Decent red from BODEGAS CASTANO.

Portugal

Abrigada, Quinta da Alenquer r w res ★★ **90 92** 94 95 96 Family estate: characterful light whites, cherry-like Castelão Francês (PERIQUITA). Best: oaked GARRAFEIRAS.

Adega A cellar or winery.

Alenquer r w Aromatic reds, whites from IPR just N of Lisbon. Good estate wines from QUINTAS DE ABRIGADA and PANCAS.

Alentejo r (w) ★ ·★★★ **92 93 94** 95 96 97 Vast tract of SE Portugal with only sparse v'yds, over the R Tagus from Lisbon, but rapidly emerging potential for excellent wine. To date, the great bulk has been coop-made. Estate wines from CARTUXA, Cortes de Cima, HERDADE DE MOUCHAO, João Ramos, JOSE DE SOUSA, QUINTA DO CARMO (now part Rothschild-owned), Tapada do Chaves and ESPORAO have potency and style. Best coops are at BORBA, REDONDO and REGUENGOS. Growing excitement here. Now classified as a VINHO REGIONAL subdivided into 5 DOCs: BORBA, REDONDO, REGUENGOS, PORTALEGRE, VIDIGUEIRA; and 3 IPRs: Granja-Amareleja, Moura, EVORA.

Algarve r w ★ Wines of the holiday area are covered by DOCs Lagos, Tavira, Lagoa and Portimão. Nothing to write home about.

Aliança, Caves Bair r w sp res ★★ ·★★★ Large BAIRRADA-based firm making classic method sp. Reds and whites incl gd Bairrada wines and mature DAOS.

Almeirim Ribatejo r w ★ Large new IPR east of ALENQUER. Its coop makes the inexpensive Lezíria.

Alta Mesa See Estremadura.

Arinto White grape best from central and S Portugal where it retains acidity and produces fragrant crisp dry white wines.

Arrábida Terras do Sado r w IPR. Reds mostly from CASTELAO FRANCES (or PERIQUITA) some Cab S and Chard allowed.

Arruda, Adega Cooperativa de Est r res ★ DYA Vinho Tinto Arruda is a best buy, but avoid the Reserva. (Arruda is now an IPR.)

Aveleda, Quinta da VV w ★★ DYA Reliable VINHO VERDES made on the Aveleda estate of the Guedes family. Sold dry in Portugal but slightly sw for export. Also gd varietal wines from LOUREIRO and Trajadura.

Azevedo, Quinta do VV w ★★ DYA Superior VINHO VERDE from SOGRAPE. 100% LOUREIRO grapes.

Bacalhôa, Quinta da Set r res ★★★ **91 92 93** 94 95 96 Estate nr SETUBAL. Its fruity mid-weight Cab is made by J P VINHOS.

Bairrada Bair r w sp ★ ·★★★ **88 89 90** 91 92 94 95 DOC for excellent red GARRAFEIRAS. Also good classic method sparkling. Now an export hit.

Barca Velha Douro r res ★★★★ 78 81 82 83 85 **91** Perhaps Portugal's most renowned red, made in v limited quantities in the high DOURO by the port firm of FERREIRA (now owned by SOGRAPE). Powerful resonant wine with deep bouquet, but being challenged by younger rivals (see Redoma).

Beiras VINHO REGIONAL including DAO, BAIRRADA and granite mt ranges of central Portugal. IPRS: CASTELO RODRIGO, COVA DE BEIRA, LAFOES, PINHEL.

Boavista, Quinta da Est DYA Large property nr ALENQUER making increasingly gd range of r and w: Palha Canas, Quinta das Sete Encostas, Espiga and a Chard, Casa Santos Lima.

Borba Alen r ★·★★ Small DOC nr EVORA; some of the best ALENTEJO wine.

Borba, Adega Cooperativa de Alen r (w) res ★ ·★★ DYA Leading ALENTEJO coop modernized with stainless steel and oak by EC funding. Big fruity Vinho Do Ano red and vg Reserva.

Borges & Irmão Merchants of port and table wines at Vila Nova de Gaia, incl GATAO and (better) Gamba VINHOS VERDES, sparkling Fita Azul.

Branco White.

Brejoeira, Palacio de VV w (r) ★★★ Outstanding estate-made VINHO VERDE from MONÇAO: fragrant with full flavour. 100% Alvarinho grapes.

Bright Brothers (r) 92 93 **94 95 96 97** Australian flying winemaker based in Portugal: interests as far-flung as Argentina, Sicily and Spain. Range of well-made wines from DOURO, RIBATEJO, ESTREMADURA and BEIRAS. See also Fiuza Bright.

Buçaco Beiras r w (p) res ★★★★ (r) **53 59 62' 63** 70 78 82 85 89 **92** (w) 91 **92** Legendary speciality of the Palace Hotel at Buçaco nr Coimbra, not seen elsewhere. At best incredible quality, worth journey. So are palace and park.

A choice for 2000 from Portugal

Douro Redoma 95, Quinta do Crasto Reserva 95, Quinta do Côtto Grande Escolha 94, Quinta da Gaivosa (red) 95

Dão Quinta dos Roques Reserva 96 (and 96 Touriga Nacional and Alfrocheiro Preto varietal wines)

Bairrada Luis Pato Quinta do Ribeirinho Pé Franco 95, Casa da Saima Garrafeira 95

Estremadura Quinta de Pancas Reserva Touriga Nacional

Terras do Sado Periquita Classico 92

Alentejo Pera Manca 91, Cartuxa 95, Esporão red 95, Jose da Sousa Garrafeira 91, Mouchão 92

Moscatel de Setúbal José Maria de Fonseca 20 yr old

Bucelas Est w ★★★ Tiny demarcated region N of Lisbon in the hands of 3 producers. Quinta da Romeira make attractive wines from the ARINTO grape.

Camarate, Quinta de Est r ★★ **90 91 92** Notable red from JOSE MARIA DA FONSECA, S of Lisbon, incl detectable proportion of Cab S.

Carcavelos Est br sw ★★★ Normally NV. Minute DOC W of Lisbon. Rare sweet aperitif or dessert wines average 19% alcohol and resemble honeyed MADEIRA. The only producer is now Quinta dos Pesos, Caparide.

Carmo, Quinta do Alen r w res ★★★ 87 92 93 94 **95** Beautiful small ALENTEJO ADEGA, partly bought '92 by Rothschilds (Lafite). 125 acres, plus cork forests. Fresh white, red better. 2nd wine: Dom Martinho.

Cartaxo Ribatejo r w ★ District in RIBATEJO N of Lisbon, now an IPR area making everyday wines popular in the capital.

Cartuxa, Herdade de Alen r ★ 94 95 w 95 96 Vast estate nr EVORA (500 acres). Big reds esp Pera Manca (90 91 94), one of ALENTEJO's best (and most pricy); soft creamy whites. Also Monte de Pinheiros, Fundação Eugenio de Almeida.

Carvalho, Ribeiro & Ferreira N Lisbon r w res ★★–★★★ Have now ceased trading but Serradayres and good GARRAFEIRAS from the RIBATEJO are still seen.

Casa Cadaval Rib 95 96 Enterprising estate with wine made by João Ramos. Varietal reds incl TRINCADEIRA, Pinot N and Cab S.

Casa de Sezim VV w ★ DYA Estate-bottled VINHO VERDE from a member of the association of private producers, APEVV.

Casal Branco, Quinta de Ribatejo r ★ Big concern; gd reds: Falua (DYA) and Falcoaria (95).

Casal García VV w ★★ DYA Big-selling VINHO VERDE, made at AVELEDA.

Casal Mendes VV w ★★ DYA The VINHO VERDE from CAVES ALIANCA.

Casaleiro Trademark of Caves Dom Teodosio-João T Barbosa, who makes a variety of standard wines: DAO, VINHO VERDE etc.

Castelão Francês Red grape widely planted throughout S Portugal. Good firm-flavoured reds, often blended with Cab S. Aka PERIQUITA.

Portugal entries also cross-refer to Sherry, Port & Madeira, pages 172–179.

167

Castelo Rodrigo Beiras r w IPR reds resembling lighter style of DAO.

Cepa Velha VV w (r) ★★★ Brand name of Vinhos de Monção. Its Alvarinho is one of the best VINHOS VERDES.

Chaves Trás-os-Montes r w IPR. Sharp pale fizzy reds from granite soils. Rounder ones from schist.

Colares r ★★ Small DOC on the sandy coast W of Lisbon. Its antique-style dark-red wines, rigid with tannin, are from ungrafted vines. They need ageing, but TOTB (the older the better) no longer. See Paulo da Silva.

Consumo (vinho) Ordinary wine.

Coruche Ribatejo r w Large IPR of Sorraia River basin NE of Lisbon.

Côtto, Quinta do Douro r w res ★★★ 90 94 95′ Pioneer table wines from port country; vg red Grande Escolha (87 90 92 94 95) and also Q do Côtto are dense fruity tannic wines for long keeping. Also port.

Cova da Beira Beiras r w Largest of the IPRs nr Spanish border. Light reds best.

Crasto, Quinta de Douro r dr sw (★) 95 96 97 Top estate nr Pinhão for port and excellent oak-aged reds. Look out for excellent varietal wines (TOURIGA NACIONAL, TINTA RORIZ) and Reserva (95).

Dão r w res ★★ 90 91 92 94 95 DOC region round town of Viseu. Too many dull wines produced in the past but region is improving rapidly with single QUINTAS making headway: solid reds of some subtlety with age; substantial dry whites. Most sold under brand names. But see Roques, Maias, Saes, Fonte do Ouro, Terras Altas, Porta dos Cavalheiros, Grao Vasco, Duque de Viseu etc.

DOC (Denominaçâo de Origem Controlada) Official wine region. There are 18 in Portugal, incl BAIRRADA, COLARES, DAO, DOURO, SETUBAL, VINHO VERDE; and new in '95: BORBA, PORTALEGRE, REDONDO, REGUENGOS, VIDIGUEIRA (in the ALENTEJO). See also IPR, Vinhos Regionals.

Doce (vinho) Sweet (wine).

Douro r w 85 87 90 91 92 94 95 96 97 Northern river whose valley produces port and some of Portugal's most exciting new table wines. See Barca Velha, Quinta do Côtto, Redoma, etc. Watch this space.

Duas Quintas Douro r ★★ 92 94 95 96 Rich red from port shipper RAMOS PINTO. Vg Reserva (92).

Duque de Viseu Dão r 90 92 94 95 High quality red DAO from SOGRAPE.

Esporão, Herdade do Alen w r ★★→★★★ 93 94 95 96 Impressive estate owned by Finagra. Wines are made (since '92) by Australian David Baverstock: light fresh Roupeiro white, fruity young red Alandra, superior (91 92) Cab S – Esporão, with a touch of Cab S, is one of ALENTEJO's best reds. Also incl Monte Velho gently oaked reds and fruity whites. Gd varietal wines from Aragonez, TRINCADEIRA and Cab S.

Espumante Sparkling.

Esteva Douro r ★ DYA V drinkable DOURO red from port firm FERREIRA.

Estremadura VINHO REGIONAL on Portugal's W coast, s'times called 'Oeste'. Large coops. Alta Mesa from São Marmade de Ventosa coop is good. IPRS: ALENQUER, ARRUDA, Encostas d'Aire, Obidos, TORRES VEDRAS.

Evelita Douro r ★★ Reliable middle-weight red made near Vila Real by REAL COMPANHIA VINICOLA DO NORTE DE PORTUGAL.

Evora Alen r w Large new IPR south of Lisbon.

Fernão Pires White grape making ripe-flavoured slightly spicy whites in RIBATEJO. (Known as Maria Gomes in BAIRRADA.)

Ferreirinha Reserva Especial Douro r ★★★ 84 86 90 Second wine to BARCA VELHA, made in less than ideal vintages.

Fonseca, José Maria da Est r w dr sw sp res ★★ Venerable firm in Azeitão nr Lisbon. One of biggest and best ranges in Portugal, incl dry white PASMADOS, PORTALEGRE and QUINTA DE CAMARATE; red PERIQUITA, PASMADOS, TERRAS ALTAS, DAO, several GARRAFEIRAS; and famous dessert SETUBAL. Fonseca also owns JOSE DE SOUSA. LANCERS rosé is less distinguished, but Lancers Brut is a surprisingly drinkable sp wine made by a continuous process of Russian invention.

Fonte do Ouro Dão r ★ **92** Good balanced red from well-run single estate. Second wine: Quinta da Giesta.

Foz do Arouce, Quinta da Beiras r ★★ **91 92 95** 96 Big cask-aged red from heart of BEIRAS.

Franqueira, Quinta da VV w ★ Typically dry, fragrant VINHO VERDE made by Englishman Piers Gallie.

Fuiza Bright Ribatejo r w ★ **96 97** DYA Joint venture with Peter Bright (BRIGHT BROS). Good Chard, Sauv, Merlot and Cab S.

Gaivosa, Quinta de Douro r ★ **94 95** Important estate near Regua. Deep concentrated cask-aged reds from port grapes. Quinta do Vale da Raposa (95) is lighter fruity red from same producer. Also Quinta da Estação.

Garrafeira Label term: merchant's 'private reserve', aged for minimum of 2 years in cask and 1 in bottle, but often much longer. Usually their best, though traditionally often of indeterminate origin. Now has to show origin on label.

Gatão VV w ★ DYA Standard BORGES & IRMAO VINHO V; fragrant but sweetened.

Gazela VV w ★★ DYA Reliable VINHO VERDE made at Barcelos by SOGRAPE since the AVELEDA estate went to a different branch of the Guedes family.

Generoso Aperitif or dessert wine rich in alcohol.

Grão Vasco Dão r w res ★★ **94 95 96** One of the best and largest brands of DAO, from a new high-tech ADEGA at Viseu. Fine red GARRAFEIRA (**90 91**); fresh young white (DYA). Owned by SOGRAPE.

IPR Indicação de Proveniência Regulamentada. See below.

Portuguese wines to look for in the early 2000s

Redoma Niepoort's red Douro wine

Vinha do Fojo the red wine of Quinta do Fojo in the Douro

Vallado the red wine from Quinta do Vallado in the Douro

Quinta dos Roques finely crafted red wines from the Dão

Herdade de Mouchão Alentejo red in minute quantities

José de Sousa Alen r res ★★ **91 92 94 95** (was Rosado Fernandes) Small firm recently acquired by J M DA FONSECA. The most sophisticated of the full-bodied wines from ALENTEJO (solid foot-trodden GARRAFEIRAS, although now slightly lighter in style), fermented in earthenware amphoras and aged in oak.

J P Vinhos Set r w sp res ★★ Enterprising well-equipped winery making wide range of wines incl João Pires Dry Muscat and reds: Meia Pipa, TINTO DA ANFORA and QUINTA DA BACALHOA. Cova da Ursa is a barrel-fermented Chard.

Lafões Beiras r w IPR between DAO and VINHO VERDE.

Lagosta VV w DYA VINHO VERDE white from the REAL COMPANHIA VINICOLA DO NORTE DE PORTUGAL.

Lancers Est p w sp ★ Sweet carbonated rosé and sparkling white extensively shipped to the US by J M DA FONSECA.

Lagoalva, Quinta da r w ★ **92 94 95** Important RIBATEJO property making gd reds from local grapes and from Syrah. Second label: Monte da Casta.

Lezíria See Almeirim.

Loureiro Best VINHO VERDE grape variety: crisp fragrant white wines.

Madeira br dr sw ★★→★★★★ Portugal's Atlantic island making famous fortified dessert and aperitif wines. See pages 172–179.

Maduro (vinho) A mature table wine – as opposed to a VINHO VERDE.

NB Vintages in colour are those you should choose first for drinking in 2000.

Maias, Quinta das Dão ★★ 94 95 96 New-wave quinta: solid reds to age.

Mateus Rosé Bair p (w) ★ World's biggest-selling medium-sweet carbonated rosé, from SOGRAPE at Vila Real and Anadia in BAIRRADA.

Monção N subregion of VINHO VERDE on River Minho: best wines from the Alvarinho grape. See Palacio de Brejoeira.

Morgadio de Torre VV w ★★ DYA Top vv from SOGRAPE. Largely Alvarinho.

Mouchão, Herdade de Alen r res ★★★ 74 82 89 90 91 92 Perhaps top ALENTEJO estate, ruined in '74 revolution; since replanted and fully recovered.

Palmela Terras do Sado r w Sandy soil IPR. Reds can be long-lived.

Pancas, Quinta das Est r w res ★★ 94 95 96 Mainly Cab S and Chard from go-ahead estate nr ALENQUER. Dense Cab and balanced oaked Chard. Outstanding TOURIGA N Res (**95**), vg dry white ARINTO: Quinta Dom Carlos.

Pasmados 91 92 94 V tasty JOSE MARIA DA FONSECA red from SETUBAL peninsula.

Pato, Luis Bair r sp ★★→★★★ 85 89 90 91 92 94 95' 96 Some of top estate-grown BAIRRADA incl tremendous red QUINTA DE RIBEIRINHO and João Pato. '95 reds notable, esp Quinta do Ribeirinho Pé Franco. Also classic method sparkling.

Paulo da Silva, Antonio Bernardino Colares r (w) res ★★→★★★ 84 85 87 88 His COLARES Chitas is one of the v few of these classics still made.

Pedralvites, Quinta de Bair w ★→★★ DYA Pleasant BAIRRADA white with apple and apricot flavours from the Maria Gomes grape, by SOGRAPE.

Periquita Est r ★★ 94 95 96 Enjoyable robust reds, made by JOSE MARIA DA FONSECA at Azeitão S of Lisbon. Periquita is an alias of CASTELAO FRANCES, a grape much grown in the RIBATEJO.

Pinhel Beiras w (r) sp ★ IPR region E of DAO: similar white, mostly sparkling.

Pires, Vinhos João See J P Vinhos.

Planalto Douro w ★★ DYA Good white wine from SOGRAPE.

Planalto Mirandês Trás-os-Montes r w Large IPR NE of DOURO. Port grapes in reds. Verdelho in whites.

Ponte de Lima, Cooperativa de VV r w ★★ Maker of one of the best bone-dry red VINHOS VERDES, and first-rate dry and fruity white.

Porta dos Cavalheiros Dão ★★ 85 88 91 92 94 One of the best red DAOS, matured by CAVES SAO JOAO in BAIRRADA.

Portalegre Alen r w DOC on Spanish border. Strong fragrant reds with potential to age. Alcoholic whites.

Quinta Estate.

Ramada Est r w ★ DYA Modestly-priced red from the São Mamede de Ventosa coop: fruity and v drinkable.

Raposeira Douro w sp ★★ Well-known fizz made by the classic method at Lamego. Ask for the Bruto. An outpost of Seagram.

Real Companhia Vinícola do Norte de Portugal Giant of the port trade (see page 177); also produces EVELITA, LAGOSTA, etc.

Redoma ★★★ 91 94 95 Amazing mouthfilling red from port-shipper NIEPOORT (**91**). And remarkable nutty, old-style white; real satisfaction after ultra-grapey, young productions.

Redondo Alen r w Nr Spanish border. One of Portugal's best large coops. Newly granted DOC status.

Reguengos Alen r (w) res ★→★★★ Important DOC nr Spanish border. Incl JOSE DE SOUSA and ESPORAO estates, plus large coop for good reds.

Ribatejo r w DYA VINHO REGIONAL on R Tagus north of Lisbon. Good GARRAFEIRAS and younger wines from ALMEIRIM coop, FUIZA BRIGHT and BRIGHT BROS. IPRS: ALMEIRIM, CARTAXO, Chamusca, Coruche, Santarém, Tomar.

A general rule for Portugal: choose youngest vintages of whites available.

Ribeirinho, Quinta do Bair r sp ★★→★★★ 85 92 95' 96 Vg tannic, concentrated reds from LUIS PATO. Pé Franco 95 is outstanding.

Rios do Minho VINHO REGIONAL covering NW – similar area to VINHO VERDE.

Roques, Quinta dos Dão r ★ 94 95 96 Promising estate for big solid oaked reds.

Rosa, Quinta de la Douro r ★★ 92 94 95 96 Firm oaky red from old port v'yds and young peppery Quinta das Lamelas made by Australian David Baverstock.

Rosado Rosé.

Rosado Fernandes See José de Sousa.

Saes, Quinta de Dão r w ★★ 92 94 95 96 Small mountain v'yd making refined wines. Quinta de Pellada also making gd wines under same ownership.

Saima, Casa de Bair r w ★★ 90 91 94 95 Small trad estate; big, long-lasting tannic reds (esp GARRAFEIRAS) and some astounding whites.

São Domingos, Comp dos Vinhos de Est r ★ 95 Reds (Espiga, Palha-Canas), from estate managed by José Neiva, maker of ALTA MESA.

São João, Caves Bair r w sp res ★★ →★★★ 83 85 90 91 92 94 95 One of region's top firms. Fruity, full r BAIRRADA: Frei João, PORTA DOS CAVALHEIROS DAO. Also fizz.

Seco Dry.

Entre Serras r w ★ DYA BEIRAS property. Sound barrel-fermented Chard (DYA) and soft light reds.

Setúbal Set br (r w) sw (dr) ★★★ Tiny demarcated region S of River Tagus, where FONSECA make aromatic Muscat-based sw wine usually sold at 6 and 20 yrs old.

Sogrape Sociedad Comercial dos Vinhos de Mesa de Portugal. Largest wine concern in the country, making VINHOS VERDES, DAO, BAIRRADA, ALENTEJO, MATEUS ROSE, Terra Franca, Vila Real red etc, and now owners of FERREIRA and OFFLEY port. Revamped Vila Regia is a pleasant, light Douro red.

Tamariz, Quinta do VV w ★ Fragrant VINHO VERDE from Loureiro grapes only.

Terras Altas Dão r w res ★ DYA Brand of r and w DAO from J M DA FONSECA.

Terras do Sado VINHO REGIONAL covering sandy plains around Sado estuary. IPRS: ARRABIDA and PALMELA.

Tinta Roriz Major port grape (variant of Tempranillo) making gd DOURO table wines. Increasingly planted for similarly full reds. AKA Aragonez in ALENTEJO.

Tinto Red.

Tinto da Anfora Est r ★★ 90 91 92 94 Deservedly popular juicy and fruity red from J P VINHOS.

Torres Vedras Est r w IPR area N of Lisbon famous for Wellington's 'lines'. Major supplier of bulk wine; one of biggest coops in Portugal.

Touriga Nacional Top red grape used for port and DOURO table wines; now increasingly elsewhere, esp DAO, ALENTEJO, ESTREMADURA.

Trás-os-Montes VINHO REGIONAL covering mountains of NE Portugal. Light reds and rosés. IPRS: CHAVES, PLANALTO-MIRANDES, Valpacos.

Trincadeira Vg red grape in ALENTEJO for spicy single-varietal wines.

Velhas, Caves Bucelas r w res ★ Until very recently the only maker of BUCELAS; also good DAO and Romeira GARRAFEIRAS.

Verde Green (see Vinhos Verdes).

Vidigueira Alen w r ★ DOC for traditionally-made unmatured whites from volcanic soils and some plummy reds.

Vinho Regional Larger provincial wine region, with same status as French vin de pays: they are: ALGARVE, ALENTEJO, BEIRAS, ESTREMADURA, RIBATEJO, RIOS DO MINHO, TRAS-OS-MONTES, TERRAS DO SADO. See also DOC, IPR.

Vinhos Verdes VV w ★→★★★ r ★ DOC between R Douro and N frontier with Spain, for 'green wines' (white or red): made from grapes with high acidity and (originally) undergoing a special secondary fermentation to leave them with a slight sparkle. Today the fizz is usually just added CO_2. Ready for drinking in spring after harvest.

Sherry, Port & Madeira

Sherry, port and Madeira are the world's great classic fortified wines: reinforced with alcohol up to between 15 percent (for a light sherry) and 22 (for vintage port). No others have ever supplanted them for quality or value – despite many attempts.

The late '90s are witnessing a significant upturn in port exports and sales with shipments continuing to exceed all previous records (esp in '98). The price of recently declared vintages (which includes 97 for most shippers) is rising in line with demand. While for sherry 1996 was a historic year – its name was at last legally recognized as belonging to Spain alone. The Cape, Cyprus and other imitators of this great wine have had to find other names.

The map on pages 154–55 locates the port (Douro) and sherry (Jerez) districts. Madeira is an island 400 miles out in the Atlantic off the coast of Morocco, a port of call for west-bound sailing ships: hence its historical market in North America.

Shippers (that is producers, blenders and bottlers) are still far more important than growers in these industries. This section lists both types of wines and shippers' names with the names and vintages (if any) of their best wines. NB: some 1985 vintage port is drinking unpredictably – best to wait and see.

Abad, Tomás Small sherry BODEGA owned by LUSTAU. Vg light FINO.

Almacenista Individual matured but unblended sherry; usually dark dry wines for connoisseurs. Often superb quality and value. See Lustau.

Alvear Mont-M g ★★★ The largest producer of excellent sherry-like aperitif and dessert wines in MONTILLA-MORILES.

Amontillado A FINO aged in cask beyond its normal span to become darker, more powerful and pungent. The best are natural dry wines.

Amoroso Type of sweet sherry, v similar to a sweet OLOROSO.

Barbadillo, Antonio Much the largest SANLUCAR firm, with a wide range of MANZANILLAS and sherries mostly excellent of their type, including Sanlúcar FINO, superb SOLERA manzanilla PASADA, Fino de Balbaina, austere Príncipe dry AMONTILLADO. Also young Castillo de San Diego table wines.

Barbeito One of the last independent MADEIRA shipping firms, now Japanese controlled. Wines incl rare vintages, eg MALMSEY 1901 and the latest, BUAL 1960.

Barros Almeida Large family-owned port house with several brands (incl Feist, Feuerheerd, KOPKE): excellent 20-yr-old TAWNY and many COLHEITAS.

Barros e Sousa Tiny family-owned Madeira producer with old lodges in centre of Funchal. Extremely fine but now rare vintages, plus gd 10 yr old wines.

Blandy One of two top names used by MADEIRA WINE CO. Duke of Clarence Rich Madeira is their most famous wine. 10-year-old reserves (VERDELHO, BUAL, MALMSEY) are good. Many glorious old vintages can be seen (eg Malmsey '54, Bual '20 and Sercial '40), though mostly nowadays at auctions.

Blázquez DOMECQ-owned BODEGA at PUERTO DE S MARIA. Outstanding FINO, Carta Blanca, v old SOLERA OLOROSO Extra; Carta Oro AMONTILLADO al natural (unsweetened).

Bobadilla Large JEREZ BODEGA, recently bought by OSBORNE and best known for v dry Victoria FINO and Bobadilla 103 brandy, esp among Spanish connoisseurs.

Borges, H M Independent MADEIRA shipper of old repute.

Brown sherry British term for a style of budget dark sweet sherry.

Bual One of the best grapes of MADEIRA, making a soft smoky sweet wine, usually lighter and not as rich as MALMSEY. (See panel on page 179.)

Burdon English-founded sherry BODEGA owned by CABALLERO. Puerto FINO, Don Luis AMONTILLADO and raisiny Heavenly Cream are top lines.

Burmester Old, small, family port house with fine soft sweet 20-yr-old TAWNY; also vg range of COLHEITAS and single-QUINTA: Quinta Nossa Sra do Carmo. Vintages: **70 77 80 85 89** 91 92 94 95.

Caballero Important sherry shipper at PUERTO DE SANTA MARIA, best known for Pavón FINO, Mayoral Cream OLOROSO, excellent BURDON sherries and PONCHE orange liqueur. Also owners of LUSTAU.

Cálem Old Portuguese house; had fine reputation, but recent vintages not as gd. Vintages: **50 55 58 60 63 66 70 75 77** 80 83 85 91 94. Reliable light TAWNY; gd range of COLHEITAS: **48 50 52 57 60 62 65 78 84** 86. Sold in '98, but family still owns Quinta da Foz (**84 86 87 88 89 90** 92 95).

Churchill **82 85** 91 94 The only recently founded port shipper, already highly respected. Vg traditional LBV. Quinta da Agua Alta is Churchill's single-QUINTA port: **83 87** 90 92 95.

Cockburn British-owned (Allied-DOMECQ) port shipper with a range of gd wines incl v popular fruity Special Res. Fine VINTAGE PORT from high v'yds: deceptively light when young, but has great lasting power. Vintages: **55 60 63 67 70 75 83 85** 91 94. Note: for many shippers, 85 generally not as gd as first thought.

A choice of port and Madeira for 2000

White Churchill

Premium Ruby Warre's Warrior, Fonseca Bin 27

LBV Graham, Niepoort, Smith Woodhouse, Taylor

Tawny Ferreira Duque de Braganca 20-Yr-Old, Taylor's Over 40 Yrs Old

Single Quinta Vintage Dow's Quinta do Bomfim 1987, Taylor's Quinta de Vargellas 1987, Martinez Quinta da Eira Velha 1992

Vintage Croft 1963, Fonseca 1963, Taylor 1963, Dow 1966, Graham 1970, Smith Woodhouse 1977

Sercial Barros e Sousa Reserve, Leacock 1950

Verdelho Henriques and Henriques 10-Year-Old, Blandy's 1968, Pereira d'Oliviera 1905

Bual Henriques and Henriques 15-Year-Old, Blandy's 1954, Cossart Gordon 1908

Malmsey Blandy's 15-Year-Old, Pereira d'Oliviera 1900

Colheita Vintage-dated port of a single yr, but aged at least 7 winters in wood: in effect a vintage TAWNY. The bottling date is also shown on the label. Excellent examples come from KOPKE, CALEM, NIEPOORT and Krohn.

Cossart Gordon One time-leading MADEIRA shipper, founded 1745, with BLANDY now one of the two top-quality labels of the MADEIRA WINE CO. Wines slightly less rich than Blandy's. Best-known for Good Company Finest Medium Rich. Also 5-yr-old reserves, old vintages (latest 74) and SOLERAS (esp BUAL 1845).

Crasto, Quinta do Well-situated estate producing ports improving in quality, esp LBV. Vintages: **85 87** 91 94 95 (for long keeping).

Cream Sherry A style of amber sweet sherry made by sweetening a blend of well-aged OLOROSOS. It originated in Bristol, England.

Croft One of the oldest firms shipping VINTAGE PORT: since 1678; now owned by Diageo. Well-balanced vintage wines tend to mature early (since 66). Vintages: **55 60 63' 66 67 70 75 77 82 85** 91 94; and lighter vintage wines: Quinta da Roeda in several other years (**78 80 83 87** 95). 'Distinction': most popular blend. Morgan: sm separate co (also DELAFORCE). Also sherries: Croft Original (PALE CREAM), Particular (medium), Delicado (FINO, also medium); gd PALO CORTADO.

Crusted Term for vintage-style port, usually blended from several vintages not one. Bottled young, then aged so it forms a 'crust'. Needs decanting.

Cruz Huge brand and market leader in France. (The French take 40% of all port exports.) Standard TAWNY in French style – not brilliant quality. Owned by French co La Martiniquaise.

Delaforce Port shipper owned by CROFT, best known in Germany. His Eminence's Choice is a v pleasant 10 yr old TAWNY; VINTAGE CHARACTER is also good. Vintage wines are v fine, among the lighter kind: **55 58 60 63 66 70 75 77 82 85** 94; Quinta da Côrte in **78 80 84** 87 91 95.

Delgado, Zuleta Old-est'd SANLUCAR firm best known for marvellous La Goya MANZANILLA PASADA.

Diez-Merito SA Sherry house famous for FINO Imperial and Victoria Regina OLOROSO. Bought by Rumasa and incorporated into BODEGAS INTERNACIONALES. Control passed to Marcos Eguizabal (of PATERNINA in RIOJA). Now apparently exists as little more than a name. Its excellent DON ZOILO sherry has been sold to the MEDINA group, and Gran Duque de Alba brandy to WILLIAMS & HUMBERT.

Domecq Giant family-run sherry BODEGA at JEREZ, recently merged with Allied-Lyons as Allied-Domecq, famous also for Fundador and other brandies. Double Century Original OLOROSO, its biggest brand, now replaced by Pedro Cream Sherry; La Ina is excellent FINO. Other famous wines incl Celebration CREAM, Botaina (old AMONTILLADO) and magnificent Rio Viejo (v dry oloroso) and Sibarita (PALO CORTADO). Recently: a range of wonderful old SOLERA sherries (Sibarita, Amontillado 51-1a and Venerable Oloroso). Also in RIOJA and Mexico.

> Top-quality sherry is now the best-value wine in the world. Supreme old dry wines cost less than Another Chardonnay.

Don Zoilo Luxury sherries, including velvety FINO, recently sold by BODEGAS INTERNACIONALES to the MEDINA group.

Dow Brand name of Silva and Cozens, celebrated their bicentenary in '98, now belonging to the Symington family alongside GRAHAM, WARRE, SMITH WOODHOUSE, GOULD CAMPBELL, QUARLES HARRIS and QUINTA DO VESUVIO. Style deliberately slightly drier than other shippers in group. Vg range of ports incl single-QUINTA Bomfim (**78 79 82 84** 86 87 88 89 90 92 95) and outstanding vintages: **55 60 63 66 70 72 75 77 80 83** 85 91 94.

Duff Gordon Sherry shipper best known for El Cid AMONTILLADO. Gd FINO Feria; Nina Medium OLOROSO. OSBORNE-owned; name also used as 2nd label for their ports.

Eira Velha, Quinta da Small port estate with old-style vintage wines shipped by MARTINEZ. Vintages: **78 82** 87 92 94 95.

Ferreira One of the biggest Portuguese-owned port growers and shippers (since 1751). Largest selling brand in P. Well-known for old TAWNIES and juicily sweet, relatively light vintages: **60 63 66 70 75 77 78 80 82** 85 87 91 94 95. Also Dona Antónia Personal Reserve, splendidly rich tawny Duque de Bragança and single-QUINTA wines Quinta do Seixo (**83**) and Q da Leda (90).

Fino, Fina Term for lightest, finest sherries and MONTILLAS, completely dry, v pale, delicate but pungent. Fino should always be drunk cool and fresh: it deteriorates rapidly once opened. TIO PEPE: the classic. Use half bottles if possible.

Flor A floating yeast peculiar to FINO sherry and certain other wines that oxidize slowly and tastily under its influence.

Fonseca Guimaraens British-owned port shipper with a stellar reputation; connected with TAYLOR'S. Robust deeply coloured vintage wine, among the v best. Vintages: Fonseca **60 63 66 70 75** 77 **80 83 85** 92 94; Fonseca Guimaraens 76 78 82 84 **86 87 88** 91 94 95. Quinta do Panascal **78** is a single-QUINTA wine. Also delicious VINTAGE CHARACTER Bin 27.

Forrester Port shipper and owner of the famous Quinta da Boa Vista, now owned by SOGRAPE. The vintage wines tend to be round, 'fat' and sweet, good for relatively early drinking. Baron de Forrester is vg TAWNY. Vintages: (Offley Forrester) 55 60 62 63 66 67 70 72 75 77 80 82 83 85 87 89 94 95.

Garvey Famous old sherry shipper at JEREZ, now owned by José María Ruiz Mateos. The finest wines are deep-flavoured FINO San Patricio, Tio Guillermo Dry AMONTILLADO and Ochavico Dry OLOROSO. San Angelo Medium amontillado is the most popular. Also Bicentenary PALE CREAM.

González Byass Enormous family-run firm shipping the world's most famous and one of v best FINO sherries: TIO PEPE. Brands include La Concha medium AMONTILLADO, Elegante dry fino and new El Rocío MANZANILLA Fina, San Domingo PALE CREAM, Nectar CREAM and Alfonso Dry OLOROSO. Amontillado del Duque is on a higher plane, as are Matusalem and Apostoles: respectively sweet and dry old olorosos of rare quality. Also makers of top-selling Soberano and exquisite Lepanto brandies.

Gould Campbell See Smith Woodhouse.

Gracia Hermanos Mont-M Firm within the same group as PEREZ BARQUERO and Compañia Vinícola del Sur making gd quality MONTILLAS. Its labels incl María del Valle FINO, Montearruit AMONTILLADO, OLOROSO CREAM and Dulce Viejo PX.

Graham Port shipper famous for some of the richest, sweetest and best of VINTAGE PORTS, largely from its own Quinta dos Malvedos (52 57 58 61 65 68 76 78 79 80 82 84 86 87 88 90 92 95). Also excellent brands, incl Six Grapes RUBY, LBV, and 10- and 20-yr-old TAWNIES. Vintages: 55 60 63 66 70 75 77 80 83 85 91 94.

Guita, La Famous old SANLUCAR BODEGA noteworthy for its particularly fine MANZANILLA PASADA.

Hartley & Gibson See Valdespino.

Sherry: which to choose

The sherry industry has recently been so badly depleted that a list of truly excellent wines still being made is needed to keep it in focus. They incl: Barbadillo manzanillas; Blázquez Carta Blanca fino; Domecq La Ina fino, Rio Viejo oloroso, Sibarita palo cortado; González Byass Tio Pepe fino, Amontillado del Duque, Matusalem and Apostoles sweet and dry olorosos; Hidalgo La Gitana manzanilla fino, Jerez Cortado and La Pastrana; the Lustau Almacenista range; Osborne Fino Quinta and 'Rare' range (esp Alonso del Sabio); Medina Don Zoilo fino; Sandeman Don fino; Royal Corregidor sw oloroso; de Soto Soto fino; Valdespino Inocente fino, Don Tomás amontillado; Williams & Humbert Pando fino and palo cortado.

Harvey's Important pillar of the Allied-DOMECQ empire, along with TERRY. World-famous Bristol shippers of Bristol Cream and Bristol Milk (sweet), Club AMONTILLADO and Bristol Dry (medium), Luncheon Dry and Bristol FINO (not v dry). More to the point is its very good '1796' range of high quality sherries comprising Fine Old Amontillado, PALO CORTADO and Rich Old OLOROSO. Harvey's also controls COCKBURN.

Henriques & Henriques The biggest independent MADEIRA shipper, at Câmara de Lobos, now with the largest, most modern cellars on the island: wide range of well-structured, rich, toothsome wines – the 10 year-olds are gold and platinum medal winners. Also a good extra-dry aperitif, Monte Seco, and v fine old reserves and vintages.

Sherry, Port & Madeira entries also cross-refer to Spain and Portugal sections, respectively pages 154–165 and 166–171.

Hidalgo, Vinícola Old family firm based in SANLUCAR DE BARRAMEDA, one of the region's best known for top quality sherries: pale MANZANILLA La Gitana, fine OLOROSO Seco, lovely soft and deep Jerez CORTADO and first-rate new Pastrana MANZANILLA PASADA.

Internacionales, Bodegas Once the pride of the now-defunct Rumasa and with such famous houses as BERTOLA, VARELA and DIEZ-MERITO, the company was taken over by the entrepreneur Marcos Eguizabal. See MEDINA.

Jerez de la Frontera Centre of the sherry industry, between Cádiz and Seville in southern Spain. The word 'sherry' is a corruption of the name, pronounced in Spanish 'hereth'. In French, Xérès.

Kopke The oldest port house, founded by a German in 1638. Now belongs to BARROS ALMEIDA. Fair-quality vintage wines (**70 74 75 77 78 79 80 82 83 85 87 89** 91 94) and excellent COLHEITAS.

Late-bottled vintage (LBV) Port from a single vintage kept in wood for twice as long as VINTAGE PORT (about 5 years), therefore lighter when bottled and ages more quickly. 'Traditional' (unfiltered) LBV now has to spend an extra 3 yrs in bottle to qualify (WARRE, SMITH WOODHOUSE, NIEPOORT, CHURCHILL, FERREIRA, NOVAL).

Leacock One of the oldest MADEIRA shippers, now a label of the MADEIRA WINE CO. Basic St-John range is v fair; 10-yr-old Special Res MALMSEY and 15-yr-old BUAL are excellent. Older vintages also available: Bual '34, Verdelho '54.

Lustau One of the largest family-run sherry BODEGAS in JEREZ (now controlled by CABALLERO), making many wines for other shippers, but with a vg Dry Lustau range (esp FINO and OLOROSO) and Jerez Lustau PALO CORTADO. Pioneer shipper of excellent ALMACENISTA and 'landed age' wines; AMONTILLADOS and olorosos aged in elegant bottles before shipping. See also Abad.

Macharnudo One of the best parts of the sherry v'yds, N of JEREZ, famous for wines of the highest quality, both FINO and OLOROSO.

Madeira Wine Company Formed in 1913 by two firms as the Madeira Wine Association, subsequently to include all the British MADEIRA firms (26 in total) amalgamated to survive hard times. Remarkably, three generations later the wines, though cellared together, preserve their house styles. BLANDY and COSSART GORDON: top labels. Now controlled by the Symington group (see Dow).

Malmsey The sweetest and richest form of MADEIRA; dark amber, rich and honeyed yet with Madeira's unique sharp tang. Word is English corruption of 'Malvasia' qv. See panel on page 179.

Manzanilla A pale dry sherry, usually more delicate than a FINO, matured in the cooler maritime conditions of SANCULAR DE BARRAMEDA (as opposed to JEREZ which is inland).

Manzanilla Pasada A mature MANZANILLA, half-way to an AMONTILLADO-style wine. At its best (eg LA GUITA) one of the most appetizing of all sherries.

Marqués del Real Tesoro Old sherry firm, famous for its MANZANILLA and AMONTILLADO, bought by the enterprising José Estévez. Shrugging off the current slump in sales he has built a spanking new BODEGA – the first in years. Tío Mateo, for which the SOLERA was acquired from the now defunct Palomino & Vergara via HARVEY'S, is a vg FINO (now histamine-free!).

Martinez Gassiot Port firm, subsidiary of COCKBURN, known esp for excellent rich and pungent Directors 20-yr-old TAWNY, CRUSTED and LBV. Vintages: **55 60 63 67 70 75 82 85 87** 91 94.

Medina, José Originally a SANLUCAR family BODEGA, now a major exporter, especially to the Low Countries. By taking over the buildings and huge sherry stocks of the former BODEGAS INTERNACIONALES and by the more recent acquisition of WILLIAMS & HUMBERT, the Medina group, which also embraces Pérez Megia and Luis Paez, has probably become the biggest sherry grower and shipper, with some 25% of total volume.

Miles Formerly Rutherford & Miles. MADEIRA shipper famed for Old Trinity House Medium Rich etc. Latest vintage 73 VERDELHO. Now a MADEIRA WINE CO label.

Montecristo Mont-M ★★ Brand name of big-selling MONTILLAS made by Compañía Vinicola del Sur.

Montilla-Moriles Mont-M g ★★→★★★ DO nr Córdoba. Its crisp sherry-like FINO and AMONTILLADO contain 14–17.5% natural alcohol and remain unfortified. At best, singularly toothsome aperitifs.

Niepoort Small (Dutch) family-run port house with long record of fine vintages (**42 45 55 60** 63 66 70 **75 77 78** 80 **82** 83 85 87 91 92 94) and exceptional COLHEITAS. Also excellent single-QUINTA port, Quinta do Passadouro (91 92 94 95).

Noval, Quinta do Historic port house now French (AXA) owned. Intensely fruity structured and elegant VINTAGE PORT; a few ungrafted vines still at the QUINTA make a small quantity of Nacional – extraordinarily dark, full, velvety, slow-maturing wine. Vg 20-yr-old TAWNY. Vintages: **55 58 60** 63 66 **67** 70 **75 78** 82 85 87 91 94 95. Also 'traditional' (unfiltered) LBV.

Offley Forrester See Forrester.

Oloroso Style of sherry, heavier and less brilliant than FINO when young, but maturing to greater richness and pungency. Dry, but often sweetened for sale.

Osborne Enormous Spanish firm with well-known brandies but also gd sherries incl Fino Quinta, Coquinero dry AMONTILLADO, 10 RF (or Reserva Familiare) Medium OLOROSO. Now also a quality-conscious port shipper following purchase of old NOVAL lodges. NB: a range of v fine 'Rare' sherries, top quality with numbered bottles. See also Duff Gordon.

Pale Cream Popular style of sherry made by sweetening FINO (cf CROFT's Original).

Palo Cortado A style of sherry close to OLOROSO but with some of the character of an AMONTILLADO. Dry but rich and soft. Worth looking for.

Pasada Style of FINO or MANZANILLA which is closer to AMONTILLADO: a slightly stronger, more pungent wine retaining some of its FLOR character.

Pedro Barquero Mont-M Another firm like GARCIA HERMANOS once part of Rumasa. Its excellent MONTILLAS incl Gran Barquero FINO, AMONTILLADO and OLOROSO.

Pereira d'Oliveira Vinhos Family-owned MADEIRA CO est'd 1850. V gd basic range as well as 5 and 10 yr olds; fine old reserve VERDELHO 1890, BUAL 1908 and Malvasia 1895.

Pinhão Small town at the heart of port country, in the upper DOURO.

Poças Junior Family port firm specializing in TAWNIES and COLHEITAS.

Ponche An aromatic digestif made with old sherry and brandy, flavoured with herbs and presented in eye-catching silvered bottles. See Caballero, de Soto.

Puerto de Santa María Second city and former port of the sherry area, with important BODEGAS.

PX Short for Pedro Ximénez, grape part sun-dried: used in JEREZ for sweetening.

Quarles Harris One of the oldest port houses, since 1680, now owned by the Symingtons (see Dow). Small quantities of LBV, mellow and well-balanced. Vintages: **60** 63 66 70 **75** 77 80 **83 85** 91 **94**.

Quinta Portuguese for 'estate'. Also traditionally used to denote VINTAGE PORTS which are usually (legislation says 100%) from estate's v'yds, made in good but not exceptional vintages. Now several excellent QUINTAS produce wines from top vintages in their own right, esp VESUVIO, LA ROSA and Passadouro.

Rainwater A fairly light, medium dry blend of MADEIRA – traditional in US.

Ramos-Pinto Dynamic small port house specializing in single-QUINTA TAWNIES of style and elegance; now owned by champagne house Louis Roederer.

Real Companhia Vinícola do Norte de Portugal Aka Royal Oporto Wine Co and Real Companhia Velha; large port house, with a long political history. Many brands and several QUINTAS, incl Quinta dos Carvalhas for TAWNIES and COLHEITAS. Vintage wines generally dismal, but some aged tawnies are gd.

Rebello Valente See Robertson.

Régua Main town in Douro Valley, centre for port producers and growers.

Robertson Brand owned by SANDEMAN. Name continues to be used for sales to the Netherlands. Rebello Valente: brand-name for vintage ports. These once had a gd reputation (**63 66 67 70**) but they are now light and early maturing.

Rosa, Quinta de la Fine single-QUINTA port from the Bergqvist family at PINHÃO. Recent return to traditional methods and stone lagares. Look for **85 88 90** 91 92 94 95 96 vintages.

Royal Oporto See Real Companhia Vinícola do Norte de Portugal.

Rozès Port shipper controlled by Moët-Hennessy. RUBY v popular in France; also TAWNY. Vintages: **63 67 77' 78 82** 83 85 87 91 94' 95.

Ruby Youngest (and cheapest) port style: simple, sweet and red. The best are vigorous, full of flavour; others can be merely strong and rather thin.

Sanchez Romate Family firm in JEREZ since 1781. Best known in Spanish-speaking world, esp for brandy Cardenal Mendoza. Good sherry: FINO Cristal, OLOROSO Don Antonio, AMONTILLADO NPU ('Non Plus Ultra').

Sandeman A giant of the port trade and a major figure in the sherry one, owned by Seagram. Founder's Reserve is their well-known VINTAGE CHARACTER; TAWNIES are much better. Partners' RUBY is new (94). Vintage wines have been at least adequate – some of the old vintages were superlative (**55 57 58 60 62 63 65 66 67 68 70 72 75 77 80 82** 85 94) but recent vintages are on the light side. Of the sherries, Medium Dry AMONTILLADO is top-seller, Don FINO is vg; also two excellent CREAM SHERRIES: Armada, and rare de luxe Royal Corregidor. Also shippers of MADEIRA since 1790 (elegant RAINWATER, fine Rich).

Sanlúcar de Barrameda Seaside sherry town (see Manzanilla).

Sercial MADEIRA grape for driest of the island's wines – a supreme aperitif. (See panel on the next page.)

Silva Vinhos New Madeira producer (founded '90) with modern lodges at Estreito de Camara de Lobos. Gd basic wines from Tinta Negra Mole grapes.

Silva, C da Port shipper owned by Ruiz Mateos of GARVEY fame. Mostly inexpensive RUBIES and TAWNIES, but gd aged tawnies and COLHEITAS under Dalva label.

Smith Woodhouse Port firm founded in 1784, now owned by Symington family (see Dow). Gould Campbell is a subsidiary. Relatively light and easy wines incl Old Lodge TAWNY, Lodge Reserve VINTAGE CHARACTER (widely sold in US). Vintages (v fine): **60 63 66 70 75 77 80 83 85** 91 92 94. Gould Campbell Vintages: **60 63 66 70 75 77** 80 83 85 91 94. Single quinta wine: Madalena (95).

Solera System used in making both sherry and (in modified form) MADEIRA. It consists of topping up progressively more mature barrels with slightly younger wine of the same sort, the object being to attain continuity in the final wine. Most sherries when sold are blends of several solera wines.

Soto, José de Best known for inventing PONCHE, this family firm, which now belongs to the former owner of Rumasa, José María Ruiz Mateos, also makes a range of gd sherries, esp delicate FINO and fuller-bodied FINO Ranchero.

Tawny Style of port aged for many yrs in wood (VINTAGE PORT is aged in bottle) until tawny in colour. Many of the best are 20 yrs old. Low-price tawnies are blends of red and white ports. Taste the difference.

Taylor, Fladgate & Yeatman (Taylor's) Often considered the best of the port shippers, esp for full rich long-lived VINTAGE wine and TAWNIES of stated age (40-yr-old, 20-yr-old etc). Their VARGELLAS estate is said to give Taylor's its distinctive scent of violets. Vintages: **55 60 63 66 70 75** 77 80 83 85 92 94. QUINTA DE VARGELLAS is shipped unblended in certain (lesser) years (**67 72 74 76 78 82 84 86** 87 88 91 95). Also now Terra Feita single-QUINTA wine (**82 86 87 88** 91 95 96). Their LBV is also better than most.

Terry, Fernando A de Magnificent BODEGA at PUERTO DE SANTA MARIA, now part of Allied-Domecq. Makers of Maruja MANZANILLA and a range of popular brandies. The blending and bottling of all HARVEY'S sherries is carried out at the vast modern El Pino plant.

Tío Pepe The most famous of FINO sherries (see González Byass).

Toro Albalá, Bodegas Mont-M ★★★ Family firm located in a 1920s power station and appropriately making Eléctrico FINOS, AMONTILLADOS and a PX among the best in MONTILLA and Spain.

Valdespino Famous family BODEGA at JEREZ, owner of the Inocente vineyard and making the excellent aged FINO of that name. Tío Diego is its dry AMONTILLADO, Solera 1842 an OLOROSO, Don Tomás its best amontillado. Matador is the name of Valdespino's popular range. In the US, where their sherries rank No 2 in sales volume, they are still sold as 'Hartley & Gibson'.

Since 1993, Madeiras labelled Sercial, Verdelho, Bual or Malmsey must be at least 85% from that grape variety. The majority, made using the chameleon Tinta Negra Mole grape, which easily imitates each of these grape styles, may only be called Seco (Dry), Meio Seco (Medium Dry), Meio Doce (Medium Rich) or Doce (Rich) respectively. Meanwhile replanting is building up supplies of the (rare) classic varieties.

Vargellas, Quinta de Hub of the TAYLOR'S empire, giving its very finest ports. The label for in-between vintages. See Taylor Fladgate & Yeatman.

Verdelho MADEIRA grape for medium-dry wines, pungent but without the searing austerity of SERCIAL. A pleasant aperitif and a good all-purpose Madeira. Some glorious old vintage wines. (See panel on above.)

Vesuvio, Quinta de Enormous 19th-C FERREIRA estate in the high DOURO. Bought '89 by Symington family. 130 acres planted. Esp **89** 90 91 92 94.

Vila Nova de Gaia City on the S. side of the River Douro from Oporto where the major port shippers mature their wines in 'lodges'.

Vintage Character Somewhat misleading term used for a good quality, full and meaty port like a premium RUBY. Lacks the splendid 'nose' of VINTAGE PORT.

Vintage Port The best port of exceptional vintages is bottled after only 2 yrs in wood and matures very slowly for up to 20 or more in bottle. Always leaves a heavy deposit and therefore needs decanting.

Warre The oldest of all British port shippers (since 1670), owned by the Symington family (see Dow) since 1905. Fine elegant long-maturing vintage wines, a good TAWNY (Nimrod), VINTAGE CHARACTER (Warrior), and excellent LBV. Single-v'yd Quinta da Cavadinha is a new departure (**78 79 82 84 86 87 88 89 90** 92 95). Vintages: **55 58 60 63 66 70 75** 77' **80 83** 85 91 94.

White Port Port made of white grapes, golden in colour. Formerly made sweet, now more often dry: a fair aperitif but a heavy one. Try with tonic water.

Williams & Humbert Famous first class sherry BODEGA, now owned by the MEDINA group. Dry Sack (medium AMONTILLADO) is its best-seller; Pando an excellent FINO; Canasta CREAM and Walnut BROWN are good in their class; Dos Cortados is its famous dry old PALO CORTADO. Also the famous Gran Duque de Alba brandy acquired from DIEZ-MERITO.

Wisdom & Warter Not a magic formula for free wine, but an old BODEGA (controlled by GONZALEZ BYASS) with good sherries, especially AMONTILLADO Tizón and v rare SOLERA. Also FINO Olivar.

Switzerland

Heavier shaded areas are the wine growing regions

Bodensee

Rhein **THURGAU**

Zürich○ **ST-GALLEN**

Aare *Zürichsee*

NEUCHATEL *Zugersee*

Luzern○ *Vierwaldstättersee*

L de Neuchâtel

○ **Bern**

Rhein

VAUD ○ Lausanne

L Léman **GRISONS**
(L de Genève) ○ Montreux

Rhône

○ Geneva Sion○

TICINO

VALAIS Lugano○

Switzerland continues to be handicapped as an exporter by high prices and the fact that her top wines come from tiny estates. Few are seen outside the country. Yet almost all Swiss wines (especially whites) are enjoyable and satisfying – if expensive. Switzerland has some of the world's most intensive wine production, with high labour and fertilizer costs. The most important vineyards (28,550 out of 37,280 acres) are in French-speaking areas: along the south-facing slopes of the upper Rhône Valley (Valais) and Lake Geneva (Vaud). Wines from German- and Italian-speaking zones are treasured and mostly drunk locally. Wines are known by place, grape names and legally controlled type names and tend to be drunk young. The Swiss cantonal and federal appellation system was set up in 1988 and still governs wine production here.

Aargau Wine-growing canton in E Switz (976 acres). Best for fragrant Müller-Thurgau and rich BLAUBURGUNDER.

Aigle Vaud r w ★★→★★★ Well-known for elegant whites and supple reds.

Aligoté White burgundy variety performing well in the VALAIS and GENEVA.

Amigne Trad VALAIS white grape, esp of VETROZ. Full-bodied tasty, often sweet.

Ardon Valais r w ★★→★★★ Wine commune between SION and MARTIGNY.

Arvine Old VALAIS white grape (also 'Petite Arvine'): dry and sweet, elegant long-lasting wines with characteristic salty finish. Best in SIERRE, SION, Granges, FULLY.

Auvernier NE r p w ★★→★★★ Old wine village on Lake NEUCHATEL and biggest wine-growing commune of the canton.

Basel Second-largest Swiss town and canton with many vines: divided into Basel-Stadt and Baselland. Best wines: Müller-Thurgau, BLAUBURGUNDER, CHASSELAS.

Beerliwein Originally wine of destemmed BLAUBURG'R (E). Today name for wine fermented on skins traditionally rather than SUSSDRUCK. Drink young.

Bern Swiss capital and canton of same name. V'yds in W (BIELERSEE: CHASSELAS, PINOT N, white SPECIALITIES) and E (Thunersee: BLAUBURGUNDER, Müller-Thurgau); 648 acres. Prized by Germanic Swiss.

Bex Vaud r w ★★ CHABLAIS appellation, mostly white wines; some good reds.

Bielersee r p w ★→★★ Wine region on N shore of the Bielersee (dry light CHASSELAS, PINOT N) and at the foot of Jolimont (SPECIALITIES).

Blauburgunder German-Swiss name for PINOT N. (Aka Clevner.)

Bonvillars Vaud r p w ★→★★ Characterful red AC of upper end of L NEUCHATEL.

Bündner Herrschaft Grisons r p w ★★→★★★ Best German-Swiss region incl top villages: Fläsch, Jenins, Maienfeld, Malans. Serious BLAUB'R ripens esp well due to warm Föhn wind, cask-aged vg. Also CHARD, Müller-T, SPECIALITIES.

Recent vintages

1998 Damp summer, but very warm autumn. Again, high quality wines.

1997 Low yields due to problems with fruit set, but very high quality.

1996 Similar to 1995: rainy September followed by sunny October led to good quality fruit.

1995 Variable year: sunny harvest led to very good wines with some excellent reds.

Calamin Vaud w ★★→★★★ LAVAUX v'yds next to DEZALEY: lush fragrant whites.

Chablais Vaud r w ★★→★★★ Sunny wine region on right bank of Rhône and upper end of L GENEVA, incl VILLAGES: AIGLE, BEX, Ollon, VILLENEUVE, YVORNE. Robust full-bodied reds and whites

Chamoson Valais r w ★★→★★★ Largest VALAIS wine commune, esp for SYLVANER.

Chardonnay Long-est'd in French Switzerland, now elsewhere in the country.

Chasselas (Gutedel) Top white grape of French cantons: neutral in flavour, so takes on local character: elegant (GENEVA), refined and full (VAUD), potent and racy (VALAIS), pleasantly pétillant (lakes Bienne, NEUCHATEL, Murtensee). In E only in BASEL. In VALAIS it is called FENDANT. 37% of Swiss wines are Chasselas.

Completer Native white grape, mostly used in GRISONS making aromatic generous wines that keep well. Winemakers are increasingly experimenting with this grape. ('Complet' was a monk's final daily prayer, or 'nightcap'.)

Cornalin Local VALAIS speciality; dark spicy v strong red. Best: Salgesch, SIERRE, Conthey, Leytron, Leuk.

Cortaillod Neuchâtel r (w) ★★ Small village S of Lake N: esp PINOT N, OEIL DE P.

Côte, La Vaud r p w ★→★★★ Largest VAUD wine area between LAUSANNE and GENEVA (N shore of Lake). Whites with elegant finesse; fruity harmonious reds. Esp from MONT-SUR-ROLLE, Vinzel, Luins, FECHY, MORGES etc.

Côtes de l'Orbe Vaud r p w ★→★★ N VAUD appellation between Lake NEUCHATEL and Lake GENEVA esp for light fruity reds .

Dézaley Vaud w (r) ★★★ Celebrated LAVAUX v'yd on slopes above L GENEVA, once tended by Cistercian monks. Unusually potent CHASSELAS, develops esp after ageing. Red Dézaley is a GAMAY-PINOT N-MERLOT-Syrah rarity.

Dôle Valais r ★★→★★★ Appellation for PINOT N, can also be blend of PINOT, GAMAY and other varieties (85% from Pinot N and Gamay. Rest can be any r from the VALAIS): full, supple, often vg. Lightly pink Dôle Blanche is pressed immediately after harvest. Eg from MARTIGNY, SIERRE, SION, VETROZ, etc.

Epesses Vaud w (r) ★★→★★★ LAVAUX appellation: supple full-bodied whites.

Ermitage Alias the Marsanne grape; a VALAIS SPECIALITE. Concentrated full-bodied dry white, s'times with residual sugar. Esp from FULLY, SION, Noble Contrée.

Féchy Vaud ★★→★★★ Famous appellation of LA COTE, esp elegant whites.

Federweisser German-Swiss name for white wine from BLAUBURGUNDER.

Fendant Valais w ★→★★★ VALAIS appellation for CHASSELAS. Wide range of wines. Better ones now use village names only (FULLY, SION etc).

Flétri/Mi-flétri Late-harvested grapes for sw/slightly sw wine (respectively).

Fribourg Smallest French-Swiss wine canton (285 acres, nr Jura). Esp for CHASSELAS, PINOT N, GAMAY, SPECIALITES from VULLY, L Murten, S Lake NEUCHATEL.

Fully Valais r w ★★→★★★ Village nr MARTIGNY: excellent ERMITAGE and GAMAY.

Gamay Beaujolais grape; abounds in French cantons but forbidden in German. Mainy thin wine used in blends (SALVAGNIN, DOLE). Gamay: 14% of grapes in Switz.

Geneva Capital, and French-Swiss wine canton; the third largest (3,370 acres). Key areas: MANDEMENT, Entre Arve et Rhône, Entre Arve et Lac. Mostly CHASSELAS, GAMAY. Also lately CHARD, Cab, PINOT, Muscat and good ALIGOTE.

Gewürztraminer Grown in Switzerland as a SPECIALITY variety esp in VALAIS.

Glacier, Vin du (Gletscherwein) Fabled oxidized wooded white from rare Rèze grape of Val d'Anniviers; offered by the thimbleful to visiting dignitaries.

Goron Valais r ★ AC for pleasant reds and DOLE that fails to make the grade.

Grand Cru Quality designation. Implication differs by canton: in VALAIS, GENEVA and VAUD used where set requirements fulfilled.

Grisons (Graubünden) Mountain canton, mainly in German Switz (BUNDNER HERRSCHAFT, Churer Rheintal; esp BLAUBURGUNDER) and partly S of Alps (Misox, esp MERLOT). 928 acres, primarily for red, also Müller-Thurgau and SPECIALITIES.

Heida (Païen) Old VALAIS white grape (Jura's Savagnin) for country wine of upper Valais (Visperterminen v'yds 1,000+ m). Successful in lower VALAIS, too.

Humagne Strong native white grape (VALAIS SPECIALITY). Humagne Rouge (unrelated, from Aosta Valley) also. Esp from CHAMOSON, LEYTRON, MARTIGNY.

Johannisberger Synomyn for SYLVANER in the VALAIS.

Landwein (Vin de pays) Trad light easy white and esp red BLAUB'R from east.

Lausanne Capital of VAUD. No longer with v'yds in town area, but long-time owner of classics: Abbaye de Mont, Château Rochefort (LA COTE); Clos des Moines, Clos des Abbayes, Dom de Burignon (LAVAUX). Pricey.

Lavaux Vaud w (r) ★→★★★ Scenic region on N shore of L GENEVA between Montreux and Lausanne. Delicate refined whites, good reds. Best: CALAMIN, Chardonne, DEZALEY, EPESSES, Lutry, ST-SAPHORIN, VEVEY-MONTREUX and Villette.

Leytron Valais r w ★★→★★★ Commune nr SION/MARTIGNY, esp Le Grand Brûlé.

Malvoisie See Pinot Gris.

Mandement r w ★→★★ GENEVA wine area incl Satigny, largest wine commune of Switzerland. Wines of local interest only; CHASSELAS and GAMAY.

Martigny Valais r w ★★ Lower VALAIS commune esp for HUMAGNE ROUGE.

Merlot Grown in Italian Switzerland (TICINO) since 1907 (after phylloxera destroyed local varieties): aromatic, soft, successful. Also used with Cab.

Mont d'Or, Domaine du Valais w s/sw sw ★★→★★★ Well-sited property nr SION: rich concentrated demi-sec and sweet wines, notable SYLVANER.

Mont-sur-Rolle Vaud w (r) ★★ Important appellation within LA COTE.

Morges Vaud r p w ★→★★ Largest LA COTE/VAUD AOC: CHASSELAS, fruity reds.

Neuchâtel City and canton. V'yds (1,519 acres) from Lake N to BIELERSEE. CHASSELAS: fragrant lively (sur lie, sp). Also gd PINOT N (esp OEIL DE PERDRIX), PINOT GR, CHARD.

Nostrano Word meaning 'ours', applied to red wine of TICINO, made from native and Italian grapes (Bondola, Freisa, Bonarda etc).

Oeil de Perdrix Pale PINOT rosé. Esp (originally NEUCHÂTEL's; also VALAIS, VAUD.

Pinot Blanc (Weissburgunder) Newly introduced grape variety producing full-bodied elegant wines.

Pinot Gris (Malvoisie) Widely planted white grape for dry and residually sweet wines. Makes v fine late-gathered wines in VALAIS (called Malvoisie).

Pinot Noir (Blauburgunder) Top red grape (31% of Swiss v'yds). Esp: BUNDNER H, NEUCHÂTEL, VALAIS.

Rauschling Old white ZURICH grape; esp for discreet fruit, elegant acidity.

Riesling (Petit Rhin) Mainly in the VALAIS. Excellent botrytis wines.

Riesling-Sylvaner Old name for Müller-THURGAU (top white of E; a SPECIALITY in W). Typically elegant wines with nutmeg aroma and some acidity.

St-Gallen E wine canton nr L Constance (553 acres). Esp for BLAUBURG'R (full-bodied), Müller-Thurgau, SPECIALITIES. Incl Rhine Valley, Oberland, upper L ZURICH.

St-Leonard Valais r w ★★→★★★ Wine commune between SIERRE and SION.

St-Saphorin Vaud w (r) ★★→★★★ Famous LAVAUX AC for fine light whites.

Salvagnin Vaud r ★→★★ GAMAY and/or PINOT N appellation. (See also Dôle.)

Schaffhausen German-Swiss canton and wine town on River Rhine. Esp BLAUBURGUNDER; also some Müller-Thurgau and SPECIALITIES.

Schafis Bern r p w ★→★★ Top BIELERSEE village and name for wines of its N shore.

Schenk Europe-wide wine giant, founded and based in Rolle (VAUD). Owns firms in Burgundy, Bordeaux, Germany, Italy, Spain.

Sierre Valais r w ★★→★★★ Sunny resort and famous wine town. Known for FENDANT, PINOT N, ERMITAGE, Malvoisie. Vg DOLE.

Sion Valais r w ★★→★★★ Capital/wine centre of VALAIS. Esp FENDANT de Sion.

Sylvaner (Johannisberg, Gros Rhin) White grape esp in warm VALAIS v'yds. Heady, spicy: some with residual sweetness.

Spécialités (Spezialitäten) Wines of unusual grapes: vanishing local Gwäss, Himbertscha, Elbling, Bondola, etc, ARVINE and AMIGNE, or modish Chenin Bl, Sauv, Cab, Syrah. Eg VALAIS: 43 of its 47 varieties are considered 'specialities'.

Süssdruck Dry rosé/bright red wine: grapes pressed before fermentation.

Thurgau German-Swiss canton beside Bodensee (678 acres). Wines from Thur Valley: Weinfelden, Seebach, Nussbaum and Rhine. S shore of the Untersee. Typical: BLAUBURGUNDER, also gd RIES-SYLVANER (aka Müller-Thurgau: Dr Müller was born in the region). SPECIALITES incl Kerner, PINOT GR, Regent.

Ticino Italian-speaking S Switzerland (with Misox), growing mainly MERLOT (good from mountainous Sopraceneri region) and SPECIALITIES. Trying out Cab (oaked Bordeaux style), Sauv, Sém, CHARD, Merlot white and rosé. (2,347 acres.)

Valais (Wallis) Rhône Valley from German-speaking upper-V to French lower-V. Largest and most varied wine canton in French Switz (13,162 acres; source of 30% Swiss wine), now seeing a revival of quality, and ancient grapes. Near-perfect climatic conditions. Wide range: 47 grape varieties incl GAMAY, PINOT N, CHASSELAS, RIES plus many SPECIALITIES. Esp white; FLETRI/MI-FLETRI wines.

Vaud (Waadt) Region of L GENEVA and the Rhône. French Switzerland's 2nd largest wine canton (9,591 acres) incl CHABLAIS, LA COTE, LAVAUX and BONVILLARS, COTES DE L'ORBE, VULLY. CHASSELAS stronghold. Also GAMAY, PINOT N etc.

Vétroz Valais w r ★★→★★★ Top village nr SION, esp famous for AMIGNE.

Vevey-Montreux Vaud r w ★★ Up-and-coming appellation of LAVAUX. Famous wine festival held about every 30 years; latest one in 1999.

Villeneuve Vaud w (r) ★★→★★ Nr L Geneva: powerful yet refined whites.

Vispertal Valais w (r) ★→★★ Upper VALAIS v'yds esp for SPECIALITIES.

Vully Vaud w (r) ★→★★ Refreshing white from L Murten/FRIBOURG area.

Yvorne Vaud w (r) ★★★ Top CHABLAIS appellation for strong fragrant wines.

Zürich Capital of largest German-speaking wine canton (same name). Mostly BLAUBURGUNDER; also PINOT GR, GEWURZ, and esp Müller-T, RAUSCHLING (1,591 acres).

Austria

Heavier shaded areas are the wine growing regions

In 14 stirring years Austria has emerged as a vigorous, innovative producer of dry white and dessert wines up to the very finest quality. Her red wines (20 percent of vineyards) are starting to make an international reputation too. New laws, passed in 1985 and revised for the 1993 vintage, include curbs on yields (Germany: please copy) and impose higher levels of ripeness for each category than their German counterparts. Many regional names, introduced under the 1985 law, are still unfamiliar outside Austria. All are worth trying; there are dramatic discoveries to be had.

Ausbruch PRADIKAT wine (v sweet) between Beerenauslese and Trockenbeeren-auslese in quality. Traditionally produced in RUST.

Ausg'steckt ('hung up') HEURIGEN are not open all year. To show potential visitors wine is being served, a green bush is hung up above the door.

Bergwein Legal designation for wines made from grapes grown on slopes with an incline of over 26%.

Blauburger Austrian red grape variety. A cross between BLAUER PORTUGIESER and BLAUFRANKISCH. Dark-coloured but light-bodied; simple wines.

Blauer Burgunder (Pinot Noir) A rarity. Vintages fluctuate greatly. Best in BURGENLAND, KAMPTAL and the THERMENREGION (from growers Achs, BRUNDLMAYER, STIEGELMAR, UMATHUM and WIENINGER).

Blauer Portugieser Light, fruity wines to drink slightly chilled when young. Mostly made for local consumption. Top producers: Fischer, Lust.

Blauer Wildbacher Red grape used to make SCHILCHER wines.

Blauer Zweigelt BLAUFRANKISCH-ST-LAURENT cross: high yields and rich colour. Top producers (especially HEINRICH, Nittnaus, Pitnauer, Pöckl, UMATHUM) are making a reputation for it.

Blaufränkisch (Lemberger in Germany, Kékfrankos in Hungary) Austria's red grape variety with the most potential, much planted in MITTELBURGENLAND: wines with good body, peppery acidity and a fruity taste of cherries. Often blended with CAB S. Best from Gesellmann, HEINRICH Iby, Igler, Krutzler, Nittnaus, TRIEBAUMER and WIENINGER.

Bouvier Indigenous grape, generally producing light wines with low acidity but plenty of aroma, esp good for Beeren- and Trockenbeerenauslese.

Bründlmayer, Willi r w sp ★★→★★★★ **90 92 93 94 95 97 98** Leading LANGENLOIS–KAMPTAL estate. Vg wines: both local (RIES, GRUNER V) and international styles, incl CHARD and reds. Also Austria's best Sekt.

Recent vintages

1998 A superb vintage for late-harvest wines, a very good one for the dry whites, but rather disappointing for reds.

1997 Very few late-harvest wines (wrong conditions for botrytis), but top dry whites and reds are rich and powerful.

1996 Small crop of variable quality. Generally light and fresh wines for drinking young, but more serious wines from top sites.

1995 Rain threatened to ruin the harvest, but late pickers and dessert winemakers hit the jackpot.

1994 Unusually hot summer and fine autumn resulted in very ripe grapes. An excellent vintage.

1993 Frost damage caused a smaller-than-average yield which produced excellent rich wines.

1990 One of the best vintages of the last 50 yrs.

Burgenland Province and wine area (40,000 acres) in east next to Hungarian border. Warm climate. Ideal conditions, esp for botrytis wines near NEUSIEDLERSEE, also reds. Four wine regions: MITTELBURGENLAND, NEUSIEDLER SEE, NEUSIEDLERSEE-HUGELLAND and SUDBURGENLAND.

Buschenschank The same as HEURIGE; often a country cousin.

Cabernet Sauvignon Increasingly cultivated in Austria; used esp in blends.

Carnuntum r w Wine region since '94, E of Vienna, bordered by the Danube to the north. Best producers: Glatzer, Pitnauer.

Chardonnay Increasingly grown, mainly oaked. Also trad in STYRIA as MORILLON; FEINBURGUNDER in WACHAU (unoaked): strong fruit taste, lively acidity. Esp BRUNDL-MAYER, Loimer, Malat, POLZ, SATTLER, STIEGELMAR, TEMENT, Topfl, VELICH, WIENINGER.

Deutschkreutz r (w) MITTELBURGENLAND red wine area, esp for BLAUFRANKISCH.

Donauland (Danube) w (r) Wine region since '94, just W of Vienna. Includes KLOSTERNEUBURG south of Danube and WAGRAM north of the river. Mainly whites, esp GRUNER VELTLINER. Best producers include: Fritsch, Chorherren Klosterneuburg, Leth, Wimmer-Cerny, R Zimmermann.

Dürnstein w Wine centre of the WACHAU with famous ruined castle. Mainly GRUNER V, RIES. Top growers: FREIE WEINGARTNER WACHAU, KNOLL, PICHLER, Schmidl.

Eisenstadt r w dr sw Capital of BURGENLAND and historic seat of Esterházy family. Major producer: Esterházy.

Falkenstein w Wine centre in the eastern WEINVIERTEL nr Czech border. Good GRUNER VELTLINER. Best producers: Jauk, Luckner, HEINRICH and Josef Salomon.

Federspiel Medium quality level of the VINEA WACHAU categories, roughly corresponding to Kabinett. Fruity, elegant, dry wines.

Feiler-Artinger r w sw ★★★ →★★★★ **91 92 93 94 95 96 97 98** Considered the outstanding RUST estate. Top AUSBRUCH dessert wines since '93. Also good dry whites and reds.

185

Feinburgunder Synonym for CHARDONNAY, in the WACHAU where the wines do not see oak. They are full and crisp, but seldom exciting.

Freie Weingärtner Wachau w (r) ★★★ 92 93 94 95 96 97 98 Important and vg growers' cooperative in DURNSTEIN. Excellent GRUNER VELTLINER, RIES.

Gamlitz w Town in southern STYRIA. Growers incl Lackner-Tinnacher, SATTLER.

Gemischter Satz A blend of grapes (mostly white) grown, harvested and vinified together. Traditional wine, still served in HEURIGEN.

Gols r w dr sw Largest BURGENLAND wine commune (N shore of NEUSIEDLER SEE). Best producers: Beck, HEINRICH, Leitner, Nittnaus, Renner, STIEGELMAR.

Grüner Veltliner Austria's national white grape (over a third of total v'yd area). Fruity, racy, lively young wines. Distinguished age-worthy Spätlesen. Best producers: BRUNDLMAYER, FREIE WEING'R WACHAU, HIRTZBERGER, Högl, KNOLL, MANTLER, NEUMAYER, NIGL, NIKOLAIHOF, PFAFFL, F X PICHLER, PRAGER, Schmelz, Walzer.

G'spritzer Popular refreshing summer drink, usually white wine-based; made sparkling by adding soda or mineral water. Esp in HEURIGEN.

Gumpoldskirchen w r dr sw Resort village S of VIENNA, famous for HEURIGEN. Centre of THERMENREGION. Distinctive, tasty, sometimes sweet wines from ZIERFANDLER and ROTGIPFLER grapes. Best producers: Biegler, Schellmann.

Heinrich, Gernot r w dr sw ★★→★★★ 92 93 94 96 97 98 Young modern estate in GOLS with Pannobile and (esp) red Gabarinza labels.

Heurige Wine of the most recent harvest, called 'new wine' for one yr, then classified as 'old'. Heurigen are wine houses where growers-cum-patrons serve wine by glass/bottle with simple local food – an institution, esp in VIENNA.

Hirtzberger, Franz w ★★★★ 90 92 93 94 95 96 97 98 Leading producer with 22 acres at SPITZ AN DER DONAU, WACHAU. Fine dry RIES and GRUNER VELTLINER.

Horitschon MITTELBURGENLAND region for reds. Best: Anton Iby, WIENINGER.

Illmitz w (r) dr sw SEEWINKEL region famous for Beeren- and Trockenbeeren-auslese. Best from KRACHER, Martin Haider, Alois and Helmut Lang, OPITZ.

Jamek, Josef w ★★ 92 93 94 95 96 97 98 Well-known estate and restaurant at Joching, WACHAU. Pioneer of dry whites since '50s. Recently back on form.

Jurtschitsch/Sonnhof w (r) dr (sw) ★→★★★ 92 93 94 95 97 Domaine run by three brothers: good whites (RIES, GRUNER VELTLINER, CHARD).

Kamptal r w Wine region since '94, along R Kamp N of WACHAU. Top v'yds: LANGENLOIS, STRASS, Zöbing. Best growers: BRUNDLMAYER, Dolle, Ehn, Schloss Gobelsburg, Hiedler, Hirsch, JURTSCHITSCH, Loimer, Metternich-Sandor, Topf.

Kattus ★→★★ Producer of traditional Sekt in VIENNA.

Kellergassen Picturesque alleyways lined with wine presses and cellars, devoted exclusively to the production, storage and consumption of wine. Situated outside the town, typical of the WEINVIERTEL region.

Klöch w W STYRIA wine town famous for Traminer. Best from Stürgkh.

Kloster Und W'tasting centre in restored monastery nr KREMS, run by E SALOMON.

Klosterneuburg r w Main wine town of DONAULAND. Rich in tradition with a famous Benedictine monastery and a wine college founded in 1860. Best producers: Chorherren Klosterneuburg, Zimmermann.

KMW Abbreviation for 'Klosterneuburger Mostwaage' (must level), the unit used in Austria to measure the sugar content in grape juice.

Knoll, Emmerich w ★★★★ 92 93 94 95 96 97 98 V traditional, highly regarded estate in LOIBEN, WACHAU, producing showpiece GRUNER VELTLINER and RIESLING.

Kollwentz-Römerhof w r dr (sw) ★★→★★★ 90 92 93 94 95 96 97 98 Innovative wine producer in Grosshöflein nr EISENSTADT: Sauv Bl, Eiswein and reds.

Kracher, Alois w (r) dr (sw) ★★★★ 81 89 91 92 93 94 95 96 97 98 1st class small ILLMITZ producer; speciality: PRADIKATS (dessert wines), some barrique-aged (Nouvelle Vague), others not (Zwischen der Seen).

Krems w (r) dr (sw) Ancient town, W of VIENNA. Capital of KREMSTAL. Best from Forstreiter, SALOMON, Weingut Stadt Krems, Walzer.

Kremstal w (r) Wine region since '94 esp for GRUNER V and RIES. Top growers: MALAT, MANTLER, Nigl, SALOMON, Weingut Stadt Krems.

Langenlois r w ★★→★★★ Wine town and region in KAMPTAL with 5,000 acres. Best producers: BRUNDLMAYER, Ehn, Hiedler, JURTSCHITSCH, Loimer.

Lenz Moser ★★→★★★ Producer nr KREMS. LM III invented high-vine system. Also incl wines from Schlossweingut Malteser Ritterorden (wine estate of Knights of Malta): Mailberg (WEINVIERTEL), Klosterkeller Siegendorf (BURGENLAND).

Loiben w In lower, wider part of Danube Valley (WACHAU). Ideal conditions for RIES and GRUNER V. Top: Alzinger, FREIE WEINGARTNER, KNOLL, F X PICHLER.

Mantler, Josef w ★★→★★★ 90 92 93 95 96 97 Leading estate in Gedersdorf nr KREMS. Vg trad RIES, GRUNER V, CHARD and rare Roter Veltliner (Malvasia).

Mayer, Franz w With 60 acres, the largest producer in VIENNA. Traditional jug wines (at picturesque HEURIGE Beethovenhaus – yes, he drank here), plus in contrast, excellent 'older-vintage' (20–30 yrs) RIESLING and Traminer.

Messwein Mass wine: must have ecclesiastical approval (and natural must).

Mittelburgenland r (w) dr (sw) Wine region on Hungarian border protected by three hill ranges. Makes large quantities of red (esp BLAUFRANKISCH). Producers: Gesellmann, Iby, Igler, WIENINGER.

Mörbisch r w dr sw Region on W shore of NEUSIEDLER SEE. Schindler is good.

Morillon Name given in STYRIA to CHARDONNAY.

Müller-Thurgau See Riesling-Sylvaner.

Muskat-Ottonel Grape for fragrant, often dry whites, interesting PRADIKATS.

Muskateller Rare aromatic grape, popular again. Best from STYRIA and WACHAU. Top growers: Gross, HIRTZBERGER, Lackner-Tinnacher, F X PICHLER, POLZ, SATTLER.

Neuburger Indigenous white grape: nutty flavour; mainly in the WACHAU (elegant, flowery), in the THERMENREGION (mellow, well-developed) and in N BURGENLAND (strong, full). Best from Beck, FREIE WEINGARTNER, HIRTZBERGER.

Neumayer ★★★ 93 94 95 96 97 98 The Neumayer brothers make powerful, pithy dry GRUNER VELTLINER at the best estate in new TRAISENTAL region.

Neusiedler See V shallow (max 1.5m deep) BURGENLAND lake on Hungarian border. Warm temperatures, autumn mists encourage botrytis. Gives name to wine regions of NEUSIEDLERSEE-HUGELLAND and NEUSIEDLERSEE.

Neusiedlersee r w dr sw Region N and E of NEUSIEDLER SEE. Best growers: Beck, HEINRICH, KRACHER, Nittnaus, OPITZ, Pöckl, UMATHUM, VELICH.

Neusiedlersee-Hügelland r w dr sw Wine region W of NEUSIEDLER SEE based around OGGAU, RUST and MORBISCH on the lake shores, and EISENSTADT in the foothills of the Leitha Mts. Best producers: FEILER-ARTINGER, KOLLWENTZ, Mad, Prieler, Schandl, Schröck, ERNST TRIEBAUMER, Wenzel.

Niederösterreich (Lower Austria) With 58% of Austria's v'yds: CARNUNTUM, DONAULAND, KAMPTAL, KREMSTAL, THERMENREGION, TRAISENTAL, WACHAU, WEINVIERTEL.

Nigl ★★★ w 92 93 94 95 96 97 98 Top grower of KREMSTAL making sophisticated dry RIESLING and GRUNER VELTLINER capable of long ageing.

Nikolaihof w ★★★ 90 91 92 94 95 96 97 98 Estate built on Roman foundations. Superb RIESLING from Steiner Hund site, other wines v good and v traditional in style.

Nussdorf VIENNA district famous for HEURIGEN and vg Ried Nussberg.

Oggau Wine region on the W shore of NEUSIEDLER SEE.

Opitz, Willi ★★★★ Tiny ILLMITZ estate specialising in late-harvest wines, incl 'Schilfmandl' and 'Opitz One' from grapes dried on reeds from NEUSIEDLER SEE.

Pfaffl ★★★★ 90 92 93 94 95 96 97 98 WEINVIERTEL estate in Stretten nr VIENNA. Best known for blended red 'Excellence', but racy dry GRUNER VELTLINERS are no less impressive.

Pichler, Franz Xavier w ★★★★ 90 92 93 94 95 96 97 98 Top WACHAU producer with v intense rich RIES, GRUNER V (esp Kellerberg) and MUSKATELLER of great breed. Widely recognized as Austria's No 1 grower for dry wines.

Polz, Erich and Walter w ★★★ 92 93 94 95 96 97 98 S STYRIAN (Weinstrasse) growers; esp Hochgrassnitzberg: Sauv, CHARD, Grauburgunder, WEISSBURGUNDER.

Prädikat, Prädikatswein Quality graded wines from Spätlese upwards (Spätlese, Auslese, Eiswein, Strohwein, Beerenauslese, AUSBRUCH and Trockenbeerenauslese). See Germany, page 141.

Prager, Franz w ★★★★ 90 91 92 93 94 95 96 97 98 Together with JOSEF JAMEK, pioneer of top-quality WACHAU dry white. Introducing new RIESLING clones and great PRADIKAT wines.

Renomierte Weingüter Burgenland Assoc founded '95 by nine top BURGENLAND producers to promote region's top wines; incl KRACHER, TRIEBAUMER, UMATHUM.

Retz r w Important region in W WEINVIERTEL. Esp Weinbauschule Retz.

Ried Single v'yd.

Riesling On its own always means German RIES. WELSCHRIES (unrelated) is labelled as such. Top growers: Alzinger, BRUNDLMAYER, FREIE W WACHAU, HIRTZBERGER, Högl, KNOLL, NIGL, NIKOLAIHOF, F X PICHLER, PRAGER, SALOMON.

Riesling-Sylvaner Name used for Müller-T (about 10% of Austria's grapes). Best producers: HIRTZBERGER, JURTSCHITSCH.

Rotgipfler Fragrant indigenous grape of THERMENREGION. With ZIERFANDLER, makes lively, interesting wine. Esp Biegler, Schellmann, Stadelmann.

Rust w r dr sw BURGENLAND region, famous since 17th C for dessert AUSBRUCH; now also for r and dr w. Esp from FEILER-ARTINGER, Schandl, Heidi Schröck, ERNST TRIEBAUMER, Paul Triebaumer, Wenzel. The Cercle Ruster Ausbruch is a group of a dozen producers set on re-establishing pre-eminence of their powerful Sauternes-like wines from a wide range of grapes. Standards already v high.

St-Laurent Traditional red wine grape, potentially vg, with cherry aroma, believed to be related to Pinot N. Esp from Fischer, Mad, STIEGELMAR, UMATHUM.

Salomon-Undhof w ★★★ Vg producer of RIES, WEISSBURGUNDER, Traminer in KREMS. Erich Salomon also owns/runs KLOSTER UND winetasting centre.

Sattler, Willi w ★★→★★★ 92 93 94 95 96 97 98 Top S STYRIA grower. Esp for Sauvignon, MORILLON. Some wines too strongly oaked.

Schilcher Rosé wine from indigenous BLAUER WILDBACHER grapes (sharp, dry; high acidity). Speciality of W STYRIA. Try: Klug, Lukas, Reiterer, Strohmeier.

Schlumberger Largest sparkling winemaker in Austria (VIENNA); wine is bottle-fermented by unique 'Méthode Schlumberger'. Delicate and fruity.

Seewinkel ('Lake corner'.) Name given to the part of NEUSIEDLERSEE incl Apetlon, ILLMITZ and Podersdorf. Ideal conditions for botrytis.

Sepp Moser ★★★ 93 94 95 96 97 98 KREMSTAL estate (Rohrendorf) founded with original LENZ MOSER v'yds. Richly aromatic, elegant dry RIES, GRUNER V, CHARD, SAUV.

Servus w BURGENLAND everyday light and mild dry white wine brand.

Smaragd Highest-quality category of VINEA WACHAU, similar to dry Spätlese.

Spätrot-Rotgipfler Typical THERMENREGION (Spätrot and ROTGIPFLER) wine.

Spitz an der Donau w W WACHAU region with cool microclimate: esp from Singerriedel v'yd. Top growers are: HIRTZBERGER, FREIE WEINGARTEN, Högl, Lagler.

Steinfeder VINEA WACHAU quality category for very light fragrant dry wines.

Stiegelmar, Georg w r dr sw ★→★★★ 92 93 94 95 96 97 98 GOLS grower: CHARD, Sauv Bl, red wine and unusual specialities. Whites currently dull.

Strass w (r) Wine centre in the KAMPTAL region for good Qualität white wines. Best producers: Dolle, Metternich-Sandor, Topf.

To decipher codes, please refer to 'Key to symbols' on front flap of jacket, or to 'How to use this book' on page 6.

Styria (Steiermark) The southernmost wine region of Austria, bordering Slovenia. Its dry whites are gaining real prestige. Incl SUDSTEIERMARK, SUD-OSTSTEIERMARK and WESTSTEIERMARK (S, SE and W Styria).

Süd-Oststeiermark (SE Styria) w (r) STYRIAN region with islands of excellent v'yds. Best producers: Neumeister, Winkler-Hermaden.

Südburgenland r w Small S BURGENLAND wine region: good red wines. Best producers: Krutzler, Wachter, Wiesler.

Südsteiermark (S Styria) w Best wine region of STYRIA: makes v popular whites (MORILLON, MUSKATELLER, WELSCHRIESLING and Sauv Bl). Top producers: Gross, Lackner-Tinnacher, Muster, POLZ, SATTLER, Skoff, TEMENT, Wohlmuth.

Tement, Manfred w ★★★ ·★★★★ 90 92 93 94 95 96 97 98 Vg and renowned estate on S STYRIA Weinstrasse for beautifully made traditional 'Steirisch Klassik' and international whites.

Thermenregion r w dr sw Wine/hot-springs region, S of VIENNA. Indigenous grapes (eg ZIERFANDLER, ROTGIPFLER) and gd reds from Baden, GUMPOLDSKIRCHEN Tattendorf, Traiskirchen areas. Top producers: Alphart, Biegler, Fischer, Reinisch, Schafler, Schellmann, Stadelmann.

Traditionsweingüter Assoc of KAMPTAL and KREMSTAL wine estates, committed to quality and v'yd classification. Incl BRUNDLMAYER, Loimer, G Malat, Nigl, SALOMON.

Traisental New region: 1,750 acres just south of KREMS on Danube. Mostly dry whites in style similar to WACHAU. Top producer: NEUMAYER.

Triebaumer, Ernst r (w) dr sw ★★★ 90 91 92 93 94 95 96 97 98 RUST producer; some of Austria's best reds: BLAUFRANKISCH (Mariental), CAB-Merlot. Vg AUSBRUCH.

Umathum, Josef w r dr sw ★★★ 90 91 92 94 95 96 97 98 Distinguished NEUSIEDLERSEE producer for vg reds; also BLAUER BURGUNDER whites.

Velich w sw BURGENLAND ★★★ The brothers Velich make burgundian-style 'Tiglat' CHARDONNAY and since '95 some of top PRADIKATS in the SEEWINKEL.

Vienna w (r) ('Wien' in German and on labels.) The Austrian capital is a wine region in its own right (1,500 v'yd acres in suburbs). Simple lively wines, served in HEURIGEN: esp Bernreiter, MAYER, Schilling, WIENINGER.

Vinea Wachau WACHAU appellation started by winemakers in '83 with three categories of dry wine: STEINFEDER, FEDERSPIEL and SMARAGD.

Wachau w Danube wine region W of KREMS: some of Austria's best wines, incl RIES, GRUNER V. Top producers: Alzinger, FREIE WEINGARTNER, HIRTZBERGER, Högl, JAMEK, KNOLL, NIKOLAIHOF, F X PICHLER, PRAGER.

Wagram r w Large wine region with loess terraces in DONAULAND. Best producers: Fritsch, Leth, Wimmer-Cerny.

Weinviertel 'Wine Quarter' w (r) Largest Austrian wine region, between Danube and Czech border. Mostly light refreshing w esp from Falkenstein, Poysdorf, RETZ. Best producers: Hardegg, Jauk, Luckner, Lust, Malteser Ritterorden, PFAFFL, Taubenschuss, Zull.

Weissburgunder (Pinot Bl) Ubiquitous: good dry wines and PRADIKATS. Esp Beck, Fischer, Gross, HEINRICH, HIRTZBERGER, Jement, POLZ, TEMENT.

Welschriesling White grape, not related to RIESLING, grown in all wine regions: light, fragrant, young-drinking dry wines and good PRADIKATS.

Weststeiermark (West Styria) p Small Austrian wine region specializing in SCHILCHER. Esp from Klug, Lukas, Reiterer, Strohmeier.

Wien See Vienna.

Wieninger, Fritz w r ★★·★★★★ 92 93 94 95 96 97 98 Vg VIENNA-Stammersdorf grower: HEURIGE, CHARD, BLAUER BURGUNDER reds and esp gd GRUNER V and RIES.

Winzer Krems Wine growers' cooperative in KREMS: dependable solid whites.

Zierfandler (Spätrot) White grape variety grown almost exclusively in the THERMENREGION. Blended with ROTGIPFLER: robust lively ageworthy wines. Best producers: Biegler, Schellmann, Stadelmann.

Central & Southeast Europe

Heavier shaded areas are
the wine growing regions

Prague O

CZECH REPUBLIC

Bratislava O

Danu

Ljubljana

SLOVENIA   Zagreb

Drava

CROATIA

Sava

**BOSNIA-
HERZEGOVINA**

Split

Sarajevo

Adriatic Sea

Dubrovnik

To say that parts of this region are in transition is an understatement.
But new regional autonomies and new statehoods are being
followed closely in many cases by higher aspirations in winemaking.

In a few much-publicized cases this takes the form of international
'flying winemakers' pitching their tents at vintage-time, usually to
make wines acceptable to Western supermarkets from predictable
grape varieties. But this affects indigenous winemaking, too; often
with happy results, making fresher and fruitier wines of intriguingly
different flavours.

The decade since Communism has witnessed the decline of
state firms and the emergence of new, family and corporate-
owned wineries. These newer wineries are now establishing their
winemaking styles and market positions with either fresh and fruity
or complex, aged wines. So far, Hungary, Bulgaria, and perhaps
Moldova, as well as Slovenia and the Czech Republic, have taken
the lead in what has become an area to follow with fascination.
The potential of other ex-Communist states has still to emerge,
with Romania in particular to watch. But about Greece there is no
doubt: the new age of wine has arrived.

In this section, references are arranged country by country, each
shown on the map on this page. Included alongside regions are
producers and other terms in the alphabetical listings.

Hungary

Hungary entered the Communist era with Eastern Europe's finest and most individual wines. It emerged with traditions battered and modern alternatives still half-baked. Progress has been rapid. Winemakers have invested new capital and earnings into improving cellar equipment and procedures and expanding plantings of certain grapes. Very drinkable standard varietals are now easy to find. The initial years of experiment have given way to proven winemaking techniques and definite wine styles. This is especially true for the reds of Villány, Szekszárd (the 'z's are silent) and Eger. Tokay, the one undisputed great wine of Central European history, remains in full renaissance and native grapes (mainly white) provide the backbone for the more traditional preference for fiery, hearty, full-bodied wines.

Alföld Hungary's Great Plain: much everyday wine (mostly Western grapes) and some better, esp at HAJOS-Vaskut, HELVECIA/KECSKEMET, KISKUNSAG, Szeged.

Aszár-Neszmély White wine district in NW Hungary nr Danube. Native and western grapes grown.

Aszú Botrytis-shrivelled grapes and the sweet wine made from them, as in Sauternes (see p102). Used to designate both wine and shrivelled berries.

Aszú Eszencia Tokaji br sw ★★★★ 57 63 93 Second TOKAY quality (see Eszencia). 7 PUTTONYOS plus; superb amber elixir, like celestial butterscotch.

Badacsony Balaton w dr sw ★★ →★★★ Famous 426-m hill on the N shore of Lake BALATON, home to the native variety KEKNYELU. The basalt soil can give rich, highly flavoured white wines, but the majority recently has been sweet SZURKEBARAT for tourists. Watch for Szent Orbán Winery.

Balaton Balaton r w dr sw ★→★★★ Hungary's inland sea and Europe's largest (50 miles long) freshwater lake. Many good wines take its name. The ending 'i' (eg Balatoni, Egri) is the equivalent of -er in Londoner.

Balatonboglár Large winery from communist era on S shore of Lake BALATON, with wide range of quality white wines, incl sp. Now owned by HUNGAROVIN.

Bátaapáti Kastélyborok 250-acre nr SZEKSZARD part-owned by Antinori of Italy. TIBOR GAL makes vg Sauv Bl, Chard, TRAMINI, KEKFRANKOS and other reds.

Bikavér Eger r ★ 'Bull's Blood', the historic name of the best-selling red wine of EGER: at best full-bodied and well-balanced, but highly variable in its export version today. A three-variety (minimum) blend, mostly KEKFRANKOS, Cab, KEKOPORTO and some Merlot. Now also made in SZEKSZARD. Happily, some wineries (see Eger) are returning to the basics with quality blends.

Bock, József Family winemaker in VILLANY. Hearty reds, both varietal and blends.

Bodvin Private 16-acre TOKAY estate in MAD exporting ASZU and other wines mainly to US.

Bór Wine. Vörös is red, Fehér is white, Asztali is table.

Csopák Village next to Balatonfured, with similar wines but drier whites.

Czárfás Royal TOKAY v'yd, still state-owned, at Tarcal; one of the top classic sites.

Dégenfeld, Count Large (150-acre) TOKAY producer in Tarcal, gearing up for full production.

Dél-Balaton Balaton r w p ★→★★ Progressive area south of Lake BALATON: sound wines, esp whites (Chard, Sémillon, Muscat). Also cuve close sparkling. Dominated by BALATONBOGLAR winery owners of Chapel Hill brand. Try also Legli, Szt Donatus, Oregbaglas.

Disznókö Important first-class TOKAY estate of 247 acres, owned by AXA (French insurance) since '92, directed by J-M Cazes. ASZU and other wines should be top class; first vintage ('93) v rich with a Sauternes touch.

Edes Sweet wine (but not as luscious as ASZU).

Eger Eger district r w dr sw ★→★★ Best-known red-wine centre of N Hungary; a baroque city of cellars full of BIKAVER. Also fresh white LEANYKA (perhaps its best product today), OLASZRIZLING, Chard and Cab. Top producers: Vilmos Thummerer (consistent Bikaver), TIBOR GAL, Ostoros Bor, Béla Vineze and potentially the enormous Egervin.

Eszencia ★★★★ The fabulous quintessence of TOKAY: intensely sweet and aromatic from grapes wizened by botrytis. Properly grape juice of v low, if any, alcoholic strength, reputed to have miraculous properties: its sugar content can be over 750 grams per litre.

Etyek Nr Budapest. Source of modern standard wines, esp Chard, Sauv Bl, esp from HUNGAROVIN.

Ezerjó ('Thousand blessings') Widespread variety but at MOR makes one of Hungary's top dry whites; great potential: fragrant with hint of grapefruit.

François President French founded (1882) sparkling wine producer at Budafok, nr Budapest. Vintage wine: President is v drinkable.

Furmint The classic grape of TOKAY, with great flavour and fire, also grown for table wine at Lake BALATON and in SOMLO.

Gál, Tibor EGER winemaker for barrique-aged BIKAVER, also oaked Chard under GIA label.

Gere, Attila Family winemaker in VILLANY with good forward-looking reds, esp oak aged Cab S (93). Gere & Wenninger is another label (Cuvée Phoenix).

Hajós Pincék Alföld r ★ Charming village in S Hungary with 1,500 cellars. Mostly traditional, family production. Some quality lighter red wines can be found.

Hárslevelű 'Linden-leaved' grape used at Debro and as second main grape of TOKAY (cf Sém/Sauv in Sauternes). Gentle mellow wine with a peach aroma.

Helvécia (Kecskemét) Historic ALFOLD cellars. V'yds ungrafted: phylloxera bugs cannot negotiate sandy soil. Whites and rosés modernist; reds traditional.

Hétszőlő Noble first-growth 116-acre estate at TOKAJI owned by Grands Millésimes de France and Suntory. V fine ASZU. Second label: Dessewffy.

Hungarovin Traders/producers with huge cellars at Budafok nr Budapest: mainly 'Western varietals', also cuve close, transfer and classic sparkling. Now owned by German Sekt specialist, Henkell.

Kadarka Red grape for vast quantities in S, but can produce ample flavour and interesting maturity (eg esp at SZEKSZARD and VILLANY) and considered by some as an essential component of BIKAVER.

Kecskemét Major town of the ALFOLD. Much everyday wine, some better.

Kékfrankos Hungarian for Blaufränkisch; reputedly related to Gamay. Good light or full-bodied reds, esp at SOPRON. Used in BIKAVER at EGER.

Kéknyelü ('Blue stalk') High-flavoured, low-yielding white grape making the best and 'stiffest' wine of Mt BADACSONY. It should be fiery and spicy stuff.

Kékoporto Often best red in Hungarian restaurants. 'Kék' means blue (so could be German Portugieser). Concentrated red; esp from VILLANY, s'times in BIKAVER.

Kisburgundi Kék German Spätburgunder: Pinot Noir.

Kiskunság Largest region in Great Plain. Gd KADARKA esp from Kiskunhalas.

Különleges Minöség Special quality: highest official grading.

Lauder-Lang Partnership of famous international Hungarians to make TOKAY at MAD. Also v'yds and cellar at EGER and famous Gundel's restaurant in Budapest.

Leányka or Király ('Little girl') Old Hungarian white grape. Makes admirable aromatic light dry white. Király ('Royal') Leányka is supposedly superior.

Mád Old commercial centre of the TOKAY region. Growers incl ROYAL TOKAJI, SZEPSY, Vince Gergely.

Mátraalja w (r) ★★ District in foothills of Mátra range in N, nr Gyöngyös (site of huge modernised winery) incl Debro, Nagyrede. Promising dry SZURKEBARAT, Chard, MUSKOTALY, Sauv Bl. French, Australian and now German investment.

Mecsekalja S Hungary district, known for good whites of PECS esp sparkling.

Médoc Noir The Merlot grape, esp in EGER (but for how long?).

Mégas Maj (or Mály) This and CSARFAS are historically the two greatest v'yds of the TOKAY region.

Megyer, Château Joint venture estate between TOKAY TRADING HOUSE and French investors Saros-Patak. See also Ch Pajzos. Excellent ASZU.

Minöségi Bor Quality wine. Hungary's appellation contrôlée.

Mór N Hungary w ★★→★★★ Region long-famous for fresh dry EZERJO. Now also Riesling and Sauvignon. Wines now mostly exported.

Muskotály The yellow Muscat. Makes light, though long-lived, wine in Tokáji and EGER. A little goes into the TOKAY blend (cf Muscadelle in Sauternes). V occasionally makes a wonderful ASZU wine solo.

Nagyburgundi Literally 'great burgundy': indigenous grape, not Pinot N as sometimes thought. Sound solid wine, esp around VILLANY and SZEKSZARD.

Neszmély Winery in ASZAR-NESZMELY; Western-style wines with award-winning Woodcutters White from homegrown Czerszegi Fuszeres hybrid.

Olaszrizling Hungarian name for the Italian Riesling or Welschriesling. Better examples can have a burnt-almond aroma.

Oportó Red grape increasingly used for soft jammy wines to drink young.

Oremus Ancient TOKAJI v'yd of founding Rakóczi family reconstituted by owners of Spain's Vega Sicilia with HQ now at Tolczva. First-rate ASZU.

Oremus A cross of Bouvier and FURMINT used by some in ASZU production, also as varietal with a pear/green-apple flavour, but production waning.

Pajzos, Château TOKAY estate and part of TOKAY TRADING HOUSE/Sárospatak joint venture. See also Ch Megyer. Excellent ASZU.

Pécs Mecsek w (r) ★→★★★ Major S wine city. Esp sp, OLASZRIZLING, Pinot Bl, etc.

Pinot Noir Normally means NAGYBURGUNDI.

Puttonyos Measure of sweetness in TOKAJI ASZU. A 'putt' is a 25 kilo measure, traditionally a hod of Aszù grapes. The number of 'putts' per barrel (136 litres) of dry base wine determines the final richness of the wine, from 3 putts to 7. 3 is equal to 60 grams of sugar per litre, 4: 90, 5: 120, 6: 150. ASZU ESZENCIA must have 180. See Eszencia for the *really* sticky stuff.

Royal Tokáji Wine Co Pioneer Anglo-Danish-Hungarian venture at MAD. 200 acres, mainly first or second growth. First wine (90) a revelation: 91 and (esp) 93 led renaissance of TOKAJI. 95s to follow. I have to declare an interest as a founder.

Siklós City in S Hungary; part of VILLANY-SIKLOS. Mainly sm producers, known for whites: esp HARSLEVELU. Ripe fruity Chard: promising; also TRAMINI, OLASZRIZLING.

Somló N Hungary w ★★ Isolated small district N of BALATON: whites (formerly of high repute) from FURMINT and Juhfark (Sheep's tail) varieties in both traditional, barrel-fermented and fresh, fruity styles. Top prods incl Fekete, Inhauser.

Sopron W Hungary r ★★ Historic enclave S of Neusiedlersee (see Austria). Traditionally known for lighter red wines like KEKFRANKOS and Austrian-style sweet wines but showing promise for whites such as Sauv Bl.

Szamorodni Word meaning 'self-made'; describes TOKAY not sorted in the v'yd. Dry or (fairly) sweet, depending upon proportion of ASZU grapes naturally present. Sold as an aperitif. In vintage TOKAY ASZU yrs, the sweet style can offer some Aszú character at much less cost. Dry Szamorodni is Hungary's sherry.

Száraz Dry, esp of TOKAY SZAMORODNI.

Szekszárd r ★★ District in south-central part of Hungary; some of country's top reds from Cab and Merlot. Also KADARKA red wine which needs age (say 3–4 yrs); can also be botrytised ('Nemes Kadar'). Good organic wines, BIKAVER and good Chard and OLASZRIZLING too. Quality wines are lighter, more delicate than those from VILLANY. Producers incl Vesztergombi, Peter Vida, Heimann.

Szepsy, Istvan Family TOKAY estate in MAD and Tarcal with highest standards: now with a Chinese partner. The Szepsy family 'invented' Tokay in 1630.

Szürkebarát Literally means 'grey friar': Pinot Gr. Too many are sweet tourist wines from BALATON. But this is one of Hungary's best: wait for great dry wines.

Tiffán, Ede VILLANY grower producing full-bodied oaked red wines.

Tokay (Tokáji) Tokáji w dr sw ★★ →★★★★ The ASZU is Hungary's famous liquorous sw wine (since circa 1660), comparable to a highly aromatic, dramatically vital Sauternes with a searing finish, from hills in NE nr Ukraine border. Appellation covers 13,500 acres. See Aszú, Eszencia, Furmint, Puttonyos, Szamorodni. Also dry table wine of character.

Tokay Trading House The state-owned TOKAY CO, with 180 acres of the magnificent Czárfás v'yd and many others. Sales 60% in Hungary.

Tramini Gewürztraminer, esp in SIKLOS.

Villány r p (w) ★★ Major region for full-bodied reds, based in this town. Villányi Burgundi: largely KEKFRANKOS can be good. Cabs S and F and Pinot N: v promising. Dependable wines. See also Nagyburgundi. A region on the move.

Villány-Siklós Southern wine region named after the two towns. High-quality producers incl BOCK, ATTILA GERE, TIFFAN. Watch for Vylyan Winery.

Zweigelt Indigenous (S) red grape: deep-coloured spicy flavoursome wine.

Bulgaria

In the last 15 years Bulgaria has become the world's sixth largest exporter of wine in volume terms. A recent EBRD investment of over 30 million dollars to Domaine Boyar will help to introduce state of the art technology, and further improve both the quality and efficiency of winemaking. Likewise, investment in existing vineyards and the planting of new ones (made possible by the settlement of the majority of land restitution disputes) should increase and improve the supply of grapes.

The main wine regions are in the south and east, in the Danube Valley, along the Black Sea coast and in the southwest. Seventy percent of grapes come from the southeastern area between Stara Zagora, Haskovo, Sliven and Iambol. 'Controliran' wines were approved in 1978, and were joined by oak-matured Reserves, wines of Declared Geographical Origin and simpler Country Wines.

Great value for money continues to be synonymous with Bulgarian wine, but since privatization there is an increasing trend to develop higher quality wines from both indigenous and international grapes. Regional characteristics are valued, but advice from overseas (especially Australian) winemakers has also had an influence, particularly on white wines. The fusion of a long tradition of winemaking with new ideas and methods promises excellent results.

Assenovgrad Main MAVRUD-producing cellar near PLOVDIV – stainless steel being introduced. Mavrud and CAB can last well.

Burgas Black Sea resort and source of rosé (the speciality), easy whites and, increasingly, reds, too.

Bulgarian Vintners Co, The Early importer of Bulgarian wines into the UK. Founded in 1980 and representing six wineries.

Cabernet Sauvignon Highly successful (with four times California's acreage). Dark vigorous fruity wine, v drinkable young; best quality wines age well.

Chardonnay Previously less successful than CABERNET. Better results now from N and E. V dry, full-flavoured wine. Recent oaky examples are promising.

Controliran Like DOCG and AOC. Bulgarian Controliran Region wines have distinct characters based on specific natural conditions. Production must comply with government regulations.

Country Wines Regional wines (cf French Vins de Pays), often 2-variety blends.

Damianitza MELNIK winery specializing in native Melnik grape.

Danube River dividing Bulgaria and Romania. ROUSSE and SVISHTOV regions benefit from its proximity, esp for reds.

Dimiat The common native white grape, grown in the E towards the coast.

Domaine Boyar Bulgaria's first independent wine merchant for almost 50 years, and now also Bulgaria's biggest producer. Set up in '91, exports worldwide. Owns IAMBOL, SHUMEN and DB SLIVEN wineries.

Gamza Red grape (Kadarka of Hungary) with potential esp from N region.

Harsovo Southwest region, esp for MELNIK.

Haskovo Recently privatized, forward-looking winery (with v'yds) in S region specializing in MERLOT; STAMBOLOVO and SAKAR are satellite wineries.

Iambol Winery owned by DOM BOYAR specializing in CAB S and MERLOT, and following new investment, now marketing Premium Oak and Premium Reserve wine ranges.

Karlovo Town famous for its Valley of the Roses. Whites, esp MISKET.

Khan Krum Satellite cellar of PRESLAV, whites esp Reserve CHARD.

Korten Subregion of SLIVEN. Korten's CAB is more tannic than most.

Lovico Suhindol Neighbour of PAVLIKENI, site of Bulgaria's first coop (1909). Good GAMZA, CAB, MERLOT blends, CHARD and SAUV. Privatized '91.

Mavrud Grape variety and darkly plummy red from S Bulgaria, esp ASSENOVGRAD. Can mature 20 yrs⁺. Considered the country's best indigenous variety.

Melnik Village in SW and highly prized grape. Dense red; locals say it can be carried in a handkerchief. Needs 5 yrs⁺; lasts 15. Also ripe age-worthy CAB.

Merlot Soft red grape variety grown mainly in HASKOVO in the S.

Misket Mildly aromatic indigenous grape; the basis for most country whites.

Muscat Ottonel Normal Muscat grape, grown in E for mid-sweet fruity white.

Novi Pazar Winery nr VARNA making finer wines, esp CHARD.

Novo Selo Good red GAMZA from the north.

Oriachovitza Satellite cellar of STARA ZAGORA. Major S area for CONTROLIRAN CAB-MERLOT. Rich savoury red best at 4–5 yrs. Recent RESERVE CAB releases have been good.

Pamid The light soft everyday red of the southeast and northwest.

Pavlikeni Northern region winery owned by SUHINDOL specializing in MERLOT and CAB of high quality.

Peruschitza Winery nr PLOVDIV. Reds only, esp MAVRUD, CAB and RUBIN grapes.

Pleven N cellar for PAMID, GAMZA, CAB. Also Bulgaria's wine research station.

Plovdiv City in southern wine region source of good CAB and MAVRUD. Winemaking mostly at ASSENOVGRAD and PERUSCHITZA. The university's Dept of Food Technology is where most Bulgarian oenologists study.

Pomorie Black Sea Gold Winery in E, whites and reds, esp CHARD and MUSKAT.

Preslav Well-known white wine cellar, in E region.Also good brandy.

Reserve Used on labels of selected and oak-aged wines. Whites for a minimum of two years and reds for at least three years in oak vats.

Riesling Some Rhine Riesling is grown. But most is Italian (Welschriesling) used for medium and dry whites.

Rkatziteli One of the most widely grown grapes in the world, known as Rikat in Bulgaria. Widely used in dry and medium whites wine blends in NE.

Rousse Large winery in N on the DANUBE. Now owned by the American Seaboard Corporation. Fresh high-tech whites esp CHARD, SAUV BL. V gd reds, incl YANTRA VALLEY CAB, and young vintage wines.

Rubin Bulgarian cross (Nebbiolo x Syrah); often blended with CAB or MERLOT.

Sakar SE wine area for MERLOT, some of Bulgaria's best.

Sauvignon Blanc Grown in E and N Bulgaria esp at SHUMEN, PRESLAV and TARGOVISHTE.

Shumen E region and winery (owned by DOM BOYAR), esp whites and New World-style reds. New Premium Oak and Premium Cuvée ranges.

Slaviantsi Winery in Sub-Balkan region. Mainly whites, esp MUSCAT, CHARD, MISKET, and UGNI BLANC. Increasingly also reds, esp CAB.

Sliven Big producing S region, esp for CAB. Also MERLOT and Pinot N (which are blended in a COUNTRY WINE), MISKET and CHARD. Vini Sliven produces red and white wines. Promising barrique-aged CAB. The new DOM BOYAR green-field winery DB SLIVEN, Australian designed, will focus on high quality and not mass production

Sofia The country's capital.

Stambolovo Satellite cell of HASKOVO, MERLOT specialist, eg Stambolovo Merlot Reserve.

Stara Planina Balkan mountain region of central Bulgaria, incl KARLOVO.

Stara Zagora S region winery: reds, esp CAB and MERLOT to RESERVE quality.

Sungarlare Satellite of SLAVIANTSI, its MISKET is noted for its distinctive delicate fragrance. Also CHARD.

Svishtov N region winery on DANUBE. Reds only, esp finely balanced CAB.

Targovishte Winery in E region, quality whites esp CHARD (incl barrel fermented) and SAUV BL.

Varna Black Sea coast region for whites, esp CHARD (buttery or unoaked), SAUV. DIMIAT, ALIGOTE and UGNI BL (sometimes blended).

Zar Simeon Top CAB selection 'by appointment' to King Simeon of Bulgaria.

The former Yugoslav states

Before its disintegration in 1991, Yugoslavia was well-established as a supplier of wines of international calibre, if not generally of exciting quality. Now the newly formed states are again working on export. Current political disarray and competition from other East European countries makes commercial contacts difficult (except in Slovenia, whose 'Riesling' was the pioneer export, since followed by Cab, Pinot Bl, Traminer and others). All regions, except the central Bosnian highlands, make wine, almost entirely in giant coops, although many small private producers are emerging with the '90s. The Dalmatian (Croatian) coast and Macedonia have good indigenous wines whose roots go deep into the ancient world. In Dalmatia, for example, new investment and Western technology promise interesting results with some of these indigenous wines. Problems remain with distribution and storage. Best results come directly from the producer's cellar.

Slovenia

Barbera Vg sparkling from Janez Istenic and family in BIZELJSKO.

Bela Krajina SAVA area, esp 'Ledeno LASKI RIZLING' (late-harvest frozen grapes).

Beli Pinot Pinot Bl, a popular grape variety. Belo is white.

Bizeljsko-Sremic In SAVA district. Full-flavoured local-variety reds and LASKI R.

Brda Slovene upper part of Collio DOC (Italy). Many estates on both sides.

Crno vino Red (literally 'black') wine.

Curin-Prapotnik Pioneer Slovenian white-wine trader.

Cvicek Traditional rosé or pale red esp from DOLENJSKA. ('Schilcher' in Austria.)

Dolenjska SAVA region: CVICEK, LASKI RIZLING and Modra Frankinja (dry red).

Drava Valley (Podravski) Slovene wine region. Mainly whites from aromatic (WELSCHRIES, Muscat Ottonel) to flamboyant (RIES and SAUV); also Eisweins and Beerenauslesen as in neighbouring Austria.

Drustvo Vinogradnikov BRDA assoc of 45 growers/winemakers (with SAVA, DRAVA and Moravia equivalents).

Gorna Radgona Winery for sp, late-harvest sw and Eiswein (Ledeno vino).

Grasevina Slovenian for Italian RIES. The normal 'Riesling' of the region.

Hlupic Producer of fine whites from around Haloze.

Jeruzalem Slovenia's most famous v'yd, at LJUTOMER. Its best wines are late-picked RENSKI RIZLING and LASKI RIZLING. Also makes tank-fermented sparklers.

Kakovostno Vino Quality wine (one step down from VRHUNSKO).

Kontrolirano poreklo Appellation. Wine must be 80% from that region.

Koper Hottest area of LITTORAL, between Trieste and Piran. Full rich MERLOTS and B'x-like Rdeci Capris blend.

Kmetijska Zadruga Wine farmers' cooperative.

Kraski Means grown on the coastal limestone or Karst. A region famous for REFOSCO wines, eg Kraski Teran and oak-aged Teranton.

Laski Rizling Yet another name for Italian RIES. Best-known Slovene wine, not best quality. Top export brand: 'Cloburg' from Podravski (DRAVA) region.

Littoral (Primorje) Coastal region bordering Italy (Collio) and the Med. Esp good reds: Cab, MERLOT (aged in Slovene oak), Barbera and REFOSK.

Ljutomer (or Lutomer)-Ormoz Slovenia's best-known, probably best white-wine district, in NE (DRAVA); esp LASKI RIZLING, at its best rich and satisfying. Ormoz winery also has sparkling and late-harvest wines.

Malvazija Ancient Greek white grape for luscious (now also lively fresh) wine.

Maribor Important centre in NE (DRAVA). White wines, mainly from VINAG, incl LASKI RIZLING, RIES, SAUV, Pinot Bl and Traminer; also the blend Mariborcan.

Merlot Reasonable in Slovenia. Comparable with neighbouring NE Italian.

Metlika BELA KRAJINA wine centre with warm Kolpa River v'yds.

Namizno Vino Table wine.

Pozna Trgatev Late harvest.

Ptuj Historic wine town with trad-based coop: wines clean, mostly white.

Radgona-Kapela DRAVA district next to Austrian border, esp late-harvest wines, eg RADGONSKA RANINA, also classic method sparkling.

Radgonska Ranina Ranina is Austria's Bouvier grape. Radgonska is nr MARIBOR. The wine is sweet. Trade name is Tigrovo Mljeko (Tiger's Milk).

Refosk Vg Italian red ('Refosco') grape in E and in ISTRIA (Croatia) as TERAN.

Renski Rizling Rhine RIES: rare here, but a little in LJUTOMER-ORMOZ.

Riesling Formerly meant Italian Ries. Now legally limited to real Rhine Riesling.

Sauvignon Blanc Vg with the resources to make it well; otherwise horrid.

Sava Valley Central Slovenia: light dry reds, eg CVICEK. Northern bank is for whites, eg LASKI RIZLING, Silvaner and recent Chard and SAUV BL.

Sipon Name for Furmint of Hungary – locally prized, p'haps has a future.

Slamnak A late-harvest LJUTOMER estate RIES.

Slovenijavino Slovenia's largest exporter. Wines (esp WELSCHRIES) bought in and blended with care for Slovin, Ashewood and Avia brands.

Tigrovo Mljeko See Radgonska Ranina.

Tokaj The Pinot Gr, making rather heavy white wine.

Vinag Huge production cellars at MARIBOR. Top wine: Cloburg LASKI RIZLING.

Vinakras Sezana v'yds for deep-purple fresh-tasting TERAN.

Vipava Forward-looking LITTORAL region with tradition of export to Austria and Germany: good Cab, MERLOT, Barbera, Chard and Vrtovcan blend.

Vrhunsko Vino Top-quality wine.

Croatia (includes Dalmatia)

Babic Standard red of DALMATIA, ages better than ordinary PLAVAC.

Badel Top négociant of Croatian wines.

Banat Region partly in Romania: up-to-date wineries making adequate RIES.

Baranjske Planote SLAVONIA area for RIES and BIJELI BURGUNDAC.

Benkovac Town and wine cellar: looking gd (esp rosé) as it emerges from war.

Bogdanusa Local white grape of the DALMATIAN islands, esp Hvar and Brac. Round, like Chard, refreshing faintly fragrant wine.

Bolski Plavac Top-quality vigorous red from Bol on the island of Brac.

Burgundac Bijeli Chard, grown in SLAVONIA.

Dalmacijavino Coop at Split: full range of DALMATIAN coastal/island wines.

Dalmatia The coast of Croatia, from Rijeka to Dubrovnik. Variety of characterful wines. High-alcohol wines are traditional, but fruitier styles are emerging.

Dingac V'yard designation on Peljesac's steep western slopes (mid-DALMATIAN coast). Traditionally produces heavy sweetish wine from PLAVAC MALI grape, but emerging as a robust, dry red that supports oak and bottle ageing.

Faros Substantial age-worthy PLAVAC red from the island of Hvar.

Grasevina Local name for ubiquitous Laski Rizling. Best from Kutjevo.

Grk White grape, speciality of the island of Korcula, giving strong, even sherry-like wine, and also a lighter pale one.

Grgich, Miljenko California winemaker (cf Grgich Hills), returns to Croatian roots. Western-style cellar scheme on Peljesac peninsular (DALMATIAN coast).

Istravino Rijeka Oldest wine négociant of Croatia.

Istria Peninsula in the N Adriatic, Porec its centre: a variety of pleasant wines, Merlot as good as any. V dry TERAN is perfect with local truffles.

Ivan Dolac A good quality dry, fruity, aromatic red.

Kontinentalna Hrvatska Inland Croatia. Mostly for whites (GRASEVINA).

Marastina Strong herbal dry DALMATIAN white, best from Lastovo.

Opol Pleasant light pale PLAVAC red from Split, Sibenik and Hvar and Brac islands.

Plavac Mali DALMATIA red grape; wine of body, strength, age-ability. Current thinking has it as Zinfandel. See Dingac, Opol, Postup. Also white, Plavac Beli.

Plenkovic Zlatan-Hvar-based winemaker producing quality red and white wines. Bogdanusa shows promise as varietal, but is generally blended.

Polu Semi... Polu-slatko is semi-sweet, polu-suho is semi-dry.

Portugizac Austria's Blauer Portugieser: plain red wine.

Posip Pleasant white of the DALMATIAN islands, notably Korcula.

Postup Soft heavy DALMATIAN red of Peljesac peninsula. Highly esteemed.

Prosek Dessert wine from ISTRIA and DALMATIA: 15% (can be almost port-like).

Slavonija N Croatia, on Hungarian border between Slovenia and Serbia. Big producer. Standard wines, esp white, incl most of former 'Yugoslav RIES'.

Stolno vino Table wine.

Teran Stout dark red of ISTRIA. See Refosk (Slovenia).

Vrhunsko Vino New origin-based designation for quality wines.

Vugava Viska Rare w grape of Vis (DALMATIA). Linked (allegedly) with Viognier.

Bosnia and Herzegovina

Blatina Ancient MOSTAR red grape and wine from pebbled W bank of Neretva.

Kameno Vino White wine of unique irrigated desert v'yd in Neretva Valley.

Mostar Means 'old bridge'. Was Herzegovina's Islamic-looking wine centre, but cellars destroyed during the civil war. Ljubuski and Citluk are rebuilding. Potentially admirable ZILAVKA white and BLATINA red.

Samotok Light red (rosé/'ruzica') wine from run-off juice (and no pressing).

Zilavka White grape of MOSTAR, making wines rather neutral when exported, but can be dry pungent and memorably fruity with a faint flavour of apricots.

Serbia

Serbia in times of peace is a potential supplier of v good quality wines, esp from Zupa in the centre and Fruska Gora in the north. Kosovo can make gd Cab.

Montenegro

13 July State-controlled coop (mainly, but not just grapes) with high-tech Italian equipment, outside PODGORICA. VRANAC is high quality.

Cemovsko Polje Vast pebbled semi-desert plain; esp VRANAC. Awaits discovery.

Crmnica Lakeside/coastal v'yds esp for Kadarka grape (see Macedonia).

Crna Gora Black Mountains.

Duklja Late-picked semi-sweet version of VRANAC.

Krstac Montenegro's top white grape and wine; esp from CRMNICA.

Merlot Since '80: good wood-aged results.

Podgorica Ancient name reintroduced for capital Titograd.

Vranac Local vigorous and abundant red grape and wine. Value.

Macedonia

Belan White Grenache. Makes neutral Gemischt wine.

Crna Reka River with many artificial lakes for irrigation.

Crveno suvo vino Red dry wine.

Kadarka Major red grape of Hungary; here closer to its origins around L Ohrid.

Kratosija Locally favoured red grape; sound wines.

Plovdina Native (S) grape for mild red, white; esp blended with tastier PROKUPAC.

Prokupac Serbian and Macedonian top red grape. Makes dark rosé (RUZICA) and full red of character, esp at Zupa. PLOVDINA often added for smoothness.

Rkatsiteli Russian (white) grape often used in blends.

Temjanika Grape for spicy semi-sweet whites. (Tamianka in Bulgaria.)

Teran Transferred from Istria, but Macedonia's version is less stylish.

Tikves Much-favoured hilly v'yd region (20,000 acres). Esp for pleasant dark red Kratosija; fresh dry Smederevka (see Serbia) – locally mixed with soda.

Traminac The Traminer. Also grown in Vojvodina and Slovenia.

Vardar Valley Brings the benefits of the Aegean Sea to inland v'yds.

Vranec Local name for Vranac of Montenegro (qv).

Vrvno Vino Controlled origin designation for quality wines.

Former Czechoslovakia

The country was re-established in January '93 as the Czech (Moravia and Bohemia) and Slovak republics. While there was little or no tradition of exporting from this mainly white-wine region, good wines have emerged since 1989. Labels will say whether they are blended or from single grape varieties. All offer good value. Privatization, foreign investment and advice bode well for the future.

Moravia Favourite wines in Prague: variety and value. V'yds situated along Danube tributaries. Many wines from Austrian border: similar grapes, Grüner V, Müller-T, Sauv, Traminer, St-Laurent, Pinot N, Blauer Portugieser, Frankovka, etc; and similar wines, eg from **Mikulov** (white, red, dry, sw classic-method sp; especially popular Valtice Cellars, est'd 1430, and traditional Vino Mikulov), **Satov** (modern, mostly white – incl Sauv, Grüner Veltliner, Müller-Thurgau – grapes from local farms and coops) and **Znojmo** (long-est'd, ideal limestone soil; local white grapes, Grüner-V, Müller-T, Sauv, 'Tramín' and sweetish prize-winning Pinot Gr 93 from Sobes). Other regions: Jaroslavice (oak-aged reds), Prímetice (full aromatic whites), Blatnice, Hustopece, sunny Pálava, Saldorf (esp Sauv, 'Rynsky' Ries) and Velké Pavlovice (good Ruländer, Traminer, St-Laurent and award-winning Cab 92, still expanding). Moravia also has sp.

Bohemia Winemaking since 9th C. Same latitude and similar wines to eastern Germany. Best: N of Prague, in Elbe Valley, and (best-known) nr Melník (King Karel IV bought in Burgundian vines in 15th C; today Ries, Ruländer and Traminer predominate). 'Bohemia Sekt' is growing, eg increasingly popular from STARY PLZENEC: tank-fermented (mostly), some oak used, with grapes from SLOVAKIA and MORAVIA, too; French advice. Also some interesting Pinot N. Top wineries: **Lobkowitz** (at Melnik), **Roudnice**, **Litomerice**, **Karlstein**.

Slovakia Warmest climatic conditions and most of former Czechoslovakia's wine. Best in eastern v'yds neighbouring Hungary's Tokay region. Slovakia uses Hungarian varieties, international varieties (Ries, Gewürz, Pinot Bl, Sauv Bl and Cab S) and makes a little Tokay, too. Key districts: Malo-Karpatská Oblast (largest region, in foothills of the Little Carpathians, incl Ruländer, Ries, Traminer, Limberger, etc), Malá Trna, Nové Mesto, Skalice (small area, mainly reds), and (in Tatra foothills) Bratislava, Pezinok, Modra.

Romania

Romania has a long winemaking tradition, but potential for quality was wasted during decades of supplying the Soviet Union with cheap sweet wine. The political situation has allowed little progress. Quantity is still the goal, despite some superbly sited vineyards. But with modern methods, advice of visiting winemakers and increasing exports, Romania's wine industry could rival that of Bulgaria. The full, soft reds from Dealul Mare (esp Pinot N) are already gaining international recognition as excellent. It will be good to watch the effect on quality of less greedy yields.

Alba Iulia Town in warm TIRNAVE area of TRANSYLVANIA, known for off-dry white (Italian RIES, FETEASCA, MUSKAT-OTTONEL), bottle-fermented sparkling.

Aligoté Pleasantly fresh white from 11,000 acres (2nd only to France).

Băbească Neagra Traditional red grape of the FOCSANI area: agreeably sharp wine tasting slightly of cloves. (Means 'grandmother grape'.)

Banat Plain on border with Serbia. Workaday Italian RIES, SAUV BL, MUSKAT-OTTONEL and local RIES de Banat; light red Cadarca, CABERNET and Merlot.

Baratca Gentle slopes around PAULIS for good Merlot and CABERNET.

Burgund Mare Name linked to Burgenland (Austria) where grape is called Blaufrankish (Kekfrankos in Hungary).

Buzau Hills Gd reds (CAB, Merlot, BURGUND M) from continuation of DEALUL MARE.

Cabernet Sauvignon Increasingly grown, esp at DEALUL MARE; dark intense wines.

Chardonnay Some sweet styles but modern dry and oak-aged styles esp from MURFATLAR and TRANSYLVANIA increasingly available.

Cotesti Warmer part of FOCSANI; deep-coloured PINOT N, Merlot etc and dry whites.

Cotnari Region at Moldavia's N v'yd limit; good botrytis. Famous (rarely seen) historical wine: light dessert white from local GRASA, FETEASCA ALBA, TAMAIIOASA, rather like v delicate Tokay, gold with tints of green.

Crisana W region including historical MiniS area (since 15th-C: reds, esp Cadarca, and crisp white Mustoasa), Silvania (esp FETEASCA), Diosig, Valea lui Mihai.

Dealul Mare 'The big hill'. Important up-to-date well-sited area in SE Carpathian foothills. Reds from FETEASCA NEAGRA, CAB, Merlot, PINOT N, etc. Whites from TAMIIOASA, etc. French investment. Look out for Dionis label (fine reds).

Dobrudja Sunny dry Black Sea region. Incl MURFATLAR. Quality is good.

DOC New classification for higher quality wines replacing VS, VSO.

DOCG (Was VSOC) Top-range wines. CMD: late harvest, CMI: late harvest with noble rot, CIB is from selected nobly rotten grapes (like Beerenauslese).

Drăgăşani Region on River Olt S of Carpathian Mountains, since Roman times. Traditional and 'modern' grapes (esp Sauv). Gd MUSKAT-OTTONEL, reds (CAB).

Fetească Romanian white grape with spicy, faintly Muscat aroma. Two types: F Alba (same as Hungary's Leányka, ageworthy and with better potential esp when carefully handled; base for sp and sw COTNARI) and F Regala (gd for sp).

Fetească Neagră Red Feteasca. Difficult to handle, but can give deep, full-bodied reds with gd character and ageing potential.

Focsani Important MOLDAVIA region, incl COTESTI, NICORESTI and ODOBESTI.

Grasă A form of the Hungarian Furmint grape grown in Romania and used in, among other wines, COTNARI. Prone to botrytis. Grasa means 'fat'.

Iaşi Region for fresh acidic whites (F ALBA, also Welschries, ALIGOTE, spumante-style MUSKAT O): Bucium, Copu, Tomesti. Reds: Merlot, CAB; top BABEASCA.

Jidvei Winery in the cool Carpathians (TIRNAVE) among Romania's N-most v'yds. Good whites: FETEASCA, Furmint, RIES, SAUV BL.

Lechinta Transylvanian wine area. Wines noted for bouquet (local grapes).

Moldavia NE province. Largest Romanian wine area with 12 subregions, incl IASI, FOCSANI, PANCIU. Temperate, with good v'yd potential.

Murfatlar V'yds nr Black Sea, 2nd-best botrytis conditions (see Cotnari): esp sweet CHARD, late-harvest CAB. Now also full dry wines and sparkling.

Muscat Ottonel The E European Muscat, a speciality of Romania, esp in cool-climate TRANSYLVANIA and dry wines in MOLDAVIA.

OdobeSti The central part of FOCSANI; white wines of FETEASCA, RIES, etc.

Panciu Cool MOLDAVIA region N of ODOBESTI. Good still and sparkling white.

Paulis Small estate cellar in town of same name. Oak-aged Merlot a treasure.

Perla Semi-sw speciality of TIRNAVE: Italian RIES, FETEASCA and MUSKAT-OTTONEL.

Pinot Gris Widely grown in TRANSYLVANIA and MURFATLAR. Full slightly aromatic wines, closer to Alsace than Italian Pinot Grigio in style.

Pinot Noir Grown in the south: can surprise with taste and character.

Premiat Reliable range of higher-quality wines for export.

Riesling (Italian Riesling) Widely planted. Most poorly made, but has potential.

Sauvignon Blanc Romania's tastiest white, esp blended with FETEASCA.

Tamiioasa Romaneasca Traditional white grape known as 'frankincense' for its exotic scent and flavour. Pungent sweet wines often affected by botrytis.

Tirnave Transylvanian wine region (Romania's coolest), known for its PERLA and much FETEASCA R. Dry and aromatic wines (esp Pinot Gr, Gewürz) and sp.

Transylvania See Alba Iulia, Lechinta, Tirnave.

Valea Călugărească 'Valley of the Monks', part of DEALUL MARE with go-ahead research station. Currently proposing new AC-style rules. CAB (esp Special Reserve 85), Merlot, PINOT are admirable, as are Italian RIES, Pinot Gr.

Vin de Masa Most basic wine classification – for local drinking only.

Vinexport Est' '90, fast developing co marketing and exporting wines (80% of Romania's wine exports).

Greece

Since Greece's entry into the EC in 1981, its antique wine industry has moved into higher gear. Some is still fairly primitive, but a new system of appellations is in place and recent years have seen much investment in equipment and expertise. Modern, well-made, but still authentically Greek wines are well worth tasting.

Achaia-Clauss Long-established wine merchant with cellars at PATRAS, in north PELOPONNESE. Most wines are exported, incl the well-known Demestica.

Agiorgitiko Widely planted NEMEA red-wine grape. Very high potential.

Agioritikos (AC) Good medium white and rosé from Agios Oros on Mt Athos, Halkidiki's monastic peninsula. Source of Cab, etc, for TSANTALI.

Antonopoulos ★★→★★★ Highly reputed MANTINIA producer. Popular w, buttery Chard, oaky Cab S.

Argyros ★★★ Top SANTORINI producer with delicious (and expensive) Visanto aged 20 yrs in cask. Current vintages: 79, 80.

Attica Ancient wine region round Athens, the chief source of RETSINA.

Boutaris, J and Son ★★→★★★ Merchants and makers with high standards in MACEDONIA. Large range from all over Greece. Single v'yd varietal wines can be excellent. Top wine: XYNOMAVRO-Merlot. Also Grande Réserve.

Boutaris, Yannis Two sm estates: high quality. Ktima Kyr-Yannis: Merlot, Syrah, Merlot-XYNOMAVRO; top quality NAOUSSA: Ramnista. Also see Vegoritis.

Calliga ★ Brand name now KOURTAKIS-owned. Gd AGIORGITIKO sourced for Montenero and Rubis.

Cambas, Andrew ★→★★ Brand name owned by J BOUTARIS AND SON.

Carras, Domaine ★★★ Estate at Sithonia, Halkidiki with its own AC (COTES DE MELITON). Sadly, no longer in family hands; future at present unknown.

Cava Legal term for blended aged red and white. Eg Cava BOUTARI (NAOUSSA-NEMEA).

Cephalonia (Kephalonia) Ionian island: good white ROBOLA.

Côtes de Meliton Appellation (since '81) of CARRAS estate.

Crete Island with potential for excellent wine. Best from BOUTARI, KOURTAKIS.

Emery An historic RHODES producer, specializing in Athiri and Mandelaria under brand names of Villare and GrandRose. Also gd quality trad method sp wine.

Gaia ★★→★★★ Top quality NEMEA estate; v fine wine under Notios label. Also Thalassitis from SANTORINI. To watch.

Gentilini ★★★ Up market white ROBOLA from CEPHALONIA. 'Fumé': oak-aged.

Gerovassiliou ★★★ Perfectionist miniature estate nr Salonika. Rhône-influenced reds and whites of unique style, esp fine Viognier.

Goumenissa (AC) ★→★★ Oaked red from W MACEDONIA. Esp BOUTARI, Aïdarini.

Hatzimichalis, Domaine ★★★ Small Atalanti estate. High standards; Greek and French varieties, incl Chard, Cab S. Top wine: Merlot; better r than w.

Katogi Well-known, popular Cabernet-AGIORGITIKO from Avera estate high in mountains nr Epirus. Also Traminer and other whites. Top wine: Ktima Averof.

Katsaros ★★★ Small winery of v high standards on Mt Olympus. Top wine: Cab S esp after '93, ages 10 yrs. To follow.

Kokkineli The rosé version of RETSINA: like the white. Drink cold.

Kouros ★★ Reliable, well-marketed white PATRAS and red NEMEA from KOURTAKIS.

Kourtakis, D ★★ Athenian merchant with mild RETSINA and good dark NEMEA.

Lazaridis, Château ★★★ Family estate NE of Salonika. Fine wines. Top wine: Magico Vouno a claret-style red to age 15 years. New winery in '97. To watch.

Lazaridis, Domaine Kostas ★★★ Not to be confused with CH LAZARIDIS. High quality reds and whites and best Greek rosé. Vg new red CAVA.

Lemnos (AC) Aegean island: RETSINA, KOKKINELI; delicious sweet golden Muscat.

Macedonia Quality wine region in the north, for XYNOMAVRO, esp NAOUSSA.

Malagousia Rediscovered white grape variety capable of giving intense wines. Major producers CARRAS, GEROVASSILIOU, MATSA.

Malvasia White grape said to be from Monemvasia (south PELOPONNESE).

Mantinia (AC) PELOPONNESE region. Fresh aromatic intense MOSCOPHILERO.

Matsa, Château ★★→★★★ Small ATTICA producer exploiting potential of native Greek varieties. Top wine: SAVATIANO Vieilles Vignes. Also stylish Laoutari and excellent MALAGOUSIA.

Mavro Black – the word for dark (often sweet) red wine.

Mavrodaphne (AC) 'Black laurel'. Dark, sweet, port/recioto-like, concentrated red; fortified to 15–22%. Speciality of PATRAS, N PELOPONNESE. To age.

Mercouri ★★→★★★ PELOPONNESE family estate. V fine Refosco, delicious RODITIS. Experiments with new varieties and ageing vines promise great things.

Moscophilero Rose-scented high quality, high acid grape.

Naoussa (AC) r High quality region for XYNOMAVRO. The only Greek region where 'cru' notion may soon develop. Excellent vintages, incl 90, 94, 97.

Nemea (AC) r Region in E PELOPONNESE producing dark, spicy AGIORGITIKO wines. Often also the backbone of many (not always Greek) blends. New High Nemea Reserves gd; Koutsi front-runner for cru status.

Oenoforos ★★ Good PELOPONNESE producer of Asprolithi white. Chard, Cab and rare red Volitsa To watch.

Oktana Newly formed marketing group of four producers: ANTONOPOULOS, KATOGI, MERCOURI and STROFILIA.

Papaïoannou ★★→★★★ Top NEMEA grower. V classy reds, incl Pinot N; elegant oaky whites.

Patras (AC) White wine (eg plentiful dry RODITIS and rarer Muscats) and wine town on the Gulf of Corinth. Home of MAVRODAPHNE.

Pegasus, Château ★★ NAOUSSA estate for good red to age 10 yrs. Organic.

Peloponnese Southern land mass of mainland Greece, with half of the country's v'yds, incl NEMEA and PATRAS.

Rapsani Interesting oaked red from Mt Ossa. Rasping until rescued by TSANTALI.

Retsina ATTICA speciality white: with Aleppo pine resin added; oddly appropriate with Greek food. Modern retsina is often too mild.

Rhodes Easternmost Greek island. Chevalier de Rhodes is a pleasant red. Also good sp by Caïr (coop).

Robola Good quality lemony white grape, originating from CEPHALONIA.

Roditis White grape grown all over Greece. Good when yields are low.

Samos (AC) Island nr Turkey famed for sweet pale golden Muscat. Esp (fortified) Anthemis, (sun-dried) Nectar. Rare old bottlings can be outstanding.

Santorini Volcanic island N of CRETE: sweet Visanto (sun-dried grapes), v dry white from high potential Assyrtico grape. Oaked examples: promising. Top producers: Sigalas, ARGYROS, Santo Wines, GAIA.

Savatiano White grape of RETSINA. Often considered dull, but see CH MATSAS.

Semeli, Château ★★ Estate nr Athens. Good white and red, incl Cab S.

Skouras ★★→★★★ Innovative PELOPONNESE wines. Viognier (Cuvée Eclectic). Top NEMEA (St George). Best wine: Megas Oenos red (**92 93** 94 95; 96 97 to follow).

Spiropoulos, Domaine ★★→★★★ Organic high quality producer in MANTINIA. Top wine: MOSCOPHILERO w. Oaky red Porfyros and sp Odi show potential.

Strofilia ★★ Small modern ATTICA winery. Good whites, rosé; reds incl Cab. New winery for reds at Asprokambos, NEMEA with OKTANA partners.

Tsantali ★★ Merchant/producer at Agios Pavlos. Wide range of country and AC wines, incl MACEDONIAN and wine from the monks of Mt Athos, NEMEA, NAOUSSA, RAPSANI, CAVA and Muscats from SAMOS and LEMNOS.

Tselepos ★★ Top quality MANTINIA producer and Greece's first Gewürz. Also promising red and tasty classic method sparkling. New varietal range incl Syrah and Merlot-XYNOMAVRO.

Xynomavro The tastiest of many indigenous Greek red grapes – though name means acidic-black. Grown purely in the north it is the basis for NAOUSSA and other reds. High potential.

Vegoritis New enterprise by YANNIS BOUTARIS AND ASSOCIATES. Gd white varietals: Sauvignon, Gewürztraminer, etc, plus red rosé. Nr lake at Amindeo.

Zitsa Mountainous N Epirius AC. Delicate Debina white, still or fizzy.

Cyprus

Cyprus's main exports are strong, reasonable reds and less significantly fortified liqueur wines (former 'Cyprus Sherry' a term banned by the EU since 1995), though treacly Commandaria is the island's finest product. Exports are significant, with over two million tourists per annum and local consumption is on the up. Cyprus has now to compete against European standards, and progress has been made in vineyard management and the introduction of up-to-date winemaking technology by large producers. Until recently, only two local grapes were grown, now another 12 have emerged, including the inevitable international favourites. Significantly Cyprus has never had phylloxera.

Afames Village at foot of Mt Olympus and a dry tangy r (MAVRO) from SODAP.

Alkion Light dry KEO w (early picked XYNISTERI grapes from Akamas, Paphos).

Aphrodite Consistent medium-dry XYNISTERI white from KEO.

Arsinoë Dry white wine from SODAP, named after an unfortunate female whom the last entry turned to stone.

Bellapais Fizzy med-sw white from KEO. Essential refreshment for holiday-makers.

Commandaria Good-quality brown sw wine since ancient times in hills N of LIMASSOL. Delimited area of 14 villages; named after crusading order of knights. Made by solera maturation of sun-dried XYNISTERI and MAVRO grapes. Best (as old as 100 yrs) is superb: incredible sweetness, fragrance, concentration: a jewel to seek out. But most is just standard Communion wine.

Domaine d'Ahera Modern lighter red from KEO: Grenache and local Lefkas grape.

Emva Brand name of well-made fino, medium and cream SHERRIES.

ETKO See Haggipavlu.

Haggipavlu LIMASSOL wine merchant since 1844. Trades as ETKO. Emva range, and quality table wines in tiny quantities.

Heritage A KEO rich, oaked dry r from rare indigenous Pambakina grape.

Kalokhorio Principal COMMANDARIA village, growing only XYNISTERI.

KEO The biggest and most go-ahead firm at LIMASSOL. Standard KEO Dry White and Dry Red are vg value. See also Othello, Heritage and Aphrodite.

Kokkineli Rosé: the name is related to 'cochineal'.

Kolossi Crusaders' castle nr Limassol; gives name to table wines from SODAP.

Laona The largest of the small independent regional wineries at Arsos, now owned by KEO. Good range, incl an oak-aged red and a fruity dry white.

Limassol 'The Bordeaux of Cyprus'. Southern wine port (and its region).

Loel Major producer. Red 'Hermes', Commandaria 'Alasia' and brandies.

Mavro The black grape of Cyprus and its dark wine.

Monte Roya Modern regional winery at Chryssoroyiatissa Monastery.

Muscat All major firms produce pleasant low-price (15% alcohol) Muscats.

Opthalmo Black grape (red/rosé): lighter, sharper than MAVRO. Not native.

Othello A good standard dry red (MAVRO and OPTHALMO grapes from the PITSILIA region). Solid and satisfying version from KEO. Best drunk at 3–4 yrs.

Palomino Soft dry w (LOEL, SODAP). V drinkable ice-cold. Imported for SHERRY-style.

Pitsilia Region S of Mt Olympus. Some of best white and COMMANDARIA wines.

Rosella Light dry fragrant rosé from KEO. OPTHALMO from PITSILIA.

St-Panteleimon Brand of medium-sweet white from KEO.

Semeli Good traditional red from HAGGIPAVLU. Best at 3–4 years old.

Sherry Sherry-style is an island staple: best dry. Term banned by EU since '95.

SODAP Major wine coop at LIMASSOL. Top wine: red AFAMES.

Thisbe Fruity medium-dry light KEO wine (of XYNISTERI grapes from LIMASSOL).

Xynisteri The native aromatic white grape of Cyprus.

Asia & North Africa

Algeria As a combined result of Islam and the EC, once-massive v'yds have dwindled from 860,000 acres to about 150,000; many vines are 40+ yrs old and won't be replaced. Red, white and esp rosé of some quality and power are still made in coastal hills of Tlemcen, Mascara (gd red and white), Haut-Dahra (strong red, rosé), Zaccar, Tessala, Médéa and Aïn-Bessem (Bouira esp gd). Sidi Brahim: drinkable red brand. These had VDQS status in French colonial days. Despite all, wine is still the fourth-largest export. Cork also produced.

China Vinegrowing and wine drinking have had a small place in China for centuries. The major regions are in NE (esp Shandong, Hebei, Jiangsu, Beijing and Tianjin). Main grape varieties are the native Lonyan (Dragon's Eye) and Beichun. A modern industry began in the early '80s and has developed rapidly. Rémy Martin led the way. Its joint venture Dynasty label (Muscat blend) quickly de-throned the longer est'd Great Wall (Dragon's Eye) as market leader among Western-style wines. Recent Chard from Hebei is v fair. Allied Domecq's Huadong winery set new standards with Chard, followed by Ries and Gamay. Pernod Ricard's Dragon Seal and Seagram's Summer Palace are more recent ventures adding classic varietals (incl Cab S, Sauv Bl); Rémy launched Imperial Court, China's first serious classic method sparkler in '92. Expansion has quickened through the '90s to meet huge growth in demand esp for red wine.

India Tiny industry dominated by Indage, SE of Bombay, with surprising international recognition for Chard- and Pinot N-based sparkling wines: Omar Khayyám, Marquise de Pompadour (sweeter) and Celèbre (vintage). Still wines incl straight European varietals as well as blends incorporating local varieties. Labels are Chantilli, Soma, Chhabri, Anarkali, Riviera and Vin Ballet.

Japan Japan's wine industry is based in the central Honshu prefecture of Yamanashi, W of Tokyo. Nagano and Yamagata prefectures (N of Tokyo) and the northern island of Hokkaido are the other significant regions.

The sentimental favourite of the Japanese is the Koshu grape, upon which the industry was founded. But 80% of the 65,000 acres under vine in Japan is planted with the V labrusca varieties or V labrusca-based hybrids (eg Delaware, Kyoho, Campbell's Early Muscat and Muscat Bailey A). The grapes are mainly intended for the table but are also used by winemakers. Fairly new plantings of Chard, Cab S, Cab F and Merlot have created a new de luxe market for Japanese wines, but quantities are tiny.

To compensate for inappropriate varieties, tricky conditions and high costs, concentrates, must, (even grapes) and bulk wine are imported and used for fermenting or blending locally. Labelling laws have permitted a small amount of genuine domestic wine to go a long way! Low-priced 'domestic' wine has predominantly imported content; even premium wines receive a boost.

Five drinks giants account for ¾ total production: Suntory, Sanraku (Mercian), Manns, Sapporo (Polaire) and Kyowa Hakko Kogyo (Ste-Neige).

The most interesting (and expensive) of the big makers wines are Mercian's Kikyogahara Merlot, Suntory's Ch Lion and Jyonohira Cab of great density and quality. The Tokachi Winery does interesting things with wild vines native to Hokkaido. Smaller operations making leading examples of Koshu and/ or classic European varieties include Marufuji (Rubaiyat), Grace, Kizan, Katsunuma Jozo, Alps, Takeda, Okuizomo, and Kobe Wines.

Lebanon The small Lebanese industry (7,500 acres) is based in Ksara in Beka'a Valley NE of Beirut; wines of vigour and quality. Three wineries of note. Ch Musar (★★★), the heroic survivor of yrs of civil war: splendid claret-like matured r, mainly Cab; a full-blooded oaked w, from indigenous Obaideh grapes (like Chard), can age 10–15 yrs; lighter r, Tradition: Cinsault-Cab S. Ch Kefraya makes Rouge de K Cinsault-Carignan; fragrant Ch Kefraya: best yrs only; also rosé, w; all early-drinking. Ch Ksara: oldest Lebanese winery (est'd 1857 by Jesuits): Cab S, Merlot, Syrah, Chard, Sauv, Sém, Grenache, Carignan, Cinsault.

Malta Imported grapes are generally used to avoid duties. Look out for the first genuine Maltese wine on the market: Marnisi – it's well worth tasting.

Morocco Morocco makes North Africa's best wine (85% r: Cinsaut, Grenache, Carignan), from v'yds along Atlantic coast (Rabat to Casablanca, light, fruity with speciality w – 'Gris' – from r grapes) and around Meknès and Fèz (solid, best-known). Also further E around Berkane and Angad (tangy, earthy) and in Gharb and Doukkalas regions. Recently v'yds have declined from 190,000 to 35,000 acres. Look for Dom de Sahari (nr Meknès, French investment, est'd '93: Cab S and Merlot vines and local grapes), Celliers de Meknès (state-owned coop: recent investment, clean, modern wines), Chaudsoleil and Sincomar. Chantebled, Tarik, Toulal: drinkable reds. Vin Gris (10% of production) esp de Boulaoune – ideal for hot-day refreshment. Also cork production.

Tunisia Tunisia now has 37,000 v'yd acres (there were 120,000 15 yrs ago). Her speciality was sw Muscat (more recently: dry Muscat de Kelibia); drinkable reds and light rosés now predominate from Cap Bon, Carthage, Mornag, Tébourba and Tunis. Improving quality. Best producers: Ch Thibar, Mornag, Royal Tardi.

Turkey Most of Turkey's 1.5 million acres of v'yds produce table grapes; only 3% are for wine. Wines from Thrace, Anatolia and the Aegean: v drinkable. Many indigenous varieties: 60 are commercial, eg Emir, Narince (w) and Bogazkere, Oküzgözü (r) and used with Ries, Sém, Pinot N, Grenache, Carignan and Gamay. Trakya (Thrace) w (light Sém) and Buzbag (E Anatolian) r: well-known standards of state producer Tekel (21 state wineries). Diren, Doluca, Karmen, Kavaklidere, Taskobirlik: private firms; fair quality. Doluca's Villa Neva r from Thrace: well made, as is Villa Doluca. Kavaklidere: gd Primeurs (w Cankaya, r Yakut) from local grapes. Buzbag: T's most original and striking wine.

The old Russian Empire

Some 2.2 million acres of vineyards make the 16 republics of the former USSR collectively the world's fourth-biggest wine producer. Russia is the largest of the 12 producing wine, followed by Moldova, the Ukraine (including top Crimea region) and Georgia. Russians have a sweet tooth for table, dessert and sparkling wines.

Russia Makes fair Ries (Anapa, Arbau, Beshtau) and sw sparkling Tsimlanskoye Champanski. Abrau Durso (speciality): classic sparkling (since 1870) from Pinot, Chard, Cab F (climate like Champagne's). Also Chard, Sauv, Welschriesling (heavy, often oxidized) from state wineries nr Moscow, St-Petersburg, etc. Best: Don Valley v'yds (Black Sea Coast of the Caucasus), for Ries, Aligoté, Cab.

Moldova The most temperate climate (as in N France); now most modern outlook. High potential: esp w from centre, r from S, r and fortified nr Black Sea (W). Grapes incl Cab, Pinot N, Merlot, Saperavi (fruity), Ries, Chard, Pinot

Gr, Aligoté, Rkatsiteli. Former Moscow bottling: disastrous. A startling glimpse of potential was given in '92 by release of '63 Negru de Purkar. Purkar: top winery; also gd: Krikova: esp Kodru 'Claret' blend, Krasny Res Pinot-Merlot-Malbec, sp. Romanesti winery (since '82) has French varieties; Yavloveni, fino- and oloroso-style 'flor sherries'. Gd old-vine Cab from Tarakliya. Western and antipodean (Penfolds since '93) investment at Hincesti: local clean bottling, better winemaking, future improvements; (to date) Moldova's most modern-tasting wines: Ryman's Chard: vg. Half v'yds: state farmed: progress (and privatization) not smooth, but worth following. Appellation system in pipeline.

Crimea (Ukraine) Crimea's first-class dessert and fortified wines were revealed in '90 by the sale of old wines from the Tsar's Crimean cellars at Massandra, nr Yalta. Alupka Palace fortified (European grapes, since 1820s), adequate classic sp from Novi Svet and Grand Duchess (from Odessa Winery founded 1896 by H Roederer). Reds have potential (eg Alushta from Massandra). State monopoly still in control. Also Aligoté and Artemosk sp (Romanian grapes). To watch.

Georgia Uses antique methods for tannic wines for local drinking, newer techniques for exports (Mukuzani, Tsinandali); Georgians are reluctant to modernize. Kakhetià (E): famed for big red, acceptable white. Imeretia (W): milder, highly original, oddly-fermented wines. Kartli: central area. Cheap, drinkable sp attracts investment from Champagne and cava companies. As equipment, techniques and attiudes evolve, Georgia could be an export hit.

Israel

Since Edmond de Rothschild re-established the wine industry during the 1880's, the Israeli wine industry produced mainly kosher sweet wine, that is until recently when Cab, Merlot, Sauv Bl and Chard were introduced. Traditionally vines were planted in coastal Samson and Shomron regions, but new cooler Golan Heights vineyards (1,200-metre altitude) have resulted in great improvements.

Barkan Large winery with potential, good Cab S, Merlot, Sauv Bl and others.
Binyamina Winery to watch with improving Cab S, Chard, Sauv Bl: gd value.
Carmel The largest winery in Israel. Top wines: Private Collection Cab S, Merlot, Chard, Sauv Bl, Muscat. 'Selected Vineyards' range is gd everyday drinking.
Castel Small family estate in Judean Hills. Very good subtle Cab-Merlot.
Dalton Young winery with established vineyards. Quality Chard.
Efrat Old winery est. 1870 near Jerusalem.
Galilee Region incl Upper Galilee and Golan Heights (Israel's top v'yd area).
Gamla Soft fruity Cab S. Full delicately oaked Chard and grassy Sauv Bl from Golan Heights Winery (See Yarden.).
Margalit Boutique winery. Full-bodied Cab S; intense but rare Merlot.
Samson Central coastal plain wine region (SE of Tel Aviv to W of Jerusalem).
Segal Family winery. Raisiny Cab S in collaboration with Wente of California.
Shomron Wine region in valleys around Zichron-Yaacov, S of Haifa.
Tishbi Estate aka Baron. Family grower in Binyamina. Gd Sauv Bl, Chard, soft fruity Cab S. New Merlot as well as new Reserve label.
Tzora Kibbutz winery nr Jerusalem, good value reds and whites to watch.
Yarden Modern ('83) Golan Heights winery with California winemaker setting highest standards. Full-bodied oaky Cab (**90 93 95 96**), complex Merlot, barrel-fermented Chard; gd classic method sp.

England & Wales

Well over two million bottles a year are now being made here from over 300 vineyards, amounting to some 2,000 acres. Although most wines are white and made from fruity German crosses, an increasing number of interesting reds come from Pinot Noir and Dornfelder, as well as from a new hybrid, Rondo. Bottle-fermented sparkling wines proving to be one of England's great successes, made of Chardonnay and Pinot Noir and closely modelled on Champagne. Since 1994 an EU approved 'Quality Wine Scheme' has been run by the United Kingdom Vineyards Association. Unfortunately it is only open to vinifera varieties so growers of the (v worthy) Seyval Blanc (and other hybrids) may not apply. NB: Beware 'British Wine' – neither British nor indeed, wine and has nothing to do with the following.

Adgestone nr Sandown (Isle of Wight) Prize-winning 8.5-acre v'yd on chalky hill site. Est'd '68. New owners; new winemaker.

Astley Stourport-on-Severn (Hereford and Worcester) 5 acres; some fair wines. Madeleine Angevine, Kerner and Huxelvaner are prize-winning.

Barkham Manor E Sussex 34 acres since '85. Wide range. Modern winery. Wines consistent award-winners, often in a sweeter style.

Battle Wine Estate Battle (E Sussex) 50 acres; New Zealand-trained winemaker. Wines winning medals. Late-harvest and reds of special interest.

Bearsted Maidstone (Kent) 4 acres est'd '86. Good Bacchus and dessert wine.

Beaulieu Abbey Brockenhurst (Hampshire) 4.6-acre v'yd, established '58 by Gore-Browne family on old monastic site. Good rosé and sparkling.

Beenleigh Manor Totnes (Devon) Top award-winning oak-aged Cab-Merlot blend grown under polythene tunnels continue to show well.

Biddenden nr Tenterden (Kent) 18-acre v'yd planted '69: wide range includes Ortega and Dornfelder. Good cider, too.

Bookers Bolney (W Sussex) 5 acres of Müller-T and others. Wines improving.

Bothy Abingdon (Oxfordshire) 3 acre. Good range of well-made wines esp Ortega-Optima. Sparkling well thought of and sweet wine winning awards.

Boze Down Whitchurch-on-Thames (Oxfordshire) 4.5 acres. Wide range of high-quality wines. Reds worth trying.

Breaky Bottom Lewes (E Sussex) 5.5-acre v'yd with cult following. Good dry wines, esp award-winning oaked Seyval Bl, Müller-T. Sparkling: v good.

Brecon Court Usk (Monmouthshire) Wales's largest v'yd with 8 acres. Wines improving. Made at THREE CHOIRS.

Bruisyard Saxmundham (Suffolk) 10 acres Müller-T. Est'd '74: oaked and sp worth trying. Winery and herb garden for visitors.

Camel Valley Bodmin (Cornwall) 2-acre v'yd; improving quality Seyval and sp.

Cane End Reading (Berkshire) 12 acres; mixed vines. Late-harvest sweet gd.

Carr Taylor Hastings (E Sussex) 21 acres, est'd '73. Pioneer of UK classic method sp. Some lively, intense, balanced wines which win awards.

Carters Colchester (Essex) 6 acres. Wines now making a mark. Award-winning Dornfelder and good sparkling.

Chapel Down Wines Tenterden (Kent) Largest wine producer in UK, buying grapes from all over southeast. Epoch Brut sp, Epoch red and Bacchus best wines. British Airways, House of Commons and major multiples supplied.

Chiddingstone Edenbridge (Kent) 66-acre v'yd; stress on dry wines, esp oaked. Gd Pinot Bl de Noir. New French winemaker should improve wines.

Chilford Hundred Linton (Cambridgeshire) 18 acres: fairly dry wines since '74.

Chiltern Valley Henley-on-Thames (Oxfordshire) 3 acres of own v'yds high up on chalk: incl Old Luxters Dry Reserve. Sp showing well.

Danebury Stockbridge (Hants) 6 acres: Auxerrois, Bacchus, etc. Improving wines.

Davenport Rotherfield (E Sussex) Vines here and in Kent. Young winery: serious wines. Australian-trained winemaker. Started to win medals and awards.

Denbies Dorking (Surrey) 250-acre v'yd (England's biggest); first harvest '89. Impressive winery: worth a visit. Wines settling down. Dessert wine esp good.

Eglantine Loughborough (Leicestershire) 3.3 acre v'yd with many varieties.

Elmham Park East Dereham (Norfolk) 4.5-acre v'yd, est '66. Light flowery wines (with ageing potential), Madeleine Angevine esp good. Also apple wine.

Frithsden Hemel Hempstead (Herts) 2.8-acre v'yd: mainly Müller-T, Ortega.

Gifford's Hall Bury St-Edmunds (Suffolk) 12 acre-v'yd for interesting wines (incl oak-aged) and visitor facilities.

Gildridge Lewes (E Sussex) About 2 acres of mixed varieties. Wines improving.

Great Stocks Billericay (Essex) Young v'yd with interesting wines, esp '95 Symphony blend and oak-aged Orion. Wines made at DAVENPORT.

Hale Valley Wendover (Bucks) Small 1.5-acre v'yd: wines of interest. To watch.

Halfpenny Green (Staffordshire) 20 acres; esp gd Madeleine Angevine and sp.

Hambledon nr Petersfield (Hampshire) The first modern English v'yd, planted in '51 by Sir Guy Salisbury-Jones. Now reduced to 3 acres; Seyval Blanc and Pinot Meunier.

Harden Farm Penshurst (Kent) 12 acres. Bacchus and Schönburger gd; major supplier to CHAPEL DOWN.

Harling Norwich (Norfolk) 6.7 acres Müller-T and Bacchus under new ownership. Wines made at SHAWSGATE.

Hidden Spring Horam (E Sussex) 9 acres with new owners. Wines v gd, esp Dark Fields red and Sunset Rosé. Wines made at VALLEY.

Horton Estate Wimborne (Dorset) 9 acres. Bacchus, Reichensteiner and selection of reds. Wines showing promise.

Kent's Green Taynton (Gloucestershire) Tiny v'yd of Müller-T and Huxelrebe. Award-winning wines produced at THREE CHOIRS.

La Mare Jersey (Channel Islands) New owners and new ex-LAMBERHURST winemaker. Wines fair but set to improve.

Lamberhurst (Kent) 25 acres A long-est'd name with new owners in '96. Bacchus gd and winning plaudits.

Leeds Castle Maidstone (Kent) Long-est'd 2.7 acres of vines. Müller-T and Seyval Blanc. Wines sold only at Castle outlets. Made at TENTERDEN.

Lillibrook Manor Maidenhead (Berkshire) 1 acre of Müller-T, Schönburger and Bacchus. Improving wines. Wines made at VALLEY and improving.

Llanerch S Glamorgan (Wales) 5.5 acres, est'd '86. Wines sold under Cariad label. Individual style developing, worth its awards. Good rosé.

Meon Valley Southampton (Hampshire) 25 acres. Under new ownership.

Milton Keynes Milton Keynes (Bucks) New 4-acre v'yd. Wines produced under Woughton Park label. To watch.

Moorlynch Bridgewater (Somerset) 16 acres of an idyllic farm. Good wines, esp Estate Dry and sparkling.

New Hall nr Maldon (Essex) 90+ acres on mixed farm; Huxelrebe, Müller-T and Pinot N, etc. Grape supplier to other wineries incl CHAPEL DOWN.

Northbrook Springs Bishops Waltham (Hampshire) 13 acres. Improving wines winning medals. Sp starting to show well.

Nutbourne Manor nr Pulborough (W Sussex) 18.5 acres: elegant and tasty Schönburger and Bacchus. Medal-winner; wines made at TENTERDEN.

Nyetimber West Chiltington (W Sussex) 42-acres, planted '88: Chard, Pinots N and Meunier for classic sp. First vintage '92 well received. V high quality.

Partridge Blandford (Dorset) 5 acres. Good Bacchus.

Paunton Court Bishop's Frome (Worcestershire) 3.75-acre young v'yd. Wine made at THREE CHOIRS.

Penshurst Tunbridge Wells (Kent) 12 acres, since '72, incl good Seyval Bl and Müller-T. Fine modern winery.

Pilton Manor Shepton Mallet (Somerset) Down to 1 acre of Pinot N for r and sp.

Plumpton College Lewes (E Sussex) Experimental v'yd attached to college running courses on viticulture and winemaking. Sm winery; wines improving.

Priors Dean Alton (Hampshire) Sm 1.5 acre v'yd. Med-dry 97 of high quality.

Ridge View Ditchling Common (E Sussex) New 16-acre v'yd planted: Chard, Pinots N and Meunier for classic sp (SOUTH RIDGE). First vintage well received.

Rock Lodge nr Haywards Heath (Sussex) 6.2-acre v'yd since '65. Oak-aged Ortega (Fumé) gd. Wines made at TENTERDEN.

Rosemary Ryde (Isle of Wight) Largest v'yd on I of W. Wines improving slowly.

St Augustine's Aust (Gloucestershire) Wines made at THREE CHOIRS.

St George's Waldron, Heathfield (E Sussex) Well-known as tourist attraction. Currently up for sale. V'yd to be leased out.

St Sampson Golant (Cornwall) 4 acres; some of the county's better wines.

Sandhurst Cranbrook (Kent) 16 acres of vines on mixed farm. High quality Bacchus and sp. Wines made at TENTERDEN.

Scott's Hall Ashford (Kent) Boutique v'yd: sp rosé and still white gd.

Seddlescombe Organic Robertsbridge (E Sussex) 15 acres; UK's main organic v'yd. Range of wines with quite a following. Some of interest.

Sharpham Totnes (Devon) 5 acres. Now own winery: getting interesting – barrel-aged wines now showing well. All wines keep improving.

Shawsgate Framlingham (Suffolk) 17 acres: good Seyval-Müller-T. Wins awards.

South Ridge Pinot N/Chard sp brand among leaders. Made by RIDGE VIEW.

Standen East Grinstead (W Sussex) Young 2.2-acre v'yd. Shows promise.

Staple St James nr Canterbury (Kent) 7 acres planted '74. Excellent quality. Müller-T, Reichensteiner and Huxelrebe especially interesting.

Sugar Loaf Abergavenny (Wales) 5 acres. Wines made at THREE CHOIRS.

Tenterden (Kent) 18.5 acres, planted '77. Wines very dry to sweet, gd Müller-T, prize-winning oak-aged Seyval, rosé. Consistent.

Thorncroft Leatherhead (Surrey) 8 acres making interesting late-harvest botrytis wine from Ortega. Also makes range of elderflower products.

Three Choirs Newent (Gloucestershire) 64 acres, est'd '74. Müller-T, Seyval Bl, Schönburger, Reichensteiner, and esp Bacchus Dry, Huxelrebe. Recent new £1-million winery. English Nouveau is popular. UK's 2nd-largest producer.

Tiltridge Upton-upon-Severn (Worcestershire) Small 1-acre v'yd with good local following. Wines of interest.

Titchfield Titchfield (Hampshire) Young 2-acre v'yd starting to make fair wines.

Valley Twyford (Berkshire) 25-acre v'yd: all styles of wine. Serious oak-matured Fumé, red (esp top award-winning Pinot N '95 and '97); classic-method sp Heritage and late-harvest sweet. One of UK's 'First Growths'.

Wellow Romsey (Hampshire) 45-acre v'yd with chequered financial history, now starting to reorganise itself. Should make some gd wines on this site.

Wickham Shedfield (Hampshire) 12-acre v'yd (since '84): consistently showing style and quality. Oak-aged Fumé and sp wines v interesting. Worth trying.

Wooldings Whitchurch (Hampshire) 8-acre v'yd. Gold medal winning Schönburger-Faberrebe; interesting sp and Bacchus.

Wroxeter Roman Shrewsbury (Shropshire) Young ('91) 6-acre v'yd planned on site of Roman town (but no v'yd). One to watch.

Wyken Bury-St-Edmunds (Suffolk) Range starting to look good, esp dry Bacchus white and full dark red. Vg restaurant, too.

North America

WASHINGTON

OREGON

CALIFORNIA

EASTERN STATES

California

Sierra Foothills

NEVADA

Anderson Valley

Clear Lake

Sacramento

Clear Lake

Alexander Valley

El Dorado

Russian River Valley

Napa Valley

Sacramento

Sonoma Valley

Carneros

Lodi

San Francisco

Livermore Valley

Santa Clara Valley

Santa Cruz Mountains

San Joaquin

Salinas

Fresno

Arroyo Seco

San Lucas

Pacific Ocean

Paso Robles

CALIFORNIA

Edna Valley

Santa Maria Valley

SANTA BARBARA

Santa Ynez Valley

Heavier shaded areas are the wine growing regions

Santa Barbara

Los Angeles

Temecu

An ever-volatile United States wine market encourages California's tradition-free vintners to revolutionize themselves again and again; perhaps it's required. Today, the reigning style is gigantism, on grounds that the prosperous, mobile, hurried young population called Generation X demands heroic size and nothing else.

California's natural endowments permit, and recent vintages have achieved, high alcohol contents (13.9 percent is modest, 15 percent is not at all rare) in hugely ripe wines. Hearty oak fills any blank spots. The market at home and abroad seems unafraid.

New wineries are sprouting up even faster than new vineyards, which is very fast indeed. Phylloxera caused a pause in new plantings after the explosive growth of the 1970s and 1980s, but replantings are now being overshadowed by new ones, especially on the Central Coast, where great expanses of open land beckon.

Phylloxera was once held out as a golden opportunity to put exactly the proper varieties in all the right places. But such subtleties as terroir have been trampled in the rush. Chardonnay (83,000 acres) swallowed up all the other white varieties. Merlot (38,500 acres) came from nowhere to challenge Cabernet Sauvignon (45,000 acres) as the red of choice.

That said appellation areas (AVAs) are now an important fact of life, with more than 120 already registered and more on the way. The first stirrings of serious meaning are with us, in – for example – the forms of Russian River Valley and Santa Maria Valley Pinot Noirs. But it still much too soon to use AVAs as a general guide to style. Listed below are the most commonly mentioned regions. Grapes and makers' names, though, remain the key.

Principal vineyard areas

Central Coast

A long sweep of coast with scattered though increasing wine activity, from San Francisco Bay south to Santa Barbara.

Carmel Valley On Monterey coast; tiny, but s'times impressive Cab and Chard.

Livermore Long famous for white wines (esp Sauv Bl). Though largely built over, v'yds and wineries: surprisingly resilient. 1,600 acres.

Monterey Primarily the huge Salinas Valley running SE inland from Monterey. Cool northern end includes Arroyo Seco AVA (esp Chard, Ries) and Santa Lucia Highlands AVA (Chard, perhaps Pinot N). Warm to hot southern end much bigger, for steady commercial wines (esp Cab S). In total 32,500 acres.

San Luis Obispo Biggest, warmest district is Paso Robles (9,000 acres of esp Zin, Cab S); finest is Edna Valley (2,000 acres, esp Chard); newest is Arroyo Grande (500 acres, esp Pinot N).

Santa Barbara Santa Maria Valley AVA dominates, (esp for vg Chard and Pinot N). Smaller Santa Ynez Valley AVA also good for Burgundian varieties at foggy seaward end, B'x or Rhône varieties better inland. 11,000 acres.

Santa Cruz Mts Wineries (though few v'yds) are scattered round the Santa Cruz Mts S of San Francisco Bay, from Woodside down to Gilroy.

South Coast

Temecula (Rancho California) In S California, 25 miles inland, halfway between San Diego and Riverside. Mainly whites. 2,000 acres of vines.

North Coast
Encompasses Lake, Mendocino, Napa and Sonoma counties, all N of SF.

Carneros, Los Important cool region on N shore of San Francisco Bay, shared between NAPA and SONOMA counties. 5,000 acres mostly in Chard and Pinot N.

Lake Clear Lake and Guenoc Valley AVAs both warm. Most impressive for Sauv Bl, good for Cab S. 3,900 acres.

Mendocino Perfectly schizoid split between cool Anderson Valley nr the coast (Gewürz, Pinot N, sparkling), warm to hot inland around Ukiah Sauv Bl, Zin). 13,500 acres.

Napa The oldest and most honoured of California wine valleys busily fragmenting itself yet sticking mainly to Cab S. Valley floor (Oakville, Rutherford, St Helena AVAs) built the reputation, Mt Veeder AVA in W Hills, Howell Mtn, Atlas Peak AVAs in E hills are enlarging it, and also doing well with Chard. Zin much under-praised. CARNEROS AVA (shared with SONOMA) much cooler. In all 36,000 acres.

Sonoma Caught between NAPA and the deep blue sea. Has a dozen AVAs in two separate drainage basins: (1) tipped to SF Bay: Sonoma Valley AVA (versatile, includes Sonoma Mountain and part of CARNEROS); (2) oriented to ocean: Russian River drainage: includes warmer inland AVAs Alexander, Knights (Cab, Italian red varieties), Dry Creek (Zin, Rhône varieties), – and cooler seaward Russian River AVA (and its sub-zones Chalk Hill, Sonoma-Green Valley) mainly for, Chard, Pinot N, sparkling). 40,500 acres.

The Interior
Amador Main county in SIERRA FOOTHILLS.

Lodi Town and district at N end of the SAN JOAQUIN VALLEY, its climate modified by a westerly air-stream from SF Bay. Traditionally for Zin, now primarily a source of many commodity Chards, Cabs. About 58,000 acres of vines.

San Joaquin Valley The great central valley of California, fertile and hot, the source of most of the jug and dessert wines in the state. (Incl LODI AVA and the Clarksburg AVA on the Sacramento River delta.) 233,000 acres.

Sierra Foothills Encompasses AMADOR (Shenandoah Valley, Fiddletown AVAs), El Dorado (AVA of the same name), Calaveras counties, among others. Zin is universal grape; Rhône and Italian varieties seen more and more. 3,800 acres.

Recent vintages

California's climate is rarely as consistent as its 'land of sunshine' reputation. Although grapes ripen regularly, they are often subject to spring frosts, sometimes a wet harvest-time and (too often) drought.

Wines from the San Joaquin Valley tend to be most consistent year by year. The vintage date on these, where there is one, is more important for telling the age of the wine than its character.

Vineyards in the Central Coast region are widely scattered; there is little pattern. The Napa and Sonoma valleys are the areas where comment can usefully be made on the last dozen or more vintages of the most popular varietal wines: Cabernet Sauvignon and Chardonnay.

Chardonnay
NB These ageing assessments work as well for Pinot N as Chard. They are based on well-balanced wines with fruit flavours dominant. Very rich and oaky examples tend to be v short-lived: 2 yrs for most Chards. Marker wines for good ageing qualities incl Acacia, Bouchaine, Davis Bynum, Navarro, Silverado, Trefethen.

1998 Stutter-stepping vintage was bewildering, but uneven ripening and slow harvest do not permit optimism. Small crop.

1997 Huge crop, strong flavours, stunningly high alcohols. To drink soonest.

1996 Smaller crop than '95 but offfering attractive fruit flavours early. With overripe style fully in vogue, many now fading. Known agers doing v well indeed.

1995 Small crop. Most now on the down-slope. Seek only known agers.

1994 Most age-worthy vintage since '90. The few who capitalized remain in excellent form.

1993 Serviceable early. Should have been drunk.

1992 Always spotty. Should have been drunk.

1991 Superior year. Few finest still of interest, but even they totter.

1990 Superior year. Few finest are holding just slightly better than the '91s.

Cabernet Sauvignon

NB As with Chardonnays, over-rich and over-oaky wines usually collapse quickly. The markers for the assessments below are not Reserves, but fine standard Cabernets from eg Caymus, Clos du Val, Freemark Abbey, Hafner, Jordan, Laurel Glen, Louis M Martini (Monte Rosso), Pine Ridge, Silverado.

1998 Erratic harvest stumbled into November. Prospects uncertain at best; optimism hard to find.

1997 Huge crop, strong flavours, stunningly high alcohol levels. Probably best drunk young for youthful exuberance.

1996 Tiny crop, intense flavours and more structure than first seemed. Great 10-year wines in vein of fabled 68s.

1995 Tiny crop, great vitality but slow to unfold. Best vintage for cellaring since 91.

1994 A bit plain-faced but servicable, with some durability.

1993 Mute? Or another 88? Suspect the latter.

1992 Oddly inconsistent. Some empty. Some flavourful and vital.

1991 After latest harvest ever, leanest, raciest, best-focused wines in years. Coming out of reticent phase.

1990 Picture-perfect California vintage: ripe, enveloping, still showing ample fruit though maturity is creeping into the flavours.

1989 Dark, flavoursome, but early promise of age-worthiness fading, even in the best. Drink up.

1988 Bland, lacking focus and structure.

1989 Dark, flavoursome, but early promise of age-worthiness fading, even in the best. Drink up.

1988 Bland, lacking focus and structure.

1987 Clearly the finest of their decade, and still in good fettle.

1986 Easy, approachable. Early baby fat now adult fat.

1985 Tendency to hardness a virtue in the known agers, a liability in the rest.

1984 Showy early. Drink up now except only proven agers.

1983 Most have faded badly.

1982 Long written off, yet many Napas now wonderfully harmonious, complex. However, even best v fragile. Hurry.

1981 Even the best from a hot harvest are well on the down-slope.

1980 High reputation but merely good and solid. Over-tannic. Should drink up.

1979 Only the three or four best still in form.

1978 Wonderful early; even the best have faded now.

California wineries

Acacia Napa ★★★ (Chard) 94 96 97 98 (Pinot N) **91 92 93** 94 95 **96** 97 98 Long-time specialist in durable, deep CARNEROS Chard and Pinot is returning to single v'yd wines after phylloxera-induced interlude of extra-oaky Reserves.

Adelaida Cellars San Luis Obispo ★★ Supple Cab, vigorous Zin the mainstays, now joined by Sangiovese and Rhône varieties.

Alban San Luis Obispo ★★ Ambitious promising Edna Valley estate given over entirely to Rhône varieties esp Syrah, Viognier.

Alderbrook Sonoma ★★ Winemakers playing musical chairs but new-in-'94 owner resolutely pursuing accessible styles in esp Chard, Syrah, Zin.

Alexander Valley Vineyards Sonoma ★★ Cab S most likely of 6 wines to live up to promise of fine v'yd. Whites quirky at best.

Almaden San Joaquin ★ Famous pioneer name, now a CANANDAIGUA-owned everyday brand, operated from Madera. 1 million+ cases.

S Anderson Vineyard Napa ★★★ (Cab) **90 91 92 93** 94 95 **96** 97(Brut) Vigorous sparkling, toasty Chard, but star of show is silky Cab from STAG'S LEAP neighbour.

Araujo Napa ★★★ Eisele v'yd, now an estate, its Cab as dark and tannic as when JOE PHELPS made it famous.

Arrowood Sonoma ★★→★★★ (Chard) 97 98 (Cab) 85 87 **90 91 92 94** 95 96 97 Long-time CHATEAU ST JEAN winemaker Dick A on peak form with supple, age-worthy Cab S. Chard (esp Res) for oak-lovers.

Artisans and Estates Polyglot of wineries bought or built by Jess Jackson of KENDALL-JACKSON fame: CAMBRIA, Camelot (CENTRAL COAST), CARDINALE, LA CREMA, Edmeades (MENDO), Hartford Court (SON), R Pepi, J Stonestreet (Son).

Atlas Peak Napa ★★ Allied-Domecq owned winery to seek for Sangiovese and Sangio-Cab Consenso from Antinori-owned v'yds in east hills.

Au Bon Climat Sta Barbara ★★★ (Chard) **91 92 93 94 95** 96 97 98 (Pinot N) **90 91 92 93** 94 95 Jim Clendenen listens to his private drummer: ultra-toasty Chard, flavourful Pinot N, light-hearted Pinot Bl. VITA NOVA label for B'x varieties, Podere dellos Olivos for Italianates. See also Qupé.

Babcock Vineyards Santa Barbara ★★ Individualistic approach to wide range of varietals. Estate Pinot N, Pinot Gris of particular note.

Barnett Napa ★★ Intriguing Cabs from tiny estate high on Spring Mtn.

Beaucanon Napa ★★ Bordeaux owner Lebègue turning out consistently supple stylish Cab S, Merlot and improving Chard from own 250 acres. La Crosse is second label.

Beaulieu Vineyard Napa ★★ (Cab) **45 49 65 91** 95 UDV's crown jewel is, rightly, best known for ageable, American-oaked Georges Delatour Private Reserve Cabernet Sauvignon. CARNEROS Chard worth a look. Commodity line is Beautour, experimental one Signet.

Belvedere Sonoma ★★ William Hambrecht uses mostly his own grapes for Alexander Valley Cab S, Dry Creek Valley Zin, Russian River Chard.

Benziger Family Winery Sonoma ★★ Called Benziger of Glen Ellen until Proprietors Reserve sold to UDV (then HEUBLEIN). Now all SONOMA grapes and dotty for oak across whole range.

Beringer Napa ★★→★★★ (Chard) **97 98** (Cab S) 80 81 84 87 **90 91** 92 94 95 96 97 98 A publicly-held corporation since '97, century-old winery persues larger-than-life style from top of line (Reserve, single v'yd Cabs) to recently introduced commodity range called Beringer Founder's Estate (originally named Hudson Estate). Also owns CHATEAU ST-JEAN, CHATEAU SOUVERAIN, MERIDIAN, NAPA RIDGE and STAG'S LEAP WINERY.

Boeger El Dorado ★★ Mostly estate wines. Attractive Merlot, Barbera, Zin; all less bold than many neighbours.

Bonny Doon Sta Cruz Mtns ★★★ Mad punster Randall Grahm still resolutely Rhôneist with white Le Sophiste, pink Vin Gris de Cigare, red Cigare Volant and Grenache Village. Medit-ations now extend to Italianates, too.

Bouchaine Carneros ★★★ (Chard) 94 95 96 97 (Pinot) 92 **93** 94 95 96 97 98 Long somnolent, recently inspired or close to it. Chard and Pinot N both in upper ranks of region. Renovated cellars may have helped.

Brander Vineyard, The Sta Barbara ★★ Estate producer in Sta Ynez Valley recently prefers power to finesse in Sauv Bl, Cab-blend.

Bronco Wine Company San Joaquin ★→★★ Umbrella label for firm owning LAURIER (cream of crop), Forest Glen, Grand Cru, Hacienda, Napa Creek, and Rutherford Vintners, plus penny-savers under CC Vineyard and JFJ Bronco.

When in California: look these up
Los Angeles: Duke of Bourbon, Wally's **Orange County:** The Wine Club **San Francisco:** Jug Shop, The Wine Club **San Francisco Peninsula:** Draeger's, Beltramo's **Sacramento:** Corti Bros **Santa Barbara:** The Wine Cask

---

Bruce, David Sta Cruz Mts ★★★ (Pinot) 95 96 97 98 Long-time source of eccentric bruiser (now moderated) Chard. Pinot N (from own and SONOMA vines) is forte.

Buehler Napa ★★ (Chard) **94** 95 96 97 98 (Cab S) 91 **92 93** 94 95 96 97 In E hills recently 'repositioned' with upscale prices on unchanged estate Cab S, Zin and Russian River Chard.

Buena Vista Carneros ★★ (Chard) **96** 97 98 (Cab S) 91 92 **93** 94 95 96 97 Has swapped an earlier taste-the-grapes style for one more heavily marked by winemaking: esp Chard.

Burgess Cellars Napa ★★ Emphasis on dark weighty well-oaked reds; Cab rather plain-faced, Zin begins to be more out-sized.

BV Abbreviation of BEAULIEU VINEYARD used on its labels.

Bynum, Davis Sonoma ★★ (Chard) **96** 97 98 (Pinot N) 91 92 **93** 94 95 96 97 98 Long-underrated but beginning to draw attention for characterful single v'yd wines, esp Pinot Ns from RRV.

Byron Vineyards Sta Barbara ★★★ (Chard) **96 97** 98 (Pinot) **93** 94 95 96 97 98 Prospering under R MONDAVI ownership; estate Pinot N leads with Chard not far behind.

Cain Cellars Napa ★★★ (Cain Five) 85 **86** 87 90 **91** 92 94 95 96 97 Stylish, supple Cain Five anchored in estate plantings of Cab S and four cousins on Spring Mtn; Cain Cuvée (declassified Cain Five) can rival the big brother. Monterey Sauvignon Musqué also fine.

Cafaro Napa ★★★ Winemaker label for sturdy-to-solid Cab and Merlot.

Cakebread Napa ★★ (Chard) **96** 97 98 (Cab S) 85 87 90 91 92 94 95 97 Now up to three bottlings of Cab all hearty and heartily-oaked.

Calera San Benito ★★★ (Chard) 97 98 (Pinot) 91 92 93 **94 95** 96 98 97 Dry sunny chalky hills nr Chalone lead to booming Rhône-weight estate Pinot Ns named after individual v'yd blocks (Reed, Selleck, Jensen). Also for perfumiest Viognier.

Callaway Temecula ★★ (Chard) 90 91 92 **94 95** 96 97 98 Oak-free, lees-aged Chard is a triumph from this warm dry region; Fumé Blanc also good.

Cambria Sta Barbara ★★ Part of KENDALL-JACKSON'S ARTISANS AND ESTATES group. Chard routinely toasty, Pinot N more enticing.

CALIFORNIA

Canandaigua Huge NY firm now No 2 to GALLO in California and long a power in bottom tier of market (Richard's Wild Irish Rose, Taylor California Cellars, etc). Lately reaching up, first with DUNNEWOOD, now with '99 purchase of SIMI.

Cardinale Napa ★★→★★★ (Cab S blend) **90 91 92 94** 95 **96** 97 98 Top-of-the-line red in KENDALL-JACKSON'S ARTISANS AND ESTATES, newly ensconced in former Robert Pepi winery.

Carmenet Sonoma ★★→★★★ (Cab S blend) 87 **90** 91 **92 94** 95 96 97 Fancifully-named variations on ripe Cab (eg Moon Mountain, Dynamite, Vin de Garde) all from mountaintop v'yd. CHALONE-owned.

Carneros Creek Carneros ★★→★★★ (Pinot N) **91 92 93 94** 95 96 97 98 Resolute explorer of climates and clones in CARNEROS offers five Pinots each yr: lightsome Fleur de Carneros, Côte de Carneros: darker, richer Estate, Reserve, Francis Mahoney Estate. Single v'yd Las Brisas coming.

Castoro San Luis Obispo ★★ Paso Robles estate, as substantial as its wines (Cab S and Zin).

Caymus Napa ★★★→★★★★ (Cab S) 87 **90 91 92 94** 95 96 97 Dark quick-to-mature American-oaked Cab Special Selection is the celebrated core; slightly lighter, regular basic bottling not far behind. Developing v'yds in MONTEREY, SONOMA for other varieties.

Cedar Mountain Livermore ★★ One of most ambitous in new wave of estate wineries: Cab and Chard.

Chalk Hill Sonoma ★★ Large estate nr Windsor, forever changing styles for Chard, Sauv Bl, Cab.

Chalone Monterey ★★★ (Chard) **94 95** 96 97 98 Unique estate high in Gavilan Mts; source of flinty Chard and dark tannic Pinot N, both slow-to-open burgundy imitations (Pinot N can go 15 yrs). Pinot Bl and Chenin styled after Chard. Also owns ACACIA, CARMENET, EDNA VALLEY VINEYARD, Echelon Gavilan and Canoe Ridge (Washington). Has links with (Lafite) Rothschilds.

Chappellet Napa ★★★ (Cab S) 75 **76 78 82 84** 86 87 **90** 91 92 94 95 96 97 98 Beautiful amphitheatrical hill v'yd. Always age-worthy Cab S has new grace-notes esp in Signature label. Chenin Bl a NAPA classic, now touched with oak. Chard gentle; now easy Sangio too, Cab Franc, Merlot, Tocai Friuilano and dessert Moelleux too.

Château Montelena Napa ★★★ (Chard) **96** 97 98 (Cab) **90 91 92** 94 95 96 97 98 Understated age-worthy Chard and recently modified (91 92) but still tannic potent Calistoga-estate Cab to age for ever.

Château Potelle Napa ★★ Expat French couple produce quietly impressive Chard (Reserve edition toastier) and vigorous Cab from Mt Veeder estate, outright aggressive VGS Zin from AMADOR.

Château St Jean Sonoma ★★→★★★ (Chard) **96 97** 98 Style always bold, heady; more so since bought from Suntory in '96 by BERINGER owners. Known for single-v'yd Chards (Robert Young, Belle Terre); now pushing reds.

Château Souverain Sonoma ★★ (Cab S) 87 **90 91 94** 95 96 Top-of-the-line CARNEROS Chard, Alexander Valley Cab and Dry Creek Valley Zin, all with lots of oak. So too basic SONOMA bottlings. Same owner as BERINGER.

Château Woltner Napa ★★→★★★ Excellent Howell Mountain estate Chards (incl expensive Frederique) joined in '95 by Cab-based red. From ex-owners of Ch La Mission Haut-Brion.

Chimney Rock Napa ★★→★★★ (Cab S) 87 **90** 91 92 94 95 **96** 97 98 Once racy Stags Leap District Cab now fleshier. Watch out for CARNEROS Chard.

Christian Brothers, The Madera (San Joaquin Valley) ★ One-time NAPA Valley institution, now mainly Diageo brandy label.

Christopher Creek Sonoma ★★ Expat Briton pouring heart and soul into Syrah and Petite Sirah in small lots from the Russian River Valley.

Cline Cellars Carneros ★★ Originally Contra Costa (imp't v'yds still there), now in SONOMA/CARNEROS and still dedicated mostly to husky Rhône Rangers (blends and varietals), eg Côtes d'Oakley, Mourvèdre.

Clos du Bois Sonoma ★★→★★★ (Chard) 96 97 98 (Cab) 87 **90** 91 92 94 95 **96** 97 98 Sizeable (400,000 case) Allied-Domecq firm at Healdsburg. Winemaker Margaret Davenport hitting impressive stride with Cab S, Pinot N, Chard. Top are single-v'yd incl Cab Briarcrest, Chard Calcaire.

Clos Pegase Napa ★★★ (Chard) 95 **96** 97 98(Cab S) **87** 90 91 **92** 94 95 96 97 98 Post-modernist winery-cum-museum (or vice versa) intelligently grows Chard in CARNEROS and Cab in Calistoga.

Clos du Val Napa ★★★ (Chard) **94 95 96** 97 98 (Cab) 75 77 81 82 85 87 **90** 91 92 94 95 96 97 98 French-run. Cab S, Cab Reserve perhaps NAPA's best agers of all, yet accessible early. Merlot also sure-footed. Silky CARNEROS Chard is best white. 60,000 cases.

Codorníu Carneros ★★★ California arm of great Catalan cava co, in bow to market, has turned away from fizz in favour of still wines.

Cohn, B R Sonoma ★★→★★★ One-time SONOMA estate Cab S specialist now buying grapes as far afield as Paso Robles, thus far to uncertain effect.

Concannon Livermore ★★ WENTE VINEYARDS now owns this historically famous source of Petite Sirah. Also Bx varieties and, of course, Chard.

Conn Creek Napa ★★ Stimson Lane owned sibling of VILLA MT EDEN makes only Cab S, Cab-based Anthology.

Cooks Penny-saving 'Cooks Champagne' and others from San Joaquin; belongs to CANANDAIGUA.

Corbett Canyon San Luis Obispo/San Joaquin Commodity varietals bottled either at SAN LUIS OBISPO or Ripon.

Corison Napa ★★→★★★ (Cab) **87** 90 91 92 94 95 **96** 97 98 Long-time winemaker at CHAPPELLET on her own making supple flavoursome Cab promising to age well.

Cosentino Napa ★★ (Pinot N) **94 95 96** 97 98 Irrepressible winemaker-owner always full-tilt. Results s'times odd, sometimes brilliant, never dull. CARNEROS Pinot Ns are to seek first.

Cottonwood Canyon Sta Barbara Good and improving wines from estate v'yd in Sta Maria Valley. Pinot N the one to watch.

Crichton Hall Napa ★★ Began as estate Chard specialist aiming to ape Meursault; has added CARNEROS Merlot, Pinot N.

Cronin Sta Cruz Mtns ★★ Lilliputian cult producer of Brobdignagian buttered toast Chards from varied sources.

Curtis (Formerly Carey) Sta Barbara ★★ With same owner as FIRESTONE. Evolving into Rhône varieties specialist.

Cuvaison Napa ★★★ (Chard) 96 97 98 (Merlot) 85 86 87 **90** 91 94 95 96 97 98 Estate CARNEROS Chard steadily top rank though fleshier, oakier than formerly. Recent estate Cab begins to outshine Merlot.

Dalla Valle Napa ★★→★★★ Hilly estate steadily moving up the ranks with newly supple reds (Cab-based Maya, Sangio-based Pietre Rosso).

Dehlinger Sonoma ★★★ (Pinot) **94 95** 96 97 98 Tom D focuses on ever-plummier estate Russian River Valley Pinot Noirs, and rightly. Also Chard, Syrah.

DeLoach Vineyards Sonoma ★★★ (Chard) **94 95** 96 97 96 97 98 Fruit-rich Chard ever the mainstay of reliable Russian River Valley winery. Gargantuan single-v'yd Zins (Papera, Pelletti) finding an audience.

de Lorimier Sonoma ★★ Alexander Valley estate winery at best with reds from B'x varieties.

Diamond Creek Napa ★★★★ (Cab S) 77 79 80 82 83 84 85 86 87 90 91 92 93 94 95 96 97 98 Austere, stunningly high-priced cult Cabs from hilly v'yd nr Calistoga go by names of v'yd blocks, eg Gravelly Meadow, Volcanic Hill. 3,000 cases.

Domaine Carneros Carneros (★★★) Showy US outpost of Taittinger in CARNEROS echoes austere style of its parent in Champagne. Vintage Blanc de Blancs the luxury cuvée. Still Pinot Noir also impressive.

Domaine Chandon Napa ★★→★★★ Maturing v'yds, maturing style, broadening range taking Moët & Chandon's California arm to new heights. Look esp for NV Reserve, Etoile Rosé. Still wines a recent addition.

Domaine Saint-Gregory Mendocino ★★ Companion label to MONTE VOLPE for wines from French grape varieties.

Dominus Napa ★★★★ 83 84 85 86 87 88 89 90 91 92 93 94 95 96 97 98 Christian Moueix of Pomerol is now sole owner of the fine Napanook v'yd and elegantly autere winery ('98). Massively tannic Cab-based blend up to 88, now looks amazingly like fine B'x (tannins softer since 90 91).

Dry Creek Vineyard Sonoma ★★ Unimpeachable source of dry tasty whites, esp Chard and Fumé Blanc, but also Chenin Bl. Cab S and Zinfandel rather underrated. 110,000 cases.

Duckhorn Vineyards Napa ★★★ (Merlot) 87 90 91 91 92 94 95 96 97 98 Known for dark, tannic, almost plummy-ripe single-v'yd Merlots (esp Three Palms, and Cab-based blend Howell Mountain. Owner recently invested in Anderson Valley.

Dunn Vineyards Napa ★★★ (Cab) 87 89 90 91 92 94 95 96 97 98 Owner-winemaker Randall Dunn makes dark tannic austere Cab from Howell Mt, slightly milder from valley floor. 4,000 cases.

Dunnewood Mendocino ★→★★ CANANDAIGUA-owned producer of reliably good value NORTH COAST varietals.

Durney Vineyard Monterey ★★→★★★ (Cab) 83 95 96 New owners reviving estate after the death of eponymous founder. Esp look for dark robust CARMEL VALLEY Cab, rich Chard. Cachagua line is ★★. Avoid sickly Chenin Blanc.

Eberle Winery San Luis Obispo ★★ Burly ex-footballer makes Cab and Zin in his own image. Also look for his polar opposite: Muscat Canelli.

Edna Valley Vineyard San Luis Obispo ★★ (Chard) 96 97 98 Decidedly toasty Chard from a joint venture of local grower and CHALONE. Pinot best drunk soon after vintage. 48,000 cases.

Estancia FRANCISCAN label for good value MONTEREY Chard, Sauvignon, Pinot N and Alexander Cab S all made in NAPA.

Etude Napa ★★★ (Pinot N) 92 94 95 96 97 98 Winemaker-owned cellar of highly respected consultant Tony Soter. V gd NAPA Cab overshadowed by burnished CARNEROS Pinot N. Engaging experiments in Pinots Blanc, Gris and Meunier.

Famiglia di Robert Mondavi, La ★★ Separate arm of famous NAPA innovator for Italianate varietals (Sangiovese, Barbera, and others) in former Vichon. Bottles weird, wines conventional.

Far Niente Napa ★★★ (Chard) 96 97 98 (Cab S) 91 92 94 95 96 97 98 Opulence appears to be the goal in both Cab S and Chard from luxury mid-NAPA estate.

Farrell, Gary Sonoma ★★★ After years in shared space, maker of brilliant, age-worthy RRV Pinot N is building his own cellar. Also excellent Merlot, Zinfandel, ultra-toasty Chard.

Ferrari-Carano Sonoma ★★ Showcase winery draws on far-flung estate v'yds for broad range of unexpectedly modest wines.

Fetzer Mendocino ★★ 3M case, Brown-Forman owned. Consistently good value from least expensive range (Sun Dial, Valley Oaks) to most (Reserve). V'yds increasingly organic.

Ficklin San Joaquin ★★ First in California to use Douro grape varieties. Since 1948, Tinta California's best 'port'. Sometimes vintages.

Field Stone Sonoma ★★ Flavourful estate-grown Alexander Valley Cab S too often overlooked. Old-vine Petite Sirah can be impressive.

California wines to try in 2000

Domaine Carneros Blanc de Blancs
Navarro Anderson Valley Gewürztraminer
Handley Anderson Valley Chardonnay
Clos du Val Stags Leap District Cabernet Sauvignon
Ridge Santa Cruz Mountains Cabernet Sauvignon 'Monte Bello'
Gary Farrell Russian River Valley Pinot Noir
Marimar Torres Estate Sonoma-Green Valley Pinot Noir 'Don Miguel V'yd'
Foxen Santa Maria Valley Pinot Noir
Lane Tanner Santa Maria Valley Pinot Noir
Nalle Dry Creek Valley Zinfandel

Firestone Sta Barbara ★★→★★★ (Chard) 96 97 98 (Merlot) 94 95 96 97 98 Fine Chard overshadows but does not outshine delicious Ries. Merlot good; Cab one of region's best. Owns CURTIS.

Fisher Sonoma ★★ Hill-top SONOMA grapes for often-fine Chard; NAPA grapes dominate steady Cab. 10,000 cases.

Flora Springs Wine Co Napa ★★ (Chard) 96 97 98 (Trilogy) 85 86 87 90 91 92 94 95 96 97 98 Old stone cellar full of oak. So are wines, esp proprietory Sauvignon called Soliloquy, Cab blend called Trilogy and varietal Sangiovese.

Fogarty, Thomas Sta Cruz Mts ★★ Fine Gewürz from VENTANA sets the pace; whole line is well made.

Folie à Deux Napa ★★ Veteran winemaker Dr Richard Peterson heads the revival of a small winery once known for fine Chard.

Foppiano Sonoma ★★ Long-est'd wine family turns out fine reds (esp Petite Sirah, Zin) under family name. Whites labelled Fox Mountain.

Forman Napa ★★★ The winemaker who brought STERLING its first fame in the '70s now makes excellent Cab and Chard on his own. 15,000 cases.

Foxen Sta Barbara ★★★ (Pinot N) 91 92 93 94 95 96 97 Tiny winery nestled between the Santa Ynez and Santa Maria valleys. Always bold, frequently brilliant Pinot N.

Franciscan Vineyard Napa ★★★ (Cab) 85 87 89 90 91 92 94 95 96 97 98 Big v'yd at Oakville for stylish Cab, Zin, ultra-oaky Chard. Sister labels: QUINTESSA and, in Chile Veramonte.

Franzia San Joaquin ★ Penny-saver wines under Franzia Corbett Canyon and many other labels. 'Bottled in Ripon' is the tip off.

Freemark Abbey Napa ★★★ (Chard) 94 96 97 98 (Cab S) 75 80 81 82 85 87 91 92 94 95 96 97 98 Underrated today, but consistent for inexhaustible stylish Cabernet Sauvignons (esp single-v'yd Sycamore and Bosché) of great depth. Vg deliciously true-to-variety Chardonnay. Also late-harvest Riesling Edelwein, infrequent but always among California's finest.

Fritz, J Sonoma ★★ With '95s new winemaker abruptly changed style from fruit-first and racy to oaky and fat, esp in whites.

To decipher codes, please refer to 'Key to symbols' on front flap of jacket, or to 'How to use this book' on page 6.

CALIFORNIA

Frog's Leap Napa ★★→★★★ (Cab S) **82 87 90 91 92** 94 95 96 Small winery, charming as its name (and T-shirts) and organic to boot. Lean racy Sauv, toasty Chard quite the reverse. Zin. Cab, Merlot all take to age.

Gabrielli Mendocino ★★ Essentially a winemaker label for good value varietals from Ukiah region.

Gainey Vineyard, The Sta Barbara ★★ Pinot N leads the list but Chard, Sauv, Cab worth a look. 12,000 cases.

Gallo, E & J San Joaquin ★→★★ Having mastered the world of commodity wines (with eponymously labelled 'Hearty Burgundy', Pink Chablis, etc) this 40M-case family firm (the world's biggest) is now unleashing a blizzard of regional varietals under such names as Anapauma, Marcellina, Turning Leaf, Zabaco and more, some from Modesto, some via GALLO SONOMA.

Gallo Sonoma Sonoma ★★→★★★ (Chard) **96 97 98**(Cab S) **91 92 94 95 96** 97 98 Increasingly distinct arm of E & J GALLO emphasizing single v'yd varietals from huge holdings throughout SONOMA county. Thus far styled (and priced) to win ratings points from those who tolerate plentiful alcohol and oak.

Gan Eden Sonoma ★★ Kosher producer of traditional single-grape wines has won substantial praise for Chards.

Geyser Peak Sonoma ★★→★★★★ Bought from Henry Trione in 1999 by distiller Jim Beam. Aussie winemaker Daryl Groom (who came when Penfolds was a partner) stays aboard, making good Chard, crackerjack Sauv and Syrah outright superior Reserve Alexandre.

Glen Ellen Proprietor's Reserve With sister commodity label M G Vallejo, the UDV bargain basement to BEAULIEU.

Gloria Ferrer Carneros ★★ Original goal of Spain's Freixenet was nothing but classic sparkling. Now smoky CARNEROS Chard and silky Pinot N on equal footing, maybe in forefront.

Greenwood Ridge Mendocino ★★ (Pinot) **94 95 96** 97 98 Est'd specialist in racy Anderson Valley Ries more recently appreciable for melony Sauv, herby Merlot. Pinot N begins to convince, too. 4,000 cases.

Grgich Hills Cellars Napa ★★★ (Chard) **95 96** 97 98 (Cab S) **80 81 83 85 86 87 90 91** 92 94 95 96 97 98 Winemaker Grgich and grower Hills join forces on pure Sauv, deftly oaked Chard long-ageing Cab, and – too little noticed – Spätlese-sweet Ries. Also plummy SONOMA Zin. 60,000 cases.

Groth Vineyards Napa ★★→★★★★ (Cab S) **85 86 87 90 91 92 94** 95 96 97 98 Oakville estate challenges leaders among NAPA Cab and Sauv Bl. Also vg Chard.

Guenoc Vineyards Lake County ★★ Ambitious winery/v'yd in its own AVA just N of NAPA county line. Property once Lillie Langtry's challenge to Bordeaux. Wines currently most riveting for flavours of oak.

Gundlach-Bundschu Sonoma ★★ (Chard) **96 97** 98 (Cab) **90 91 92 94** 95 96 97 98 Pioneer name solidly revived by fifth generation. Versatile Rhinefarm v'yd signals memorably individual Gewürz, Merlot, Zin, Pinot N. 50,000 cases.

Hafner Sonoma ★★ (Cab S) **87 90 91 92 94** 95 **96** 97 98 Semi-secretive Alexander V winery for flavourful age-able Cab. Also agreeable Chard. 8,000 cases.

Hagafen Napa ★★ First and perhaps still finest of the serious kosher producers. Esp Chard and Johannisberg Ries. 6,000 cases.

Handley Cellars Mendocino ★★ (Chard) **94 95 96** 97 98 (Pinot N) **94 96 97 98** Winemaker-owned producer of excellent Anderson Valley Chard, Gewürz, Pinot N and (tiny lots) classic sparkling. Also vg Dry Creek Valley Sauv, Chard from her family's vines.

Hanna Winery Sonoma ★★ 600 acres of Russian River and Alexander valleys v'yds producing sound middle-of-the-road Chard, Cab, Sauv. Another new winemaker in '98.

Hanzell Sonoma ★★★ (Chard) **96 97** 98 (Pinot N) **94 95 96** 97 98 The late founder revolutionized California Chards, Pinot Ns with French oak in late '50s. Three owners later, the estate v'yd produces powerhouses from same two varieties.

Harlan Estate Napa ★★★ Cab **91 92 93 94** 95 **96** 97 98 Racy Cabs from small estate in hills W of Oakville earning their right to luxury prices.

Hartford Court Sonoma ★★→★★★ Specialist in KENDALL JACKSON'S ARTISANS & ESTATES group shows promise with single v'yd Pinot Ns esp Arrendell.

Haywood Vineyard Sonoma ★★ Signature is heady SONOMA Valley estate Zin Los Chamizal. Vintner Select a commodity line. BUENA VISTA owned.

Heitz Napa ★★★→★★★★ (Cab) **74 78 79 80 84 87 91 92** 94 95 96 97 98 On dark, deep-flavoured Cab S, esp Martha's Vineyard, rests the fame of the place. So it has since the 1960s, when the individualist winemaker-owner set new standards for his peers. The newer Trailside Vineyard even rivals Martha.

> The vigorous strain of phylloxera that is forcing Napa and Sonoma to replant about half of their 60,000 acres of vineyard on new rootstocks is being combated: Napa is now well past its planting halfway mark, Sonoma is certainly close to it now.

Hess Collection, The Napa ★★ →★★★ (Chard) **94 95** 96 97 (Cab S) **87 91 92 94** 95 96 A Swiss art collector's winery-cum-museum in former Mont La Salle winery of CHRISTIAN BROTHERS. Ever more impressive Mt Veeder Cab S. Chard newly from American Canyon. 60,000 cases. More broadly sourced 300,000 case Hess Selection label gives vg value.

Heublein Former name of UDV/Diageo.

Hidden Cellars Mendocino ★★ Ukiah producer anchored in Zin, but producing worthy examples of nr-lost varieties eg Chauche Gris, Carignane, etc.

Hill Winery, William Napa ★★ Allied-Domecq property on the rise with subtle (for California) Chard; even more with flavourful, silky Cab.

Hill & Thoma Partnership Mendocino ★★ Partners cast nets widely from MENDOCINO base; labels include CARNEROS Bighorn (Chard, Pinot N), Dom Clos du Fontaine (NAPA Cab), Parducci (wide range), Van Duzer (Oregon Chard, Pinot N). Others coming.

Hop Kiln Sonoma ★★ Source of sometimes startlingly fine 'Valdiguie' (aka Napa Gamay). Russian River Gewürz is full-flavoured and large-scale.

Husch Vineyards Mendocino ★★ Has Anderson Valley v'yd for often fine Pinot N, Ukiah one for s'times good Sauv, Cab S.

Inglenook Famous old NAPA name in mothballs under CANANDAIGUA ownership. History-rich NAPA estate now NIEBAUM-COPPOLA.

Iron Horse Vineyards Sonoma ★★→★★★(Chard) **95 96 97** 98 (Brut) Substantial Russian River property at its best with classic-method fizz that hovers between fine and bold. Chard can excel. Cab-Sangiovese from affiliated Alexander Valley property.

J Sonoma ★★★ Born as a part of JORDAN now on its own in former PIPER-SONOMA cellars. Creamy classic-method Brut (**89 90 91 92**) the foundation. Recently still Pinot N, too.

Jade Mountain Napa ★★ Pursuing lofty goals using Rhône varieties, esp Syrah.

Jekel Vineyards Monterey ★★ (Chard) **96 97** 98 Jekel's ripe juicy Ries is most successful wine from Salinas v'yds. Chard begins to rival it. Cab intensely regional (capsicum-flavoured).

Jepson Vineyards Mendocino ★★ Sound steady Chard, Sauv Bl and classic sparkling from estate in Ukiah area. Also pot-still brandy.

Jordan Sonoma ★★★ (Cab S) 85 87 **90 91 92 94** 95 **96** 97 98 Extravagant Alexander Valley estate models its Cab on supplest Bordeaux. And it lasts. Chard typical California-toasty.

Karly Amador ★★ Among more ambitious sources of SIERRA FOOTHILLS Zin.

Keenan Winery, Robert Napa ★★ Winery on Spring Mountain: supple, restrained Cab, Merlot; also Chard.

Kendall-Jackson Lake County ★★→★★★ Staggeringly successful with style aimed at widest market: esp broadly sourced off-dry toasty Chard. Even more noteworthy for the development of a diversity of wineries under the umbrella of ARTISANS & ESTATES.

Kenwood Vineyards Sonoma ★★→★★★ (Chard) 97 98 (Cab S) 87 90 91 95 96 97 98 Single-v'yd Cab (Jack London), Zin (several) the high points. Recently the same owner as KORBEL.

Kistler Vineyards Sonoma ★★★ (Chard) 95 96 97 98 Ever more chasing the Burgundian model of single v'yd Pinot N, most from Russian River (greatest successes), Chards v much the toasty, buttery school.

Korbel Sonoma ★★ Long-est'd classic-method sparkling specialist emphazises bold fruit flavours, intense fizz; Natural tops the line.

Krug, Charles Napa ★→★★(Cab S) 85 91 **92 94** 95 96 97 98 Historically important winery with generally sound wines. Cabs at head of list, CARNEROS Pinot N not far behind. CK-Mondavi is relentlessly sweet commodity brand.

Kunde Estate Sonoma ★★ (Chard) 96 97 98 Long-time large grower has emerged as winemaking force with buttery Chard, flavourful Sauv (lightly touched with Viognier). Reds still finding a footing.

La Crema Sonoma ★★ (Chard) 97 98 (Pinot N) 93 94 95 96 97 98 Part of K-J's ARTISANS AND ESTATES group. Steadily impressive SONOMA Coast Chard, even better Pinot N.

La Jota Napa ★★ Tannic Cab S from small estate on Howell Mountain.

Laetitia San Luis Obispo ★★ Former MAISON DEUTZ now concentrating on estate still wines. Pinot N scintillating, Pinot B maybe. Also Chard.

Lakespring One-time NAPA winery now a label owned by Frederick Wildman. Attractive wines esp Cab S.

Lambert Bridge Sonoma ★★ Revival of briefly defunct Dry Creek Valley winery so far sound more than exciting.

Landmark Sonoma ★★ (Chard) 96 97 98 Long-time Chard specialist now in the me-too toasty-buttery school.

Laurel Glen Sonoma ★★★ (Cab S) 85 86 90 91 92 94 95 96 97 98 Big, austere distinctly regional Cab from steep v'yd in SONOMA Mtn sub-AVA. 5,000 cases. Counterpart good-value, higher-volume second label.

Laurier Sonoma ★★ (Chard) 96 97 98 Crown-jewel label of BRONCO WINE CO. Currently aiming high with Chard. Pinot N began with 93.

Lava Cap El Dorado ★★ Where bold styles rule, a source of singularly understated, intriguing Zins and Cabs.

Lazy Creek Mendocino ★★ 'Retirement hobby' of a long-time restaurant waiter yields serious Anderson Valley Gewürz and Chard. Also Pinot N.

Leeward Winery Ventura ★★ (Chard) 97 98 Ultra-toasty CENTRAL COAST Chards are the mainstay. 18,000 cases.

Liberty School San Luis Obispo ★→★★ Ex-second label of CAMUS bought in '96 by its primary supplier of Cab S and moved to his v'yd at Paso Robles.

Lockwood Monterey ★★ Huge v'yd (1,650 acres) in S Salinas Valley. Lockwood, Shale Creek labels virtually indistinguishable by style, but Lockwood ranges wider.

Lohr, J Central Coast ★→★★ Large, wide-reaching firm at peak with Paso Robles Cab S Seven Oaks. Commodity line sub-titled Cypress.

Lolonis Mendocino ★★ Substantial grower at Ukiah with range of consistently attractive varietals from own vines.

Long Vineyards Napa ★★★ (Chard) 96 97 98 (Cab) 80 84 85 86 87 90 91 92 94 95 96 96 97 98 Tiny neighbour of CHAPPELLET: lush Chard, flavourful Cab, luxury prices.

Longoria Winery Santa Barbara (★★→★★★) Long-time GAINEY winemaker now on own, and brilliant with Pinot N.

Lyeth Vineyard Sonoma ★★ Former estate, now a négociant label for Burgundian J C Boisset's California arm. MERITAGE red is the one to seek. Boisset also owns Christophe, WHEELER labels.

MacRostie Carneros ★★ Buttery Chard, is the flagship. Also well-oaked Merlot, Pinot N.

Madrona El Dorado ★★ Loftiest v'yds in SIERRA FOOTHILLS, good for steady Chards (among others). 10,000 cases.

Maison Deutz See Laetitia.

Mark West Vineyards Sonoma ★★ Gewürztraminer grows best in Russian River Valley estate owned by Associated Vintners Group. Also Chard, Pinot N.

Markham Napa ★★★ (Cab S) 87 90 91 92 94 95 96 97 98 Recently good to excellent, esp Merlot and Cab S grown in own v'yds. Sauv also to note.

Martin Bros San Luis Obispo ★★ Entirely dedicated to Italian varieties (Nebbiolo, Sangiovese), or styles ('Vin Santo', chestnut-aged Chard).

Martini, Louis M Napa ★★ Resolute insistence on making truly age-worthy Reserve Cab S, Merlot, Zin and Barbera from fine v'yds (Monte Rosso, Los Vinedos, Glen Oaks, etc) finally begins to recapture public attention.

Masson Vineyards Monterey ★→★★ CANANDAIGUA's mid-range label

Matanzas Creek Sonoma ★★★ (Chard) 96 97 98 (Merlot) 91 94 95 96 97 98 Fine ripe toasty-oaky Chard, Sauv, and renowned ultra-fleshy Merlot. Once-clear style drifting just a bit of late.

Maurice Car'rie Temecula ★★ Setting standards for its region with reliable, approachable Chard, Sauv and others.

Mayacamas Napa ★★★ (Chard) 95 96 97 98 (Cab S) 78 81 85 87 90 91 92 94 95 96 97 Vg small v'yd with rich Chard and firm (but no longer steel-hard) Cab. Some Sauv, Pinot. 5,000 cases.

Mazzocco Sonoma ★★ Good and improving Chard, Cab from Alexander and Dry Creek Valley estate v'yds.

McDowell Valley Vineyards Mendocino ★★ Grower-label for family with hearts set on Rhône varieties, esp ancient-vine Syrah and Grenache.

Meridian San Luis Obispo ★★ Fast-growing sibling to BERINGER making mark with single-vineyard Edna Valley Chard, Paso Robles Syrah. Also STA BARBARA Chard, Pinot N, Paso Robles Cab S. 300,000 cases.

Meritage Trademarked name for reds or whites using Bordeaux grape varieties. Aiming for 'varietal' status and gaining ground.

Merryvale Napa ★★ Oak aplenty in red, white MERITAGES, Chard. Cab S more middle of the road.

Michael, Peter Sonoma ★★→★★★ Partly Knights Valley estate-v'yd and partly bought-in Howell Mountain: larger-than-life, Frenchified Chard, Merlot, Cab.

Michel-Schlumberger Sonoma ★★ Reinvigorated Dry Creek Valley winery at its best with Cab S.

Mill Creek Sonoma ★★ Dry Creek Valley winery can wobble, but Cab, Merlot always worth a look.

Mirassou Central Coast ★★ Fifth-generation grower and pioneer in MONTEREY (SALINAS) gets highest marks for Pinot Bl classic sp. Chard, Pinot worth a look.

CALIFORNIA

Mondavi, Robert Napa ★★→★★★★ Tireless, brilliant innovator now applying lessons to varietals for every purse. From top: NAPA Valley Reserves (bold, prices to match), Napa Valley appellation series (eg CARNEROS Chard, Oakville Cab, etc), Napa Valley (basic production), Coastal Series (eg CENTRAL COAST Chard, North Coast Zin etc), RM-Woodbridge (California appellation for basic production, also pricier 'Twin Oaks' line). Also FAMIGLIA DI ROBERT MONDAVI, OPUS ONE, BYRON, Caliterra (Chile), Luce (Italy), Vichon (France).

Mont St John Carneros ★★ Old NAPA wine family makes good value Pinot N, Chard from own v'yd; buys in for solid Cab.

Monte Volpe Mendocino ★★ Greg Graziano looks to his heritage and wins with brisk Pinot Bianco, tart Barbera, juicy Sangiovese. French varieties separately labelled as DOM ST-GREGORY.

Monterey Peninsula Monterey ★★ Now part of Rutherford Benchmarks stable (see Quail Ridge), still making bold wines from SALINAS Valley.

Monterey Vineyard, The Monterey ★→★★ Seagram-owned label for good-value SALINAS Valley Chard, Pinot N, Cab.

Monteviña Amador ★★ Owned by SUTTER HOME. Turning more to Italian varieties (30 trial plantings) but hearty SIERRA Zin still the foundation stone.

Monticello Cellars Napa ★★ (Cab S) **87 90 91 92 94** 95 **96** 97 98 Basic line under Monticello label, reserves under Corley. Both incl Chard, Cab S. Reserve Pinot is the most intriguing.

Morgan Monterey ★★→★★★ (Pinot) **92 93 94** 95 96 Winemaker-owner. Basic Pinot N blends MONTEREY, CARNEROS but deep earthy possibly age-worthy Reserve is all Monterey now. Also toasty Chard.

Mount Eden Vineyards Sta Cruz Mts ★★ (Chard) **96 97** 98 Big expensive Chard from old Martin Ray v'yds; gentler MONTEREY version. Also Pinot N, Cab.

Mount Veeder Napa ★★ Once steel-hard Mt Veeder Cab now merely austere, as is more recent red MERITAGE. FRANCISCAN-owned.

Mumm Napa Valley Napa ★★★ G H Mumm-Seagram joint venture Range includes cheery Blanc de Noirs, distinctive single-v'yd Winery Lake and opulent luxury DVX.

Murphy-Goode Sonoma ★★ Large Alexander V estate. Sauv, Merlot, Cab S. to explore. Reserves lavishly oaked.

Nalle Sonoma ★★→★★★ (Zin) **90 91 92 93 94 95** 96 97 98 Winemaker-owned Dry Creek cellar getting to the very heart of Zin: wonderfully berryish young; that and more with age. 2,500 cases.

Napa Ridge Sonoma ★ Modest-priced part of BERINGER stable; recently everything lumbered with oak. Single v'yd wines new.

Navarro Vineyards Mendocino ★★→★★★ (Chard) **93 94 95 96** 97 98 From Anderson Valley, splendidly age-worthy Chard, perhaps the grandest Gewürz in state. Even more special: late-harvest Ries, Gewürz. Pinot N not to be ignored. Only self-deprecating prices keep this from being cult favourite of big-shot collectors.

Newton Vineyards Napa ★★→★★★ (Chard) **96 97** 98 (Cab S) **87 91** 92 94 95 **96** 97 98 Luxurious estate growing more so; formerly ponderous style now reined back to the merely opulent for Chard, Cab, Merlot.

Niebaum-Coppola Estate Napa ★★★ (Rubicon) **91 92 94** 95 96 97 98 Movie-man Coppola's luxuriously wayward hobby much invigorated since acquisition of INGLENOOK winery and 220-acre v'yd (but not name). Flagship wine (Cab-based) Rubicon beginning to take form; more accessible Coppola Family varietals quicker to show upturn.

Opus One Napa ★★★★ (Cab S) **85 87 90 91 92 93 94** 95 **96** 97 98 Joint venture of R MONDAVI and Baronne Philippine de Rothschild. Spectacular winery a proper advert for showy wines. 10,000 cases.

Parducci Mendocino ★★ Now part of HILL & THOMA; NORTH COAST varietal reds often gd value.

Pecota, Robert Napa ★★ Drink-young Cab, Sauv, Chard, Gamay.

Pedroncelli Sonoma ★★ Old-hand in Dry Creek. Reds incl single v'yd, too austere for easy enjoyment. Whites more agreeable.

Phelps, Joseph Napa ★★★ (Chard) 95 96 97 98 (Cab S) 75 85 87 90 91 92 94 95 96 97 98 Deluxe winery, beautiful v'yd: impeccable standards. Vg Chard, Cab S (esp Backus) and Cabernet-based Insignia. Splendid late-harvest Ries and Sém. Also look for promising Rhône series under Vin du Mistral label.

Philips, R H Yolo, Sacramento Valley ★→★★ Pioneer in Dunnigan Hills NW of Sacramento trying everything on huge property, succeeding best with Syrah, Viognier and pretty good Chard.

Pine Ridge Napa ★★→★★★ Gentlemanly, commune-labelled Cabs are best (Rutherford, Stags Leap, etc), Merlot not bad either. Dry oak-aged Chenin Petite Vigne is intriguing and there is Chard too, of course.

Piper Sonoma Sonoma ★★ Sold properties to J in '97.

Preston Sonoma ★★ One of California's pioneer 'terroiristes' concentrating on wines best suited to his Dry Creek v'yds: esp. Zin, Barbera, and several Rhône varieties.

Quady Winery San Joaquin ★★ Imaginative Madera Muscat dessert wines, including celebrated orangey Essencia, dark Elysium and Moscato d'Asti-like Electra. Starboard is a play on port; a better name than wine.

Quartet See Roederer Estate.

Quail Ridge Napa ★★ Third owner (Rutherford Benchmarks) has installed winery at Rutherford (ex-Domaine Napa); for toasty Chard, rich Sauv. Also Cab, Merlot.

Quintessa Napa ★★★ Splendid new estate of Huneeus family, on Silverado Trail linked to FRANCISCAN. Predictably v high standards.

Quivira Sonoma ★★ Sauv, Zin, others, from Dry Creek Valley estate. More enamoured of oak than v'yd in recent vintages.

Qupé Sta Barbara ★★→★★★ Never-a-dull-moment cellar-mate of AU BON CLIMAT. Marsanne, Pinot Bl, Syrah are all well worth trying.

Rafanelli, A Sonoma ★★ (Cab) 90 91 92 94 95 96 97 98 (Zin) 90 91 93 94 95 96 97 98 Hearty, fetchingly rustic Dry Creek Zin; Cab of striking intensity.

Rancho Sisquoc Sta Barbara ★★ Long-time friends-and-family winery edging onto larger stage with broadening range from 250-acre estate.

Ravenswood Sonoma ★★★ Major critical success for (or despite) single-v'yd Zins of skull-rattling power.

Raymond Vineyards and Cellar Napa ★★ (Chard) 97 98 (Cab S) 87 90 91 92 94 95 96 97 98 Old NAPA wine family now with Japanese partners. Generations signifies well-oaked top-of-the-line Chard, Cab. Amberhill is consistent good value commodity second label.

Renwood Amador ★ Ambitious new player in SIERRA FOOTHILLS Zin game, esp with sev'l single-v'yd bottlings. Also Barbera.

Ridge Sta Cruz Mts ★★★★ (Cab S) 83 85 86 87 89 90 91 92 93 94 95 96 97 98 Winery of highest repute among connoisseurs. Drawing from NAPA (York Creek) and its own mountain v'yd (Monte Bello) for concentrated Cabs, worthy of long maturing in bottle but needing less than formerly (MB 90 91 more approachable than 80). But power remains in SONOMA (Lytton Springs) and SAN LUIS OBISPO (Dusi) Zinfandels and other red wines. Also v pleasant Chardonnays from SANTA CRUZ.

Rochioli, J Sonoma ★★★ (Pinot N) 94 95 96 97 98 Long-time Russian River grower making 4 distinct Pinot Ns from sizeable v'yd long-celebrated under own, other labels. Also vg Sauv Bl.

CALIFORNIA

Roederer Estate Mendocino ★★★ Anderson Valley branch of Champagne house (est '88). Resonant Roederer style apparent esp in luxury cuvée l'Ermitage. Still stuns the Champenois. 25,000 cases, poised to triple. Sold as Quartet in Europe.

Rombauer Vineyards Napa ★★ Well-oaked Chard, dark Cab S (esp reserve-style Meilleur du Chai). Now also owner of the revived Hanns Kornell sparkling wine cellars and NAPA cellars.

Round Hill Napa ★★ In throes of rebirth as Van Asperen Family of Wineries, renamed after the owners. Offering 3 lines: Van Asperen (top-end NAPA), RUTHERFORD RANCH (modest-priced Napa), Round Hill (CA appellation commodities). Watch, esp for Cab S, Zin.

Rutherford Hill Napa ★★ After '96 purchase by Paterno Imports of Chicago, sources broadened to other regions, eg MENDOCINO Gewürz, but NAPA Merlot remains the mainstay.

Count on typical Napa Valley and other North Coast Cabernet Sauvignons to last eight years in good form. Do not expect any but famously durable ones to stay at their peak beyond 15.

Rutherford Ranch See Round Hill.

St Clement Napa ★★→★★★ (Chard) **96 97** 98 (Cab) **85 87 90 91 92 94** 95 96 97 98 Japanese-owned turning towards burlier, oakier style in recent vintages of NAPA Sauv Bl, Cab, Merlot and CARNEROS Chard.

St Francis Sonoma ★★ (Chard) **96 97** 98 (Cab S) **87 90 91 92 94** 95 96 97 98 Tasty Chard (Reserve far oakier). Merlot and Cab both subtly aged in American oak.

St-Supéry Napa ★★ French-owned (Skalli qv) and much activity since arrival of Michel Rolland as consulting oenologist. Chard, Sauv Bl still pallid but Cab newly richer, deeper-flavoured.

Saintsbury Carneros ★★★ (Chard) 91 **94 95 96** 97 98 (Pinot N) **91 93** 94 95 96 97 98 Contends as AVA's finest and longest-lived Pinot N. Lighter Pinot Garnet and oaky Chard also vg. 60,000 cases.

Sanford Sta Barbara ★★★ (Pinot N) **84 86 87** 89 92 **94 95** 96 97 98 Bold to over-the-top, esp Barrel Select but never dull Chard, Pinot N. Intensely regional Sauv worth a look.

Santa Barbara Winery Sta Barbara ★★ (Chard) **96 97** 98 (Pinot N) **94 95** 96 97 98 Former jug-wine producer, now among regional leaders, esp for Reserve Chard, Pinot N. Also Sauv Bl, Ries.

Santa Cruz Mountain V'yd Sta Cruz Mts ★★ Huge, tannic, heady Pinot N and subtler Rhône-variety reds. 2,500 cases.

Sattui, V Napa ★★ King of direct-only sales (ie winery door or mail order). Lusty Cab, more refined Ries are the wines to seek.

Sausal Sonoma ★★ Steady large-scale Alexander Valley estate esp notable for its Zin and Cabs.

Scharffenberger Mendocino ★★ Although technically still the name of local sparkling wine pioneer, owner Veuve Clicquot now labels everything as Pacific Echo.

Schramsberg Napa ★★★★ Dedicated specialist: California's best sparkling. Historic caves. Reserve splendid; Bl de Noir outstanding, deserves 2–10 yrs. Luxury cuvée J Schram is America's Krug. Founder Jack Davies died '98: his family presses on.

Schug Cellars Carneros ★★ German-born and trained owner-winemaker dabbles in other types, but CARNEROS Chard, Pinot N are his deepest interests and deepest wines.

Screaming Eagle Napa Exemplar of the new NAPA paradigm: Cab S grower + consulting oenologist + leased cellar space = small lots of cult wine at luxury prices.

Sebastiani Sonoma ★→★★ Substantial old family firm working low end of market (August Sebastiani Country, Vendange, Talus) but able to compete above this price level, esp with Sonoma Cask. 4 million cases.

Seghesio Sonoma ★★ Concentrating now on superb, age-worthy Zins from own old v'yds in Alexander, Dry Creek valleys, but don't overlook smaller lots of Sangiovese Vitigno Toscano, Pinot N.

Sequoia Grove Napa ★★ NAPA Cabs (Napa, Estate): dark and firm. Chards recently firmer, fresher, longer-lasting.

Shadow Creek Export label for DOMAINE CHANDON.

Shafer Vineyards Napa ★★★ (Chard) **97** 98 (Cab S) **90 91 92 94 95 96** 97 98 With '95, oak overshadows grape in single-v'yd Red Shoulder Ranch Chard (CARNEROS), and begins to do in Hillside Select Cab S (Stags Leap District), Sangiovese-based Firebreak.

Sierra Vista El Dorado ★★ Dedicated Rhôneist in SIERRA FOOTHILLS.

Silver Oak Napa/Sonoma ★★★ Separate wineries in NAPA and Alexander Valleys make Cab S only. Owners have ridden extreme American-oaked style to pinnacle of critical acclaim.

Names to look for in the early 2000s

Fiddlehead Sta Barbara: big plantings and big plans for Pinot Noir

Jaffurs Sta Barbara: tiny winemaker-owned specialist in Rhône varieties

Luna Napa: big hopes for Sangiovese on old St Andrews site

Lynmar Sonoma: ambitious try with Russian River Valley Pinot Noir

Seven Hills San Luis Obispo: joint venture (Penfolds-Paragon V'yds) for Edna Valley Chardonnay

Wattle Creek Sonoma: serious matching of Rhône varieties with Alexander Valley

Wild Hog Sonoma: to watch for Pinot Noir from Sonoma Coast

Silverado Vineyards Napa ★★→★★★ (Chard) **95 96** 97 98 (Cab S) **85 87 90 91 92** 94 95 **96** 97 98 Showy hilltop Stags Leap district winery with major v'yds there and elsewhere in NAPA. Cab, Chard, Sauv, Sangiovese all consistently refined.

Simi Sonoma ★★→★★★ After trimming line to a select few historic winery is back to making a wide range of varietals. Long-lived Cab S, vg Chard still the heart of the matter. Reserves (like most) try too hard.

Sinskey Vineyards, Robert Napa ★★ Winery in Stags Leap, v'yds in CARNEROS for boldly oaked, firm Chard, Merlot, Pinot N.

Smith & Hook Monterey ★★ (Cab S) **86 88 90** 91 92 **95** Specialist in dark age-worthy Salinas Valley Cabs. Regional flavour so herbaceous you can taste dill (fades with time).

Smith-Madrone Napa ★★ 95 **96 97** 98 Chard from Spring Mtn estate has had ups and downs; now up. Riesling admirably supports an almost-lost NAPA tradition. Don't miss it.

Sonoma-Cutrer Vineyards Sonoma ★★→★★★ (Chard) **95 96** 97 98 Ultimate Chard specialist at its somewhat diminished best with single-v'yd Les Pierres, Cutrer. FETZER owner Brown-Forman acquired 80% interest in 1999.

Spottswoode Napa ★★★→★★★★ (Cab S) **87 89 91 94** 95 **96** 97 98 Firm resonant luxury Cab from small estate v'yd in St Helena town. Also supple polished Sauv. 3,500 cases.

Stags Leap Wine Cellars Napa ★★★★ (Chard) **94 95 96** 97 98 (Cab S) **75 77 78 84 86 87 89 90 91 93 94** 95 96 97 98 Celebrated v'yd for silky, seductive Cabs (SLV, Fay, top-of-line Cask 23), Merlots; non-estate vg; also Chard, Sauv, Ries. 50,000 cases.

Stag's Leap Winery Napa ★★ Since '97 purchase by owners of BERINGER, abandoned old reliance on Chenin B., Petit Sirah in favour of Cab S. and Chard.

Staglin Napa (★★★) (Cab S) **90 91 92 93 94** 95 96 97 98 From small Rutherford v'yd designed by the late André Tchelistcheff, consistently superior, startlingly silky Cab S, ditto Sangiovese.

Steele Wines Lake (★★→★★★) Long-time K-J winemaker patrols whole coast for esp single v'yd Chards. Boldly oaked, pricey. Second label called Shooting Star.

Stemmler, Robert Sonoma ★★ BUENA VISTA label for fleshy SONOMA County Pinot N.

Sterling Napa ★★→★★★ Scenic Seagram-owned winery with extensive v'yds and inexplicable ups and downs. Tart Sauv and firm basic bottling of Cab S most reliably attractive.

Stony Hill Napa ★★★ (Chard) **93 94 95** 96 97 98 Hilly v'yd and winery for many of California's v best whites over past 30 yrs. Founder Fred McCrea died in '77, widow Eleanor in '91; son Peter carries on powerful tradition. Chard (both estate and non-estate SHV) is less steely, more fleshy than before. Oak-tinged Riesling and Gewürz are understated but age-worthy.

Storybook Mountain Napa ★★ NAPA's only dedicated Zin specialist makes oaky Estate and Reserve wines from Calistoga v'yd.

Strong Vineyard, Rodney Sonoma ★★ (Chard) **96 97** 98 (Cab) **90 91 92 94 95** 96 97 98 Formerly Sonoma V'yds; produces good basic bottlings, better single-v'yd ones (Alexander's Crown Cab, Chalk Hill Chard, Charlotte's Home Sauv, River East Pinot N).

Sutter Home Napa ★★★★ Famous for sweet white Zin, heady AMADOR Zinfandel. Branching out and reaching up with Signature Series and M Trinchero line for mid-priced NAPA varietals.

Swan, Joseph Sonoma ★★ (Zin) **85 86 87 90 91 92 93 94 95** 96 97 98 The son-in-law of late Joe Swan makes equally ultra-bold Zin, Pinot N.

Swanson Napa ★★→★★★ (Cab S) **91 92 94 95** 96 97 98 Reds are the measure of the house, esp heartily oaked Cab, Sangio, Syrah.

Taft Street Sonoma ★★ After muddling along, has hit an impressive stride with esp good-value Russian River Chards, Merlots. 18,000 cases.

Talbott, R Monterey Wealthy owner doing well with big toasty Chards from Santa Lucia, Highlands and CARMEL VALLEY AVAs.

Talley Vineyards San Luis Obispo ★★ Estate in Arroyo Grande (nr SANTA BARBARA boundary) growing exceptional Pinot N. Chard too.

Tanner, Lane Santa Barbara ★★★ (Pinot N) **93 94 95 96** 97 98 Owner-winemaker with often superb single-v'yd Pinot Noirs (Bien Nacido, Sierra Madre Plateau). Drink immediately or keep. Now Syrah too.

Tobin James San Luis Obispo ★★ Typically large-scaled Paso Robles Zins are the mainstays.

Torres Estate, Marimar Sonoma ★★★ (Pinot N) **91 92 93 94 95 96** 97 98 Sister of Catalan hero makes ultra-buttery Chard, lovely Pinot N from Russian River Valley estate.

Trefethen Napa ★★★ (Chard) **87 90 91 92 93 94 95** 96 97 98 (Cab) **79 80 84 85 87** 90 91 92 94 95 96 Respected family winery. Vg dry Ries, tense Chard for ageing (late-released Library wines show how well). Cab shows increasing depths. Lower priced wines labelled Eshcol.

Truchard Carneros ★★→★★★ From warmer, inner-end of CARNEROS comes one of the flavoury, firmly built Merlots that give the AVA identity. Cab even better.

Tudal Napa ★★ (Cab S) **87 90 91 92** 94 95 **96** 97 98 Tiny estate winery N of St Helena; steady source of dark firm ageable Cabs.

Turley Napa ★ Former partner in FROG'S LEAP, now specializing in hefty, heady single v'yd Zin, Petite Sirah from old vines.

Tulocay Napa ★★ (Pinot N) **90 91 92 94 95** 96 97 98 Tiny winery at Napa City. Pinot esp can be v accomplished. Cab is also worth attention.

Turnbull Wine Cellars Napa ★★ Once extra-minty Cab now (95 96) more classical, restrained. New (95) Sangio looks bright too. Estate faces MONDAVI winery.

UDV New Diageo name for ex-HEUBLEIN still encompasses BEAULIEU, GLEN ELLEN, etc.

Ventana Monterey ★★ '78 winery, showcase for owner's v'yds: watch for Chard and esp Sauv from Musqué clone.

Viader Napa ★★ (Cab blend) **94 95** 96 97 Argentine Delia Viader fled to California to do her own thing: dark Cab-based blend from estate in hills above St Helena.

Viansa Sonoma ★★ After obligatory Chard, Merlot, roster pays homage to Sam SEBASTIANI's ancestors with blended varietal Italianates incl such rarities (for California) as Arneis, Dolcetto, Freisa.

Villa Mount Eden Napa ★★ Lynch-pin in powerful push into California by Washington's Stimson Lane/Ch Ste Michelle; new v'yd acquisitions incl 240 acres in Napa, 195 in MONTEREY, 500 in Paso Robles. Conventional wines ever-more appellation-oriented.

Vine Cliff Napa ★★★ New well-heeled family winery in E hills above Oakville. V ambitious with estate Chard, Cab S. Shows promise.

Vino Noceto Amador ★★ California's truest-to-type Sangiovese shifted from grower-label to estate winery in 1999.

Vita Nova Sta Barbara ★★ In AU BON CLIMAT stable, the label for wines from Bordeaux varieties. Strong regional identities.

Wente Vineyards Livermore and Monterey ★★★ Historic specialist in whites, esp LIVERMORE Sauv and Sém. MONTEREY sweet Ries can be exceptional. A little classic sparkling. Also owns CONCANNON. 300,000 cases.

Whaler Mendocino ★★ Family-owned estate winery producing deep dark Zin from E hills of Ukiah Valley.

Wheeler Sonoma ★★ Was William Wheeler until bought by J C Boisset (see France). Steady source of middle-of-the-road Chard, Cab.

White Rock Napa ★★★ French owner placing faith in impressive vineyard-foremost Cab-based red, full of finesse, called simply 'Claret'. Also Chard.

White Oak Sonoma ★★ (Zin) **94 95** 96 97 98 Vibrant Zin dominates; fruit-rich Alexander Valley Chard and Sauv underrated.

Whitehall Lane Napa ★★ Boldly oaked Chard and heady Cab head short list. San Francisco family the third owner in 25 years.

Wild Horse Winery San Luis Obispo ★★→★★★ (Pinot) **92 93 94 95** 96 97 98 Owner-winemaker has a particular gift for Pinot N (mostly SAN LOUIS OBISPO and STA BARBARA GRAPES). Also worthy Chard, Merlot.

Williams Selyem Sonoma ★★★★ (Pinot) **90 91 92 93 94 96** 96 97 98 Intense smoky Russian River Pinot esp Rochioli and Allen v'yds. Now reaching to SONOMA coast, MENDOCINO, too. Followers get in line to pay high prices for emphatic individuality. New majority owner ('98) hopes to hold course.

Zaca Mesa Sta Barbara ★★ Turning away from Chard and Pinot to concentrate on Rhône varieties (especially Marsanne and Syrah) and blends (Cuvée Z) grown on estate.

ZD Napa ★★→★★★ (Pinot) **93 95** 96 97 98 Lusty Chard tattooed by American oak is ZD signature wine. Pinot N is often finer. 18,000 cases.

NB Vintages in colour are those you should choose first for drinking in 2000.

The Pacific Northwest

The largest wineries of the Pacific Northwest seem small in comparison to those in California. Most of the nearly 300 wineries in Oregon and Washington (a number that increases every year) produce fewer than 30,000 cases of wine annually and many wineries make only 2-5,000 cases each year.

Wines grown in Oregon, Washington and Idaho (Pacific Northwest) plus neighbouring British Columbia share few similarities except geographic proximity. Oregon's vineyards lie primarily in the temperate Willamette Valley and warmer Southern Umpqua Valley between the Pacific Ocean and Coast and Cascade mountain ranges. The warm days and cool nights make the Willamette Valley ideal for Burgundian and Alsatian varieties. Bordeaux varieties are grown in the warmer southern part of the state.

Across the Columbia River in Eastern Washington, the dry and continental climate of the Columbia Valley allows thicker-skinned varieties (Merlot, Cabernets and the hot favourite Syrah) to ripen well.

Weather plays an important role in each region; wet and cool harvests in Oregon from 1995-1997 resulted in a trio of disappointing vintages and wines after a run of fine vintages since 1988. Washington's warmer climate consistently ripens grapes and allows a harvest without much difficulty. Only a winter freeze in 1996 caused any hardship; (many vineyards, especially Merlot, were killed off).

The 1998 vintage looks outstanding across the region. In Oregon this vintage also marks an abundance of young, early-ripening, brighter-flavoured Pinot Noir clones from Burgundy planted over the last ten years. Poor spring weather in Oregon reduced yields by 40-50%, but the quality of the 1998 wines should be exceptional.

Oregon

Acme Wineworks (John Thomas) Yamhill County ★★ 94 95 96 Consistent, good-value NV Pinot N from small producer; excellent Pinot also under John Thomas label. Very limited supply.

Adelsheim Vineyard Yamhill County ★★★ (Pinot) 91 92 93 94 **95** 96 97 Smoothly balanced Pinot Noir, Chard best early. Riesling, Pinots Gris and Blanc are clean, bracing. Also fruity Merlot.

Amity Willamette ★★ (w) 96 97 Excellent Gewürz, Riesling and Pinot Bl. Inconsistent Pinot N.

Andrew Rich (Tabula Rasa) Willamette ★★ Small producer; wide range: Pinot N, Washington Cab S, Chenin-Sauv Bl, rosé and Gewürz ice wine.

Archery Summit Yamhill County ★★★ **93 94 95'** 96 97 Flashy operation of NAPA owner Gary Andrus. Impressive Pinot N; Vireton (Pinot Gr blend).

Argyle Yamhill County ★★★ (sp) 91 **93 94** Oregon's best classic bubbly (incl NV), consistently well made. Also fine Riesling, Chard and increasingly gd Pinot N.

Beaux Frères Yamhill County ★★★ **91 92 93** 94 95 96 97 Excellent big, extracted, new oak-style Pinot N. Part-owned by wine critic Robert Parker.

Bethel Heights Willamette ★★★ (Pinot N) 91 92 93 94 **95 96** 97 Deftly made Pinot N (Early Release, Vintage and Selected) from estate nr Salem. Chard vg since '93, notable Pinot Bl.

Brick House Yamhill County ★★★ **93 94 95** 96 97 Dynamic, organic property operated by former CBS news correspondent. V Burgundian style. Small quantities of v gd Pinot N, Gamay and barrel-ferm Chard.

Cameron Yamhill County ★★★ (Pinot N) 92 93 **94 95** 96 97 Eclectic producer of Pinot N, Chard: some great, others conversation pieces. Vg Pinot Bl.

Chehalem Yamhill County ★★★ (Pinot N) 91 92 93 **94** 95 96 97 Premium estate winery. Top quality Pinot N, Chard, Pinot Gr, Ries. Reserve Pinot N: collaborations with Burgundian winemaker Patrice Rion.

Cristom N Willamette ★★★ (Pinot N) 92' 93 **94** 95 95 96 97 Delicious Pinot N and buttery smooth Chard.

Domaine Drouhin Willamette ★★★★ 91 92 93 94 **95 95 96 97** Superb estate-grown Pinot N from one of the first families of Burgundy. Laurène Reserve superb: equally fine Chard **96 97**.

Domaine Serene Willamette ★★ Big jammy Pinot N. Very small production; look for Evenstead Reserve.

Elk Cove Vineyards Willamette ★★ Fairly consistent range of wines featuring Pinot N, Pinot Gr, Chard, Ries. Excellent dessert wines called Ultima.

Erath Vineyards Yamhill County ★★★ (Pinot) 93 94 95 **96** 97 Excellent Chard, Pinot Gr, Gewürz, Pinot Bl. Esp lovely are some of the old Pinots, 76 and Ries 76.

Evesham Wood Nr Salem Willamette ★★★ Sm family winery; fine Pinot N (**91 92** 93 94 95 96 97), Pinot Gr and dry Gewürz. Ltd production of Cuvée J in high demand.

Eyrie Vineyards, The Willamette ★★ Pioneer ('65) winery with Burgundian convictions. Older vintages of Pinot N are treasures (**75 76 80 83 86 89 90**); Chards and Pinot Gr: rich yet crisp and age beautifully.

Firesteed ★★ Large-volume producer of value-priced Pinot N and a fine DOC Barbera d'Asti (made in Italy). Look for other varietals in the future.

Foris Vineyards Rogue Valley ★★ Range of wines (Pinot N, Chard, etc) from warmer southern Oregon. Merlot and Gewürz are esp good.

A choice of Pacific Northwest wines for 2000

Col Solare (Washington joint effort of Chateau Ste-Michelle and Antinori of Italy)

Domaine Drouhin Chardonnay (Oregon)

Quilceda Creek Cabernet (Washington)

DeLille Chaleur Blanc (Washington)

Willamette Valley Vyds Joe Dobbes Signature Cuvée Pinot N (Oregon)

Panther Creek Freedom Hill Pinot Noir (Oregon)

Griffin Creek Rogue Valley ★★ New label from WILLAMETTE VALLEY VINEYARDS, vg Merlot and Pinot Gris.

Hinman Vineyards/Silvan Ridge S Willamette ★→★★ Wide range of varietals; good value.

Ken Wright Cellars Yamhill County ★★★ 93 94 **95 96** 97 Big, forward Pinot N that has a cult following. Also vg Chard and Melon de Bourgogne.

King Estate S Willamette ★★ **94** 95 96 97 Huge beautiful Napa-like estate. Vg Pinot Gr; Chard and Pinot N improving; fruit not estate-grown.

Lange Winery Yamhill County ★★ Small family winery; look for reserve Pinot N; Pinot Gr is solid but Res reveals a heavy hand with oak.

Oak Knoll Willamette ★★ Started with fruit wines; now one of Oregon's larger Pinot N producers.

Panther Creek Willamette ★★★ (Pinot N) 91 92 94' 95 96 Concentrated, meaty Pinot N and pleasant Melon de Bourgogne. Same winemaker as ST-INNOCENT. Freedom Hill Vineyard top cuvée.

Ponzi Vineyards Willamette Valley ★★★ (Pinot N) 89 90 91 92 **93** 94 **95** 96 97 Small winery almost in Portland, well-known for Riesling, Pinot Gr, Chard, Pinot N. Experimenting with Italian grapes.

Rex Hill Willamette ★★★ (Pinot N) 91 **92** 93 **93** 94 **95** 96 97 Excellent Pinot N, Pinot Gr and Chard from several N Willamette v'yds. Reserves are among Oregon's best; King's Ridge label is great value.

St-Innocent Willamette ★★ Gaining reputation for delicious, forward Pinot N; pleasant but slightly bitter Chard.

Sokol Blosser Willamette ★★ (Pinot N) 93 **94 95 96** 97 Consistently gd, easy Pinot N, Chard; Redland (res) Pinot N and Chard: excellent. Often vg Ries.

Torii Mor Yamhill County ★★ 93 **94 95 96** 97 Established Pinot N v'yd (planted 1977) in Dundee Hills; gd Pinot Gr. Several gd single v'yd Pinot N bottlings.

Tualatin Vineyards Willamette ★★ (Pinot) 93 **94 95** 96 97 Pioneer estate winery, vg Chard, Pinot N vg, also gd Ries and Gewürz. Winery now owned by WILLAMETTE VALLEY VINEYARDS.

Tyee S Willamette ★★ Small, family-owned and -run winery is especially good with dry Gewürz, Riesling and Pinot Bl. Pinot N improving.

Valley View Vineyards Rogue Valley ★★ Family-owned estate saw leap in quality with '90 vintage. Cabernet, Merlot, Chard and Sauvignon Bl are gd, sometimes exciting. Jazz series less gd.

Willakenzie Estate Yamhill County ★★★ First wines released '96; delicious Pinots Gr, Bl, Chard, Pinot N. Well-financed, state-of-the-art facility; French winemaker.

Willamette Valley Vineyards Willamette ★★→★★★ Big winery nr Salem. Moderate- to very high-quality Chard, Ries, Pinot N. Amazing range from commercial to top flight.

Witness Tree Willamette ★★ S'times lovely but inconsistent Pinot N; vg rich Chard.

Yamhill Valley Vineyards ★ Gd Pinot Gr, Chard, Pinot N. New Pinot Blanc.

Washington & Idaho

Andrew Will Puget Sound (Washington) ★★★ 89 90 91 **92 93 94** 95 96 97 Exceptional Cab S, Merlot and barrel-fermented Chard from E Washington grapes.

Arbor Crest Spokane (Washington) ★★ Est'd mid-size winery; dependable Chard, Sauv Bl, Merlot and late-harvest Ries.

Barnard Griffin Pasco, Columbia Valley (Washington) ★★★ Small producer: well-made Merlot, Chard (esp barrel-fermented), Sem, Sauv Bl. Very consistent.

Canoe Ridge Walla Walla (Columbia Valley) ★★★ Newer winery owned by Chalone Group (California). Impressive 93 **94 95 96** 97 Chard and Merlot.

Cascade Ridge Woodinville ★★ New label produced by Corus (see Columbia Winery), small production well-made Cab, Merlot and Chard.

Château Ste-Michelle Woodinville (Washington) ★★★ Ubiquitous regional giant is Washington's largest winery; also owns COLUMBIA CREST and Snoqualmie. Major E Washington v'yd holdings, first-rate equipment and skilled winemakers keep Chard Sém, Sauv Bl, Ries, Cab (**91 92 93** 94 95 96 97) and Merlot in front ranks. V'yd-designated Cab and Chard. Newer top-of-the-range Artists Series B'x blend.

Chinook Wines Yakima Valley (Washington) ★★ Owner-winemakers purchase local grapes for sturdy Chard, Sauv and Merlot.

Columbia Crest Columbia Valley ★★★ Separately run CHATEAU STE-MICHELLE label for delicious well-made accessible good value wines. Cab, Merlot, Syrah and Sauvignon Bl are best. V gd reserve wines too.

Columbia Winery Woodinville ★★→★★★ (Cab) 79 83 85 **87 88 89 90 91 92 93** 94 95 96 97 Pioneer ('62, as Associated Vintners now Corus) and still a leader. Balanced stylish understated single-v'yd wines, esp Syrah. Very good oak-fermented Chard, vg fruity long-lived Sém, Gewürz and late-harvest Ries.

Covey Run Yakima Valley ★★(Chard) 92 93 94 95 96 97 Consistent, large-scale producer. Heady Merlot, Cab. Purchased '96 by Corus (See Columbia Winery).

DeLille Cellars/Chaleur Estate Woodinville ★★★★ Exciting winery for vg red B'dx blends: age-worthy Chaleur Estate 92 93 94 95 96 97, D2 (more forward, affordable). Excellent barrel fermented white (Sauv-Sém). Look out for new Syrah.

Dunham Wines Walla Walla ★★★ 95 96 97 Young exciting wines from the L'ECOLE NO 41 (see below) assistant winemaker. Cabs and Sém-Chard all well extracted and elegant

Gordon Brothers Columbia Valley ★★→★★★ Tiny cellar; consistent Chard (Reserve 91), Merlot, Cab. Recently improving: new young French winemaker.

Hedges Cellars Yakima Valley ★★★ Made its name exporting its wines to Europe and Scandinavia. Now boasts fine v'yd (Red Mountain), château-style winery, delicious Cab, Merlot, Sauv Bl.

Hogue Cellars, The Yakima Valley ★★★ Large producer known for excellent wines, esp Ries, Chard, Merlot, Cab. Produces quintessential Washington Sauv Bl.

Tracking down Northwest wines

Portland Wildwood (1221 NW 21st Avenue, tel 503-248-9663)
The quintessential Northwest restaurant, where the seasonal cuisine hits the Oregon Trail. The all-West Coast wine list features a number of top notch Oregon and Washington producers.
Liner & Elsen (202 NW 21st Avenue, tel 503-241-9463) Irreverent small wine shop, but the knowledge and service are unbeatable.

Dundee Ponzi Wine Bar (100 7th Street, tel 503-554-1500) A very attractive stop in the epicentre of wine country (45 mins from Portland). While the focus of wines to taste and buy is Ponzi, of course, you'll also find a broad selection of current releases from other top producers.

Seattle Ray's Boathouse (6049 Seaview Avenue NW, tel 206-789-3770) The longtime favourite for fabulous seafood and an encyclopedic (and global) wine list heavy on the top Washington producers. This is the place to get those hard-to-find reds, including the Leonetti and Quilceda Creek line-up.

Leonetti Walla Walla ★★★★ 91 92 93 94 95 96 97 The Washington estate in highest demand – one of America's gems. Harmonious individualistic Cab; fine big-boned, yet succulent Merlot: bold, ageworthy.

L'Ecole No 41 Walla Walla ★★★ 91 92 93 94 95 96 97 Blockbuster reds (Merlot, Cab and Meritage blend) with jammy, age-worthy fruit. Good barrel-fermented Sémillon

Matthews Cellars Woodinville ★★★ Smaller producer of mouth-filling Bordeaux blends since 1993. New Sém wort hunting down.

McCrea Puget Sound ★★ Small winery for good Viognier and Grenache. Experiments with Rhône blends continue.

Paul Thomas Yakima Valley ★★ Forward and sensibly priced Chard, Sauv Bl, Chenin, Cab, Merlot. Part of Corus Group (see Columbia Winery)

Quilceda Creek Vintners Puget Sound ★★★★ (Cab) 87 88 89 90 91 92 93 94 95 96 97 Expertly crafted ripe well-oaked Cab S from Columbia Valley grapes is the speciality. Exceptional finesse.

Rose Creek Vineyards S Idaho ★★ Small family winery; good esp for Chard.

Ste Chapelle Caldwell (Idaho) ★★ Pleasant, forward Chard, Ries, Cab, Merlot, Syrah from local and E Washington v'yds. Attractive sparkling wine: good value and improving quality.

Thurston Wolfe Yakima Valley ★★★ Tiny eclectic winery: excellent Lemberger (red), late-harvest Sauv, Black Muscat, Cabernet 'port style'.

Washington Hills Cellars/Apex Yakima Valley ★★ Solid line incl Sém, Fumé, Cab, Chard, Merlot and late-harvest Ries, Gewürz. Apex label: higher quality.

Waterbrook Walla Walla ★★★ 89 90 91 **92** 93 94 95 96 97 Stylish, distinctive Chard, Sauv, Cab, Merlot from a winery that has hit its stride.

Woodward Canyon Walla Walla ★★★ **90** 91 92 93 94 95 96 97 Solid, quality-driven producer; loyally followed ripe, intense, v oaky Cab, Chard and blends.

British Columbia

This small but significant part of the Canadian wine industry has developed since the '70s in the splendid Okanagan Valley, 150 miles east of Vancouver, in climatic conditions not very different from eastern Washington.

Blue Mountain ★★ 95 **96 97** 98' Sm property. Vg Pinot Gr, v fair Pinot N and sp.

Calona Vineyards ★★ 95 **96 97** 98' Large winery. Gd Pinot Bl, Sém and Merlot.

Gray Monk ★★ **96 97** 98' Gd Okanagan Auxerrois, Gewürz and Pinot Blanc.

Lang Vineyards 94 95 **96 97** 98' Juicy Pinot Meunier.

Mission Hill ★→★★★ 94 95 **96 97** 98' Caused a gold medal stir in '94. Esp for Grand Reserve Chard, Pinot Blanc.

Quails' Gate ★★ 94 95 **96 97** 98' Chard, Chenin Bl, Pinot N, Ries Ice Wine all worth trying.

Sumac Ridge ★★ 94 95 **96 97** 98' Gewürz, Pinot Bl, sp among region's best.

East of the Rockies & Ontario

Producers in New York (there are now 125 in 6 AVAs) and other eastern states, as well as Ohio (56 in 4 AVAs) and Canada's Ontario (35), traditionally made wine from hardy native grapes, varieties of *Vitis labrusca* whose wine has strong 'foxy' flavour, off-putting to non-initiates. Growers then turned to less pungent French-American hybrids. Today, consumer taste plus cellar and vineyard technology have largely bypassed these, although Seyval Blanc and Vidal keep their fans, and Norton, an intense red, is gathering contemporary devotees. Chard, Ries, Cab S and Merlot are now firmly established. Pinot N and Cab F are emerging with some notable results. Progress, from Virginia to Ontario, is accelerating as the wines gain recognition outside their own immediate region.

Major Northeastern grape varieties

Chambourcin Red hybrid of French origin: under-appreciated Loire-like reds and agreeable rosé.

Concord *Labrusca* variety. Heavy 'foxy' sweet one-dimensional red wines and dessert wines, but mostly grape juice and jelly.

Norton AKA Cynthiana. Hybrid producing intense reds; gaining in popularity.

Seyval Popular French-American hybrid that can produce stylish dry whites.

Vidal Mainstay French-American hybrid grape for full-bodied personable dry white wines and late-harvest dessert wines.

Wineries and vineyards

Allegro ★★ **97'** 98' Pennsylvania maker of worthy Chard, Cab.

Andres Second-largest Canadian winery; gd B'dx-style red. Owns HILLEBRAND.

Bedell ★★★ 93 **94** 95 96 97 LONG ISLAND winery; excellent Merlot and Cab S.

Biltmore Estate ★★ 93 **94** 95 96 97 North Carolina winery on 8,500 acres with Vanderbilt mansion, America's largest. Chard and sparkling.

Canandaigua Wine Co No longer a winery; now owns Widmer's Wine Cellars; full range of sherry-style wines, and table and sparkling (250,000 cases).

Cave Spring ★★★ 96 97 98' ONTARIO boutique: sophisticated Chard and Ries. Big restaurant, popular tourist stop.

Chaddsford ★★ 96 97 **98** Solid Pennsylvania producer since '82: esp for burgundy-style Chard and B'dx-style red blend.

Chamard ★★ 95 96 97' **98** Connecticut's best winery, owned by Tiffany chairman. Top Chard. AVA is Southeastern New England.

Château des Charmes ★★→★★★ 93 94 95 96 97 98' Show-place château-style ONTARIO winery. Fine Chard, Viognier, Cab, sparkling.

Clinton Vineyards ★★ 95 96 97 98 HUDSON RIVER winery; clean dry SEYVAL and spirited sp Seyval.

Chalet Debonné Vineyards ★★ 94 96 97 98 Popular OHIO estate (in Lake Erie AVA): hybrids, eg CHAMBOURCIN and VIDAL; and vinifera, eg Chard, Ries.

Finger Lakes Beautiful historic upstate New York cool-climate v'yd region, source of most of the state's wines. Also the seat of New York State's 'vinifera revolution'. Top wineries: DR FRANK, FOX RUN, GLENORA, STANDING STONE, HERMANN WEIMER, Treleaven/Kings Perry.

Firelands ★★ 95 96 97 98 Ohio estate in LAKE ERIE AVA, growing Chard, Cab, Gewürz, Pinot Gr, Ries and Pinot N.

Fox Run ★★★ 93 94 95 96 97 98 Now leader of the new generation of FINGER LAKES winemaking; some of the region's best Chard, Ries, Pinot N and sp.

Frank, Dr Konstantin (Vinifera Wine Cellars) ★★ 95 **96** 97 98 Sm, influential winery. The late Dr F was a pioneer in growing European vines in the FINGER LAKES. Good Ries, Gewürz, Chard, Cab S and Pinot N. Vg Chateau Frank sp.

Glenora Wine Cellars ★★ 94 95 96 97 FINGER LAKES producer of good sparkling wine, Chard, Ries and Pinot Bl.

Gristina ★★ 93 94 95 **96** 97 Solid winery on LONG ISLAND'S N FORK AVA with Chard, Cab, Merlot and Pinot N.

Hamptons (Aka South Fork) LONG ISLAND AVA. The top winery is moneyed WOLLFER ESTATE SAGAPOND. Duck Walk is up and coming. Brand-new Channing Daughters bears watching.

Hargrave Vineyard ★★★ 93 94 95 96 97 LONG ISLAND'S pioneering winery, v'yds since '72 on NORTH FORK. Good Chard, Cab S and Cab F.

Henry of Pelham ★★★ 95 96 97 Elegant ONTARIO Chard and Ries; distinctive Baco Noir.

Hillebrand Estates ★→★★★ 95 96 97 98' Dynamic ONTARIO producer attracting attention with Ries, Gewürz and B'dx-style red blend. New restaurant.

Hudson River Region America's oldest winegrowing district (25 producers) and NY's first AVA. Straddles the river, two hours' drive N of Manhattan.

Inniskillin ★★★ 93 94 95 **96** 97 98' Outstanding (VINCOR-owned) producer that spear-headed birth of modern ONTARIO wine industry. Skilful burgundy-style Chard and Pinot N. Vg Ries, VIDAL ice wine, Pinot Gris and Auxerrois.

Knapp ★→★★ 95 **96** 97 98 Versatile FINGER LAKES winery. Tasty Bordeaux-style blend, Cab, Ries, sp Brut. Only Finger Lakes producer making Sangiovese.

Lake Erie The biggest grape-growing district in the eastern US; 25,000 acres along the shore of Lake Erie, incl portions of New York, Pennsylvania and OHIO. 90% is CONCORD (mostly used for commercial juice and jelly), generally from New York's Chautauqua County. Also the name of a tri-state AVA: NY's sector has 8 wineries, Pennsylvania's 5 and Ohio's 24. Ohio's Harpersfield sets standards for quality.

Lakeview ★★ 93 94 95 97 98' ONTARIO producer with gd reputation for full-flavoured reds and Ries.

Lamoreaux Landing ★★ 94 95 96 97 98 Stylish FINGER LAKES house: promising Chard and Ries from striking Greek-revival winery.

Lenz ★★★ 94 95 96 97 Classy winery of NORTH FORK AVA. Fine austere Chard in the Chablis mode, also Gewürz, Merlot and sparkling wine.

Long Island Exciting wine region E of Rockies and a hothouse of experimentation. Currently 2,000⁺ acres, all vinifera (47% Chard) and 2 AVAs (NORTH FORK and HAMPTONS). Most of its 17 wineries are on the North Fork. Best varieties: Chard, Cab, Merlot. A long growing season; almost frost-free.

Michigan One of America's finest cool-climate Ries areas; 21 commercial wineries (+3 new ones this year) and 4 AVAs. Best incl: St-Julien Wine Co, Ch Grand Traverse and Tabor Hill. Mawby Vyds and Ch Chantal known for sparkling wine from Chard, Pinot N and Pinot Meunier. Fenn Valley and Good Harbour have large local following. To watch: Peninsula Cellars.

Millbrook ★★★ 93 94 95 96 97 98 Top HUDSON RIVER REGION winery. Money-no-object viticulture and savvy marketing has lifted spiffy whitewashed Millbrook in big old barn into New York's firmament. Burgundian Chards; splendid, Cab F can be delicious.

North Fork LONG ISLAND AVA (of 2). Top wineries: Bedell, Gristina, LENZ, PALMER, PAUMANOK, PELLEGRINI, PINDAR. 2½ hrs' drive from Manhattan.

The Big Apple has local wines – where to find them:

An American Place All-American wine list to match all-American food (Michigan cheeses, New York venison, etc).

Home and **Drovers Tap Room** Two cosy Greenwich Village spots where Long Island wines complement 'American Neighbourhood' cuisine.

Hudson River Club NY wines and NY foods such as Hudson Valley foie gras and Fishers Island oysters.

March American cuisine gets a personal twist in an elegant Eastside townhouse. The impressive wine list includes a few Eastern selections.

Quilties Chic Soho refuge for foodies who appreciate Virginia and New York wines as well as New American cuisine with a French accent.

Union Square Café Place to experiment and be seen (food less fun than people).

Windows on the World Stunning arial views of Manhattan. A few regional wines to go with New American cuisine.

Ohio 4 AVAs notably LAKE ERIE and Ohio Valley .

Ontario Main E Canada wine region, on Niagara Peninsula and LAKE ERIE north shore: 56 wineries. Heavy investment and glimmerings of great future. Riesling, Gewürz, Chard, even Pinot N show incipient longevity, esp Pelee Island. Ice wine is flagship of region.

Palmer ★★★ 94 95 96 97 Superior LONG ISLAND (N FORK) producer and byword in Darwinian metropolitan market. High profile due to perpetual-motion marketing; fast growth. Tasty Chard, Sauv Bl and Chinon-like Cab F.

Paumanok ★★★ 95 96 97 98 Rising fine LONG ISLAND (N FORK) winery; promising Cab, Merlot, Ries, Chard, outstanding Chenin and savoury late-harvest Sauv.

Pellegrini ★★★ 93 94 95 96 97 LONG ISLAND's most enchantingly designed winery (on N FORK), opened '93. Opulent Merlot, stylish Chard, B'x-like Cab. Inspired winemaking. Exceptionally flavourful wines.

Pindar Vineyards ★★→★★★ 93 94 95 96 97 Huge 287-acre mini-Gallo winery of N FORK, LONG ISLAND. Wide range of toothsome blends and popular varietals, incl Chard, Merlot, and esp gd Bordeaux-type red blend, Mythology.

Sakonnet ★★ 94 95 96 97 98 Largest New England winery, based in Little Compton, Rhode Island (SE New Eng AVA). V drinkable wines incl Chard, VIDAL, dry Gewürz, with Cab Fr and Pinot N. Delicious new sp Brut cuvée.

Standing Stone ★★★ 94 95 96 97 One of FINGER LAKES finest wineries with v good Ries, Gewürz and Cab Franc.

Tomasello ★★ 93 94 95 96 97 Est'd New Jersey winery. Gd CHAMBOURCIN. Promising Cab S and Merlot.

Unionville Vineyards ★★→★★★ 95 96 97 One of New Jersey's best wineries, est '93. Lovely Ries, French-American hybrids elevated to near-vinifera status.

Vincor International ★→★★ Canada's biggest winery (formerly Brights-Cartier), in ONTARIO, BC, Quebec, New Brunswick. Mass-market and premium wines; varietals, blends, Canadian and imported grapes. Owns INNISKILLIN. Also Jackson-Triggs (premium Chard, Cab) and Sawmill Creek labels.

Vineland Estates ★★ 94 95 96 97 Gd ONTARIO producer; dry and semi-dry Ries much admired. VIDAL ice wine: gd, Chard, Cab. Restaurant and tasting room.

The Vintners Quality Alliance Canada's voluntary appellation body, started in ONTARIO but now incl BRITISH COLUMBIA. Its self-policing of standards has rapidly raised respect and awareness of Canadian wines to high levels (Ontario will be legalised as of '99).

Wagner Vineyards ★★ 95 96 97 Famous FINGER LAKES winery. Barrel-fermented Chard, dry and sw Riesling and ice wine. Attracts many visitors.

Westport Rivers ★★ 95 96 97 Massachusetts house est'd '89. Good Chard and sparkling. (Southeastern New England AVA.)

Wiemer, Hermann J ★★→★★★ 95 97' 98' Creative German-born FINGER LAKES winemaker. Interesting Ries incl vg sparkling and 'late harvest'. Vg Chard.

Wolffer Estate SagaPond Vyds ★★★ 94 95' 96 97' 98' In operation since '87, has come of age with modish Chard, Merlot and sp from German-born winemaker. Proof that gd wine can be made on LONG ISLAND's South Fork.

Wollersheim ★★ Wisconsin winery specializing in variations of Maréchal Foch. Prairie Fumé (Seyval Bl) is a commercial success.

Southern and central states

Virginia Emerged as an important wine state since '72. Whites, esp Chard, lead. 53 wineries (in 6 AVAs). Gd Ries, Gewürz, Viognier, Cabs and Merlot (and newly introduced Pinot Gr and Barbera) from 1,500 acres of grapes. Top producers incl: Prince Michel (Chard, Merlot, Cab), Jefferson (nr Monticello; gd Chard). Other top producers: Horton (Viognier, other Rhône-style wines), Linden, Oasis (sp), Piedmont, Barboursville (Malvasia Res is inspired: an American original), Williamsburg, Ch Morrisette. Also Piedmont, Tarara, Ingleside Plantation. Whitehall, Breaux and Landwirt exciting newcomers.

Missouri A blossoming industry with 35 producers in 3 AVAs: Augusta (first in the US), Hermann, Ozark Highlands. In-state sales catching fire. Best wines are SEYVAL BL, VIDAL, Vignoles (sw and dry versions). Top estate is Stone Hill, in Hermann (since 1847): rich red from NORTON (or Cynthiana) grape variety; Hermannhof (1852) is drawing notice for the same. St James for both Vignoles and Norton; Mount Pleasant, in Augusta: rich 'port' and nice sparkling wine. To watch are Augusta Winery, Blumenhof, Les Bourgeois, Montelle, Röbler.

Maryland 9 wineries, 2 AVAs. Basignani makes gd Cab S, Chard, SEYVAL. Elk Run's Chard and Cab can be delicious. Best-known Boordy V'yds: gd Seyval Bl (esp Res) and sp. Woodhall for Seyval, Cab. Fiore's CHAMBOURCIN is interesting. Catoctin AVA: main Cab and Chard area. Linganore is second AVA.

The Southwest and the Rockies

Texas

Since the '70s, the Texas wine industry has continued to grow and make its voice heard. Over two dozen wineries and over 450 growers have made wine a visible part of the Texas economy. The best wines compare favourably with northern California's.

Becker Vineyards Stonewall. New and very promising. Vg Cab, gd Chard.

Bell Mountain Vineyards Bell Mountain AVA winery at Fredericksburg. Consistently good Cab S and Chard.

Cap Rock Nr Lubbock. Since '90 reliably good varietals: Cab S, Chard, Muscat Canelli. Well-crafted blends, esp Cabernet Royale: v good.

Delaney Vineyards Nr Dallas. Very good Chard, Cab S and Muscat Canelli. Good sparkling wine.

Fall Creek Vineyards Texas Hill Country. Consistently good Cab S, Chard and Carnelian.

Hidden Springs Winery Very good Cab S and good blends.

Llano Estacado Nr Lubbock. The pioneer (since '76) continues on award-winning track with Cab S and blends, esp Signature red. Good Zinfandel and Rhône-style wines.

Messina Hof Wine Cellars nr Bryan. One of the largest producers of speciality boutique wines. Excellent late-harvest Johannisberg Riesling Angel and consistently good Cab S, Sauv Bl and Muscat Canelli.

Ste-Genevieve Largest Texas winery, linked with Domaines Cordier (France). Well-made, mostly NV wines. V good Chard. Look out for Zin and Pinot N along with good blends.

Sister Creek Texas Hill Country. Tiny with particularly good Pinot N.

Spicewood Good Merlot and Sauvignon Blanc.

New Mexico etc

New Mexico continues to show promise with more emphasis now on vinifera grapes, though some French hybrids are still used (historic Mission grape is produced at Tularosa Winery). There are now three AVAs and 22 wineries. Blue Teal V'yd: good Cab S; Casa Rondeña: Bordeaux-style wines and gd Cab F Gruet (region's largest winery) has good sp wines and excellent Chard. La Chiripada has v good blends, some with hybrids and gd port-style wine. Los Locos: new and v promising. V good Baco Noir and Chard. Mademoiselle: Gd Sauv Bl. Madison V'yds and Winery: gd Baco Noir and blends, esp Pecos Wild Flower. Ponderosa Valley: award-winning Riesling, gd Chard, vg blends esp Summer Sage. St-Claire: Gd Cab S. La Viña: fine Chard and good Zin.

Colorado and **Arizona** focus on vinifera grapes. Colorado (21 wineries) is growing rapidly esp Grand Junction area: Chard and Merlots leading the planting. Family-owned Carlson Cellars (Pallisade): vg blends esp Prairie Dog White series, Ries and Chard. Grande River V'yds (Pallisade): gd Viognier. New and promising Canyon Wind Cellars: V gd Chard, Merlot, Cab S. Cottonwood Cellars: bold flavours, Cab S, Merlot. Small excellent Terror Creek: Riesling, Gewürz, Chard. Trail Ridge (Front Range): gd Ries. Arizona (10 wineries) is highlighting Rhône varieties (eg Dos Cabezas: Sangiovese, Syrah; Kokopelli: Cab S and Callaghan V'yds) with Cab S from Kokopelli Winery looking gd.

Oklahoma has two wineries (and increasing interest in grape growing). **Utah** will be the next to emerge – the state's four wineries all focus on vinifera esp Merlot, Cab S and Chenin. **Nevada**'s one winery is nr Las Vegas: Pahrump Valley V'yd (Chard and Symphony).

South America

Chile

Now firmly established as a supplier of excellent value everyday wines, especially reds, it is understandable that Chile wants to move upmarket. But wines now sporting price tags in line with classed-growth claret have still to show that they are good enough to deserve a place in such company. The news for fans of Chilean Merlot is that most of it (60-90%) might not be Merlot at all, but the rare Bordeaux variety, Carmenère. The Chileans have only recently recognised Carmenère as an official variety for making wines, and, at the time of writing, the EU has yet to do so. Disentangling the two varieties will take years, but already some wineries offer versions of both. Even so, many winemakers feel that the best wines will be from vineyards where the varieties are interplanted. Watch this space... Conditions are ideal for vines (all irrigated) in the Maipo Valley near Santiago and for 300 miles south. The more recent Casablanca region between Santiago and Valparaiso offers excellent terroirs for Chard and Sauv Bl. Many long-time growers are no longer supplying the big bodegas but making their own wines. Major regions, from north to south, are Aconcagua, Maipo, Rapel, Curicó, Maule and southern Itata, and Bío Bío.

Aconcagua Northernmost quality wine region. Incl CASABLANCA, Panquehue.

Agrícola Aquitania ★★→★★★ 60-acre joint venture of Paul Pontallier and Bruno Prats from Bordeaux with Felipé de Solminihac. Premium wine is Paul Bruno: slowly improving as vines age. Also gd value Uno Fuera Cab S 93.

Almaviva ★★★★ MAIPO joint venture between CONCH Y TORO and Mouton Rothschild, first v'tage '96; classy wine matching the hype and almost the price.

Bío-Bío Sthnmost quality wine region. Wet. Potential for gd whites and Pinot N.

Calina, Viña ★★→★★★ Kendall-Jackson (see California) venture. Better reds (esp Selección de Las Lomas Cab S) than whites.

Caliterra ★★→★★★ Sister winery of ERRAZURIZ, now half-owned by Mondavi (California). Chard and Sauv Bl improving (higher proportions of CASABLANCA grapes), reds becoming less one-dimensional. Reserva range excellent.

Cánepa, José ★★→★★★ Historically gd reds but shaken up by recent co upheavals. However, fine reds and white of the Mapocho range made with Australia's BRL Hardy group augur well for future.

Carmen, Viña ★★→★★★ MAIPO winery under same ownership as SANTA RITA. Ripe, fresh Special Res (CASABLANCA) Chard and deliciously light Late Harvest Maipo Sém top whites. Reds even better; esp RAPEL Merlots, Maipo Petite Sirah and Cabs, esp Gold Reserve. Now does vg Maipo Syrah.

Carta Vieja ★★ MAULE winery owned by one family for six generations. Reds, esp Cab and Merlot better than whites, though Antigua Selección Chard is gd.

Casa Lapostolle ★★→★★★ Well-healed venture incl Marnier-Lapostolle family, owners of Grand Marnier. Michel Rolland-inspired. Supple spicy Merlot (Cuvée Alexandre possibly Chile's best), plummy Cab, fleshy Chard, B'dx style Sauv.

Casablanca Cool-climate region between Santiago and coast. V little water: drip irrigation essential. Top-class Chard and Sauv; promising Merlot and Pinot N.

Casablanca, Viña ★★★ Sister winery to SANTA CAROLINA. Ignacio Recabarren makes some of Chile's best wines. RAPEL and MAIPO fruit used for some reds, Santa Isabel Estate in CASABLANCA already producing vg Sauv, Chard and Gewürz. Barrel samples of Cab and Merlot look promising.

Concha y Toro ★→★★★ Mammoth operation; bodegas and v'yds all over Chile. Top wines: mealy Amelia CASABLANCA Chard, rich chocolatey Marques de Casa Concha Merlot (RAPEL) and Don Melchor Cab (Rapel); also l Recabarren's Trio range. Promising Explorer range: Alicante Bouschet, Pinot N, Cab/Syrah, etc. Recent agreement with Mouton-Rothschild to produce a premium MAIPO red.

Cono Sur ★★→★★★ Chimbarongo winery owned by CONCHA Y TORO for vg Pinots (local and CASABLANCA fruit). Also dense fruity Cabs. Second labels Tocornal and Isla Negra (latter incl wines from Argentina).

Cousiño Macul ★★→★★★ Distinguished, beautiful old MAIPO estate. Long-lived Antiguas Res Cab; top wine Finis Terrae (B'x blend). Also: supple Merlot and old-fashioned, v dry Sém, Chard.

Domaine Oriental ★★ Gd MAULE reds, esp Clos Centenaire Cab; French-owned.

Domus ★★★ MAIPO single v'yd venture from Ignacio Recabarren (see Viña Casablanca) and Ricardo Peña, making good Chard and vg Cab.

Echeverría ★★ Boutique Curicó (MAULE) winery producing intense complex Reserve Cabs, v gd oaked and unoaked Chard and rapidly improving Sauv.

Edwards, Luís Felipé ★★ Colchagua (RAPEL) winery; citrussy Chard, silky Res Cab.

Errázuriz ★★★ Sole winery in Panquehue district of ACONCAGUA. First class whites, (CASABLANCA fruit), esp rich yet elegant Chard Res, complex, mealy Wild Ferment Chard. Reds just as gd: brooding Syrah; earthy, plummy Merlot; fine Cabs topped by Don Maximiano Reserve. Also top-flight Seña: Cab S-Merlot-Carmenère produced with CALITERRA and Mondavi of California, launched '98.

La Fortuna, Viña ★★ Old-est'd winery in Lontué Valley. Range of attractive varietal wines, esp chunky Malbec, without fertilisers or herbicides.

Francisco de Aguirre, Viña ★★ Promising Cabs S and F and Chard from new winery in the northerly region of Valle de Limari.

Gracia, Viña ★★→★★★ Newcomer with v'yds from ACONCAGUA down to BIO BIO. Cab S Reserva R is best; gd Pinot N and Chard. Plans for Mourvèdre and Syrah.

La Rosa, Viña ★★ Impressive RAPEL Chards, Merlots, Cabs aided by new winery. Consultant: Ignacio Recabarren. Labels: La Palma and Casa Leona.

de la Rose, Viña ★★ RAPEL venture by Médoc Ch Larose-Trintaudon under the Las Casas del Toqui and Viña Alamosa labels.

Maipo Oldest wine region, nr Santiago. Quite warm. Source of Chile's top Cabs.

Maule S'most region in Central Valley. Incl Claro, Loncomilla, Tutuven Valleys.

Mont Gras ★★★ State-of-the-art winery in Colchagua Valley capable of top class Merlot and Cab. Best wines under Ninquen label.

Montes ★★→★★★ Label of Discover Wines nr Curicó. Montes Alpha Cab can be brilliant, Merlot and Malbec also fine; whites steady. New B'x blend Montes M is not special enough for its price.

Morande Aventura ★★ New venture. Reds already show potential (incl César, Malbec, Cinsault, Bouschet, Carignan). See also Argentina.

Paul Bruno See Agrícola Aquitania.

Porta, Viña ★★→★★★ MAIPO winery; mainly Cachapoal (RAPEL) grapes. Known for Cab (Unfiltered Res), Chard. Also plummy Merlot and gd 2nd label Casa Porta.

Portal del Alto, Viña ★★★ Sm bodega; excellent Cab-Merlot blend from own v'yds in MAIPO and RAPEL.

Rapel Central quality region divided into Colchagua and Cachapoal valleys. Source of great Merlot.

San Pedro ★★→★★★ Third-largest Chilean producer based at Molina, Curicó. Gato Negro and Gato Blanco: top sellers. Best wines: Castillo de Molina and Sta Helena Seleccíon de Director. Jacques Lurton of B'dx is consultant.

Santa Carolina, Viña ★★→★★★ Impressive old Santiago bodega; increasingly impressive and complex wines. All MAIPO Reserve wines are v gd, inc a rich limey Sauv Bl. Also excellent oak-aged Late Harvest Sém/Sauv blend.

Santa Emiliana ★★ A division of CONCHA Y TORO. V'yds in RAPEL and CASABLANCA. Second labels Andes Peak and Walnut Crest are v gd value.

Santa Inés ★★ Successful small family winery in Isla de MAIPO making ripe, blackcurranty Legado de Armida Cab Sauv. Also labelled as De Martino.

Santa Mónica ★★ Rancagua (RAPEL) winery; the best label is Tierra del Sol. Ries, Sém and Merlot under Santa Mónica label also gd.

Santa Rita, Viña ★★→★★★ Long est'd MAIPO bodega improving steadily. Range in ascending quality: 120, Reserva, Medalla Real, Casa Real. Best: Casa Real Maipo Cab S, but Medalla Real CASABLANCA Merlot and Chard, and Maipo Cab nearly as gd. Also promising experiments with Pinot N, Petite Sirah, Syrah.

Seña See Errázuriz.

Tarapacá, Viña ★★→★★★ Traditionally rather stolid, but well-equipped bodega; vastly improved (imput from Calif's Beringer). Millenium red blend: excellent.

Terra Mater ★★→★★★ Wines made by Australian David Morrison from sources throughout the Central Valley incl v gd Altum range. The v'yds used to belong to the CANEPA winery until a recent family feud.

Terra Noble ★★ Talca winery with oenologist from the Loire. Grassy Sauv and light, peppery Merlot are only wines.

Torreón de Paredes ★★→★★★ Attractive crisp Chard, age-worthy Res Cab from this modern RAPEL bodega.

Torres, Miguel ★★★ Curicó winery now back on form with fresh whites and gd reds esp sturdy Manso del Velasco single-v'yd Cab. See also Spain.

Undurraga ★★→★★★ Traditional MAIPO estate known for its (rather dilute) Pinot. Top wines: Reserva Chard, refreshing limey Gewürz; peachy Late Harvest Sém.

Valdivieso ★★→★★★ Known in Chile for sp wines. New Lontué winery. Major investments and new talent have led to impressive range, esp reds: Cab F, Merlot, Malbec, Pinot N, Cab S. Also eclectic but superb nv blend Caballo Loco.

Vascos, Los ★★ Lafite-Rothschild-SANTA RITA operation, but no Chilean first growth. Wines: fair but neglect Chile's lovely fruit flavours in favour of firm structures.

Veramonte ★★★ CASABLANCA-based operation of California winery Franciscan; whites from Casablanca fruit, red from Central Valley grapes all good.

Villard ★★★ French enterprize in CASABLANCA. Gd RAPEL reds, esp heady Merlot and Casablanca whites. Also v alluring Casablanca Pinot N.

Argentina

While Argentina grows Cab, Chard and friends, and with success, it is the refreshingly different array of quality grapes that currently makes it such an exciting wine country. The list is headed by the chunky Malbec and spicy Torrontés, and includes Syrah, Tempranillo and Italian grapes such as Sangiovese, Barbera and Bonarda. A warm, dry climate, watered by snow-melt from the Andes makes grape-growing relatively easy. Vineyard conditions are determined not as much by latitude as by altitude, with Salta, one of the most northerly regions, also being one of the coolest. Mendoza, with over 90 percent of the vineyards, is by far the most important province. But the search is on for cooler climates. Over-irrigation remains a problem, as does a reluctance to address hygiene problems in the 2,000 plus bodegas, and the vineyards have been compared with those of Eastern Europe. Fortunately, foreign influence from France, Spain and the US is increasing, and more and more top-flight wines are appearing with each vintage.

SOUTH AMERICA

Arizu, Leoncio ★★★ Makers of Luigi Bosca wines: Chard, Malbec, Cab, Syrah; small Mendoza (Maipu) bodega; all vg. Also promising Sauv, Pinot N and Ries.

Balbi, Bodegas ★→★★★ Allied-Domecq-owned San Raphael producer. Juicy Malbec, Chard, delicious Syrah rosé. Whites fair. Red blend Barbaro vg.

Bianchi, Bodegas ★→★★ Seagram-owned San Rafael producer, now country's third largest. Reserva Malbec, Elsa's V'yd Cab: among Argentina's best.

Bosca, L See Arizu.

Canale, Bodegas Humberto ★★ Premier Río Negro winery with v gd Sauv Bl and Pinot N and improving Merlot and Malbec.

Catena ★★→★★★ Dynamic Dr Nicolas Catena owns Bodegas Esmerelda which makes wines as Alamos Ridge (gd value Cab, Chard, Malbec), Catena (v gd Cab, Chard, Malbec) and Alta Catena (top Cab, Malbec, stunning Chard).

Esmerelda, Bodegas See CATENA.

Etchart ★★→★★★ Pernod-Ricard owned, two wineries in SALTA and MENDOZA. Fresh, spicy Torrontés from Cafayate in Salta, reds from both regions gd, topped by plummy Cafayate Cab S.

Fabre Montmayou ★★★ Promising French-owned Luján de Cujo (MENDOZA) bodega; fine reds and advice from Michel Rolland of B'dx. Also decent Chard.

Finca La Anita ★★★ Syrah, Malbec and Cuarto de Milla (Syrah-Malbec blend) are best wines from this MENDOZA boutique winery.

Finca Colomé ★★★ SALTA bodega managing to turn out very Rhône-like Cab-Merlot blend in primitive conditions.

Finca Flichman ★★ Old co: two wineries in Mendoza now owned by bank investing heavily. Varietal range topped by Private Res Cab S. Gd value Syrah.

Finca El Retiro ★★ MENDOZA bodega making gd reds under guidance of Alberto Antonini, former technical director at Antinori (cf Italy).

La Agrícola ★★ Large privately-owned MENDOZA estate producing gd value wines under the Picajuan Peak, Santa Julia and Viejo Surco labels.

Lagarde ★→★★ Revived old bodega now making gd reds, esp Syrah and whites. Viognier and Sauv Bl still need working on.

Lurton, Bodegas J & F ★★→★★★ MENDOZA joint venture between Jacques and François Lurton and Escorihuela Winery (part of CATENA group). Gd whites and reds, esp Chard, Gran Lurton Cab S and Bonarda. Also Corazon label.

M Chandon ★→★★★ Makers of Baron B and M Chandon sparklers under Moët & Chandon supervision; new promising Pinot N-Chard blend. Large range of labels for domestic market, much better export wines under Paul Galard label.

Marqués de Griñon ★★ Spanish producer. Impressive range: Malbec and Temp.

Mendoza Most important province for wine (over 70% of plantings). Best sub-regions: Agrelo, Tupungato, Luján de Cuyo and Maipú.

Morande, Viña ★★ Trans-Andean efforts by Chilean Pablo Morande (qv) under Vista Andes label look gd on first showing, esp Malbec and Syrah.

Navarro Correas ★★→★★★ Gd if s'times over-oaked reds, esp Col Privada Cab S. Also reasonable whites, inc v oaky Chard and Deutz-inspired fizz.

Nieto & Senetiner ★★★ Luján de Cuyo-based bodega. Good value wines under Valle de Vistalba label, plus recently introduced top-of-the-range Cadus reds.

Norton, Bodegas ★★★ Old bodega, now Austrian-owned. Good whites and v gd reds, esp chunky, fruity Malbec and Privada blend (Merlot-Cab S-Malbec).

Peñaflor ★→★★★ Argentina's biggest wine co, reputedly the world's third largest. Bulk wines for domestic market incl Andean V'yds, Fond de Cave (Chard, Cab) labels and for finer wines, TRAPICHE.

Rafael Estate ★★ MENDOZA estate where Hugh Ryman made good commercial range of 97s and 98s, notably Tempranillo and Malbec.

Río Negro Promising new area in Patagonia.

Rural, Bodegas La ★★→★★★ CATENA-inspired. Gd commercial modern wines. Best: Malbec, Merlot. Fair Chard. 2nd label Libertad less intense but still gd.

Salta Northerly province with the world's highest v'yds. Sub-region Cafayate renowned for Torrontés.

San Telmo ★★→★★★ Modern winery making fresh full-flavoured Chard, Chenin Bl, Merlot and esp Malbec and Cab Cruz de Piedra-Maipú.

Santa Ana, Bodegas ★→★★★ Old-est'd family firm at Guaymallen, MENDOZA now controlled by Chile's Santa Carolina. Wide range incl good Syrah, Merlot-Malbec, Pinot Gr 'blush' and sparkling (Chenin-Chard) Villeneuve.

Torino, Michel ★★→★★★ Rapidly improving (and organic) Cafayate enterprise with particularly gd Cab.

Trapiche ★★→★★★ Premium label of PENAFLOR aided by French consultant Michel Rolland. Best wines: Merlot, Malbec, Cab, Chard. Top-of-the-range Medalla is v gd, Oak Cask range good value.

Vistalba, Viña y Cava ★★→★★★ See Nieto & Senetiner.

Weinert, Bodegas ★★★ The Malbec, Cab and Cavas de Weinert blend (Cab-Merlot-Malbec) are among the best reds from Argentina.

Other Southern American wines

Brazil New plantings of better grapes are transforming a big and booming industry with an increasing home market. International investments, esp in Río Grande do Sul and Santana do Liuramento, esp from France (eg Moët & Chandon) and Italy (Martini & Rossi), are significant, and point to possible exports. The new sandy Frontera region (bordering Argentina and Uruguay) and Sierra Gaucha hills (Italian-style sp) are to watch. Exports are beginning. Equatorial v'yds (eg nr Recife) can have two crops a year – or even five in two years. Not a recommendation. Of the wines that do leave Brazil, 95% are made by the massive Vinicola Aurora (Bento Gonçalves). Look out for Amazon label.

Mexico Oldest American wine industry is reviving, with investment from abroad (eg Freixenet, Martell, Domecq) and California influence via UC-Davis. Best in Baja California (85% of total), Querétaro and on the Aguascalientes and Zacatecas plateaux. Top Baja C producers are L A Cetto (Valle de Guadaloupe, the largest, esp for Cab, Nebbiolo, Petite Sirah), Bodegas Santo Tomás (since 1888, Mexico's oldest), Monte Xanic (with Napa-award winning Cab), Bodegas San Antonio, and Cavas de Valmar. The premium Chard and Cab S from Monterrey-based Casa Madero are also good. Marqués de Aguayo is the oldest (1593), now only for brandy.

Peru Viña Tacama near Ica (top wine region) exports some promising wines, esp the Gran Vino Blanco white; also Cab S and classic-method sparkling. Chincha, Moquegua and Tacha regions are slowly making progress. But phylloxera is a serious problem.

Uruguay Argentina has the sturdy Malbec, Uruguay has the even more rugged and tannic Tannat (from SW France), which occupies around a third of vinifera plantings in the country. Some producers are learning to handle it in such a way as to enhance the rather rustic, plummy flavours, and blending with more supple varieties such as Merlot is becoming more common. Other fashionable grapes are being grown, and the 98 Sauvignon made by flying winemaker John Worontschak in conjunction with Bodegas Castillo Viejo is delicious. Five different viticultural regions were established in 1992: south (Montevideo, San José, Florida), southwest (Colonia), northwest (Paysandú, Salto and Artigas), northeast (Rivera-Tacuarembo) and central (Durazno). Wineries to look out for are Stagnari (Tannat, Gewürz), Castel Pujol (Tannat, Muséo 1752) and Juanicó (Tannat).

Australia

Heavier shaded areas are the wine growing regions

The influence of Australia in the modern wine world is out of all proportion to the size of its vineyards. They represent less than two percent of global production, yet Australian ideas and names are on all wine-lovers' lips. In 14 years, her exports have grown from 8 to 200 million litres and the number of wineries has climbed to over 1,100. Even growers in the south of France listen carefully to Australian winemakers. Australia has mastered easy-drinking wine and is making some of the world's very best.

Her long-term classics are Shiraz, Semillon and Riesling. In the seventies they were joined by Cabernet and Merlot, Chardonnay, Pinot Noir and other varieties. Then, in the nineties, Grenache and Mourvèdre were rediscovered. At the same time, cool fermentation and the use of new barrels accompanied a general move to cooler areas. For a while, excessive oak flavour was a common problem. It still happens, but moderation is now the fashion – and sparkling wine of startling quality is a new achievement.

The problem with Australian wines today is under-supply of red grapes and a looming surplus of Chardonnay. A massive planting programme is underway (75,000 acres) with the aim of doubling production and trebling exports. Coupled with this is the ongoing, exhaustive process of formally mapping Australia into zones, regions and sub-regions (all called geographic indications) with legislatively drawn borders. Value for money, though, is still high.

Wine regions

Adelaide Hills (SA) Spearheaded by PETALUMA: 21 wineries at v cool, 450-metre sites in the Mt Lofty ranges.

Barossa (SA) Australia's most important winery (though not v'yd) area; grapes from diverse sources (local, to MURRAY VALLEY; high-quality, cool regions: from adjacent hills, to COONAWARRA far S) make diverse wines. Local specialities: SHIRAZ, SEMILLON, GRENACHE, etc. 46 wineries.

Bendigo/Ballarat (Vic) Widespread small v'yds, some of vg quality, re-creating glories of the gold rush. 27 wineries incl BALGOWNIE, JASPER HILL, Heathcote.

Canberra District (ACT) 15 wineries now sell 'cellar door'. Quality is variable, as is style.

Central Ranges Zone (NSW) Encompasses MUDGEE, Orange and Cowra regions, expanding at breakneck pace in high altitude, moderately cool to warm climates. To south (in Southern NSW Zone) are Hilltops, CANBERRA DISTRICT and Tumbarumba, also growing rapidly.

Clare Valley (SA) Small, high-quality area 90 miles north of Adelaide, best for Riesling; also SHIRAZ and CABERNET. 31 wineries spill over into new subdistrict, Polish Hill River.

Coonawarra (SA) Southernmost and finest v'yd of state: most of Australia's best CAB, successful CHARD, RIES and SHIRAZ. Newer arrivals incl Balnaves, Majella, PARKER ESTATE, PENLEY ESTATE. 22 wineries.

Eden Valley (SA) Now formally separated from both the ADELAIDE HILLS and BAROSSA VALLEY; 9 wineries incl HENSCHKE and MOUNTADAM.

Geelong (Vic) Once-famous area destroyed by phylloxera, re-established mid-'60s. Very cool, dry climate: firm table wines from good-quality grapes. Names incl BANNOCKBURN, IDYLL, SCOTCHMAN'S HILL. 16 wineries.

Goulburn Valley (Vic) Very old (eg CH TAHBILK) and relatively new (eg MITCHELTON) wineries in temperate mid-Victoria region; full-bodied table wines. 15 wineries.

Grampians (Vic) Region previously known as Great Western. Temperate region in central W of state. High quality (esp sparkling). 8 wineries, 6 of relatively recent origin.

Granite Belt (Qld) High altitude, (relatively) cool region just N of NSW border; 21 wineries. Esp spicy SHIRAZ and rich SEM-CHARD.

Great Southern (WA) Remote cool area in S of state; GOUNDREY and PLANTAGENET are biggest wineries, from 31 in all.

Hunter Valley (NSW) Great name in NSW. Broad soft earthy SHIRAZ and SEM that live for 30 years. CABERNET not important; CHARD increasingly so. 90 wineries.

King Valley (Vic) Increasingly important alpine region producing 10,000 tonnes chiefly for purchasers outside the region, but now with 12 wineries of its own. High yields, moderate quality.

Limestone Coast Zone (SA) Important zone including COONAWARRA, PADTHAWAY and rapidly expanding Robe, Mount Benson, Wrattonbully and Bordertown regions of southeast South Australia.

Macedon and Sunbury (Vic) Two adjacent regions, Macedon at much higher elevation, Sunbury 10 minutes from Melbourne airport. 27 wineries incl CRAIGLEE, HANGING ROCK, VIRGIN HILLS.

Margaret River (WA) Temperate coastal area with superbly elegant wines 174 miles S of Perth. 51 operating wineries; others planned for Australia's most vibrant tourist wine region.

McLaren Vale (SA) Historic region on the southern outskirts of Adelaide. Big reds now rapidly improving; also vg CHARD. 52 wineries.

Mornington Peninsula (Vic) Exciting wines in new cool coastal area 25 miles S of Melbourne. 2,500 acres. 39 commercial wineries incl DROMANA, STONIERS.

Mudgee (NSW) Small isolated area 168 miles NW of Sydney. Big reds, full CHARDS; from 24 wineries.

Murray Valley (SA, Vic & NSW) Vast irrigated v'yds nr Mildara, Swan Hill (Vic and NSW), Berri, Loxton, Morgan, Renmark and Waikerie (S Aus). Principally making 'cask' table wines. 40 per cent of total Australian wine production

Ovens Valley (Vic) Similar topography and climate to KING VALLEY and similar use of grapes, all with notable exception of GIACONDA. 5 wineries.

Padthaway (SA) Large vineyard area developed as an over-spill of COONAWARRA. Cool climate; some good PINOT N is produced and excellent CHARDONNAY (esp LINDEMANS and HARDY'S), also Chard-Pinot N sparkling wines. 3 wineries.

Pemberton (WA) New and rapidly growing region between MARGARET RIVER and GREAT SOUTHERN; initial enthusiasm for PINOT N and CHARD replaced by MERLOT and SHIRAZ. 22 wineries have appeared overnight.

Perth Hills (WA) Fledgling area 19 miles E of Perth with 13 wineries and a larger number of growers on mild hillside sites.

Pyrenees (Vic) Central Vic region with 12 wineries: rich minty reds and some interesting whites, esp Fumé Bl.

Riverina (NSW) NV Large-volume irrigated zone centred around Griffith; gd-quality 'cask' wines (especially white), great sw botrytised SEM. 15 wineries.

Rutherglen and Glenrowan (Vic) Two of four regions in the Northeast Victorian Zone justly famous for weighty reds and magnificently sweet fortified dessert wines. 21 wineries.

Swan Valley (WA) The birthplace of wine in the west, on the N outskirts of Perth. Hot climate makes strong low-acid table wines but good dessert wines. Declining in importance viticulturally. 23 wineries.

Tasmania 50 vineyards now offering wine for commercial sale: over 700,000 litres in all. Great potential for CHARD, PINOT N and RIES grapes in cool climate.

Upper Hunter (NSW) Est'd in early '60s; irrigated vines (mainly whites), lighter and quicker-developing than Lower Hunter's. Often value. 10 wineries.

Yarra Valley Superb historic area nr Melbourne: 45 wineries. Growing emphasis on v successful PINOT NOIR and sparkling.

Grape varieties in Australia

The most important grape varieties grown in Australia are as follows:

Cabernet Sauvignon (95,000 tonnes) Grown in all of Australia's wine regions, best in COONAWARRA. Flavour ranges from herbaceous green pepper in coolest regions to blackcurrant and mulberry in Coonawarra, and dark chocolate and redcurrant in warmer areas such as MCLAREN VALE and BAROSSA. Used both on its own and blended with Merlot or more traditionally with SHIRAZ. Reaching 145,000 tonnes in 2001.

Chardonnay (165,000 tonnes) Has come from nowhere since '70. Best known for fast-developing buttery, peachy, s'times syrupy wines, but cooler regions such as PADTHAWAY, S Victoria and ADELAIDE HILLS can produce more elegant, tightly structured, age-worthy examples. Oak, too, is now less heavy-handed.

Chateau Reynella McL Vale ★★→★★★★ ('Vintage Port') **75' 77'** 82 87 88 Historic winery serving as HQ for BRL HARDY group. VG 'Basket-pressed' red table wines, superb vintage 'Port', now under Reynell label.

Chateau Tahbilk Goulburn Valley ★★→★★★ (Marsanne) **89 90 92' 93** 94 96 96 97' (Shiraz) **84'** 86 88 91' 92' 94 (Cab) 80 86' 88 90 92' 94 Beautiful historic family estate: reds for long ageing, also RIES and Marsanne. Reserve CAB outstanding; value for money ditto. Rare 1860 vines SHIRAZ, too.

Coldstream Hills Yarra Valley ★★★ (Chard) 88' **90 91 92' 94'** 96' 97' 98 (Pinot N) **91 92' 94'** 96' 97' 98 (Cab S) 88 **90 91'** 92' 93' 94' 97 Estate winery est'd '85 by wine critic James Halliday. Delicious PINOT N to drink young and Reserve to age lead Australia. Vg CHARD (esp Reserve wines), fruity CAB and Cab-Merlot and (from '97) Merlot. Acquired by SOUTHCORP in '96.

Conti, Paul Swan Valley ★→★★ One of the doyens of the SWAN VALLEY, s'times exceptionally elegant SHIRAZ and intensely grapey Frontignac.

Coriole McLaren Vale ★★→★★★ (Shiraz) **89 90'** 91 92 94' 95 96 To watch, especially for old-vine SHIRAZ Lloyd Reserve; best when nicely balanced by oak. Other wines are worthy.

Craiglee Macedon (Vic) ★★★ (Shiraz) **86' 88' 90' 91'** 92 93 94' 97' (98) Recreation of famous 19th-C estate: fragrant peppery SHIRAZ, CHARD.

Croser Adelaide Hills ★★★→★★★★★ 92 **93 94'** 95 Now Australia's top sparkling CHARD-PINOT N blend. Offshoot of PETALUMA with Bollinger as partner. Lean, fine, with splendid backbone from Pinot N.

Cullen Wines Margaret River ★★★ (Chard) **93' 94** 95' 96' (Cab S-Merlot) **90'** 91' 92 94' 95' 96 Mother-daughter team pioneered the region with strongly structured CAB-Merlot (Australia's best), substantial but subtle SAUV and bold CHARD: all real characters.

> **Australian wines to look for in early 2000s**
> **Brangayne of Orange** – Orange, New South Wales
> **Chain of Ponds** – Adelaide Hills, South Australia
> **Nepenthe** – Adelaide Hills, South Australia
> **Notley Gorge** – Tamar River, Northern Tasmania
> **Yering Station/Yarrabank** – Yarra Valley, Victoria

Dalwhinnie Pyrenees ★★→★★★ (Chard) **92' 93'** 95 96' 97 (Cab S) **86' 88** 90' 91' 92 93 94' 95' 96 4,500-case producer of concentrated rich CHARD, SHIRAZ and CAB S, arguably the best in PYRENEES.

d'Arenberg McLaren Vale ★★→★★★ Old firm with new lease of life; sumptuous SHIRAZ and GRENACHE, fine CHARD with a cascade of garrulous new labels.

De Bortoli Griffith (NSW) ★→★★★ (Noble Sem) 87' **90 91 92'** 93' 94'95 96 97 Irrigation-area winery. Standard reds and whites but magnificent sweet botrytised Sauternes-style Noble SEM. See also next entry.

De Bortoli Yarra Valley ★★→★★★ (Chard) **92' 93** 94' 96 97 98 (Cab S) **88 90 91** 92' 94' 95 97' (98') Formerly Chateau Yarrinya: bought by DE BORTOLI and now YARRA VALLEY's largest producer. Main label is more than adequate; second label Gulf Station and third label Windy Peak vg value.

Delatite Central Vic ★★★ (Ries) **90 92 93 94** 96 97 98 Winemaker Rosalind Ritchie makes appropriately willowy and feminine RIES, Gewürz, PINOT N and CAB from this v cool mountainside v'yd.

Devil's Lair Margaret River ★★→★★★ 100 acres of estate vineyards for opulently concentrated CHARD, PINOT N and CAB-MERLOT. Production is 10,000 cases annually. Acquired by SOUTHCORP early '97.

NB Vintages in colour are those you should choose first for drinking in 2000.

251

Diamond Valley Yarra Valley ★★→★★★ (Pinot) 92 94 96' 97 98 Outstanding PINOT N in significant quantities; other wines good, esp CHARD.

Domaine Chandon Yarra Valley ★★★ The showpiece of the YARRA VALLEY, leading Oz in fizz. Classic sparkling wine from grapes grown in all the cooler wine regions of Australia, with strong support from owner Moët & Chandon in France. Immediate success in UK under GREEN POINT label.

Drayton's Bellevue Hunter Valley ★★ ('Hermitage') Traditional 'Hermitage' and SEM, occasionally gd CHARD; recent quality improvements after a lapse.

Dromana Estate Mornington Peninsula ★★→★★★ (Chard) 92 94 97' 98' (Cab S-Merlot) 90 92 94 97' 98' Led energetically by Gary Crittenden: light fragrant CAB, PINOT, CHARD; sudden interest in Italian varieties (grown elsewhere).

Evans Family Hunter Valley ★★★ (Chard) 88 91 93 94 95' 96 97 98' Excellent CHARD from small vineyard owned by family of Len Evans. Fermented in new oak. Repays cellaring.

Elderton Barossa ★★ Old v'yds; flashy rich American-oaked CAB and SHIRAZ.

Evans and Tate Margaret River ★★★ (Sem) 92 93' 95' 96 (Cab) 88 91' 94' 95' 96 Fine elegant SEM, CHARD, CAB, Merlot from MARGARET RIVER, Redbrook. Going from strength to strength at 100,000 cases.

Freycinet Tasmania ★★→★★★ (Pinot N) 93' 94' 95 96' 98' East coast winery producing voluptuous rich PINOT N, good CHARD.

Geoff Merrill McLaren Vale ★→★★★ (Sem-Chard) 88' 91' 94' 95' (Cab) 90' 92 94' 95 Ebullient maker of Geoff Merrill, Mount Hurtle and Cockatoo Ridge wines. A questing enthusiast; his best wines are excellent, others unashamedly mass-market oriented. 50% owned by CH TAHBILK.

Giaconda Central Vic ★★★ (Chard) 88 90 91 92 93 94' 95 96' 97' (Pinot N) 89 91 92' 93' 96' 97' Very small ultra-fashionable winery near Beechworth: popular CHARDONNAY and PINOT N.

Goundrey Wines Great Southern (WA) ★★★ (Ries) 90 91 92 94' 95' 96 (Cab S) 88 89 90' 91' 94' 95 Recent expansion and quality upgrade. Now in top rank: esp good Res CAB, CHARD and SAUV BL.

Grant Burge Wines Barossa ★★→★★★ Solid output of silky-smooth reds and whites from the best grapes of Burge's large v'yd holdings. Burge was founder of KRONDORF. 70,000 cases.

Green Point See Domaine Chandon.

Grosset Clare ★★★→★★★★ (Ries) 88 90' 92 93' 94 95' 96' 97' 98' (Gaia) 86 90 91 92 93' 94' 95' 96 Fastidious winemaker: very elegant RIES, spectacular Gaia CAB-Merlot.

Hanging Rock Macedon (Vic) ★→★★★ (Shiraz) 87 88 90' 91' 92 93 94' Eclectic range: budget Picnic wines; huge Heathcote SHIRAZ; complex sparkling.

Hardy's McLaren Vale, Barossa, Keppoch etc ★→★★★★ (Eileen Chard) 92 93' 94 95 96' 97 98 ('Vintage Port') 45' 51' 54 56 69 71 73 75' 81' 87 88' Historic company using and blending wines from several areas. Best are Eileen Hardy and Thomas Hardy series and (Australia's greatest) 'Vintage Ports'. CHATEAU REYNELLA's beautifully restored buildings are now group headquarters. '92 merger with Berry-Renmano and public ownership (BRL HARDY) makes this Australia's second-largest wine co.

Heggies Adelaide Hills ★★ (Ries) 90' 91 92' 95 96 97 (Chard) 92' 93 94 96 Vineyard at 500 metres in eastern BAROSSA Ranges owned by S SMITH & SONS. The wines are separately marketed.

Henschke Barossa ★★★★ (Shiraz) 58' 60 61' 62 66 67' 68' 72 73 75 76 79 80' 81' 83 84' 86' 88' 90' 91' 92' 93' 96' (Cab S) 78 80 81 84 85 86 88 90' 91' 92 93' 94' 95 125-year-old family business, perhaps Australia's best, known for delectable SHIRAZ (especially Hill of Grace), vg CAB and red blends. New high-country Lenswood v'yds on ADELAIDE HILLS add excitement.

Hill-Smith Estate Adelaide Hills ★★→★★★ Another separate brand of s SMITH & SONS; CHARD, SAUV and CAB-SHIRAZ can be vg value.

Hillstowe Adelaide Hills ★★ Recent small winery using excellent fruit for intense vivid CHARD, PINOT N; also CAB-Merlot, SAUV BL.

Hollick Coonawarra ★★ (Chard) **92 93 94** 96 (Cab-Merlot) **86 90** 91' 92' 93 96' Gd CHARD, RIES; much-followed reds, esp Ravenswood. Terra is trendy second label.

Houghton Swan Valley ★→★★★ (Supreme) **84 86 87 89' 91' 93'** 94 95 96 97 The most famous old winery of WA. Soft ripe Supreme is top wine; a national classic. Also excellent CAB, Verdelho, etc. See Hardy's.

Howard Park Mount Barker ★★★ (Ries) **86' 88'** 90' 91 93 94' **95'** 96 97' (Cab S) **86 88** (89) 90' 91 92' 93 94' 95' John Wade (formerly of WYNNS, hand-crafts tiny quantities of scented RIES, CHARD and spicy CAB S. Major winery expansion is underway with flourishing contract-winemaking business for others. Second label: Madfish Bay.

Huntington Estate Mudgee ★★★ (Cab S) **81 83 84 86** 89 **91' 93** 94 95' 96 Small winery; the best in MUDGEE. Fine CAB, vg SHIRAZ. Invariably underpriced.

Idyll Geelong ★→★★ Small winery making Gewürz and CAB in v individual style. A pioneer exporter.

Jasper Hill Bendigo ★★★→★★★★★ (Shiraz) 83' **85' 86'** 90' 91' 92' 94' 96' 97' Emily's Paddock SHIRAZ-Cab F blend and George's Paddock Shiraz from dry land estate are intense, long-lived and much admired. BENDIGO's best.

Jim Barry Clare ★→★★★ Some great v'yds provide good RIES, McCrae Wood SHIRAZ and convincing Grange pretender The Armagh.

Katnook Estate Coonawarra ★★★ (Chard) 86 **90 92' 94' 96'** 97 (Cab S) **85 86 90'** 91' 92 93 94 Excellent and pricey CAB and CHARD; also SAUV.

Knappstein Wines Clare ★★★ Reliable RIESLING, Fumé Blanc, CAB-Merlot and Cab Franc wines. Owned by PETALUMA.

Krondorf Wines Barossa ★★ Part of MILDARA-BLASS group with niche market brands: Show Reserve wines are best, esp CHARD. Fairly dull, though.

Lake's Folly Hunter Valley ★★★★ (Chard) **86 89 91** 92' 93' 94 95 96' **96** 98 (Cab S) **69 72 75 78 81' 85 87** 88 91' **91'** 92 93' 94 95 Small family winery of Max Lake, the pioneer of HUNTER CAB. Cab is v fine, complex. CHARD exciting and age-worthy.

Lark Hill Canberra District ★★ Most consistent CANBERRA producer, making esp attractive RIES, pleasant CHARD and surprising PINOT.

Leasingham Clare ★→★★★ Important medium-sized quality winery bought by HARDY's in '87. Good RIES, SEM, CHARD and CAB-Malbec. Various labels.

Leconfield Coonawarra ★★→★★★ (Cab S) **80 82 84 88** 90' 91' 92' 93' 94 COONAWARRA SHIRAZ and CAB of great style. CHARD not as good.

Leeuwin Estate Margaret River ★★★★ (Chard) **82' 83' 85' 86** 87' **89** 90 91 92' **95'** 96 (Cab) **81 82 84 85** 87 88 89 90 91 92 93 94 Leading W Australia estate, lavishly equipped. Superb (and v expensive) CHARD; vg RIES, SAUV and CAB.

Lenswood Vineyards ★★★ Estate now sole occupation of Tim KNAPPSTEIN making subtle SAUV BL and powerful CHARD, PINOT N.

Lindemans originally Hunter Valley, now everywhere ★→★★★ (Hunter Sem) **66 67' 70' 72 75 79'** 86' **87'** 91 92 94 96 98' (Hunter Shiraz) **59' 65' 66' 70 73 75** 79 82 83 86 87 91' **94** 96 97' (Padthaway Chard) **85 88 90** 91 92 93 **94'** 95 96' 97' (Coonawarra Red) **82 86'** 90' 91' **92** 94 96 One of the oldest firms, now a giant owned by PENFOLDS. Owns BURING (BAROSSA), ROUGE HOMME (COONAWARRA), and important v'yds at PADTHAWAY. Vg CHARD and Coonawarra reds (eg Limestone Ridge, Pyrus). Pioneer of new styles, yet still makes fat, old-style 'Hunters'. Bin-number Classics can be vg.

McWilliam's Hunter Valley and Riverina ★→★★★ (Elizabeth Sem) **79'** 80 **81 82 84'** 86' 87' 88 **89 91' 92** 93' 94 (96) (98') Famous family of HUNTER VALLEY winemakers at Mount Pleasant: SHIRAZ and SEM. McWilliam's is also a pioneer in RIVERINA with CAB S and sweet white Lexia. Recent show results demonstrate high standards. 'Elizabeth' (sold at 6 yrs) and 'Lovedale' (10 yrs) Sems are now Australia's best. Honest RIVERINA wines at low prices.

Mildara Coonawarra and Murray Valley ★→★★★ (Coonawarra Cab) 63' **64 80' 82 85 86' 88 90'** 91' 93 94 96' 'Sherry' and brandy specialists at Mildara on the MURRAY RIVER, also make fine CAB S and RIESLING at COONAWARRA. Now has BAILEY'S, BALGOWNIE, BLASS, KRONDORF, ROTHBURY, SALTRAM and YELLOWGLEN, too, all acquired in '96 by Fosters Brewing Group.

Miramar Mudgee ★★ Some of MUDGEE's best white wines, especially CHARD; long-lived CAB and SHIRAZ.

Mitchells Clare ★★★ (Ries) 78' **84' 86 90'** 92 93 **94'** 95 96 97 (Cab S) **80' 82 84 86'** 90' 92' 93 94 96 Small family winery for excellent CAB and v stylish dry RIES.

Mitchelton Goulburn Valley ★★→★★★ Substantial winery, acquired by PETALUMA in '92. A wide range incl a vg wood-matured Marsanne, SHIRAZ; classic Blackwood Park RIES from GOULBURN VALLEY is one of Australia's v best-value wines. Many enterprising blends and labels.

Montrose Mudgee ★★ Reliable underrated producer of CHARD and CAB blends. Now part of the ORLANDO group.

Moondah Brook Estate Gingin (WA) ★★ HOUGHTON v'yd 80km NW of Perth: v smooth flavourful CHARD, Chenin Bl, Verdelho and CAB.

Moorilla Estate Tasmania ★★★ (Ries) **88 89 90** 91 93 94' **95'** 97 98' Senior winery on outskirts of Hobart on Derwent River: vg RIESLING (**94'** superb), Traminer and CHARD; PINOT N now in the ascendant.

Morris NE Vic ★★→★★★★ Old winery at Rutherglen for Australia's greatest dessert Muscats and 'TOKAYS'; also recently vg low-price table wine.

Moss Wood Margaret River ★★★★ (Sem) **83' 86' 87' 91 92'** 94' 95' 96 (Chard) **89 90 92** 93 95' 96 (Cab S) **77' 80' 83 86** 87 90 91 92 93 94' 95' 96 To many, the best MARGARET RIVER winery (only 29 v'yd acres). SEM, CAB, PINOT N and CHARD, all with rich fruit flavours, not unlike some of the top California wines.

Mount Hurtle See Geoff Merrill.

Mount Langi Ghiran Grampians ★★★ (Shiraz) **86 88 90'** 91' 92' 93 94' 95 96' Esp for superb rich peppery Rhône-like SHIRAZ, one of Australia's best cool-climate versions.

Mount Mary Yarra Valley ★★★★ (Pinot N) **83 85 86 89 90 91' 92'** 94' 95 96' 97 (Cab S-Cab F-Merlot) **79 80 82 84' 85 86' 88'** 90' 91' 92' 94 (97) Dr John Middleton is a perfectionist making tiny amounts of suave CHARD, vivid PINOT N, and (best of all) CAB S-Cab F-Merlot. All will age impeccably.

Mountadam Barossa ★★★ (Chard) **89 90 91 92** 93 94 96' High EDEN VALLEY winery of Adam Wynn. CHARD is rich, voluptuous and long. Other labels include David Wynn, Eden Ridge.

Nepenthe Adelaide Hills First winery to be built here for 10 yrs (since PETALUMA); severe restrictions apply in water-catchment zone. State-of-the-art kit, excellent v'yds, skilled winemaking: sophisticated wines esp SAUV, CHARD, SEM.

Normans McLaren Vale ★→★★★ Public listing in late '94 lifted the profile of this winery, but premium Chais Clarendon has always been excellent.

Notley Gorge N Tasmania Newly opened spectacularly sited winery/ restaurant complex by Tamar river. Wines incl CHARD, PINOT N and CAB-Merlot.

Orlando (Gramp's) Barossa ★★→★★★ (St Hugo Cab) **80 86 88 90** 91' 92 94 96' Great pioneering company, bought by management in '88 but now owned by Pernod-Ricard. Full range from huge-selling Jacob's Creek 'Claret' to excellent Jacaranda Ridge CAB S from COONAWARRA. See Wyndham Estate.

Paringa Estate Mornington Peninsula ★★★ Maker of quite spectacular CHARD, PINOT N and (late-picked) SHIRAZ winning innumerable trophies with tiny output of 2,000 cases.

Parker Estate Coonawarra ★★★ Young estate making v good CAB, esp Terra Rossa First Growth.

Penfolds orig Adelaide, now everywhere ★★→★★★★ (Grange) **52' 53' 55' 62 63' 66' 67 71' 75 76** 80 **82** 83 **85 86'** 88' 90' 91' 92 93 (Bin 707) **64 65 66' 78 80 83 84 86' 88** 90' 91' 92' 93 94' 96' (Bin 389) 66 **70 71 82 83** 86' **87 88' 90'** 91' 92 93 94' 96' Ubiquitous and excellent: in BAROSSA VALLEY, CLARE, COONAWARRA, RIVERINA, etc. Consistently Australia's best red wine company. Bought LINDEMANS in '90. Its Grange (was called 'Hermitage') is deservedly ★★★★. P's Yattarna CHARD, the long-awaited 'White Grange', released April '98. Bin 707 CABERNET not far behind. Other bin-numbered wines (eg Cab-SHIRAZ 389, Kalimna Bin 28 Shiraz) can be outstanding, though prices are rising. Grandfather 'Port' is often excellent. The Penfolds/Lindemans group was taken over by SOUTHCORP, already owner of SEPPELT, in '90.

Where to drink wine in Australia

One of the great advances of the past decade have been the evolution of serious wine-by-the-glass programs by restaurants, picking up on the trail-blazing work done by places such as Willi's Wine Bar in Paris. A list of restaurants with specially extensive or innovative lists follows.

Melbourne France-Soir has Australia's finest wine list, while Walter's Wine Bar was one of the first to take its cue from Willi's. Foodier places incl Blake's, Charcoal Grill on the Hill, Est Est Est, Jacques Reymond, Stella and Mask of China – all among the best.

Sydney Belmondo, Bistro Moncur, Cicada, Darling Mills, Forty One Restaurant (great views of the harbour) and the Bathers Pavillion (on the harbour shoreline).

Brisbane The Grape Food and Wine Bar is the first choice, but La Fontaine, Marco Polo and (on coast s of Brisbane) Tables of Toowong.

Adelaide boasts Michael Hill-Smith's MW's Universal Wine Bar, not only an Adelaide institution, but a national one. Chesser Cellars, Grange Restaurant with Cheong Liew (in the Hilton Hotel) and Chloe's Restaurant are all outstanding.

Perth Dear Friends at the Hyatt Hotel complex is simply great, as good as the east coast can offer; Alto's, Stephenie's (sic spelling), No 44 King Street and San Lorenzo Restaurant are all excellent.

Penley Estate Coonawarra ★★★ High-profile, no-expense-spared new-comer winery: rich, textured, fruit-and-oak CAB; also SHIRAZ-Cab blend and CHARD.

Petaluma Adelaide Hills ★★★★ (Ries) **79 80' 82 84 86' 88 90'** 91 93 94' 95' **96 97'** (Chard) **77 86 87 90'** 93 94 **95' 96'** (Cab S) **79 86' 88' 90'** 91 92' 93' 94 A rocket-like '80s success with COONAWARRA CAB, ADELAIDE HILLS CHARD, CLARE VALLEY RIES, all processed at winery in Adelaide Hills. Red wines have become richer from '88 on. New Tiers CHARD challenges PENFOLDS' Yattarna and LEEUWIN ESTATE. Also: BRIDGEWATER MILL. Now owns KNAPPSTEIN and MITCHELTON. See also Croser.

Peter Lehmann Wines Barossa ★★→★★★ Defender of BAROSSA faith, Peter Lehmann makes vast quantities of wine, with v fine 'special cuvées' under own label; now publicly listed and flourishing. NB Stonewell SHIRAZ (tastes of blackberries and rum) and dry RIES.

AUSTRALIA

Pierro Margaret River ★★★ (Chard) **90 91'** 93' **94** 95' 96 Highly rated maker of expensive, tangy SEM, SAUV BL and vg barrel-fermented CHARD.

Piper's Brook Tasmania ★★★ (Ries) **79' 82' 84' 85' 89** 91 **92'** 93' 94 96 97' 98' (Chard) **84 86 88** 91' 92' 93 94' 97' 98' Cool-area pioneer; vg RIES, PINOT N, excellent CHARD from Tamar Valley. Lovely labels. Second label: Ninth Island. Acquired HEEMSKERK, Rochecombe '98; now controls 35% of Tasmanian wine industry.

Plantagenet Mount Barker ★★★ (Chard) **90' 92 94'** 95 96 97 (Shiraz) **86 88 90' 91'** 92 94' (Cab S) **85' 86' 88** 90' 93 94 95' The region's elder statesman: wide range of varieties, especially rich CHARD, SHIRAZ and vibrant potent CAB S.

Primo Estate Adelaide Plains ★★★ Joe Grilli is a miracle-worker given the climate; successes incl vg botrytised RIES, tangy Colombard, potent Joseph CAB-Merlot (aka Moda Amarone).

Redman Coonawarra ★→★★ (Cab S) **69' 70 72 71 87 90' 91'** 92 93' 94' 96 The most famous old name in COONAWARRA; red wine specialist: SHIRAZ, CAB S, Cab-Merlot. Quality slowly reviving after a disappointing period.

Renmano Murray Valley ★→★★ Enormous coop now part of BRL Hardy (see Hardy's). 'Chairman's Selection' CHARD offers value.

Reynold's Yarraman Estate Upper Hunter ★★ Former stone prison building to watch: winery of ex-HOUGHTON/WYNDHAM winemaker Jon Reynolds.

Rockford Barossa ★★→★★★★ Small producer, wide range of thoroughly individual wines, often made from v old, low-yielding v'yds; reds best. Sparkling Black SHIRAZ has super-cult status.

Rosemount Upper Hunter, McLaren Vale, Coonawarra ★★→★★★ Rich and unctuous HUNTER 'Show' CHARD is international smash. This, MCLAREN VALE Balmoral Syrah, MUDGEE Mountain Blue CAB-SHIRAZ and COONAWARRA Cab lead the wide range, which gets better every year.

Rothbury Estate Hunter Valley ★★ Fell prey to Fosters/MILDARA in '96 after long bitter fight by original founder Len Evans (since departed). Has made long-lived SEM and SHIRAZ and rich, buttery, early-drinking COWRA CHARD to good effect. Old Evans fans should see Evans Family (above).

Rouge Homme Coonawarra ★★ (Shiraz-Cab S) **80 81 85 86' 90' 91'** 92 94' 96' Separately branded and promoted arm of LINDEMANS with keenly priced CHARD and SHIRAZ-CAB leaders.

Rymill Coonawarra ★★ Descendants of John Riddoch carrying on the gd work of the founder of COONAWARRA. Strong dense SHIRAZ and CAB esp noteworthy.

St Hallett Barossa ★★★ (Old Block) **83 84' 86 88 90' 91' 92'** 93 94 96 Rejuvenated winery. 60⁺-yr-old vines give splendid Old Block SHIRAZ. Rest of range (eg CHARD, SAUV-SEM) is smooth and stylish.

St Huberts Yarra Valley ★★→★★★ (Chard) **92' 93 94'** 96 97' (Cab) **77' 86 88** 90 91' 92 94 97' Acquired by ROTHBURY in late '92; accent on fine dry CHARD and smooth berryish CAB. Now part of Fosters/MILDARA.

St Sheila's SA p sw sp **36 22 38** Full-bodied fizzer. Ripper grog.

Saltram Barossa (Merged with ROTHBURY in '94.) Mamre Brook (SHIRAZ, CAB, CHARD) and No 1 Shiraz are leaders. Metala is assoc Stonyfell label for old-style Langhorne Creek Cab-Shiraz.

Sandalford Swan Valley ★→★★ Fine old winery with contrasting styles of red and white single-grape wines from SWAN and MARGARET RIVER areas.

Scotchman's Hill Geelong ★★ Newcomer making significant quantities of stylish PINOT N and good CHARD at modest prices.

To decipher codes, please refer to 'Key to symbols' on front flap of jacket, or to 'How to use this book' on page 6.

Seaview McLaren Vale ★★→★★★ Old winery now owned by SOUTHCORP. CHARD, SHIRAZ-CABERNET and single-grape CAB S frequently rise above their station in life, while the sparkling wines are among Australia's best – now based on PINOT N and Chard. Premium label: Edwards & Chaffey.

Seppelt Barossa, Grampians, Padthaway etc ★★★ (Shiraz) 71' **85' 86'** 90 91' 92 93' 94 (Salinger) **88 90 91 92** 93' Far-flung producers of Australia's most popular sparkling (Great Western Brut); also new range of Victoria-sourced table wines. Top sparkling is highly regarded 'Salinger'. Another part of SOUTHCORP, Australia's biggest wine company.

Sevenhill Clare ★★ Owned by the Jesuitical Manresa Society since 1851; consistently good wine; reds (esp SHIRAZ) can be outstanding.

Seville Estate Yarra Valley ★★★ (Chard) 91 92 94' 97' (Shiraz) 85 86 88 90 91 92 93 94 97' Tiny winery acquired by BROKENWOOD '97; CHARD, SHIRAZ, PINOT N, CAB.

Shaw & Smith McLaren Vale ★★★ Trendy young venture of flying winemaker Martin Shaw and Australia's first MW, Michael Hill-Smith. Crisp SAUV, vg unoaked CHARD, complex barrel-fermented Reserve Chard are the 3 wines.

Southcorp The giant of the industry, despite its naff name: owns PENFOLDS, LINDEMANS, SEPPELT, SEAVIEW, WYNNS, etc, etc (17 in all!).

S Smith & Sons (alias Yalumba) Barossa ★★→★★★ Big old family firm with considerable verve. Full spectrum of high-quality wines, incl HILL-SMITH ESTATE. HEGGIES and YALUMBA Signature Reserve are best. Angas Brut, a good-value sparkling wine, and Oxford Landing CHARD are now world brands.

Stafford Ridge Adelaide Hills ★★→★★★ 20-acre estate of former HARDY'S winemaker Geoff Weaver, at Lenswood. V fine SAUV, CHARD, RIES and CAB-Merlot blend. Marvellous new label design.

Stoniers Mornington Peninsula ★★★ (Chard) 92 93' 94' 95 97 98' (Pinot) **91' 92 93' 94 95'** 97' Has overtaken DROMANA ESTATE for pride of place on the Peninsula. CHARD, PINOT are consistently vg; Reserves outstanding. 70% owned by PETALUMA since '88.

Taltarni Grampians/Avoca ★★→★★★ (Shiraz) 79 82 84 86 **88** 89 90 91 92 94 96 (Cab S) **79 81 82 84 86** 88 89 90 91 92 94 Huge but balanced reds for long ageing; good SAUV and adequate sparkling.

Tarrawarra Yarra Valley ★★★ (Chard) 91' 92 93 94' 95 97 (Pinot N) **88' 91 92 94'** 96' 97' Multimillion-dollar investment with limited quantities of idiosyncratic expensive CHARD and robust long-lived PINOT N. Tunnel Hill is the second label.

Taylors Wines Clare ★→★★ Large inexpensive range of table wines seeking to improve.

'Tokay' Speciality of northeast Victoria. An aged intense sweet fortified Muscadelle wine; less aromatic than Muscat but at best superb. Under EU rules the Hungarian name will have to go.

Tollana Barossa ★★→★★★ Old company once famous for brandy. Has latterly made some fine CABS, CHARD and RIES. Acquired by PENFOLDS in '87.

Tulloch Hunter Valley ★→★★★ Old name at Pokolbin with reputation for dry red wines, CHARDONNAY and Verdelho. Now part of the SOUTHCORP group but a shadow of its former self.

Tyrrell Hunter Valley ★★★ (Sem Vat 1) 75 76 77' **79 86' 87' 89'** 90 91' 92' **93 94** 96' 97' (Chard Vat 47) **79' 82 84' 85 89** 90 92' 94' 95' 96 97 (Shiraz Vats) **73 75 77 79 80 81' 83 85** 87' **89'** 91' 93 94' 96 97' Some of the v best traditional HUNTER VALLEY wines, SHIRAZ and SEM. Pioneered CHARD with big rich Vat 47 – still a classic. Also PINOT N.

Vasse Felix Margaret River ★★★ (Cab S) **79 83 85** 88 89 91 92 95' 96 With CULLEN, pioneer of the MARGARET RIVER. Elegant CAB, notable for mid-weight balance. Major expansion underway. Second label: Forest Hills (esp RIES, CHARD).

Virgin Hills Bendigo/Ballarat ★★★★ **73' 74' 76' 81' 82' 84'** 88' 91' 92' 95 97' Tiny supplies of one red (a CABERNET-SHIRAZ-Malbec blend) of legendary style and balance. Acquired late '98 by new-listed co Vincorp.

Wendouree Clare ★★★★ 78 **79 83** 86 89' 90' 91' 92' 93 94 96' Treasured maker (in tiny quantities) of some of Australia's most powerful and concentrated reds based on SHIRAZ, CAB S, MOURVEDRE and Malbec; immensely long-lived.

Westfield Swan Valley ★→★★ John Kosovich's CAB, CHARD and Verdelho show particular finesse for a hot climate, but he is now developing a new v'yd in the much cooler PEMBERTON region.

Wignalls Great Southern (WA) ★★→★★★ In the far southwest corner of Australia (near Albany), Bill Wignall makes sometimes ethereal, always stylish PINOT NOIR.

Wirra Wirra McLaren Vale ★★★ (Chard) **90 91 92 93** 96 97 (Cab S) **87' 90' 91'** 92' 94'95 96' High-quality, beautifully-packaged wines making a big impact. Angelus is superb top-of-the-range CAB, ditto RSW SHIRAZ. Dr Tony Jordan (ex DOMAINE CHANDON) is new managing director – watch this space.

Woodleys Barossa ★ Well-known for low-price 'Queen Adelaide'.

Woodstock McLaren Vale ★★ Ever-reliable maker of chunky, highly flavoured reds in regional style and luscious botrytis wines from esoteric varieties. 20,000 cases.

Wyndham Estate Mudgee (NSW) ★→★★ Aggressive large HUNTER and MUDGEE group with brands: Craigmoor, Hunter Estate, MONTROSE, Richmond Grove and Saxonvale. Acquired by ORLANDO in '90.

Wynns Coonawarra ★★★ (Shiraz) **53' 54' 55' 63 65 82 85** 86' 88 **90' 91'** 92 93 94' 95 96' (Cab S) **57' 58' 59' 60 62 82' 85** 86' **88 90'** 91' 92 93 94' 96' SOUTHCORP-owned COONAWARRA classic. RIES, CHARD, SHIRAZ and CAB are all very good, esp John Riddoch Cab, and Michael 'Hermitage'.

Yalumba See S Smith & Sons.

Yarra Burn Yarra Valley ★★→★★★ Estate making SEM, SAUV, CHARD, sparkling PINOT, Pinot N, CAB; acquired by BRL HARDY in '95, with changes now under way. Bastard Hill Chard and Pinot N legitimate flag-bearers.

Yarra Ridge Yarra Valley ★★→★★★ Expanding young (70,000-case) winery, v successful CHARD, CAB, SAUV BL, PINOT N, all with flavour and finesse at relatively modest prices. Now fully owned by MILDARA BLASS.

Yarra Yering Yarra Valley ★★★→★★★★ (Dry Reds) 78 79 80' **81' 82' 83 84 85 90' 91** 92' 93' 94' 95 97' Best-known Lilydale boutique winery. Esp racy powerful PINOT N, deep herby CAB (Dry Red No 1) and SHIRAZ (Dry Red No 2). Luscious daring flavours in red and white. Also fortified port-sorts from the correct grapes.

Yellowglen Bendigo/Ballarat ★★→★★★ High-flying sparkling winemaker owned by MILDARA-BLASS. Recent improvement in quality, with top-end brands like Vintage Brut, Cuvée Victoria and 'Y'.

Yeringberg Yarra Valley ★★★ (Marsanne) **90 91'** 92 93 94' 95 97' 98 (Cab) **74' 75 76 79 80' 81' 82** 84 86 87 88' 90' 91' 92 94' 97' Dreamlike historic estate still in the hands of the founding family, now again producing v high-quality Marsanne, Roussanne, CHARD, CAB and PINOT N, in minute quantities.

Yering Station/Yarrabank Yarra Valley On site of Victoria's first v'yd; replanted after 80 yr gap. Extraordinary joint venture: Yering Station table wines (Reserve CHARD, PINOT N, SHIRAZ); Yarrabank (esp fine sp wines for Champagne Devaux).

Zema Estate Coonawarra ★★→★★★ One of last bastions of hand-pruning and -picking in COONAWARRA; silkily powerful, disarmingly straightforward reds.

For key to grape variety abbreviations, see pages 7–13.

New Zealand

Heavier shaded areas are
the wine growing regions

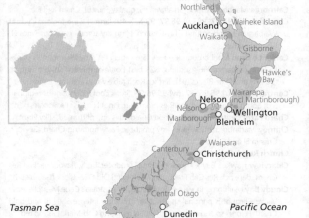

Northland

Auckland ○   Waiheke Island
Waikato

Gisborne

Hawke's
Bay

Wairarapa
Nelson **○** (incl Martinborough)
Nelson ○ ○**Wellington**
Marlborough **Blenheim**

Waipara
Canterbury ○**Christchurch**

Tasman Sea

Central Otago
○**Dunedin** *Pacific Ocean*

Since the mid-1980s, New Zealand has made a worldwide name for wines (mainly white) of startling quality, well able to compete with those of Australia or California, or indeed France. In 1982 it exported 12,000 cases; in 1998, almost 1.7 million. There are now over 22,000 vineyard acres.

White grapes prevail. The most extensively planted are: Chardonnay, Sauvignon Blanc (these two cover over half of the national vineyard), Pinot Noir, Cabernet Sauvignon, Merlot (soon to overtake Cabernet), Riesling and Müller-Thurgau.

Intensity of fruit and crisp acidity are the hallmarks of New Zealand. Nowhere can match Marlborough Sauvignon for pungency. Chardonnay has shone throughout the country, but Riesling's stronghold is the South Island. Marlborough has also proved its worth with excellent fizz. The relatively warm Hawke's Bay and Auckland regions are now succeeding with Cabernet and Merlot-based reds, but Pinot Noir thrives in the cooler climates of Martinborough and the South Island. The principal regions and producers follow.

Allan Scott Marlborough ★★ Attract Ries, Chard and Sauv Bl.

Ata Rangi Martinborough ★★★ V small but highly respected winery. Outstanding Pinot N and Chard; also gd Cab-Merlot-Syrah blend (Célèbre).

Auckland (r) **91 93 94 97'** (w) **96 97'** Largest city in NZ. Location of head offices of major wineries. Some of NZ's top Cab-based reds. Incl Henderson, Huapai, Kumeu and Waiheke Island districts.

Babich Henderson (Auckland) ★★ →★★★ Med-sized family firm, est'd 1916; quality, value. AUCK, H BAY and MARLB v'yds. Rare premium wines: The Patriarch. Fine Irongate Chard, Cab-Merlot (single v'yd). Mara Estate varietals: value.

Black Ridge (Central Otago) ★→★★ World's southernmost winery. Noted for rich, soft Pinot N, also gd Chard, Ries and Gewurz.

Brancott Vineyards ★★→★★★ Brand used by MONTANA in US market.

Brookfields Hawke's Bay ★★→★★★ One of region's top v'yds: outstanding 'gold label' Cab-Merlot and Reserve Chard, gd Sauv Bl.

Cairnbrae Marlborough ★★ Small winery; quality Sauv Bl, Chard and Ries.

Canterbury (r) 95 97' 98 (w) 96 97' 98 NZ's 4th-largest wine region; v'yds at Waipara in N and around Christchurch. Long dry summers favour Pinot N, Chard and Ries.

Cellier Le Brun Marlborough ★→★★★ Sm winery est'd by Champenois Daniel Le Brun (departed '96): some of NZ's best bottle-fermented sp, esp vintage (90' 91) and Bl de Blancs (91). Terrace Road table wines less impressive.

Central Otago (r) 95 96' 97' (w) 95 96 97' Small cool mountainous region in S of South Island. Chard and Ries promising, Pinot N rivals M'BOROUGH's best.

Chard Farm Central Otago ★★ Good Chard, Ries and perfumed, silky Pinot N.

Chifney Martinborough ★→★★ Tiny producer. Fast-improving Chard, Gewürz, Chenin Bl and Cab S.

Church Road See McDonald Winery.

Clearview Hawke's Bay ★★→★★★ V small producer. Burly, flavour-packed Res Chard, dark rich Res Cab Franc, Res Merlot and Old Olive Block (Cab blend).

Cloudy Bay Marlborough ★★★★ Founded by W Australia's Cape Mentelle; now Veuve Clicquot is principal shareholder. Thrillingly intense Sauv Bl and bold Chard. Pelorus sp also impressive. Pinot N replacing Cab-Merlot as top red.

A choice from New Zealand for 2000

Cabernet-Merlot blends Te Mata Coleraine (91), Goldwater (93), Stoneyridge Larose (93)

Pinot Noir Ata Rangi (96), Martinborough Vineyard Reserve (94), Dry River (96), Felton Road Block 3 (97)

Chardonnay Clearview (96), Neudorf Moutere (97), Babich The Patriarch (96), Isabel Estate (97)

Sauvignon Blanc Grove Mill (98), Hunter's (98), Villa Maria Reserve (98)

Riesling Stoneleigh (96), Pegasus Bay (95), Dry River (97)

Bottle-fermented sparkling wines Deutz Marlborough Cuvée NV, Pelorus (94), Domaine Chandon Marlborough Brut (94)

Sweet wines Villa Maria Reserve Noble Riesling (96), Ngatarawa Glazebrook Noble Harvest (96), Shingle Peak Botrytised Riesling (97)

Collard Brothers Henderson (Auckland) ★★→★★★ Long-est'd sm family winery. Whites esp Rothesay V'yd Chard and Sauv Bl, H BAY Chenin Bl, MARLB Ries.

Cooks Hawke's Bay ★→★★ Lge firm merged with McWilliams (NZ) in '84 and absorbed by CORBANS in '87. Now principally an export brand. Good HAWKE'S BAY Chard and Cab S: Winemakers Res label.

Coopers Creek Huapai (Auckland) ★★→★★★ Medium-sized producer, highly successful in NZ competitions, but recently involved in mis-labelling scandal affecting '95 and '96 vintages. Excellent Swamp Res Chard, H BAY Ries and MARLB Sauv Bl.

Corbans Henderson (Auckland) ★→★★★ Est'd 1902, now NZ's 2nd-largest wine company. Key brands: Corbans (top wines: Cottage Block); next: Private Bin; Huntaway Res, COOKS, Stoneleigh (MARLB), Longridge (H BAY), Robard & Butler. Top GISBORNE Chards, South Island Ries and sp wines can be superb.

Cross Roads Hawke's Bay ★★ Sm winery. Satisfying Chard, Ries, Cab S, Pinot N.

De Redcliffe Waikato (S of Auckland) ★→★★ Small Japanese-owned winery; 'Hotel du Vin' attached. Good Chard, Sém blends, Ries and Sauv Bl, plain reds.

Delegat's Henderson (Auckland) ★★→★★★ Med-sized family winery. V'yds at H BAY and MARLB. Proprietor's Reserve label recently dropped; now replaced by less oaky Chard, Merlot and Cab S under new Reserve label. Oyster Bay brand: deep flavoured Marlb Chard and Sauv Bl.

Deutz Auckland ★★★ Champagne firm gives name and technical aid to fine sp wines produced in MARLB by MONTANA. NV: lively, yeasty and flinty; vintage Bl de Blancs: rich and creamy.

Domaine Chandon (Blenheim) ★★★ One of NZ's most intense and refined sp wines made at MARLB winery by Oz subsidiary of Moët et Chandon.

Dry River (Martinborough) ★★★ Tiny winery. Penetrating long-lived Chard, Ries, Pinot Gr (NZ's finest), Gewürz (ditto) and Pinot N.

Esk Valley (Hawke's Bay) ★★→★★★ Former lge family firm, now owned by VILLA MARIA. Some of NZ's most voluptuous Merlot-based reds (esp Res label), v gd dry Merlot rosé, oak-aged Chenin Bl, satisfying Chards and Sauv Bl.

Felton Road (Central Otago) ★★ Star new winery in warm Bannockburn area. Debut '97 Pinot N Block 3, barrel-fermented Chard and Dry Ries all outstanding.

Forrest Marlborough ★★ Small winery; fragrant, ripe Chard (non-wooded) Sauv Bl and Ries; stylish H BAY Cornerstone V'yd Cab-Merlot.

Fromm Marlborough ★★ Small winery, Swiss-founded, focussing on red wines. Fine Pinot N, esp under La Strada Res label.

Gibbston Valley Central Otago ★★ Pioneer winery with popular restaurant. Greatest strength Pinot N (esp Res, 1st vintage '95). Racy local whites (Chard, Ries, Pinot Gr, Sauv Bl). In some vintages a top MARLB Sauv.

Giesen Estate Canterbury ★→★★★ German family winery, now region's largest. Known for Ries, esp honey-sweet well-structured Res Botrytised. Grapes now from CANTERBURY except Chard, Sauv Bl (MARLB). Chard and Pinot N gd esp Res.

Gillan Marlborough ★★ Small winery producing fresh, vibrant Sauv Bl and Chard, promising sparkling wine and leafy Merlot.

Gisborne (r) **94** 98 (w) **96** 98 NZ's third-largest region. Strengths in Chard (typically fragrant ripe and appealing in its youth), and Gewürz (highly perfumed and peppery). Abundant rain and fertile soils ideal for heavy croppers, esp Müller-T. Reds typically light but Merlot shows promise.

Glover's (Nelson) ★→★★★ V small winery producing freshly acidic Ries and Sauv Bl, muscular Pinot N and Cab S.

Goldwater Waiheke I (Auckland) ★★★ Region's pioneer Cab S-Merlot (first vintage '82) still one of NZ's finest: Médoc-like concentration and structure. Also crisp citrussy Chard and pungent Sauv Bl, both grown in MARLB.

Grove Mill Marlborough ★★→★★★ Attractive whites incl several Chards esp fully oak-ferm'd Lansdowne and vibrant MARLB Chard; excellent Ries, Gewürz, Sauv, slightly sweet Pinot Gr. Dark chunky tannic reds.

Hawke's Bay (r) **91'** 94 **95'** 98 (w) **95 96** 97' 98 NZ's 2nd-largest region. Long history of table wine making in sunny climate, shingly and heavier soils. Full rich Cab S and Merlot-based reds in gd vintages; powerful Chard; rounded Sauv.

Heron's Flight Matakana (nr Auckland) ★★ Tiny producer with sturdy brambly Cab S-Merlot (esp 91 and 94).

Highfield Marlborough ★★ After hesitant start, rich oaked Chard and Sauv Bl; promising sp under premium Elstree label. Opulent botrytised Ries. Solid lower-tier Sauv Bl, Ries, Chard and leafy Merlot.

Hunter's Marlborough ★★→★★★ Top name in intense immaculate Sauv (oaked and not). Fine delicate Chard. Excellent sp, Ries, Gewürz; reds less notable.

Isabel Estate Marlborough ★★ Small family estate with limey clay soil. Vg Pinot Noir, Sauv Bl and Chard.

Jackson Estate Blenheim ★★→★★★ Large v'yd, no winery. Rich Sauv Bl, good Chard (esp weighty Res). Outstanding sp, gorgeous sw whites.

Kemblefield Hawke's Bay ★ Sizable new American-owned winery. Initial releases (93 on) incl solid Sauv Bl, Chard, Gewürz, Merlot and Cab S-Merlot.

Kim Crawford Auckland ★★ Personal label of COOPER'S CREEK winemaker, launched '96. Rich oaked GISBORNE Chard, robust unwooded MARLB Chard, weighty steely MARLB Sauv Bl.

Kumeu River Kumeu (NW of Auckland) ★★★ AUCKLAND grapes, v rich, mealy Kumeu Chard; single v'yd Mate's V'yd Chard even more opulent. Rest of range solid. Brajkovich is second label.

Lawson's Dry Hills Blenheim ★★→★★★ Top recent arrival. Weighty wines with rich intense flavours. Distinguished Sauv Bl, Chard, Gewürz and Ries.

Lincoln Henderson (Auckland) Long est'd medium-sized family winery. Gd value sound varietals: buttery GISBORNE Chard (esp Parklands and Vintage Sel).

Lintz Martinborough ★★ Sm characterful producer: floral tangy sp Ries, treacly botrytised Optima. Weighty Sauv. Chunky Pinot N, Cab S, Cab-Merlot, Shiraz.

Longridge See Corbans

McDonald Winery Hawke's Bay ★★→★★★ MONTANA'S H BAY winery: wines under Church Road label. Rich ripe Chard (Res more oaky). Elegant Cab S-Merlot made with technical input from Bordeaux house of Cordier.

Marlborough (r) **97' 98** (w) **96 97 98** NZ's largest region. Sunny warm days and cool nights give intensely flavoured crisp whites. Extraordinarily intense Sauv, from sharp green capsicum to riper tropical fruit character. Fresh limey Ries. High-quality sp. Too cool for Cab S, but Pinot N and Merlot promising.

Martinborough (r) **96 97'** 98 (w) **96 97'** 98 Sm high quality area in S WAIRARAPA (foot of North Island). Warm summers, dry autumns and gravelly soils. Success with white grapes (Chard, Sauv Bl, Ries, Gewürz, Pinot Gris) but principally renowned for intensely varietal Pinot N.

Martinborough Vineyard Martinborough ★★★ Distinguished sm winery; one of NZ's top Pinot N (Res 91, 94, 96). Rich biscuity Chard. Also Ries, Sauv.

Matawhero Gisborne ★→★★ Formerly NZ's top Gewürz specialist. Now has wide range (also Chard, Sauv Bl, Cab-Merlot) of varying but often gd quality.

Matua Valley Waimauku (Auckland) ★★→★★★ Highly rated, middle-sized winery with large estate v'yd. Excellent oaked Res Sauv Bl. Top wines labelled Ararimu incl fat savoury Chard and dark rich Merlot-Cab S. Numerous well-priced, attractive GISBORNE (esp Judd Chard), H BAY and MARLB wines (the latter branded Shingle Peak).

Mills Reef Bay of Plenty (SE of Auckland) ★★ The Preston family produces impressive wines from H BAY grapes. Top Elspeth range incl lush barrel-ferm'd Chard and Sauv Bl. Middle-tier Res range also impressive. Two quality sparkling wines: Mills Reef and Charisma.

Millton nr Gisborne ★★→★★★ Region's top sm winery: organic. Top-flight med-sw Opou V'yd Ries. Soft, savoury Chard Barrel Ferm'd. Robust, complex Chenin Bl Dry.

Mission Greenmeadows (Hawke's Bay) ★→★★ NZ's oldest wine producer, est'd 1851, still run by Catholic Society of Mary. Solid varietals: sweetish intensely perfumed Ries esp gd value. Top Jewelstone range incl rich complex Chard, deep-flavoured Cab-Merlot and botrytised sw Ries.

Montana Auckland ★→★★★★ NZ wine giant, approx. 40% mkt share. Wineries in AUCKLAND, GISBORNE, H BAY (see McDonald Winery) and MARLB. Extensive co-owned v'yds. Famous for Marlb whites, incl top-value Sauv Bl, Ries and Chard. Strength in sp, incl DEUTZ and stylish, fine value Lindauer. Elegant H Bay Church Road reds and quality Chard.

Morton Estate Bay of Plenty (S of Auckland) ★★→★★★ Respected med-sized producer with v'yds in H BAY and MARLB. Refined rich Black Label Chard one of NZ's best, but mid-tier White Label Chard also gd.

Nautilus (Marlborough) ★★ Small range of distributors Negociants (NZ), owned by S Smith & Son of Australia (cf Yalumba). Top wines incl classic Sauv Bl and fragrant yeasty smooth sp. Lower tier wines: Twin Islands.

Nelson (r) **97' 98** (w) **96 97 98** Small region west of MARLBOROUGH; similar climate but little wetter. Clay soils of Upper Moutere hills and silty Waimea Plains. Strengths in whites, esp Ries, Sauv Bl, Chard. Reds can lack ripeness.

Neudorf Nelson ★★★ One of NZ's top boutique wineries. Strapping creamy-rich Chard, one of NZ's best. Fine Pinot N, Sauv Bl and Ries.

Nga Waka Martinborough ★★→★★★ Emerging star. Dry steely whites of v high quality. Outstanding Sauv Bl; piercingly flavoured Ries; robust savoury Chard.

Ngatarawa Hawke's Bay ★★→★★★ Boutique winery in old stables. Top Glazebrook range incl deep-flavoured citrussy Chard, sw Noble Harvest and v supple and attractive Cab-Merlot. Solid mid-range 'Stables' varietals.

Nobilo Auckland ★→★★ NZ's 4th-largest winery still family-run. Acquired SELAKS '98; now part-owned by BRL Hardy). Early reputation for reds faded. Off-dry White Cloud (Müller-T-based) worldwide success. Gd GISBORNE Chard (in British Airways ¼ bottles). MARLB Sauv: gd, sharply priced. Top label: Grand Reserve.

Okahu Estate Northland (N of Auckland) ★→★★ NZ's northernmost winery, at Kaitaia. Hot, humid climate. Reds: stuffing and warm ripe flavours. Kaz Shiraz 94 NZ's first gold medal Shiraz.

Omaka Springs Marlborough ★ Small new producer with solid Sauv Bl, Ries, Sém, Chard and Merlot.

Oyster Bay See Delegats.

Palliser Estate Martinborough ★★→★★★ One of area's largest and best wineries. Superb tropical fruit-flavoured Sauv Bl, excellent Chard, Ries and Pinot N. Top wines: Palliser Estate; lower-tier: Pencarrow.

Pask, C J Hawke's Bay ★→★★ Smallish winery, extensive v'yds. Gd, sometimes excellent Chard (esp Res). Cab S and Merlot-based reds vary from light, herbaceous to rich, complex Res releases.

Pegasus Bay Waipara (N Canterbury) ★★→★★★ Small but distinguished range, notably taut cool-climate Chard, lush complex oaked Sauv/Sém; and zingy, high flavoured Ries. Cab S-based reds: region's finest. Pinot N v promising.

Mark Rattray Canterbury ★★ Stylish Pinot N, Chard and Sauv Bl.

Rippon Vineyard Central Otago ★★ Stunning v'yd. Fine-scented v fruity Pinot N and slowly evolving whites, incl steely appley Chard.

Robard & Butler See Corbans.

Rongopai Waikato (S of Auckland) ★★ Small winery using local, GISBORNE and H BAY fruit. Softly mouthfilling, ripe Sauv Bl and Chard. Renowned for botrytised sw whites, esp Res Ries and weightier Res Chard.

Sacred Hill Hawke's Bay ★★ Sound 'Whitecliff' varietals; gd, oaked Res Sauv Bl (Barrel Fermented and Sauvage). Gd Basket Press Cab S and Merlot-Cab.

St Clair Marlborough ★★ Fast-growing export-led producer. Substantial v'yds. Fragrant full Ries, Sauv Bl, easy Chard. Plummy early-drinking Merlot.

St Helena Canterbury ★→★★ The region's oldest winery, founded nr Christchurch in '78. Light, supple Pinot N (Res is bolder). Chard variable but gd in better vintages. Cheap, earthy, savoury Pinot Bl is fine value.

St Jerome Estate Henderson (nr Auckland) ★→★★ Small producer of average whites and estate-grown dark flavour-crammed tannic Cab-Merlot.

Seifried Estate Upper Moutere (nr Nelson) ★→★★ Region's only medium-sized winery, founded by Austrian. Known initially for well-priced Ries, but now also producing gd-value, often excellent Sauv Bl and Chard. Light reds.

Selaks Kumeu (NW of Auckland) ★★→★★★ Med-sized family firm bought by NOBILO '98. V'yds and 2nd winery: MARLB. Sauv Bl: strength, esp superb lightly oaked Sauv/Sém. Powerful yet refined Founders Chard. Reds plain; sp gd.

Seresin Marlborough ★★ Est'd by expatriate NZ film producer Michael Seresin. First vintage '96. Stylish immaculate Sauv and Chard (esp Res), Pinot Gr, Pinot N, Ries and Noble Ries.

Sherwood Canterbury ★→★★ Tart, austere Ries and Chard and two Pinot Noirs, notably robust, meaty and tannic Res model.

Shingle Peak See Matua Valley.

Soljans Henderson (Auckland) ★→★★ Long-est'd small family winery. Steadily improving whites and reds, most distinctively a supple meaty Pinotage.

Spencer Hill Nelson ★★ Known for Chard (soft fragrant lemony): 1st vintage '94. 'Tasman Bay': regional blending. 'Spencer Hill': v'yd-designated and oaky.

Stonecroft Hawke's Bay ★★→★★★ Sm winery. Dark concentrated Syrah, more Rhône than Oz. Also v gd Cab-Merlot ('Ruhanui'), Chard, Gewürz, Sauv Bl.

Stoneleigh See Corbans.

Stonyridge Waiheke Island ★★★★ Boutique winery. Two Bordeaux-style reds: Larose exceptional (esp 87 89 91 93 94' 96 97); Airfield: second label.

Te Awa Farm Hawke's Bay ★★ New winery (since '94) with large estate v'yd. Classy Chard, Cab-Merlot and Merlot under top Boundary and larger volume Longlands labels.

Te Kairanga Martinborough ★→★★ One of district's larger wineries. Big flinty Chard (Res: richer), perfumed supple Pinot N (Res: complex powerful).

Te Mata Hawke's Bay ★★★★ HB's most prestigious winery. Fine powerful Elston Chard; v gd oaked Cape Crest Sauv Bl; stylish Coleraine Cab-Merlot (89 90 91 95'). Awatea Cab-Merlot (v gd): 2nd label, less oak. Cab-Merlot: 3rd label.

Te Motu Waiheke I (Auckland) ★★→★★★ Top wine of Waiheke V'yds, owned by the Dunleavy and Buffalora families. Dark, concentrated, brambly red of v high quality, first vintage 93. Dunleavy Cab-Merlot is second label.

Torlesse Waipara (N Canterbury) ★★ Flavour-packed tangy Sauv Bl, robust rich Chard from MARLB; zesty Ries Dry and v characterful Waipara Pinot Gr.

Trinity Hill (Hawke's Bay) ★★ Part-owned by John Hancock (ex-MORTON ESTATE). Impressively dark, firm, concentrated reds since '96 and tight, elegant Chard.

Vavasour Marlborough ★★→★★★ Based in Awatere Valley. Immaculate intense Single V'yd Chard and Sauv Bl; promising Pinot N. Dashwood: second label.

Vidal Hawke's Bay ★★→★★★ Est'd 1905 by Spaniard, now part of VILLA MARIA. Reserve range (Chard, Cab S, Cab-Merlot) uniformly high std. Other varietals gd and well-priced.

Villa Maria Mangere (Auckland) ★★→★★★ NZ's 3rd-largest wine company, incl VIDAL and ESK VALLEY. Top range: Reserve (Noble Ries NZ's most awarded sw white); Cellar Sel: middle-tier (less oak); third-tier Private Bin wines can be excellent and top value (esp Ries, Sauv Bl, Gewürz).

Waimarama Hawke's Bay ★★ Small producer specialising in high-quality reds; v gd Merlot, Cab S and Cab-Merlot.

Waipara Springs Canterbury ★→★★ Small N CANTERBURY producer with lively cool climate Ries, Sauv Bl and Chard; reds promising.

Wairarapa NZ's fifth-largest wine region. See Martinborough.

Wairau River Marlborough ★★ Small, export-orientated producer of highly flavoured Sauv Bl and succulent toasty Chard.

Wellington (r) 96 97' 98 (w) 96 97' 98 Capital city and official name of the region which includes WAIRARAPA, Te Horo and MARTINBOROUGH.

West Brook Auckland ★★ Long-est'd, underrated producer of immaculate, full-flavoured Chard, Sauv Bl and Ries.

Whitehaven Marlborough ★★ Emerging firm (first vintage 94); excellent wines: racy Ries, scented delicate lively Sauv Bl, flavourful easy Chard.

Wither Hills Marlborough ★★★ V'yd owned by former DELEGAT's winemaker Brent Marris. Exceptional Chard and Sauv Bl since '92.

South Africa

President Nelson Mandela called South Africa the 'Rainbow Nation' after the diversity of races crowded into southern Africa. With the help of a Mediterranean climate at the continent's southern tip, Cape wine seems to mirror that diversity in the styles of its wines. Within a 700-mile east-west arc north of Cape Town, linking the Atlantic with the Indian oceans over steep mountains and alluvial river beds, are vineyards producing every imaginable kind – and quality – of wine. There is a lively revival under way now – and much searching for an 'inimitable Cape style'. Whatever that might turn out to be, it's still way off an agreed definition, let alone an appellation on a bottle.

Unsurprisingly, after decades of long apartheid isolation and boycotts, South African wines re-entered international markets in the early 1990s with a confused image. There was the 300-year history and faded glory of the intense Constantia dessert wines of the 18th Century. But then the sudden appearance on the world's supermarket shelves of hundreds of unknown Cape brands, often unconnected with a specific Cape wine region or winery, made for a wobbly re-introduction. Fair value, perhaps, but 'cheap' also crept into image. That's changing. The Cape wine industry has been revitalized by a new-generation approach, boosted by a steady influx of foreign capital and expertise led by the demands of modern consumers. The volume of South Africa's 'outflow' has slackened, but quality has begun to pick up significantly – with riper, less tannic fruit, more experienced oaking, better organized vineyard management, less dowdy packaging. Mandela's successor, Thabo Mbeki, has coined a term which might apply: 'The South African Renaissance.'

Agusta Wines r w ★★→★★★ Rising star at Franschhoek with excellent CAB S (95 96 97). Also Sémillon, CHARD. Formerly Haute Provence.

Allesverloren r ★→★★★ Old family estate in hot wheatlands W of Cape Town, best known for port-style (89 90 96 97). Also hefty CAB and Shiraz (94 96).

Alto r ★★ 250-acre mountain v'yds S of S'BOSCH. Sturdy, long-lived CAB (95) Cab-based blend Alto Rouge (95).

Altydgedacht r w ★★ (Cab S) 94 Durbanville estate just outside Cape Town; also gutsy Tintoretto blend of Barbera and Shiraz. Rich PINOTAGE.

Avontuur r w ★★ 200-acre ST'BOSCH v'yd. Soft NV B'x-style blend, Avon Rouge plus range of dry to sw wines incl quirky sw red (Dolcetto).

Backsberg r w ★★→★★★ (r) 92 94 95 Prize-winning 395-acre PAARL estate. Leader in modern v'yd management systems and worker participation schemes. Also joint venture with California's Zelma Long (of Simi qv). Delicious B'x blend Klein Babylonstoren (95 96); also reliable, gd value PINOTAGE, CAB (96 97), Shiraz and mid-weight CHARD.

Beaumont r w ★★ Walker Bay v'yds, family-run, recently restored old winery: v gd PINOTAGE Res (97), CHARD and CHENIN BL.

Bellingham r w ★★→★★★ Big-selling, sound brand r (95 97), popular w, esp sw soft Cape RIES-based Johannisberger wines (exported as Cape Gold), CHARD, SAUV BL and Chard-Sauv 'Sauvenay'. Outstanding Cab F (95 97), PINOTAGE (97).

Berg and Brook Big new PAARL-based vintners sourcing grapes and wines widely, mainly for premium range Savanah; best is Merlot Res (98). French links, with technical input from Alain Moueix of Pomerol.

Bergkelder Big STELLENBOSCH CO, member of Oude Meester-Rembrandt group, making/distributing many brands (FLEUR DU CAP, Grunberger), 12 estate wines.

Beyerskloof r ★★★ (Cab S) 94 95 96 Small STELLENBOSCH property, deep-flavoured CAB S and PINOTAGE (96).

Blaauwklippen r w ★★ (r) 94 96 STELLENBOSCH winery: bold reds, esp CAB Reserve and Shiraz 95. Also good Zin (93 95).

Bloemendal r w ★★ (Cab) 93 96 Sea-cooled Durbanville estate. Fragrant CAB, Merlot. Good CHARD CAP CLASSIQUE.

Boekenhoutskloof r w ★★→★★★ New FRANSCHOEK winery, launched with vg Shiraz 97, CAB S 96 and Sémillon 97. Gd value second label Porcupine Ridge.

Bon Courage w sw ★→★★ ROBERTSON estate; gd dessert Gewürz and CHARD.

Boplaas r w ★★ Estate in dry hot Karoo. Earthy deep Vintage Reserve port-style esp (94 96), fortified Muscadels. Links with Grahams in Portugal. 'Reserve port-style' incl Touriga Nacional from '95.

Boschendal r w sp ★★ 617-acre estate nr Franschhoek. Gd CHARD and METHODE CAP CLASSIQUE (Chard and Pinot); improving reds, sp B'x-style blend (97) Merlot (95), Shiraz (97).

Bouchard-Finlayson r w ★★★ Excellent (CHARD) 97 (Sauv) 97 Emphatic firm PINOT NOIRS sp Galpin Peak (96 97) 95 First French-Cape partnership (Paul Bouchard of Burgundy, Peter Finlayson at Hermanus, Walker Bay).

Brampton See Rustenberg.

Breede River Valley Fortified and white wine region E of Drakensberg Mts.

Buitenverwachting r w sp ★★★ Exceptional, German owned, replanted CONSTANTIA v'yds. Outstanding Sauv (95 96), CHARD, B'x blend 'Christine' (89 90 91 92 95), CAB S (91 92). Lively clean CAP CLASSIQUE. Fine restaurant.

Cabernet Sauvignon Successful in coastal region. Range of styles: sturdy long-lived, sometimes too tannic, to elegant fruity. More recently use of new French oak is giving great improvements. Best recent vintages: 91 94 95 97.

Cabrière Estate ★★→★★★ Franschhoek growers of gd NV CAP CLASSIQUE under Pierre Jordan label (Brut Sauvage, CHARD-PINOT N and Belle Rose Pinot N). Also promising 'new clone' Pinot N (96 98).

Cap Classique, Méthode South African term for classic method sp wine.

Chardonnay S Africa came to Chard late, beginning mid-'80s. Now offering many styles, incl unwooded and blended – with Sauv. More than 200 labels; a decade ago, just 3.

Chateau Libertas ★ Big-selling blend of mainly CAB S made by SFW.

Chenin Blanc Most widely planted grape of the Cape; still almost one vine in three. Adaptable, s'times vg; much upgrading by leading growers, incl barrel-fermented examples. See also Steen.

Constantia Once the world's most famous sweet Muscat-based wine (both red and white), from the Cape. See Klein Constantia.

Cordoba r w ★★→★★★ Promising sea-facing mountain v'yds – new winery on Helderberg, STELLENBOSCH. Stylish CAB F-based claret blend – labelled Crescendo (95), plus ripe rich Merlot (95) and Shiraz (94)

De Wetshof w sw ★★ ROBERTSON estate specializing in CHARDS of varying oakiness. Also dessert Gewürz, 'Danie de Wet' Rhine RIES, own-brand CHARDS for British supermarkets.

Delaire Winery r w ★→★★ (CHARD) 97 (Merlot-CAB blend) High v'yds at Helshoogte Pass above STELLENBOSCH.

Delheim r w dr sw ★★ Big winery; mountain v'yds nr STELLENBOSCH. Gd barrel-aged CAB S, Merlot, Cab F Grand Res (91 95). Value Cab (95 96), PINOTAGE, Shiraz (95 97); also CHARD, Sauv. Sw wines: Gewurz, outstanding botrytis STEEN.

NB Vintages in colour are those you should choose first for drinking in 2000.

266

Die Krans Estate ★★ Karoo semi-desert v'yds making rich full Vintage Reserve port-style. Best are **91 94 95 97**. Also traditional fortified sweet Muscadels.

Dieu Donné Vineyards r w ★★ Franschhoek CO: CHARD (**96**), CAB (**95**).

Edelkeur ★★★★ Excellent intensely sweet noble rot white by NEDERBURG.

Eikendal Vineyards r w ★★→★★★ Swiss-owned 100-acre v'yds and winery nr STELLENBOSCH. Merlot (**96 97**). Vg CHARD (**97 98**); CAB S Reserve.

Estate Wine Official term for wines grown and made (not necessarily bottled) exclusively on registered estates. Not a quality designation.

Fairview r w dr sw ★★→★★★ (CHARD) **97 98** Enterprising PAARL estate; wide range (Viognier new '98). Best: Shiraz Res (**93 95 97**) Res Merlot (**93 95 97**). Powerful Zin **97**. Barrel-fermented CHENIN. Consistently gd range of sw wines. One of SA's leaders in softer, fruitier wines. Also v interesting Sém.

Fleur du Cap r w sw ★★ Value range from BERGKELDER at STELLENBOSCH: good CAB (**95**). Also Merlot (**95 96**), Shiraz (**94 96**), fine Gewürz, botrytis CHENIN.

Fredericksburg, R & de R r w ★★ Joint venture by Benjamin de Rothschild and Anthonij Rupert, from Cape's wealthiest wine family. Lavish cellar v'yds at PAARL. CAB S-Merlot (**97**), Sauv Bl (**98**).

Glen Carlou r w ★★★ (r) **95 96 97** (CHARD) **96 97** Top Cape winery, v'yds at PAARL. Since '97 has ties with Donald Hess of Napa, California (qv). Outstanding CHARD sp Res (**97 98**), full PINOT N, good B'x blend Grande Classique (**93 95 97**).

A choice for 2000 from South Africa

Cabernet Sauvignon Thelema, Rustenberg, Brampton, Agusta (Haute Provence), Eikendal Res

Cabernet Sauvignon-Merlot Hartenberg, Veenwouden Classic, Meerlust Rubicon, Rozendal, Backsberg (Klein Babylonstoren)

Merlot Veenwouden, Hartenburg, Cordoba, Spice Route

Shiraz Boekenhoutskloof, Fairview, Saxenburg

Pinotage Kaapzicht, L'Avenir, Kanonkop, Grangehurst, Warwick, Uiterwyk

Pinot Noir Bouchard-Finlayson (Galpin Peak), Meerlust

Chardonnay Vergelegen, Thelema, Hamilton Russell Vineyards

Sauvignon Blanc Vergelegen, Thelema, Villiera

Chenin Blanc L'Avenir, Villiera, Ken Forrester

Sémillon Boekenhoutskloof

Viognier Fairview

Port-style J-P Bredell

Dessert Vergelegen Noble Late Harvest Sémillon

Sparkling Graham Beck (Méthode Cap Classique: bottle fermented)

Graham Beck Winery w sp ★★→★★★ Avant-garde ROBERTSON winery (350 acres); METHODE CAP CLASSIQUE Brut RD NV, Blanc de Blancs sp (**92**); still Lone Hill CHARD (**97**) well regarded. Big vg Merlot, Shiraz in pipeline.

Grand Cru (or Premier Grand Cru) Term for a totally dry white, with no quality implications. Generally to be avoided.

Grangehurst Wines r ★★★ Small top STELLENBOSCH winery, buying in grapes. Specializing in PINOTAGE (**95 97**), and concentrated Res CAB-Merlot (**95 97**).

Groot Constantia r w ★★ Historic gov't-owned estate nr Cape Town. Superlative Muscat in early 19th C. Gd CAB (esp Cab-Merlot Gouverneur's Reserve (**91 95 96**). CHARD Res (**97**). PINOTAGE, Weisser (Rhine) RIES-Gewürz Botrytis, sw Muscat.

Hamilton Russell Vineyards r w ★★★ (Pinot N) **91 97** (CHARD) **95 96 97** A pioneer, still at the cutting edge of quality. Good PINOT N vineyards and cellar. Small yields, French-inspired vinification in cool Walker Bay. Many awards.

Hanepoot Local name for the sweet Muscat of Alexandria grape.

Hartenberg r w ★★★ STELLENBOSCH estate. Among Cape's very top red producers, restyled since '93. Shiraz (**93 95 97**) and Merlot from (**93 95 97**). V individual Pontac (95) and Zinfandel (95); (95) and sw Weisser RIESLING.

Hazendal r w ★★ Dramatic revival underway at this old STELLENBOSCH estate. Now owned by Moscow-born Mark Voloshin, Cape wine's first such investor. V gd CHARD (**98**) and Shiraz-CAB (**97**).

Jordan Vineyards ★★→★★★ Top property in SW STELLENBOSCH hills: vg SAUV BL, CHARD (**96 97**) and CAB S (**93 95**). Husband-and-wife team, California-trained.

J P Bredell ★★★ STELLENBOSCH v'yds. Rich dark deep Vintage Reserve port-style from Tinta Barocca and Souzão grapes. Also rich PINOTAGE, Shiraz.

Kanonkop r ★★★ N STELLENBOSCH estate with grand local status. Individual powerful CAB (**89 91 94 95**) and B'x-style blend Paul Sauer (**89 91 94 95**). PINOTAGE (**89 91 94 97**), oak-finished since '89.

Ken Forrester Vineyards ★★ Imaginative STELLENBOSCH-Helderberg producer. Full CHENIN (**97 98**) and Sauv Bl. Also Grenache-Syrah. Emphasis on bush vines.

Klein Constantia r w sw ★★★ Subdivision of famous GROOT CONSTANTIA neighbour. Emphatic CHARD, Sauv (**97 98**). Big CAB, B'x-style blend Marlbrook (**91 94 95**). From '86, Vin de Constance revived the 18th-C Constantia legend, scintillating sw wine from Muscat de Frontignan.

KWV The Kooperatieve Wijnbouwers Vereniging, S Africa's national wine coop created in 1917 as a quasi-govt control body until privatization in '97. Vast premises in PAARL, a range of gd to s'times excellent wines, esp Cathedral Cellars reds, La Borie RIES, 'Sherries', sweet dessert wines. In '92, gave up widely criticized quota restrictions, freeing growers to plant v'yds at will.

La Motte r w ★★→★★★ (r) **91 92** Lavish Rupert family estate nr Franschhoek. Lean but stylish reds: Merlot, B'x-style blend Millennium (**93 95**), top Shiraz and CAB S (**93 95** 97). Gd CHARD (**97**).

L'Avenir ★★→★★★ Excellent recent STELLENBOSCH estate. Top Cape CHENIN (**97 98**) PINOTAGE (**95 96**), CAB S (**96**), CHARD (**97**). Also botrytis dessert Vinde Meuveur (97).

Landgoed Afrikaans for 'estate': on official seals and ESTATE WINE labels.

Landskroon r w ★→★★ Old family estate in PAARL. Gd dry reds, esp Shiraz, CAB S, Cab F.

Late Harvest Term for a mildly sweet wine. 'Special Late Harvest' must be naturally sweet. 'Noble Late Harvest' is highest quality dessert wine.

Le Bonheur r w ★★→★★★ (r) STELLENBOSCH estate often producing classic tannic minerally CAB (**95**); big-bodied Sauv Bl.

Leroux, JC ★★ Old brand revived as BERGKELDER's sparkling wine house. Sauv (Charmat), PINOT (top METHODE CAP CLASSIQUE is well-aged). Also CHARD.

Lievland r w ★★→★★★ (r) STELLENBOSCH estate: leading Cape Shiraz (**95 97**), gd CAB S, Merlot and Cab S-F 'DVB' (**91 94 95 96**). Also gd Cinsault-based blend 'Lievlander' 95.

Linton Park r w ★★ Impressive brand-new 1,000-ton winery at Wellington, a British investment (Linton Park is listed on The London Stock Exchange). Promising CAB S (98) also Sauv Bl and CHARD.

Long Mountain ★★ Pernod-Ricard label, buying grapes from coops under Australian direction (Robin Day, formerly of Orlando). V gd well-priced CAB S, Ruby Cab, Cab S-Merlot Res plus CHARD, CHENIN.

Longridge Winery ★★→★★★ Quality winery in STELLENBOSCH; grapes and wines from many sources. Incl CHARD (**97 98**), CAB S, Shiraz-Merlot (**96**), PINOTAGE. Also gd CAP CLASSIQUE sp. Consultants: Dom Jacques Prieur of Burgundy (qv).

L'Ormarins r w sw ★★→★★★ 89 91 94 One of two Rupert family estates nr Franschhoek. CAB (**91 94**) and vg claret-style Optima (**89 94 95**), also Shiraz (**91 93**). Fresh lemony CHARD, forward oak-aged Sauv; outstanding Gewürz-Bukketraube botrytis dessert wine.

Louisvale w ★★→★★★ (CHARD) 97 STELLENBOSCH winery. Gd CAB-Merlot (from '94).

Meerlust r w ★★★ (r) 89 90 91 92 95 Prestigious old family estate nr STELLENBOSCH; Cape's only Italian winemaker. Outstanding Rubicon (Médoc-style blend 89 91 92 95), CAB (91), Merlot (89 91 93 94), PINOT (89 91 95 96). Toasty CHARD (95 96 97). Also first SA estate grappa.

Middelvlei r ★★ STELLENBOSCH estate: good PINOTAGE (94 95), CAB (91 94), Shiraz (91 95 97) and CHARD (93).

Monis ★→★★ Well-known wine co of PAARL, with fine Special Reserve port-style.

Morgenhof r w dr s/sw ★★→★★★ Refurbished s'BOSCH estate. French owners; CAB, Merlot (96), B'x blend (95 96); dry white, (excellent Sauv, CHARD), s/sw whites; port-style.

Mulderbosch Vineyards w ★★★ Penetrating Sauv from mountain v'yds nr s'BOSCH: one oak-fermented, another fresh bold. Also CHARD and B'x-style blend Faithful Hound (95).

Muratie Ancient STELLENBOSCH estate, esp port-style. Revival with excellent B'x blend Ansela (94 95).Now also PINOT N (97).

Nederburg r w p dr sw s/sw sp ★★→★★★★ (r) 94 95 (CHARD) 96 98 Well-known large modern PAARL winery (6–700,000 cases pa; 50 different wines). Own grapes and suppliers. Sound CAB, Shiraz, CHARD, RIES, blends in regular range. Limited Vintages, Private Bins often outstanding. '70s pioneer of botrytis dessert wines, now benchmarks. Stages Cape's biggest annual wine event, the Nederburg Auction. See also Edelkeur.

Neethlingshof r w sw ★★→★★★ (r) 91 93 94 95 s'BOSCH estate: replanted with classic grapes, cellar revamped. Run jointly with nearby STELLENZICHT. Vg CAB S (94), Merlot (95), Shiraz (95), CHARD, fresh Sauv Bl, excellent Gewürz and blush Bl de Noirs. Consistently judged national champion botrytis wines from RIES (97), and Sauv Bl. B'x-blend Lord Neethling Res (93 94).

Neil Ellis Wines r w ★★★ (r) 91 94 95 96 Full forthright wines vinified at Jonkershoek Valley nr STELLENBOSCH (16 widely spread coastal v'yds). Spicy structured CAB S and Cab-Merlot, also PINOT N (97); excellent Sauv from various sites, sp Groenkloof; full bold CHARD.

Nelson Wine Estate r w ★★ PAARL winery, v'yds: gd CAB S (95), CHARD (97). Among first Cape grower-worker partnerships, with Klein Begin (Small Beginning) label.

Nuy Cooperative Winery r w dr sw sp ★★ Small Worcester coop, frequent local award-winner. Outstanding dessert wines; fortified Muscadels.

Overgaauw r w ★★ Old family estate nr STELLENBOSCH; Merlot v gd (94 95 97), and Bordeaux-style blend Tria Corda (95). Also Cape Vintage (a Cape port-style 88 92 93), incl Tourriga Nacional in '94 – South Africa's first.

Paarl Town 30 miles NE of Cape Town and the demarcated wine district around it.

Paul Cluver w ★★ First modern winery, v'yds in cooler Elgin coastal region, E of Cape Town. V gd Sauv (98), CHARD also Rhine RIES.

Pinot Noir Like counterparts in California and Australia, Cape producers struggle for fine, burgundy-like complexity. They're getting closer to it. Best from CABRIERE, BOUCHARD-FINLAYSON, GLEN CARLOU, HAMILTON RUSSELL, MEERLUST.

Pinotage S African red grape cross of PINOT N and CINSAULT, useful for high yields and hardiness. Can be delicious but overstated flamboyant esters often dominate. Experiments/oak-ageing show potential for finesse.

Plaisir de Merle r w ★★★ New SFW-owned cellar nr PAARL producing v gd CAB-Merlot (94 95) and Merlot (95) also CHARD. Paul Pontallier of Château Margaux is a consultant.

Pongrácz ★★ Successful value non-vintage sp METHODE CAP CLASSIQUE from PINOT N (75%) and CHARD, produced by the BERGKELDER.

Rhebokskloof r w ★→★★ 200-acre estate behind PAARL mountains: sound small range. CAB is promising (esp 95).

Riesling S African or Cape Riesling is actually France's Crouchen Blanc, very different (neutral, simple) from Rhine or Weisser Riesling, the German grape producing spicy – sometimes pungent – and mainly off-dry, sweet white wines in the Cape.

Robertson District inland from Cape. Mainly dessert wines (notably Muscat); white table wines on increase. Few reds. Irrigated v'yds.

Rooiberg Cooperative Winery ★ Big-selling ROBERTSON range of more than 30 labels. Good CHENIN BL, Colombard and fortified dessert wines.

Rozendal r ★★★ Small STELLENBOSCH v'yd: outstanding, sumptuous in some yrs (esp 94 95 96) mainly Merlot with CAB S.

Rust en Vrede r ★★→★★★ Well-known estate just E of STELLENBOSCH: red only. Good CAB (91 94 96), Shiraz (90 91 94 96), Rust en Vrede blend (mainly Cab S 89 91 94).

Rustenberg r w ★★★→★★★★ Old STELLENBOSCH estate, founded 300 yrs ago, making wine continuously for last 100. Determined revamp since mid '90s. Striking new flagship CAB S (96) Peter Barlow, Rustenberg B'x blend (96), v gd CHARD (98). Also top class Brampton label, Cab S (95), Chard (97), Sauv bl (98).

Saxenburg Wines r w dr sw ★★★ Prize-winning STELLENBOSCH v'yds and winery. Distinctive powerful reds under Private Collection labels; robust deep-flavoured PINOTAGE (96); CAB (91 92 94 95), Shiraz (91 93 94 95). Also Merlot (94 95), CHARD and Sauv Bl.

Simonsig r w sp sw ★★→★★★ Malan family estate at S'BOSCH with extensive range: CAB-Merlot Tiara (91 92 93 95). vg Cab, PINOTAGE Cab blend (95), Pinotage (93 95 96), CHARD (97) dessert-style Gewürz. First Cape METHODE CAP CLASSIQUE.

Simonsvlei r w p sw sp ★ One of S Africa's best-known coop cellars, just outside PAARL. A prize-winner with PINOTAGE under 'Reserve' label. Vast gd value range.

Spice Route Wine Company r w ★★→★★★ New S African winery-v'yds at Malmesbury, newly fashionable Cape west coast: v intense, dark Shiraz, Merlot, PINOTAGE, CAB S-Merlot (98). A partnership of two well-known winemakers, Gyles Webb (THELEMA), Charles Back (FAIRVIEW) with Zulu oenophile (ex-US exile) Jabulani Ntshangase and wine writer John Platter.

Springfield Estate Robertson ★★→★★★ Long-est'd ROBERTSON growers; began own bottling in '95. Drawing attention for super crisp Sauv Bl (98); rich CHARD (98); distinctive nutty soft-textured CAB S (95 97).

Steen S Africa's most common white grape, often-used local synonym for CHENIN BL. It gives youthful short-lived tasty lively wine when dry; lasts better when off-dry or sweet.

Steenberg r w ★★→★★★ Serious new CONSTANTIA winery v'yds set in a Cape Town golf course. V gd inaugural Merlot (97), with Sauv Bl and Sémillon.

Stellenbosch Town and demarcated district 30 miles E of Cape Town (2nd oldest town in S Africa after Cape Town). Heart of wine industry, with the 3 largest companies. Many top estates, esp for reds, are in mountain foothills.

Stellenbosch Farmers' Winery (SFW) The world's fifth-largest winery, South Africa's biggest after KWV: equivalent of 14M cases pa. Range incls NEDERBURG; top is ZONNEBLOEM. Wide selection of mid-/low-price wines.

Stellenbosch Vineyards New regional venture in '97 by some 150 S'BOSCH growers; first releases are re-styled improved labels from former S'bosch coops Welmoed, Eertserivier, Helderberg and Bottelary.

Stellenryck Collection r w ★★★ Top-quality BERGKELDER range. Rhine RIES, Fumé Blanc, CAB (89 91 92 93).

Stellenzicht ★★★ Replanted STELLENBOSCH v'yds and modern winery; outstanding wines across wide range: B'x blend (**94 95**), CAB (**94 95**), Syrah (**94 95**), Sauv, Sém Res; remarkable noble late harvest botrytis dessert wines.

Swartland Wine Cellar r w dr s/sw sw sp ★→★★ Vast range of wines from hot, dry wheatland: big-selling and low-price, esp CHENIN and dry, off-dry or sweet, but (recently) penetrating, Sauv, also big no-nonsense PINOTAGE.

Thelema r w ★★★★ (Cab S) **91 92 93 94 95** (CHARD) **93 94 95 96 97** Heavy-hitting v'yds and winery at Helshoogte, above S'BOSCH. Impressive, individual fruity-minty CAB and B'x blend (starting with vg **91**) and Merlot (since '92). Excellent CHARD and unoaked Sauv. American v'yd advice is giving winemaker Gyles Webb (festooned with awards) fab fruit.

Twee Jongegezellen w sp ★★ Old Tulbagh estate, still in Krone family (18th-C founder). Whites, best known: popular dry TJ39 (blend of a dozen varieties), Schanderl off-dry Muscat-Gewürz. CAP CLASSIQUE Cuvée Krone Borealis Brut.

Uiterwyk r w ★→★★ Old estate SW of S'BOSCH. PINOTAGE-based blend (**96**) Cab F and Merlot, v gd PINOTAGE Reserve (**96**). Also sw whites

Uitkyk r w ★★ (r) Old estate (400 acres) W of STELLENBOSCH esp for Carlonet (big gutsy CAB, **89 92 93 94**). Also CHARD (**97**).

Van Loveren r w sw sp ★★ Go-ahead ROBERTSON estate: range incl muscular CHARD (since '95), good Pinot Gr; scarcer Fernão Pires, Hárslevelü.

Veenwouden ★★★ Outstanding Merlot (**95 96 97**), dense B'x blend (**95 96 97**) from PAARL property owned by Geneva-based opera tenor, Deon Van der Walt soliciting advice from Pomerol's ubiquitous wine consultant Michel Rolland.

Vergelegen r w ★★★ One of Cape's oldest wine farms, founded 1700. Spectacularly restored. Outstanding Merlot (**95**). Superb CHARD Res (**96 97**) and v gd Sauv Bl (**98**).

Vergenoegd r w sw ★→★★ Old family estate in S S'BOSCH bottling CAB S, Shiraz. New B'x-style blend 'Reserve' (**92 94 96**).

Villiera r w ★★→★★★ PAARL estate with popular NV METHODE CAP CLASSIQUE 'Tradition'. Top Sauv Bl (**98**), CHENIN, good Rhine RIES, fine B'x-style blend CAB-Merlot 'Cru Monro' (**94 95**). Recently exceptional Merlot (**91 94 95 97**).

Vredendal Cooperative r w dr sw ★ S Africa's largest coop winery in hot Olifants River region. Big range: mostly white.

Vriesenhof r w ★★→★★★ (Cab) **91 94 95** (Chard) **97** Highly rated B'x blend Kalista (**91 93 94** 95). V gd PINOTAGE (**97**). Vg CHARD (**98**) Also Pinotage under sister Paradyskloof label.

Warwick r w ★★→★★★ STELLENBOSCH estate; one of Cape's few female winemakers. Vg B'x blend Trilogy (**92 93 94 95**), individual Cab F (**94 95 97**). One of top SA PINOTAGES (**95 96 97**) from 24-yr-old bush vines. CHARD (**97 98**).

Welgemeend r w ★★→★★★ Boutique PAARL estate: Médoc-style blends (**93 94 95**). Also Duelle, a mainly Malbec blend.

Wine of Origin The Cape's appellation contrôlée, but without French crop yield restrictions. Demarcated regions are described on these pages.

Worcester Demarcated wine district round BREEDE and Hex river valleys, E of PAARL. Many co-op cellars. Mainly dessert wines, brandy, dry whites.

Zandvliet r ★★ Estate in ROBERTSON area making recently improved Shiraz (**96**) and CHARD. V promising Merlot (**96**).

Zevenwacht r w ★★ STELLENBOSCH. Excellent Shiraz (96 97) Vg CAB-Merlot (**96 97**), CHARD. PINOTAGE improved from '96. Unusually spicy elegant CHENIN (**96 98**).

Zonnebloem r w ★★ (Cab S) Quality SFW range incl CAB S, Merlot (**94 95**), B'x blend Laureat (**91 93 94 96**), Shiraz, PINOTAGE (**91 94 95**), Sauv Bl, CHARD plus Sauv-Chard blend. Bl de Bl one of Cape's best and most available dry CHENINS.

A little learning...

A few technical words

The jargon of laboratory analysis is often seen on back-labels of New World wines. It has crept menacingly into newspapers and magazines. What does it mean? This hard-edged wine-talk, unsympathetic as it is to most lovers of wine, is very briefly explained below.

The most frequent technical references are to the ripeness of grapes at picking; the resultant alcohol and sugar content of the wine; various measures of its acidity; the amount of sulphur dioxide used as a preservative; and occasionally the amount of 'dry extract' – the sum of all the things that give wine its character.

The **sugar** in wine is mainly glucose and fructose, with traces of arabinose, xylose and other sugars that are not fermentable by yeast, but can be attacked by bacteria. Each country has its own system for measuring the sugar content or ripeness of grapes, known in English as the '**must weight**'. The chart below relates the three principal ones (German, French and American) to each other, to specific gravity, and to the potential alcohol of the wine if all the sugar is fermented.

Sugar to alcohol: potential strength

Specific Gravity	°Oechsle	Baumé	Brix	% Potential Alcohol v/v
1.065	65	8.8	15.8	8.1
1.070	70	9.4	17.0	8.8
1.075	75	10.1	18.1	9.4
1.080	80	10.7	19.3	10.0
1.085	85	11.3	20.4	10.6
1.090	90	11.9	21.5	12.1
1.095	95	12.5	22.5	13.0
1.100	100	13.1	23.7	13.6
1.105	105	13.7	24.8	14.3
1.110	110	14.3	25.8	15.1
1.115	115	14.9	26.9	15.7
1.120	120	15.5	28.0	16.4

Residual sugar is the sugar left after fermentation has finished or been artificially stopped, measured in grams per litre.

Alcohol content (mainly ethyl alcohol) is expressed in percent by volume of the total liquid. (Also known as 'degrees'.)

Acidity is both fixed and volatile. **Fixed acidity** consists principally of tartaric, malic and citric acids which are all found in the grape, and lactic and succinic acids which are produced during fermentation. **Volatile acidity** consists mainly of acetic acid, which is rapidly formed by bacteria in the presence of oxygen. A small amount of volatile acidity is inevitable and even attractive. With a larger amount the wine becomes 'pricked' – to use the graphic Shakespearian term. It starts to turn to vinegar.

Total acidity is fixed and volatile acidity combined. As a rule of thumb for a well-balanced wine it should be in the region of one gram per thousand for each 10°Oechsle (see above).

pH is a measure of the strength of the acidity, rather than its volume. The lower the figure the more acid. Wine usually ranges from pH 2.8 to 3.8. Winemakers in hot climates can have problems getting the pH low enough. Lower pH gives better colour, helps stop bacterial spoilage and allows more of the SO_2 to be free and active as a preservative.

Sulphur dioxide (SO_2) is added to prevent oxidation and other accidents in winemaking. Some of it combines with sugars etc and is known as '**bound**'. Only the '**free**' SO_2 that remains in the wine is effective as a preservative. **Total SO_2** is controlled by law according to the level of residual sugar: the more sugar, the more SO_2 needed.

A few words about words

In the shorthand essential for this little book (and often in bigger books and magazines as well) wines are often described by adjectives that can seem irrelevant, inane – or just silly. What do 'fat', 'round', 'full', 'lean' and so on mean when used about wine? Some of the more irritatingly vague and some of the more common 'technical' terms are expanded in the following list:

Acid To laymen often a term of reproval, meaning 'too sharp'. But various acids are vital to the quality and preservation of wine (especially white) and give it its power to refresh. For those on the advanced course, malolactic, or secondary, fermentation is the natural conversion of tart malic (apple) acid to lactic, replacing the immediate bite of a wine with milder, more complex tastes. The undesirable acid is acetic, smells of vinegar and is referred to as 'volatile'. Too much and the wine is on its way out.

Astringent One of the characters of certain tannins, producing a mouth-drying effect. Can be highly appetizing, as in Chianti.

Attack The first impression of the wine in your mouth. It should 'strike' positively, if not necessarily with force. Without attack it is feeble or too bland.

Attractive Means 'I like it, anyway'. A slight put-down for expensive wines; encouragement for juniors. At least refreshing.

Balance See Well-balanced.

Big Concerns the whole flavour, including the alcohol content. Sometimes implies clumsiness, the opposite of elegance. Generally positive, but big is easy in California and less usual in, say, Bordeaux. So the context matters.

Bitterness Another tannic flavour, usually from lack of full ripeness. Much appreciated in N Italy but looked on askance in most regions.

Body The 'weight', the volume of flavour and alcohol in wine. See Big and Full.

Botrytis See page 102.

Charming Rather patronizing when said of wines that should have more impressive qualities. Implies lightness and possibly a slight sweetness. A standard comment regarding Loire Valley wines.

Corky A musty taint derived (far too often) from an infected cork. Can be faint or blatant, but is always unacceptable.

Crisp With pronounced but pleasing acidity on the palate; fresh and eager.

Deep/depth This wine is worth tasting with attention. There is more to it than the first impression; it fills your mouth with developing flavours as though it had an extra dimension. ('Deep colour' simply means hard to see through.) All really fine wines have depth.

Earthy Used of a sense that the soil itself has entered into the flavour of the wine. Often positive, as in the flavour of red Graves.

Easy Used in the sense of 'easy come, easy go'. An easy wine makes no demand on your palate (or your intellect). The implication is that it drinks smoothly, doesn't need maturing, and all you remember is a pleasant drink.

Elegant A professional taster's favourite term when he or she is stuck to describe a wine whose proportions (of strength, flavour, aroma), whose attack, middle and finish, whose texture and whose overall qualities call for comparison with other forms of natural beauty.

Extract The components of wine (apart from water, alcohol, sugar, acids, etc) that make up its flavour. Usually the more the better, but 'over-extracted' means harsh, left too long extracting matter from the grape skins.

Fat Wine with a flavour and texture that fills your mouth, but without aggression. Obviously inappropriate in eg a light Moselle, but what you pay your money for in Sauternes.

Finesse See Elegant.

Finish See Length.

Firm Flavour that strikes the palate fairly hard, with fairly high acidity or tannic astringency giving the impression that the wine is in youthful vigour and will age to gentler things. An excellent quality with highly flavoured foods, and almost always positive.

Flesh Refers to both substance and texture. A fleshy wine is fatter than a 'meaty' wine, more unctuous if less vigorous. The term is often used of good Pomerols, whose texture is notably smooth.

Flowery Often used as though synonymous with fruity, but really meaning floral, like the fragrance of flowers. Roses, violets etc are some of those specified.

Fresh Implies a good degree of fruity acidity, even a little nip of sharpness, as well as the zip and zing of youth. All young whites should be fresh: the alternative is flatness, staleness. . . ugh.

Fruity Used for almost any quality, but really refers to the body and richness of wine made from good ripe grapes. A fruity aroma is not the same as a flowery one. Fruitiness usually implies at least a slight degree of sweetness. Attempts at specifying which fruit the wine resembles can be helpful. Eg grapefruit, lemon, plum, lychee. On the other hand writers' imaginations freqently run riot, flinging basketfuls of fruit and flowers at wines which could well be more modestly described.

Full Interchangeable with 'full-bodied'. Lots of 'vinosity' or wineyness: the mouth-filling flavours of alcohol and 'extract' (all the flavouring components) combined.

Heady The sense that the alcohol content is out of proportion.

Hollow Lacking a satisfying middle flavour. Something seems to be missing between the first flavour and the last. Characteristic of wines from greedy proprietors who let their vines produce too many grapes. A very hollow wine is 'empty'.

Honey A smell and flavour found especially in botrytis-affected wines, but often noticeable to a small and seductive degree in any mature wine of a ripe vintage.

Lean More flesh would be an improvement. Lack of mouth-filling flavours; often astringent as well. Occasionally a term of appreciation of a distinct and enjoyable style.

Length The flavours and aromas that linger after swallowing. In principle the greater the length, the better the wine. One second of flavour after swallowing = one 'caudalie'. Twenty caudalies is good; fifty terrific.

Light With relatively little alcohol and body, as in most German wines. A very desirable quality in the right wines but a dismissive term in eg reds where something more intense/ weighty is desired.

Maderized Means oxidized until it smells/tastes like Madeira. A serious fault unless intentional.

Meaty Savoury in effect with enough substance to chew. The inference is lean meat; leaner than in 'fleshy'.

Oaky Smelling or tasting of fresh-sawn oak, eg a new barrel. Appropriate in a fine wine destined for ageing in bottle, but currently often wildly overdone by winemakers to persuade a gullible public that a simple wine is something more grandiose. Over-oaky wines are both boring and tiring to drink.

Plump The diminutive of fat, implying a degree of charm as well.

Rich Not necessarily sweet, but giving an opulent impression.

Robust In good heart, vigorous, and on a fairly big scale.

Rough Flavour and texture give no pleasure. Acidity and/or tannin are dominant and coarse.

Round Almost the same as fat, but with more approval.

Structure The 'plan' or architecture of the flavour, as it were. Without structure wine is bland, dull, and won't last.

Stylish Style is bold and definite; wears its cap on its ear.

Supple Often used of young red wines that might be expected to be more aggressive. More lively than 'easy' wine, with good quality implications.

Well-balanced   Contains all the desirable elements (acid, alcohol, flavours, etc) in appropriate and pleasing proportions.

The options game

Like-minded wine-lovers who enjoy discussing wines together to improve their knowledge cannot do better than to play the 'Options Game'. The game was devised by the MC of the wine world, Australian Len Evans of Rothbury Estate. It is played during a meal and needs only a chairman who knows what the wine is, and any number of players who don't. Each player is given a glass of the same wine. The chairman asks a series of questions: one choice is the truth.

For example: 'Is this wine from California, France or Australia?' France is correct. Any player who has said France collects a point. 'Is it from Bordeaux, the Rhône or Provence?' Bordeaux is correct; another point. 'Is it from St-Emilion, Graves or the Haut-Médoc?' Haut-Médoc is correct; another point. 'Is it from Pauillac, St-Julien or Margaux?' Pauillac is right; another point. 'Is it a first, second or fifth growth?' Fifth is right; another point. 'Is it Grand-Puy-Lacoste, Lynch-Bages or Batailley?' Grand-Puy-Lacoste is right. 'Is it from 1982, 1983 or 1985?' The answer is 1985: the wine is identified.

Each time a player answers correctly he or she scores a point. There is no penalty for being wrong. So you can start by believing it was a California wine and still be in at the kill. There are many possible variations, including a knock-out version which can be played with a ballroom full of guests, who stand so long as they are answering correctly, and sit when they drop out. 'Options' is a great game for the competitive, and a wonderful way to learn about wine.

Wines for toasting the millennium

Red Bordeaux
Top growths of 90, 88, 85, 83, 82, 78, 75, 70, 66, 61, 59, 49, 47, 45
Other crus classés of 90, 89, 88, 86, 85, 83, 82, 81, 70, 61
Petits châteaux of 96, 95, 90, 89

Red Burgundy
Top growths of 90, 89, 88, 85, 78, 69, 64, 59
Premiers Crus of 93, 90, 89, 85, 78
Village wines of 96, 95, 93, 90

White Burgundy
Top growths of 95, 92, 90, 89, 86, 85
Premiers Crus of 96, 95, 92, 89, 86
Village wines of 97, 96, 95

Rhône reds
Hermitage/top northern Rhône reds of 95, 91, 90, 89, 88, 85, 83, 78
Châteauneuf-du-Pape of 95, 93, 90, 89, 88, 85, 83

Sauternes
Top growths of 90, 89, 88, 86, 85, 83, 82, 81, 79, 76, 75, 71, 70, 67
Other wines of 95, 90, 89, 88, 86, 85, 83

Alsace
Grands Crus and late-harvest wines of 93, 92, 90, 89, 88, 85, 83, 78, 76, 67
Standard wines of 97, 96, 95, 94, 92, 91, 90, 89, 88

Sweet Loire wines
Top growths (Anjou/Vouvray) of 90, 88, 86, 85, 78, 76, 75, 71, 64, 59

Champagne
Top wines of 90, 89, 88, 86, 85, 83, 82, 79, 76, 75

German wines
Great sweet wines of 94, 92, 90, 89, 88, 86, 85, 83, 76, 71, 67
Auslesen of 95 94, 93, 92, 90, 89, 88, 86, 85, 83, 76, 71
Spätlesen of 97 96, 95, 94, 93, 92, 91, 90, 89, 88, 86, 85, 83, 76
Kabinett and QbA wines of 98 97, 96, 95, 94, 93, 92, 91, 90, 89

Italian wines
Top Tuscan reds of 93, 91, 90, 88, 86, 85, 82
Top Piedmont reds of 91, 90, 89, 88, 87, 86, 85, 83, 82, 79

California wines
Top Cabs, Zins, Pinot N of 96, 95, 91, 90, 87, 86, 84, 75
Most Cabernets etc of 97, 96, 95, 91, 90, 87, 86
Top Chardonnays of 97, 96, 95, 94, 89
Most Chardonnays of 97, 96, 95

Australian wines
Top Cabs, Shiraz, Pinot N of 91, 90, 88, 84, 82, 80, 75
Most Cabernets etc of 95, 94, 91, 90, 88
Top Chardonnays of 96, 95, 94, 92, 90, 89, 88, 86
Most Chardonnays of 96, 95, 94
Top Semillons and Rieslings of 95, 94, 93, 92, 90, 89, 88, 86, 84, 83, 79, 78

Vintage Port
83, 82, 80, 70, 66, 63, 60, 55, 48, 45…

And the score is...

It seems that America and the rest of the world will never agree about the idea of scoring wines. America is besotted with the 100-point scale devised by Robert Parker, based on the strange US school system in which 50 = 0. Arguments that taste is too various, too subtle, too evanescent, too wonderful to be reduced to a pseudo-scientific set of numbers fall on deaf ears. Arguments that the accuracy implied by giving one wine a score of 87 and another 88 is a chimera don't get much further.

America likes numbers (and so do salesmen) because they are simpler than words. When it comes to words America likes superlatives. The best joke of 1997 – at least I hope it was a joke – was the critic who came up with a 150-point scoring system. He argued that if 50 was no score at all you needed 150 to reach 100. Logical, but if it catches on there will be chaos. It might just ridicule the whole unreal business to death.

The Johnson System

Very cautiously, therefore, I offer an alternative way of registering how much *you* like a wine. The Johnson System reflects the enjoyment (or lack of it) that each wine offered at the time it was tasted or drunk with inescapable honesty. Here it is:

> The minimum score is 1 sniff
>
> One step up is 1 sip
>
> 2 sips = faint interest
>
> A half glass = slight hesitation
>
> 1 glass = tolerance, even general approval

Individuals will vary in their scoring after this (they do with points systems, too). You should assume that you are drinking without compunction – without your host pressing you or the winemaker glowering at you.

> **Two glasses means you quite like it** (or there is nothing else to drink);
>
> **Three glasses – you find it more than acceptable;**
>
> **Four – it tickles your fancy;**
>
> **One bottle means thorough satisfaction;**
>
> **Two, it is irresistible.** The steps grow higher now:
>
> **A full case means you are not going to miss out on this one...** and so on.
>
> **The logical top score in the Johnson System is, of course, the whole vineyard.**

The right temperature

No single aspect of serving wine makes or mars it so easily as getting the temperature right. White wines almost invariably taste dull and insipid served warm and red wines have disappointingly little scent or flavour served cold. The chart below gives an indication of what is generally found to be the most satisfactory temperature for serving each class of wine.

		°F	°C	
		68	20	
		66	19	
Room temperature		64	18	Best red wines
		63	17	especially Bordeaux
	Red burgundy	61	16	
	Best white burgundy	59	15	Chianti, Zinfandel
	Port, Madeira	57	14	Côtes du Rhône
		55	13	*Ordinaires*
		54	12	Lighter red wines
Ideal cellar	Sherry	52	11	eg Beaujolais
	Fino sherry	50	10	
	Most dry white wines	48	9	Rosés
	Champagne	46	8	Lambrusco
Domestic fridge		45	7	
		43	6	Most sweet white wines
		41	5	Sparkling wines
		39	4	
		37	3	
		35	2	
		33	1	
		32	0	

Quick reference vintage charts

These charts give a picture of the range of qualities made in the principal 'classic' areas (every year has its relative successes and failures) and a guide to whether the wine is ready to drink or should be kept.

I	drink up	—	needs keeping
/	can be drunk with pleasure now, but the better wines will continue to improve	六	avoid
		0	no good
		10	the best

France

Red Bordeaux / White Bordeaux / Alsace

	Médoc/Graves	Pom/St-Em	Sauternes & SW	Graves & dry	Alsace	
98	5-8 —	6-10 —	5-8 —	5-9 ∠	7-9 ∠	98
97	4-7 ∠	4-7 ∠	5-8 —	4-7 V	7-9 ∠	97
96	6-8 ∠	5-8 ∠	7-9 —	7-10 ∠	6-9 ∠	96
95	6-9 ∠	6-9 ∠	6-9 —	5-9 V	5-8 ∠	95
94	5-8 ∠	5-9 ∠	4-6 ∠	5-8 V	4-8 ∠	94
93	4-7 ∠	5-8 ∠	2-5 I	5-7 V	6-8 V	93
92	3-7 V	3-5 I	3-5 ∠	4-8 I	7-9 V	92
91	3-6 V	2-4 I	2-5 V	6-8 I	5-7 I	91
90	7-10 ∠	8-10 ∠	7-10 ∠	7-8 V	7-9 V	90
89	6-9 ∠	7-9 ∠	7-9 ∠	6-8 I	7-10 V	89
88	6-9 ∠	7-9 ∠	6-10 V	7-9 I	8-10 V	88
87	3-6 I	3-6 I	2-5 六	7-10 I	7-8 六	87
86	6-9 ∠	5-8 V	7-10 ∠	5-8 I	7-8 I	86
85	7-9 ∠	7-9 ∠	6-8 V	5-8 I	7-10 I	85
83	6-9 ∠	6-9 I	6-10 ∠	7-9 I	8-10 六	83
82	8-10 ∠	7-9 I	3-7 V	7-8 I	6-8 六	82
81	5-8 I	6-9 I	6-8 V	7-8 I	7-8 I	81
79	5-8 I	5-7 I	6-8 ∠	4-6 六	7-8 六	79

Burgundy / Rhône

	Côte d'Or red	Côte d'Or white	Chablis	Rhône (N)	Rhône (S)	
98	6-8 ∠	6-8 ∠	6-9 ∠	6-8 ∠	7-9 ∠	98
97	7-9 ∠	6-9 ∠	7-9 ∠	7-9 ∠	5-8 ∠	97
96	7-10 ∠	7-10 ∠	7-10 ∠	5-7 ∠	4-6 V	96
95	7-9 ∠	5-8 ∠	5-8 V	6-8 ∠	6-8 ∠	95
94	5-7 V	5-8 ∠	6-8 V	6-7 V	5-7 V	94
93	6-9 ∠	4-6 I	4-7 I	3-6 I	4-9 V	93
92	4-7 I	6-8 V	5-8 I	4-6 I	3-6 I	92
91	5-7 I	4-6 V	4-6 I	6-9 ∠	4-5 I	91
90	7-10 ∠	7-9 V	6-9 I	6-9 V	7-9 V	90
89	6-9 ∠	6-9 V	7-10 I	6-8 V	6-8 V	89
88	7-10 ∠	7-9 V	7-9 I	7-9 V	5-8 V	88
87	6-8 I	4-7 六	5-7 I	3-6 I	3-5 I	87
86	5-8 I	7-10 I	7-9 I	5-8 I	4-7 I	86

Beaujolais 98, 97, 96, 95 Crus will keep, 93 vg. **Mâcon-Villages** (white) Drink 98, 97, 96, 95 now or can wait. **Loire** (Sweet Anjou and Touraine) best recent vintages: 97, 96, 95, 93, 90, 89, 88, 85; Bourgueil, Chinon, Saumur-Champigny: 98, 97, 96, 95, 93, 90. **Upper Loire** (Sancerre, Pouilly-Fumé): 98, 97, 96 and 95 vg; 94 and 93 drink up. **Muscadet** 98, 97, 96 vg: DYA.

Germany / Italy / USA (California)

	Rhine	Mosel	Tuscan reds	Cabs	Chards	
98	6-9 ∠	6-9 ∠	6-8 ∠	5-8 ∠	5-9 ∠	98
97	7-10 ∠	7-10 ∠	8-10 ∠	6-8 ∠	5-8 V	97
96	7-9 V	6-8 V	6-8 ∠	5-7 ∠	6-8 V	96
95	7-10 V	8-10 V	4-8 ∠	4-6 V	4-6 V	95
94	5-7 V	6-10 V	6-7 V	6-9 ∠	4-7 I	94
93	5-8 V	6-9 V	7-9 V	5-7 V	5-8 I	93
92	5-9 V	5-9 V	3-6 I	7-9 V	6-8 I	92
91	5-7 V	5-7 V	4-6 I	8-10 V	5-7 I	91
90	8-10 ∠	8-10 V	7-9 V	8-9 V	6-9 I	90
89	7-10 V	8-10 V	5-8 V	6-9 I	5-9 I	89
88	6-8 I	7-9 V	6-9 V	4-6 I	6-8 六	88
87	4-7 I	5-7 I	4-7 I	7-10 V	7-9 六	87
86	4-8 I	5-8 I	5-8 I	5-8 I	6-8 六	86